CITY CENTER TO REGIONAL MALL

CITY CENTER TO REGIONAL MALL

Architecture, the Automobile, and Retailing in Los Angeles, 1920–1950

RICHARD LONGSTRETH

THE MIT PRESS
CAMBRIDGE, MASSACHUSETTS
LONDON, ENGLAND

Published with the assistance of the Getty Grant Program.

This book was set in Bembo by Graphic Composition, Inc., and was printed and bound in the United States of America.

Library of Congress Cataloging-in-Publication Data
Longstreth, Richard W.
    City center to regional mall : architecture, the automobile, and retailing in Los Angeles, 1920–1950 / Richard Longstreth.
       p.   cm.
    Includes bibliographical references and index.
    ISBN 0-262-12200-6 (hc : alk. paper)
    1. Central business districts—California—Los Angeles Metropolitan Area—History.   2. Retail trade—California—Los Angeles Metropolitan Area—History.   3. Automobiles—Social aspects—California—Los Angeles Metropolitan Area—History.
4. City and town life—California—Los Angeles Metropolitan Area—History.   I. Title.
HF5429.5.L7L66   1997
381.1'0979494—dc20   96-25115
                                                   CIP

for Bob, and in memory of Brinck, David, and John

ACKNOWLEDGMENTS

I was born in southern California, San Marino to be precise, but returned with my family to the East after a year's residence, so while I can claim native status, I am hardly a Californian. I did not come to the region again until twenty years later, in 1966, when I had the good fortune to secure summer employment in the office of Richard and Dion Neutra. My tasks included sifting through records to identify material to be sent to the then nascent Neutra archive at UCLA, affording an unusual contact with a primary component of Los Angeles's architectural legacy. I began to sense how extraordinarily rich and varied that legacy was through the contents of the just published guide to architecture in southern California by David Gebhard and Robert Winter. Office work and field work together consumed most of my waking hours. By the end of two months, I realized the metropolitan area boasted one of the nation's greatest yields of modern architecture. Yet I did not enjoy Los Angeles as an urban setting. Like many visitors, I found it hard to accept the place as a real city.

My attitude toward the metropolis changed over the next half-dozen years. With repeated visits, I began to understand the city on its own terms and all the extraordinary things it had to offer. Los Angeles has more than a great collection of modernist and arts and crafts residences sequestered behind lush foliage. The fabric of the city, its public no less than its private worlds, possesses much from which we can learn. A central factor in this change of perspective was a rapidly growing interest in commercial architecture, in its vernacular as well as its high-style mani-

festations. Perhaps more than anything else the change stemmed from thousands of hours spent behind the wheel traversing the Philadelphia metropolitan area to gather material for a guide, and many hours more driving through other parts of the country, gradually looking at things I had been told were trivial as well as those generally considered significant. Moving to Berkeley in 1971 furthered the process. At a time when most colleagues regarded studying commercial architecture, especially that of the recent past, as sheer nonsense, I received insight and encouragement from John Beach, David Gebhard, and J. B. Jackson.

Few people possess both the great range of interests in the built environment and the depth of perception that were characteristic of John Beach. Through him I finally understood LA. David Gebhard opened many doors, conceptually, for myself and for a generation of architects, historians, and the lay public. His contribution to our understanding of California architecture is inestimable. His untimely death, like John's a decade ago, is a great professional as well as personal loss. Brinck Jackson has revealed the imperative of understanding things so commonplace as to be taken for granted and of doing so with a minimum of polemical baggage. His example has been a constant reminder that the modern metropolis is a significant part of our culture and our history. Once this project was under way, Brinck and David were both supportive in many ways, but I owe a special debt to Robert Winter for insisting that this project become a history of Los Angeles when I was making an exploratory probe of the subject in 1986. For these reasons, among others, I dedicate this book to them.

Many people have provided assistance along the way. Robert Bruegmann, Howard Gillette, Thomas Hines, Chester Liebs, and Dell Upton read an early draft and offered numerous valuable suggestions for its improvement—advice that I hope is reflected in the revisions. Ed Whittington facilitated my efforts in many ways, including permitting me to examine his vast collection of negatives—perhaps the single largest pictorial resource for the city—while they were housed in the library at California State University, Long Beach, prior to their deposit at the University of Southern California's special collections. Brent Howell of Coldwell Banker gave me introductions to a number of senior members of the real estate community, which proved invaluable to understanding the intricacies of postwar commercial development.

The architects, developers, planners, real estate brokers, and others who permitted me to interview them offered insights that would have been impossible to glean otherwise. I am thus indebted to Eaton Ballard, Howard B. Drollinger, Joseph Eichenbaum, Albert Frey, the late Regula Fybel, the late Frederick Gutheim, Calvin Hamilton, the late S. Charles Lee, Walter Leimert, Jr., Philip Lyon, William McAdam, Fred Marlow, A. C. Martin, Jr., Ben Schwartz, Bill Symonds, and Julian Whittlesey. The late Robert Alexander, the late Pietro Belluschi, and Whitney Smith were kind enough to respond to my questions through correspondence.

Many others have helped in ways too numerous to mention: Carson Anderson, Scott Bottles, Kenneth Breisch, Lauren Weiss Bricker, David Cameron, Meredith Clausen, Margaret Crawford, David De Long, William Scott Field, Douglas Gomery, Thomas Hanchett, Greg Hise, Preston Kaufmann, Steven Levin, Christy McAvoy, Brita Mack, Megs Merriwether, Frank Mittlebach, the late Dione Neutra, Tom Owen, K. C. Parsons, Anna Pehoushek, Eric Sandweiss, Richard and Sarah Striner, Dace Taube, Michael Tomlan, Richard Wagner, Mary Jo Winder, and David Zeidberg. Kenneth Caldwell of A. C. Martin Associates, Vicki Cwiok of Sears Merchandise Group, Lee Fowler and Barbara Barrickman of the J. C. Nichols Company, Stuart Lottman of Gruen Associates, Dana Prettyman of Bullock's Pasadena, and Shirley Wilson of I. Magnin allowed me access to material in company archives.

I am grateful to the staffs of the many institutions in which my research was conducted. Without the vast collections of the Library of Congress—including those in the Geography and Maps, Newspapers and Current Periodicals, and Prints and Photographs divisions—the task would have been far more difficult, time-consuming, and expensive. In southern California, the Los Angeles Public Library, the Los Angeles Municipal Library, the Sever Center at the Los Angeles County Museum of Natural History, and several libraries each at the University of Southern California and the University of California, Los Angeles, were major sources. Others in the region include the public libraries of Anaheim, Beverly Hills, Culver City, Glendale, Inglewood, Long Beach, Pasadena, Palos Verdes, and Santa Ana as well as the Huntington Library, and the Architectural Drawing Collection at the University of California, Santa Barbara. Elsewhere, the special collections at Cornell University's library and the public libraries of Jenkintown, Pennsylvania, Greenwich, Connecticut, New Rochelle, New York, and Philadelphia were utilized.

The stock at the Book Castle in Burbank allowed me to acquire original copies of the Los Angeles Times, *without which many of the illustrations in this book would have been impossible to use.*

The initial trip to Los Angeles for this study was underwritten by the National Main Street Center of the National Trust for Historic Preservation. Lectures at the Foundation for San Francisco's Architectural Heritage, California State University at San Luis Obispo, Southern California Institute of Architecture, and UCLA facilitated additional trips. Generous funding for the illustrations and other facets of my research was provided by several grants from George Washington University.

Time spent in southern California was greatly enhanced by the hospitality of friends, including Kenneth Breisch and Judy Keller, David Cameron, John and Nadine Dillon, the late Hans and Regula Fybel, the late David Gebhard, Thomas Hines, Tom Owen, Gene Waddell, and Robert Winter. Randell Makinson and Edward Bosley, directors of the Gamble House, greatly facilitated the project by allowing me to reside at that remarkable dwelling on several occasions. Time there helped me keep a balanced perspective and gave respite. Caesar, J.J., and other staff

at the Pantry restaurant ensured an abundance of good food and humor as a routine part of my visits.

I am grateful to Roger Conover and his staff at the MIT Press, most especially Matthew Abbate and James McWethy, for the care they have lavished on the manuscript and for making the whole production process a pleasure.

My father, Thaddeus Longstreth, as always has been enthusiastic and encouraging. My wife, Cinda, and daughter, Elizabeth, have been more than tolerant throughout a decade of research and writing, particularly since they do not share my interest in LA.

ACKNOWLEDGMENTS

xii

INTRODUCTION

The emergence of major business centers in multiple locations within metropolitan areas represents one of the most significant changes to the structure of settlement in the United States during the twentieth century. Large concentrations of offices, stores, and other businesses far removed from the traditional urban core, often in places that supported little development before, have profoundly affected both the shape of the land and the routine patterns of social interaction. "Suburb" in any traditional sense of the term carries little meaning in this context, for workplace no less than homeplace is likely to lie some distance from established locales of a generation ago. Moreover, movement from residence to places of employment and shopping is now seldom from outskirts toward the center but rather in multiple directions, crisscrossing the metropolitan area. Much commented on in recent years, the trend has generated reactions ranging from advocacy to derision.[1] However the results are viewed, there can be no question that the modern metropolis is very different from that of even a half-century ago and that these changes will have a basic impact for decades to come.

The creation of major retail centers on the urban periphery after World War II lay in the forefront of this business dispersal, pioneering locations as well as locational techniques subsequently used for other, more diverse forms of business development. Large new retail complexes were the first to challenge the hegemony of downtown functions, attracting a sizable share of the public away from the core on a regular basis.[2] While

retail decentralization took many forms, the key component was the regional shopping center, which was planned to operate as a unified business entity and provide an alternative to major established marketplaces, including downtown.[3] Without the orchestrated gathering of emporia found at a regional center, it is not clear that many outlying business districts would have gained the critical mass of stores necessary to compete with the quantity and range of outlets in the urban core.

When the regional shopping center became a primary thrust of commercial development nationwide during the 1950s and 1960s, it seemed an invention of the postwar era that had little precedent. Prior to the war, downtown had been the major destination for all but routine shopping needs in the great majority of American cities. The new regional center, by contrast, lay near the periphery, well removed from established local business areas and often set apart even from new residential tracts. The regional center's siting was defined by acres of space for cars, the polar opposite of the highly restricted confines of the core. At the same time, most regional centers were inward-looking, with stores oriented to a sequestered pedestrian way, a mall, that invited a quiet, leisurely pace. The regional center was clean and neatly maintained; it was new, sporting a cool, nonreferential modernist vocabulary; it lacked vehicular congestion, jostling crowds, street noise, the "wrong" social elements, and crime—all departures from qualities associated with downtown. The regional center was a bastion of middle-class ingenuity, respectability, and order; it was touted as a cure for the purportedly ailing condition and antiquated arrangement of the core.

But neither the regional center nor the tendencies that propelled it into the limelight manifested themselves in the span of just a few years. Shifts in residential development, consumer, and merchandising patterns, and corresponding trends in planning retail enclaves and in creating major destinations far afield from the city center, had begun decades earlier. The origins of the regional shopping center and, with it, of modern metropolitan structure lie not with sudden radical change in a few conspicuous arenas, but rather with numerous changes, some abrupt, many others gradual, that over time established significant new directions. This book examines that process, focusing on three decades of formative development, from 1920 to 1950. Only through scrutiny of these origins can the major shifts of the postwar period be understood.

In analyzing the emergence of the regional center, I have avoided a study of architectural typology in the usual sense, in part because these complexes are defined less by a fixed set of physical attributes than by ones of ownership, management, tenancy, and merchandising. Even more importantly, the broader context of urban retail development is essential to understanding how and why the regional center became such a significant phenomenon during the second half of the twentieth century. The climax and decline of downtown as the dominant shopping district and the rise of myriad subordinate forms in outlying areas figure significantly in this equation, as does the nature of residential growth and consumer mobility.

The emergence of the regional center examined as an integral part of urban growth and change reveals no neat, linear sequence of events. Numerous parties were involved—retailers, real estate developers, architects, and planners among them—for a variety of reasons, some of them conflicting. Locating outside the city center was often seen as a highly risky venture, and was propelled as much by reaction to competing interests as it was by the aim of taking new directions. Views about how a new shopping district should be developed and what its basic character should be differed to a considerable extent. Innovation could be deferred, even subsumed, by a persistent conservatism. Features that might appear vestigial could continue with remarkable tenacity. At the same time, a combination of features that might seem inevitable in retrospect occurred only through unanticipated intermediaries. The emergence of the regional center in a sense describes the process of city building itself.

The complexity of the subject resists a broad study, covering cities in the United States generally. Furthermore, during the formative decades prior to the 1950s, the nature and timing of events differed significantly from one major city to another. Profiles of Chicago, New York, Boston, and Philadelphia are marked as much by singularity as by commonality. To provide the level of detail that does the subject justice and to afford a perspective with more than local implications, I have focused on Los Angeles as a case study.

The choice was not difficult. Los Angeles is unusually fertile ground for inquiry on several counts. No other city came close to doing so much so early and so often to spur the transformation from the downtown core to the regional center. In 1900, Los Angeles's retail structure remained highly centralized. Beginning some two decades later, the upstart metropolis far exceeded others in the range of innovative approaches to outlying retail development, the scale at which many of these trends matured at an early date, and the cumulative effect of these changes on the urban landscape. At the same time, Los Angeles gave ample evidence of resistance to change, such as partiality to traditional streetfront orientation of buildings and disdain of conspicuous parking lots, that shaped practices into the mid-twentieth century. Such attitudes help explain why southern California was not to be the foremost proving ground for the mall as the organizing component of the regional center, even though in preceding developments it often set the pace nationally.

Los Angeles begs attention for another reason. By 1930, this metropolis not only ranked among the largest in the United States but also began to be recognized as a harbinger of the modern American city. In recent years, a growing corpus of scholars has examined Los Angeles's role as a prototype for the American metropolis of the late twentieth century.[4] No better demonstration of this role exists than in the retail sphere, where between the 1920s and 1950s Los Angeles functioned much as Chicago or New York had for the development of the tall commercial building. Correlating the study of place with that of retail development is important if the circumstances under which Los Angeles served as an incubator for new

ideas in the field are to be understood. Furthermore, most historical studies of how the automobile has affected the landscape imply, at least, that the process was un- or even anti-urban, ultimately leading to decline and decay in the city. Such characterizations, however, ignore the inherently urban circumstances affecting change in the commercial sphere. Los Angeles reveals that the automobile was not an isolated cause but one of several factors that contributed to a recasting of metropolitan form rather than to its destruction.

The extent to which the region functioned as a crucible for innovative approaches to retail development becomes clear only when placed in national perspective. Key innovations and general trends elsewhere in the United States thus form an essential part of my framework, particularly in chapters devoted to the shopping center. I have devoted space to seminal shopping center developments in the Boston, Chicago, Kansas City, Seattle, and Washington areas, among others, because they help clarify how southern California often was, and sometimes was not, on the front line of new conceptual approaches.

The appeal of Los Angeles as a case study is matched by the challenge. The city is among the least researched of major American centers, a situation that is only somewhat less glaring today than it was in 1900 or 1950. No less a challenge is the fact that mythmaking has been endemic to Los Angeles for over a century. Boosters and detractors alike have spun such a rich tapestry of lore that the imagination often has overwhelmed reality in depicting the city's past and in molding its sense of identity.[5] The city has few solid histories. Journalistic critiques, some of which are as sophisticated as they are engaging, frequently are taken as substitutes, even though they may rely heavily on vignettes and assumptions. An underlying thesis of many such accounts is that Los Angeles is not a real city, that its urbanism is "counterfeit," as Mike Davis has recently reminded us.[6] Even admiring chroniclers tend to portray the city as being so different as to be an anomaly. Intellectuals along with purveyors of popular descriptions, novels, and films have long typecast Los Angeles as a curious, eccentric place.

I have tried to focus on historical realities instead. I do not speculate as to whether the forces that shaped Los Angeles during the first half of the twentieth century were inherently detrimental or otherwise. Likewise, I avoid qualitative debate over the basic attributes of the shopping center, which also has received scant historical study while attracting much commentary and criticism outside the business arena.[7] My concern lies with taking both city and shopping center as serious subjects of inquiry, so that value judgments may be founded on understanding rather than on presumption and prejudice.[8] Just as Los Angeles is one of the major population, business, and cultural centers of the nation, so retail development is a key indicator of urban form and identity. No other single component of the city attracts so many people so frequently and for so many reasons. No other more frankly reveals current attitudes toward public assembly and decorum. No other so clearly reflects change in both market conditions and

consumer taste. No other embodies more fully the unyielding impact of motor vehicles on the landscape.

I have concentrated on the physical dimension and the economic factors that directly influenced retail development as a foundation for broader inquiry. Too often, sweeping cultural generalizations are offered without a solid grasp of the actual places that both shape and are shaped by human values. Most of the printed sources on which I have relied possess some kind of business orientation—to architecture, to urban planning and development, to real estate practice, and to retailing. Yet I have attempted to maintain sufficient balance to delineate an accurate historical picture. Fieldwork made an essential contribution to this perspective. During the course of this study, I drove some 5,000 miles within the Los Angeles basin to examine both buildings and the urban fabric that helps give them meaning.

The subject does not lend itself to a strict architectural, urban, or business history in the traditional sense of those terms. Instead, I have sought to integrate these spheres. Social and cultural factors are introduced when possible, though I have exercised caution in this realm, owing to the difficulties of accurately portraying complex and often elusive issues. An account that transcends assumptions and that documents in detail how retail development relates to people's lives, habits, values, and attitudes toward community will require at least as much research as I have undertaken in laying some groundwork here.

To do justice to the complexity of the subject and at the same time achieve an acceptable level of coherence, I have organized the text more or less chronologically, modifying the structure somewhat to give adequate emphasis to type and to district.

Chapter 1 affords an overview of Los Angeles's rise as a major metropolis during the early twentieth century. Chapter 2 analyzes the importance of downtown Los Angeles, in both functional and symbolic terms. After delineating how the city's major department stores helped define the modern city center, the chapter focuses on the building boom of the 1920s, which at once strengthened downtown's importance and led to the growth of outlying centers.

Chapter 3 examines the initial stage of decentralization prior to and just after World War I, when development was small in scale and localized in orientation, supplementing rather than competing with downtown. Chapter 4 addresses what was then often viewed as the next logical step, chronicling the rise of Hollywood during the 1920s as the region's first major outlying business center, one that sought to replicate downtown in its basic form while surpassing it in retail function. Chapter 5 is devoted to the growth of new commercial districts along Wilshire Boulevard during the late 1920s and 1930s, which introduced the idea of building in the center of residential areas while selecting sites easily accessible to the motorist. By this means, the Wilshire precincts challenged Hollywood's bid for supremacy and to a significant degree succeeded within a remarkably short span of time.

Chapter 6 introduces the shopping center as an integrated business development, a place where control was a paramount concern and which eschewed metropolitan allusions. After tracing the type's origins as a component of comprehensively planned elite residential enclaves, the chapter examines how, beginning in the late 1920s, the shopping center became a more independent and consequential factor in urban growth as a compelling alternative to the Hollywood and Wilshire models.

The problem of accommodating large numbers of automobiles in retail districts is discussed in most of the previous chapters but is the focus of the next. On the eve of World War II, Beverly Hills illustrated how the best planned of campaigns to meet motorists' needs in a retail district failed due to the problems inherent in orchestrating change among a multitude of property owners. Concurrently, a more feasible course was charted at modest, locally oriented shopping centers, setting a key precedent for practices in the postwar era.

Chapter 8 discusses the decline of the city center during the 1930s and 1940s, attempts to bolster downtown, and circumstances that made reversing the downward trend so difficult. While competition from outlying districts contributed to the situation, significant problems were posed by the size, arrangement, and density of the core itself.

Chapter 9 turns to the postwar period, examining the factors that spawned a new wave of retail development in outlying areas, unprecedented in its extent, and why the regional shopping center lay at the forefront of this program. Experimental in nature, these complexes seemed wholly new in location, character, and arrangement. Yet they were marked by a strong, persistent conservatism as well, driven perhaps more by habit than by conscious efforts to retain ties to the past.

Chapter 10 backtracks to discuss the origins of an alternative approach that oriented retail complexes to a pedestrian mall. This approach had little appeal during the interwar decades save for specialty stores. The mall was resisted as a component of shopping centers; only through the unusual circumstances of federal sponsorship during the late 1930s and early 1940s were prototypical examples realized.

The last chapter examines the tentative acceptance of the mall in business circles during the late 1940s, thence its meteoric rise as the optimal solution for large-scale undertakings. The prevailing attitude in Los Angeles was cautious at first; what could have been pacesetting designs never materialized. The first to be constructed in the region drew from examples elsewhere. Thereafter, beginning in the mid-1950s, acceptance was rapid and widespread.

Like many studies that focus on neglected subjects, this book cannot begin to be definitive. Its ultimate value may lie in the questions it raises concerning both the seminal period it addresses and how the results have contributed to the sweeping changes in metropolitan growth patterns during the second half of the twentieth century. At a time when "sprawl" is becoming a code word for urban ills, much as "congestion" and "overcrowding" were two generations ago, we need to be careful not to condemn

in wholesale fashion the environment created in recent decades.[9] My argument is not to defend all that has been developed in the recent past, nor is it against current strategies for change, but only that we should not repeat the mistake of previous generations who dismissed cities of the nineteenth and early twentieth centuries as wastelands. Only through understanding the modern metropolis can our choices for the future be informed, rational, and productive.

M A P S

MAP 1

Los Angeles metropolitan area. "1920 Motor Map of Los Angeles Vicinity," Touring Guide Publishing Company, 1920.

(Geography and Maps Division, Library of Congress)

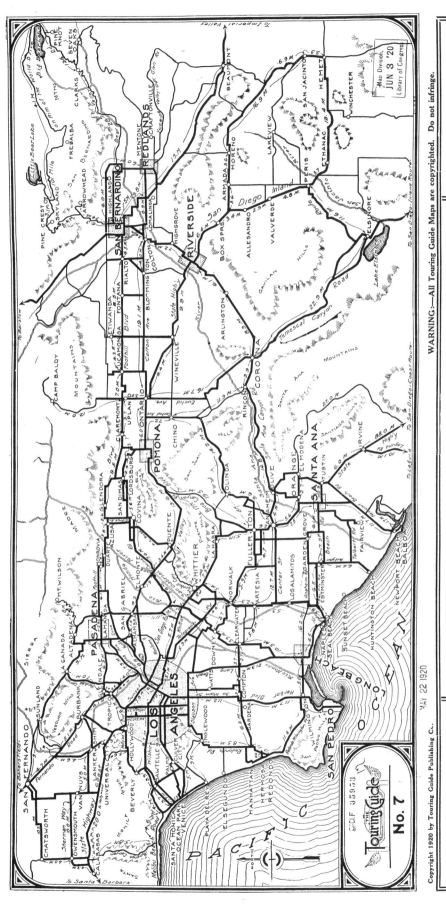

There is a series of Maps showing California Highways in detail. There is one Map showing the entire State. Throughout the West you will find a series of TOURING GUIDE Maps. They are always FREE. In using them, bear in mind that they are made for you at the expense of our advertisers. This is their way of rendering service to you and of seeking your patronage.

Copyright 1920 by Touring Guide Publishing Co..   MAY 22 1920

1920 MOTOR MAP
—OF—
Los Angeles Vicinity

All TOURING GUIDE Maps are FREE when obtained from any of our advertisers, but owing to the ever increasing demand for them, all requests sent us by mail must be accompanied by 10 cents for each Map desired.

© CLF 359-53

The Touring Guide

No. 7

Major downtown department stores as of 1900 (dark gray) and 1920 (light gray).

(Geography and Maps Division, Library of Congress)

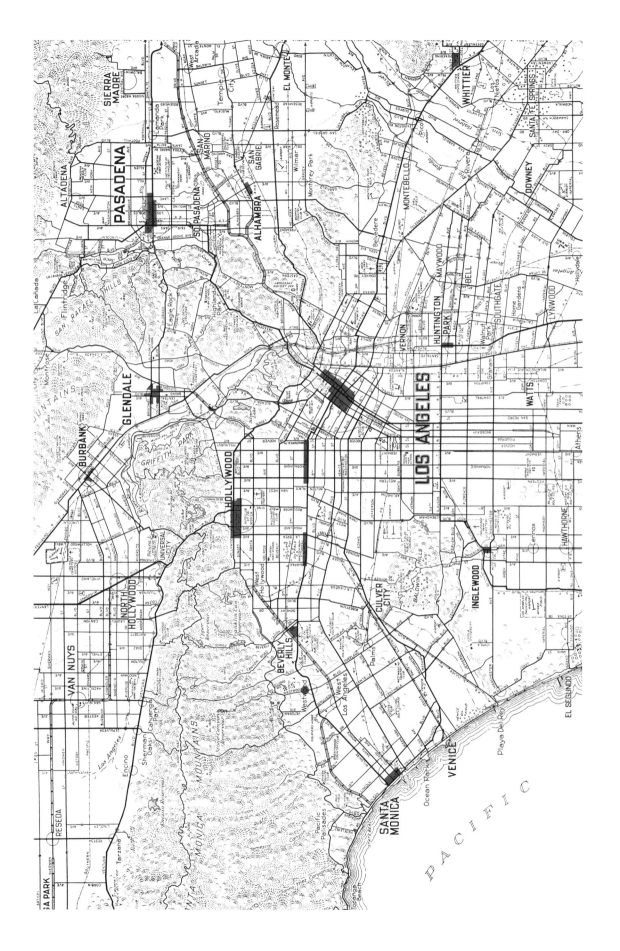

Branches of major downtown department stores (dark gray) and Sears, Roebuck stores (black) operating or under construction in the Los Angeles metropolitan area as of 1950. Based on "Automobile Road Map of Metropolitan Los Angeles," Automobile Club of Southern California, ca. 1931.

(Geography and Maps Division, Library of Congress)

MAP 5

xxx

Regional shopping centers built in the Los Angeles metropolitan area between 1945 and 1960. Based on "Map of Los Angeles County and Vicinity, California," Map Company of America, 1959.

(Geography and Maps Division, Library of Congress)

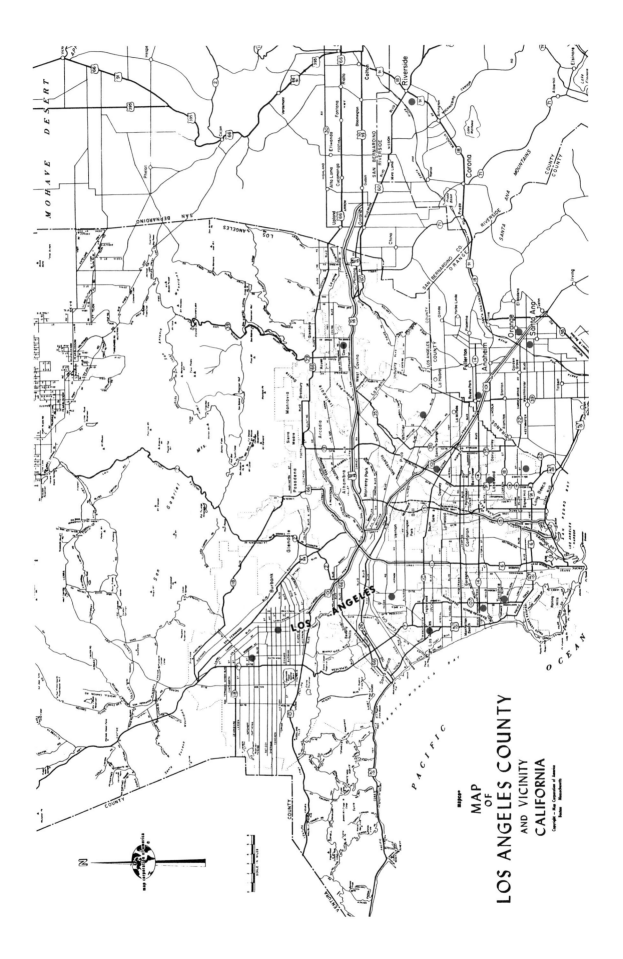

MAP
OF
LOS ANGELES COUNTY
AND VICINITY
CALIFORNIA

CITY CENTER TO REGIONAL MALL

I

THE PERILS OF A PARKLESS TOWN

In February 1920 the Los Angeles City Council was about to act on as pressing a matter as it had faced in recent years: traffic congestion. The commercial center was inundated with automobiles to the point that movement through its streets was severely impaired, especially during the late afternoon rush period. The solution the council sought to implement was to ban curbside parking in the core area for most of the day and limit parking time to one hour along surrounding blocks. Proponents of this ordinance charged that while the percentage of the main business district's automobile commuters was small, they created havoc for the great majority of citizens, who still came by streetcar. The ordinance was intended to allow trolleys to move freely again and spur the development of off-street parking facilities for the prosperous minority who drove.[1]

The measure passed, but some of its critics remained skeptical about the effects. Among the most vocal opposition came from the *Los Angeles Times,* which forecast in a piece entitled "The Perils of a Parkless Town" that the ordinance would do nothing short of revolutionize the city's growth patterns (figure 1). Many shoppers and workers alike depended upon automobiles. If they were prevented from using their cars, they would take their business elsewhere. The tone was ominous:

Big mercantile establishments, to cater to automobile-using shoppers, banned by the ordinance . . . , are already being arranged for in Hollywood, on Wilshire Boulevard, and other sections outside the no-parking area. The city's old "main business district" will be supplemented . . . by half a dozen smaller but otherwise similar districts in all parts of the city. The "congested area" will become a thing of the past.

Editorial Section
VIEWS, NEWS, PICTURES.

Los Angeles Sunday Times

Part II: 16 Pages
THE CITY AND SUBURBS.

VOL. XXXIX. SUNDAY MORNING, FEBRUARY 29, 1920. POPULATION { By the City Directory—(1920)—671,000 / By the Federal Census—(1910)—319,198

THE PERILS OF A PARKLESS TOWN.

Law Barring Standing Autos on Downtown Streets will Create New Shopping and Theater Districts, Jam Street Cars to Impossible Point and Hurt Trade.

In the view of experts who have made a careful study of the situation, the no-parking ordinance, which will go into effect six weeks hence, will work a revolution in the manner of Los Angeles' growth.

It will inevitably force the creation of new shopping districts outside the present congested area. Big mercantile establishments to cater to automobile-using shoppers, banned by the ordinance from downtown, are already being arranged for in Hollywood, on Wilshire boulevard and other sections outside the no-parking area. The city's old "main business district" will be supplemented, as in New York, by half a dozen smaller but otherwise similar districts in all parts of the city. The "congested area" will become a thing of the past.

Similarly, a second theater district will arise outside the no-parking areas to cater to the matinee crowds, who customarily leave their cars downtown while attending the afternoon show but who will be prevented from so doing by the new law. As in the case of stores, these new theaters will have the advantage of cheaper sites, but will be in no wise inferior to the present big Broadway playhouses. Such theaters are already in contemplation. In each case, the patronage of the outside stores and show houses will represent net loss to the present ones.

Of the immediate effects of the ordinance, the following are noteworthy:

ON THE STREET CARS.

The 30,000 autos, which daily park in the to-be-forbidden area represent 82,500 people, who will be forced to do one of three things: Stay at home, leave their cars outside the no-parking area (thereby creating as much congestion on its edges as now exists downtown) and walk in or take the street cars, or use the street cars all the way from home. In any case the big load will fall on the street cars. To the man familiar with the present congestion of our street cars, not only in the rush hours but most of the time, the addition of 80,000 passengers each way is an appalling prospect. The car company plans to add more cars and run them faster. How many cars and how much faster will be necessary to accommodate 80,000 more people than now hang on by their eyebrows? Can they do it? Question! The projected rerouting of the street cars, which may be expected to help out some, cannot be put into effect before May 1, the railway officials say.

When thousands of cars are parked a mile or so from their respective owners' places of business or visiting, the auto-stealer's trade is expected to boom. Several big storage garages planned for downtown locations will care for a thousand cars or so and the rest will stand out, far from their drivers' eye.

The taxi business, representing about $60,000 income a year, will be driven out of the downtown area, to the grave loss of the stand-owners and the serious inconvenience of the public.

The police courts will be flooded with cases of unfortunate drivers who accidentally stopped for more than two minutes in the forbidden area.

There is, finally, no question but that the law will relieve downtown congestion, but it will do it on the same principle by which there was no congestion in the Los Angeles streets of 1870.

All of which are some of the reasons why 15,000 people have so far signed the referendum petition against the no-parking law.

HOLLYWOOD DEPT. STORE.

While details of his project are not as yet available for publication, a wealthy eastern merchandiser who retired from business and came to Southern California a few years ago is now planning to build in Hollywood at once a department store which he says will be the equal of anything in the city.

The promoter of this project has a four-acre site, well located, and he plans to put up a store building which will cover about one acre, reserving the other three acres for parking space. It is his intention to maintain a regular auto-checking system. Customers can glide up in their cars, step out, and turn their machines over to experienced chauffeurs, who will remove them to the parking area, and drive them back to the store entrance upon call. The backer of the plan believes that such a store in Hollywood will catch the bulk of the worth-while motor-driving patronage in the Wilshire, Westlake, Hollywood and southwestern districts.

OTHER MOVES.

Willard George, the furrier, and Eddie Schmidt, the tailor, are already planning to move their stocks of goods from the business district of the city, where they have long been located, to new stores on Wilshire boulevard. Mr. George expresses the opinion that Wilshire boulevard is destined to be another Fifth avenue, and he plans to get in on the ground floor.

The disintegrating effect of the no-parking ordinance upon the business district is also reflected in the fact that at least two new and pretentious theaters for Sunset boulevard are already being planned. The Little Theater on Figueroa, just south of Pico, which has long been dark, has just been leased by Frank Egan and opened as a stock house, with splendid prospects for patronage.

Another shift from the congested business district is that which has just been made by Madame Piche Wood, the milliner. She has long been established at 704 West Seventh street, and now she is opening up a second store at 1721 West Seventh, near the corner of Seventh and Burlington.

One and two-story business blocks in great number have been springing up in the outlying districts with startling rapidity in recent weeks. There are many good reasons why stores are being established at some distance from downtown Los Angeles just now. Sites are much cheaper and the no-parking ordinance is quite generally expected to act as a business scattering agency of great potency.

WHERE WILL AUTOS GO?

The disposition of the 30,000 or more automobiles now parked in the business district of the city every day between 9 a.m. and 4:30 p.m. is a grave phase of the problem.

It is true that hundreds of machines are now parked each day on the hilly streets northwest from Pershing Square, and yet there is a limit to the parking capacity of those thoroughfares, and the overflow will naturally have to go elsewhere. It can't well go beyond Pico, nor beyond San Pedro street, nor can it get inside those limits because, at the present time, with the vast amount of parking on Broadway, Hill, Spring, Main and their downtown cross-streets, the parked cars extend clear to Ninth on the south and San Pedro on the east.

Some relief will be afforded by the construction of gigantic storage garages within the business district. Last year the first garage of this sort was erected at the corner of Fourth and Olive streets by the Clark Hotel management. It is so situated on a side hill that machines can drive in off the inclines of two streets onto all four floors, and a runway from the fourth floor affords access to the roof, where machines are washed and repaired, as well as parked in case of emergency. This garage accommodates about 375 machines.

Another building of this type is soon to be erected at the southeast corner of Fifth street and Grand avenue by the Grand Central Garage Company, at a cost of $650,000. It will be 168x180 feet, with eight floors for storing automobiles. Five floors of the building will be accessible from the two streets, and the others can be reached by runways from the fifth floor. The building will be capable of housing 1082 cars, all of which can reach their stalls on their own power. For the accommodation of patrons passenger elevators will be installed.

Perhaps it will ultimately be necessary for automobilists to leave their cars in their garages at home and form themselves into neighborhood roller skating clubs. There might, before long, come into popular use here a power-driven roller skate of the Henry Ford type, which would come so near solving the problem that citizens would be seen coming up Broadway ten and twenty abreast, on their way to office and store, blithely singing "Merrily We Roll Along, Roll Along, Roll Along," and then, but not till then, would the "old skates" make their appearance on Broadway again.

If somebody would invent a tin lizzard that could be folded up and swung on the arm like some of these baby perambulators the women folk carry with them on shopping trips the auto parking problem could be solved before church time today, but it looks now as though nothing but power skates will save Los Angeles from the stupidity of her City Council.

Should roller skates come into sudden popularity their users would not dare to leave them on the streets, because of the no-parking ordinance, and the prevalence of automobile thieves, but the safety deposit boxes of local banks suggest a maximum of safety and convenience at a minimum cost. Most of them are just about the right size to house a pair of roller skates.

THE PASSENGER PROBLEM.

Can the street railway handle twice a day the majority of the people who are now parking their machines down town? Figuring that 60,000 of them will ride the street cars each way the street car company will have 120,000 extra passengers to handle each day. Can it do it? R. B. Hill, superintendent of operation for the Los Angeles Railway, says it can. A lot of business men in this city say it can't by any stretch of the imagination, adding that it can't adequately handle even the present traffic.

Supt. Hill contends that when the autos get out of the way his com-

(Continued on Tenth Page.)

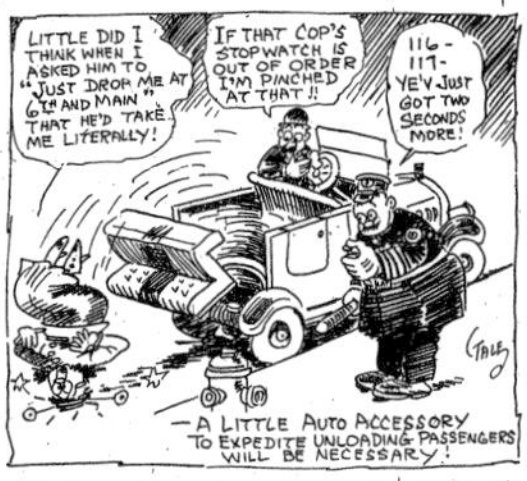
LITTLE DID I THINK WHEN I ASKED HIM TO "JUST DROP ME AT 6TH AND MAIN" THAT HE'D TAKE ME LITERALLY!
IF THAT COP'S STOPWATCH IS OUT OF ORDER I'M PINCHED AT THAT!!
116-117- YE'V JUST GOT TWO SECONDS MORE!
GALE
—A LITTLE AUTO ACCESSORY TO EXPEDITE UNLOADING PASSENGERS WILL BE NECESSARY!

A Few Little Prophecies for Los Angeles on and After April 10 Next.

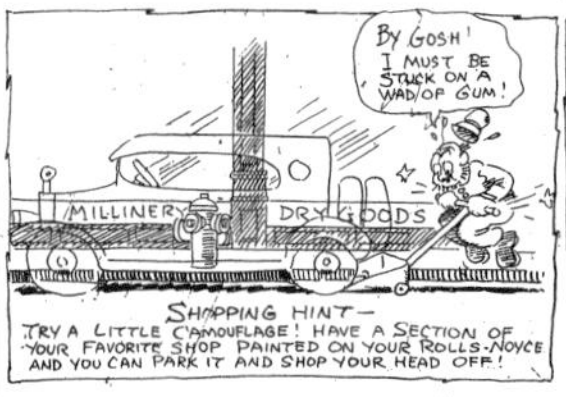
BY GOSH! I MUST BE STUCK ON A WAD OF GUM!
MILLINERY
DRY GOODS
SHOPPING HINT—
TRY A LITTLE CAMOUFLAGE! HAVE A SECTION OF YOUR FAVORITE SHOP PAINTED ON YOUR ROLLS-NOYCE AND YOU CAN PARK IT AND SHOP YOUR HEAD OFF!

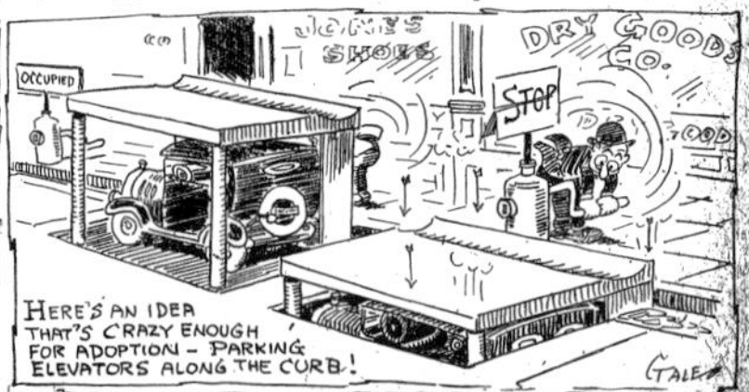
OCCUPIED
SHOES
DRY GOODS CO.
STOP
HERE'S AN IDEA THAT'S CRAZY ENOUGH FOR ADOPTION - PARKING ELEVATORS ALONG THE CURB!
GALE

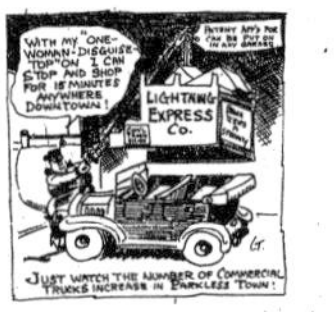
WITH MY "ONE-WOMAN-DISGUISE-TOP" ON I CAN STOP AND SHOP FOR 15 MINUTES ANYWHERE DOWNTOWN!
LIGHTNING EXPRESS CO.
JUST WATCH THE NUMBER OF COMMERCIAL TRUCKS INCREASE IN PARKLESS TOWN!

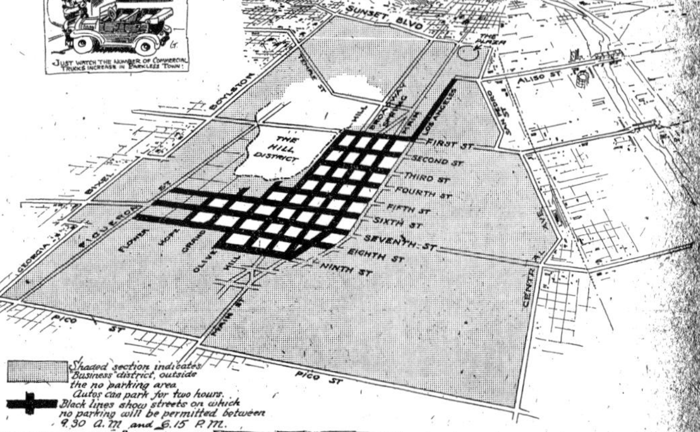
SUNSET BLVD
THE PLAZA
ALISO ST
BOYLSTON
TEMPLE ST
THE HILL DISTRICT
HILL
BROADWAY
SPRING
MAIN
LOS ANGELES
SAN PEDRO ST
FIRST ST
SECOND ST
THIRD ST
FOURTH ST
FIFTH ST
SIXTH ST
SEVENTH ST
EIGHTH ST
NINTH ST
BIXEL
FIGUEROA
GEORGIA
FLOWER
HOPE
GRAND
OLIVE
HILL
MAIN ST
CENTRAL AVE
PICO ST
Shaded section indicates "Business" district, outside the no parking area. Autos can park for two hours.
Black lines show streets on which no parking will be permitted between 9.30 A.M. and 6.15 P.M.

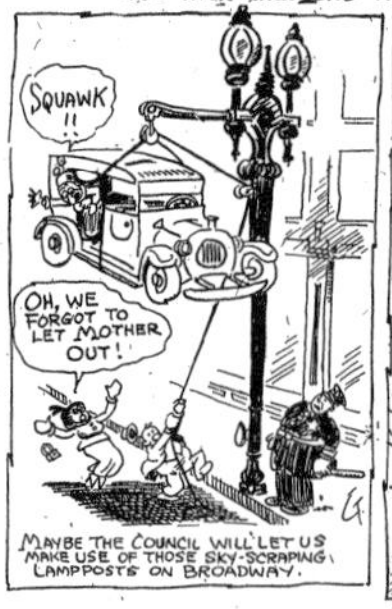
SQUAWK !!
OH, WE FORGOT TO LET MOTHER OUT!
MAYBE THE COUNCIL WILL LET US MAKE USE OF THOSE SKY-SCRAPING LAMPPOSTS ON BROADWAY.

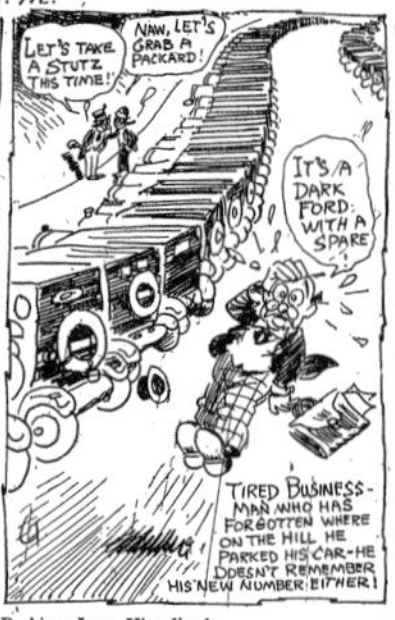
LET'S TAKE A STUTZ THIS TIME!
NAW, LET'S GRAB A PACKARD!
IT'S A DARK FORD WITH A SPARE
TIRED BUSINESS-MAN WHO HAS FORGOTTEN WHERE ON THE HILL HE PARKED HIS CAR-HE DOESN'T REMEMBER HIS NEW NUMBER EITHER!

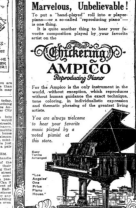

Our New Anti-Automobile-Parking Law Visualized.

The map, drawn by Charles H. Owens, shows at a glance where you may not park at all, where you are allowed to leave your car for two hours and where you must leave it if you expect to do more than two hours' work before returning to it. The sketches, by Gale, are only a few of the things which may happen.

HERE'S THE NO-PARKING LAW.

The no-parking ordinance, effective April 10, creates three circles in what is known as downtown Los Angeles. In what is known as the congested district—the area embraced by Main, Spring, Broadway and Hill streets, from First to Ninth streets—automobiles cannot park between 11 a.m. and 6:15 p.m., certain areas of the hill regions being excepted. Outside this congested district, and within the business district proper, which is bounded on the north by Sunset boulevard, on the east by San Pedro street and Central avenue, on the south by Pico street, and on the west by Georgia, Bixel and Boylston streets, the automobile owner can park his car for two hours at a stretch without being cited into police court. Anywhere outside the boundary of the so-called business district it will be safe to park an auto till the cows come home, providing auto thieves don't happen along.

The new ordinance prohibits the use of the left-hand turn during the no-parking hours at the Fifth, Sixth and Seventh-street crossings of Main, Spring, Broadway and Hill street.

Commercial deliveries are to be made from alleys whenever conditions permit.

The new styles this spring as developed by our artists and craftsmen are fascinating in their charming lines and beautiful finish. Concealed in them is a wonderful ease and comfort, and a serviceability given only by REEDCRAFT.

Our trade mark guides the way to supreme furniture satisfaction. REEDCRAFT is sold only at our shop, 939 So. Broadway.

THE REEDCRAFT CO.

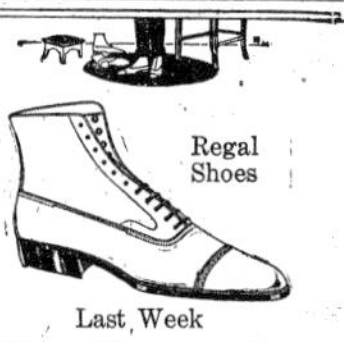
Regal Shoes

Last Week
After-Inventory Sale
High Shoes, Oxfords and Pumps
For Men, Women and Children at Extreme Reductions
Values $10.00 to $18.00
Now $7.85 to $12.85
Reductions are up to one-half less than present values.
You get "Regal" Shoes, standardized in price and quality, of national reputation, at extraordinary reductions.

All styles in the smaller sizes at Third and Broadway Store only.	$3.85
Men's 4½ to 7½.	and
Women's 2½ to 4½.	$4.85

Store at 3rd and Broadway open Saturdays until 10 p.m.
AGENCY REGAL SHOES
VAN DEGRIFT'S
802 SOUTH BROADWAY
224 W. THIRD STREET
749 SOUTH BROADWAY
Standard and Finest Footwear for Men, Women and Children.

ESTABLISHED 1880
FRANK J. HART SOUTHERN CALIFORNIA MUSIC COMPANY
332-334 SOUTH BROADWAY, LOS ANGELES.

Marvelous, Unbelievable!
To put a "hand-played" roll into a player-piano—or a so-called "reproducing piano"—is one thing.
It is quite another thing to hear your favorite composition played by your favorite artist on the
Chickering
AMPICO
Reproducing Piano
For the Ampico is the only instrument in the world, without exception, which reproduces without human guidance the exact technique, tone coloring, in individualistic expression and thematic phrasing of the greatest living artists.
You are always welcome to hear your favorite music played by a noted pianist at this store.
Easy Terms Arranged
"Los Angeles' One Price Piano House."

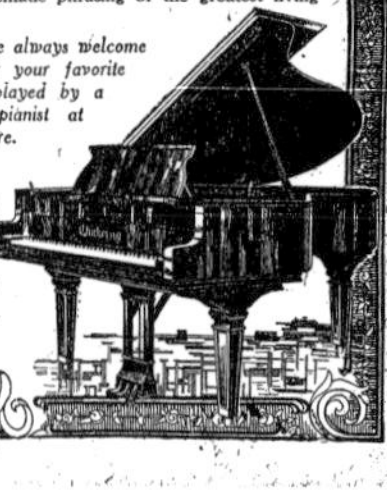

Similarly, a second theater district will arise outside the no-parking area to cater to the matinee crowds, who customarily leave their cars downtown while attending the afternoon show. . . . These new theaters will have the advantage of cheaper sites, but will be in no wise inferior to the present big Broadway [in Los Angeles] playhouses. Such theaters are already in contemplation.[2]

The enormous investment represented by downtown real estate would, in short, be devastated—a dire prediction at a time when most Angelenos, like other Americans, believed that the very essence of the city in symbol and function was a great center where tall office buildings, stores, hotels, and an array of public facilities offered every conceivable product and service.

Not long after the ordinance took effect that April 10, the *Times*'s unthinkable scenario began to unfold. Street congestion was significantly reduced, but a sharp decline in banking and retail transactions also occurred. Many businessmen feared swift financial ruin, and a mounting sector of the public came to regard the ordinance as a draconian one, perpetrated by the much despised Los Angeles Railway Company to force the use of its streetcars instead of automobiles. An amendment was soon passed on April 29. Curbside parking was reinstated, now with a 45-minute limit, between 10:00 A.M. and 4:00 P.M., banning parked cars only when traffic was at its worst from 4:00 to 6:15 P.M. The *Times* admonished the council for its previous mistakes, declaring that "the only good thing that can be said for the no-parking law is that it served once and for all to demonstrate the extent to which the automobile has become a part of our every day life." The paper quoted extensively from remarks made by Gilbert Woodill of the Motor Car Dealers Association: "What people seem slow to realize is that anything tending to speed up transportation, business or any other human activity is bound to be accepted and become absolutely essential to everyday life, even before the users themselves realize it."[3]

No episode prior to that time had made Angelenos so aware of the degree to which they depended on their cars and the influence this had in shaping their city. Over the following two decades no less than in the post–World War II years, that consciousness became a central factor in the undertakings of business and real estate interests, planners, architects, and the general public in southern California. By the late 1920s, considering the motorist in the development of new areas was so commonplace as to be almost taken for granted. Ten years later, the cumulative result of this work had profoundly affected the configuration and appearance of the metropolitan area. Much of what the *Times* had foreseen in 1920 became a reality, despite the still ubiquitous presence of cars downtown. The core area was by no means "a thing of the past," but its hegemony over the commercial life of the region was broken. Most specialized goods and services could be found in other parts of the city as well. Symbolically no less than in function the central district ceased to be of central import to the experience of many area residents.

Los Angeles was hardly unique among American cities in the widespread use of the automobile and in the rapid changes that use fostered. Many other cities experienced the same kind of problems with downtown congestion and rapid dispersal of business.[4] What distinguished Los Angeles was its newness as a major metropolis. In 1880 it had been a town of about 11,000 people. The speculative real estate boom that occurred over the ensuing decade generated a 351 percent population increase, followed by one of 103 percent during the 1890s. Still, by 1900 Los Angeles had only 102,000 inhabitants, fewer than Kansas City or Denver, less than one-third of San Francisco's, one-fifth of St. Louis's, one-tenth of Philadelphia's. Then the population increased by more than five times during the next twenty years. By 1930 the city reached fifth place among those in the United States, with over 1.2 million residents. Development of the surrounding area, inextricably tied to the city in its identity and economic life, made the figures even more impressive. Los Angeles County had over 936,000 people by 1920, 2,200,000 by 1927. The more than tenfold rise within the county limits during the first three decades of the twentieth century was by far the greatest rate of increase in any major metropolitan area of the United States at that time. In sharp contrast to other places with over one million people—New York, Chicago, Philadelphia, and Detroit—the shape, character, and routines of Los Angeles were primarily determined by twentieth-century forces, including the automobile.[5]

The upstart metropolis's stature stemmed not just from the number of its residents but from dramatic increases in its territory, trade, finance, and manufacture. Completion of the Owens Valley Aqueduct in 1913 ensured an ample water supply for future development, spurring annexation of the San Fernando Valley among other areas.[6] The land encompassed by the city's corporate limits increased 300 percent during the 1910s, from 89.6 to 363.9 square miles, with another 77.8 square miles added by 1930, making Los Angeles the world's largest city in area. Development spread through incorporated and unincorporated precincts alike to encompass dozens of theretofore isolated settlements, rendering them functionally, perceptually, and often physically parts of a vast whole. These changes did not just emanate from the Los Angeles city center outward. Other communities such as Long Beach, Pasadena, and Glendale also rapidly expanded during the period.[7]

A sharp rise in the region's economic base, especially in manufacture and other forms of production, was a key stimulus both to attracting newcomers and to decentralization. By the early twentieth century, Los Angeles County led the nation in agricultural output; however, the value of manufactured goods remained relatively modest at $15 million for the city in 1899. A concerted effort to lure industries to the region during the 1910s and 1920s, coupled with the availability of large areas of undeveloped land, abundant natural resources, and nonunion labor, contributed to altering the situation radically. By 1923, the value of manufactured goods was recorded at $417 million for the city, $1.2 billion for the metro-

politan area as a whole. Los Angeles ranked as the largest industrial center on the west coast and eighth in the country by the decade's end. Further impetus for industrial development came from improvements in both overland and overseas connections. The Port of Los Angeles, greatly expanded during the early twentieth century, handled almost as much freight as all other west coast ports combined, with gross tonnage transfers exceeded only by those of the Port of New York during the 1920s.[8] Large-scale industrial expansion, decentralized from the start, coupled with a major port facility situated twenty miles south of downtown, significantly furthered the diffusion of residential growth areas.

Rapid economic development was also an underlying factor in the widespread prosperity enjoyed throughout the metropolitan area, but it was not the only cause. Unlike most large American cities, still filled with contingents of poor, foreign-born immigrants, Los Angeles was comprised overwhelmingly of U.S. natives—85 percent of the white population in 1930.[9] Furthermore, many people came to the region after acquiring sufficient resources to enjoy the fruits of their labors. The newcomers, emphasized one observer in 1924, "had made their more or less modest stake, [and] sought not opportunity but comfort and health in a mild climate and beautiful surroundings." Most were not rich; yet, as a journalist quipped, "Los Angeles has small use for poor people."[10] The idle life of "comfort and health" could breed restlessness. Many gained employment; others started ventures of their own; thousands invested, especially in real estate. The unusual degree of capital and skills that newcomers brought fueled the economy and fostered an optimistic, expansive mood.

A very sizable portion of the newcomers moved from central portions of the country—from northern states such as Ohio, Illinois, and Iowa, and also from southern ones such as Oklahoma and Texas. Equally important was the preponderance of this "middle-aged middle class from the Middle West" with roots in small cities, towns, and rural areas. If financial gain did not initially loom large among their goals, neither did a quest for radical change in their living patterns. The yearning to savor the fast pace, the intrigue, the cultural stimulus, or the diversity associated with most metropolises seemed noticeably less pronounced in Los Angeles. One chronicler noted that while New York held the lure of an escape from a provincial home environment, Los Angeles was often seen as a place to enrich a way of life to which one had become accustomed. The newcomer "arrives there, not out of dissatisfaction with his own, not out of a dominant conviction that he must find a new place on which to scamper untrammeled. . . . He . . . stays . . . because the physical circumstances—the climate principally—permit him to live more fully the life he has always led." As a result, "the town is merely an overgrown boy, precocious in mechanical bent. It remains a small town in atmosphere, in outlook, in activity, in its very self-consciousness, in all those attributes that give a community character. . . . [It] has become a magnified crossing of Dubuque and Kansas City." Thus, while one of the largest cities in the nation, Los Angeles was felt to stand quite apart from places such as New York or Chicago.[11]

Not everyone found such an atmosphere agreeable. By the 1920s numerous critics caricatured Los Angeles as a haven for farmers and boosters, a place possessing no semblance of sophisticated culture. One of the best-known accounts of the period was written by Morrow Mayo, whose acerbic prose surely delighted eastern urbanites. Mayo cast Los Angeles as

> an artificial city which has been pumped up under forced draught, inflated like a balloon, stuffed with rural humanity like a goose with corn. . . . It has never imparted an urban character to its incoming population for the simple reason that it has never had an urban character to impart. On the other hand, the place has retained the manners, culture, and general outlook of a huge country village . . . of a million population, a remarkable sociological phenomenon; and that is precisely what Los Angeles is.[12]

To some observers, attitude was as much a problem as size. One account showed no mercy:

> The new Greece has its own established values. What it reads in Mr. Coolidge's column is Wisdom. What it sees in the spectacular super-production is Art. The combination of these is Culture.
> The new Greece is an amalgam of the Middle West and the movies—each, whether we like it or not, a dominant element in contemporary American life.[13]

Many writers admitted that "of all American cities [Los Angeles] is the easiest to poke fun at." Yet even some of those who scorned its cultural aspirations could admit that "Los Angeles is the most 'American' city." Whatever the subject of disdain, it probably could be applied to much of the nation. One observer saw virtue in Los Angeles as "the great American mirror," asserting that "as New York is the melting-pot for the peoples of Europe, so Los Angeles is the melting-pot for the peoples of the United States." The city "is unique by virtue of her very universality, of the fact that she is typical of us all. Nothing is so rare as a perfect type." That type was filled with contradictions:

> Its mushroom growth, its sprawling hugeness, its madcap speed, its splurge of lights and noise and color and money; and, against all this boisterous crudity, the amazing contrast of its cultured charm, its mature discrimination, its intellectual activities—this is sprung from American soil, and could come from no other. If we are a nation of extremes, Los Angeles is an extreme among us.[14]

By the 1920s Los Angeles was at once typical and atypical. Like any other city, it had no shortage of prosaic people bent on pursuing limited, predictable routines. It had eccentrics and banal figures, who captured more than their share of the limelight in the press. But the incessant typecasting belied the city's complex nature and, most importantly, the dynamics that made it far more than an inflated town. Southern California proved fertile ground for many persons capable of distinguished achievement—from the business figures whose cumulative endeavors became a major force in the national economy to professionals who gave Los Angeles national and international renown in fields as varied as film, architecture, and women's apparel. Even critics who assailed the local tendency to conform often focused on aspects of the city's life and landscape that resisted conformity. Angelenos in fact wanted their city to be like and unlike others at the same time.

The interplay of opposites was evident in many components of the urban fabric. The city's basic development patterns derived from well-established models, yet the scale, the combination, and an array of unconventional departures yielded results that made Los Angeles seem unique. The product often was heralded as preferable to the norm elsewhere, and often, too, had a significant influence on national practices.

SETTLEMENT

Perceived and actual differences played a major role in attracting newcomers. Accounts depicting the region as an Eden—salubrious in climate, lush in vegetation, abundant in space, dramatic in scenery, absent the crowding, the filth, the slums, the poverty, the corrupt politics, the crime associated with large American cities—had proliferated for decades. The selling of southern California as a superior place became a standard practice during the boom of the 1880s. Half a century later, the promoters' hyperbole was so integral to how visitors and residents alike viewed the region that it was widely assumed to be a self-evident truth: here even a person of modest means could settle in agreeable surroundings—very likely a house with a yard and garden—partake in an outdoor life amid almost perpetual sunshine, and still have all the amenities of a city. For many, Los Angeles was the essence of the American dream.

In southern California the dream was realized on a large scale. Carey McWilliams, outspoken in deriding what he considered the prevailing parochial aura, nonetheless saw merit in Los Angeles as the least citified of American cities—a place that was "neither city nor country, but everywhere a mixture of both."[15] What made the region so unusual in this respect was not the particulars of its urban form but the extent of low-density settlement. Newcomers could tour the metropolitan area for days and see the freestanding house as the predominant residential type. Ample space existed in which to build more. In 1930 over 50 percent of the lots in the county remained vacant, and vast acreage had yet to be platted. The opportunities for development seemed limitless. The ways in which this space was used reflected both the prosperity of the populace and the time in which expansion took place. Occuring at a rate experienced decades earlier by most large cities, Los Angeles's growth during the early twentieth century was shaped by new forms of transportation. Widespread use of the streetcar beginning in the 1880s, then of the automobile beginning in the 1910s, induced low-density development. As a result, the number of persons per square mile was markedly smaller than in other places of equivalent size.[16]

The freestanding, single-family house dominated the landscape of Los Angeles as it did no other American metropolis, continuing a pattern established well before 1900 when the community functioned more as a seasonal retreat.[17] By 1930, single-family residences comprised 93 percent of the city's residential buildings, almost twice that in Chicago and sur-

passing those found in Philadelphia and Washington. Well under half as many families lived in apartment buildings as in houses despite the substantial increase in multiple-unit construction during the 1920s. At the decade's end, single-family houses stood on more than 60 percent of all occupied lots within the city limits.[18]

Equally important to the character of the area's residential districts was the sense of openness they imparted. Attached dwellings were almost nonexistent. Many houses were low in mass, containing one or one and a half stories. Yards tended to be more generously dimensioned than those common to large eastern or midwestern cities; so were setbacks. Lots with a 40 to 50-foot frontage and a 130 to 150-foot depth were the norm in many parts of the city. Except in a few concentrated areas, apartment buildings were modest in scale and scattered intermittently, even along arterial routes, rather than forming the dense corridors characteristic of numerous major urban areas of the period. Many had a few units on two levels set off by a sizable yard on at least one side. The ambience projected by these tracts was much like that of a small city or town in one of the central states whence so many newcomers came—no doubt a key reason Los Angeles was so stereotyped by outsiders. The vastness far more than the character of its domestic territory differentiated Los Angeles from communities in the heartland (figure 2).[19]

Among the most striking contrasts between residential areas of Los Angeles and those of most other large cities was afforded by the tracts of workers' housing developed to serve the large, decentralized industrial districts, begun after the first world war, that lay to the east and south of the city center. In communities such as South Gate, Maywood, Belvedere,

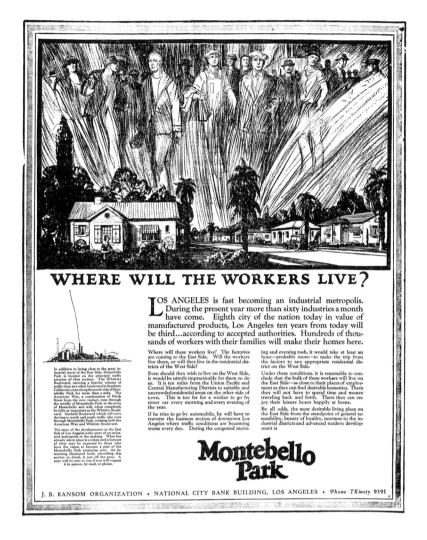

2

Residential area, Hollywood district, Los Angeles, looking southeast from Rossmore and Rosewood avenues. Photo C. C. Pierce, ca. late 1920s. (California Historical Society Collection, Department of Special Collections, University of Southern California.)

3

"Where Will the Workers Live?" Montebello Park advertisement. (*Los Angeles Times*, 24 May 1925, V-4.)

and Montebello, the freestanding house set in a verdant yard along a quiet street, rather that the tenement or flat, became the standard. Realtors promoted the difference strenuously and sometimes with élan (figure 3). Yet the idyllic image advertised often did not stray far from the actuality. A significant portion of the skilled blue-collar populace could live much like their white-collar counterparts—more modestly but otherwise in the same mode, partaking of a spacious environment, tied to municipal services, often agreeably removed from the workplace, commuting by streetcar or by automobile.[20]

Patterns of residential development and automobile use acquired a symbiotic relationship by the early 1920s. As Los Angeles grew into a major city, maintaining a high percentage of single-family houses and modestly scaled neighborhoods necessitated a reliance on cars for routine transportation. Southern Californians' early acceptance of motor vehicles gave impetus to yet further decentralization. As the automobile began to play an integral role in people's lives, real estate interests were forced to make hard decisions in meeting the appetite for buildable land. The region's municipal and intercity streetcar systems had created the initial matrix for de-

centralization between the 1880s and 1910s by extending over much of the Los Angeles basin. The size of this network now led to its obsolescence as the primary carrier. Streetcar line construction incurred so great a debt by 1914 that scant capital could be raised either for expanding lines or for building new ones.[21] Limited funds, combined with what seemed to be unending operational problems, fueled public dislike for the Los Angeles Municipal Railway in particular. During the 1920s many Angelenos came to see mass transit as a nuisance more than a transportation lifeline. The *Times* and other influential organs repeatedly cast streetcars as relics whose demise would not be mourned (figure 4).[22]

Before World War I, real estate development was closely tied to the streetcar in Los Angeles no less than in other cities; yet by the decade's end, many of the choicest locations, convenient to streetcar lines, had been consumed. To meet the swelling demand for housing during the 1920s, two basic options were available. Established areas could be more densely developed, but the cost would be high and the process difficult, especially as most of the building stock was of recent vintage. The results

would destroy the openness that made the region so appealing and would rely on a disliked mode of transportation. The other choice was to continue to build at a low density by breaking the bond between land subdivision and rail transit. Scores of developers did just that by the early 1920s, opening tracts distant from existing streetcar lines.[23] The abundance of vacant land combined with the soaring market afforded ample temptation to initiate such projects, despite the risks. The proliferation of these tracts indicated that a substantial number of people were in fact willing to drive on a daily basis.

AUTOMOBILES

"The automobile," proclaimed one local car dealer in 1921, "is 10 per cent pleasure, 90 per cent utility and 100 per cent necessity." His perspective, while clearly biased, was not much of an exaggeration. Growth in car ownership ranked among the most striking of many such trends in Los Angeles. Countywide, automobile registrations soared from about 16,000 in 1910 to 110,000 in 1918; by 1923 they had increased by another 300 percent to 430,000; and several years later more cars were registered in the county than in any one of thirty-nine states. One car existed for every 8.2 Angelenos in 1915 (compared with one for every 61 Chicagoans and one for 43.1 people nationwide). By 1920 the ratio stood at one for every 3.6 Angelenos (versus 30 Chicagoans or 13.1 people nationwide), an average

4
"More Rerouting," editorial cartoon by Gale. (*Los Angeles Times,* 11 May 1920, II-1.)

5
"Madam—how do YOU get around?" advertisement for *Los Angeles Times* want ads. (*Los Angeles Times,* 8 May 1928, I-14.) Copyright 1928, Los Angeles Times. Reprinted by permission.

Madam ~ how do YOU get around?

Nine-thirty in the morning. The family car somewhere downtown. A day's round of marketing, social duties, club meetings . . . What a comfort--what economy--to have a car for yourself! And why not? Excellent used cars, ideal for women drivers, are offered by local dealers at prices and terms that enable any average family to enjoy two cars instead of one. And Times Want Ads show you the choicest, selected offerings. Dealers advertising in The Times welcome feminine car buyers. You are assured considerate service, help in making a wise selection---and you will be given courteous demonstrations without being urged to buy. Study the used car columns in today's Times---if hubby cannot go with you, go by yourself and ask for a demonstration of any car advertised in

World's Greatest Want Ad Service

that was maintained with minor variations throughout the decade.[24] Thus the two-car family became a common feature of the region shortly after World War I. A budding used-car market was bolstered by married women constrained by family budgets yet determined to have a car of their own (figure 5).[25] The practice of wage earners driving to work while their spouses drove to conduct errands and other everyday pursuits was not unusual. Everyone drove for pleasure as well. the habits of retired newcomers were vividly portrayed in one period account:

> After almost a lifetime of gruelling hardship and toil they have enough to live in what they deem luxury for the remainder of their days, and they are making the most of it. They drive, drive, drive in lusty holiday fury—to the beach, to Hollywood, to anywhere or nowhere, as a carousel ceaselessly circles. They fill the streets, gaping at the sights; they "eat out," an unspeakable luxury to the women after years of making pies and "baking hens" for the harvest crew; they rush for every sensational amusement, whether it be the pre-view of a hair-raising film, Peaches Browning in vaudeville, Aimee Semple McPhearson's Sunday service, or the Ostrich farm. . . . The incessant craze for driving seems to epitomize the whole psychological situation.[26]

Numerous factors contributed to southern California's national leadership in automobile use. The prosperity enjoyed by the established and incoming populace alike was a central cause. Many newcomers had already acquired the automotive habit in their towns and rural areas of former residence, where routine driving was easier than in cities. The move to Los Angeles after World War I was frequently accomplished by car, constituting what Carey McWilliams described as "the first migration of the automobile age."[27] Climate further encouraged use. At a time when many cars were still open to the elements, mild weather the year round was conducive to ongoing rather than seasonal driving. The array of places one could reach without difficulty further shaped motoring patterns. Miles of wide, straight boulevards were being extended like a sectional grid, more or less concurrently with new development. During the 1920s, the Los Angeles street network was considered among the best in the United States. Aggressive public works campaigns greatly added to the infrastructure; 300 to 500 miles' worth of street improvements annually was not unusual. By 1927, the city engineering department proclaimed that, if laid end to end, improved streets would reach Chicago.[28] As a result, motorists traversed distances in the metropolitan area with relative ease as long as they avoided the city center. The eleven-mile drive, for example, from the Silver Lake district, four miles north of downtown, to Westwood, near Santa Monica, could be accomplished without hurrying in about thirty minutes—less time than is now required with the freeway system.[29] Whether for business or pleasure, such areawide trips became commonplace.

The direct correlation between driving habits and urban form was recognized locally at an early date. Gordon Whitnall, director of the Los Angeles City Planning Department and an advocate of decentralization, stressed to members of the Municipal League in 1927 that the impact of driving was already widespread. The advent of the automobile occurred

when cities [in southern California] also were new . . . before [they] became stereo-typed. Cities began to grow with the automobile. Instead of the automobile conform-ing . . . to the limitations of the cities, the cities began to conform . . . to the necessities and services of the automobile. That is the BIG thing that has happened here in the Southland. It has just begun.

Here for the first time in history, the efficient travel radius of the individual has been stretched. . . . So prevalent is the use of the motor vehicle here that it might almost be said that Southern Californians have added wheels to their anatomy . . . that our popula-tion has become FLUID.[30]

Well before that time, local realtors began to view the automobile note just as an agent in broadening the geographic limits of development but as an index to the most preferable forms of development in new and old areas alike. In 1922, a member of the real estate community observed: "Economists agree that there is perhaps no better indicator of the purchas-ing power . . . and . . . the wealth of the community, than the number of automobiles."[31]

The proliferation of cars exacted a toll as well. Pedestrians down-town had to battle a seemingly endless stream of automobiles and trucks as well as electric rail cars. Since car tracks lay in the middle of the street, pas-sengers were forced to scurry across one or more lanes of moving vehicles to get to the curb (figure 6). At a time when traffic controls were new in the city center and almost nonexistent elsewhere, pedestrians in outlying areas also found the new torrent of automobiles unpleasant and sometimes dangerous (figure 7).

Motorists, too, encountered frustrations. No matter how exten-sive, street improvements never seemed to keep pace with demand. The long distances many motorists drove to work imposed burdens on the ci-ty's thoroughfares during peak commuting periods. A large share of public

6
"Popular Nightmares, No. 1," editorial cartoon by Gale. (*Los Angeles Times,* 26 January 1924, I-1.)

7
"The Pedestrian's Nightmare," editorial cartoon. (*Hollywood Daily Citizen,* 11 August 1927, 12.)

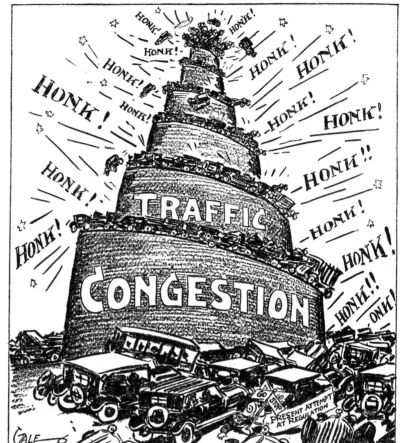

8

"The Modern Tower of Babel," editorial
cartoon by Gale. (*Los Angeles Times,*
13 December 1923, II-1.)

works allocations went to straightening, widening, realigning, and creating
new streets as well as to constructing bridges and tunnels—all to foster
access to downtown. Still, the volume of traffic mounted at a formidable
rate. In 1920, an estimated 22,000 cars entered the city center and its immediate environs between six in the morning and eight in the evening
on a given work day. Four years later, well over ten times that number
entered the business district during a twenty-four-hour period—fully
three quarters of the total number of cars then registered in Los Angeles
County. The number of persons commuting by automobile was almost as
great as that using public transportation.[32] For adults, most of whom re-
membered cities without cars and for whom streets with only a few cars
at any time of day remained a recent memory, traffic conditions assumed
an apocalyptic aura (figure 8). Most of Los Angeles was a motorist's paradise, but downtown the perils were real and abundant.

II

THE PROBLEM SOLVED

The growth of traffic problems associated with downtown Los Angeles during the 1920s was a source of widespread concern. Despite the enormous territorial spread of the metropolitan area, despite the diffuse, low-density character of residential development, despite the fact that outside chroniclers scarcely took notice, the city structure retained strong centralized characteristics. Downtown continued as the focus of major business activities, except in the industrial sphere, and attracted by far the greatest flow of vehicles. No other part of the metropolis began to challenge this hegemony until the decade's end, and even then few business leaders could envision a time when downtown's dominance might cease.

Automobile trips to and from downtown Los Angeles became so numerous in the decade after World War I in part because of the exponential increase of motorists who used their cars to commute, but also because the district grew at an even faster pace. The 1920s comprised the most intense period of the downtown's development, rendering it one of the largest in the nation. At the same time, the structure remained that of the typical large, centralized city, forming an intensely used, compact area, little of which was given to ground-level circulation. As more automobiles entered the city center, space for them came at an ever greater premium.

"The problem solved" was one of many entrepreneurial claims made during the 1920s regarding the mounting perils of a parkless town. In this case, the purported solution was to build a series of immense office

blocks, each with an 1,800-car parking garage through its core.[1] Bold proposals failed to materialize as instruments of change, however. Downtown Los Angeles was much like others in the United States in its function, form, and dependence upon uncoordinated, incremental, and expeditious responses to space pressures wrought by widespread automobile use. The spectacular rise of downtown Los Angeles, and the success it enjoyed, brought with it a problem that seemed insoluble.

SKYSCRAPERS

While Angelenos took pride in their city's abundance of low-density residential areas and understood the automobile's pivotal role in shaping their routines and environment, they likewise placed great value on having a large commercial core as the metropolitan centerpiece. The *Times* reflected broad sentiments in championing at once the freedom of the motorist and the growth of the business center, which was continually used to illustrate the city's achievements and potential. Downtown development during the first three decades of the twentieth century seemed as

spectacular as any advance Los Angeles had made. The small-city character that still prevailed around 1900 was replaced by that of a great city center, with new primary retail and office locations created in what had been peripheral, low-density areas (figure 9).[2] Despite ongoing traffic problems, downtown building construction continued at a fast pace during the 1920s. Sixteen buildings reaching the maximum allowable height limit stood downtown in 1918, seventy-two in 1925, one hundred three in 1929. At the decade's end, Los Angeles boasted one of the most extensive business cores of any American city, exceeded only by those few with larger populations (figure 10).[3]

For members of the business community and no doubt for many others among an intensely boosterish populace, downtown was the most visible and impressive image of collective attainment. Well before 1920, visions of the future city were fashioned after those of New York, including extravagant fantasies presented as means to alleviate nascent traffic problems (figure 11). Similarly expansive images of a giant skyscraper metropolis were advanced until the depression.[4] Tall buildings—planned, under way, and completed—received foremost attention in issue after issue of the *Times* real estate section as well as in dozens of promotional publications of the 1910s and 1920s. The incantations of Irving Hellman, one of the city's prominent financiers and real estate investors, were typical: skyscrapers "express in the spirit of our city a challenge that invites us to time progress to the needs of the hour, to build on and on . . . [they] stand impressively as monuments of principal progress and as strongly reflecting our faith in the city's future."[5] Hellman's view, of course, was shared by

9
Broadway between Sixth and Seventh streets, Los Angeles. Photo ca. late 1920s. (Los Angeles County Museum of Natural History.)

10
Downtown Los Angeles, looking south from City Hall. Photo ca. 1930s. (Los Angeles County Museum of Natural History.)

Los Angeles' Advanced
Plan for Relief of
Overcrowded Streets.

many Americans who considered the urban core the primary emblem of their cities and the skyscraper its ultimate manifestation. In their determination to make Los Angeles a great metropolis, businessmen and the general public alike were especially conscious of having an enormous downtown, filled with tall buildings. Low-density residential districts were considered a great asset, not in isolation but as part of the support system for a big city, the heart of which must emulate Chicago and New York rather than suggest a Dubuque or an Omaha.

At the same time, there was a conspicuous distinction between downtown Los Angeles and many other American cities: the height of buildings was restricted to 150 feet, or about thirteen stories. The limit was not quite as low as Boston's 125 feet or Washington's 130 feet but was much less than Chicago's 260 feet.[6] The Los Angeles "skyscraper" thus was a height-limit building, not a towered mass but a blocky one whose verticality often was self-consciously emphasized. The restriction was first enacted in 1905 as a precaution against the dangers of being in a seismically active zone. The maximum height was changed in 1911 from 130 to 150 feet and then remained steadfast until the 1950s. Maintaining the height limit became a concern among the business community after World War I. Most leaders opposed increases, arguing that the status quo encouraged the lateral spread of the commercial center, increasing the value of more land. Economic factors were also cited: construction costs were lower, rentals on floors near the street higher. There was also a mounting fear that the now large stock of height-limit buildings would plunge in value were taller ones allowed. The need to avoid even greater traffic congestion than currently existed was yet another argument. The business community wanted the urban core to look metropolitan; however, spokesmen seldom failed to remark that the height limit made their downtown a better place than those of most cities—more conducive to human occupancy and more profitable to property owners.[7]

The area occupied by downtown ranked along the height limit's most dramatic effects. In 1900, the core was modest in size and scale, covering less than twenty square blocks. Main Street was the city's thoroughfare. Retail activity concentrated along Spring Street, although some merchants remained in their older Main Street locations and a number of the most prominent stores had recently relocated to Broadway.

By 1920, large business buildings rose far to the south and west of the old center, covering over fifty square blocks. A pronounced shift in the siting of key functions had also occurred. Third Street, which had crossed the heart of downtown, now stood at the periphery. South of Third, Spring Street was now the spine of the financial district, Broadway the retail and theater core. Other sizable buildings were situated further west, facing both north-south and east-west arteries. Among these, Seventh Street was the most prominent for stores as well as for office buildings. The intersection of Seventh and Broadway was considered the hub of the metropolis.

11
"Los Angeles' Advanced Plan for Relief of Overcrowded Streets," hypothetical view of the urban core in 1937. (*Los Angeles Times, Midwinter Number*, 1 January 1912, 132.)

The height limit worked in conjunction with topography. The downtown that emerged during the late nineteenth century was configured like the neck of an hourglass, bounded to the east and northeast by lowlands and railroad tracks and to the immediate west by the precipitous slopes of Bunker Hill, which extended south to Fifth Street. Expansion to the north would have to overcome a narrow, irregular street pattern and rolling terrain. To the south and southwest, on the other hand, the existing grid of streets was straighter and wider, the land nearly flat. These distinctions continued for a considerable distance: hilly terrain lay to the north and northwest of the established city while seemingly limitless flatlands extended in a broad arc from south to west. After 1900, the first great thrust of residential development occurred within this latter sphere, where the terrain enabled lower costs for the construction of houses and, most importantly, of streetcar lines. Barring unusual circumstances, downtown was likely to grow in the same direction as the city itself.

DEPARTMENT STORES

Beyond the limits of height and direction, a factor that proved key to the specific form of downtown's expansion was the rise of the large department store. No other kind of business activity and no infrastructural project appears to have matched the impact of this commercial enterprise in setting the main paths and parameters of downtown into the mid-twentieth century.

Department stores in the modern sense did not exist in Los Angeles until the century's end, and even then they were of relatively modest size. The process began in 1890 when a dry goods emporium, A. Hamburger & Sons, expanded its operation by moving into the four-story Phillips Block (built 1887) at Spring and Franklin streets. One of the largest, most ornate business buildings then in the city, the latter contained around 40,000 square feet. Fifteen years later, Hamburger's had more than trebled in size, adding to the rear and acquiring the use of an adjacent building (1896, 1899). The store's only rival was the Broadway, founded in 1896 as a small enterprise situated close to the then southwestern edge of downtown at Fourth Street and Broadway. That store was enlarged in 1901 and twice in 1905 to encompass over 145,000 square feet, likewise by adapting contiguous space. These were the sole full-fledged department stores in 1906. Only seven other retailers occupied more than 50,000 square feet: four dry goods houses (Coulter's, Ville de Paris, Boston Dry Goods Store, and Jacoby Brothers) and three furniture stores (Barker Brothers, California Furniture Company, and Los Angeles Furniture Company), all of which likewise had expanded in recent years. The average store size remained much less; most occupied under 5,000 square feet.[8]

Department store growth between 1890 and 1906 was very modest compared to what occurred over the next decade, when four enormous buildings were erected. In appearance and appointments, they

compared favorably to counterparts nationwide and were outpaced only by the most venerable operations, such as John Wanamaker in Philadelphia, R. H. Macy in New York, and Marshall Field in Chicago. This transformation took place during a significant period of change for the department store business generally: retail operations were eclipsing those of the wholesale trade, the range of goods and services available greatly expanded, and shopping at such places became at once a frequent pastime and ritual indulgence among millions of consumers, especially middle-class women. To accommodate these changes, a new wave of department store construction began in some U.S. cities as early as the 1890s and was particularly intense in the years before World War I. Buildings were much larger and far more sumptuous than most of their forebears. The new department store was a latter-day palace—the most ornate and luxurious environment to which many consumers had ready access.[9]

The Los Angeles merchants who took the ambitious leap from modest-sized stores to grand emporia understood the national phenomenon of which they were a part. Each studied firsthand contemporary developments in the field in major cities while preparing plans at home. Each also seems to have realized that Los Angeles was a metropolis in the making and that by redefining their own businesses they would have a significant impact on the city itself.

The first project was the most audacious. In April 1906 D. A. Hamburger announced plans to build an enormous store containing

12

A. Hamburger & Sons (later May Company) department store, 801–829 S. Broadway, Los Angeles, 1906–1908, A. F. Rosenheim, architect. Photo ca. 1908. (Security Pacific Historical Photograph Collection, Los Angeles Public Library.)

nearly 500,000 square feet, over two-thirds of which was to be selling space—purportedly the largest building of its type west of Chicago. The exterior possessed much the same purposeful character—its composition at once classicizing the reflective of the structural frame beneath—as Marshall Field's new State Street store (1900–1902, 1905–1907), while carrying more embellishment (figure 12). Inside, its vast selling floors were elaborately appointed and boasted choice wares. A suite of intimate showrooms was set aside for gowns and millinery. Departments specialized in sporting goods, glass, china, pianos, rugs, wallpaper, furniture, and upholstery. A restaurant, together with a market carrying basic and fancy foods, occupied the entire fourth floor. Besides staffed retiring rooms for women customers, there were offices for doctors and dentists, a 1,000-seat auditorium, and, for several years, the public library.[10] The scale of operation combined with the array of amenities was impressive for any city, and would make almost everything else in the western half of the nation seem dated. So big an enterprise depended upon a huge clientele; this palace would serve the area's swelling middle-class population. But Hamburger's

also was clearly targeted to the elite, catering to its needs and whims as did no other store then operating in southern California.

The most remarkable aspect of Hamburger's plan was the location. The site extended from Broadway to Hill Street on the south side of Eighth, several blocks away from the edge of the business district, in a precinct occupied by modest houses, flats, and neighborhood shops.[11] In the process of creating a new kind of store for the region, Hamburger was determined to reshape the city. He was not the first department store owner to "pioneer" a location, as members of the trade referred to the strategy. A. T. Stewart and R. H. Macy had made similarly unprecedented moves in New York during the mid-nineteenth century, with stores that in turn became catalysts for a new "uptown" shopping district known as the Ladies Mile. Now the process there was repeating itself, with major new stores erected further north on Fifth Avenue. Yet in both phases of relocation the target districts in New York were already well established, first as fashionable places of residence and later as locations of important institutions, houses of worship, hotels, and clubs.[12] Hamburger's site, on the other hand, was marginal in both stature and function.

Perhaps the closest historical analogy to the Los Angeles enterprise had occurred along State Street in Chicago shortly after the Civil War, when Potter Palmer acquired extensive landholdings in what until then had been considered an undesirable precinct. Palmer convinced his former associates, Marshall Field and Levi Leiter, to erect a large new store on one of the blocks. That move, in turn, triggered a shift in the retail center from Lake Street to State, of which Field himself was a principal beneficiary through his real estate transactions.[13]

Whether Hamburger knew of this precedent or not, he pursued much the same course. While assembling the land for his store, he purchased numerous additional lots in the vicinity, and soon after plans for the building were announced began an aggressive campaign to sell sixteen parcels valued at nearly $1.8 million (figure 13). The financial opportunities the store would provide investors were trumpeted in advertisements:

The remarkable growth of Los Angeles has forced the retail district southward. Those who anticipated . . . the trend . . . and invested wisely, have rolled up fortunes. Those who are *now* buying in advance of the present retail growth will reap big rewards. The gigantic Hamburger store . . . will be the backbone of the new commercial center. Investments made anywhere . . . [near] this building will bring wealth to the . . . buyers.[14]

By combining real estate speculation with retail development, Hamburger reduced the risks of breaking from the fold. He also secured a means to finance the dramatic enlargement of his business. Furthermore, the new site was much less expensive than any in the established business district. But the location was also strategic, lying close to where a number of the car lines from middle-class residential tracts approached the city center. Riders would reach the big new store before others downtown and might decide to remain, perusing the acres of floor space, rather than traipsing several blocks afield to comparison-shop.

13
Hamburger Realty & Trust Company advertisement. (*Los Angeles Times,* 22 July 1906, V-19.)

Hamburger's enterprise succeeded. From the time it opened in August 1908, the store functioned as a magnet of trade. Development southward was accelerated. If the store first rose in splendid isolation, it was joined by many other retail establishments, office blocks, and theaters over the next decade. By the late 1920s, Broadway and Spring Street south to Eleventh formed the most densely developed axis in the metropolitan area. Yet the store never became a true centerpiece. Building activity to its west was sporadic. Hill Street did not grow to be the "Fifth Avenue of Los Angeles" as Hamburger had predicted. The main shopping district never extended far beyond his store to the south, west, or east. Part of the problem was that Hamburger failed to attain the hegemony he sought. Almost at once competitors entered the scene who likewise understood the potential rewards of pioneering location.

The first rival initiative was launched just two weeks after Hamburger announced his plans. Undertaken by east coast entrepreneurs, the project entailed a seven-story emporium of nearly 200,000 square feet and located just one block north at Seventh Street and Broadway (figure 14). When construction was well under way, the syndicate collapsed. Soon, however, the lease was assumed by Arthur Letts, owner of the Broadway department store. Apparently, Letts sought to safeguard against being unable to renew the lease of his own building on favorable terms. He turned the project over to an employee, John Bullock, giving him complete freedom to establish a separate store.[15] Opened in March 1907, Bullock's proved an enormous success by concentrating ever more on high-caliber

merchandise and ever less on run-of-the-mill stock. Even before Hamburger's opened, Bullock's was attracting widespread patronage. The demand for prestigious goods surpassed all expectations, fueled by the prosperous middle class more than the carriage trade. To accommodate its growing clientele, Bullock's opened a ten-story addition in 1912. Large adjacent buildings were purchased in 1917 and 1919, bringing the store's floor area to nearly 460,000 square feet.[16]

Letts's apparent munificence toward Bullock was probably motivated by trying to keep Hamburger's expansive program at bay as well as blocking competitors from acquiring the site. Moreover, Bullock's location might inhibit any tendency for merchants to relocate yet further south around Hamburger's. Bullock's profile as an exclusive establishment complemented rather than posed a threat to Lett's principal operation. The Broadway's own swift rise as one of the region's biggest retail establishments stemmed from merchandising aimed at budget-conscious shoppers. Advertisements continually stressed low price and good value in a store that was "always giving a little more for a little less than any one else . . . a lonesome landmark on the road to economy," at once a center of style and "a museum of cheapness."[17]

Once Bullock's future seemed secure, a second salvo in the campaign to hold Hamburger's in check was launched by the Broadway itself. In December 1912, Letts unveiled plans for a mammoth new building of some 460,000 square feet, nearly equaling Hamburger's dimensions (figure 15).[18] But rivalry was by no means the sole cause for expansion. Only through growth could the seemingly insatiable demand for consumer goods be met. Perhaps even more important was the need to maintain the high volume/low price equation relative to other stores. Without a significant increase in the scale of its operation, the Broadway could not remain competitive.

One aspect of Letts's scheme that resisted change, however, was its location. The decision to stay at Fourth and Broadway, which necessitated a phased, four-year construction program, was defended on fiscal grounds. Letts explained that "it is very easy to move" but difficult to generate enough new revenue to justify the change. If the store is well run, it need not relocate: "I have visited a great many cities and I have never seen them take business away from an established corner having a modern store of the size that the new Broadway will be." On the other hand, leap-frogging merchants "are injuring the city, . . . creating an upheaval in . . . real estate values that will make it very difficult to get reasonable loans . . . for improvements; they are creating a doubt in the minds of property owners . . . north of Fourth street whether or not it will be wise to improve."[19] The business core, in other words, should not shift from one part to another as it periodically had done in many cities during the second half of the nineteenth century. But Letts stood in the minority among the downtown business interests. During the rapid pace of the city center's expansion before World War I, most major retailers moved their stores at least once, always in a more or less southwesterly direction; few significant

14

Bullock's department store, 639–657 S. Broadway, Los Angeles, 1906–1907, Parkinson & Bergstrom, architects. Photo ca. 1907–1908. (Whittington Collection, Department of Special Collections, University of Southern California.)

15

The Broadway department store, 401–423 S. Broadway, Los Angeles, 1912–1915, Parkinson & Bergstrom, architects. Advertisement. (*Los Angeles Times,* 1 January 1913, II-11.)

16

J. W. Robinson Company department store, 600–632 W. Seventh Street, Los Angeles 1914–1915, Noonan & Richards, architects; exterior completely resurfaced 1934. Photo ca. 1915. (Whittington Collection, Department of Special Collections, University of Southern California.)

projects were launched north of Fourth Street.

The final setback to retaining the old business district's primacy came in May 1914, with the announcement by the J. W. Robinson Company that it would erect a palatial new store of some 400,000 square feet. Robinson's had been one of the first major retailers to relocate on Broadway, opening its store there in 1895. Now the firm was moving further afield, three blocks west of Bullock's, to Seven Street between Grand and Hope.[20] Like Hamburger's site a decade earlier, this one lay on the very edge of downtown, beyond dense development (figure 16). The location differed, however, in that it stood away from the primary axis of commercial growth. The choice was no doubt affected by those already made by competitors. Robinson's was traditionally considered the most fashionable among the city's big stores—a prominence now challenged by Hamburger's and by Bullock's. Robinson's new site stood closest to the city's affluent neighborhoods along the Figueroa Street and Adams Avenue corridors to the southwest and also to the fast-growing ones in the Wilshire district due west. With Seventh Street becoming the major access route from these places to the city center, Robinson's would be the first downtown store reached by many well-to-do shoppers.

Yet far more consequential than the few blocks' difference in space was the relative absence of vehicular congestion, which was already starting to plague Broadway.[21] Traffic jams were irritating enough to the streetcar rider, far more so to the motorist. Robinson's president, J. M. Schneider, may have been the first merchant to recognize that a site slightly away from the center of trade could appeal to drivers because it was much easier to reach. He was quite aware that an increasing percentage of this well-heeled clientele was using the automobile for shopping trips. The new store provided an amenity then perhaps unique among re-

tail establishments nationwide: a basement parking garage, from which patrons could reach the selling floors directly by elevator.[22]

Little public comment had arisen over Hamburger's plans to move during the previous decade, perhaps because most observers thought them unrealistic. Robinson's project, on the other hand, generated considerable controversy because it seemed to accelerate what was now recognized as a serious trend. The *Times* editorialized on the ostensible damage initiated by the "Hamburger hegira" to a "country" location, which propelled business development "southward like an ever thinning string of molasses taffy" and could leave "a portion . . . detached for years from the rest."

Many thoughtful observers have long deplored the fact that . . . instead of spreading out into a conveniently located, compact and well-built-up area, [businesses] have constantly tended to straggle southward in a ribbon-like band of ragged development. . . . The region already given up to business covers sufficient ground for a city three times the size of this.[23]

Robinson's decision was the last straw. It "crystallized a consciousness that has been waxing and waning and waxing again in an endless cycle for many years." Now enough interested parties had begun to realize that "the business district . . . has too long been a thing on wheels. . . . Unanimity of purpose in the building of Los Angeles along modern and rational lines has been lost sight of in the scramble to create new business

centers and to make new killings for individual investors and financial cliques." Such freewheeling forces served to destabilize conditions throughout the city center.[24]

In the event, Robinson's impact on the shape of downtown was greater than, but different from, what the *Times* predicted. The emporium became the catalyst for a cross-axial corridor that began almost at once to check the advance of new building projects to the south along Broadway by affording a sound and for some a preferable alternative. Soon after the store opened in September 1915, plans were under way for two of the region's most prestigious dry goods firms, Coulter's and the Ville de Paris, to relocate in large new buildings opposite one another at Seventh and Olive streets. Smaller specialty shops came as well, many of them situated on the lower floors of multistory office buildings, themselves following the retailers' lead, just as had occurred on Broadway.[25] By 1920, Bullock's and Robinson's functioned as anchors to an elite shopping precinct that was unprecedented in Los Angeles (figure 17).

At the turn of the twentieth century, stores catering to any and all segments of the consumer public had been close to one another in a relatively confined area. The dispersal of retailing through the development of large department stores not only greatly extended the business district's boundaries but stimulated a hierarchical division of precincts within those boundaries. Each area possessed much the same character as its largest stores. If Seventh Street represented the high end of this order, Broadway encompassed a much greater range. Some of its stores (N. B. Blackstone Company, Mullen & Bluett, Silverwood's), from the Sixth Street intersection south, directly competed with those on Seventh or were strong, second-string counterparts.[26] Established stores oriented toward the lower end of the market (J. M. Hale Company, Jacoby Brothers) generally retained their sites north of Fourth Street. Newcomers to the bargain trade (Fifth Street Store) took sites nearby.

The locational tugs-of-war that occurred in downtown Los Angeles during the early twentieth century would be repeated by the major department store companies in the development of branches during the late 1920s and 1930s and again, with greater intensity, after World War II. More than any other kind of establishment, these emporia proved crucial to attaining prominence as an important locus of trade among the metropolitan area's many outlying business districts. The introduction of such a facility could help secure the stature of an existing district, but more often these stores were instrumental in creating new hubs, echoing the reconfiguration of downtown spurred by Hamburger's, Bullock's, and Robinson's. Likewise, too, the choice of a new site that came with expansion was driven not primarily by a search for cheap land or to realize an increase in land values for collateral real estate investments, but to provide the most convenient access for store patrons, a measure that included avoiding congested areas.

Arthur Letts correctly understood the power of a big store to generate business. Size, combined with quality of merchandise, service, and

17

W. Seventh Street, looking east from Olive Street, Ville de Paris (later Dyas) department store (1916–1917) at right. Photo ca. 1926. (California Historical Society Collection, Department of Special Collections, University of Southern California.)

price, could create a prime location, but not just anywhere. A major reason for Hamburger's and Robinson's success in attracting trade and additional development was that each lay on a major approach route to
downtown and thus functioned somewhat as a gateway; Bullock's site at
the juncture of those routes was no less important to its success. Letts's call
for a rebuilding of the old city center might have been valid were the locations there equally strategic. But since the blocks north of Sixth Street
were hemmed in by Bunker Hill on the west side, the area was too constrained to accommodate the needs of a rapidly growing metropolis.

EXPANSION

Downtown Los Angeles's boom during the 1920s intensified patterns of
the previous two decades but did not generate significant new ones, despite the proliferation of automobiles. Broadway remained a major spine
for development as far south as Tenth Street (now Olympic Boulevard).
Spring Street became identified almost entirely with the leading financial
institutions that continued to erect grand quarters along the blocks between Fourth and Eighth streets. To the east, Main Street harbored less
prestigious businesses, while Los Angeles Street became lined with a number of large wholesaling and light manufacturing companies, especially
those engaged in the garment and accessories trades. On the other side
of Broadway, Seventh Street attracted ever more premier retail and office
functions. Some of the most concentrated activity occurred in the area
west of Broadway and north of Seventh, which, by the decade's end,
boasted new theaters, hotels, and clubs as well as numerous tall office
buildings. The area directly south of Seventh grew much more sporadi-

cally; most multistory construction rose amid smaller buildings of the previous generation or amid newly vacant lots used for commercial parking.[27]

Retail development was among the most active contributors to downtown's progress. Floor space in shopping facilities probably doubled between the war and the depression. But, like the district generally, retail growth occurred as a result of increased density rather than significant territorial expansion. Virtually all new building of consequence took place between Fourth and Ninth streets on Broadway and between Broadway and Flower Street (one block west of Robinson's) on Seventh. Most new retail activity on side streets was situated no more than a block away from the two principal corridors. Hill Street emerged as an important secondary spine, but only for a short distance, close to the Broadway and Seventh intersection. Office buildings erected beyond these blocks seldom attracted retail functions save those that were convenience-oriented or so specialized that they could operate independently. Geographic stability characterized not only the district as a whole but also the location of its stores. Many prominent merchants remained at their established addresses. When movement did occur, it was usually within a block or two of the former site.

18
Bullock's department store, showing additions (left to right): 630 S. Hill Street (1933–1934), 638 S. Hill (1923), 640 S. Hill (built for Pease Furniture Company, purchased 1917), 650 S. Hill (1924), 660 S. Hill (1927–1928), 325 W. Seventh Street (built 1908 as Gerard Eastman Building, purchased 1919), and original building. Not shown: 639–641 S. Broadway, 1911–1912. All but purchased buildings by John and Donald B. Parkinson, architects. Photo "Dick" Whittington, 1955. (Whittington Collection, Department of Special Collections, University of Southern California.)

19
Fifth Street Store (later Milliron's), 501–515 S. Broadway, Los Angeles, 1921–1924, Aleck Curlett, architect. Photo "Dick" Whittington, 1940. (Whittington Collection, Department of Special Collections, University of Southern California.)

The near absence of lateral growth in the shopping district was partly attributable to the city's department stores having demarcated a core area with ample room for dense new building. This arrangement, combined with the newness of their plants, gave department store executives no reason to redirect the course of development as the consumer market swelled. Instead, they expanded their buildings, which collectively stood as the largest single component of downtown's retail growth during the 1920s. Hamburger's again set the pace. Soon after the store's purchase by the St. Louis–based May Company in 1923, a new section was built, followed by a larger one in 1929, together more than doubling floor space. Bullock's undertook three additions between 1923 and 1928, adding a total of nearly 400,000 square feet, and purchased two adjacent buildings as well. The aggregate seemed like a city in itself and dwarfed the original section (figure 18).[28] Robinson's and the Broadway also erected additions in 1923 of some 158,000 and 130,000 square feet, respectively. Between 1921 and 1924, the Fifth Street Store embarked on a phased replacement of its facility, much as the Broadway had done a decade earlier, with a new building more than three times the size of its predecessor (figure 19).[29] Together, these programs represented over 1.5 million square feet of floor space, an area that came close to matching the total of the five big stores when originally built.

If seldom as large, new buildings for more specialized retailers were even more conspicuous elements in the shopping district's growth during the 1920s. By remaining close to the department stores, these establishments reinforced the existing structure, further inhibiting any thought of relocation. Clothing stores played an especially prominent role in the consolidating trend. Prior to World War I, most of these outlets were housed either in modest-sized, single-purpose buildings or in the lower floors of office blocks. A pronounced change began in 1920 when F. B. Silverwood opened a five-story emporium at Sixth and Broadway, with over 115,000 square feet to hold a vast stock of men's wear and accessories, arranged on multiple floors like a small department store (figure 20). Two leading rivals, Desmond's and Harris & Frank, followed suit, with new stores of 65,000 and 71,000 square feet opening in 1924 and 1925, respectively. Specialty shops for women's wear tended to remain much smaller, yet one prominent firm, Myer Siegel, constructed a six-story, 52,000-square-foot building in 1926–1927.[30] All these facilities were designed to project a memorable image inside and out (figure 21). Exterior treatment was more individualistic than that of earlier department and dry goods stores. Rather than sheer mass, they employed a decorous use of composition, materials, and detail to gain a strong public identity.

Music stores also acquired a conspicuous presence, with elaborate new buildings constructed to house bulky traditional wares such as pianos but also a wide selection of new items such as phonographs and radios, whose popularity was growing rapidly.[31] The configuration of these emporia—typically five to seven stories, encompassing 50,000 to 80,000 square feet—was much like that of furniture stores, which had enjoyed visual prominence since the 1890s owing to the space requirements of main-

20

F. B. Silverwood store, 555–559 S. Broadway, Los Angeles, 1920, Walker & Eisen, architects; altered. Advertisement. (*Los Angeles Times,* 21 November 1927, I-9.)

21

Desmond's store, 616 S. Broadway, Los Angeles, 1923–1924, A. C. Martin, architect. Opening advertisement. (*Los Angeles Times,* 16 September 1924, I-5.)

taining an adequate stock.[32] Furniture store expansion was limited during the 1920s save for the ambitious program of Barker Brothers, which claimed to be the largest in the trade west of Chicago and took aggressive steps to dominate the local market. Situated on Broadway between Bullock's and Hamburger's, its complex was the product of five building campaigns and encompassed nearly 335,000 square feet when the last addition was completed in 1922.[33] Lacking room to expand further, the company soon prepared plans to relocate on Seventh Street in a block-long behemoth of 500,000 square feet, rivaling the major department stores as a landmark of the retail district (figure 22).[34] The exterior offered a marked contrast to those emporia, however, with an understated dignity and palatial references more characteristic of premier office buildings of the period. Both the principal entrance and the lobby extended three stories high, the former suggestive of a large governmental seat, the latter of an enormous movie house.

The rising cost of space in what remained the most desirable downtown locations led some retailers to erect multistory buildings in which they occupied a small portion of the space, deriving rental income from the rest. Alexander & Oviatt, a fashionable men's store, announced plans for such a venture as early as 1923. Implementation was delayed,

however, and the design was recast in a more stylish tone four years later (figure 23). Thus configured, the store's presence was fostered not only by a soaring, twelve-story mass but also by an unusually extravagant external display area, one of the first in Los Angeles to emulate the modernism of the 1925 Paris decorative arts exposition, with intricate glasswork from René Lalique's studio. The store-office combination was not limited to upper-end establishments, however. Foreman & Clark, a budget-oriented men's clothier, announced plans for a height-limit building before the

22
Barker Brothers store, 840 W. Seventh Street, Los Angeles, 1924–1926, Curlett & Beelman, architects. Photo "Dick" Whittington, 1930. (Whittington Collection, Department of Special Collections, University of Southern California.)

23
James Oviatt Building, 617 S. Olive Street, Los Angeles, 1927–1928, Walker & Eisen, architects. (*Los Angeles Times,* 25 May 1927, I-7).

Oviatt was completed. Occupying over 56,000 square feet, the store
proper was situated on the second, third, and fourth floors so that the
lucrative ground-level spaces could be leased to others. The savings incurred, advertisements noted, were important in keeping prices low.[35]

The opportunity for smaller retail operations to occupy buildings
of their own in the business core diminished steadily with the construction of ever more multistory buildings. Nevertheless, some merchants
found parcels of land that were deemed unsuitable for intense development, most of them scattered on residual lots between large-scale projects.[36] More pronounced was the emergence of an exclusive specialty shop

zone at downtown's western edge, along Flower Street to either side of
Seventh. Like that of Robinson's, a Flower Street location carried appeal
because of its position on the fringe.[37] Well-heeled consumers could reach
Flower Street without encountering the worst downtown congestion.
Flower was not a major thoroughfare and had no streetcar lines between
Sixth and Tenth streets, facilitating automobile movement and curbside
parking as well as keeping the price of land relatively low. The cost factor
was particularly appealing to some Seventh Street merchants who were
seeing their rental rates rapidly increase as available property along that
corridor came ever more at a premium.

Flower Street's transformation began at the start of the new decade. Initially the tone was set by Chappell, a stylish women's clothing
store that had to vacate its Seventh Street quarters to make way for
construction of a height-limit office block.[38] When it opened in 1921,
Chappell's new store contrasted with most commercial buildings in the
city (figure 24). The front was cast in a historicizing mode evocative of the
vernacular fabric of Hispanic towns, creating an intimately scaled, quasi-
domestic ambience antithetical to that of the contemporary urban core.
Even more unusual was the provision for customer parking on the rear
third of the site—probably the earliest case in the metropolitan area in
which a surface car lot was created as part of a new retail facility. Other
posh stores soon located nearby.[39] This trend, in turn, may have influenced
the decision by Barker Brothers to situate at Seventh and Flower, two
blocks west of Robinson's—the one case in which a major store expanded
the perimeter of the shopping district.

Barker Brothers greatly enhanced Flower Street's standing as a
retail location but also changed its attributes, for with prestige came a rise
in land values. A new scale and urban density was introduced in 1926,
the year Barker Brothers opened, with the six-story emporium for Myer
Siegel half a block to the south. Soon Parmelee-Dohrmann, a store purveying costly china, silver, and glassware as well as objects of art, started
building large quarters next door (figure 25).[40] These initiatives, along
with public works projects extending the street to make it more accessible, led some observers to predict that Flower would replace Seventh as
"the street of smart shops," an exclusive precinct much like that emerging
along Chicago's North Michigan Avenue.[41] Flower Street's prominence
proved short-lived, however. Development came to a halt in 1931, ar-
rested both by the depressed economy and by competition from new outlying retail centers. Most stores either closed or relocated. Even in its brief
heydey, Flower Street functioned as a subsidiary extension of a unified
retail core rather than as a precinct in its own right. Unlike Chicago and
some other large cities, Los Angeles never developed a fashionable shopping area tangent to, yet distinct from, the core. Instead, its downtown
structure remained more analogous to those of smaller urban centers—
an Indianapolis or a Denver—tightly knit and closely tied to the drawing
power of the major department stores.

24
Chappell store, 645 S. Flower Street, Los
Angeles, 1921, Richard D. King, architect; no longer standing. Opening advertisement. (*Los Angeles Times,* 4 September
1921, III-2.)

The hegemony enjoyed by Los Angeles department stores helped ensure that the basic form, complexion, and character of the shopping district continued to be shaped by local interests during the 1920s. Furthermore, almost all leading retail business had reached a mature stage of development. Bullock's ranked among the newest; most were founded before 1900 and some dated to the mid–nineteenth century, when Anglo-American development was still in its infancy.[42] While many of these mercantile houses drew analogies between themselves and the youth, energy, and seemingly limitless potential for growth of Los Angeles itself, the retail

community was dominated by long-standing organizations, not upstarts.

Outsiders barely existed among the city's store owners before World War I. The situation began to change thereafter, but without significant effect on local practices. After purchasing Hamburger's in 1923, May Company executives took pains to retain its strong local identity. Acquisition of the California Furniture Company by W. & J. Sloane five years later gave Barker Brothers a strong new competitor but did not upset its dominant position. By that time, a number of other national firms had established outlets downtown. A few of these ventures were on a large scale. Bedell, a chain of women's clothing stores, opened its fourteenth unit in a six-story building at Sixth and Broadway in 1920. Others, such as Young's Shoe Company, operated with a string of tiny outlets. The success and standing of these stories varied, but none of them contributed in any significant way to local tendencies in the siting, scale of operation, or design of stores. Outside interests were more discreet followers, adapting to regional trends and tastes, than pacesetters.[43]

Companies based far afield did alter one aspect of retailing in Los Angeles during the 1920s: the selling of inexpensive, everyday items. As early as 1912, F. W. Woolworth opened three modest-sized units downtown in the shopping districts. S. H. Kress entered the local arena with a store in 1920. A decade later, these and two other national variety store firms were operating a total of nine facilities, all but one of them concentrated along a seven-block stretch of Broadway.[44] Such stores captured a major share of their market, and no doubt many local merchants in neighborhood settings as well as downtown saw their businesses erode as a result. On the other hand, the chain variety store reinforced the local spatial pattern by strengthening Broadway's primary over Spring and Main streets as the locus of mass market trade.

25

Flower Street, Los Angeles, looking north toward Seventh, showing (left to right): Parmelee-Dohrmann store, 741–747 S. Flower, 1926–1927, Ashley & Evers, architects; Myer Siegel store, 733–737 S. Flower, 1926–1927, Ashley & Evers, architects; Ranschoff's store, 729 S. Flower, 1926, Myron Hunt, architect; Wetherby-Kayser store, 715–719 S. Flower, 1925–1926, Charles F. Plummer, architect; all no longer standing; Barker Brothers at rear. Photo "Dick Whittington, ca. 1930. (Whittington Collection, Department of Special Collections, University of Southern California.)

PARKING

Local interests were less than effective in attempts to meet the demand for off-street parking. While public agencies focused on upgrading downtown streets, improving access to the precinct, and regulations designed to enhance traffic flow, parking was left to the private sector. Projects were created on a piecemeal basis, each directed to immediate concerns. Conditions never deteriorated to the point of threatening the business district's viability, but marked overall improvements did not occur either. Instead, the somewhat chaotic status quo was maintained, with new parking facilities more or less keeping abreast of increased demand. The perils envisioned in 1920 had abated little a decade later.[45]

Part of the problem lay with the disparate needs among patrons, workers, and property owners. Many executives wanted convenient parking for themselves. Major business owners focused on provisions for their own customers rather than for the shopping district as a whole. Small-scale merchants, for the most part, believed the problem lay beyond their

abilities to change. Patrons wanted to park as close as possible to their destinations, but some might only remain for a short period, while others spent the better part of the day downtown. The overriding objective of property owners, on the other hand, was the most profitable use of their land, which seldom entailed parking on more than a temporary basis. Finally, doubts were harbored by some parties as to how long parking might remain an issue. In 1928, the executive secretary of the Los Angeles Building Owners and Managers Association proclaimed that downtown streets would soon be congestion-free. Evidence was mounting, he asserted, that deliveries would be restricted to nighttime and streetcars would either run underground or encircle the city center. Most cars would be confined to the periphery. Specially designed mass transit vehicles would carry people "beyond easy walking distance" within the core.[46]

For those less optimistic, there was the exasperating fact that automobiles consumed so much space, when parked and while maneuvering, relative to the number of pesons they carried. Accommodating any significant number of vehicles was a costly enterprise. Yet the greatest need for parking occurred where land values were highest. These opposing factors intensified during the 1920s when downtown Los Angeles, like other cities, continued to grow in a concentrated form once predicated on mass transit as the near universal carrier.

The most common off-street parking facility was the surface lot. At an early date, the parking business became profitable enough to warrant the demolition of small buildings, deemed obsolete, on blocks surrounding prime downtown locations. As a result, a patchwork of car lots took hold in all but the centermost part of the business district in the late 1910s (figure 26). While fewer than five such lots existed in the 102-square-block area between First, Eleventh, Figueroa, and Wall streets in 1915, over forty could be found in 1920. The most intense period of growth occurred over the next five years, in the aftermath of the city's first major parking crisis, raising the total to over one hundred in 1925. Expansion slowed thereafter; about twenty additional lots were operating in 1930. Combined, these facilities had a capacity of about 12,000 cars at a time, one of the largest then found in the nation. Slightly fewer automobiles were accommodated at curbside spaces and in sheltered parking structures combined.[47]

Car lots, as a rule, were developed by parties independent of the businesses they served. Coordination between the two often did not exist at the outset. Lot operators sought proximity to major businesses, of course, but had to convince property owners that a more profitable use of their land was not imminent. From the owner's perspective a parking lot was no more than a holding action—a temporary method of deriving income until the land was densely developed. Downtown Los Angeles's rapid growth during the 1920s made the situation especially unstable. Even if the geographic area consumed by new buildings did not reach the proportions often predicted, the pace was fast enough to render any one car lot a short-lived enterprise. Approximately three-quarters of those operating downtown in 1920 became sites of construction over the next five-year period. Much the same rate occurred between 1925 and 1930. Only five of the lots that existed at the start of the decade were still operating at the end.[48]

The factors that affected parking lot location often ran counter to the convenience of patrons. Facilities close to key portions of the shopping district were relatively few. Many shoppers, some eighty percent of

26

Parking lots, downtown Los Angeles, looking south on Flower Street from top of Richfield Building. Photo "Dick" Whittington, 1930. (Whittington Collection, Department of Special Collections, University of Southern California.)

27

Grand Central Garage, 525–555 W. Fifth Street and 440–460 S. Grand Avenue, Los Angeles, 1920–1921, Reed & Hibbard, architects; demolished 1988. (*Los Angeles Times,* 15 February 1920, V-2.)

whom were women, resisted walking even two or three blocks to a store from their car. Driving was still a new experience to most consumers and widely perceived as liberating and facilitating. The circuitous route taken, coupled with the time entailed in finding a car lot with space available, then in reaching one's destination, seemed like an ordeal. Moreover, in many people's minds, mobility was viewed as a right; one should not have to pay to park. As an exasperated realtor noted in 1930, women especially resented deducting the cost of automobile storage from their shopping budget and frequently spent considerable time searching for curbside space instead. In a survey conducted by a prominent local real estate firm, the great majority of respondents patronized downtown stores far less than they would have liked due to the parking conditions.[49]

Besides the car lot, the most important kind of off-street parking facility was the multistory garage. These buildings enabled much more efficient use of land, but at a high cost, owing to the strength required of the structure and the complex layouts needed for efficient vehicular circulation. Parking garages also necessitated a sizable staff if cars were to be stored and retrieved with any speed. In sharp contrast to the car lot, the multistory garage represented a major investment, designed to last for a considerable length of time. Yet these behemoths did not generate as much revenue as did well-situated office buildings, hotels, or major stores. Thus the number of large garages in Los Angeles and other cities prior to the depression was relatively small. Like the car lot, garages tended to be on peripheral sites not far from the edge of concentrated development.[50]

While no sizable parking garages existed in Los Angeles prior to World War I, ambitious projects began soon thereafter. In February 1920, plans were unveiled for the Grand Central Garage, boasting eight levels that would hold over 1,000 cars in addition to an accessories store, gasoline pumps, repair and paint shops, wash racks, and a chauffeur's lounge (figure 27). When it opened, the facility ranked among the most capacious of its kind in the nation.[51] The building stood on the edge of Bunker Hill, at Fifth and Grand streets, then some distance from the main business blocks but close to where intense building activity was predicted—a forecast that soon proved accurate.

Six other multilevel garages were constructed downtown between 1923 and 1928, though none exceeded the Grand Central's size and most carried 500 cars or fewer.[52] The first two successors rose nearby at Fourth and Olive streets, where the terrain likewise was so irregular that it held no appeal for office building construction. On the other hand, these peripheral sites enabled patrons to skirt the most congested areas when entering and leaving. Operators often emphasized accessibility so that motorists would see their garages as convenient destination points rather than the places of last resort (figure 28). Women customers were actively courted in at least several cases. Publicity emphasized the care with which cars were handled and the rooms provided for personal comfort. Irrespective of gender, the garage's clientele probably differed somewhat from that of many car lots. Minimum charges at a garage could run twice that of a

28
Mutual Garage, 354–363 S. Olive Street,
Los Angeles 1923–1924; demolished
1980s. Opening advertisement. (*Los
Angeles Times,* 12 January 1924, I-8.)

car lot and monthly storage exceeded twelve dollars in the mid-1920s.
While such fees held, only a small portion of the motoring public could
afford to utilize the facilities on a regular basis.[53]

Only one large parking structure, Hill's Garage, was built in a
truly central location, on Spring Street between Fourth and Fifth. When

it opened in March 1928, the facility was heralded as a source of much-needed relief both to the financial district and to the main shopping blocks nearby. The venture was an extravagant one. Thirteen levels were served by three vehicular elevators, rather than the usual ramps, in response to site constraints. The facade was decorously festooned to rival its ornate neighbors (figure 29). While the capacity of Hill's nearly equaled that of the Grand Central, the project cost considerably more. The sponsors hoped their initiative would set a precedent: if enough garages comparable in capacity and convenience were erected, curbside parking could be eliminated and downtown streets would be relatively congestion-free.[54] The governing trend in the field, however, was less altruistic. The blocks west of Hill Street between Fifth and Ninth—where ample land existed

and where the need was considerable—harbored only two garages at the decade's end. Holding out for more profitable development remained the norm. Hill's was the most splendid, but also the last, example of its kind built in the city.[55]

Like car lots, most parking garages were developed by parties specializing in that field and were not directly tied to other downtown businesses. Only on rare occasions did one of the latter build a garage to sustain or expand its clientele. Such facilities could generate some revenue if open to general use, but most of their space was customarily reserved for patrons, who could park without charge or at a greatly reduced one. Hotels were among the most frequent businesses to initiate such projects in the United States, due to the rapidly increasing number of motorist travelers. The earliest multilevel garage in Los Angeles opened in 1919 to serve the Hotel Clark upon its completion.[56]

Department stores were the other leaders in this limited field. Among the pioneers nationally was Scruggs, Vandervoort, Barney of St. Louis, which opened a 296-car garage in 1922 where customers could park free for as long as two hours.[57] Not long after the St. Louis–based May Company purchased Hamburger's, it embarked on one of the most elaborate garages of its kind. Completed in 1927, the building housed 535

29
Hill's Garage, 413 S. Spring Street, Los Angeles, 1926–1928, Kenneth MacDonald, Jr., architect; altered. Opening advertisement. (*Saturday Night,* 3 March 1928, 2.)

30
May Company Garage, 218–228 W. Ninth Street, Los Angeles, 1926–1927, Curlett & Beelman, architects. Photo "Dick" Whittington, ca. 1940. (Whittington Collection, Department of Special Collections, University of Southern California.)

cars on six levels (figure 30).[58] Unlike most such facilities, it lay less than a block away from the store and was designed as a closely related part of the shopping district. Ground-floor space was leased to convenience stores, and the main elevations were composed to match embellished Broadway neighbors. Beyond accommodating loyal customers, the main reason for the venture was to draw others away from emporia on Seventh Street. Perhaps for that reason, the building was sited to the south of the May Company store rather than to the west, where it might enhance competing outlets. Soon thereafter, the Broadway department store joined the fray, purchasing the five-year-old Mutual Garage, the third largest in the city, and allowing patrons two hours of free parking (versus the May Company's one hour) with a one-dollar minimum purchase (figure 31). By that time a number of merchants were striking agreements with car lot opera-

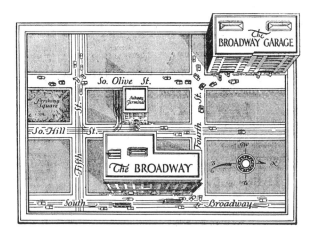

A New BROADWAY Service

Free Auto Parking

For BROADWAY Customers

KEEPING pace with modern merchandising service requirements, and with the problems of automobile parking in the metropolitan district, The Broadway has acquired a modern 7-Story fireproof garage at the north-west corner of Fourth and Olive Streets, for the convenience of its customers.

This spacious, modern garage (formerly the Mutual) is built with staggered floors, approached by ramps. It is close to the Store, easy to enter, and provides the most modern parking facilities. Gas and oil are available, and courteous attendants will handle your car with utmost care.

Two Hours' Free Parking
in a Convenient Garage

A merchandise purchase of $1.00 or more entitles customers to two hours' free parking service. A charge of 5c being made for each additional hour or fraction thereof.

Customers will simply have their garage check validated at the Information desk on our Street Floor, and this check presented to the Garage attendant will entitle you to the two hours' parking without charge.

Locate Your Business in *the Path of Progress!*

— *The "Fifth Avenue"*
of Los Angeles

ONE of the many important features of the Roosevelt Building at 7th and Flower is a modern 450 car garage in the basements. Elevators connect garage serving every floor. Monthly rental is only $10.00.

Every modern convenience, — advantageous location and added prestige — at moderate rates.

One Hour
FREE Parking for
Clients of
Roosevelt Building
Tenants

A conference with our leasing department will incur no obligation

Telephone
TRinity 3343

SUN REALTY CO., Owners
LEASING *and* BUSINESS OFFICE

720 Roosevelt Building ⇒⇐ 727 West Seventh Street

31
The Broadway (formerly Mutual) Garage, advertisement. (*Los Angeles Times,* 20 November 1929, I-4.)

32
Roosevelt Building, 727 W. Seventh Street, Los Angeles, 1926–1927, Curlett & Beelman, architects. Leasing advertisement, showing basement garage. (*Southern California Business,* July 1927, 19.)

tors so that patrons likewise could park for little or no money if they made the minimum purchase.[59]

A far more expensive method of providing off-street space was to incorporate it in the business building itself. Space used for this purpose was limited to one or two basement floors or, less often and never in Los Angeles, to lower above-ground floors. The number of cars thus sheltered tended to be less than in multistory garages while use fees were greater. Robinson's basement garage was a pioneering experiment, but one not repeated by the city's other retail establishments due to the high cost and the fact that customer demand quickly outstripped the space that could be allocated to the purpose. After World War I, however, the concept began to gain favor with the developers of tall office buildings. In this context, the limited confines of a basement could be transformed into an amenity for executives who wanted the convenience of on-site parking for themselves and for their clients (figure 32). The earliest Los Angeles example was constructed in 1920–1921 for the Pacific Mutual Life Insurance Com-

Centrally Located OFFICES

BUS LINES:
WILSHIRE
SUNSET
FIGUEROA

YELLOW CARS:
A·C·D·U·2·3

RED CARS . . Subway Terminal:
HOLLYWOOD .. GLENDALE-BURBANK
SAN FERNANDO LINES.. SANTA MONICA BLVD.
SANTA MONICA-BEVERLY HILLS
VENICE SHORT LINE
HERMOSA & REDONDO *via* DEL REY

In New TITLE GUARANTEE *Bldg.*
(*FACING PERSHING SQUARE*)

CONVENIENT transportation facilities...a
veritable downtown "crossroads." ❧ Many
neighborhood auto parks. ❧ Lots of sunshine
and fresh air. ❧ A good location in which to
increase your business. ❧ One, two and three
room suites facing Pershing Square. ❧ Apply
to Case Bradford. TRinity 3741.

TITLE GUARANTEE & TRUST
COMPANY
TITLE GUARANTEE BUILDING
HILL *at* FIFTH, LOS ANGELES
Capital and Surplus $7,500,000.00

pany at Sixth and Grand streets. Land just behind the building harbored
an underground garage for 200 tenant cars and a street-level lot for visitors—provisions that were depicted as novelties for any city at the time
of completion.[60] Within a few years, however, the practice became more
widespread, if hardly commonplace. Between 1924 and 1930 at least eight
other downtown Los Angeles office blocks were constructed with subterranean parking, now always placed directly under the building's occupied
floors due to the soaring cost of land. Most facilities contained space for
around 120 cars, but the enormous Roosevelt Building (1926–1927) on
Seventh Street could hold up to 350.[61]

The appeal of on-site parking was sufficiently great that at least one property owner adapted the basement of an extant building to garage purposes. Located at Sixth and Broadway, the W. P. Story Building (1908–1910) was one of the first height-limit structures in a then still new part of downtown. The conversion some two decades later was likely made to retain tenants who might otherwise be lured to recent facilities with on-site parking, most of which lay several blocks to the west.[62]

Competition also led several office building owners to follow the example of garage operators and promote peripheral locations. As early as 1927, advertisements for the new Western Pacific Building, which rose at the southern tip of the business district on Broadway below Tenth, claimed occupants could save twenty to forty minutes daily by avoiding congested streets and utilizing several nearby car lots. When the Title Insurance Building opened at Fifth and Hill streets four years later, the owners published maps emphasizing its "central" location, set not in the traditional terms of concentrated development and pedestrian circulation, but rather in relation to off-street parking (figure 33). Among the most extreme measures were taken by the developers of the Beaux-Arts Building (1926–1927), situated on Eighth Street more than ten blocks to the west of Flower in an area then containing little more than scattered neighborhood commercial services amid blocks of houses and apartment buildings. The pile had its own adjacent car lot; the management boasted low rents as well as accessibility. But while the building lay "only 5 minutes from downtown," such complete removal from concentrated business development remained very much of the exception. The advantages of centrality outweighed all others for the bulk of office functions.[63]

An even more unorthodox scheme was revealed in 1924, incorporating a multistory garage as a centerpiece of an office building (figure 34).[64] Not only would there be parking space for tenants and visitors alike, but that space lay immediately adjacent to the office to which each party was destined. Parking thus would be self-service rather than by attendants; all pedestrian movement was internalized, including entry to the thirty-one shops lining an arcade. To accommodate these features, the plan approached titanic dimensions: over 109,000 square feet of ground area; a total square footage of 1.4 million—the largest area under one roof in the city at that time; 670 office suites; space for 1,800 cars—about the same as the total capacity of basement garages constructed downtown during the decade.

No precedent existed for what its promoters dubbed the Mammoth Office Building and Garage, although Howard Putnam Sturges, the Chicago architect responsible for its design, may have known of the more or less concurrent scheme, employing an automatic parking system in its core, for the Jewelers Building in his own city.[65] The Los Angeles syndicate that developed the proposal intended it to be a prototype for at least four others in the city. Ambitiously billing it as "The Problem Solved," announcements indicated that construction was imminent; however, the high cost (four million dollars) relative to the projected return, combined

with the fact that its footprint did not conform to the block sizes in the area where it was to be built, probably contributed to the venture's demise.[66] A more modest plan for a garage, with the front quarter of each floor devoted to offices, was unveiled two years later, but likewise never left the planning stage.[67]

Abrupt departures from the norm elicited interest, but never affected the formative tendencies of real estate development for downtown buildings. Most developers ignored the problem. On-site parking was, after all, a luxury of which only a small fraction of a building's workforce could partake. However appealing such provisions, they were seldom considered an essential factor in a new business building's success. At the height of its growth and stature, downtown Los Angeles remained conspicuously congested, scarcely better equipped than it had been a decade before to deal with the specter of a "parkless town." But parking, as it turned out, was only one of the perils facing downtown Los Angeles. Even as the central shopping district was reaching new heights in size and prestige, its regional dominance was beginning to be challenged by new outlying centers that were growing at a much faster rate.

34
"Mammoth Office Building and Garage," Los Angeles, 1924, Howard Putnam Sturges, architect; project. (*Los Angeles Times,* 27 March 1924, I-11.)

III

WESTWARD HO FOR BUSINESS

Before World War I, when building several blocks from the established
core area was a source of controversy in business circles, no major Los
Angeles retailer would have contemplated a site outside downtown. The
belief was universal that only a center city location could tap a sufficient
consumer market to sustain large stores and many types of small ones as
well. The development of ever more ambitious retail outlets reinforced
this view. During the early twentieth century, the construction of enormous department stores and complementary emporia consolidated the
regional market, attracting ever greater crowds from ever increasing
distances. So strong was downtown's hold on the metropolitan area's consumer public that it is doubtful whether many Angelenos really believed
the *Times*'s warning in 1920 that major stores would relocate outside the
city center if the parking problem was not satisfactorily resolved.

Yet attitudes soon began to change as a result of the fast pace of
both residential and business growth in areas some distance from downtown. The greatest concentration of new development now lay along a
broad path extending toward the Pacific Ocean, giving rise to forecasts
that the metropolis would occupy the entire intermediate area within the
foreseeable future. Predictions such as that made in 1922 that La Brea Avenue, located five miles west of downtown, would become a major commercial artery in ten years no longer seemed far-fetched. Already one real
estate veteran had asserted that "in Los Angeles it is 'Westward, Ho, for
Business.' City builders are in a progressive trek toward the sea."[1] Within

the next decade many such speculative claims were realized; sometimes they were exceeded. By 1930 several large shopping districts had emerged between the city center and the coast, all but one of them located in areas where there had been virtually no commercial development at the end of World War I. Dozens of other business centers, more modest in size, could be found throughout the metropolitan area. Prior to the depression, the capacity for continued growth in this sphere seemed limitless.

ORIGINS

Commercial decentralization did not begin in Los Angeles until the early twentieth century. Prior to then most types of consumer goods and services were predominantly or exclusively found in the urban core.[2] Downtown enterprises included stores for clothing and accessories, household goods, and a variety of other items such as books, stationery, novelties, plumbing supplies, and photographic equipment. Financial services were quartered downtown, as were most physicians, dentists, tailors, florists, hairdressers, laundries, restaurants, and places of entertainment. Even some kinds of food stores, such as those specializing in candy, fish, and poultry as well as ones selling tobacco and beverages, were concentrated in the core. The principal exceptions were groceries, meat markets, and about a third of the city's drug stores. Other types were rare. The collective total of dry goods, millinery, and hardware stores within the city limits but outside the city center, for example, numbered twelve in 1900. Significant changes in this pattern were under way in 1910. Not only had the quantity of establishments increased (fivefold for dry goods and hardware stores, fourfold for millinery, threefold for furniture), but a marked rise occurred in the proportion of them located outside downtown (60 percent in 1910 versus 15 percent in 1900 for dry goods stores, 68 percent versus 31 percent for hardware, 38 percent versus 11 percent for millinery). Some functions quartered only downtown in 1900 now had a sizable share (33 percent of furniture stores) in outlying areas. Nodes containing about thirty to forty businesses each rose in at least seven locations ringing the city center.[3]

The dispersal of business continued to intensify over the next decade. By 1920 the proportion of outlying stores relative to those downtown had not increased so much as their numbers and their tendency to form sizable groupings. At least ten outlying centers now contained eighty or more businesses, and probably a greater number contained forty to sixty.[4] Outlets purveying convenience goods—those purchased on a routine basis, such as food and pharmaceuticals—and everyday services—including cleaners, laundries, dressmakers, tailors, hairdressers, barbers—comprised the majority. Yet a wide variety of shopping goods—those purchased less frequently and often on a comparison basis—were available in these nucleations as well. Indeed, relatively few basic types of goods and services could not be found within the largest outlying centers.

Among the approximately 180 businesses located along the 4200 to 4900 blocks of South Broadway, for example, were stores selling dry goods, jewelry, notions (two each), shoes, men's wear, millinery (one each), hardware (five), furniture, plumbing supplies, paint (two each), and stationery (one). The precinct also contained a bank, twelve restaurants, three movie theaters, and two automobile repair shops.

No matter how large, the outlying centers that had developed by 1920 complemented more than competed with the city center. Nothing approached the selection of goods offered by the large downtown department, apparel, and furniture stores, whose items were also often of higher quality and sold at lower prices. The spectrum of downtown specialty shops far exceeded what could be found in all outlying centers combined. More than 80 percent of stores selling jewelry, hats, shoes, toilet articles, electrical appliances and supplies, books, stationery, musical instruments, photographic equipment, automobiles, and tires remained downtown, as did virtually all establishments concentrating on articles of high fashion. The best restaurants were downtown as were all first-run movies and stage performances. Despite the operation of twenty branch banks in Los Angeles by 1920, many financial transactions could occur only in the city center. Professional services in outlying areas likewise remained limited.

Both the extent and the distribution of the largest outlying centers indicate that they catered primarily to a localized clientele. All these nucleations were, of course, along streetcar lines, and their placement reflected the well-developed residential sections of the city. Their greatest concentration lay within the arc of most intense residential growth during the first two decades of the new century, extending from south to west of downtown. Smaller outlying centers, containing forty to sixty businesses each, were located along the same or nearby arteries. The great majority of the city's residents lived within a mile or at most two of a sizable outlying center.

The area occupied by an outlying center was considerable. Those with from forty to ninety businesses typically extended four to five blocks along an artery. All but one of the seven centers containing more than 100 businesses extended six to thirteen blocks. Each of the latter group had a core zone, two to three blocks in length, that was the most intensely developed, but many important functions within the center lay outside this zone. Indeed, there was seldom much hierarchy in the distribution of businesses. Major facilities such as a furniture store or movie theater could be located at the edge of the center where land was less expensive just as frequently as within its core.[5] Purchase of more than one or two types of goods often entailed traversing a distance of several blocks, perhaps the whole length of the center. The great majority of businesses faced the main street, and the exceptions seldom stood more than 100 feet away from that thoroughfare. Linearity was matched by modesty of scale. Even in the core zones, more street frontage was occupied by one- than by two-story buildings (figure 35).[6] Anything taller was virtually nonexistent save for a few neighborhood movie houses. Beyond the core, the density

was lower, with flats, houses, and vacant lots interspersed among business buildings (figure 36). When two or more centers arose along a single artery, the distance between them seldom was much greater than their respective lengths. To observers, the impression was probably of more or less continuous development, varying in density but with few real breaks, rather than of separate nucleations that defined one neighborhood from another.[7]

Early outlying center development in Los Angeles differed somewhat from the norm for large cities of the period. Typically such places were more compact, with few breaks in business frontage along the main artery and with two or three stories of residential units above the stores. Large outlying centers also generally served consumers of modest means who seldom had the time or the money to go downtown. By the 1910s, business centers in middle-income neighborhoods of major cities could be just as dense. For medium-sized cities, on the other hand, businesses tended to be either on thinly scattered sites or in smaller nucleations.[8]

The low density of the Los Angeles examples reflected the residential tracts they served. Fewer households per acre on average meant lower demand for businesses in any one precinct, and hence relatively low prices for arterial frontage. Furthermore, both the prosperity and the free time enjoyed by many local citizens enabled frequent trips to the city center. For most Angelenos, outlying centers were probably not their principal marketplaces other than for routine purchases. Only in the mid-1920s

would some centers begin to compete with downtown.

Whatever the differences, the early twentieth-century outlying centers of Los Angeles were like those of other U.S. cities in being piecemeal accretions owned and operated by myriad individual parties. Often little or no coordination occurred among property owners. Projects within a center might be complementary or might be redundant. Oftentimes insufficient attention was given to the type or quality of merchandise purveyed. Some outlying centers were overbuilt, with too many stores of a certain kind or just too many vacant store units.

Yet if laissez-faire practices prevailed, the process was sometimes guided by a degree of order, even control. How an outlying center developed depended in part on the nature of property ownership. A single party holding a large tract, especially one intended for residential development, was in a good position to orchestrate the creation of a business cluster that would serve the area. Much of the relatively small commercial node at Main Street and Washington Boulevard, for example, was built by members of a syndicate, Central Pacific Improvement Corporation, that also owned the adjacent Prager Park tract. Begun in 1912, the business center included three sizable buildings, each with between five and twelve stores at ground level and around sixty small apartments above (figure 37).[9] The size of these buildings reflected their proximity to downtown (about twelve blocks from Seventh Street) and thus the demand for modest living quarters easily accessible to it. The syndicate's head, Robert H.

35
Vermont Avenue at Twenty-third Street, Los Angeles. Photo "Dick" Whittington, 1929. (Whittington Collection, Department of Special Collections, University of Southern California.)

36
Pico Boulevard at Ardmore Avenue, Los Angeles. Photo "Dick" Whittington, 1929. (Whittington Collection, Department of Special Collections, University of Southern California.)

Raphael, owned a large building supply company and was active in lobbying for public improvements that would stimulate development toward
Prager Park.

Between 1900 and 1920, numerous residential buildings with
ground-level stores like those at Washington and Main were erected along
arteries within a two-mile radius of downtown, but such intense use of
property seldom extended further. The costs of land and construction
alike were sufficiently low that many people with moderate incomes could
purchase a house for about the same amount per month as they paid in
rent.[10] As a result, subdivisions located as far as four to five miles from the
city center were undertaken well before 1910. Purchasers were willing
to endure a thirty-minute streetcar commute to work rather than a thirty-
minute walk or ten-minute streetcar trip; however, they were loath to
travel long distances for convenience goods. The small, temporary
stands—selling a few basic items, sometimes of questionable quality, often
at high prices—that appeared in tracts before retail services were developed were not considered an adequate substitute (figure 38). Proximity to
bona fide stores was a distinct asset in marketing residential subdivisions,
one often mentioned and sometimes prominently featured in advertisements (figure 39). At a time when most new subdivision sales were for un-
improved lots rather than completed houses, neighborhood stores could
help reassure prospective buyers that the area would develop according to
expectations. One writer for the *Times* noted in 1910 that "when a new
section of scattering houses gets to the point where it can support a small
mercantile establishment the first step in the growth of a permanent community has been taken."[11]

The value of businesses in stimulating residential sales prompted some developers of remote tracts to erect commercial buildings, just as the Central Pacific Improvement Corporation did on its more costly, close-in location. Frederick W. Braun undertook such a project, which included a theater and service garage as well as a range of stores, next to his forty-acre subdivision at Vermont and Slauson avenues. However, such coordinated development strategies were rare.[12] The norm was for the tract owner to promote the sale of lots to those wishing to build commercial facilities no less than to those wishing to build houses (figure 40).

DEVELOPMENT

Just as boulevard frontage was treated as neutral space, available for a potentially wide range of commercial functions, so most store buildings were designed as shells that could be easily adapted to suit the needs of individual tenants. Called taxpayer blocks in many parts of the country, these unassuming and, by the 1910s, ubiquitous components of outlying urban areas might contain only two or three units; many had around six; few had more than ten. Often there was a second level for offices or apartments, but one-story buildings became even more common after World War I when mounting automobile traffic made arterial routes less agreeable places to live and apartment dwellers increasingly expected some off-street space for their cars. The great majority of taxpayers were built as speculative enterprises by property owners wishing the most profitable use for their land. On average, the per-square-foot cost of a one-story taxpayer did not differ significantly from that of a two-story apartment building, but income could be substantially greater. Base construction cost was quite low; $10,000 for a block with four or five units was typical in the late 1920s. If many owners believed their land would soon rise in value to the point that they might sell it at a handsome profit, many others prob-

ably realized that change might not be so rapid and were content with the income from their investment. A taxpayer filled with successful stores generated more revenue than the carrying costs of the property; it could be a lucrative enterprise in itself, earning a 15–20 percent return, and for that reason the supply of such buildings more than kept up with the demand.[13]

Flexible space was important to the taxpayer's plan because the nature of the tenants was generally unknown at the design stage, and, once the building was erected, tenancy could change, perhaps at frequent intervals. A real estate broker worked to secure tenants on the owner's behalf. If circumstances were favorable, the units could be fully leased before construction, but often leasing progressed at a slower rate, and many taxpayers remained partially vacant well after completion. The broker's aim was to get tenants as quickly and on as good terms as possible. Securing a drug or grocery store might be the first priority because these businesses were likely to attract numerous customers on a frequent basis and thus provide an added incentive to other merchants to locate close by. Beyond such measures, little thought appears to have been given to the types of establishments in a taxpayer. These projects were almost never conceived as integrated business developments where tenants were selected as complementary parts, each reinforcing the presence of the others.

Taxpayers were not intended as long-term investments. One account of the type in New York put the maximum profitable life expec-

tancy at ten years.[14] Both the design and the construction of the buildings therefore tended to be of an elementary kind. Yet some embellishment often was considered helpful in attracting tenants and customers alike (figure 41). A somewhat comparable balance characterized construction. By the early 1920s, wood frame commercial buildings—which in southern California were then almost always sheathed in stucco and referred to by that material—were seen as distinctly inferior to those of masonry. Brick or hollow-tile terra cotta exterior walls became the norm after World War I, if not earlier, due to public preference as well as, perhaps, lower insurance premiums. The typical Los Angeles taxpayer block of the 1920s represented standards that were conspicuously higher than the norm twenty years previous or than what was still the standard in many small towns outside the metropolitan area (figure 42). These new buildings represented more than basic shelter. They were a benchmark of neighborhood progress. However, after being welcomed as an addition to the precinct, they were subsequently taken for granted. Architectural features, no matter how ornate, almost at once began to be overshadowed by a panoply of signs. Conceived as neither permanent nor transitory, taxpayers had a useful purpose but almost never contributed to a sense of singular identity for the places they served (figure 43).

Even when many parties were involved in the development of an outlying center, some order could be brought to the process by one or a small group of property owners who solicited the involvement of others

39
Whitmore Park advertisement, 1909. (*Los Angeles Times,* 22 August 1909, V-12.)

40
Commercial building, 2521–2535 S. Hill Street, Los Angeles, ca. late 1920s. Photo "Dick" Whittington, 1929. (Whittington Collection, Department of Special Collections, University of Southern California.)

and who sought to guide the general course of work. Such orchestration
appears to have become especially pronounced after World War I, when
the patterns of outlying center development established over the previous
decade intensified throughout the metropolitan area. The underlying aim
of this involvement was to increase the value of one's own holdings. Arterial frontage in outlying areas cost a small fraction of prime frontage downtown, but could yield substantially greater profits. Between 1917 and
1927, business property values rose as much as 850 percent in the Southwest district, 833 percent, on South Broadway in the South Central, 586
percent along the Pico and Washington Boulevard corridors. These figures were modest compared to those for property at key intersections.
During almost the same time period, land at Western Avenue and Fifty-
fourth Street rose over 2,100 percent at Western and Slauson over 3,600
percent. By contrast, increases at Seventh Street and Broadway were 171
percent, at Ninth and Broadway 18 percent. The rise in dollar value remained much higher downtown, but investment required huge sums of
capital and opportunities were limited in comparison to the miles of potentially lucrative business property in outlying areas. The ideal situation was
to select a site prior to substantial growth in the area when the purchase
price was low. The assessed value of the land at the northeast corner of
San Fernando Road and Los Feliz Boulevard, just beyond the Los Angeles
city limits in Glendale, was only $680 in 1919, for example. A decade
later the value had risen to $12,000.[15]

But choosing sites that would increase exponentially in value was a risky proposition. Miles of undeveloped boulevard frontage existed, the vast majority of it deemed suitable only for commercial use well before such thinking was codified by the city's 1921 zoning ordinance (figure 44).[16] One of the most dependable indicators of good business location in outlying areas of older cities such as Chicago was a transfer point between streetcar lines.[17] However, few such places existed in Los Angeles. Beyond the periphery of downtown, the municipal railway network had few intersecting paths in 1910, and almost none that did exist became host to a business center of consequence.[18] Crossings were more numerous a decade later and in some cases afforded stimulus to commercial growth, yet the automobile was now eclipsing public transportation as a barometer of human movement. By the mid-1920s, counting the number of cars that crossed an intersection daily seems to have become a conventional means of gauging the strength of adjacent property for business purposes.[19]

The mobility afforded by cars fueled the competition between established and nascent outlying business centers alike, for if one close at hand did not fully suit a customer's wishes, it was easy to drive somewhere else. Sustaining a critical mass of businesses that provided the products desired by a local market was thus crucial to a center's success. Property owners could not afford to remain passive under the circumstances; without an ongoing effort to secure good merchants, the outlying center could fall far short of realizing its potential. There was no better example of the dynamics of this process in Los Angeles during the early 1920s than along Western Avenue between Wilshire and Hollywood boulevards.

So named because it once formed a western boundary for the city, Western Avenue experienced little real estate activity of any sort before World War I. Residential development in the area was just beginning in 1913. But less than a decade later Western was heralded as the "Wonder Street"—a magnet for commerce that would become an unbroken

41

Commercial buildings, 742–772 S. Vermont Avenue, Los Angeles, ca. late 1920s; 742–758 altered, 760–772 no longer standing. Photo "Dick" Whittington, 1931. (Whittington Collection, Department of Special Collections, University of Southern California.)

42

Commercial buildings, 1501–1525 W. Seventh Street, Los Angeles, ca. 1920s; altered. Photo "Dick" Whittington, 1929. (Whittington Collection, Department of Special Collections, University of Southern California.)

shopping corridor second only to downtown.[20] The transformation began abruptly. Between 1918 and 1921 at least seven business centers emerged along the two-and-a-half-mile path. The size to which several of these nodes grew in a short period provided ample ammunition to boosters' claims that Western was destined to become another Broadway. One business center, located just north of Wilshire Boulevard around the Sixth Street intersection, boasted some eighty stores by the early months of 1922.[21] The blocks between First and Third streets were even more intensely developed, with close to one hundred businesses (figure 45).

The scope of enterprises found in such a node by the mid-1920s increased from that of the decade previous, in part because many small-scale, independent business owners were moving from downtown due to rising rents. Operational costs outside the city center, even in a prime location such as Western Avenue, were significantly lower. Furthermore, these sites lay closer to the prosperous clientele many merchants hoped to attract, a factor that rapidly became predominant. The same reasons induced

WE TOLD YOU SO!

The Business Lots We Offered Last Week Are Going Fast and Inquiry Is Increasing Every Day. The Number is Limited, So Don't Delay. These are

BOULEVARD BUSINESS LOTS

On a Los Angeles Paved Main Artery

THE BIG PROFITS ARE IN COMMUNITY CENTER BUSINESS LOTS

They are the inspiration, the heart and the keystone of real estate activity today. You want to make money. See these lots. Bring a deposit.

Terms as Low as
$125 Down

$1250

$15 Monthly
Including Interest

No Reservation Will Be Made Without a Deposit. Get an Early Start. Our Salesmen Will Be on the Ground at 8 A. M.

BUY LOS ANGELES

It Is Better to Be Glad You Did Than to Be Sorry You Didn't

TO GET THERE
By Auto:
Go West on Slauson Avenue to Tract Office at Slauson Ave. and Mesa Drive.

ANGELES MESA LAND CO.
W. P. JEFFRIES, PRESIDENT
OWNERS & BUILDERS
612-15 PANTAGES THEATRE B'L'D'G.
411 W. 7TH ST. PHONE -66015

TO GET THERE
By Street Car:
Take Grand Avenue-Mesa Drive Car or Hawthorne-Inglewood Car to Tract Office at 54th Street and Mesa Drive.

43
Angeles Mesa Land Company advertisement for commercial property fronting Slauson Avenue. (*Los Angeles Times,* 22 January 1922, V-10.)

44
Undeveloped boulevard frontage, La Brea and Willoughby avenues, Los Angeles. Photo "Dick" Whittington, 1931. (Whittington Collection, Department of Special Collections, University of Southern California.)

45
Western Avenue, looking north at W. Second Street intersection, Los Angeles. Photo C. C. Pierce, ca. 1924. (California Historical Society Collection Department of Special Collections, University of Southern California.)

many entrepreneurs to start businesses in outlying areas. At the decade's end, a veteran Los Angeles real estate broker summarized the mood: "Nearby customers are the best customers. The neighborhood store draws from about a mile. The store in a sub-center [such as Sixth and Western] of 50,000 people draws from about two to three miles, and the nearer its customers live the oftener they come and the more they buy."[22]

A principal force behind Sixth and Western's prosperity was the Lilly-Fletcher Company, a construction firm that started purchasing land along the thoroughfare in 1919. Within a year, Lilly moved its offices to Western and concentrated on developing the area. The firm expanded its scope to include departments in real estate brokerage, rental, insurance, and architecture so that it could design, construct, finance, and secure tenants for both apartment and business buildings. Many projects were done for others, but about a third were undertaken on land Lilly owned or controlled. The firm also helped launch the Western Avenue Improvement Association, comprised of merchants and property owners, which lobbied for public improvements. Lilly's professed aim was to have the area "constitute a complete community."[23]

Much the same objective was pursued through somewhat different means at Western and Santa Monica under the auspices of A. Z. Taft. While still in his early thirties, Taft rose to regional prominence as a real estate developer. He was first vice-president of two family enterprises— Taft Realty and Taft Land and Development companies—and involved in two others—Taft Building and Taft Mining and Exploration companies.

Much of his energy was directed toward Hollywood, where all these concerns were based. During the 1920s he became a central figure in the development of Hollywood Boulevard, but he also had an interest in smaller commercial centers as well.[24]

Taft's work at Western and Santa Monica began modestly enough in 1917, with the construction of a block containing five store units and offices above—the first commercial building in the vicinity and one of the first along Western. When the property was sold in 1925, it was part of a booming center that contained over 200 businesses (figure 46). Land Taft had purchased for $50 per front foot now fetched $2,240, an increase of nearly 4,500 percent.[25] The success of this venture stemmed not from large-scale holdings by Taft himself, but rather from a six-year campaign to make the area attractive for development. Taft first improved access by securing an extension of the municipal railway line in 1920—one of the few occasions when the creation of a transfer point proved successful in stimulating retail growth. The underlying aim was to attract other investors, whose projects the Taft Realty Company could finance and build. Many additional parties undertook projects on their own, convinced that the location was opportune. Some participants were in the real estate field as brokers or as developers, including Martin Kane, an associate of Taft's who built the Palomar Hotel in the precinct. Others were merchants, including P. A. BeHannessey, a supplier of movie props who expanded his business into the retail furniture trade; L. Felix, a Pasadena furrier who opened a branch store; or the Ries brothers, who left a motion picture studio to establish a photography business. Yet others were investors who employed third parties to realize the project.[26]

Taft also seems to have sensed the advantages afforded by two new phenomena: the chain store and the branch bank. A lease for one of the first units of the Owl Drug Company to be situated away from the city center was secured for Taft's building in 1922. About three years earlier a store operated by Sam Seelig, then the largest chain grocer in the metropolitan area, opened across the street. Branches of the Los Angeles Trust & Savings Banks and the Security Trust & Savings Bank were completed in 1922 and 1923, respectively.[27] Together, these businesses were as important as any other factor in stimulating growth.

46
Santa Monica Boulevard, looking east toward Western Avenue intersection, Los Angeles. Photo "Dick" Whittington, 1930. (Whittington Collection, Department of Special Collections, University of Southern California.)

CHAIN STORES

The proliferation of chain stores during the early twentieth century was among the most significant developments in national retailing practices and one that ultimately had a profound effect on the nature of outlying business centers. Although the first chain store system in the United States—the Great Atlantic and Pacific Tea Company—originated during the Civil War era, the phenomenon as a whole remained in a nascent stage at the century's end. By 1929, however, chains accounted for 22 percent of gross sales in the retail trade, including about 40 percent of the

retail grocery business and over 18 percent of the retail drug business. The most spectacular period of growth occurred during the decade after World War I. Between 1919 and 1928, chain grocery store sales increased 366 percent, chain drug store sales 159 percent.[28] To many observers, it seemed as if chain companies were not only transforming the nature of retail business but becoming monopolies that would displace the independent merchant.

Chroniclers of the phenomenon during the interwar decades generally defined a chain as any company having two or more stores, based on the fact that many of the largest enterprises started with a single unit and at first gradually expanded with a few additional ones. Yet the characteristics that made chain store operation significant were more numerous and complex. Around 1930 one analyst estimated that for chain methods to be fully effective in the grocery field a company needed at least fifty stores and could get the best results with at least two hundred.[29] A true chain operation had centralized management that included accounting, advertising, purchasing of stock, price and policy setting, and warehousing. The system entailed no main store, but rather multiple outlets of more or less equal statute, with standardized goods, pricing, hours, and other operational components.[30]

The primary reason for the chain stores' rapid growth was that they offered merchandise of sound quality at lower cost than many independent merchants. An estimate made in 1930 found an average difference in grocery store prices of 11.2 percent.[31] The savings stemmed from a series of practices implemented or considerably refined during the 1910s. Chain stores enjoyed greater buying power than most independent retailers and thus could command lower prices from manufacturers and wholesalers alike. Many chains developed their own wholesaling functions, eliminating an array of costs traditionally incurred at that middle stage of distribution. Costs were further reduced through operating efficiencies. Credit and delivery services were eliminated; all items were sold on a cash-and-carry basis. Stock was pruned to goods that enjoyed mass appeal to promote rapid turnover (an item that sold once a month generated one eighth of the profit of one at the same price that sold twice a week). Rapid turnover also ensured that goods always appeared new, an important factor in customer appeal even when items were nonperishable. Many small independent merchants had a considerable amount of seldom-purchased stock and lacked the time, and often the expertise, to develop efficient operational methods. A sizable chain could lure well-trained personnel who worked in specialized areas of management. Chains also could afford advertising in city newspapers, an expense too great for most retailers save the largest ones downtown.

Physical attributes of chain stores further contributed to their widespread appeal. Through the 1920s, chains generally avoided having elaborate stores; most sought to minimize the investment per outlet. At the same time, considerable attention was given to appearance. Chains did much to raise the standard for a clean, orderly environment among small

and moderate-sized stores. Good lighting and ventilation were deemed essential. Store layout was under constant study both to improve its convenience to customers and to induce greater purchasing.[32]

Chains spent no less time studying those factors that made the best sites for their outlets. Initially, when most chain stores were concentrated in the city centers, the focus was on analyzing the optimal places within the retail core. Mass transit stations and transfer points, as well as other generators of extensive pedestrian movement such as a grouping of theaters, were key elements in determining the most advantageous site—what was termed a 100 percent location. The prices chain companies were willing to pay for purchase of, or a long-term lease on, a 100 percent location were enormous by the standards of the time and effectively preempted independent competitors.[33]

During the 1920s a significant portion of chain store growth occurred in outlying areas, which theretofore had been almost exclusively the domain of the small, independent retailer. From the chain's perspective, this program's purpose was to maintain proximity to the target audience. But the impact chains had on outlying areas was considerable. The high prices chain companies were willing to pay for a good location accelerated the rise of values on neighboring property. The very presence of a chain store led other parties to deduce that the area was advantageous for retailing. Chain store companies added fuel to this tendency by often locating near competing chains.[34] As a result, chain stores became a central factor in the expansion of established outlying areas and the emergence of new ones. By the late 1920s, the extent and range of chain stores in a given center could be a valuable measure of its importance.

Just as with the large downtown department store, the development of major chain companies occurred relatively late in southern California. The type was virtually nonexistent there in 1910, when a handful of drug and grocery firms operated from two to six stores each, all of them situated in or close to the city center. By 1920 the situation had begun to change in the grocery business, with two companies operating thirty-nine and twenty-four units, respectively. The expansion rate was enormous over the next five years, with six major chains operating between fifty and 260 stores in the metropolitan area. All but one, Piggly Wiggly, were locally owned, and all but one other, H. G. Chaffee Company, either had a single store or did not exist at all in 1914.[35] The most units belonged to Sam Seelig, who had opened his first store in 1911 and two more in 1915. Three years later he had seventeen. By the time he sold his business to the northern California-based Safeway Stores in 1925, Seelig had 263 units. Expanding into the Los Angeles market was a major early step in the growth of Safeway to become a national chain. Growth through acquisition became a distinct pattern by the decade's end. In 1931 Safeway acquired MacMarr Stores, which had entered the region three years earlier by taking over more than 200 units of two Los Angeles chains (E. A. Morrison and Von's) and one in Pasadena (Crown Emporium).[36]

Between 1920 and 1930, the number of grocery outlets owned by chains with twenty or more units in Los Angeles proper rose from 63 to 418; their share of the groceries in the city rose from 03.8 percent of the total of 12.9 percent. Just two companies owned chains of this size in 1920; a decade later four did. Most other grocers with multiple units had only two or three and could hardly operate as full-fledged chains. Irrespective of chain size, the overwhelming majority of this expansion occurred outside the city center.

To independent retailers, a development program such as Safeway's, or Seelig's before it, must have seemed like an all-out assault. Safeway operated small units, requiring no more than 2,100 square feet to house its mix of grocery, produce, and meat departments. This size enabled the company to adapt space in taxpayer blocks rather than commission its own facilities (figure 47). Expansion in a precinct was accomplished by opening additional units—as many as four in all—because Safeway executives believed most patrons walked to their stores and as a rule would go no further than about five blocks or a quarter-mile. This saturation strategy carried with it the assumption that some units might not succeed. Closing an unprofitable store did not incur significant loss, however, due to the scale of the chain operation and the modest investment in each unit.[37]

The emergence of a few firms controlling a substantial number of units also came to characterize the local drug store business during the 1920s. Here, however, expansion occurred at a much slower rate, in part because the cost of establishing a drug store was eight times greater on average than of establishing a grocery.[38] At the start of the decade, only two chains of any size existed in Los Angeles: the Sun Drug Company (thirteen units) and the San Francisco-based Owl Drug Company (six units). Five years later Owl had absorbed Sun and had thirty-seven units. The next largest competitor was Court Drug Company with nine units. Thirty-seven others had two or three stores. By 1930 Owl had not increased its base by much (to forty units), but remained well ahead of the others (Liggett had twelve units, Court eleven).[39] Besides numbers, the most conspicuous difference between the major grocery and drug chains was that the latter were predominantly situated downtown—39 out of 46 units in 1925; 42 out of 63 in 1930. Strong consumer identification with the individual druggists in a neighborhood made the position of independent operators far stronger than that of their counterparts in the grocery business. During the 1920s chain drug companies generally fared best downtown where their clientele was transient.[40] But Owl in particular was seeking to make inroads into the lucrative neighborhood trade. The Santa Monica and Western branch was one of the first outside the city center. Between 1925 and 1930 most of the firm's expansion occurred in similar places. Growth accelerated over the next decade, so that chain drug stores were a standard component of outlying business centers by the eve of World War II.

The pattern varied with other types of chain establishments. Among the fifteen shoe stores with multiple units in 1920, the largest had five, two others had four. Out of a total of forty chain units, only one was situated beyond the city center. A decade later, the largest shoe chain had ten units, the next nine, and eight others between four and six. The number of chain units had more than doubled to eighty-two, over a third of which now lay in outlying areas. Although no chain variety stores appear to have been operating in Los Angeles in 1920, at mid-decade there were at least fourteen, eight of which were in outlying areas. By 1930, twenty-three units out of a total of thirty-three were outside the city center. Both types illustrate the fact that, irrespective of particular differences, many prominent chain companies had targeted outlying areas as principal places of expansion by the decade's end. Yet chains seldom if ever initiated the development of Los Angeles's outlying centers prior to the depression. Aside from groceries, most chains came to these nodes after they were on their way to assuming a distinctive form. Chains thus helped validate the mercantile strength of those centers in which they located, chosen over many others that might seem just as good in a period of fast-paced metropolitan growth.

The branch bank was often a more important catalyst in the initial stages of an outlying center's development. Los Angeles differed from many other cities in this regard because it was a national leader in decentralized banking activities. State legislation passed in 1909 enabled state banks to establish branches in the same community as their respective home offices. While this provision was not unique, it was among the most favorable in the country. Los Angeles became the center of this activity due to the city's large geographic area, downtown congestion, and the considerable amounts of capital brought by newcomers, and the local practice

47
Commercial building, 2168–2170 Venice Boulevard, Los Angeles, ca. early/mid-1920s; altered. Photo 1925. (Hearst Collection, Department of Special Collections, University of Southern California.)

of the bank serving as an intermediary in real estate transactions. The success of a few initial ventures spawned a proliferation of branches after World War I. By 1925, nearly 140 branch offices could be found among Los Angeles-based banks. Five years later, the total approached 200.[41]

More than most early chain stores in Los Angeles, the branch bank was cast as a pioneer in providing services theretofore associated with the city center. These major financial institutions could instill a greater sense of confidence among depositors and had far greater resources from which customers could secure loans than small, independent banks.[42] Branch banks were seen as a major stimulus to retail growth in their vicinity. Furthermore, at a time when elaborate commercial buildings outside downtown were still the exception, the branch bank became a local landmark, adding distinction and a sense of legitimacy to an emerging business node. Before the 1920s, small storefront quarters, much like those of retail establishments, were commonplace for neighborhood banks in cities nationwide. As branch expansion became more competitive, designs changed markedly. In 1926, the senior vice-president of Security Trust indicated his objective "to erect a building that will stand out as the best in the locality. . . . It is good business for the bank, . . . a good-looking building adds to its prestige and attracts the best class of people; it inspires other property owners to follow suit; and it serves in both a commercial and cultural sense to raise the whole tone of the community" (figure 48).[43] In both its physical embellishment and its broadening of choices available to consumers in outlying areas, the branch bank prefigured the branch of the major downtown store, which had a key impact on the rise of new shopping districts by the decade's end.

In its scale and character, Western Avenue typified arterial development in Los Angeles during the 1920s. The rate of growth was now quicker than in previous years, the competition among business nodes was greater, and the advantages some such places had over others could be more conclusively demonstrated when they were selected for branch banks and chain store outlets. However, the basic physical pattern was no more than an extension of what was well established in the decade prior to World War I.

By the early 1920s, a number of real estate speculators sought undertakings of a larger scale. Based on anticipated growth, they believed that market demand soon would be great enough to spawn multistory business centers throughout the metropolitan area—places that were substantial "downtowns" in their own right. Most projections were inflated. One firm exhorted *Times* readers to "visualize tomorrow," when adjacent

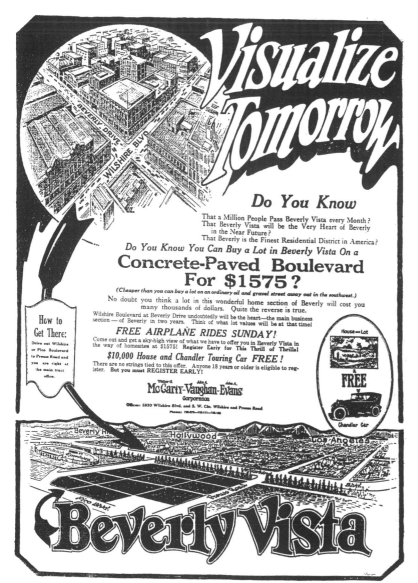

48
Security Trust & Savings Bank, 2100 W. Pico Boulevard, Los Angeles, ca. 1923, John and Donald B. Parkinson, architects; burned 1992. (*Shapes of Clay,* January 1926, V.)

49
"Visualize Tomorrow," Beverly Vista advertisement. (*Los Angeles Times,* 29 April 1928, V-11.)

Oliver & Carver

Are selling the heart of

the ATLANTIC CITY

of the Pacific Coast

Venice

NEW BUSINESS DISTRICT

F IRST STEPS are now being taken to make Venice the ATLANTIC CITY of the Pacific Coast.

This community is the NEAREST beach to the heart of Los Angeles. It is now included within the Los Angeles city limits and has been definitely chosen for intensive development by the Los Angeles City Planning Commission and Playground Commission.

Today a NEW and MODERN business center is being developed in the exact center of the present business district.

Here will be erected the best of the new office buildings, hotels and shopping centers that are already necessary to meet the existing needs of Venice.

Here TODAY you may still secure FULLY IMPROVED business property at low OPENING PRICES to be increased 10% or more on November 1st, in line with the rapid increase in values that is now occurring.

The purchase to date of more than $500,000 worth of this property by leading Los Angeles business men is sufficient reason for giving careful consideration to the unusual opportunity for profitable investment now presented.

Drive to Venice today over Washington and Venice Boulevards and see for yourself the actual situation.

OLIVER & CARVER
Fred H Oliver   Roy L Carver
608 PACIFIC FINANCE BLDG.
Tract office: Windward & Trolley Way
VENICE
Phones   Santa Monica 64,479
Tucker 8476

Jones & Norell
Hollywood Representatives
Suite 912 Guaranty Building
Telephone GRanite 6718

blocks of Wilshire Boulevard (then still open land) would become the core of a major business district (figure 49). Now was the time to buy house lots, the advertisement coaxed, before the building boom that surely would soon occur. Industrial development was also seen as a stimulus. Boulevard frontage along one thoroughfare extending southeast of downtown into the new Central Manufacturing District was promoted as the "key to millions"; the profits made from office and retail development there would be comparable to those made in the expansion of the urban core a decade or two earlier. The ocean was yet another draw. The beach community of Venice was destined to become "the Atlantic City of the Pacific Coast," according to another firm, presenting a vision of skyscrapers well above the Los Angeles height limit in an area that had persistently failed to attract a stable population (figure 50). Sometimes no pretext was used other than the implied one that all major arterial intersections would one day become latter-day Times Squares. A tract along Pico Boulevard at the fringe of the metropolis, thirteen miles from downtown, was heralded as the future "Great White Way of Western Los Angeles." "There'll be skyscrapers at Imperial Center," its promoters insisted.[44]

While such speculative visions were improbable, the idea of future dense urban growth in outlying areas was shared by many respected business interests as well. Even the depression failed to extinguish the idea fully. Writing in 1935, Charles Cohan, long-standing real estate editor of the *Times,* described at length how the city a hundred years hence would extend from Santa Barbara to San Diego and be laced with skyscraper business centers at frequent intervals.[45] Los Angeles was to be not just a lateral metropolis of enormous proportion, but also a multicentered vertical one. The intense building program that had transformed downtown was forecast to occur again and again, if not always at the same magnitude. Just as the business community projected images of the core area as a mighty forest of skyscrapers, equivalent to those of New York and Chicago, so they were fond of depicting the whole region in a similarly titanic, urban cast. To justify such dreams, boosters had more than wildly optimistic projections; they had the example of Hollywood.

50

Real estate advertisement for Venice business district. (*Los Angeles Times,* 24 October 1926, V-7.)

IV

HOLLYWOOD—LOS ANGELES'S OTHER HALF

Just as the term "parkless" was used by the press to discuss parking problems rather than a dearth of municipal open space, so the "other half" referred not to the city's poor, as Jacob Riis had popularized the term among east coast reformers, but rather to potential area of real estate growth. "Hollywood," gloated a 1927 account in the *Los Angeles Realtor,* was rapidly becoming "a gateway between . . . new and old Los Angeles." Lying to the northwest of downtown in an area roughly bounded by Vermont Avenue on the east, Beverly Boulevard on the south, La Brea Avenue on the west, and the Santa Monica Mountains on the north, the Hollywood district "has for a decade played the leading role in the suburban growth of Los Angeles during [the city's] most remarkable period of development." But this surge in metropolitan expansion "simply foreshadow[s] the big activity that is yet to come." The author asked his readership to imagine a giant fan, its handle positioned near Hollywood's business heart. If oriented to the southeast, the fan's ribs "will point to everything that Los Angeles' present 'half' has done in the last fifty years. Turn the fan around and it will spread over the San Fernando Valley, Los Angeles' 'other half,' and Hollywood thus becomes the connecting link or gateway between the two."[1]

This buoyant prophecy did not materialize to a significant extent until the late 1940s; prior to then most of Los Angeles's growth took place west and south of Hollywood. Yet the idea that Hollywood was destined

to be the new metropolitan hub was widely believed and helped propel the intense development of its commercial center up to the depression. By 1930 Hollywood Boulevard boasted a "skyscraper mile" that formed the second largest business district in Los Angeles and one of the largest outlying centers in the United States.

ALADDIN CITIES

For all of its aura as a unique center of filmmaking and stardom, Hollywood was in fact part of a national phenomenon in urban development that represented the initial challenge to downtown's hegemony as a retail center. During the 1920s, most large cities spawned at least one such outlying center, more ambitious in size and scope than preceding examples, that functioned as an alternative to downtown for many shopping and related needs. These new magnets of trade—such as Upper Darby outside Philadelphia, Englewood in Chicago, and Midtown in St. Louis—were well removed from their city centers, and it was this distance upon which their rise was predicated.[2] Residential developments of the 1910s and 1920s placed so many middle-class people far afield from downtown that a substitute business district could flourish amid their new tracts. Typically located where little or no concentrated settlement had existed a generation previous, these Aladdin cities, as one observer termed Upper Darby, seemed like miniature downtowns, providing an array of stores, restaurants, financial and professional services, as well as entertainment facilities, many of which theretofore had been rare or unavailable outside the urban core.[3] In layout and appearance, these places also echoed city center characteristics, with buildings densely congregated along a main street, the largest tending to form clusters around one or two intersections. Construction of a building over four or five stories was seen as a benchmark for the precinct coming into its own.

Yet Hollywood differed from most major outlying centers of the 1920s in several important ways. Even with the inflated expectations of the period, boosters seldom thought they would wrest commercial dominance from the city center, as a number of parties in Hollywood believed. Most Aladdin cities were targeted to people of moderate income. Hollywood merchants courted this audience but also sought to cultivate a sense of exclusiveness, capitalizing on patronage by movie stars and the more traditional urban elite. Finally, most Aladdin cities were tied to strategic locations along public transportation routes. Hollywood was well served by streetcars, but its principal attraction was to the motorist. Many well-to-do households were now locating nearby in the hills where public transit did not reach. The car, too, made Hollywood conveniently accessible from areas further afield. Boosters even claimed that driving to Hollywood from Glendale and Pasadena was easier than going downtown. At first, its business precinct also lacked congestion.

During the 1920s, Angelenos saw Hollywood as a model for decentralization and credited the automobile with spurring the district's meteoric rise. When Hollywood was incorporated as a third-class city in 1903, approximately 700 people resided within its limits; when annexed to Los Angeles seven years later, the population was at 10,000. The increase was more than sevenfold over the next decade and thereafter climbed at an average of 10,000 people a year, the total exceeding 153,000 in 1930.[4] The rise of the motion picture industry to a position of national leadership during the same twenty-year period helped transform Hollywood into one of the fastest-growing parts of the region. The large amounts of capital generated by that industry also fostered the rise of a major new business district in its midst. But Hollywood's economic strength was beholden to no one source. Many residents worked in downtown Los Angeles. The most frequently cited reason for Hollywood's success was its appeal as a place to live, using the automobile as a routine mode of conveyance. The most prestigious residential areas of previous decades, lying on more or less level terrain west and southwest of the city center, began to lose ground. Further removed from downtown, more varied topographically, and tinged with the glamour of the movies, tracts in and around Hollywood were now the places of choice for many prosperous commuters. A large affluent populace and an even larger middle class made the average income in Hollywood considerably higher than that citywide, an extremely appealing market for many businesses.

STORES

At the end of World War I, Hollywood's commercial landscape combined features typical of new outlying districts and of large town centers found in many parts of the United States. Small clusters of modest one- and two-story buildings were scattered along Hollywood Boulevard, the main east-west artery and streetcar route from downtown Los Angeles. Toward the western end of the car line, extending for eight blocks between Cahuenga Boulevard and Highland Avenue, lay the largest of the city's first-generation outlying centers, with more than 200 stores by 1920 (figure 51). These outlets purveyed routine goods and services used by middle-income households. Almost all the businesses were locally based. Selection was limited; a trip downtown was necessary for specialized needs and for comparison shopping.

By the mid-1920s, conspicuous changes began to affect the size, composition, and character of Hollywood's business core. New commercial buildings were rising at a rapid rate on lots previously vacant or occupied by houses and smaller store blocks. Many new retail outlets opened, joined by others that were expanding. The range of available goods increased, particularly in clothing and accessories. Spurred by the film industry, Hollywood was emerging as a center of fashion, with shops that sought to rival ones in New York and Chicago as purveyors of stylish

women's wear.[5] The most decisive factor in Hollywood's rise as a magnet
of trade was the first wave of branch store development among prominent
local and national downtown-based retailers. Specialty stores in apparel
and accessories led the way, among them Schwab's (1921) and Mullen &
Bluett (1922) in men's clothes, Myer Siegel (1925) in women's clothes,
Innes (1923), Young's (1923), Wetherby-Kayser (1923), and C. H. Baker
(1925) in shoes, and the New York Hat Store (1924).[6] Hollywood boasted
the first branch of the distinguished San Francisco emporium I. Magnin,
which opened in 1923. A second Bay Area clothier, Roos Brothers, followed six years later.[7]

Numerous other well-known businesses built Hollywood outlets
as well. The paint manufacturer W. P. Fuller erected a large store in 1921.
Barker Brothers opened a multistory, 50,000-square-foot facility in 1927,
for a brief period southern California's largest branch outlet. Showrooms
were built for Maytag (ca. 1925), Frigidaire (1927), and General Electric
(1928) at a time when major household appliances were still regarded as
new emblems of attainment.[8] Yet other branches such as the Platt Music
Company (ca. 1922) catered to the recreational pursuits of the well-to-do.
Fancy restaurants of the sort then primarily identified with downtown also
appeared: Paulais (1924), the Elite Catering Company (ca. 1926), and Pig
N' Whistle (1927). Chain drug and food stores could be found in considerable number by 1926; variety stores (F. W. Grand, J. J. Newberry) somewhat later (1928–1930).[9]

By 1930 Hollywood had some 300 stores along the heart of
"The Boulevard" and probably 100 more along nearby side streets. Promotional efforts emphasized the small-scale ambience of the district's stores,
where one could purchase goods in an intimate, convivial atmosphere.

Hollywood not only lacked the traffic of downtown Los Angeles, boosters claimed; it also lacked the pressing crowds, particularly those segments of the population that a well-heeled clientele found undesirable.[10] Most stores were of modest dimensions and many were boutiques. Hollywood Boulevard was cast as a great collection of specialty shops unsurpassed anywhere in the region. Some leading branch and chain stores looked the part, with buildings that were considerably more elaborate—inside and out—than facilities in other outlying centers prior to the late 1920s (figure 52). Yet the majority of buildings were of a conventional cut.[11] Hollywood's distinction lay with the scope of its businesses, not with their physical attributes. At the end of the boom, the commercial center no longer resembled that of a midwestern town, but rather that of a moderate-sized midwestern city (figure 53).

Just as with a city, the specialty store was only one part of the equation. While promoters stressed exclusiveness, they also cultivated the mass-market appeal of a metropolitan center. Soon after the first world war, business leaders began to pursue the development of a large department store as a catalyst for retail growth. By October 1921, Charles E. Toberman, a major landholder along Hollywood Boulevard and a key figure in advancing its business development, announced plans for a large emporium. When the building opened ten months later, Toberman noted that he had tried to interest prominent Los Angeles businesses in Hollywood but was always rebuffed due to a lack of distinction in local outlets. Thus, "I determined to build a department store, . . . not only [because] . . . it would be good business . . . but because . . . it would do more to hold business in Hollywood than any other one thing."[12]

Initially called the C. R. S. Company and soon renamed Robertson's, the department store did in fact stimulate retail growth. The building rose four stories and contained some 46,000 square feet, making it by far the largest store in Hollywood and among the largest outside downtown Los Angeles when it opened. Yet the business was a new one, with-

out reputation, and while Toberman claimed that it equaled the finest emporia on Broadway, the store never approached that stature. Downtown merchants might be receptive to opening branches in Hollywood, but not to creating equivalents to their parent stores.[13] An establishment befitting the core of a great city still eluded The Boulevard.

The chance to bestow metropolitan stature on Hollywood's shopping district came five years later, in July 1927, with plans for an enormous second B. H. Dyas store at Hollywood and Vine. The program stipulated a nine-story edifice containing over 130,000 square feet, making it larger than the downtown Dyas emporium (figure 54). A syndicate of local businessmen had aggressively pursued the project, persuading Bernal Dyas to break ranks with his competitors. Los Angeles department store executives had informally agreed to resist branch development in an effort to maintain the volume of their downtown trade.[14] Dyas was a newcomer to the field, having expanded his business from sporting goods a decade previous, and may well have believed that creating a large Hollywood store was the best means of capturing a larger share of the market. The new building was not only bigger than his existing one, it was run independently, with a separate staff of buyers who targeted the affluent residents of Hollywood. Here, Dyas believed, his company could move to the forefront. When announcing the plan, he proclaimed that Hollywood and Vine would rival Forty-second Street and Broadway in New York.[15]

Dyas's move had little precedent anywhere in the United States. When the Hollywood emporium opened in March 1928, the trend toward branch development among downtown department stores was barely under way. Just as in Los Angeles, parent companies had invested millions of dollars in their physical facilities, and conventional wisdom held that a big branch would erode downtown patronage. The few branches then operating were mostly small and specialized in nature. Among the first was erected in 1925 by William Filene's Sons Company of Boston and targeted to students at Wellesley College. Over the next three years, Filene's opened two additional stores in other college towns, three in resort communities of Massachusetts and Maine, and three in small cities—Portland, Providence, and Worcester—of which the Worcester outlet was by far the largest at 28,000 square feet. Branches of New York stores were limited to tiny outlets of departmentalized stores specializing in apparel and accessories: Best & Company (1924) and Saks Fifth Avenue (1925) at Palm Beach.[16] All these units were conceived as extensions of the parent store, engaging the patronage of customers while they were at school or on vacation or enlisting a new clientele beyond the company's trading radius. An important exception to this tendency was the first known branch of a major downtown store: B. Nugent & Brother's outlet in the Midtown district of St. Louis, which opened at the remarkably early date of 1913. Adapting space in an existing facility, the store contained nearly 40,000 square feet, some 15,000 of which was at first used for selling space.[17] The only other comparable outlet constructed before Dyas Hollywood was the 50,000-square-foot branch of a small but long-established Philadelphia department

53
Hollywood Boulevard, looking east from
McCadden Street. Photo ca. late 1920s/
early 1930s. (Courtesy Christy McAvoy.)

store, George Allen, completed several months earlier. Situated in German-town, it was likewise designed to attract residents of affluent enclaves nearby as a substitute for shopping downtown.[18] Dyas's store was thus far the most ambitious of its kind and stood at the leading edge of a phenome-non that would transform urban retailing in later years.

Upon its completion, the Dyas store was heralded as a bench-mark in Hollywood's commercial ascendancy. Seeing the benefits the new emporium would bring to his own business, Robertson's manager asserted that "Hollywood Boulevard can now in every sense of the word be the 'Mecca' for the great shopping public," adding that only "a few years ago people could with some justification say, 'I can't find what I want in Holly-wood and have to go downtown anyway.' That can hardly be true now for Hollywood has not only ample stock to choose from but a great variety of stocks at prices to fit any purse."[19] Within a short period, how-ever, this purported capstone to the shopping district was experiencing financial problems. Dyas had overextended his resources. At an early stage of the depression he retrenched, consolidating assets in the downtown facility and concentrating on a more limited range of goods. Though Dyas's bid for leadership failed, it inaugurated the idea of large-scale

branch development. Even with the economic downturn, several competitors bid to take over the enterprise and, on the third anniversary of its initial opening, purchase was announced by the president of the Broadway department store.[20] What seemed like a disastrous turn of events for Hollywood was averted, the retail base strengthened in the process.

The Broadway's reputation and very name, synonymous with the retail corridor downtown, gave recognition to Hollywood in a way that Dyas could not. At the same time, the Broadway's executives followed their predecessor's strategy in using the outlet to upgrade their clientele. The Broadway had built its business upon a middle-income market. Now the company could court a more elite audience as well, featuring fashionable wares and other costly items. The attributes of store and community thus were mutually reinforcing. The Broadway Hollywood prospered, expanding to occupy three previously unused floors and, in 1938, to include a six-story addition of over 52,000 square feet.[21] For several decades, the facility fulfilled its promise as an anchor for trade in the community.

An important factor in the Broadway's decision to establish a large store outside downtown was that its competitors were contemplating, and in one case had already made, similar moves. Bullock's confirmed long-standing rumors when its president announced plans to build an elegant emporium on Wilshire Boulevard in April 1928, seven months after the company had achieved complete financial separation from the Broadway.[22] Far more ominous from the latter's perspective were indications that the archrival May Company would erect a nine-story branch on Hollywood Boulevard three blocks west of Vine Street.[23] A year earlier, Universal Pictures president Carl Laemmle had nearly succeeded in courting a "large New York department store" to establish an enormous outlet right across the street from the Dyas building. Laemmle had gone so far as to secure a design by an unnamed French architect, which, whiles somewhat schizophrenic in composition, would have been among the most arresting examples of modernism in the country at that time, making its precursor seem both small and dated by comparison (figure 55).[24] Both projects were stillborn, no doubt due to the depression, yet Hollywood's desirability as a center for large-scale retail development was now well established. Dyas's move forever changed the thinking of Los Angeles's major retailers. Not only was further downtown growth hampered by soaring land values, but fear was mounting that with ever more customers living ever further afield, fewer among them would be willing to make frequent downtown shopping journeys. A great emporium could continue to expand primarily by coming to its clientele. The fact that one department store had taken this step no doubt made it seem imperative for the others to follow.

BUSINESS DIVERSITY

Retail trade was by no means the only contributor to Hollywood's commercial boom. The range of enterprises located on or near The Boulevard did indeed resemble that of a typical city center. Together with the Broadway Hollywood store, the most conspicuous components were tall office buildings, seven of which existed by 1930. Over the previous five years Hollywood's "skyscraper" construction had outpaced that in other outlying areas of Los Angeles and elsewhere in the nation as well.[25] The impe-

54
B. H. Dyas Hollywood (later the Broadway Hollywood) department store, 6300 Hollywood Boulevard, Los Angeles, 1927–1928, Fred. H. Dorn, architect. Photo "Dick" Whittington, ca. 1953. (Whittington Collection, Department of Special Collections, University of Southern California.)

tus for this work came to a large extent from leading Los Angeles financial institutions, which proved less reluctant to develop large, full-service branches there than their retail counterparts. These companies also recognized Hollywood's potential for a concentration of professional offices, offering services theretofore primarily available downtown.

Concrete steps to make Hollywood an important financial and office center began before comparable advances materialized in the retail sphere. In 1920, Security Trust & Savings Bank, one of the largest in southern California, unveiled plans for a six-story building in the heart of the new business district, a project that Toberman later admitted was crucial to his decision to erect a department store.[26] Three years later, construction began on a height-limit (thirteen stories) block for the Guaranty Building & Loan Association, followed by one for the First National Bank in 1927.[27] Local capital began to match that from outside Hollywood at an early date. The district's largest office building project was undertaken in 1923–1924 by the Taft Realty Company, whose leadership ranked with Toberman's in fostering business growth. Work started in 1928 on the Bank of Hollywood's new headquarters, which rivaled its branch neighbors in size and embellishment.[28]

55

Department store, Hollywood Boulevard and Vine Street, northwest corner, Los Angeles, 1929–1930; project. (*Los Angeles Times,* 26 January 1930, V-2.)

56

Idealized view of Hollywood, ca. 1926. (*Hollywood Daily Citizen,* Hollywood Today Edition, 8 June 1926, I-1.)

57

"Shopping's Good in Hollywood," promotional illustration. (*Hollywood Daily Citizen,* 4 December 1928, 3.)

Collectively, the tall buildings formed Hollywood's image as a new metropolitan center. By 1926, the *Hollywood Daily Citizen* was carrying depictions of the emerging skyline, arranged to suggest a pyramidal assemblage soaring above sequestered residential enclaves (figure 56). Two years later the momentum in high-rise building had increased to the point that Hollywood Boulevard was portrayed as the heart of a great city, resembling the coveted urbanity of Fifth Avenue (figure 57).[29] But the configuration was hardly the same. Hollywood's tall commercial buildings formed clusters around the two principal north-south arteries—Vine Street and Highland Avenue—which lay close to either end rather than in the middle of the retail center (figures 58, 59). In between, few buildings exceeded four stories and most were no more than two. This configuration distinguished Hollywood from other Aladdin cities, whose tallest buildings were concentrated around one or two closely spaced intersections. Visually, the results enhanced the perceived size of the district, emphasizing its length, without disturbing the small-scale characteristics of the retail spine for most of its extent. Hollywood continued to grow according to the linear structure established well before 1920. Toberman concentrated his energies on one end of the spine, the Tafts on the other.

58
Hollywood Boulevard, looking east toward Cahuenga Boulevard intersection; tall buildings from left to right: Security Trust & Savings Bank (1920–1922, John and Donald B. Parkinson, architects), Guaranty Building (1923–1924, John C. Austin and Frederick M. Ashley, associated architects), Bank of Hollywood Building (1928–1929, Aleck Curlett, architect), and the Broadway Hollywood store. Photo "Dick" Whittington, 1939. (Whittington Collection, Department of Special Collections, University of Southern California.)

Widespread automobile use fit well with this development pattern. The distance between tall building clusters allayed the problems of traffic congestion. Not only were the greatest concentrations of tall buildings separated by a considerable distance, but many of the intervening retail blocks felt little impact from drivers destined for the two ends. An independent assessment made in 1928 found that curbside parking space in the business center could be secured most of the time without undue difficulty.[30]

Concurrent building projects in the residential and recreational spheres did much to bolster Hollywood's ascendancy as a business center. Several multistory hotels were constructed during the 1920s, most notably the Roosevelt (1925–1927), which served as a social center for the area's elite as well as a destination for well-to-do tourists.[31] On blocks north of Hollywood Boulevard rose a bumper crop of midrise apartment houses, forming the largest concentration of its kind in the metropolitan area.[32] Far more people of means lived in proximity to Hollywood's core than to downtown Los Angeles. To the south, Sunset Boulevard became home of the nine-story Hollywood Athletic Club (1923–1924) as well as the metropolitan area's second highest concentration of automobiles sales and service facilities.[33]

59

Hollywood Boulevard, looking east toward Highland Avenue intersection; tall buildings from left to right: Pacific-Southwest Trust & Savings Bank (1927–1928, Meyer & Holler, architects), Hotel Christie (1920–1921, Arthur R. Kelly, architect); and Barker Brothers Hollywood store/El Capitan Theatre (1926–1927, Morgan, Walls & Clements and G. Albert Lansburgh, associated architects). Photo "Dick" Whittington, 1939. (Whittington Collection, Department of Special Collections, University of Southern California.)

One of the most conspicuous and influential features of Hollywood's commercial center was its movie theaters, the aggregate of which posed a challenge to Broadway as the metropolitan region's focus of popular entertainment. That challenge stemmed not so much from size or elaborateness of the facilities as it did from their function as settings for lavish premieres and first-run pictures. Nationally, first-run movies were shown almost exclusively in downtown theaters throughout the interwar decades, not in neighborhood houses in outlying areas. Having first-run movies, complete with opening spectacles, made Hollywood Boulevard seem unique.[34]

Paralleling what occurred in the financial sphere, efforts to make Hollywood a center for the exhibition of motion pictures began prior to the district's rise as a leading retail area. In 1921, the redoubtable Los Angeles impresario Sid Grauman started construction of the Egyptian Theatre, which, while not large (1,760 seats), was conceived to replace his still new Million Dollar Theatre (1917–1918) on Broadway and be the new scene of his lavish premieres. Five years later, Grauman was at work on a slightly larger (2,200-seat) and much more imposing Chinese Theatre, whose front itself suggested a stage set.[35] More or less concurrently, Warner Brothers erected a 2,700-seat "palace" for the introduction of its films. Complementing this triad was the 1,500-seat El Capitan (1925–1926), probably the largest legitimate theater in the region and developed to attract major performances from New York, and the 2,800-seat Pantages (1928–1930), conceived for extravagant vaudeville shows and adapted for movies by the time it opened.[36] These enterprises, extending the full length of Hollywood's business core, elicited comparisons to Broadway in New York and were as significant as any other development in nurturing the belief that this district would become the new heart of the California metropolis.[37]

PROMOTION

By 1930, Hollywood functioned much like a metropolitan center in miniature, with an array of mutually reinforcing commercial activities. While it never approached the importance of downtown Los Angeles, it nonetheless was more than the equivalent of small satellite city centers such as in Pasadena or Glendale, for the aggregate encompassed a caliber of retail, financial, and recreational facilities seldom found in those places. Numerous parties shaped the amalgam. Real estate developers such as Toberman and the Tafts played a formative role, but there were many others with lesser resources at their command, including long-time owners of boulevard frontage who constructed single, modest buildings. Initiatives taken by businesses and investors from outside the district were as crucial to Hollywood's advance as were local concerns. Conservative banks no less than the flamboyant Grauman proved essential to transforming the street.

The results would not have been so successful without some co-operative relationship among members of the business community. Hollywood had its own Chamber of Commerce, which worked for physical improvements and generated publicity to enhance patronage. Special shopping days were staged by coalitions of merchants early in the decade, but all such efforts seemed parochial compared to "Hollywood Dresses Up," a three-day affair organized by the chamber during the 1927 Christmas season. Fusing glamorous aspects of the film industry with those of the retail trades, the event was christened by a battery of klieg lights along Hollywood Boulevard and nearby streets, which, when the master switch was thrown by Mary Pickford, set a forest of illuminating shafts skyward just after sunset (figure 60). The public could "mingle with the stars" while perusing the latest store displays. A chamber spokesman minced no words in explaining the costly program:

Much of the outside world is more prone to order things from Hollywood than the average resident of the town. We have . . . the means of setting fashions throughout the world. Many of the best people here realize this. . . . But there are enough Hollywood people going down town for all their needs to have inspired us to inaugurate this campaign.[38]

The spectacle gave the public something downtown did not offer, underscoring the idea of Hollywood as a unique destination point.[39] Property owners continued the initiative the following April when they established the Hollywood Boulevard Association, which was patterned after

60
Hollywood Boulevard, looking east from Sycamore Avenue; night view probably taken at movie premiere. Photo "Dick" Whittington, 1928. (Whittington Collection, Department of Special Collections, University of Southern California.)

organizations promoting Broadway in New York and Michigan Avenue in Chicago.[40] Among the most ambitious of the group's early projects was held in the spring of 1929 and entailed coordination of merchandise and pricing throughout the commercial center so that it would function as the "World's Largest Department Store."[41] By this point, the objective was not so much to stimulate awareness of what retailers had to offer as to demonstrate that prices were competitive with those downtown. Such programs were, of course, partly built on illusion. Hollywood never actually operated as a single store. Even for the association's event, only about a third of the merchants in the business center participated. Yet the stream of publicity emanating both from the chamber and from the association enhanced trade. These activities also helped prepare business leaders for devising strategies in response to the subsequent economic downturn, when aspirations to become another Fifth Avenue soon faded and "dressing up" for boulevard spectacles no longer had such widespread public appeal.

STRUGGLE

Hopes continued to run high for Hollywood's future during the early stages of the depression, but increasingly were directed toward recapturing what was now portrayed as a past era of elegance. In 1932, Roos Brothers placed a conspicuous advertisement in the *Hollywood Citizen News,* declaring, with some unease, "Hollywood is still Hollywood!" Appearances still counted, even if the emphasis of promotional campaigns was shifting to more basic objectives. By 1934 the *News* itself ran a full-page call for a "modern crusade," urging that "just as the Crusaders of old went in search of the Holy Grail—so we seek the modern "Holly-Goal"—a bright, gleaming, spotless town—-comparable to the Hollywood of pre-depression days! Spring is here. . . . Let Hollywood be Hollywood again!"[42]

The situation was not quite as gloomy as such accounts might suggest. 1931 saw the completion of the so-called "Five Fingers Plan," a six-million-dollar public works project. The result of intensive lobbying by the Chamber of Commerce and other local groups, the improvements included widening, straightening, and repaving six miles of arteries in the business district to make it more accessible to motorists.[43] The number of national chain store branches increased, and a more or less steady influx of new independent outlets opened along Hollywood Boulevard throughout the 1930s.[44] Some merchants expanded their quarters. Campaigns for building modernization were launched as early as 1930; by the eve of Pearl Harbor, many Hollywood Boulevard storefronts were updated or completely remade.[45] On the other hand, two major companies, I. Magnin and Mullen & Bluett, closed their branches. Robertson's went out of business. Even more ominously, Hollywood failed to attract any new stores of comparable stature.[46] Much of the mercantile growth that did occur was oriented more toward a broad, middle-income market than to-

ward an elite trade. The extent of new construction paled in comparison with that of the 1920s. Aside from the Broadway's 1938 addition, the most ambitious project of the decade was a four-story store for S. H. Kress Company, completed in 1934. Max Factor embarked on a sumptuous remodeling of his headquarters in 1935, but most of the facelifting done to stores failed to generate the aura of elegance that boosters still wished to project.[47] On the whole, Hollywood's architecture had never possessed unusual élan; now it saw restrained, sometimes minimalist modern vocabularies employed for remodeled fronts. A poignant example was provided by Nancy's, a locally based women's apparel store, whose owner in 1939 converted the vacant I. Magnin building into a scaleless box.[48]

On the eve of World War II, while Hollywood remained the second largest retail area in Los Angeles and continued to hold much of its appeal, it no longer enjoyed the prestige of the 1920s. The depression was not the primary cause of this change, however. Well before the stock market crash, the groundwork for a challenge to Hollywood's commercial prominence was being laid in other places, which would grow and flourish during the next decade. Behind attempts in the 1920s to make Hollywood the new metropolitan center lay the belief that a city would always have a single dominant business precinct, and that with growth concentrated to the north and west in Los Angeles County, Hollywood was ideally situated to be this single center. Local business leaders knew that their counterparts elsewhere were pursuing the same goal, but they assumed that, like competing communities in a metropolitan region, the relationships among them would become increasingly hierarchical. One outlying center would enjoy leadership; most others would rank well below. What Hollywood's promoters failed to foresee was that the mobility that so contributed to their center's rise as an alternative to downtown also fostered development of other outlying centers further afield, conveniently located near yet newer residential areas. One of the key factors in this struggle was adequate off-street parking space, which Hollywood's business community was slow to recognize.

Like almost every outlying commercial center developed during the 1920s, Hollywood had little space reserved for parking. Conventional wisdom held that problems with automobiles were endemic to the city center but not to areas well removed. Boosters who prophesied that Hollywood would be the new commercial heart of the metropolis ignored the potential problems that stature might bring. Programs initiated for motorists echoed those in downtown Los Angeles: widening, straightening, and otherwise improving arteries into the business district so as to facilitate traffic flow. Because adequate curbside space seemed to exist in most parts of the commercial area, it was assumed that parking, in itself, would not become a serious problem. Several stores did break from this mode by making special provision for customers. I. Magnin was the first in Hollywood, and among the earliest in Los Angeles, to have a parking area at the rear of its store when it opened in 1923 (figure 61). Additions made some five years later included a basement garage for patrons, an amenity also fea-

I. MAGNIN & CO.
Womens' and Misses' Exclusive Apparel & Accessories

6340 HOLLYWOOD BOULEVARD
HOLLYWOOD ● CALIFORNIA

LOS ANGELES
THE AMBASSADOR HOTEL

WE PARK YOUR CAR

**A gratuitous parking space service
for the exclusive use of our patrons
in the rear of the I. Magnin & Co.
shop at 6340 Hollywood Boulevard**

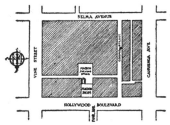

I. MAGNIN & Co. have established a commodious **free**
parking space in the rear of their shop at 6340 Hollywood
Boulevard as indicated on the above diagram.   Here their
patrons may conveniently and securely park their motors,
while shopping, free from the annoyance of parking regulations.   *If you drive your own car our uniformed attendant
will gladly park it for you* ● You are cordially
invited to avail yourself of this service.

NOTE: Our Shop at The Ambassador Hotel is likewise free from parking annoyances

tured at the Roos Brothers emporium of 1929.[49] But such provisions were
unusual. The largest stores, including Robertson's, Dyas, and Barker Brothers, had no parking lots of their own. Even when retailers recognized the
need for off-street space, most let independent parties address the matter,
just as in the city center. Thus by 1930 a few commercially operated parking lots could be found on side streets near Hollywood Boulevard, situated on land whose owners were waiting to put it to more profitable use
(figure 62).

The extent to which Hollywood actually had a parking problem in 1930 is difficult to ascertain, for almost no discussion of the matter was carried in the press. Ten years later, on the other hand, the problem was not only acknowledged but said to be acute. Off-street and curbside space alike were inadequate. The situation was exacerbated by the many motorists who cruised the streets in search of curbside parking, which was still free. The problem did not stem from new commercial development, since the business district had experienced little new growth. What had changed was the number of motorists, with automobile registrations in Los Angeles County increasing by some 300,000 between 1930 and 1940. Many shoppers had still relied on the streetcar to take them to Hollywood Boulevard during the 1920s, but public transportation had much less appeal on the eve of World War II. By 1936 it was estimated that automobile use was four times greater than that of trolleys and buses combined.[50] Finally, new residential development continued, especially after 1935, in the San Fernando Valley, which had little besides neighborhood-oriented outlets until the 1950s. Hollywood may have lost some of its prestige as a retail center during the depression, but it succeeded in sustaining patronage on a large scale.

Despite the problem, little was done to address parking needs in Hollywood until conditions became acute, and even then measures were inadequate.[51] Merchants continued to rely on others to provide the service, paying scant attention to how much space was required and where it might best be situated. Only once did a coordinated segment of the business community succeed in establishing a sizable number of new off-street parking spaces in an area where demand was greatest. That initiative occurred in 1931–1932, shortly after Hollywood's most intensive period of commercial development, under the auspices of the Vine Street Development Association, a consortium of property owners headed by A. Z. Taft. The program led to the construction of commercial car lots at the rear

61

I. Magnin & Company store, 6340 Hollywood Boulevard, Los Angeles, 1923, Myron Hunt, architect; altered. Advertisement. (*Los Angeles Times,* 2 March 1925, I-3.)

62

Theatre Auto Park, Argyle Street, Los Angeles. Photo "Dick" Whittington, 1931. (Whittington Collection, Department of Special Collections, University of Southern California.)

of the tall buildings clustered around the Hollywood and Vine intersection—an achievement, Taft claimed, that would ensure commercial viability for years to come.[52]

But what Taft and most others then involved with Hollywood's business center failed to understand was the aversion motorists had to fee parking, particularly in outlying districts, where they believed ample space should always exist for their cars along the street. The plan also was oriented to office buildings and the large workforce they housed more than to retail activities. Following the example of downtown stores, some merchants arranged to reimburse lot operators for parking charges incurred by store patrons. Yet individual agreements failed to stimulate shopping in the district as a whole. Customers were constrained by time limits on free parking and felt further inconvenienced if they wished to visit stores some blocks away on the same trip.

Concerted efforts to improve conditions did not coalesce until the decade's end. In March 1939 the Chamber of Commerce unveiled a scheme for "universal free parking." The strategy was to provide a convenience no other district offered: a unified system allowing motorists to park without charge in any lot for at least one hour if they made a one-dollar minimum purchase at any store.[53] Though quickly implemented, the plan enjoyed only limited success. Some forty percent of the merchants refused to participate and many others failed to promote it to customers, apparently due to a lack of voice in parking lot operations and improvements. Some car lot operators also resisted the plan because they believed that they could reap greater profits on their own.

The problems generated by the chamber's initial plan soon led to a more ambitious scheme aimed at centralizing management, equitably distributing expenses, and creating additional parking space. Unveiled in May 1940, the scheme called for a nonprofit corporation comprised of all boulevard property owners in the main business district—a group that on the whole had shunned responsibility for the parking issue.[54] Through the corporation, owners and their tenants would contract with car lot operators for a specified sum over a specified number of years. Theoretically, this arrangement would prove lucrative enough to develop new car lots. The project would be limited to blocks on the south side of Hollywood Boulevard between Gower Street and Highland Avenue so that over time a more or less continuous parking area would emerge, extending some 600 feet from the rear of Hollywood Boulevard buildings to Selma Avenue, the next parallel street to the south (figure 63).[55] The corporation would be empowered to acquire some or all of the lots. Total ownership would be costly, but would enable unlimited free parking without the bother of validating tickets. The corporation would oversee, but not finance, improvements to the rear elevations of tangent buildings so that they could function as new customer entrances. Chamber officials argued that the cost of the entire scheme would not be great for any one party if shared in equal proportion by all property owners, and that much greater sums

would be lost, both in store revenues and property values, if Hollywood's consumer draw continued to erode.

The chamber's proposal, soon christened the Hollywood Plan, ranked among the most sweeping of its kind prior to World War II. The national publicity it received in turn may have had some influence on numerous undertakings for the redevelopment of other existing commercial districts during the postwar era. Yet the scheme itself never advanced beyond a modest first stage, which modified the program by allowing three hours of free parking with a one-dollar minimum purchase.[56] U.S. entry into the war curtailed further steps. The quilt of individually owned car lots was never integrated, nor were rear elevations converted to new "fronts." Perhaps the Hollywood Plan's most important lesson was to underscore the difficulties in implementing such programs. No matter how pressing the needs, no matter how logical the plan devised, no matter how assertive the leadership seeking to implement change, dependence upon the full cooperation of numerous independent parties, many of whom put immediate self-interest above long-term common goals, made the outcome problematic at best. Over a decade before the issue came to a head, a more efficacious course was being pursued by individual parties along Wilshire Boulevard in two districts that would soon challenge Hollywood as principal destinations for metropolitan retail activity.

63

Plan for off-street parking proposed by Hollywood Chamber of Commerce, 1940; project. (*Architectural Record*, December 1940, 46.)

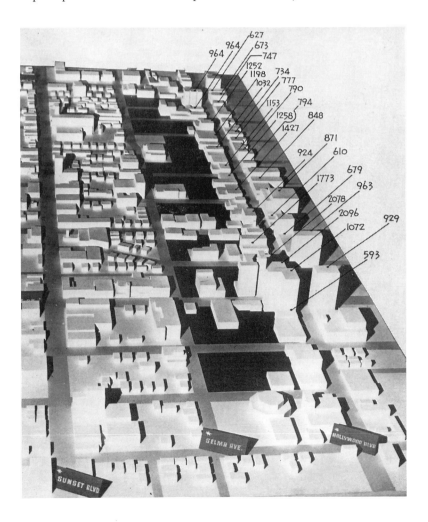

V

FABULOUS BOULEVARD

Even at an early stage, Wilshire Boulevard was assigned a leading role in Los Angeles's future. A year after the stock market crash, boosters seemed undaunted: "[Wilshire] has become, throughout the world, synonymous with Los Angeles . . . it will become the most famous lane in modern civilization . . . the Twentieth Century's super-street." Wilshire's promise did not lose its currency with the next generation. In 1949, a New York journalist, Ralph Hancock, wrote a "biography" of what he called the "Fabulous Boulevard." Hancock warned his readers that after driving Wilshire's length, one would "run out of descriptive adjectives . . . surrounded by a world so new, so kaleidoscopic that no basis of comparison exists." Yet the assemblage was hardly an alien composite: "To know the Boulevard intimately is to know the city and to know Los Angeles is to know a cross-section of the United States, for all of the currents . . . of American life . . . flow through this sunlit valley. . . . Here is a street more expressive of America's youth, its aspirations, and its daring than any other anywhere."[1]

Between the late 1920s and the 1940s Wilshire became not only one of Los Angeles's most heavily traveled arteries but the city's most touted corridor of commerce, whose prestige challenged, and in some respects eclipsed, those of downtown and Hollywood. The endless stream of hyperbole used to depict the fabulous boulevard reflected the importance it acquired as a place and as a symbol in the minds of southern Californians. Few thoroughfares ran through so many new and significant urban districts. Furthermore, the commercial centers that were the principal bea-

cons along its path differed from others of the period in their arrangement, complexion, and appearance. Probably nowhere else did Angelenos
see more conspicuous and compelling evidence that their new metropolis
was a proving ground for alternatives to the norm.

TRANSFORMATION

As with so many aspects of Los Angeles, Wilshire entered the limelight at
a rapid pace after inauspicious beginnings. In 1920, the boulevard was still
an improbable setting for significant commercial growth. Extending from
downtown to the Pacific Ocean at Santa Monica, the artery was a patchwork of connected routes, the last of which, crossing Westlake (now Mac-
Arthur) Park, was not to be completed until 1934. No streetcar line ran
this course, and because of its relative seclusion the eastern end of Wilshire developed as an enclave of the rich during the late nineteenth century. Tracts of comparable stature were platted some blocks further west
through the 1910s. Concurrently, Wilshire frontage near Westlake and
Sunset (now Lafayette) parks became a prime location for costly apartment
houses and residential hotels, generating optimistic predictions that the
street soon would be for Los Angeles what Riverside Drive was for New
York.[2] In contrast to almost every other thoroughfare in the city, Wilshire
Boulevard was zoned for residential use only. These factors, combined
with the dearth of nearby commercial or industrial activity along most of
its nearly seventeen-mile length, led to hopes that Wilshire would become
a grand avenue of residences, adorned with fountains and monuments—

Wilshire Boulevard Visualized as the Fifth Avenue of the West

a route of extravagant showiness from which the city might derive a new symbol of attainment.[3]

Yet after World War I, the notion of a great residential street fast lost its appeal due to widespread automobile use. The car made such places far less secluded as well as noisier and dirtier than they had previously been. Wilshire tracts soon found competition from more remote, topographically varied ones such as Beverly Hills, San Marino, and Flintridge. During the 1920s, residential development near Wilshire was more for the middle class than for the elite.

At the same time, Wilshire became a magnet for commercial enterprises to serve the burgeoning populace close by and also the large, mobile, and affluent trade that lay beyond in several directions. The automobile transformed the corridor into a major spine of development by making access easy. Without streetcars, travel along Wilshire was far less cumbersome for the motorist than on most parallel arteries. Organized efforts to develop Wilshire Boulevard as the "Fifth Avenue of the West" were well under way by the latter months of 1924. Over the next several years, the Wilshire Boulevard Association, comprised of area property owners, lobbied for the most part with success to have the street widened, making it a veritable "speed-way." Wilshire soon became an unofficial laboratory for new methods to enhance traffic flow. The association also secured the installation of elaborate light standards along the boulevard's length, rendering it among the best illuminated in the metropolitan area.[4]

The main agenda of the association, however, was to modify the zoning ordinance to permit commercial development. In April 1926, the first step was consummated when a more than twenty-block stretch be-

64
Wilshire Boulevard at Western Avenue, Los Angeles, hypothetical view of future development, 1926. (*Los Angeles Times,* 25 April 1926, V-1.)

65
Wilshire Boulevard looking west from Serrano Street, showing Pellissier Building at left (1930–1931, Morgan, Walls & Clements, architects) and Wilshire Professional Building at center (1929–1930, Arthur E. Harvey, architect). Photo Putnam Studios, early 1930s. (Los Angeles County Museum of Natural History.)

tween Westlake Park and Western Avenue was rezoned. Soon thereafter, association members agreed to erect commercial buildings that were at least three stories high and of "great architectural beauty" to further their dream of Wilshire as a posh shopping district. But the association harbored a much more ambitious program (figure 64).[5] Their vision of future development was thoroughly metropolitan in character, a variation of the Bellamyesque ones nurtured for downtown Los Angeles for over a decade. Wilshire's destiny should entail not just an assemblage of fashionable shops but a skyscraper center of unparalleled dimensions. The association believed its objective was attainable. Besides the redevelopment of Fifth Avenue in midtown Manhattan, which had been evolving since the late nineteenth century, precedent existed with North Michigan Avenue in Chicago, which, like Wilshire, was of recent vintage and was now rapidly becoming lined with tall buildings.[6] But while these precincts grew as extensions of core areas, the targeted blocks of Wilshire were separated from downtown by nearly two miles. More unusual was the length of the envisioned skyscraper corridor, stretching to the ocean. Equally so was the implication that such intense linear development would not disturb the low density of adjacent residential tracts. The Wilshire Boulevard of the future would be like a North Michigan Avenue reaching to Winnetka with Evanston and Highland Park situated to either side.

The association's ideal might be dismissed as promotional excess had not some of its aspects soon started to materialize. By 1930 numerous projects were completed or under way on rezoned Wilshire frontage.[7] Now extending over twenty-three blocks, between Westlake Park and Wilcox Avenue, this precinct was recognized as a major new business center. Property values soared, so that Wilshire joined the uppermost ranks of streets in the metropolitan area's frenzy of commercial real estate speculation. Although most projects were modest in size, several reached the height limit, including the Wilshire Professional (1929) and Pellissier (1930–1931) buildings (figure 65).[8] Massed as freestanding, stepped towers, with the lowest stories occupying a much larger ground area than the shaft above, these office structures seemed quite different from the closely spaced, bulky masses that defined Hollywood's skyline. The configuration carried a higher cost because of the relatively small usable floor area at each tower level. But the results brought an advantage that was important in courting tenants to the new precinct. Unlike many offices downtown, these would always be assured of ample air, light, and views, protected from encroachment by the spread of the lower stories.[9] Even with a few examples, Wilshire evoked visions of a new, linear, city.

Yet for all its ambitious overtones, commercial development along the eastern stretch of Wilshire Boulevard remained strikingly unfocused. The sudden arrest of growth by the depression, combined with the numerous competing parties involved and their collective goal of realizing a linear rather than a nodal district, contributed to this result. No intersection, no block or cluster of blocks, gained decisive prominence over the others. Indeed, most major intersections, such as that at Vermont Avenue,

66
Wilshire Boulevard looking southwest at
Vermont Avenue. Photo "Dick" Whit-
tington, 1931. (Whittington Collection,
Department of Special Collections, Uni-
versity of Southern California.)

supported little development of consequence (figure 66).[10] With stores scattered seemingly at random among churches, apartment houses, service stations, hotels, residences, and vacant lots, the order lacked a hierarchy to a
degree that made the precinct unlike other major outlying centers locally
or elsewhere.

    The retail structure of this precinct assumed an equally unusual
complexion. By the early 1930s, most stores were neither branches of
large downtown establishments nor chain units but small, independently
run concerns that catered to women's clothing and beauty needs.[11] Antique and gift shops, florists, commercial galleries, decorators' offices, and
restaurants were among the complementary businesses. Many doctors
were situated on the upper floors of buildings. Stores devoted to everyday
goods were the exception.[12] Wilshire's success hinged on its appeal as an
exclusive shopping district for the metropolitan area. Patronage of boulevard stores was only convenient when one drove to the area and also
drove from place to place while there. The scattering of outlets hindered
the pedestrian but benefited the motorist, for the arrangement reduced
traffic congestion caused by nodal centers. Travel along Wilshire was faster
and easier than along many other arteries, and the distinctiveness of store
buildings made them easy to recognize from the driver's seat.

    By the mid-1920s, the matter-of-fact building designs characteris-
tic of outlying centers of all sizes were coming under mounting criticism,
in part as a result of shifts in taste. What may have seemed sensible to one
generation was now regarded as unattractive, even banal. J. C. Nichols, a
nationally prominent developer in Kansas City, had harsh words for the
commercial architecture that lined arterials in cities across the country:

Our new outlying business centers . . . are becoming the ugliest, most unsightly and dis-
orderly spots of the entire city. . . . Buildings of every color, size, shape, and design . . .
huddled and mixed together in a most unpresentable manner . . . unrelated, unconge-
nial mixtures of shops of every type and use, with no relation to one another . . . per-
fectly square, unadorned buildings of poor design . . . are bringing about disorder,
unsightliness, and unattractiveness that threatens to mar the beauty and good appearance of residential regions of American cities.[13]

For Nichols and many others in real estate, retailing, and design, decrying the "great monotony" of stores possessing no "well defined architectural character" was not merely based on new aesthetic preferences or a sense of civic altruism; it was directly tied to business aims. Architecture was increasingly seen as a contributor to effective merchandising. The critic Harold Eberlein stressed in 1929 that "the shop front is one place where standardization of any sort will not apply; in fact it is a positive detriment. . . . It is a serious business mistake on the merchant's part to try to rid his premises of 'architecture' and to put all his faith in the utmost possible area of window display space. Appropriate architectural design is indispensable to the shop front." Architecture was touted as "the best advertising medium a retailer has," and the fact that many shoppers now drove was considered a central factor in the equation. One Buffalo merchant, describing how the automobile now made shopping easy, inferred that "the day is past when the neighborhood store may draw trade to the fullest extent and be merely a hole . . . with three walls and a show window."[14]

Distinctive stores lying outside the city center had been built since the mid-nineteenth century, but they remained the exception, principally as isolated examples in stylish bedroom and resort communities. With the growth of consumer mobility and the concurrent, by no means unrelated, rise in sophisticated marketing techniques, individualistic store designs became more common. Consumer demand also raised property values, which, in turn, gave owners greater inclination to invest in their buildings. Improving the appearance of modest-sized commercial facilities in outlying areas emerged as a significant concern in both architectural and real estate fields.[15] The initial approach was to develop historicizing qualities evocative of preindustrial eras to give buildings a sense of distinctiveness and also compatibility with surrounding residential districts. A broad-based tendency emerged that for the first time gave business houses in outlying areas a distinct and positive character different from those in the core.

In southern California, the mode that became the favorite for such commercial design during the 1920s was then described as "Spanish" or "Spanish Renaissance," and more recently as Spanish Colonial Revival.[16] By mid-decade, references to Spanish, Mexican, and early California architecture were ubiquitous in residential areas, a phenomenon widely viewed as furthering a sense of regional identity. Moreover, the mode encompassed a range of expressive possibilities, affording a romantic portrayal of the past while also seeming contemporary—a new approach deemed superior to the purportedly workaday designs then the norm or to decorative "excesses" of the nineteenth century—in effect, very "modern" (figure 67).

The sense of newness was nowhere more evident than in commercial buildings, which poignantly reflected emerging attitudes toward both the present and the past. Few contemporary accounts of Los Angeles failed to remark upon the city's rapid growth over the previous half-

67

"What Does the Word 'Modern' Mean to You?" Luther T. Mayo, Inc. advertisement. (*Los Angeles Times,* 12 June 1927, V-2.)

century and how within living memory a sleepy town with vestiges of Hispanic culture transformed into a metropolis (figure 68). This notion of progress had two complementary facets: change should be evident not just in the degree to which new buildings differed from those of the past, but also in the way they could be reminders of the past. There was little need for authenticity to achieve these ends. A vocabulary suggestive of Spanishness could keep the memory of recent progress alive by at once recalling traditions long departed and demonstrating the values of modernity. Enhancing a sense of regional distinction was a no less important aim, one that added to the boosterish claim that southern California was different from, and better than, other parts of the country.[17]

Perhaps because this domesticated commercial architecture both reflected a national trend and seemed closely identified with the region, early examples received much fanfare and exerted considerable influence on subsequent work in outlying areas. The first major concentration of such buildings occurred along the Wilshire corridor on Seventh Street near Westlake Park. Called Westlake Square, the project was undertaken by several property owners as a coordinated effort to form a new exclusive shopping district. The architectural firm of Morgan, Walls & Clements was hired to design all the buildings, seven of which saw realization, as an

1887 ~ 1925

ONLY a few years divide the Los Angeles of yesterday and today. Down in the old Plaza, the Mission looks out from behind its palm trees and wonders what the world is coming to, with all the roar and rush and people hurrying to and fro.

It was back in the eighties that the new Los Angeles began to take form. In 1887 Los Angeles Pressed Brick Company opened its first plant. Out of the fires of the kilns larger buildings began to rise, timidly at first....buildings of permanent brick.

Each year new and finer structures came, rising high above their humble neighbors.

Los Angeles is now the largest city in the west. This company feels a degree of pride in the fact that *out of its kilns have come most of the big buildings that form the city's imposing skyline today.*

Doubling and redoubling in size many times, Los Angeles Pressed Brick Company has "grown up" with Los Angeles. The service it now renders is more complete and comprehensive than that of any other similar institution in the west.

"The Standard of Quality in Clay Products"

L·A·Pressed Brick Co

ENTIRE SIXTH FLOOR...... FROST BLDG
Second and Broadway .... TRinity 5761
LOS ANGELES

FACE BRICK · HOLLOW TILE · ROOFING TILE · TERRA COTTA, ETC.

ensemble (figure 69).[18] The venture enjoyed only limited success, however. Many of the elite-oriented specialty stores, studios, and offices sought for Westlake Square located on Wilshire instead once it was rezoned for commercial uses. While store advertisements emphasized the lack of parking restrictions, the precinct was not oriented to the motorist but rather was an extension of a modest-sized outlying center developed during the previous decade. The setting was well suited to a small grouping of shops, but not to becoming a major destination point. Wilshire, on the other hand, had the space to accommodate ambitious building programs and the free movement of cars.

The architectural character of Westlake Square nevertheless set the tone for much of the small-scale commercial development along Wil-

shire and other outlying areas. Many projects were likewise by Morgan, Walls & Clements, who rapidly became leaders in designing distinguished work of this genre. In addition to its inimitable Spanish-inspired mode, the firm created an equally inventive one derived from northern French sources. This formalized, abstracted, and overtly commercial adaptation of French domestic sources conveyed a sense of old-world stylishness appropriate to fashion-oriented emporia (figure 70.)[19] Wilshire could be interpreted as a motor-age Champs-Elysées, punctuated by office towers soaring between elegant little stores that paid homage to tradition and to current haute-monde tastes. Just as with the other components of Wilshire, these store buildings were scattered, but enough examples existed to impart a distinct identity to the district. Hollywood Boulevard, by comparison, seemed more like an ordinary midwestern city center.[20]

The eastern end of Wilshire did not become a new downtown, but it offered an engaging alternative both to the urban core and to Holly-

68

Los Angeles Pressed Brick Company advertisement. (*Architect and Engineer,* February 1925, 20.)

69

Westlake Square, Los Angeles, looking southwest from Westlake Park, showing, left to right, Seventh and Grandview Building, Bilicke Estate Building, and Thorpe Building, 2214–2228, 2300–2312, 2316–2328 W. Seventh Street (all 1923–1924; Morgan, Walls & Clements architects); buildings now altered or demolished. Photo 1924. (*California Southland,* September 1924, 9.)

70

Bilicke Building, 3921–3933 Wilshire Boulevard, Los Angeles, 1929–1930, Morgan, Walls & Clements, architects; no longer standing. (Kenneth Stowell, *Modernizing Buildings for Profit,* 159.)

wood by harboring an array of elite services. The precinct's size and dispersed layout, now extending some thirty blocks, combined with its role as a decorous island of fashion, made Wilshire an unusual precinct nationally. A pronounced break with convention likewise characterized the quarter's foremost landmark, the sumptuous pile conceived as southern California's premier department store, Bullock's.

BULLOCK'S

In April 1928, ten months after plans for the Dyas Hollywood store were made public, John Bullock announced that his company would soon begin construction of a new outlet at Wilshire Boulevard and Westmorland Avenue (figure 71). Bullock took pains to assure customers that the project would complement rather than undermine the downtown store. While the Dyas branch was larger than its parent, the Wilshire building would be only a small fraction of the nearly 740,000 square feet now contained in Bullock's at Seventh and Broadway.[21] Bullock had contemplated branch expansion for some time. In 1924, his company purchased land at Wilshire and Vermont, two blocks away, to use for development once the area was rezoned. Bullock was one of several downtown business leaders who at an early date recognized Wilshire's potential as a new focus of commercial activity that might eclipse the city center itself. Archrival Tom May secured property across the street from Bullock's first site; Marshall Field officials were exploring the possibilities of having a store nearby. Bullock, May, and others agreed to develop on a large scale, with height-limit buildings that would rapidly transform the precinct into a major business

center. Within a few months, however, this vision was abandoned as too
ambitious. Apparently at that point Bullock and May agreed to refocus
their resources downtown and not plan branches at all. Only Dyas's move
to Hollywood altered that strategy.[22]

By the late summer months of 1928 Bullock changed course a
third time, now planning for a facility on the scale of the 1924 project.
Hopes for intense development no longer seemed so far-fetched. Indeed,
the immediate impetus for enlarging the plan may have come from a
scheme just announced by Haggerty's, a major downtown clothing store,
for an enormous, height-limit building at Wilshire and Vermont. Though
it never materialized, the design was the first serious proposal to build at
the scale envisioned by the Wilshire association (figure 72). The program,
Haggerty executives proclaimed, was "based upon [our] confidence that
the district is bound to become the Fifth avenue high-class shopping district sooner than is generally supposed . . . a great array of premier shops
that not only will equal but also perhaps surpass the new shops put up
near Fifth avenue and Fifty-seventh street."[23] Bullock's emporium likewise
was designed to serve the region, attracting customers from a radius of
at least fifteen miles. But other aspects of the scheme, unveiled that November, broke from earlier proposals and indeed from convention generally. The results proved catalytic to Wilshire's emergence as a unique
shopping district.[24]

As realized, Bullock's Wilshire was remarkable on many counts.[25]
Among major retail facilities in the United States, it represented a sophisticated exposition of Art Deco, combining an array of east coast and European sources with originality and élan (figure 73). The interior scheme

was lavish, with a sequence of spaces suggestive of specialty shops designed as showcases of contemporary decorative art. The ensemble was an arresting contrast to the expansive selling floors of early twentieth-century predecessors.

In its exterior form, too, Bullock's looked unlike any precedent in department store design. Rather than a planar block, it was modeled as three-dimensional sculpture, sheathed in terra cotta and copper, intricately shaped and detailed on all four sides, each massed differently with considerable variation in height. The composition culminated in a 241-foot tower, inspired by Eliel Saarinen's railroad terminal in Helsinki but here made a more integral part of the composition.

The siting of Bullock's Wilshire was no less unusual. Two-thirds
of the lot was reserved for a "motor court." Customers could drive to a
porte cochere on the south side—nominally the rear of the building, but
designed with the same refinements as the north elevation facing Wilshire—and leave their car with an attendant (figures 74, 75). Purchases
could be taken directly to the car by the staff and the car in turn brought
to meet its owner at either entrance. The car lot itself was enormous by
standards of the day, with space for 375 automobiles, its perimeter landscaped in a gesture of compatibility with the environs.[26]

In certain respects, Bullock's was part of a national trend, for the branch store concept had gained considerable headway as a national phenomenon in the short period since the Dyas Hollywood emporium had been planned. The fast pace stemmed from the sharp increase in growth of residential areas well removed from the city center. The once common fear that branches would diminish the function of the parent store was giving way to the belief that an outlet conveniently located near these new population centers not only enhanced the company's prestige but strengthened ties with customers that ultimately bolstered patronage downtown. Equally important was the competition created by other stores in outlying areas. Chain companies in particular were seen as a threat. By the close of 1930, more than a dozen major downtown department store companies elsewhere in the United States had opened branches, the great majority of them since 1927.[27] Yet the trend remained in a nascent stage. Most branches were still located in resort towns or communities outside the parent store's normal trading radius. Of the nearly twenty units situated within outlying areas of the store's home base, only seven besides Bullock's and Dyas Hollywood were of substantial size. Chicago had the largest concentration, with two big neighborhood stores acquired by the Fair Company in 1928 and 1929 and two others built by Marshall Field & Company during those same years.[28] Field's stores in Oak Park and Evanston were the largest of their kind outside Los Angeles, encompassing around 80,000 and 85,000 square feet, respectively (figure 76). Two branches built for the Bailey Company in the Cleveland area (1928–1929) enclosed about 40,000 and 60,000 square feet; Strawbridge & Clothier's Ardmore branch (1929–1930) on Philadelphia's Main Line encompassed about 40,000 square feet.[29] By contrast, Bullock's contained nearly 200,000 square feet, more than twice the floor area of its biggest counterparts elsewhere in the country.

One reason for Bullock's great size was that, unlike most examples, it was not a branch in the strict sense of the term: a physical exten-

sion of selected goods and services purveyed at the parent store. Branches were generally viewed by their owners as feeder outlets, which by sustaining patronage for a relatively small number of items in satellite locations could entice more customers to make many additional purchases downtown. Instead Bullock's followed the Dyas Hollywood model. Except at the highest executive level, the Wilshire Boulevard store was a separate operation; management and purchasing were conducted independently of the Seventh and Broadway emporium.[30] The array of goods and services at Bullock's Wilshire was narrower because the facility was targeted to the affluent. At the same time, it functioned as a full-fledged department store, a status few branches then possessed.

Bullock's further departed from the norm as a paradigm for what would later be known as the "lone-wolf" store. Throughout the interwar decades, major department store branches were almost always sited in the cores of important, well-established outlying business centers. By contrast, Bullock's stood in relative isolation. The scattering of small specialty shops nearby comprised a much less clearly defined retail area than the ones at Evanston, White Plains, or Hollywood. John Bullock may have hoped that the precinct would soon blossom into an equivalent of Fifth Avenue, but few commercial establishments existed in the area when work on the building began. Houses erected less than a generation earlier still abounded in the immediate vicinity when the store opened in September

76
Marshall Field & Company department store, 1700–1704 Sherman Avenue, Evanston, Illinois, 1928–1929, Graham, Anderson, Probst & White, architects. Photo author, 1988.

77
Bullock's Wilshire, general view with neighboring houses. Photo "Dick" Whittington, 1929. (Whittington Collection, Department of Special Collections, University of Southern California.)

1929 (figure 77). The site represented a far greater leap than those taken by Hamburger's and Robinson's half a generation earlier.

The site also lay two blocks from the nearest major intersection, Vermont Avenue (figure 78). A location at a key corner lot was an essential characteristic of downtown department stores, and was held to be just as important for outlying areas. Both Bullock and May had adhered to that pattern when securing land at the Wilshire-Vermont intersection in the mid-1920s. But now the company changed its approach, deciding that the extent of automobile traffic at a primary juncture would inhibit the motorists that were the store's target audience. Being somewhat removed from this vehicular confluence enabled motorists to enter and leave the premises apart from congestion.[31] The essential aspect of the siting was accessibility by car from the Wilshire district itself and from well-to-do areas further afield. As primary commuting routes, Wilshire Boulevard, Vermont Avenue, and Western Avenue facilitated access. The building's tower, illuminated at night, served as a beacon to guide customers and to remind everyone that the store had arrived (figure 79). Bullock's was in essence its own skyline, as if to underscore the point that when a destination was easily reached by car, a concentrated shopping district was not needed.

Such an approach to locating large stores had little precedent at the time Bullock's was planned. Some inspiration may have been derived from the Pasadena Furniture Company, which for a number of years was

the only large store outside downtown Los Angeles to advertise regularly in the area's leading papers. Among the advantages of driving to Pasadena rather than entering the Los Angeles city center, the company stressed as early as 1920, was an abundance of unrestricted parking (figure 80). All that space, however, was curbside, and while the store's location was on the edge of downtown Pasadena, it was nonetheless part of that shopping district.[32]

A more profound break from convention was inaugurated in 1925 when the Chicago mail order house Sears, Roebuck & Company entered the retail business. Sears chose outlying areas in which to situate its large, full-fledged department stores ("A" stores was the in-house term) as a direct result of increasing automobile use among its target clientele. General R. E. Wood, the company's new vice-president who conceived and directed the initiative, was explicit on the matter:

With a larger and larger proportion of the population possessing automobiles, the problem of parking space, traffic congestion and resulting inconvenience to downtown shoppers became more and more serious. The automobile made shopping mobile, and this mobility created an opportunity for the outlying store, which with lower land values, could give parking space; with lower overhead, rent and taxes, could lower operating costs, and could with its enlarged clientele created by the automobile offer effective competition to the downtown store.[33]

78

Wilshire Boulevard looking east at Vermont Avenue, Los Angeles. Photo "Dick" Whittington, 1934. (Whittington Collection Department of Special Collections, University of Southern California.)

79

Bullock's Wilshire, advertisement. (*Los Angeles Times,* 17 December 1929, II-8.)

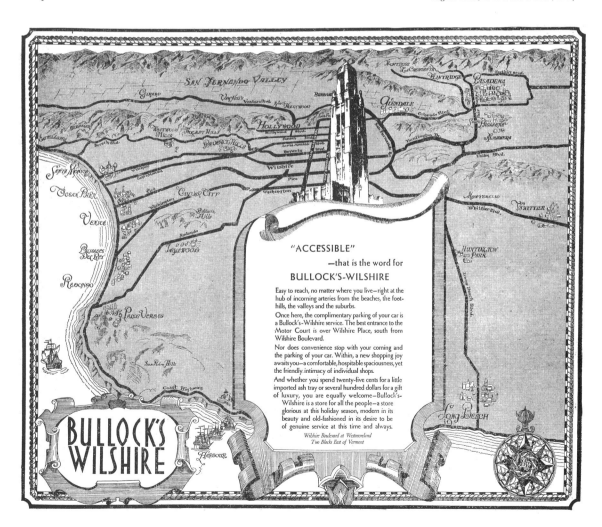

when you are up in the air

This is about the way our location appears from an airplane—notice the broad streets with plenty of room to park your car.

People from all over Southern California come here because of the convenience of our location and the completeness of our assortment—they find many things that are not shown elsewhere and they are pleased with our prices—especially during the

Reorganization Sale

now in progress, which offers an opportunity to select from our entire furniture stock at reduced prices for cash. Come and compare values. We can serve you well, no matter where you live.

Pasadena FURNITURE CO.

83 to 91 N. Raymond, Pasadena.

From the start, Sears's "A" stores were expansive buildings—many contained around 100,000 square feet—with large parking lots to the side or rear.[34] Proximity to one, even two, mass transit lines helped determine the location of early stores; the sites that were chosen, however, clearly indicate that convenient access by car was the primary consideration.

The nature of Sears's operation was, of course, entirely different from Bullock's. Sears skillfully adapted chain company methods to bring large quantities of staple goods to people of moderate means. Men initially comprised the target audience more than women. Most downtown department stores placed little or no emphasis on the kinds of merchandise that were Sears's stock in trade. Sears relied heavily on self-service. Many of Sear's first retail stores were somewhat utilitarian in character inside and out, appearing much like the warehouses from which the company's mail order business was conducted.[35] Not surprisingly, department store executives snubbed the upstart operation; only after World War II would they publicly acknowledge their debt to Sears's merchandising practices and store development program.[36] The Chicago company's performance in the retail field could hardly be judged from a long-term perspective when planning for Bullock's got under way. Yet no major retailer could help taking notice of the constant barrage of news that appeared in *Women's Wear Daily* (the *Wall Street Journal* of the apparel trades) on Sears's building program—sixteen large retail stores by the end of 1927, over fifty two years later—and the enormous profits it was yielding. Department store executives may have pretended to ignore Sears, but at least some were watching the company's meteoric rise closely.[37]

Anyone in Los Angeles who cared to study the situation could do so firsthand. Two large stores for the city were announced in December 1926 and opened the following summer as part of the first wave of

Sears's aggressive expansion program. One was an immense building east of downtown at Olympic Boulevard and Boyle Avenue; of its 425,000 square feet, 125,000 were for retail purposes, the rest for mail order operations (figure 81). The other outlet, at Vermont and Slauson avenues in the Southwest district, contained some 90,000 square feet and was designed for retail purposes only (figure 82).[38]

Beyond general similarities of size and location, the Sears and Bullock's stores shared other characteristics. Among the most obvious was the expansive car lot. Sears was the first large-scale retailer in Los Angeles to have this element as an integral part of its site plan, Bullock's the second (figure 83).[39] A prominent tower distinguished Sears's mail order buildings and became a ubiquitous feature of its "A" stores as well. These towers served the practical purpose of enclosing a water tank that supplied the building's sprinkler system, but they were also devised as landmarks for motorists, clearly identifying the relatively remote sites on which they rose (figure 84). Equally important was the strong physical presence of the Sears Olympic Boulevard facility. This exposed-concrete pile, strikingly modeled as a varied yet unified mass and resting on high ground above the railroad yards and the Los Angeles River, could be seen for miles around to an extent shared by almost no other individual building in the city.

80

Pasadena Furniture Company, 83–91 N. Raymond Avenue, Pasadena, 1914; altered. Advertisement. (*Los Angeles Times*, 4 May 1920, II-8.)

81

Sears, Roebuck & Company department store and mail order building, 2650 E. Olympic Boulevard, Los Angeles, 1926–1927, George C. Nimmons & Company, architects; altered. Photo late 1920s. (Security Pacific Historical Photograph Collection, Los Angeles Public Library.)

Bullock's Wilshire was of a thoroughly metropolitan cut—a Sears Olympic Boulevard store in formal attire. This adaptation at once placed Bullock's in a league of its own. No matter how much of the concept may have been derived from Sears, the two were never compared. If Sears was the apogee of national chain expansion, Bullock's became a symbol of Los Angeles itself, a mark of the city's coming of age. For the first time, boosters could claim a department store that ranked among the great emporia in the eyes of the nation. Likewise, the building embodied a faith in Los Angeles's future not just as a new city, but as a distinct and preferable kind of city. The building was the sole Los Angeles representative illustrated in a 1930 *Vogue* article on southern California, in which the author observed:

One becomes aware gradually of a new people living in a new country who are building for the future, unhindered by any great conservatism. In Los Angeles exists . . . perhaps the most beautiful shop in the world . . . Bullock's-Wilshire, which stands on the edge of the city a dozen stories higher than any other building. . . . It is accepted as a creation for the future when the city will have grown up to it.[40]

Bullock's further seemed to herald cultural maturation, standing as a benchmark in efforts to synthesize artistic expression with economic development. A local commentator remarked that the building "has come to embody in the public mind something more than merely an extension of an already great business . . . it has come to symbolize, not the seeking after more business, but the inculcation of beauty as an unselfish element in modern commercial enterprise."[41]

Had Wilshire Boulevard developed into a skyscraper corridor, Bullock's would have become more conventional. Locationally, it would

have paralleled emporia such as Bergdorf-Goodman and Saks Fifth Avenue in New York. Visually, it would have ceased to be an isolated monument, instead rising as part of a more or less continuous planar wall. The company anticipated such changes: the building was structured so that its entire mass could extend to the height limit and have additions occupying a portion of the car lot as well.[42] Yet the effects of the depression and subsequent shifts in development left neighboring blocks of Wilshire as a fragmented composite, unique in appearance and mix of retail functions. These circumstances made Bullock's example all the more significant in later years. The success of the operation demonstrated how a large-scale business in luxury items could be sustained on a profitable basis without an extensive supporting cast. The place could be nowhere but in a metropolis, yet was wholly unlike the standard settings for such activities.

Aside from Sears, Bullock's was an anomaly as a lone-wolf department store when it opened. The closest counterparts prior to the late 1930s were built in New York and Philadelphia. Owing to the diffuse, low-density nature of the New York metropolitan area's elite residential communities, early branches there were modestly sized outlets of stylish departmentalized stores specializing in apparel and accessories.[43] Among the first examples was a branch of some 20,000 square feet erected in 1929–1930 for Best & Company at Mamaroneck in Westchester County. Located about a half-mile from the town center along the county's principal thoroughfare, the site was chosen for its easy access from communities as far away as the Hudson River Valley and southwestern Connecticut (figure 85).[44] Precisely the same criteria determined the site of the area's second lone-wolf branch, built for Franklin Simon in 1931–1932 several blocks removed from the commercial center of Greenwich, Connecticut (figure 86). Containing nearly 40,000 square feet, the store was ranked

To the
People of Los Angeles

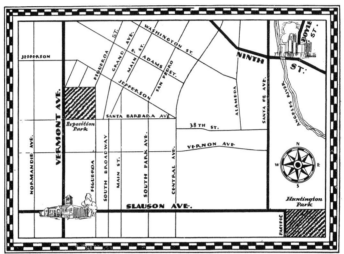

ERY soon we shall announce the opening of the first of two retail department stores which we are now building.

The first one will be at Vermont and Slauson Avenues. The second one will be at Ninth Street and Boyle Avenue.

Each location is, as you know, easy of access. It centers in a large residential area. It can be reached on convenient thoroughfares and transportation lines.

Escaping the congested traffic sections, each location appeals to the motorist. Appreciating this, we are creating ample free parking space beside each store. You can drive in, park your car as long as you wish, and do your shopping free from worry.

Each of these new stores enjoys the full advantage of our distinctive merchandising policy.

They will stand out in your mind because they will give you merchandise of dependable quality at lowest prices. This means every day in the business year. We go on record now, before the doors of either store are opened. On every article you purchase you will actually see a definite, worth while saving.

On top of that, every transaction with these stores will be covered by our unrestricted guaranty of absolute satisfaction or your money back.

When you are near either location, we invite you to watch their progress and see how we are preparing to make everything most convenient for you.

Knowing that you will appreciate the business policy which has earned for us more than eleven million families as customers, and an annual volume of three hundred million dollars, we feel that our entry into Los Angeles will be welcomed in the spirit of one of the fastest growing cities in the world.

Sears, Roebuck and Co.

*Plenty of Free
Parking Space*

among the largest New York branches of the period and also had unusually generous provisions for off-street parking: a terraced rear lot accommodating 250 cars.[45] Despite these early initiatives, the lone-wolf store failed to gain much favor during the extensive branch development program that occurred in the New York area prior to World War II.

The maverick in Philadelphia's branch development was the venerable Strawbridge & Clothier department store. Its first outlying unit was built in 1929–1930 as part of an integrated business development, later called Suburban Square, that lay directly across the Pennsylvania Railroad from the Ardmore town center, then the largest shopping district serving Philadelphia's Main Line communities.[46] The immediate success of that store prompted Strawbridge's to commission a similar but larger complex—the first major department store branch planned from the start as the anchor unit of an integrated retail complex (figure 87).[47] The site lay several blocks beyond the shopping district of Jenkintown, which func-

84
Sears, Roebuck & Company advertisement for Los Angeles stores. (*Los Angeles Times,* 19 June 1927, II-16.)

85
Best & Company store, 590 E. Boston Post Road, Mamaroneck, New York, 1929–1930, Edward Necarsulmer, architect. Photo author, 1991.

86
Franklin Simon & Company store, 95–101 W. Putnam Avenue, Greenwich, Connecticut, 1931–1932, Edward Necarsulmer, architect. Photo author, 1992.

tioned much like Ardmore as a destination point for routine needs of residents from surrounding communities north of Philadelphia. The deepening depression precluded building the scheme as a whole; however, Strawbridge's went ahead with plans for its own store, containing over 60,000 square feet. When it opened in September 1931, the building stood amid residential blocks much like Bullock's on Wilshire Boulevard.[48] The venture set an influential precedent for the Philadelphia metropolitan area, where the lone-wolf store was the standard form of branch development until the mid-1950s.[49]

From the start, branch development patterns were localized in nature, making Bullock's influence on practices outside southern California difficult to assess. Moreover, the first lone-wolf projects in the New York and Philadelphia areas were launched soon after construction of the Wilshire Boulevard store began. The initial decisions to adopt this locational approach probably were made independent of one another, based on local conditions and without benefit of a firm model. On the other hand, Bullock's was by far the most ambitious of these endeavors and quickly became the most famous. Both factors, coupled with its operational success, no doubt reinforced the validity of the lone-wolf concept among some major downtown retailers once branch expansion began to resume in the late 1930s.

Locally, Bullock's served as a direct model for the size, siting, generous off-street parking accommodations, and elegant ambience of the new I. Magnin store (1938–1939) sited on Wilshire several blocks to the west.[50] The outlet provided a second primary destination point for the precinct, whose loosely knit, low-density structure had changed little over the intervening decade. Planned as a greatly expanded replacement of Magnin's Hollywood unit, the building was the company's largest

(162,000 square feet) and underscored the merits of size in lone-wolf branch development.

Bullock's example also strengthened the understanding that conventional wisdom did not always provide the most effective response to changing needs. Well before the late 1930s, the store reinforced the inclinations of others to experiment in addressing new consumer demands. None of these ventures attracted more attention or achieved greater success during the interwar decades than did a second commercial precinct along Wilshire, three miles to the west—a place that many Angelenos embraced as a new downtown and that was universally known as the Miracle Mile.

MIRACLE MILE

During its initial years of development, the Miracle Mile appeared much like numerous other nascent low-density arterial business districts of Los Angeles. The "miracle" lay neither in its physical character nor in the complexion of its few, small retail outlets, but rather that it existed at all. Major investors considered the site too remote; municipal law excluded commercial uses. The Miracle Mile was slow to take form at first. Yet when the vision of its creator, a previously little-known real estate agent named A. W. Ross, began to coalesce into a reality, the result was a new kind of retail center, one that had a significant impact on practices in the region and beyond. Even the name, ostensibly suggested to Ross by a client when the precinct's transformation into a major center was beginning to occur, soon became a household term in the region. After World War II, "Miracle Mile" was used as a generic term nationwide to denote a form of commercial development in outlying areas that challenged the hegemony of downtown in a way seldom known before.[51]

When Ross started to assemble property along Wilshire Boulevard in 1923, his intent was to create a major business district. The location selected, extending along what became a seventeen-block stretch between La Brea and Fairfax avenues, did not seem promising for such an enterprise, since much of the area remained open land.[52] What made his venture so unusual, and at first so subject to ridicule, was the planning of a large retail center absent a surrounding community. Ross's acreage was not in a Hollywood or Beverly Hills, nor tangent to an established network of subdivisions such as along the eastern part of Wilshire. Instead the property was a hypothetical center for the western half of the metropolitan area, a position premised on extensive growth of fledgling settlements and on unplatted land. The developer sought a long-term investment, and, since he could purchase large parcels at relatively low cost, that investment would no doubt yield some future return.

Yet the anticipation of intense commercial land use was laden with risks, especially since it depended on decisions made by hundreds of other parties over whom Ross exercised no control. Like many colleagues,

87
Strawbridge & Clothier Jenkintown department store, 600 Old York Road, Jenkintown, Pennsylvania, 1930–1931, Dreher & Churchman, architects; altered. Initial design, showing unexecuted shopping complex around store. ([Jenkintown] *Times-Chronicle,* 1 October 1931, 6.)

he believed that the expansion of Los Angeles had no limits; his gamble, however, was just as much predicated on a faith in the automobile as the shopper's primary conveyance. With most of the metropolitan area's new residential tracts for upper- and middle-income groups lying within a few miles of the site, Ross was certain that people living there would prefer the drive to the Miracle Mile to the journey downtown if the right goods were available.[53] The fact that the site was isolated, with little established development close by, was seen as advantageous because it facilitated access. As Sears and Bullock's pioneered the lone-wolf store, so Ross employed this locational strategy for his entire business district.

The most remarkable aspect of Ross's vision was its early date. No major retail district had then been conceived along such lines. The gamble seemed preposterous to many colleagues, but it proved a sound one. He correctly gauged the pace of residential building in western sections of the metropolis. By 1936, almost half a million people with an estimated annual purchasing power of $600,000,000 lived within a four-mile radius.[54] What Ross did not forecast was that when most of his land was annexed by the city in 1925, it would be zoned for residential purposes only, due to the still strong commitment among some other property holders in the area that Wilshire become a grand avenue of houses and apartment buildings. Ross's subsequent efforts to change the zoning designation by voter referendum failed.

Forced to recast his plans, Ross embarked on an even more unusual, higher-risk strategy: seeking zoning variances for commercial build-

ings on a project-by-project basis.[55] His tactic was successful but entailed more time and effort than once anticipated. Working drawings and specifications for each building were submitted for review by the Planning Commission to grant a variance. However cumbersome, the process gave Ross much greater control than were he merely selling lots. Ross himself undertook the arguing of each case before the commission, and to strengthen his advocate's role he gained leverage with the client in stipulating the caliber of design, siting, and tenancy. Ross's desire to create a district of distinction thus became more readily attainable than by any other method save undertaking the entire development on his own. He found willing investors, since commercial development seemed lucrative in almost any growing part of the city. Some parties erected their own buildings, working with Ross; others hired him to develop the project for them. Ross was also consulted by owners of the few Wilshire properties he was unable to acquire. The Miracle Mile was not a fully integrated business center, since it had no overall plan or management structure, but it possessed many of the same attributes. Ross played the decisive role in determining the choice and arrangement of tenants as well as the size, location, and character of the buildings.

At first, the unorthodoxy of the development discouraged the kind of investors and tenants Ross most wanted.[56] The situation began to change in 1928 when he persuaded Desmond's, a prominent clothing

store with three locations downtown, to establish a branch on the Miracle Mile instead of in Hollywood. Even though most neighboring blocks remained vacant, the project offered advantages not available on Hollywood Boulevard. First, there was ample room; the store would contain some 17,000 square feet. Moreover, it was not housed in a conventional business block, nor in one of modest scale and quasi-domestic imagery as might be found along the eastern part of Wilshire, but rather in one arm of a ten-story office building, thoroughly metropolitan in its cast (figure 88).[57] The design did not seem at all practical, for while the main entrance suggested a skyscraper of great dimensions, the office floors contained less than half the square footage of the store. This grand gesture nevertheless worked to the retailer's advantage. With an enormous sign bearing the firm name atop of the tower, the building gave Desmond's a singular presence rivaled by few others citywide save Bullock's and Sears.

From a real estate perspective, the Wilshire Tower Building, as it was called, did offer a marketing advantage: it was the first multistory office space anywhere along the boulevard. The massing was configured so as to keep the office portion permanently unencumbered by later development. This pattern was inspired by the just completed Los Angeles City Hall (1925–1928), which at 452 feet was by far the tallest building in southern California and was at once embraced as an embodiment of the city's metropolitan aspirations (figure 89).[58] For the public, no form offered a more suggestive symbol of Wilshire as a great urban center. For the physicians and dentists who were to become the principal tenants, tower spaces offered more than panoramic views of a landscape in the making; they offered a prestige address close to many of the area's most prosperous households and at the heart of the new shopping district for that clientele—if other stores followed Desmond's lead.

Like Ross's whole enterprise, the Wilshire Tower Building was a risky venture, but perhaps only so ambitious a project could have sparked

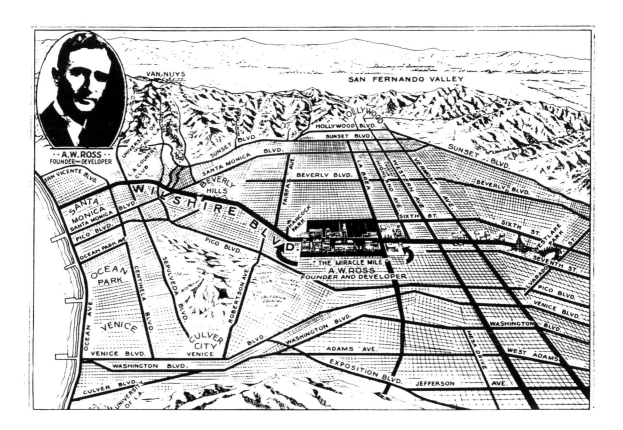

the transformation the developer sought. Before construction was completed, Silverwood's, an equally well-known downtown competitor of Desmond's, signed the lease for the building's other arm, again as an alternative to establishing a Hollywood branch. Other downtown firms that already had Hollywood outlets were lured to the Miracle Mile as well. Both Myer Siegel (women's apparel) and C. H. Baker (shoes) opened stores nearby in the Dominguez-Wilshire Building (1930–1931) which followed the Wilshire Tower model, though with a broader, more usable office floor plate. Earlier, work had begun on the E. Clem Wilson Building (1929–1930), the tallest of the three, marking the eastern end of the precinct at La Brea Avenue.[59] This rapid succession of projects transformed Ross's endeavor from one of bold promises to striking reality. The results seemed the more remarkable as the towers soared above a sea of single-story buildings and still vacant lots (figure 90).

Besides proximity to a lucrative market, the Miracle Mile became attractive to important business interests because of its absence of congestion, a point Ross emphasized unceasingly. The office towers were placed at least a block from one another rather than clustered around an intersection, which helped diffuse traffic and also made the development appear larger in its extent (figure 91). Once the Wilshire Tower Building was completed, Ross aggressively promoted the Miracle Mile as the new "downtown" for the western two-thirds of the city (figure 92).[60] The ambitiousness of this vision is tellingly revealed in a projected joint venture with a colleague, Charles Cooper. Unveiled in August 1929, the scheme

90

E. Clem Wilson Building, 5217–5231 Wilshire Boulevard, Los Angeles, 1929–1930, Meyer & Holler, architects. Photo "Dick" Whittington, 1932. (Huntington Library.)

91

Promotional diagrammatic map showing Miracle Mile's position in metropolitan Los Angeles, ca. 1929. (*Los Angeles Times, Midwinter Number,* 2 January 1930, III-2.)

called for a forty-story hotel at the precinct's western end (figure 93). Though set back from Wilshire itself, the building clearly would have become the boulevard's dominant landmark, one visible for many miles and unrivaled in the region save by City Hall, which served as an inspiration for this undertaking just as it did for the office towers.[61]

Yet this new downtown was more than a parade of soaring commercial spires. Most buildings were no higher than two stories, and the low bases of their tall neighbors combined to keep the scale a comfortable one for pedestrians. Containment was as important to Ross as conveying a sense of expansiveness. In an oblique reference to the eastern part of Wilshire, he stressed that his precinct was more compact, hence more convenient for patrons. Similar comparisons could be made with Hollywood Boulevard. The Miracle Mile more approximated the size of central shopping districts in a Quincy, Illinois, or a Topeka, Kansas. Those thousands of city dwellers who had lived in the heartland could feel right at home even as they were partaking of a big-city atmosphere. Silverwood's exploited this duality in advertisements addressed to Beverly Hills residents soon after the store's opening. While illustrations showed an interior finished in a suave Art Deco mode evocative of the most elegant new shops in New York and Paris, the text focused on "Unhurried Ease. There is an

92

Miracle Mile, looking west from Detroit Street, showing Dominguez-Wilshire (1930–1931, Morgan, Walls & Clements, architects) and Wilshire Tower buildings. Photo "Dick" Whittington, 1939. (Whittington Collection, Department of Special Collections, University of Southern California.)

93

Hotel, Wilshire Boulevard near Fairfax Avenue, Los Angeles, 1929, Kenneth MacDonald, Jr., architect; project. (*Los Angeles Times,* 16 August 1929, II-1.)

air of restfulness here. Somehow it's not like 'a store'. None of the hustle and bustle of down town. Lots of time. A neighborly atmosphere. . . . Then, too, there is a large parking area at the south entrance reserved for your use. Plenty of room at all times."[62]

The Miracle Mile codified and intensified those characteristics that made Wilshire so important to Los Angeles: a linear structure, punctuated by freestanding towers that rose amid low-density development, the whole anchored to a broad street where traffic flowed unimpeded—a place that was easy to reach, that always seemed busy but never crowded, a place permeated with natural light and air, a place that fused the best qualities of Main Street and metropolis, evoking memories of both but unlike either one.

The Miracle Mile differed from downtowns of any size and also from Hollywood in that most of its functions centered on consumption. A few small bank branches comprised the extent of the financial activities. The total office area remained relatively modest. No large theater was built along the Miracle Mile. Ross may have wished otherwise, but any effort to attract a major movie house would have been thwarted by the

presence of the Carthay Theatre (1925–1926) a few blocks to the south and the Fox Wilshire Theatre (1929–1930) several blocks to the west. Similarly, the Miracle Mile may have lain too close to the nascent commercial district of Beverly Hills to become a banking center.[63] Ross's aborted scheme for a skyscraper hotel suggests an interest in broadening the scope. For whatever reasons, the Miracle Mile remained more a single-focus district, and its success demonstrated that a major outlying center need not be a miniature downtown to thrive.

The factor that appears to have been at the heart of the Miracle Mile's success was parking. The absence of space for cars downtown was reputedly a basic reason that Ross embarked on his venture in the first place, and parking remained a paramount concern throughout the development of the Miracle Mile.[64] With Desmond's, he began to implement an idea that no Hollywood Boulevard developer could match. Like Bullock's, the Wilshire Tower Building had its own parking lot, located at the rear, with an entrance directly to the center of the building.[65]

Desmond's proved a successful trial for the overall parking plan, which ranks among the most ambitious conceived during the 1920s for any outlying center in the United States. Ross's objective was eventually to provide sufficient space for customers' automobiles at the rear of all stores. To achieve this goal, he insisted that purchasers acquire sizable parcels of land; that, with few exceptions, commercial development be excluded from side streets; and that tangent residential buildings on those streets be kept to a relatively modest size. When curbside parking no longer satisfied needs, space at the rear of the lot could be converted and, if needed at a later date, adjacent rear parcels purchased for a comparatively low cost. The scheme possessed a flexibility that must have pleased investors, since there was no need to make a large initial outlay for parking. The few car lots that were realized prior to the worst years of the depression were modest in size compared to Bullock's or Sears's (figure 94). Yet the matrix was laid for a system unrivaled in the metropolitan area until after World War II.

The extent to which Ross's idea broke with convention is suggested by comparison with the 1925 scheme devised for Bullock, May, and other property owners along Wilshire between Vermont and Western avenues. This stillborn plan called for the construction of large basement garages, with direct access to the floors above, in each tall building erected (figure 95).[66] At a time when off-street parking was rarely considered an integral part of large-scale building projects anywhere, the proposal was unusual enough, yet it was predicated upon building at a density characteristic of the city center and would necessitate substantial outlays at the start. Furthermore, many motorists resisted parking in a garage unless other options were precluded; Wilshire would have to become a high-rise corridor before such a plan could be effective. In reality, off-street parking along the eastern blocks of Wilshire was minimal except for occupants of the apartment buildings and hotels and for customers of Bullock's. Few other property owners wished to incur the expense when developing a site as

long as curbside space could be found, and provisions became much harder to make once building density reached the critical mass that rendered parking a problem.

Ross's farsighted alternative, possible only because he enjoyed so much control over the Miracle Mile's development, had its drawbacks too. Some property owners might be reluctant to initiate or expand parking lots even when the need existed. Since these facilities were individually owned and none, at first, were contiguous, patronizing several stores meant that a customer would have either to move from lot to lot or keep the car in a space for longer than the time taken in the adjacent store. Yet the supply of space was kept sufficiently close to the demand to spare the Miracle Mile from the serious parking problems faced in Hollywood at least through the mid–1940s.[67] The provision kept the boulevard unencumbered and led to a phenomenon observers were quick to note: low volume of pedestrian traffic on the sidewalks compared to that inside the stores.

Securing a relatively wide mix of retail functions was also a key aspect of Ross's program. Unlike the eastern end of Wilshire, the Miracle Mile soon boasted a number of businesses purveying everyday goods and services. Many establishments, too, were geared to the budget-conscious shopper. The affluent comprised but one part of the target audience; the much larger middle class was the backbone of trade. In these respects, too, the Miracle Mile was like a small-city Main Street. To achieve the bal-

94

Miracle Mile. Aerial view looking northeast, La Brea Avenue intersection at upper right. Photo Spence, 1931. (Photo archives, Department of Geography, University of California, Los Angeles.)

ance, Ross courted leading national and local chain companies beginning in the early years of his endeavor. In 1928, a large and very ornate building was erected for Ralphs Grocery Company, one of southern California's foremost volume food stores. When the Wilson Building opened in 1930, its ground-floor space was occupied by a variety store (J. J. Newberry) and a low-priced men's wear outlet (Brooks Clothing).[68] The biggest surge in chain development came following the worst years of the depression, when the Miracle Mile conspicuously outpaced Hollywood in new development. Between 1935 and 1938, six clothing stores, three drug stores, two variety stores, three restaurants, an auto supply store, a candy store, and a market were opened by major chain operations. These businesses were concentrated along the eastern blocks of the precinct so that the presence of each might reinforce those of the others. Many of the chains erected more ambitious quarters than would have been contemplated a decade previous. Among the first such projects was undertaken in 1935 by the Sontag Drug Company. While occupying space in a taxpayer block was still a standard practice, Sontag erected its own building, which contained some 16,000 square feet and ranked among the largest of its kind in the region (figure 96).[69]

The Sontag project also helped set a new standard for the Miracle Mile in its exuberant streamlined design, updating the use of modernist modes that Ross had embraced at an early date. The developer was concerned that the appearance of buildings embody the caliber of goods and services purveyed inside. Newness was crucial to the equation. The appeal of modernism in this respect was well summarized as early as 1929 in the *Southwest Builder and Contractor:*

With the architecture of small buildings there has also developed a demand for . . . treatment that gives individuality or distinctiveness to . . . structures. . . . This demand . . . has brought into vogue the so-called "Moderne" or "Art Nouveau" [i.e., Art Deco]. . . . Classical and Renaissance styles have failed to satisfy because of their limitations. They lose character when their motifs or lines are exaggerated. They are impossible unless given their natural modes of expression in materials. The so-called

"Moderne" has no limitations except those fixed by consistency. Motifs in endless variety may be employed. Traditions being lacking, the choice of materials and methods of treatment has no bounds.[70]

Ross may well have encouraged his clients to pursue what he believed were the most appropriate recent trends in design. Whether he helped select architects or advised on the development of a design is unknown. Yet the cumulative result was a showcase of modernist commercial work then unmatched by any other business district in the region and

95
Wilshire Boulevard, hypothetical view of future development, ca. 1925. (*Los Angeles Times,* 11 January 1925, V-5.)

96
Sontag drug store, 5401–5403 Wilshire Boulevard, Los Angeles, 1935–1936, Norstrom & Anderson, architects. *Hollywood Citizen News,* 30 April 1936, Advertising Sect.)

97
Retail, office, and apartment building for California Estates, Inc., preliminary design, 1930, Vincent Palmer, architect; project. (*Los Angeles Times,* 2 March 1930, V-1.)

by few, if any, in the United States. Ross also seems to have welcomed architectural experimentation. One scheme prepared in 1930 called for a
crystalline tower in the form of a Greek cross, set at forty-five degrees to
the street, its arms massed in a stepped, expressionistic manner (figure
97).[71] While the proposal fell victim to the depression, the realized designs
along the Miracle Mile exhibited a sense of optimistic modernity that was
much desired, but seldom so fully achieved, in the nation's shopping districts during the 1930s.

The capstone to Ross's efforts—in design as well as in real estate
development—came toward the end of the decade when he convinced
two of the city's largest retailers to erect major outlets. In November
1937, plans were announced for Coulter's, a venerable downtown establishment that still referred to itself as a dry goods store, to construct a four-
story, 124,000-square-foot building on the Miracle Mile.[72] Like Bullock's,
the new store was primarily oriented to the motorist, with an elaborate
rear entry and a sizable (150-car) parking lot. However, the most striking
aspect of the plan was that it would replace the Seventh Street quarters,
ending an almost sixty-year association with the city center. Coulter's
was probably the nation's first major downtown emporium to abandon
the core.

Coulter's new building bespoke its maverick role, showing no
overt ties to tradition. Applied decoration was virtually nonexistent; a commanding presence was achieved through the elementary aspects of its
massing and composition (figure 98). Instead of operating windows, the
exterior walls supported bands of glass block, one of the most extensive
uses of that material then to be found.[73] Natural light, diffused by the
blocks, permeated the selling areas at selected points, yet the space was
primarily internalized, with artificial means used to spotlight displays and
control the temperature year-round. Coulter's was among the earliest
large stores designed with a complete air conditioning system. In both

its appearance and features, the scheme helped set the tone nationally for the wave of department store remodeling and construction then just beginning.[74]

A month after Coulter's opened, the May Company disclosed its plans for a behemoth nine blocks to the west. Containing over 270,000 square feet, the building would replace the store at Broadway and Eighth Street as the flagship operation—another national first.[75] Like Dyas, Bullock's, and the Broadway, the May Company conceived the project as a means by which it could appeal to a more affluent trade. Perhaps for this reason, the building was oriented toward Beverly Hills and posh enclaves to the north, standing some distance from other Miracle Mile stores (figure 99). The parking area (450 cars) was the largest surface lot developed as part of a single retail facility at that time, and incorporated two novel features. An underground staging area, connected by ramp to a side street, allowed delivery vehicles and customer's automobiles to move without encumbering one another. A service station stood at the far end of the lot, enabling cars to be left for maintenance or repairs while their owners shopped. Future expansion of the store at the rear appears to have been planned from the start; consequently the elevation facing the car lot was the least embellished of the four (figure 100).[76]

Two aspects of the May Company Wilshire design were more tied to convention. The site lay at a major intersection, with Fairfax Avenue, perhaps in the belief that the area would never become congested.

98

Coulter Dry Goods Company store, 5600 Wilshire Boulevard, Los Angeles, 1937–1938, Stiles Clements, architect; demolished 1970s. (Whittington Collection, Department of Special Collections, University of Southern California.)

99

May Company Wilshire department store, 6051–6057 Wilshire Boulevard, Los Angeles, 1938–1939, Albert C. Martin and Samuel A. Marx, associate architects. Aerial view looking northwest. Photo "Dick" Whittington, ca. 1939. (Whittington Collection, Department of Special Collections, University of Southern California.)

The building also sat right at the corner, as if to capture pedestrian traffic even though almost none existed. The basic exterior form, too, was thoroughly urban in character—a scheme more suggestive of a downtown location than a lone-wolf one (figure 101). For all of its overt modernity, the streetfront composition, with a rounded corner rendered as a continuous vertical element, had been a leitmotif of department stores since the mid-nineteenth century, beginning with the celebrated Bon Marché in Paris (1867–1876). This parti was revived by Erich Mendelsohn during the 1920s in a manner that fused streamlined dynamism with emphatic massiveness, most notably at his Schocken department store in Stuttgart (1926–1928).[77] Yet the particulars of scale and arrangement at the May Company Wilshire store were new and clearly attuned to the passing motorist. Rather than being glazed, the corner element was a banded mosaic of gold-colored tiles, surrounded by an enormous concave frame sheathed in polished black granite. Probably nowhere save at world's fairs of that decade had a purely ornamental feature previously assumed such titanic proportions. Combined with the diminutive scale of the fenestration, this lavish cornerpiece expanded the perceived size of the building. Without a tower or even a sculptural mass, the store nevertheless commanded a singular distinction from the street, rivaled only by Bullock's.

Coulter's and the May Company buildings were also like Bullock's in being anomalies prior to World War II. Contemporary branch de-

100

May Company Wilshire store, aerial view looking southwest. Photo "Dick" Whittington, ca. 1939. (Whittington Collection, Department of Special Collections, University of Southern California.)

101

May Company Wilshire store, principal elevations. Photo author, 1992.

velopment elsewhere remained modest by comparison, with buildings of 40,000 to 60,000 square feet the norm. Most retailers now believed that the large branch store had been a momentary indulgence, proven ineffectual by the depression. The complexion of the New York–area branches constructed around 1930 became the prevailing pattern.[78] New construction downtown was rare until after the war; most department store companies continued to remodel and add to existing plants instead.[79]

The Miracle Mile itself remained unique among outlying business districts in Los Angeles and elsewhere. The absence of direct offspring can be partially attributed to Ross's unusual role in the precinct's development. More important, however, were the urban qualities he pursued from the outset and continued to encourage during the limited expansion that occurred after World War II.[80] By that time, both the ever more diffuse nature of metropolitan growth and changing concerns among major retailers led to new approaches even less bound to tradition. Yet Ross's work exerted considerable influence on thinking about commercial development in outlying areas. The Miracle Mile demonstrated how the arterial form, absent nodal concentrations, could effectively utilize boulevard frontage in a motorized age. The precinct further underscored the value of containment, of limiting the boundaries of development so that the designated space could be more effectively used. The provisions made for off-street parking firmly convinced many parties that special accommodation for automobiles was a necessity. The Miracle Mile further offered profound lessons concerning location. While Sears and Bullock's showed how large retail facilities could successfully operate in isolated but strategically placed sites created *de novo,* Ross's endeavors revealed how much the same ends could be achieved on a far more ambitious scale, offering a spectrum of goods and services that, at least in many people's minds, outshone the choices provided by the city center.

VI

A GUARANTEED NEIGHBORHOOD

In 1923, at the same time as A. W. Ross was beginning to purchase land along the Wilshire corridor, a small army of designers and real estate agents commissioned by New York financier Frank Vanderlip were completing plans for a "new city" far more remotely situated. Occupying the peninsula at the southwestern tip of the metropolitan area, this "new city" of Palos Verdes Estates was conceived as a haven for the well-to-do. Ninety percent of its housing stock would be comprised of single-family residences, each individually designed but conforming to communitywide guidelines to ensure a harmonious relationship between architecture and the natural terrain.

Palos Verdes Estates was to have several business districts, each quite unlike most in outlying areas. The big-city allusions cultivated along Hollywood and Wilshire boulevards were the last thing sought here, nor did the smaller-scale patchwork development of a Western Avenue hold any appeal. Kirtland Cutter, architect of the "new city's" largest business complex, described it as

an old Spanish town with balconies, winding stairways, grill iron gates and windows and arcaded walks. . . . Lots of color. . . . Soft tans, dull ivory and pinks and touches of blue—tile roofs of warm browns and terra cotta with a pink tint in the purple. Quaint lantern towers. Garden walls and the surfaces of buildings broken up irregularly. . . . Different ages will be expressed in different building . . . [which] will bring charm and defeat possibilities of . . . monotony.[1]

Beyond picturesque effects, Cutter's scheme departed from almost all of the region's commercial development in its siting. Rather than being an-

chored to an artery, the complex opened onto a secluded plaza and could extend no further than two blocks from that locus. The purpose of this arrangement was to contain commerce so that "future home surroundings are forever assured against business encroachment." The ultimate objective was to create "a 'guaranteed' neighborhood" where the "beauty of residential areas" would exist in perpetuity (figure 102).[2]

The proposal was an early manifestation of a new approach to business development in outlying areas, which was laying the groundwork for the mid-twentieth-century concept of the shopping center. Among the pioneering ventures advanced during the interwar decades, Palos Verdes was the most sweeping in its proposed territorial extent. Just before the depression, another important development was inaugurated near Beverly Hills, the first of its kind designed to compete with downtown. Through both schemes, Los Angeles made a major contribution to the concept during its formative period. That work, however, would have been inconceivable without the precedent set elsewhere in the country by several projects designed during the previous decade.

102
"A 'Guaranteed' Neighborhood," advertisement for Palos Verdes Estates showing Lunada Bay Plaza in background. (*Los Angeles Times,* 6 April 1924, V-16.)

PRECEDENTS

Through the 1930s, "shopping center" was a term by and large loosely applied to a collection of businesses irrespective of size. Downtown might be called a "shopping center," as might major outlying business districts, modest neighborhood clusters, or even a taxpayer block that contained several stores. Yet as early as the 1920s, "shopping center" began to assume a much more specific meaning, which would become the dominant one by the post–World War II era.[3] This new definition entailed comprehensive planning in both the design and business realms. In the physical dimension, a shopping center was built according to an overall program that covered all aspects of the scheme, from the fundamental nature of the site plan down to the details of exterior lighting and signs. The design process was coordinated among the parties involved to achieve a unified ensemble, both visually and functionally. Often they sought a harmonious relationship with the residential areas served by the center. Toward that end, the ambience cultivated through the 1930s and sometimes later was an idealized presentation of preindustrial communities in Europe and North America. The shopping center was tailored to meet the needs of a prosperous consumer society, including ready access by automobile, but it was in no way to suggest the physical attributes of downtown.

Unity was just as important to the operational structure of the shopping center. A complex was initiated, implemented, owned, and managed under the auspices of a single party—an individual or a syndicate—which generally established an organization for the purpose. That organization bore ultimate responsibility for every aspect of the development, including site selection, financing, design, construction, choosing tenants, maintenance, and promotion. The shopping center thus was run

as an integrated business to which a number of independent parties paid for the opportunity to participate. Tenants were picked on the basis of performance as well as how their respective businesses related to an overall merchandising plan. The optimal "mix," as it was called, enabled each tenant's presence to reinforce the others. The complexion of that mix depended upon the target audience—the number of people in a given income range residing within a specified radius of the site.[4]

So complicated a strategy for retail development did not, of course, emerge fully formed. The mature conception of the shopping center grew incrementally over a period of about seventy-five years, beginning in the post–Civil War era. One reason why projects such as that proposed for Palos Verdes were so unlike conventional patterns of commercial real estate development is because the shopping center as an idea was nurtured under wholly different circumstances.

The shopping center was born not out of a drive to achieve maximum profits from arterial frontage, but rather from reform efforts in residential development, using a holistic approach to create places that functioned as communities in their own right rather than as undefined tracts added to the urban matrix. While connected to the city by railroad lines and dependent upon it as an employment base, the first generation of planned residential enclaves was championed for their seclusion from the urban world. A few stores providing goods and services residents needed on a routine basis were important under the circumstances. On the other hand, a basic purpose of the community was to allow escape from commerce as well as from industry and crowded conditions. Barring commercial uses altogether would likely mean that a scattering of operations, perhaps marginal in caliber, would establish themselves just outside the precinct. Allocating space for stores within the community, but without controls over what or who located there, might yield no better results. Furthermore, such ventures tended to be housed in rudimentary quarters that well-heeled residents considered eyesores.[5] The alternative was more costly and complicated but would enhance the community's prestige. The developer could invest in a building that was more ornamental, one that would be regarded as commensurate with its surroundings, and choose tenants for it that were well suited to address local demands. The purpose of the undertaking, then, was not to generate profits in itself, but to do so indirectly by making the community more appealing to prospective householders.

Probably the first decorous store building realized as an integral part of a planned residential community during its initial stage of development was a five-unit block erected in 1870 at Riverside, Illinois. Few other examples materialized over the ensuing years, in part because such enclaves themselves remained anomalous.[6] The situation began to change during the early twentieth century as the result of several factors. The exponential growth of cities made escape to satellite locations the more desirable among those who could afford it. Such places also became more accessible owing to the rapid growth of far-flung streetcar lines. The swell-

ing market, in turn, made the development of elite residential enclaves a more competitive field. Amenities and safeguards against undesired forms of development were increasingly important to attracting well-off home-buyers. Planning, beyond the subdivision of lots and some basic improve-ments to the land, became a strategic means by which real estate entrepreneurs could sell house lots at substantial prices.[7]

Among the most celebrated examples, and one of the most im-portant as a model for early twentieth-century real estate practices, was Roland Park, which lay just beyond the Baltimore city limits when it was first platted in 1891. Guards against business "encroachment" were a cen-tral part of the plan. Yet because the area lay some distance from the down-town establishments patronized by the prominent families courted for the development, a building was erected for a few basic retail functions. The developer, Edward Bouton, went to great lengths to ensure that the build-ing would be viewed as an asset instead of an intrusion.[8] The exterior suggested a country house, or perhaps a country club, more than a com-mercial facility (figure 103). Bouton did not solicit tenants, but he was careful in choosing merchants (the initial group included a grocer, a phar-macist, and a confectioner) to purvey the types and caliber of goods ex-pected by his elite clientele.

After 1900, Roland Park began to attract national attention among members of both the design and real estate fields, for it repre-sented one of the most ambitious, sophisticated, and economically sound ventures of its kind on this side of the Atlantic.[9] The store block appears to have enjoyed special interest. While decorous examples could be found in an increasing number of affluent residential areas, this one was unusu-ally elaborate. The building was one of a very few that stood in isolation, not as part of an unplanned village center but surrounded by residential functions, without the possibility of enlargement.[10] No better illustration could be found of how commerce could operate in an environment fully

103
Roland Park store block, 4800–4812 Ro-land Avenue, Baltimore, Maryland, 1894, Wyatt & Nolting, architects. (*Baltimore American Souvenir Edition* 1895, courtesy Jacques Kelly.)

consonant with genteel domesticity. The Roland Park store block afforded a paradigm both in the integration of retail outlets as amenities in residential development and in the planning of those outlets to address needs of a specific clientele.

A project undertaken in 1907 by the Los Angeles Investment Company indicates the extent to which the store block gained acceptance as a component of planned residential subdivisions. Founded in 1895, this firm became a major business within fifteen years, deriving its funds from a swelling corpus of stockholders (9,000 in 1911) who wished to partake in the city's real estate bonanza. Unlike most ventures of the period, the company built and sold houses rather than just platting land. The concern operated at an enormous scale by standards of the period, having purchased over 3,100 acres in the Southwest district and constructed some 2,200 houses there by 1913. The area was improved incrementally, but even those tracts were sizable. On the eighty-acre College Tract (begun 1907), houses were first erected on every other lot so that purchasers could temporarily enjoy a side yard. Seventy houses out of the 450 planned were almost completely sold within the first fifteen months. In contrast to many nearby areas, streets were improved, utilities installed, and landscaping undertaken as part of the enterprise. Space was set aside for small parks, and also for eight store buildings, on strategic corners so that they lay within convenient reach of all residents.[11]

Much like the bungalows they were built to serve, the store blocks had a standardized design. The scheme was more pedestrian than the Roland Park facility but otherwise embodied a similar approach. The Los Angeles buildings were separated from other commercial development and were consciously designed to resemble the houses that surrounded them (figure 104). Each had four units for stores. Space above was reserved for community purposes: recreation halls, fraternal lodges, and temporary quarters for churches and schools. The company retained ownership of the buildings and presumably had an ongoing plan for their management. Not all the buildings appear to have been realized, and they

A VILLAGE STREET—BEFORE AND AFTER
JARVIS HUNT, Architect

were sold in 1914 when the company suffered setbacks due to a downturn in real estate activity.[12] Nevertheless, the venture was a precocious step locally toward establishing an integrative approach to outlying retail development.

Reform motives also led to the next, decisive move in the emergence of the shopping center concept: housing a broader range of commercial functions to serve community needs. Planning in this context entailed an ensemble of buildings that would function as a business district. Some of the earliest efforts in this vein were to remake existing centers of satellite towns that were attracting prosperous city dwellers. The urbanites' dislike of these junctions where the machine met the garden was considerable. In 1910 the editors of *House Beautiful* described the core of Wheaton, twenty-five miles west of the Chicago Loop:

The station was hopeless in its packing-box ugliness, and the street across the way even more dreary. . . . Beyond the town were miles of beautiful country . . . , but not a hint of this was revealed by the foreground. . . . It was the average outlook in the average town . . . presenting the same hit-or-miss building scheme—a sort of architectural patchwork, unrelated and depressing.

Commercial architecture was the worst of the lot: "Beautiful country houses we have long had . . . , imposing public buildings, fine churches, but these alone have not made . . . our country places . . . architecturally perfect. There has always been a blot somewhere—usually at the [town center]."[13]

There followed a scheme for recasting this alleged wasteland proposed by a prominent Chicago architect, Jarvis Hunt. Hunt had convinced property owners to underwrite a preliminary plan, replacing an assemblage "irregular and monotonous—a combination peculiarly American" with a picturesque ensemble of freely interpreted postmedieval elements—"a little English, a touch of German, all planned by a Yankee"

104

College Tract store block, 1942–1946 W. Forty-eighth Street, Los Angeles, 1907–1908, Los Angeles Investment Company, designer; altered. Photo "Dick" Whittington, 1927. (Whittington Collection, Department of Special Collections, University of Southern California.)

105

Hypothetical design for streetfront remodeling of commercial center, Wheaton, Illinois, ca. 1909–1920, Jarvis Hunt, architect. (*House Beautiful,* April 1910, 128–129.)

(figure 105). The design was practical, Hunt claimed. It would cost less than $1,000 because work entailed only few facades. While the vocabulary was by then well evident in prosperous residential areas, the scope was unprecedented in the commercial sphere. The design elicited widespread interest, the editors claimed; their own enthusiasm was overflowing: "Surely anyone who can start a movement to reform the American town, architecturally speaking, deserves . . . all kinds of monuments—and it is quite possible that [Hunt] might be remembered long after the maker of cathedrals had been forgotten. . . . The . . . scheme will be watched with keen interest, for the real story is just beginning."[14]

Hunt's proposal in fact stood little chance of materializing. The cost would have been greater than his estimate. Absent competition, property owners had little incentive to remodel. Even if some of them were willing to invest, the objective would have been lost without full participation. If nothing else, the proposal underscored the need for a single organization to undertake such an enterprise.

Perhaps the most important result of Hunt's proposal was the inspiration it almost certainly afforded for Market Square, which was built several years later and established a precedent nationally for an integrated shopping complex. Like Hunt's, the project was directed at the commercial center of a Chicago satellite town, Lake Forest. The existing fabric was similarly branded "a disgrace to civilization . . . strikingly like Sun Dance, Wyoming in the early '80s."[15] Likewise, too, the design was the brainchild of a leading Chicago architect, Howard Van Doren Shaw. But in this case, Shaw had a collaborator, Arthur Aldis, partner in one of the city's foremost real estate development and management firms. Aldis and Shaw both had "country" residences at Lake Forest, as did a number of friends who ranked among Chicago's richest families. Plans to redevelop the town center began in 1912 when Aldis persuaded several others, including Cyrus H. McCormick, Jr., to form an investment trust, of the sort

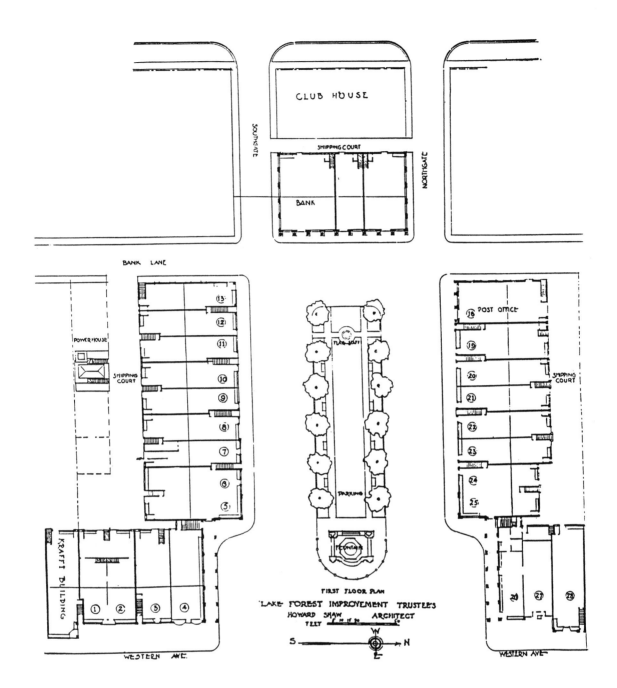

FIRST FLOOR PLAN
LAKE FOREST IMPROVEMENT TRUSTEES
HOWARD SHAW   ARCHITECT

his company had pioneered for large downtown buildings several decades earlier. Shares in the venture cost from $5,000 to $25,000; over $540,000 was raised in subscriptions and through a bond issue in two campaigns. With these funds, the trustees purchased a major portion of the business district and erected Market Square behind the range of extant buildings to minimize disruption to merchants. Once work was completed in the spring of 1916, the trust assumed the role of manager for the ensemble of twenty-eight stores, twelve office suites, thirty apartments, a gymnasium, a clubhouse, and the landscaped space that served as a centerpiece (figures 106, 107). Although initial plans called for dissolving the trust once buildings were sold with restrictive covenants, the organization did not relinquish its role as steward for over half a century.[16]

106
Market Square, Western Avenue, Lake Forest, Illinois, 1915–1916, Howard van Doren Shaw, architect. Photo author, 1988.

107
Market Square, site plan. (*Architect and Engineer,* December 1918, 82.)

Market Square might be dismissed as a millionaire's indulgence had the program not been developed on a sound financial basis by so important a figure in the real estate field. Aldis and his associates received a return of from three to four percent on their investment even though the venture was driven by aesthetic rather than monetary objectives. Shaw worked closely with Aldis to create an arrangement that served both ends. The automobile was a central factor in this planning, since most Lake Foresters had cars at an early date. Market Square was perhaps the first business district to be laid out specifically to accommodate motor vehicles. The setback not only enabled construction to proceed before existing buildings were demolished, but permitted a significant widening of the main street. This step, combined with having new streets around the square, was designed to relieve traffic congestion that often occurred when trains arrived at the depot close by. The square also was seen as a means to increase curbside parking space. Delivery vehicles were given their own service courts behind both ranges of stores. The configuration further increased the area that could be used for business purposes; the linear footage of storefronts was nearly three times that of the earlier grouping. The cost of the buildings, whose exterior treatment was as decorous as any among commercial architecture in outlying areas, was justified on the grounds of increasing trade. Providing a full range of basic goods and services in embellished surroundings, the complex was intended to raise community patronage.[17]

Market Square attracted widespread attention within a few years of its opening. Much of the interest lay in its visual attributes. Here, it seemed, was a long overdue illustration of how the spirit of the city beautiful could be manifested in a mercantile endeavor, of how business buildings, no less than public ones, could give civic focus to a community. San Francisco architect Albert Farr wrote enthusiastically for west coast colleagues tht the scheme provided an exemplar for much-needed changes in small business districts throughout California.[18] Yet it was the practical aspects of Market Square that stimulated the most interest and enthusiasm. The project demonstrated that a single organization could bring order to the supposedly chaotic commercial landscape in such a way as to improve business and generate a profit for the sponsors.

The concept of developing a commercial center with set boundaries, designed as a unified entity, and with a harmonious relationship with its residential environs received considerable reinforcement from the flurry of comprehensive plans for industrial communities prepared during the 1910s. Manufacturers commissioned such work both to mitigate labor unrest and as a positive means of advancing stability and productivity in the workforce.[19] At the same time, proponents of city planning and of housing reform seized the opportunity to realize in embryo an agenda they believed should have general application. More than most undertakings of the period, these plans presented a matrix for total communities, places containing all the components necessary to sustain a well-rounded, healthful existence. Because the intended residents had few resources and

little mobility, more attention was paid to providing a strong focal point for activity at the town center. In function as well as appearance, that center represented an idealized view of the traditional community core.[20]

Some of the most ambitious proposals for early twentieth-century industrial towns were developed for copper mining operations in the Southwest. These schemes provided a direct precedent for California work in their imaginative responses to topography and climate as well as their use of Latin-inspired forms.[21] One of the best known and most widely praised—in Los Angeles and nationally—was Bertram Grosvenor Goodhue's scheme for Tyrone, New Mexico (1914–1918), prepared for the Phelps Dodge Corporation (figure 108). Though based in New York, Goodhue spent much of his time in southern California and did much to shape its architecture, first through his plans for the Panama-California Exposition at San Diego (1911–1915), which to many observers seemed at once more worldly and sensitive to the region, more sophisticated and natural, more decorous and coherent than local work.[22] The exposition influenced design in the state through the 1920s as few individual projects did. Tyrone was an important sequel, possessing many of the same attributes, simplified in a manner conducive to residential application. The design had an unpretentious gentility coveted by the affluent during the 1920s. The town center, which was emphasized in the presentation drawings, suggested not so much an outpost for miners as the heart of an exclusive residential tract in southern California. It was likely on the minds of those planning Palos Verdes.

PALOS VERDES

When designed in 1921–1923, Palos Verdes Estates was to be one of the largest planned communities in the United States. The tract encompassed some 16,000 acres. Topographically, it was spectacular by any standard,

108
Town center, Tyrone, New Mexico, 1914, Bertram Grosvenor Goodhue, architect; partially realized, all constructed buildings destroyed. (*Bertram Grosvenor Goodhue, Master of Many Arts,* pl. clxx.)

with quasi-mountainous terrain and panoramic views of the coast in three directions.[23] Wanting to create a national model for enlightened development, Vanderlip and his associates took pains to ensure that the natural setting was used to advantage. The venerable Olmsted Brothers firm, widely considered the nation's foremost landscape architects and town planners, together with Charles H. Cheney, then one of the few nationally prominent planners on the west coast, were hired to prepare the master plan. Concurrently, they made more detailed plans of four initial subdivisions, comprising about one-fifth of the total area. More than in most such undertakings, natural features were to be protected and form the basis for development. When completed, precincts would suggest gradual growth over several centuries. In some areas indigenous vegetation would be cultivated to a degree that would make it difficult to discern the presence of settlement. Generous provisions were made for open space, much of which would be left undisturbed, with the rest allocated to recreational amenities. A strict zoning code excluded all land uses considered undesirable. Among the provisions that elicited the greatest interest nationwide was the establishment of a professionally qualified "art jury" with authority over individual projects to assure a high standard of design. Few if any precedents, save for the federal core of Washington, D.C., under the purview of the Commission of Fine Arts, were then subject to such detailed and sweeping aesthetic oversight.

Palos Verdes was envisioned as an idyllic enclave for persons of means. Controls not only mandated costly development but excluded the rise of any substantial employment base.[24] The endeavor was repeatedly promoted as a "city," to harbor 80,000 residents in a decade and eventually twice that population. Yet breadwinners would, of necessity, commute to work. Furthermore, the location was a considerable distance from centers of employment even by regional standards. Downtown Los Angeles lay twenty miles afield; downtown Long Beach ten (figure 109). Public transit connections were nonexistent. Only pesrons who could afford to spend the time driving or who did not have to work might find Palos Verdes a feasible option.[25] Probably no other planned, year-round residential community possessed a greater sense of detachment from the urban world on which it depended.

Basic characteristics of the Palos Verdes plan drew from an earlier one for a lavish resort on the same site, developed in schematic form during the early months of 1914.[26] The initial project, also undertaken by the Olmsted firm, was to create a west coast equivalent to New York's Tuxedo Park. Vanderlip and his syndicate of some fifty friends considered a number of places in both the United States and Cuba prior to choosing Palos Verdes for its climate as well as natural beauty. Large country places would be built for seasonal occupation by a coterie of the very rich, most of whom would occupy their coastal retreats for perhaps a month each year. Three "small, model villages" would provide staff quarters. Each "hamlet" would also have a few stores and community facilities arranged around a plaza and composed as a picturesque assemblage "such as that

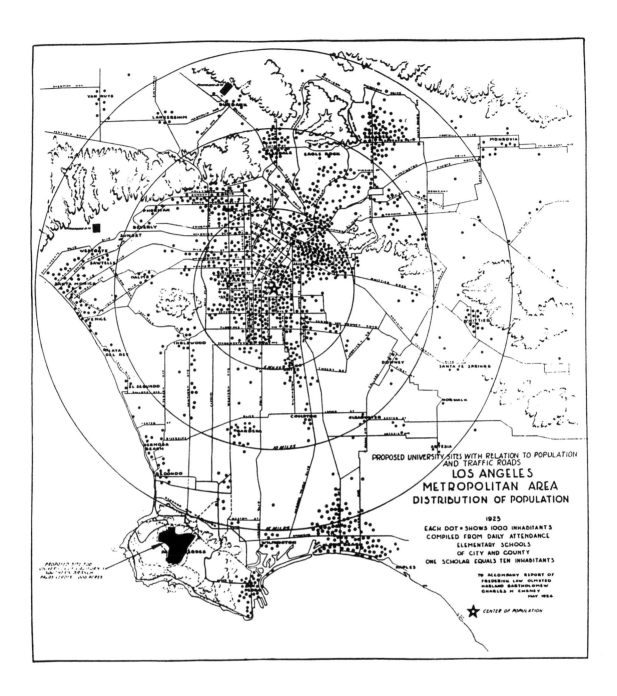

109

Map of Los Angeles metropolitan area showing relation of Palos Verdes tract (lower left) to existing population densities, 1925. (*Palos Verdes Bulletin,* February 1925, 7.)

which delights the tourist automobiling among the village districts of . . . England and Germany."[27] Distinguished east coast architects would design these ensembles; the syndicate would own them. Conceptually, the village centers were allied with Market Square in image, with Tyrone in function.

The outbreak of World War I and a depressed local economy postponed the plan. The subsequent recasting of Palos Verdes as a year-round residential area was likely influenced by the fast growth of the region and the increased mobility brought by widespread automobile use. Still, the 1914 scheme left its imprint. Nowhere was this legacy more evident than in the design of the business centers, which retained a paternalis-

tic aura. The design nevertheless indicated an attitude that was now more accepting of commerce, using it as a pretext for community focal points. The plans further acknowledged the importance of convenient automobile access. Visual appeal to the sightseer was by no means discounted, but a far more important objective now was addressing the routine use of these business centers by their well-to-do constituency.

The Olmsted-Cheney plan called for a network of commercial centers throughout Palos Verdes, a provision of unprecedented scope in comprehensively planned developments. Each subdivision was to have one such complex, which would meet all basic needs of between 10,000 and 30,000 residents. The projected size was quite large relative to that of the clientele, with a minimum of around forty stores and perhaps as many professional offices.[28] The scope no doubt extended beyond routine goods and services, such as those that occupied the majority of units at Market Square, to include some fashionable specialty shops. This range was advanced, in all likelihood, because no other places of business were permitted inside Palos Verdes and no competing ones existed for some distance beyond the boundaries. To a degree that many retailers would welcome but seldom had the luxury of experiencing, the target audience was a captive one.

The exterior of the business centers, each designed by a different, hand-picked architectural firm, was intended to help set the tone for the whole enterprise. As soon as the general plans were completed during the winter of 1923–1924, they were conspicuously featured in advertisements as part of an intensive campaign to stimulate land sales.[29] The popular appeal of these images lay in their pronounced historicizing attributes (figure 110). The ambience of a preindustrial village cultivated at Market Square and Tyrone was fully exploited, to the point of suggesting a stage set. In concert with the prescribed mode of residential design, the complexes employed a free interplay of Spanish and Italian, medieval and Renaissance, high-style and vernacular sources, idealized in character and regularized in arrangement. The results were more evocative of the past, more a departure from the conventional business district, than anything then realized in the United States. Nothing was allowed to compromise the totality of Latin allusions. Instead of a landscaped square—an amalgam of English and Yankee, not European, precedents—the center space was a paved plaza punctuated by an ornamental fountain. Storefronts and signs lay behind arcaded passages. All services related to the automobile itself were to be discreetly placed on side streets. The messiness of commerce was edited from the picture.

For all their old-world associations, these complexes differed from the historic urban patterns they emulated in being contained and inward-looking. Linear extension of commerce from the square into the streets of the community was nonexistent. A guaranteed neighborhood meant not only prohibiting business beyond a tightly defined node, but also providing a buffer zone comprised of multiunit dwellings around those nodes (see figure 102). Total segregation of trade from the preserves

110
Lunada Bay Plaza, Palos Verdes Estates,
1923, Kirtland Cutter, architect; project.
(*Architect and Engineer*, January 1930, 83.)

of single-family houses would be explicit in concrete no less than in
perceptual terms. The relationship possessed almost medieval overtones—
the business centers as latter-day fortresses—only with protection directed
toward those living outside rather than within the confines.

From a practical standpoint, on the other hand, aspects of the
business centers' layouts were innovative. The center square made an
effective parking lot, which far exceeded most provisions for cars at that
time. The plan of Malaga Cove Plaza was especially well suited to this
function, with entrances placed at the corners rather than in the middle
of the block (figures 111, 112). Even though no distinction was made
between space for moving and for stationary vehicles, the arrangement
minimized the opportunities for conflict between the two. Furthermore,
unlike in the great majority of commercial development in Los Angeles
and elsehwere, vehicular circulation was strictly local. Roads carrying
through traffic were separated from the plazas to preclude congestion.
Finally, the inward orientation of stores to the plaza, combined with the
extent of the latter's space, facilitated keeping shoppers' cars off nearby
residential streets. The results could go a long way to mitigate the visual
impact of the motor vehicle.

Greater thought was given to the physical plan and to the regulations guiding it than to the operational structure of the business centers. In
1922, blanket newspaper solicitations, differing little from those promoting boulevard frontage, were directed toward prospective merchants.[30]
Lots could be purchased and buildings erected on an individual basis; even
speculative holding of property was permissible. Not until the following

year were plans begun for unified complexes. Even then, development of a center would be undertaken by several parties, each purchasing a separate portion of the site. Participants had to adhere to the overall exterior design; however, policies governing the selection, mix, and management of tenants do not appear to have been formalized. Throughout the numerous accounts of planning at Palos Verdes, no clues were given to suggest that these centers of trade would be run as fully integrated business developments.

As it was, little need for an operational plan arose because most of the building scheme never materialized. Following the peak of residential real estate activity in the mid-1920s, public interest in Palos Verdes began to wane, dropping precipitously with the depression. Although southern Californians were driving ever greater distances to work, the tract lay too far from existing population centers to stimulate the rapid growth its sponsors envisioned. Development prior to the late 1930s was confined primarily to the northernmost subdivision, Malaga Cove. Only a small part of Malaga Cove Plaza was realized during its first decade.[31]

While mostly stillborn, the projected network of stylish business complexes at Palos Verdes came at a pivotal point in the shopping center's emergence as a significant part of planned community development. Retail facilities anticipated at Palos Verdes enjoyed a prominence—both in the plan and in promotions—never previously accorded in the residential sphere. The designs represent a capstone to the reformers' use of commerce to advance the cause of civic improvement. They had few direct offspring in part because planning on this scale required enormous capital, more than most developers of residential property could command. The

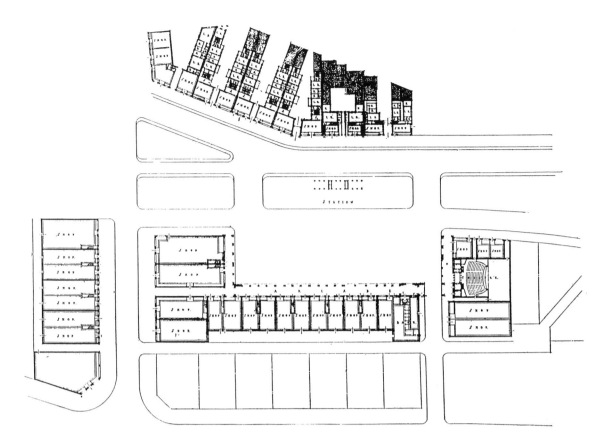

risks were high as well. All the money spent on planning and improvements to the land was for naught if a substantial part of the tract was not purchased by prospective homeowners. Attractive commercial centers were presented as part of numerous community plans in southern California during the height of the real estate boom, but few were realized.[32] In some cases, the undertaking does not seem to have attracted enough residents to sustain much retail trade. In others, competing businesses were too close at hand. Finally, unless the projected business volume was great, lenders and merchants alike were probably inclined to think of decorous buildings as a garnish they could not afford. The shopping center had to be more than an ornament to a guaranteed neighborhood; it had to succeed in strictly economic terms. The idea of an integrated business development continued to grow in sophistication not because proponents were seeking aesthetic reform in its own right, but rather because they believed their approach to be a profitable alternative to the norm. That transformation took a major step forward with the announcement of Westwood Village in 1927.

111
Malaga Cove Plaza, Palos Verdes Estates, preliminary design, 1923, Webber & Spaulding, architects. (*Architect and Engineer,* January 1930, 38.)

112
Malaga Cove Plaza, site plan. (*California Southland,* February 1924, 23.)

WESTWOOD VILLAGE

Unlike the Palos Verdes complexes, Westwood Village was conceived as a major business center and a significant generator of profit in its own right. The target audience comprised residents not only of surrounding tracts cre-

ated by the same developer, but also of communities further afield. Although the first businesses in the center opened their doors shortly after the stock market crash of 1929, Westwood Village boasted over two hundred establishments after eight years of operation. By the eve of World War II, it had achieved the stature of Hollywood and the Miracle Mile as a leading destination for shoppers in the metropolitan area. Westwood Village was also fashioned as a distinct place, possessing the intimate scale, cohesiveness, and architectural gentility cultivated at Palos Verdes. The venture demonstrated that such a shopping center could attract a large and somewhat diverse market.

Westwood Village lay in the heart of the former Rancho San Jose de Buenos Aires, a tract of nearly 3,300 acres between Beverly Hills and Santa Monica. The land remained open as late as 1919 when it was purchased by Arthur Letts, owner of the Broadway and Bullock's department stores. Letts entrusted development of this enormous area to the Janss Investment Company, run by his son-in-law, Harold Janss, Harold's brother, Edwin, and their father, Peter. Founded in 1901, the firm was perhaps the largest developer of residential real estate in southern California, platting nearly 100,000 acres by 1929. Like most such businesses in the early twentieth century, Janss focused on the subdivision and sale of land.[33] Yet the company's growth stemmed from atypical practices. The tracts purchased were unusually large—Belvedere Heights had 6,000 lots—they were improved by the company in short order, and the selling price was low. Through one of the most aggressive newspaper advertising campaigns in Los Angeles, Janss sold lots fast—1,000 in Belvedere Gardens in the first ten months. The benefits derived from this economy of scale were targeted to the lower-middle and prosperous working classes, who found the quality of the sites and prospects for quick growth of a full-fledged residential area appealing. Much like those of the Los Angeles Investment Company, Janss's undertakings could reach epic proportions because of capital derived from an army of shareholders (25,000 in 1922).

Janss began to develop Lett's tract in much the same way as it had earlier ventures: making basic improvements to, then feverishly promoting, land subdivisions. No comprehensive plan was prepared, nor was the final product envisioned as a distinct community comparable to Palos Verdes. Indeed, there was little cohesiveness to the whole. The acreage instead became a mosaic of residential areas encompassing a cross section of the income groups then in the western half of the metropolis. Westwood, the southernmost tract, lying between Pico and Santa Monica boulevards, was mostly comprised of small lots costing as little as $750 apiece (the cheapest house lot at Palos Verdes was $2,000) laid out on an orthogonal grid. At the opposite end of the spectrum were tracts such as Holmby Hills, north of Sunset Boulevard in the Santa Monica Mountains, that carried myriad restrictions and became some of the region's poshest enclaves. The 25,000 people that Janss estimated in 1939 to be inhabitants of the land Letts had purchased twenty years earlier were as diverse a group as could be found in one area developed by a single firm.

113
Janss Investment Company advertisement for commercial property at Westwood tract. (*Los Angeles Times,* 2 December 1922, V-8.)

Janss may not have conceived so variable a development at the outset. In contrast to the Vanderlip syndicate and many other large-scale real estate enterprises of the period, the company seldom revealed its intentions except on a piecemeal basis when the sale of property was about to commence. The subdivisions on Letts's rancho were most likely planned on an incremental and pragmatic basis. Similar circumstances characterized the creation of the shopping center dubbed Westwood Village. Half a dozen years earlier, when the first parts of the Westwood subdivision were opened in 1922, property along Santa Monica and Westwood boulevards was set aside for commercial development. Hoping to entice motion picture studios to locate nearby, Janss dubbed the corridor "the Second Hollywood."[34] Here, it was hoped, would quickly rise a business center similar in scale and function to the burgeoning one on Hollywood Boulevard (figure 113). Little came of the effort. Among the problems was the bisection of Santa Monica Boulevard by a Pacific Electric car line, whose more even grade imposed physical as well as psychological barriers to motorists. A decade after the scheme was launched, most of the frontage remained vacant (figure 114). The episode underscored the fact that even with considerable resources at one's command and an attractive general location for business, an outlying center could not be willed into existence. For every Miracle Mile, there were many visions soon forgotten.

By 1925, Janss began to focus on land north of Wilshire, including a very large tract named Westwood Hills, which was marketed to an affluent audience. A year later, the regents of the University of California chose a 384-acre section in the center of Westwood Hills as the permanent home of the recently created Los Angeles campus, a move Janss took vigorous steps to help consummate.[35] The university was seen as a major stimulus to surrounding development, attracting not just faculty but many persons of means who believed proximity to an institution of higher learn-

ing enhanced land values. Furthermore, the substantial enrollment of 6,000 that was projected for UCLA when it began operating its new campus in 1929 would no doubt accelerate growth of nearby subdivisions. These factors served as a catalyst in Janss's decision to create a large commercial center on adjacent land. The Santa Monica Boulevard fiasco no doubt contributed to taking an entirely different approach: the second attempt to rival Hollywood was carefully planned.[36]

Soon after the UCLA location was finalized, Janss began preparing a scheme for Westwood Village. Almost three years were given to research and programming before ground was broken on the first buildings in March 1929. To guide the process, Janss hired Harland Bartholomew, a St. Louis planner whose reputation rivaled the Olmsteds', and L. Deming Tilton, a former Bartholomew employee now living in Santa Barbara and active in the recent reconstruction of that town center. Bartholomew and Tilton worked closely with Gordon Whitnall, director of the Los Angeles City Planning Department. They also surveyed a number of new retail centers that were considered premier examples of their kind in other parts of the country.[37]

Accessibility was deemed of paramount importance to the venture's success. The site lay between Wilshire Boulevard, which had become the major route west from Beverly Hills in the previous few years, and the main entrance to the university (figure 115). Perhaps influenced by the layout of the centers at Palos Verdes, the plan excluded commercial

114
Santa Monica Boulevard looking east, vicinity of Westwood Boulevard. Photo "Dick" Whittington, 1931. (Whittington Collection, Department of Special Collections, University of Southern California.)

115
Westwood Village, Westwood Boulevard and adjacent streets between Wilshire Boulevard and Le Conte Avenue, Los Angeles, begun 1928, Harland Bartholomew and L. D. Tilton, planners. Aerial view looking north, Wilshire Boulevard in foreground. Photo ca. 1937. (Los Angeles County Museum of Natural History.)

development along Wilshire so as to avoid automobile congestion. The heart lay several blocks to the north, with Westwood Boulevard, the principal north-south route connecting Pico and Wilshire, extended through to serve as the spine. Because this street ended at the university campus, traffic would be local. Furthermore, vehicular circulation would be diffuse because Westwood Boulevard was one of an irregular grouping of streeets laid out to facilitate flow in more or less equal measure. Westwood Village stood in sharp contrast to Hollywood or the Miracle Mile in having a minimal hierarchy of streets, but it was equally dissimilar to Palos Verdes, Tyrone, or Market Square in having no clearly identified center—no plaza, no green, no singular focal point of any kind. Beyond enhancing the movement of automobiles, this arrangement maximized property values throughout the complex by having all frontage seem desirable to merchants and customers alike. Some sites would inevitably become preferable to others; nevertheless, the distinctions would be far less than under ordinary circumstances.

In order to ensure that development would occur as planned and to guard against overly rapid growth, Janss implemented the scheme incrementally, at a pace that must have seemed snaillike compared to conventional speculative practice. This approach also made it easier to respond to changes in market conditions over time, because it was based on a site plan and guidelines for growth, not on a design per se. The project was announced in December 1927. Over the succeeding months more details were made public, fueling interest and anticipation. Although the goal was to house several hundred businesses eventually, Janss noted the following June that only two or three dozen would be granted a place among the initial group. Moreover, only one establishment purveying a given type of goods or service would be allowed to operate at first. Competing stores, and other businesses generally, would be added according to market demand. Gauging that demand would rely on careful study, not assumptions. Janss established a Business Research Department in March 1929 for that purpose. The limitations intensified the eagerness of retailers. Apparently enough offers were received at the outset for the entire complex to have been built in a single campaign had Janss so chosen.[38]

Janss not only selected the merchants but determined where they would locate in the development. Initial buildings were concentrated along Westwood Boulevard to achieve a critical mass, but large spaces were left for complementary establishments to be added later. Construction also began fronting nearby streets within the first few years. To maintain flexibility and appeal, no lots were platted in the original layout. Instead, Janss worked with clients individually to determine the lot size and configuration best suited to the specific needs of each. Additional latitude was given clients in realizing projects. Janss could contract with these parties to construct the building to their requirements and lease it to them, or the land could be sold and the purchaser take responsibility for implementation. Some clients were mercantile companies; others were investors who planned to lease the parcel they held. While Janss did not

116

Janss Investment Company advertisement for Westwood Hills. (*Los Angeles Times,* 26 October 1930, V-5.)

retain ownership of all the land, the company exercised ongoing control of the other landowners through provisions on tenancy and design.

Within the first months of planning, Janss appears to have decided that Westwood Village would have an exceptional character. The ensemble would suggest a "village," not a city; it would be cohesive and meet an unusually high architectural standard. Buildings would in effect form a commercial campus that would complement the university's and be commensurate in quality of expression.[39] Like the university, too, the business village would stand out as a major community asset, not just for the convenience it offered nearby householders but for the atmosphere it conveyed and the stability it brought to the area. The undertaking was strenuously marketed as yet another means to strengthen property values over time—another way to create a guaranteed neighborhood (figure 116).

To set the tone for design, Janss itself undertook developing the first two units of the complex. Each was composed to suggest a series of small buildings erected at different times (figure 117). This treatment was likely inspired by the much-praised proposals for downtown Santa Barbara prepared in 1924 as part of a civic improvement campaign (figure 118). Though these designs were not realized, their general tone was adopted for the construction campaign, to which Tilton contributed, in the aftermath of a devastating earthquake that struck in June 1925. The local government adopted design guidelines on appearance not unlike those of Palos Verdes, with the enthusiastic support of merchants as well as civic leaders.[40] In a short period, Santa Barbara was heralded as an emblem of how planning from an aesthetic perspective could also be instrumental in enhancing business. Given this reputation and the fact that the city's business district served some of the most fashionable resort communities on the Pacific coast, it is not surprising that Janss turned to the Santa Barbara initiative as a model.

At Westwood, the guidelines Janss established for building exteriors were probably vaguer than at Santa Barbara, enabling architects to work with a loosely defined spectrum of historical sources associated with Mediterranean Europe. Variety in form, detail, and character was encouraged. Virtually all shopping centers conceived during the 1920s were the product of a single team of collaborating designers. Janss, on the other hand, appears to have sought the involvement of numerous architects. The company's own buildings were designed by Allison & Allison, a firm best known for its institutional work, including the new UCLA campus, and by Gordon Kaufmann, resident of nearby Holmby Hills and a favorite architect of the elite.[41] Other leading southern California firms soon became involved as well, including Morgan, Walls & Clements, John and Donald Parkinson, S. Charles Lee, and Paul Williams. As a consequence, Westwood Village emerged as a showcase of stylish, historicizing commercial architecture, rivaled in its extent by few places nationwide.

If variety abounded in the particulars of expression, an underlying cohesiveness was achieved through the oversight process. All building proposals had to be approved by a company-appointed Board of Architec-

tural Supervisors, which functioned much like the art jury at Palos Verdes. Here, too, guidelines existed for many aspects of design beyond the general ones on the use of historical imagery.[42] Building fronts had to be at least seventeen feet high, but no more than two or three stories—probably to avoid overconcentration of business in any one part as well as to avoid discordant streetscapes. At the same time, some buildings situated at strategic points in the complex could incorporate towers. The collective result was to enhance Westwood Village's identity as a unified complex, while each tower served as a guide to orient shoppers within the precinct. Strict control was exercised over details, including signs. Oversight did not stop when construction was completed; all later external changes to buildings came under the same scrutiny. Janss invested substantial sums on public improvements, including ornate streetlight standards (similar to those on Wilshire Boulevard further east); multicolored sidewalks (derived from those of Rio de Janeiro); a grassy median lined with palms along Westwood Boulevard (said to be inspired by one in Honolulu), and a parklike entrance zone on what normally would be the highest-priced land, fronting Wilshire Boulevard (figure 119).

The mix of businesses was as important as design. In contrast to other shopping centers developed during the interwar decades, Westwood Village was conceived from the start as a home for numerous branches of leading downtown stores. Desmond's was among the early arrivals, its premises opening in March 1930. Two years later, Bullock's completed its branch; Myer Siegel followed in 1937.[43] National chains also were courted: J. J. Newberry (1931), Sears, Roebuck (1936), and J. C. Penney (1937).[44] Yet other chains catered to routine needs, including Ralphs (1929), Safeway (1929), and A&P (1931) markets and Owl (1934) and Sontag (1937) drug companies.[45] Finally, there was a broad spectrum of in-

117

Westwood Village, 900 and 1000 blocks of Westwood Boulevard, looking south; left to right: Janss Building (1929, Allison & Allison, architects), Kelly Building (1929–1930, Paul R. Williams, architect), Desmond's store (1929–1930, John and Donald B. Parkinson, architects), Holmby Building (1929–1930, Gordon Kaufmann, architect), Campbell Building (1929, Allen Hawes, architect); numerous alterations. Photo ca. 1930. (Los Angeles County Museum of Natural History.)

dependent specialty stores, some relocated from the precinct near the university's previous campus on Vermont Avenue, others newly established.[46] The array of retail establishments was matched by few outlying centers prior to World War II, and made Westwood Village competitive locally with Hollywood and the Miracle Mile. But unlike the latter development, which was mainly a focus for retail and personal services, Westwood Village addressed a wider range of consumer needs. Besides banks and numerous professional offices, there was a bowling alley (1930) and two sizable movie theaters (1930–1931, 1937), branch offices of utility companies, and a storage facility.[47] The first business to open in the complex was a gasoline station, which was joined by three others and a large service garage over the next several years.[48] The mix was possible in part because of market diversity. Thousands of students and others with relatively modest disposable incomes lived nearby; so did more prosperous contingents and a rapidly growing concentration of the rich. Besides Janss's own foothill tracts, Brentwood, Pacific Palisades, Santa Monica, Beverly Hills, and West Hollywood were among the target communities.

The variety of shopping options also occurred because Janss eschewed what had become the prevailing Los Angeles pattern of big branch stores. Paralleling the policy to develop the complex at a gradual, more or less even pace was one that kept leading stores at a modest initial scale so that trade would hinge on an assemblage of well-known outlets rather than on a single, enormous one. The minimal hierarchy of stores was also reflected in their appearances. Quite unlike their Wilshire Boulevard branches, here Desmond's and Bullock's were not designed as con-

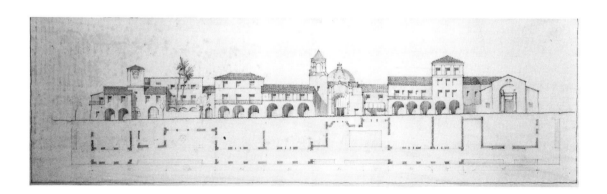

120

Desmond's store, 1001 Westwood Boulevard, Los Angeles, 1929–1930, John and Donald B. Parkinson, architects; altered. Photo "Dick" Whittington, ca. 1930. (Whittington Collection, Department of Special Collections, University of Southern California.)

121

Bullock's Westwood department store, 1000–1004 Westwood Boulevard, Los Angeles, 1932, John and Donald B. Parkinson, architects; altered. (Hearst Collection, Department of Special Collections, University of Southern California.)

spicuous beacons in their own right. Desmond's branch was just slightly smaller than that on the Miracle Mile, but it looked much like the neighboring specialty shops that surrounded it (figure 120). Containing under 17,000 square feet, Bullock's was less than a tenth the size of its Wilshire store, with a low-key exterior fusing elements derived from Tuscan villas and Andalusian farmhouses (figure 121). Sears's store was the largest in the complex (though, at 42,000 square feet, it was modest compared to others in that chain), but its massing was divided so as to elude conspicuousness. Even the tower was scaled down in deference to others in the complex—an effect quite the opposite of what the retailer sought elsewhere (figure 122). These stores were situated so that they could expand on vacant prop-

erty as market conditions warranted. Sears added 15,000 square feet in 1939; Desmond's doubled its size to approximately 30,000 square feet that same year; Bullock's was enlarged three times between 1935 and 1940.[49] Still, the ensemble far more than any of its parts remained the basis for the center's recognition and appeal.

Janss's remarkable conception did more than validate the efficacy of planned business development. The complex proved among the most successful ventures in the commercial expansion of Los Angeles during the interwar decades, despite a generally poor economic climate. Thirty-four businesses comprised the initial group that opened in 1929. Two years later, the number had nearly trebled. The expansion slowed a bit during the worst years of the depression; still, there were 172 businesses by the end of 1934, 225 by 1936. With an improved economy came a new burst of construction. Westwood Villege had 452 businesses employing 1,700 people in the spring of 1939.[50] Merchants took an active role in the process. Shortly after the first stores opened, the Westwood Village Business Association was formed to sponsor group advertising, coordinate merchandising events, and stage street festivals—all to enhance customer draw.[51] The endeavor also fundamentally changed Janss's own business. The company moved its main office to the site from downtown in 1931 because most operations now focused on the development rather than the sale of property—a complete reversal in practice from only three years previous.[52]

The pronounced shift in business orientation, and indeed the quantum leap in scale and complexion, from the centers planned for Palos

Verdes did not result from the ingenuity of Janss and its consultants alone. Though no mention was made of a link at that time, the scheme almost certainly owed a major debt to the work of Kansas City developer J. C. Nichols. By the mid-1920s, Nichols was nationally recognized by his colleagues as a leader in the use of comprehensive planning as an integral component of real estate practice. Nichols's Country Club Plaza, begun in 1922, represented a benchmark in the creation of fully intergrated business developments, unmatched in its prestige and influence during the interwar decades. Nichols also played the leading role in identifying this new form of commercial enterprise with the term "shopping center."[53] Since Bartholomew was from St. Louis, he probably would have known the Country Club Plaza firsthand, and the Jansses could not have helped knowing Nichols by reputation, if not personally. Even without such ties, the Plaza would have ranked among the principal stops for any systematic investigation of innovative retail developments such as Janss undertook around 1927.[54] The similarities between the Plaza and Westwood Village were too numerous, and the differences between them and all other examples of the period too great, for coincidence to explain the relationship.

The basic concept Westwood Village and the Plaza shared was that of a very large, integrated business development created as part of a much larger network of comprehensively planned residential subdivisions for the well-to-do. The Plaza was intended to house about 200 stores and around the same number of offices to serve Nichols's Country Club District, which encompassed 2,000 acres with over 10,000 residents by 1922. Nichols sited the Plaza off the area's main thoroughfare and planned the complex around broad streets forming relatively short, irregular blocks to facilitate traffic flow (figures 123, 124). Similarly, too, the Plaza had no distinct center, despite its name, and no strong hierarchy of locations or tenants; all portions of the complex were intended to be desirable for retail use. The plan was not a detailed three-dimensional design, but, as at Westwood, a matrix for incremental growth that would be responsive to changing circumstances. The buildings were designed in an ebullient if less suave interpretation of Spanish precedent, complete with towers at carefully chosen points to enhance collective identity and individual blocks.

122
Sears, Roebuck & Company department store, 1101–1111 Westwood Boulevard, Los Angeles, 1936, P. P. Lewis, architect; demolished. (Hearst Collection, Department of Special Collections, University of Southern California.)

123
Country Club Plaza, Kansas City, Missouri, begun 1922, Edward Buehler Delk and Edward W. Tanner, architects, Hare & Hare, landscape architects. General view looking southwest. Photo late 1930s. (Courtesy J. C. Nichols Company.)

Nichols insisted on a two-story height limit to ensure evenness in development density and vehicular traffic. His office also exercised tight control over other aspects of the operation, including the caliber and mix of tenants. As at Westwood Village, every aspects of the scheme was given careful thought so that it might contribute with maximum effectiveness toward a profitable whole.

There were also significant differences between the two endeavors. Nichols's company designed, constructed, maintained ownership of, brokered space in, and managed all buildings at the Plaza, creating the most complete retail development operation of its kind. While this operational structure became a model for large-scale retail projects as early as the 1920s and especially after World War II, it was resisted by Janss and most others in southern California until the 1950s. As landlord, Nichols reviewed almost every aspect of his tenants' businesses, including the kinds of goods they purveyed. Nichols constructed large buildings, each of which could hold numerous tenants, to provide maximum flexibility of space over an extended period of time. He assumed that both tenant needs and some of the tenants themselves would change.

Among the most pronounced differences between Westwood and the Plaza was the tenant mix. Nichols strongly preferred independent retailers, considering chains only when no alternative could be found to suit programmatic needs. He also did not court most downtown concerns to establish branch stores. Despite the great size of his project, he believed it should always function in a complementary rather than a competitive relationship to the city center. Janss, on the other hand, followed the pattern already set for developments along Hollywood and Wilshire boulevards by creating an alternative to downtown Los Angeles for the multitudes residing in the western half of the metropolitan area.

The Plaza's tenancy was primarily comprised of small specialty stores, which in Kansas City, as in Los Angeles, had been concentrated downtown at the turn of the century but were now, owing to soaring land

prices in the core and an ever more decentralized population, becoming the staple of outlying commercial districts. Many of the stores Nichols brought into his development carried luxury items catering to the upper end of the market in response to the many well-to-do Country Club District residents. Other outlets traded in routine goods and services required by a much broader segment of the population.[55] By combining these two types, Nichols sought to make the Plaza a major destination, but the range of shopping options was less than at Westwood Village by the mid-1930s. If the Plaza had greater impact nationally on integrated business practices, Westwood Village was the more precocious in its objective of functional equivalence to downtown.

Yet there was another difference that proved Janss the less far-sighted. Both the initial plan and later management policies at Westwood Village underestimated how much space customers needed for parking. When work on the Plaza started in 1922, Nichols had assumed that streets wide enough to permit diagonal curbside parking, a high ratio of street to building area, and low-density, diffuse development would address motorists' demands fully. Within a few years, however, these measures were proving insufficient. A two-story garage for both the service and storage of automobiles was built in 1928, though it appears to have been planned for employee more than for customer use since it was not well located in relation to most stores then operating. A program to provide shopper-oriented off-street parking was created at the same time, with surface lots

124
Country Club Plaza, intersection of Forty-seventh Street and Mill Creek Parkway, looking west. Photo late 1920s/early 1930s. (Courtesy J. C. Nichols Company.)

125
Country Club Plaza, general view looking northeast, showing Forty-seventh Street and Alameda parking stations (far left and foreground) and Plaza Theatre Building, 1928 (center). Photo late 1920s/early 1930s. (Courtesy J. C. Nichols Company.)

of a then unconventional sort (figure 125).[56] Two entire blocks in the complex were allocated for the purpose, their perimeters embellished with masonry walls and landscaping. Like everything else at the Plaza, these spaces were celebrated as an asset and accorded the dignified name of "parking stations." Customers would have no trouble finding them becuase their siting was conspicuous. Instead of driving to the back of the property, one could leave the car facing the storefront ranges. The generous allotment of space made maneuvering easy; one did not have to entrust an attendant with the car. For all this convenience, there was no charge.

However logical the solution might seem in retrospect, it was far from a customary one at a time when off-street parking space was seen as at best an unfortunate necessity that added to urban blight. Even at the Miracle Mile, most parking areas were utilitarian in character. Nichols took a bold leap forward in dedicating primary space for what was still generally seen as a tertiary use. The sites that were so centrally placed for the motorists were in key locations for stores, and most real estate developers would not have considered using them for any but the latter purpose. Nichols had the foresight to realize that without adequate parking space, his whole venture could be put in jeopardy. The Plaza's block configuration precluded interior lots, but it is doubtful that Nichols would have taken that option even if it had been possible. At his direction, the parking lot became a hallmark of the modern shopping center. It was not a square on which cars could park, as at Palos Verdes, but a place designed expressly for cars and for the people who drove them.

The Plaza's parking stations were completed months before the first stores opened at Westwood Village; nevertheless, Janss's approach to the situation remained akin to Nichols's initial approach half a dozen years earlier. A much-touted feature of Westwood's layout was a fifteen-foot setback of all buildings from the service alleys to create room for employee parking so that customers would have no competition in finding a diagonal space along the wide streets. But right from the start, employees resisted using the alleys, and they continued to do so despite repeated efforts by the business association. Stronger measures proved unenforceable. As early as 1932, parking space was said to be at a premium. Matters only got worse when the Los Angeles Police Department challenged the legality of diagonal parking, a matter not resolved until 1937. By the decade's end at least one store, Desmond's, had its own lot, and several other vacant parcels were appropriated for parking.[57] Still, lot sizes were small, locations were scattered, and their relation to store sites was often less than ideal. Employees continued to pose a problem. Janss gave no public sign of interest, leaving the business association to struggle for improvements. After World War II, the problem worsened.[58] More lots were created, but restrictions increased and several charged fees. New construction fueled demand. Westwood Village was in danger of becoming parkless.

Yet the importance of Westwood Village as a commercial center was not seriously eroded by its parking problems at midcentury, in large part because competing districts were faring no better. Bullock's and Sears

had achieved an effective parking solution for their lone-wolf stores, but shopping districts created in Los Angeles during the interwar decades failed to keep pace with the ever mounting demand for land where customers could conveniently and safely leave their automobiles. A. W. Ross was the most visionary of Los Angeles developers in that realm, yet he underestimated the extent of space required or how fragmenting that space undercut its value to the entire enterprise. The Janss Company neither understood the parking problem at the outset nor changed its viewpoint once the problem became more evident. Only after World War II did the idea begin to gain acceptance of creating wholly new configurations for shopping centers based upon the demands of off-street parking. This approach would not have been possible, however, without the earlier demonstration of the considerable advantages afforded by a comprehensive approach to retail development, for only through that approach could adequate space be allocated to automobiles. In the long run, it was not the guaranteed neighborhood but the imperatives of retail development that propelled the shopping center type into the mainstream. As parking problems mounted in the late 1930s, the groundwork was laid for their resolution.

VII

A HINDRANCE TO BUSINESS

Wilshire's emergence, and much of its success, as a prominent corridor of commerce from MacArthur Park to Westwood Village was in part due to Hollywood's limitations. Wilshire seemed the unassailable alternative, the street of the future no less than of the present. Despite their many differences, the Miracle Mile and Westwood Village, especially, were seen as places where there would be ample room for buildings and cars for a long time to come. In the late 1920s, no one could have imagined that parking would balloon into a significant problem within ten years, any more than one could have imagined in 1914, when Robinson's staked out new territory on Seventh Street, that the dominance of downtown stores would be challenged during the next decade by huge branches several miles afield. Yet a survey of Wilshire Boulevard, conducted in 1941 by the Automobile Club of Southern California, found a striking shortage of parking in many areas from the edge of downtown to the Santa Monica Boulevard intersection some nine miles to the west. At any given time during the workday nearly 20,000 cars were parked along the curb, over three times the number in lots and garages. Street parking extended well beyond business blocks into residential areas, much to the consternation of the inhabitants. The club's chief engineer minced no words about what he considered a harbinger of blight:

It is quite apparent that the uncontrolled growth of new business areas is slowly but surely choking the streets . . . and destroying the efficiency of the motor vehicle. . . . These new business areas are reproducing with dogged determination the identical conditions which caused the decline of the old business areas.

The problem was of epidemic proportions:

Conditions in the Wilshire district are identical with those along and adjacent to every major thoroughfare in the Los Angeles area. . . . We interviewed many business and professional men who left the central business district to escape congestion and . . . they frankly admit that the problems from which they tried to escape are already overtaking them in their new locations.[1]

A. W. Ross, of course, had taken numerous steps to ensure that enough parking would exist on the Miracle Mile, but even there shortcomings soon became noticeable. In 1948 the Los Angeles City Planning Commission estimated that existing spaces were less than half of the desirable number.[2]

As parking became a serious problem along Los Angeles's thoroughfares, adequate land in convenient locations was seldom any longer available. Only at the big downtown store branches and at Sears had significant foresight been exercised in this regard. Even when steps were initiated before the problem became acute, effective measures were almost impossible to implement because of the multitude of interests involved. Nowhere in outlying parts of the metropolitan area were the frustrations of "parklessness" so apparent as at another Wilshire destination, Beverly Hills, which lay to the east of Westwood and was becoming one of the region's most prestigious neighborhoods in the 1920s. At mid-decade, when the commercial center was just a scattering of modest-sized stores, the *Beverly Hills Citizen* fussed over supposed parking inadequacies, declaring how a lack of space posed a significant "Hindrance to Business."[3] A decade later, parking became a preoccupation in Beverly Hills to a degree probably unequaled in southern California, even in downtown Los Angeles. Perhaps more than at Westwood Village, the Miracle Mile, or Hollywood, the parking situation at Beverly Hills underscored the need for a new approach to planning business centers, one just beginning to be visible on a modest scale in a few arterial developments elsewhere in the metropolitan area at the decade's end.

BEVERLY HILLS

Conditions in Beverly Hills seemed optimal for the provision of ample parking. Unlike at Westwood Village, the need was identified early on, when the business district was still forming and curbside space remained readily at hand. In contrast to Hollywood, business leaders here were unrelenting in their drive to create a sound, comprehensive parking plan for the community. The matter dominated the activities of the local Chamber of Commerce during the pre–World War II years. Beverly Hills had the further advantage of being a separate municipality whose officials were willing to take action.

Beverly Hills was one of southern California's first communities to employ a comprehensive approach to planning. The initial tract was developed by the Rodeo Land and Water Company, which in 1907 commis-

BEVERLY HILLS

California's Model Residence Suburb

Different From Any Other

Different because it is devoted exclusively to residences.

Different because it will have a costly sewer system.

Different because there will be no waiting for gas, electricity, water, telephones.

Different because its avenues do not run at right angles, but sweep in graceful curves from the car line to the crest of the foothills.

Different because the subway will make 15 minutes time between Beverly Hills and Los Angeles.

Different because it already has more frequent car service than Hollywood (3 car lines).

Different because it has four parks costing $75,000.

Different because it is not a scheme to sell property at the maximum profit but to actually create a successful, built up suburb.

Different because it is already rapidly building up.

If you have any intention of building a home in Southern California, we cordially invite you to visit Beverly Hills at our expense and prove for yourself the truth of these assertions. Call at office for complimentary tickets.

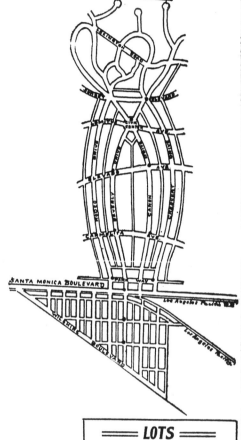

Percy H. Clark Co.

Managers

311-312 H. W. Hellman Bldg.

LOTS
$900 Up
Size 80 x 160 Up

sioned Wilbur Cook, a landscape architect from New York, and Myron Hunt, an architect recently arrived from Chicago, to prepare a detailed design.[4] While modest compared to the later Palos Verdes plan, the scheme set an important precedent in the region for the cultivation of naturalistic features, including curvilinear streets and open space reserved for parks. With development began extensive planting campaigns. Utilities were relegated to alleys bisecting the long blocks. Almost the entire section north of Santa Monica Boulevard was reserved for substantial, single-family residences, with use strictly controlled in other sections as well. The care paid to these provisions and to overall appearances of the community became an integral part of the municipal government's function once Beverly Hills

126

Percy H. Clark Company advertisement for Beverly Hills, showing business district in left half of triangular section. (*Los Angeles Times,* 22 September 1907, V-15.)

was incorporated as a city in 1914. Growth remained slow until after World War I. A population of only 674 in 1920 swelled to over 17,000 a decade later. By that point, Beverly Hills was supplanting Hollywood and the Wilshire district as an area of choice for Los Angeles's elite.

Beverly Hills also set a regional precedent by limiting commercial development to a single precinct with prescribed boundaries. The north and south borders were clearly defined by the community's two principal thoroughfares—Santa Monica and Wilshire boulevards—which converged at the western end, and by a connecting street, Crescent Drive, at the eastern end (figure 126). By virtue of its configuration, the area soon became known as the Business Triangle. Beyond containment, however, little oversight was accorded to commercial development. Lots were sold on a piecemeal basis to anyone willing to purchase them. The type and caliber of commercial enterprise as well as the character of the building that housed it were left to the discretion of the owner, perhaps because it was assumed that commercial development would reflect the upper-end market to which it catered. Construction of retail facilities began almost immediately. The first store block opened in 1907 and would not have been out of place at Roland Park or Lake Forest.[5] Subsequent work, however, was often less genteel in character; much of it was of a sort common to arteries throughout the metropolitan area.

Though probably unintentionally, the Business Triangle's layout proved conducive to diffuse development and hence a dispersal of curbside parking—an arrangement consciously planned at Westwood Village. Unlike most outlying commercial districts, it had no central intersection of major arteries, such as Hollywood and Vine, that could form a nucleus for dense building. Nor did the arrangement lend itself to concentrated arterial growth. During Beverly Hills's first major wave of business development, between the mid-1920s and the depression, both Santa Monica and Wilshire boulevards grew as automobile thoroughfares more than as commercial corridors. Wilshire did attract some large-scale projects, including the eight-story Beverly-Wilshire Hotel (1927–1928), the earliest major undertaking in the community that was distinctly urban in character and reflected the metropolitan aspirations of local boosters. Yet the hotel re-

mained in isolation, with only the smaller California Bank (1928–1929) competing for a part of the skyline.[6] Otherwise buildings were of modest size and scattered to a degree even more pronounced than in the area around Bullock's (figure 127). Retail development congregated along the wide but short streets connecting Wilshire and Santa Monica, especially Canon and Beverly drives.[7] Here, one- and two-story buildings were the norm; many lots remained vacant. Street width enabled angle parking. Space for automobiles abounded to an unusual degree (figure 128).

What prompted the initiative was a concern that the Business Triangle would fail to become a major commercial center. The erosion of Hollywood's prestige, combined with the rise in its stead of the Miracle Mile and Westwood Village, bracketing Beverly Hills to the east and west, may well have influenced the decision. Convenient access to the precinct was almost entirely by automobile. New development was on the upswing and was likely to accelerate in the immediate future. Ample space existed for new buildings, but not for more curbside parking. Furthermore, acreage in the Business Triangle was finite, and enlarging the area

Yet while Beverly Hills did not appear to have a parking problem, the need for a long-range plan was addressed as early as March 1937 when the Chamber of Commerce proposed a network of municipal parking lots on the interior of Business Triangle blocks. Most of the land was underutilized at that time; access to it would be by existing alleyways. Alteration to buildings and to the choicest land for future development would be minimal. Between 1,000 and 1,500 cars could be accommodated at any given time. The needed acreage would be condemned through the power of eminent domain, but the cost of acquisition and improvement would be equally distributed among Triangle property owners. The chamber asserted that the project would likely bolster patronage and increase land values, justifying the expense.[8]

127
Wilshire Boulevard, looking east from Santa Monica Boulevard. Photo 1929. (Hearst Collection, Department of Special Collections, University of Southern California.)

128
North Canon Drive, Beverly Hills, looking southeast, Warner Theatre (1930–1931) in background. Photo "Dick" Whittington, 1931. (Whittington Collection, Department of Special Collections, University of Southern California.)

would undermine the very premise upon which Beverly Hills had gained appeal among the affluent. If significant growth occurred without adequate parking, it was argued, decline was sure to follow.

The chamber's scheme was without precedent in southern California, and few examples existed elsewhere. A municipal car lot was established as early as 1918 in Piqua, Ohio, but fewer than thirty communities nationwide had made similar provisions when the Beverly Hills proposal was launched. Furthermore, many of these places were rural centers that established lots so that country dwellers could leave their cars for extended periods while shopping in town. Only the San Francisco Peninsula community of San Mateo shared Beverly Hills's position as a wealthy residential enclave in a metropolitan area.[9] The concept of appropriating land for cars in the center of business blocks had been suggested for Yonkers, New York, in 1932, but no scheme of this type appears to have been executed by 1937.[10] On the other hand, the fear of decline due to insufficient parking and the belief that only municipal intervention would solve the problem were becoming widespread. In the half-decade before Pearl Harbor, providing municipal parking lots became a concern among many planners, traffic engineers, and elected officials as well as business owners who felt that their future was at stake.[11]

The chamber's call for action in Beverly Hills prompted the city government to undertake a detailed study to assess existing conditions and plan for future needs. Completed the following year, the report was recast as a series of sixteen articles in the *Beverly Hills Citizen,* providing one of the most detailed accounts of parking published prior to World War II. Among presentations intended for the general public, it is perhaps unique for the period.[12]

The report echoed the basic thrust of the chamber's proposal while making recommendations that were more specific and refined. Space 116 feet wide should be procured in most block interiors for parking "courts," with two rows of diagonally parked cars on either side of the alley spine. Courts in every block where development existed would provide 1,500 spaces. But, the report continued, the courts would only meet the needs of shoppers, not of employees whose cars occupied space throughout the day. To house the latter group, using a minimal amount of land, the report recommended construction of three self-parking garages, each with six tiers and capable of supporting additional levels if needed. The capacity would equal that of the surface lots.[13]

The multistory garage's cost was so high that its use was limited at that time to the densest urban centers. Yet it was implicit in the report that the Business Triangle should remain low-density. Large buildings like those on the Miracle Mile would consume too much ground area to permit the interior courts, and the cars these behemoths attracted would overwhelm the whole system. Thus the mixture that had characterized the precinct from an early date—small, exclusive specialty shops and stores purveying everyday goods—would continue to prevail. That assumption was not borne out, however, by events then taking place.

Beverly Hills had begun to attract sizable, prestigious branch stores during the post-depression years. First and largest among them, at over 150,000 square feet, was W. & J. Sloane (1935–1936), one of the region's most distinguished purveyors of furniture, which, like Coulter's, moved its store from downtown. Soon thereafter came outlets for Chas. Levi & Sons (women's apparel) (1936–1937) and the first Saks Fifth Avenue branch on the Pacific coast (1937–1938).[14] The three lay close to one another on the south side of Wilshire Boulevard, the only place where land parcels were large enough to contain both the buildings and tangent rear parking lots. Unlike most other Wilshire stores, these had relatively narrow and tall fronts, which, coupled with the restrained character of

129
W. & J. Sloane store, 9536 Wilshire Boulevard, Beverly Hills, 1935–1936, John and Donald B. Parkinson, architects; altered. (Private collection.)

their designs, made them distinctly suggestive of elegant downtown emporia (figure 129). More than any other part of the fabulous boulevard, this
small section seemed like a nascent Fifth or North Michigan Avenue.
Both in appearance and function, these branches supported local boosters'
hopes that the most fashionable stretch of Wilshire would emerge in Beverly Hills. The stores lay some distance from the heart of the Business Triangle; however, their great success (Saks more than doubled the size of its
building in 1938–1939, making it the company's largest branch) indicated
that Beverly Hills was indeed becoming an important destination for
affluent shoppers in the metropolitan area.[15] The cars brought by these big
stores would have an impact on the small-scale business center as well.

The city's parking report was issued in July 1938, soon after the
last of the big Wilshire stores opened. Its recommendations were widely
applauded among the business community. Yet the leadership within the
Chamber of Commerce soon realized that the proposal would take years
to implement fully—too long to avoid serious problems. Once again, the
chamber took the lead in seeking an interim solution that could swiftly
materialize. Unveiled that November and approved by the city council the
following January, the new plan entailed a cooperative arrangement: available space, regardless of location, would be leased for temporary use as
parking lots; the cost of leases would be borne by the chamber, and those
of grading, surfacing, improvement, and maintenance by the municipal
government.[16] Parking would be free. The scheme got off to a promising
start: twelve lots were secured at once, and by November 1939 the total
approached twenty. Yet no sooner had these gains been made than the inherent weakness of the plan became clear: owners could terminate the
arrangement on short notice, and some were already doing so to erect
buildings on their respective sites. The supply of parking thus was diminishing in the places where the need was greatest. Calls for implementation
of a long-term plan again began to swell.[17]

The debate that ensued over a "permanent" parking solution
centered on the best means to secure land expeditiously. Some endorsed
taking advantage of the temporary plan by either purchasing the lots or securing long-term leases. Opponents of that idea argued that car lots visible
from the street were unsightly and consumed space best suited to future
building; the inner court plan developed by the city was far preferable.
The only point upon which all parties agreed was that parking garages
were too costly to contemplate in the foreseeable future. No one appears
to have opposed the court scheme on grounds other than the time and
difficulty involved in securing so many separate parcels of land. After
much further discussion from both contingents, the pro-court group
seized the initiative. City attorneys worked with their representative in the
state legislature to draft a bill enabling localities to create an assessment district, issue bonds, acquire property (through condemnation proceedings,
if necessary), and dedicate the acreage to parking. Introduced in January
1941, the bill drew widespread support from other communities across
the state, and was signed into law four months later.[18]

Soon after the bill's passage, the chamber resumed the drive to implement a long-term plan, presenting a somewhat modified version of the city's court scheme in August (figure 130).[19] The principal change was a reduction from four to two ranges of parking spaces, perhaps out of recognition that a wider area would encroach upon the space increasingly needed by many stores. Despite the fact that total capacity was about a third of what the city had proposed in 1938, the scheme was favorably received. Hopes for implementation persisted after the United States entered the war; but, as in Hollywood, the momentum eventually dissipated. After that conflict's end, an even more ambitious proposal was developed, only to remain on paper.[20] All Beverly Hills had to show for its foresight, leadership, cooperation, meticulous study, and statewide initiative to address the parking problem was a diminishing number of temporary lots on vacant parcels of land.

Even if the scheme had been realized, it probably would not have proven as beneficial as its sponsors believed. Each court would have accommodated about sixty cars, less than demand at peak shopping periods. A tight configuration invited bottlenecks as motorists searched for a vacant space. Deliveries would have to be made curbside to avoid blocking customers' cars at the rear. Converting utilitarian rear elevations to suitable store entrances would have been expensive, especially given the small number of patrons served. Finally, it is doubtful whether the well-heeled and often status-conscious clientele that frequented the Business Triangle would be enthusiastic about parking in an expanded alley corridor. Beverly Hills business leaders had a solid grasp of the problem and its implications for their community, but proved incapable of implementing a preventive strategy and were not fully aware of the kind of space needed to provide a viable solution.

The changes needed to ensure a long-term supply of parking came from forces other than legislation, zoning, Chambers of Commerce, reformers, planners, or even major real estate developers. They came rather from merchants and were based on a narrow set of pragmatic concerns. Change came slowly, incrementally, and tentatively at first, not in large-scale projects but in modest ones along boulevards less fabulous than Wilshire. The developments had no names, except sometimes informal ones that identified the intersection—much like speculative boom developments along Western Avenue in the 1920s. Yet they boasted configurations to which Beverly Hills parking advocates pointed as models, to which the planners of Hollywood's grand, stillborn parking scheme likewise looked for inspiration, and to which A. W. Ross may have turned a wistful eye, wishing he had gone so far on the Miracle Mile.

MAIN STREET

The integration of parking and retail space beyond that found at individual buildings began to occur during the late 1930s as the shopping center

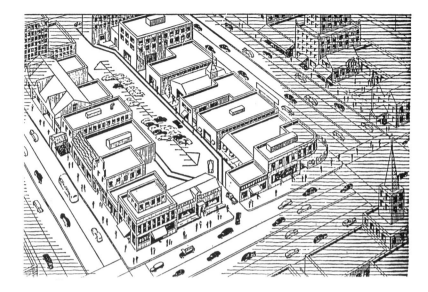

concept began to enter the general realm of speculative commercial development. These first examples contrasted markedly with Westwood Village and other ambitious projects planned in the previous decade. The new generation were smaller—"neighborhood" centers, they would soon be called—containing up to around twenty stores, with a supermarket as the anchor tenant.[21] They were oriented to routine needs, although variety, apparel, and accessory stores might be included. Their audience was local and largely middle-income.

Elsewhere in the United States, neighborhood shopping centers had emerged during the 1920s as an outgrowth of comprehensive community planning efforts generated by reform concerns, and were the direct descendants of the earlier store block.[22] But the neighborhood center as part of a planned residential enclave held little interest among Los Angeles developers. Instead the parties involved had traditionally undertaken arterial development. Their motivation was strictly to increase profit margins.

The catalyst for introducing the neighborhood center to Los Angeles appears to have been the supermarket. Between the late 1920s and mid-1930s, the city was arguably the nation's most important proving ground for this new kind of food emporium.[23] Supermarkets carried every basic kind of food product under one roof, with most, if not all, departments operated as a single business. These outlets depended heavily on brand-name goods, self-service, low staffing, and cash-and-carry sales. But what most distinguished the supermarket from earlier food stores was the large scale of its operation. Goods were stocked in quantity and sold in volume; thus prices could be kept low, lower even than at chain stores. Pioneers in the field, most notably Ralphs Grocery Company, proved the advantages of this economy of scale before the stock market crash, but the broad application of the concept, in Los Angeles and elsewhere, began after significant economic decline when competition for consumer dollars grew acute.

By 1939 the Los Angeles area boasted some 350 supermarkets, by far the largest concentration in the country. The average size of new units was around 10,000 square feet in 1935, and twice that at the decade's end.[24] These enormous plants could be found in numbers as part of middle-class and many prosperous blue-collar precincts throughout the region. They made significant inroads on the business done by other food stores, including chain outlets. The supermarket helped revolutionize the distribution system by firmly establishing low price as a transcendent factor in mass appeal, by expanding the scope of self-service shopping, and by selling food and other convenience goods at a much larger volume than previously thought possible. These buildings further accelerated the trend of business development away from established nodes, with location increasingly predicated on easy access for motorists.

    The supermarket was inconceivable without general consumer mobility. If shoppers were to buy in volume, they had to rely on their cars to carry the food home. The need to minimize the distance between the storefront and the car, combined with the sizable number of patrons at peak shopping periods, rendered curbside space inadequate almost from the start. Street congestion also was an issue. As a result, supermarkets were generally located on the fringe of neighborhood shopping districts, or in lone-wolf locations, where traffic was less and where land was rela-

130
Proposed inner-block parking plan sponsored by Beverly Hills Chamber of Commerce, 1941. (*Western City,* March 1942, 37.)

131
Von's Olympic store, 1020 S. Fairfax Avenue, Los Angeles, ca. 1934; no longer standing. Photo "Dick" Whittington, 1953. (Whittington Collection, Department of Special Collections, University of Southern California.)

tively cheap. Like Sears, the supermarket could attract enough customers to stand alone, without adjacent stores. Thus situated, these emporia could have a large floorplate and ample contiguous space for parking. A lot with a capacity of perhaps 100 to 150 automobiles was not uncommon by the mid-1930s (figure 131).

Competition among supermarkets grew to the point that many early examples had closed or were operating marginally toward the decade's end.[25] Problems stemmed not from a flawed concept but from oversaturation. Many merchants believed the only way to improve their situation was to expand through more and/or larger facilities. One of the most innovative responses came from Ben Surval, a veteran wholesaler who opened one of the first Hollywood supermarkets in 1931, and his new partners, grocers Al and Morris Wisstein. Among their initial joint ventures was a neighborhood shopping center designed to sustain trade for the immense supermarket that lay in its midst.[26]

The Wisstein Bros. & Surval complex was constructed in stages between 1936 and 1939 on South Broadway between Eighty-seventh and Eighty-eighth streets (figure 132).[27] The site was ideal for a supermarket, located at the edge of a modest-sized shopping district developed during the previous decade. Residential growth was rebounding in the area, with single-family dwellings and a few small apartment complexes occupied by persons of moderate means—a budget-conscious constituency that was the bedrock of the supermarket's success. An entire block was purchased to allow room for a critical mass of stores in the project. Collectively, these outlets would enhance the district as a whole by broadening the choices available to shoppers, but they would also compete with existing businesses. With the supermarket as its centerpiece, the ensemble would become a new locus of trade, pulling customers away from the established heart of the district one block to the north. Surval was frank about the supermarket's generative role: "You can see that the whole community develops to your [the market's] advantage. You can rent to the types of stores that will draw the kind of traffic you want."[28]

What gave the complex its merchandising strength was the clustering of chain outlets, including two drug and two variety stores, which complemented the supermarket by providing other routine goods at low prices. Many items may have been offered on especially favorable terms, given the positioning of rival companies within the same complex. Smaller shops, most of which carried apparel and accessories and were likewise chain-operated, were interspersed among the big units.[29]

Wisstein Bros. & Surval tailored their strategy to a new wave of chain store expansion that was beginning to take shape. In outlying areas of Los Angeles, chain development had largely been forged by food companies during the previous decade. Now other kinds of retailers were entering the field. Hollywood, the Miracle Mile, and Westwood Village had the greatest concentrations of newcomers, but many chains also targeted smaller, less prestigious shopping districts as well. Drug and variety stores were the most aggressive. The three principal drug companies—Owl,

Sontag, and Thrifty—had a total of eight outlying units in Los Angeles in 1930, sixty-six in 1940. Among variety chains, S. H. Kress was the exception in adding only two outlying units during the decade to the seven it had in 1930. F. W. Woolworth, on the other hand, went from nine such units in 1930 to twenty-one by 1940. Southern California's other major variety chain, J. J. Newberry, had only one outlying unit in 1930, thirteen a decade later.[30]

Chain outlets increased dramatically in size as well as in number. The supermarket afforded an important model for drug and variety stores in its large, uninterrupted floor area, emphasis on self-service, and sleek imagery—all to stimulate volume purchasing. Drug as well as variety store units were now almost always purpose-built instead of being adapted to existing retail blocks.[31] Drug stores had long been considered nearly as important to the tenant mix of a neighborhood center as a market, but most of these had been independently owned. Now securing a unit of a major drug chain was believed to significantly increase the draw of a retail complex. In a parallel vein, the expansion of variety stores in outlying areas rendered their inclusion a prized objective. As a result chain companies had enormous leverage in the planning of a project.[32]

The configuration and visual character of the Broadway and Eighty-seventh Street center reflected the circumstances of its development. The heavy reliance on well-known chains led to an emphasis on individual storefront identity to a far greater degree than at Westwood or other large shopping centers of its kind. Some coordination was evident in features such as a more or less uniform cornice line; however, the overall effect did not suggest a complex planned as a single entity. The largest and most conspicuous component was the supermarket, yet other stores held their own in attention-getting facades. The presence of each was enhanced by particularized graphics as well as by amount of frontage (for the major outlets), which was much wider than the standard a decade earlier. Store depth varied between 120 and 135 feet, again reflecting the normative size increase of the period.

Off-street parking was, of course, essential for the supermarket, and for the other stores it would be a novel feature that could only enhance patronage. The presence of those additional outlets necessitated a car lot considerably bigger than would have been needed for the supermarket alone. The grouping also prevented the car lot from being in its normal location at one side of the market. Given the circumstances, only two siting options existed: to the front or to the rear of the range. The former was inconceivable to supermarket owners, who depended heavily on the visual appeal of open-front buildings adorned with lavish produce displays. Even without this factor, both chain store companies and independent merchants in the region adamantly believed a strong streetfront orientation was essential to their success. Parking would be in back, just as at Sears and the big Wilshire stores.

So positioned, the car lot needed to extend the full length of the block if it was to function efficiently for vehicular circulation and access

132

Shopping center, 8701–8765 S. Broadway, Los Angeles, 1936–1937, 1939; altered. Photos "Dick" Whittington, 1949. (Whittington Collection, Department of Special Collections, University of Southern California.)

to all stores. It made no sense to have this space less than the depth of the property, because the residual land would have had little market value. This premise, plus the precinct's block configuration, led to a parking facility of more or less equal area to the buildings. This 1:1 ratio was unusually high at that time, permitting space for 280 cars. The demand proved commensurate, however. Reportedly, the lot was often full at peak hours. Further convenience was afforded by customer entrances at the rear of at least some of the stores. Yet despite the importance of this amenity, it was treated in a wholly utilitarian fashion. Architectural and product display were reserved for the Broadway facade; the rear elevation, which many patrons may have experienced more often, was designed as if it faced no more than the service alley that ran between it and the parking area (figure 133). For all their love of the automobile, Angelenos exhibited no love of parking lots. These spaces were seen as eyesores—unfortunate ne-

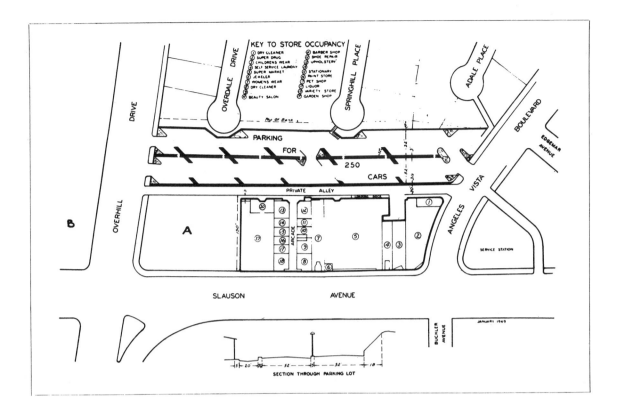

KEY TO STORE OCCUPANCY

① DRY CLEANER
② SUPER DRUG
③ CHILDRENS WEAR
④ SELF SERVICE LAUNDRY
⑤ SUPER MARKET
⑥ JEWELER
⑦ WOMENS WEAR
⑧ DRY CLEANER
⑨ BEAUTY SALON

⑩ BARBER SHOP
⑪ SHOE REPAIR UPHOLSTERY
⑫ STATIONARY PAINT STORE
⑬ PET SHOP
⑭ LIQUOR
⑮ VARIETY STORE
⑯ GARDEN SHOP

SECTION THROUGH PARKING LOT

cessities best concealed from public view. The elegance of Bullock's arrangement had no impact beyond the other big Wilshire stores. Thus the contrast between front and back of the Broadway and Eighty-seventh Street center was inconsequential to its users. What was important was that ample space existed to park at a complex that offered new options in products and pricing close to home. The streetfronts were rendered in a sleek, streamlined vocabulary that likewise carried positive associations. Collectively, these advantages made the concept a model for the region.

That model was loosely interpreted in location, arrangement, and tenant mix. Not long after the Broadway and Eighty-seventh Street center was completed, Wisstein Bros. & Surval signed a contract to build a supermarket at a somewhat similar complex whose primary function was serving the new Windsor Hills subdivision (figure 134). The site lay some nine miles southwest of downtown on the fringe of urban settlement and well removed from existing shopping districts. Windsor Hills's developer, Marlow-Burns, wanted a center that would provide basic services, more limited in scope than at the Broadway and Eighty-seventh Street center. Here the target audience was smaller and also more affluent. Presumably Windsor Hills residents would drive to Westwood, the Miracle Mile, or some other major center to satisfy additional needs. As a result, most units were occupied by small-scale, independent operations, and there was less rear parking space (figure 135). Comprising some 22,000 square feet, the supermarket was by far the biggest unit in the complex and the first to be constructed so it would be a catalyst for other businesses. Owing to the isolated location and U.S. entry into World War II, the development pro-

133
Shopping center, 8701–8765 S. Broadway, rear view. Photo author, 1989.

134
Windsor Hills Shopping Center, 4401–4435 W. Slauson Avenue, Los Angeles, 1941, 1948, Office of Stiles Clements (and others?), architect; altered. Photo ca. 1948. (*Urban Land Institute Technical Bulletin,* July 1948, 10.)

135
Windsor Hills Shopping Center, plan. (*Urban Land Institute Technical Bulletin,* July 1948, 10.)

cess took longer than anticipated, and much of the complex was not realized until 1948. By that time, the rear parking lot was so heavily used that
building on the western third of the site was never undertaken.[33]

The facade treatment at Windsor Hills was simpler than at Broadway and Eighty-seventh. Stiles Clements, whose office designed the market and probably the rest of the center as well, composed the front like a
series of billboard frames, providing large but otherwise neutral backdrops
for store signs. This configuration gave the center somewhat more the appearance of a unified ensemble, yet variation in facade height, setback and
detailing still resulted in a decidedly accretive effect. The rear elevation
was without embellishment; however, to facilitate circulation between
front and back and to house a number of merchants requiring very small
spaces, a covered pedestrian walkway, lined with shops, ran through the
building at midblock—a feature then seldom employed in retail development of any sort.

The fully integrated neighborhood shopping center was slow to
gain ground in southern California. Some ambitious proposals were made,
but most appear never to have materialized in anything approaching their
projected form (figure 136). By the eve of Pearl Harbor, perhaps as few as
a half-dozen fully developed examples could be found in Los Angeles and
adjacent counties. [34] The abundance of large new supermarkets in metropolitan Los Angeles substantially reduced the places where a shopping center anchored by yet another grand food emporium could thrive. If the
supermarket was instrumental in shaping the neighborhood centers of the
region, it likewise had a decisive effect on limiting that type's growth until
large-scale development of new residential areas occurred during the postwar years.

At the same time, the approach to retail planning embodied at
the Broadway and Eighty-seventh Street center was adapted in a number
of projects of less complete scope. For example, an eight-unit complex
was erected in 1941 by a syndicate, Southern Counties Investment Company, to complement a recently completed Ralphs supermarket lying just
to the north at Exposition and Crenshaw boulevards (figure 137). The ensemble was created as a cluster of chains, including J. J. Newberry, J. C.
Penney, Sontag, Grayson, and Karl's Shoe Company, supplemented by a
few independent stores—all served by an equally large parking lot at the
rear.[35] Similar complexes appear to have been undertaken during the same

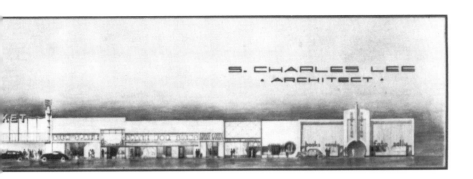

period. Some variation occurred among them in size and scope; nevertheless, the cumulative result represented the beginnings of a marked change
in the metropolitan landscape. The rapid growth of chains, now including
some that specialized in clothes, shoes, and other accessories, in many
smaller, more localized trading centers heralded a substantial increase in
the shopping choices many Angelenos could enjoy close to home. Variety
was greater, prices often were lower, the quality of goods could be better—not just because of the chains' economies of scale but because of the
opportunities they afforded for comparison shopping.

   Not all ventures were so inclusive as the Crenshaw Boulevard
complex. Some looked much the same but lacked a strong tenancy. A
complex built several years earlier (1936–1937) on South Vermont Avenue
near another Ralphs market contained neither a variety store nor major
outlets for clothing and accessories, but did have units of all three leading
drug store chains in the region (figure 138).[36] A rear parking lot was often
a feature at such places, but not always: the belief persisted that curbside
space was adequate when a supermarket or comparably sized stores were
absent. Conventional wisdom maintained that these developments functioned much like an updated Main Street, drawing from a limited trade
area. If many patrons living nearby drove, others would walk or take public transportation to shop at the local center.

   Custom also affected ownership and development practices. Numerous shopping groups were created not under the initiative of a single
firm but rather by a real estate broker, who in effect functioned as the de-

136
Shopping center, possibly for Sherman
and Van Nuys boulevards, Los Angeles,
1939, S. Charles Lee, architect; project.
(Special Collections, University of California, Los Angeles.)

137
Retail development for Southern Counties Investment Company, 3651–3695
Crenshaw Boulevard, Los Angeles, begun
1941; altered. Photo author, 1989.

veloper, working with a loose confederation of property owners and merchants. The products were not true shopping centers as they lacked central management, and many of them may not have had ongoing controls over tenancy or physical appearance. These groups also differed from the taxpayer block in that the scale was larger, stores were bigger, more types of chain companies were involved, and the structuring of an ensemble of mutually reinforcing tenants was a key objective. Yet these complexes were rooted in established practices of strip retail development in the region. New components modified those practices but did not subsume them. This orientation was aptly reflected in the name of the coterie formed shortly before World War II by about a dozen leading brokers involved in such work: the Main Streeters.

As a group, the Main Streeters had no specific agenda. Their gatherings were partly for social intercourse, partly for informal exchange of information.[37] The rare occasions when two or more members joined forces to work on a retail project stemmed from mutually advantageous circumstances, not from the objectives of the group itself. Most members had ties to a major regional or national chain company. The locational concerns that had guided chain store development in outlying parts of the metropolis for some two decades constituted a major undercurrent in the Main Streeters' thinking. As with the Broadway and Eighty-seventh Street center, the optimal site was believed to be at or close to the intersection of two major thoroughfares and surrounded by a large residential area. Multiple ownership was considered desirable because it lessened the risk taken by any single party—a factor that also led insurance companies to help underwrite such ventures. Planning and business integration were undertaken only to the extent the parties involved felt was needed to avert the high incidence of business failure and property vacancy that occurred during the 1920s. Since such centers proved to be very profitable investments, at least in the short run, the parties involved saw no reason to deviate further from established habits.

The new "Main Street" seemed at once strikingly modern yet reassuringly conventional. Little wonder that business leaders in Beverly

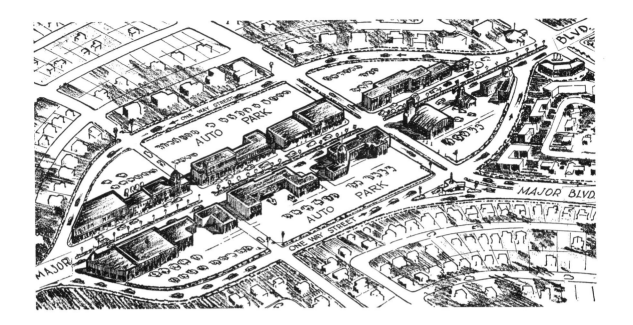

Hills were envious of these complexes.[38] What so many parties could not accomplish in Beverly Hills was materializing, if still tentatively, along thoroughfares near the urban periphery. Given both the fragmented nature of the neighborhood shopping center's emergence in Los Angeles and the level of frustration over parking as a hindrance to business throughout the metropolitan area, it is little wonder, too, that planning officials sought to codify the concept.

Unveiled by the Los Angeles Department of City Planning in February 1941, the model scheme sought to combine the aim of bringing greater order, unity, and containment to commercial growth—factors very important to the developers of guaranteed neighborhoods—with the more pragmatic, mundane concerns of the mainstream. The configuration of the Broadway and Eighty-seventh Street center was expanded to encompass both sides of the thoroughfare for three long blocks (figure 139). The shopping experience as well as vehicular circulation were to be enhanced by directing through traffic onto peripheral streets. These one-way arteries improved access to the rear car lots, while functioning as self-imposed boundaries to commercial development. The planners were optimistic that their design would resolve the dilemma of parklessness once and for all. The proposal would be widely accepted in the marketplace, not only because of its "Main Street" origins but also because it had been specifically created as a cooperative venture with a syndicate of property owners for the Westchester district, a huge tract not far from Windsor Hills.[39] United States entry into the war ten months later delayed the plans. But once peace returned, Main Street reemerged as a springboard for many of the new shopping centers that soon would be built. The relatively few, modest complexes of the post-depression era convinced ever more retail and real estate concerns that at least some form of planning was needed for new business developments, especially if shoppers were to be rid of frustration in finding a place to park.

138
Retail development, 8400–8436 S. Vermont Avenue, Los Angeles, 1936–1937; altered. Photo author, 1989.

139
Plan for development of outlying business centers, Department of City Planning, City of Los Angeles, 1941. (*Los Angeles Times,* 9 February 1941, V-3.)

VIII

HOLD ON!

"Hold on! It happened once. It will happen again." Thus did the *Los Angeles Times* editors paraphrase the 1933 New Year's message issued by the presidents of five leading financial institutions to property owners in southern California, especially to those in the city center. Many readers had grown skeptical of what the future might bring. But the *Times* incanted, as it had for decades, that the years ahead were filled with promise: "The history of real estate here through seven depressions is that from every low level it climbs to new high peaks. . . . Just as prices were once absurdly inflated, they are now absurdly deflated. Hold On!"[1]

In 1933 the hope lingered among many of those in business that a new downtown Los Angeles would take the form of a skyscraper city, punctuated with towers many times the height then permitted by law, permeated by high-speed motorways and other transportation lines at multiple levels—a futuristic update of the Bellamyesque images presented for two decades and which enjoyed special favor during the years just passed (figure 140).[2] The future city would be an even more radical departure from that of the present than the present one was from that of the late nineteenth century. If confidence remained strong, extraordinary things would occur.

Within a few years, however, such expansive visions largely were forgotten. Downtown Los Angeles did not recreate itself; indeed, it barely grew at all. Between the early 1930s and early 1950s little new construction of consequence occurred in the district. The depression did not, of

LOS ANGELES 47 YEARS HENCE

"Hear ye not the hum of mighty workings?"

LOS ANGELES is building its foundation. Its firm, bedrock foundation ... to nurture the millions that will call it "home" ... the World's Industrial Center forty-seven years hence.

Today's endeavors prophesy Tomorrow's attainments. Thriving, humming, active industries ... that wrest from Nature her gifts . . . . .

Yellow gold and oil ... metals, base and precious ... timber ... wool from countless flocks ... the products of the West—all pouring into this great industrial vortex that is Los Angeles—to be converted into the requisites of modern civilization.

Mountain streams and the ocean's waves now lend their myriad millions of horsepower to accomplish giants' tasks in foundry, factory and mill, whose products are known in every land, amongst all peoples.

Swifter and ever swifter grow the steeds of Commerce. Winged freighters and transports, their very manufacture a colossal Los Angeles industry, unload furs from the Siberias and return with the golden fruits of Southern California within twenty-four hours.

A city so great draws, like a magnet, the artisans of many Nations, the craftsmen and designers of civilization's needs and luxuries. Los Angeles, then, takes its natural place as creator and dictator of the Fashions of the day.

And yet another industry grows greater with Los Angeles. An industry that supplies the needs of the individual ... his home and his person. The May Company of 1975!

Vision now, this colossal "Mart of the West," dedicated wholly to serving a modern Los Angeles of 1975. A city within a city ... with its army of employees ... its artists who create the fashions ... its private landing decks for aircraft ... its international trade and art galleries . . . its battery of beacons and floodlights to direct night air travel ... an institution that parallels in its growth and supremacy, the growth and leadership of the future Industrial Los Angeles.

Today, looking forward to a Greater Los Angeles, The May Company pledges its allegiance to the community of Tomorrow, building on its ideals of service and helpfulness in the Present.

THE MAY COMPANY

course, destroy downtown Los Angeles; it only accelerated tendencies set in motion during the previous decade when the city center seemed indomitable.[3] Major property owners "held on," and many put new capital into their buildings. Yet significant growth failed to take place because greater demand existed for business development in outlying areas. "Hold on" became a watchword not for promises ahead but for preventing further deterioration.

REMODELING

Among the numerous factors considered important for strengthening retail trade downtown, two were cited most often as pivotal: appearances and parking. Retailers had long held that the image of an establishment was central to its success, and in particular that an appearance of newness was an essential part of customer appeal. During the rapid growth of centralized retail functions nationwide in the late nineteenth and early twentieth centuries, change for the most part occurred as a result of expansion— either through adding to the premises or through building new quarters. Beginning with the depression, however, enlargement of the main store was seldom needed, and in fact almost never occurred in downtown Los Angeles. Competition in a shrinking market wrought by economic instability thus assured remodeling a new prominence in the retail sphere. The popular acceptance of stylistic modernism was both encouraged by and further encouraged this trend. New store design could suggest innovative business practices, sound finances, concern for the customer, and confidence in the future. The updating program generally involved improvements in layout and building systems, but ultimately appearance counted as the essential product.[4]

In 1930, downtown Los Angeles's retail building stock was not very old, a condition shared with other U.S. cities. Most outlets were constructed after 1900 and many dated from the 1920s. Yet this inheritance soon came to be viewed as a relic because it was experientially so different from the newest outlying centers. Like the street railway system soon after its greatest period of expansion, downtown was now cast as outmoded, replaced by a more convenient and appealing alternative. In 1935, Egerton Shore, a local real estate analyst, advised businessmen that substantial action was necessary. The Century of Progress Exposition in Chicago "had started a revolution in business throughout the country [because] . . . it presented such a modern conception of improved designs that everything seemed out of date. . . . With streamlined automobiles, railway trains, airplanes, modernized stores . . . even the progress of the passing generation seemed obsolete." In downtown Los Angeles "first class buildings have undergone a decadence in condition and style." On the other hand, "Wilshire Boulevard has . . . introduce[d] building designs that are modern, and shops that suggest quality and originality."[5] Downtown was no longer setting the standard. Merchants and property owners had to look beyond

140
"Los Angeles 47 Years Hence," May Company advertisement. (*Los Angeles Times*, 25 July 1928, I-5.)

the city center for examples to emulate, a reversal of the relationship that had shaped commercial development in the nation for at least a century.

As Shore noted, the drive to update appearances had already begun in downtown Los Angeles. The leaders, not surprisingly, were the city's major department stores. Bullock's initiated the trend in 1933, opening several new specialty stores in its existing plant and, four months later, announcing construction of the seventh addition to the complex (see figure 18).[6] Robinson's soon followed with an interior modernization plan. The project grew to encompass a complete resurfacing of the outside in a "restrained-modernistic design" that seemed as up-to-date, but not as flashy, as Bullock's Wilshire (figure 141).[7] Other department stores were not far behind, with new specialty "shops" and other amenities.[8] New display equipment, new lighting fixtures, air conditioning, escalators, and similar improvements were added incrementally, putting the behemoths in a more or less continual state of change up to the eve of World War II.

Department store owners took every opportunity to publicize that their capital improvement programs underscored a strong faith in downtown no less than in the city itself. Upon completion of its new exterior, Robinson's management intoned that its first purpose-built store was

constructed in the mid-1890s "when financial panic swept the nation." The present facility opened "when World War I brought disaster and chaos to the entire world." Now, "with the world shaken as never before, the company again provided employment for hundreds of men and erected another monument to courage and progress."[9] However much energy may have gone into expansion through branches, the principal investments of major stores lay in the city center—investments that required aggressive measures to maintain.

Other prominent mercantile houses thus were conspicuous as well in the effort to improve downtown's image. Desmond's remodeled its storefront at ground level in 1933; Mullen & Bluett redid its store inside and out the following year, with one of the most thoroughly streamlined compositions yet realized in the metropolitan area (figure 142).[10] Many other stores initiated projects after the worst years of the depression, including substantial work undertaken by Barker Brothers, Eastern-Columbia Outfitting Company, Harris & Frank, Jacoby Brothers, and Silverwood's. Many more transformed the appearance of modest quarters.[11] The initiative taken by Los Angeles companies began to broaden toward the decade's end as a new wave of national and Pacific coast chain companies entered the local market, attracted to downtown both because of the commitment to its renewal and because it remained the largest shopping district west of the Mississippi. With these enterprises, too, remodeling an existing facility rather than new construction was now the standard practice.[12] Significant expansion programs were also undertaken by leading variety and drug store chains already established in the metropolitan area.[13] By 1941, new storefronts and, often, new sales areas inside were commonplace on the primary retail blocks of the precinct. Downtown no longer looked so old.

141
J. W. Robinson Company department store, as remodeled, 1934, Edward D. Mayberry, architect, Allison & Allison, consulting architects. Photo Mott Studios, ca. 1934. (Hearst Collection, Department of Special Collections, University of Southern California.)

142
Mullen & Bluett store, 600 S. Broadway, Los Angeles, as remodeled, 1934; altered. (Hearst Collection, Department of Special Collections, University of Southern California.)

But the city center nevertheless suffered significant losses in the retail sphere during the 1930s. The depression triggered a rash of store closings. Blackstone's six-story dry goods emporium at Ninth and Broadway folded less than a year after the stock market crash; Bedell's ended operation in 1931. Selling the big Hollywood store failed to save B. H. Dyas's business; the Seventh Street building shut its doors in July 1932. The following year brought several more failures, including Parmelee-Dohrmann and Alexander & Oviatt.[14] Some losses were quickly absorbed. Bullock's purchased Parmelee-Dohrmann's stock and name; Oviatt was reorganized and reopened within a year of the initial closing; Myer Siegel took advantage of the shaky real estate market to expand its own operation by leasing Dyas's building. Still, the situation was hardly stable. Myer Siegel closed its own doors not long after the move, and its quarters stood vacant until 1940. Likewise, the space formerly occupied by Blackstone's languished until it was remodeled as the new headquarters facility of the Famous Department Store, a business oriented toward the lower end of the market and among the last to move from Main Street.[15]

More ominous than store failures were the steps taken by leading merchants to relocate outside the city center once economic recovery was under way. W. & J. Sloane initiated the trend in 1935, but the greatest blow was the announcement two years later that Coulter's, which had been operating in a sequence of six downtown locations since 1878, would move to posh new quarters on the Miracle Mile. Adding momentum to the shift were decisions by at least two nationally known retailers not to locate downtown. In 1937, Saks Fifth Avenue chose a site near Sloane's in Beverly Hills for its first west coast store. When I. Magnin enlarged the scope of its southern California operations the following year, the move was made from Hollywood to the mid-Wilshire district.[16] Statistically, the situation was not promising either. Overall retail sales downtown accounted for 29.6 percent of the county total in 1929, 17 percent ten years later. Sales in downtown department stores fell from $106 million in 1929 to $77 million in 1939, dropping from 74.8 percent of the county total in the year of the stock market crash to 47.4 percent in 1941.[17]

Despite setbacks, the belief persisted that the core should continue as the dominant business center of the metropolitan area. The view held firm in some quarters that decentralization could affect only a limited range of enterprises. No outlying district could begin to house the extent of goods and services found in the city center, the argument ran, and many types of businesses could not operate effectively in scattered locations.

Among the most outspoken defenses of downtown came from the economist George Eberle, who had long analyzed real estate and other business trends in the region. Eberle asserted that the city center was the necessary place not just for most governmental offices but also for financial institutions, however many branches they might have. Other kinds of business, including major real estate, advertising, and insurance firms,

were best quartered downtown, as were offices of leading professional firms. A central location also was needed for many forms of retailing. Even if several department stores had established outposts away from the core, downtown remained the focal point for their business. Equally important was the collective array of goods offered by smaller establishments:

While there are some convenience goods, like groceries, drugs, and small household items, which must be retailed extensively to suit the convenience of the buyer, . . . there will also remain a large category of goods in the purchase of which the consumer will demand a large centralized stock with a wide variety of price, color, size, quality, and style at the time of selection. . . . Chain store distribution is economical and satisfactory for many of these items, but chain methods demand the high turnover of standardized items with limited variety. It is only when shopping between a number of convenient chain and independent stores that the consumer can effectively satisfy his demand for variety. Wide decentralization in retailing of shopping goods does not provide this satisfaction.

Eberle maintained that decentralization carried disadvantages as well:

The scattered location of certain large department stores on Wilshire Boulevard may appear . . . at first as a relief from the tiring trip through congested traffic to the downtown center, but experience may soon show . . . that the more convenient location is offset by a lack of variety. . . . Moreover, if one is not satisfied in one Wilshire store, he must drive several miles to another decentralized location on Wilshire or to Hollywood, Beverly Hills, or Westwood Village. By the time he has satisfied his need, he may have come to the conclusion that a trip to the downtown area would have been simpler and more economical of time, energy, and gasoline.

He concluded:

Decentralization of shopping [i.e., non-routine] goods . . . results in decreased shopping opportunities because there are fewer outlets and fewer management viewpoints and services. Moreover, the spreading of such retail service is uneconomical and fosters duplication of services and greatly increased transportation for the individual shopper.[18]

Not all business leaders may have shared Eberle's belief in the unimportance of outlying areas, but virtually everyone involved in retailing agreed on the importance of having choices in shopping. The combined extent and variety of goods available downtown was a primary reason why the district retained the greatest volume of trade in the region. Shopping days continued to attract throngs of consumers, crowding the sidewalks and stores with an intensity seldom experienced under other circumstances (figure 143). Gasoline rationing during the war further enhanced patronage since the core was the most accessible place by streetcar. And even with the return of peacetime, a sizable portion of Angelenos still resided within a few miles' radius of downtown, and many thousands of them worked there. As a result the dollar volume of downtown retail sales increased 126 percent between 1939 and 1948. Downtown department store sales rebounded after the late 1930s, reaching $189 million in 1948. Seven years later that figure had dropped to $141 million, yet even when adjusted for inflation, the amount was respectable when compared to the $106 million of 1929. As late as 1960, downtown Los Angeles stood as the fifth largest concentration of business in the United States.[19]

Yet while persistently "holding on," downtown experienced steady erosion in its prestige as a retail center. Updating appearances could

not compensate for the loss of half a dozen major stores oriented to the upper end of the market and the absence of new ones of comparable stature. The chain and local companies that expanded in or entered the district were targeted to a more budget-conscious trade. Furthermore, changes were beginning to occur in the kinds of goods that attracted shoppers downtown. The great majority of remodeling projects undertaken after 1930 were for stores purveying apparel and accessories. Very little new work occurred among other types of specialty establishments, including those in the furniture and music trades, which were prominent contributors to the precinct's richness prior to the depression. Even as shopping choices continued to grow in outlying areas, they no longer seemed as great in the city center, despite Eberle's optimistic portrayal.

The size of the core retail district also diminished somewhat during the 1930s. Flower Street was the first casualty, but other peripheral locations lost ground as well. Nearly all the remodeling done to stores was concentrated in a six-linear-block area along Broadway from Fifth to Seventh streets and on Seventh from Broadway to Hope.

The shifts in complexion of downtown retailing became more evident after World War II. The department stores and most other businesses that comprised the mercantile elite embarked on few capital improvements downtown between 1945 and 1950, even though it was a significant period of growth in the field and most of these establishments were expanding their operations in outlying centers. Even Robinson's,

which had steadfastly resisted the trend toward branch development prior to the war, announced plans for a large facility at Beverly Hills in 1947. Likewise, the Fifth Street Store's executives had decided that their business could not remain competitive without a foothold elsewhere, unveiling a scheme for a branch in the burgeoning Westchester district the previous year.[20] Several mass market chains expanded and others established units for the first time downtown, but these programs paled in comparison to chain development outside the city center.[21]

Remodeling was still championed as an essential means to enhance customer draw; however, many merchants and property owners alike seem to have lost confidence in the prospects of significant future growth. In 1950, the Downtown Business Men's Association (DBMA), organization of executives from leading firms in the district, began a campaign for a coordinated, block-by-block modernization of storefronts to impart the sense of newness and unity associated with the enormous shopping centers being built in outlying areas.[22] Yet little appears to have resulted from the initiative. Demands beyond the city center made merchants reluctant to invest substantial sums downtown, even if they had been inclined to do so. To stay abreast of the booming market, many retailers were establishing additional branch locations. Hollywood and the Wilshire corridor were no longer the only concentrations of major retail activity beyond the core. Other large business centers with a more mass market orientation were being developed or planned in the Baldwin Hills and Westchester districts to the southwest, along the Whittier Boulevard corridor to the east, in the San Fernando Valley to the northwest, and in Orange County to the southeast—places that had remained predominantly rural prior to the war.

Downtown business interests also sought to learn from the success of outlying centers through coordinated promotional campaigns. Prior to the stock market crash, cooperative ventures among merchants in downtown Los Angeles and other U.S. cities had been minimal because no need had been seen for them. Major stores drew crowds at peak shopping periods such as Christmas and Easter through lavish window displays and presentation of new merchandise. Locally, a number of stores participated in a home furnishings "exposition" held during the summer and joined in offering clearance sales—"Dollar Days"—in the spring and fall. Furthermore, each of the large stores had its own sales, anniversary celebrations, and other events. The cumulative effect was that some kind of "special" merchandising occasion could be found in at least one major emporium most weeks of the year. The DBMA was founded in 1924 principally to facilitate these existing practices, which its members had created and which had a record of success.

The status quo was sufficiently entrenched that more aggressive measures gained acceptance only in the late 1930s, when it was becoming apparent that the depression was less the root cause of decline than was the growth of outlying centers. A Christmas parade had been held downtown in 1929, perhaps to upstage a similar spectacle organized for Holly-

143
Shopping crowd, Seventh Street and S. Broadway, looking south. Photo "Dick" Whittington, 1939. (Whittington Collection, Department of Special Collections, University of Southern California.)

wood Boulevard as well as to soothe consumer nerves after "temporary" setbacks to the economy during the previous months.[23] But the event was not repeated until a decade later, now under the auspices of the DBMA. For several years previous, the group had been conspicuously promoting other events, such as Dollar Days, and sponsoring large advertisements in the *Times* to enhance public perceptions of downtown as the place best suited to consumer needs. The DBMA's efforts intensified in 1940 and 1941, with new officers, new bylaws, and a seven-point plan that included improvements to the public transit system, the civic center, car lots, "blighted" areas, streets and sidewalks, and signage, as well as building modernization and publicity. The Christmas pageant was now the most lavish in a series of attention-getting endeavors orchestrated throughout the year.[24] After the war, promotional efforts resumed at a fast pace, with a growing list of new projects. In 1948, for example, the DBMA inaugurated a cooperative venture among stores to remain open until nine P.M. on Mondays so as to encourage family shopping excursions.[25]

Gargantua

In all the DBMA campaigns, downtown was presented as a single entity in much the same way as Hollywood, the Miracle Mile, and Westwood Village were by their respective boosters. DBMA advertisements went so far as to imply that the precinct functioned like an integrated business development. Yet the very existence of such material implied that downtown's once impregnable position was no longer secure; at best, the new promotional programs could keep the core's trade from further eroding. Unlike Eberle, the DBMA never tried to advance downtown at the expense of outlying centers, for most of its leaders now had substantial businesses in both places.[26] Their objective was to find a balance that would enable both territorial expansion and core stability.

PARKING

No matter more concerned the DBMA and other parties with an interest in downtown than did parking. During the 1930s, adequate off-street space for automobiles was considered a central factor—perhaps the decisive one—in bringing renewed vitality to the precinct, a belief that was widely shared in cities coast to coast.[27] After the war, the issue seemed even more urgent. Soon after victory over Japan, the *Times* cast the parking problem as "Gargantua"—a latter-day King Kong, poised to destroy the city center as swiftly as Admiral Yamamoto had destroyed the fleet at Pearl Harbor (figure 144). Despite endless rhetoric, efforts to improve off-street facilities remained uncoordinated and piecemeal.

Throughout the 1930s the city's major department stores continued to address the matter individually. Instead of planning more multistory parking garages, however, department store executives focused on the expeditious use of car lots. The most integrated plan came from Robinson's, which, as part of its 1934 renovation program, included a new motor entrance at the rear from which attendants drove cars to an adjacent surface lot, replicating the arrangement at Bullock's Wilshire.[28] But most emporia could not expand so conveniently, and instead had to reach accords with independent lot operators. By 1935, the May Company had established such relationships with a half-dozen parking businesses to supplement its own garage, which had been designed with an excess capacity less than a decade earlier (figure 145).[29] Bullock's, whose central location in terms of pedestrian movement rendered it among the least accessible to motorists, created the most elaborate scheme among retailers, securing space at no less than twenty-five lots within a five-block radius of the store by 1940 (figure 146).

Downtown business interests were generally supportive of plans for a regional network of high-speed, limited-access freeways, which began to be advanced in the late 1930s.[30] All these proposals called for routes from every direction to converge on the city center. Since it was generally believed that improving access to the core would restore the district's competitiveness with outlying centers, retailers heralded the freeway program

as the salvation of their downtown plants (figure 147). But these results could only be realized if parking capacity was substantially augmented and parking spaces conveniently related to freeway interchanges. Calls for a regional freeway plan prompted initiatives to create a unified parking plan for downtown. The first scheme was unveiled in 1941 by a group called United Taxpayers.[31] To cure the precinct's "heart disease," the proposal required purchase of fifty adjacent blocks around the core area for surface lots. Customer charges would be minimal: $.15 per half-day of use. Work would be financed through first-mortgage bonds on the acquired property and from patron revenues. Still, it would be necessary to remove the acreage from the tax rolls, a proposition that ensured the idea a swift demise.[32]

Devising a feasible alternative preoccupied both the city's planning department and especially the DBMA during the war years. The latter commissioned what the Urban Land Institute called one of the most extensive studies of its kind in the nation. Presented in January 1945, the proposal called for establishing a single agency—public or otherwise—to create a comprehensive program to develop permanent, well-situated facilities that could hold around 45,000 cars.[33] By that November two new sur-

146

Bullock's downtown store. Advertisement showing car lots available to customers. (*Los Angeles Times,* 9 December 1940, II-3.)

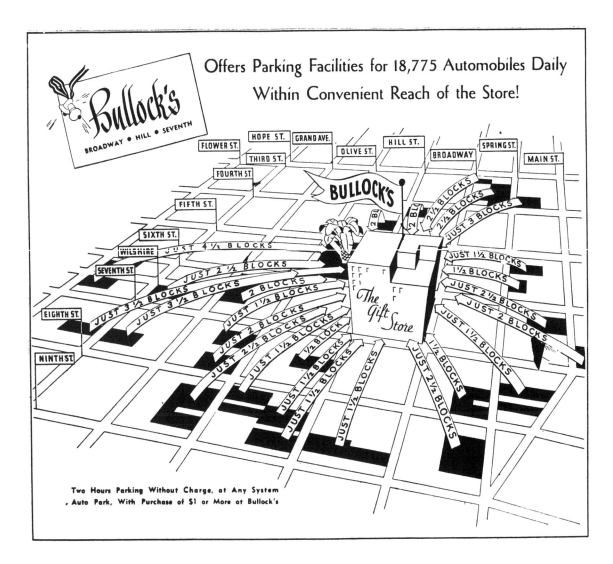

face lots, with a combined capacity of 1,300 cars, had opened under the DBMA's auspices. Two months later a meeting was convened with the mayor and civic groups to broaden the campaign; by March 1946, one of those parties, the Central Business District Association, completed a complementary plan for extensive parking areas between Flower Street and the path of the Habor Freeway, then under construction. Soon thereafter, the DBMA organized its own subsidiary group, the Los Angeles Downtown Parking Association, for purposes of implementation, vowing to create new space for 10,000 cars over the next three years.[34] The association's efforts, however, soon refocused on the creation of an enormous parking facility at Pershing Square.

Bounded by Hill, Olive, Fifth, and Sixth streets, Pershing Square had become a strategic location with the growth of downtown west of Broadway and north of Seventh during the 1920s. Most parking initiatives of the period focused on peripheral sites, which were best suited to employee parking but considered too far removed from the retail core to attract many shoppers—the group most prone to abandon downtown. By contrast, Pershing Square lay a short distance from the densest part of the city center, including three of its major department stores, yet, like several of the early multistory garages, it was close enough to the edge to enable convenient vehicular access. Proposals began to advance in the late 1920s for an underground garage there that could accommodate as many as 3,000 cars, but the huge cost combined with the economic downturn made the plans impracticable.[35] The site's appeal nevertheless grew steadily over the ensuing years as the parking situation seemed to deteriorate.

Not surprisingly, then, Pershing Square emerged as the DBMA's top priority. The association commissioned a preliminary study, which was unveiled in January 1947 and strenuously promoted in the months that fol-

147
Bullock's downtown store. Advertisement supporting implementation of freeway plan. (*Los Angeles Times,* 19 March 1945, III-3.)

148
Pershing Square Garage, Fifth, Sixth, Hill, and Olive streets, Los Angeles 1949–1952, Stiles Clements, architect. (City Planning Commission, *Accomplishments* 1950, 21.)

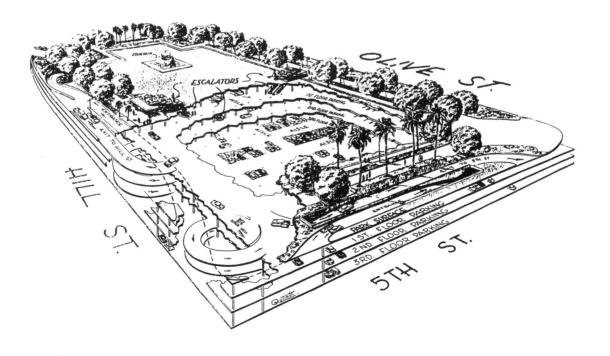

lowed. That April, voters approved an amendment enabling lease of the land beneath the square to a private-sector party for development as a garage. Yet another three years elapsed before opposition, mainly by public transit interests, and other obstacles were surmounted. The DBMA persisted tenaciously—lobbying public support, working behind the scenes, twice soliciting firms to undertake the venture. Finally, ground was broken in February 1951. When completed a year and a half later, the garage was hailed as a major achievement (figure 148). Still, the 1,500 spaces it provided, after half a decade of intense activism, fell far short of the DBMA's overall goal.[36]

Nonetheless the Pershing Square garage was almost the only such large-scale project realized locally since the 1920s. Several modest facilities housing between 100 and 200 cars each were erected during the depression decade, but contributed little to the precinct's overall needs.[37] Los Angeles even lacked examples of open-air parking garages—"parking decks," as they were often called—which began to appear in a number of U.S. cities on the eve of World War II. Generally consisting of three to four levels and comprised of little more than structure and decking surfaces, these facilities averaged around half the per-square-foot construction cost of the multilevel enclosed garages of the previous decade. Since it had no heating or ventilating and minimal lighting systems, the parking deck enjoyed substantially lower operating expenses as well. Department stores were among the earliest sponsors of such projects, but independent parking companies were quick to see their advantages as well.[38]

Aside from Pershing Square, the only major garage to be realized in downtown Los Angeles between 1928 and 1953 was the seven-level structure built for the General Petroleum Company in 1948.[39] The scheme was not conceived to address shoppers' needs, but rather was a result of a 1946 municipal ordinance, the first of its kind in the country, that required all new commercial buildings downtown to include space for one automobile per 1,000 square feet of office floor area. The facility need not be within, but could lie no further than 1,500 feet from, the parent building. General Petroleum executives took advantage of this provision, selecting a less expensive site two blocks away from their new headquarters for the garage.[40] Holding nearly 500 cars at a time, the structure was among the first in the United States to have the parking surface slope as a continuous ramp from ground to roof levels, an arrangement that reduced the area required for vehicular movement as well as construction costs (figure 149). It was also an early example of a large, multilevel structure incorporating the economies of parking deck design. The garage became a national model, yet it had little immediate impact locally. With new construction downtown remaining a rarity, the ordinance proved ineffective as a quick means of adding to the precinct's parking capacity. The only other major project to be realized before the end of the Korean War was the Statler Center (1946–1952), a hotel–office building complex, which contained underground parking for 465 cars.[41]

If strategic initiatives did little to rectify parking conditions downtown, considerable progress was made through the more traditional method of expanding the quilt of privately owned car lots. Space thus created increased nearly threefold between 1930 and 1953.[42] In sharp contrast to what had occurred during the 1920s, few lots operating at the start of this period closed over the next two decades, owing to low demand for more intense use of downtown property. New lots were added through the 1930s as untenanted vintage buildings were demolished to minimize the tax burden.[43] After the war the process continued, as demand for new building sites failed to rebound while that for more parking space persisted. As a result, off-street parking conditions markedly improved, with an overall capacity in garages and surface lots of some 43,000 spaces, more than double the total figure of approximately 20,000 in 1930. Some of the increase was offset by the few new construction projects of the period as well as ongoing increases in the number of people driving to the city center, yet the improvement was a dramatic one. Downtown became more accessible to motorists than it had been for some three decades. Furthermore, major outlying centers begun in the 1920s were now experiencing conspicuous parking difficulties of their own.[44] Public perceptions may not have changed, and business leaders and city officials alike continued to anguish over parking, but finding off-street space for one's car was no longer a deterrent of consequence to shopping downtown.

PREDICAMENT

Ultimately, the dilemma faced by those with interests in the central shopping district was not a matter of appearances, merchandising, or access, but rather one of physical configuration relative to escalating areawide needs. During a six-year period alone—1948 to 1954—retail sales in the metropolitan region rose by 50 percent, the largest such increase in the na-

149
General Petroleum Garage, 750 S. Flower Street, Los Angeles, 1948, Wurdeman & Becket, architects; altered. (*Parking—How It Is Financed,* 10.)

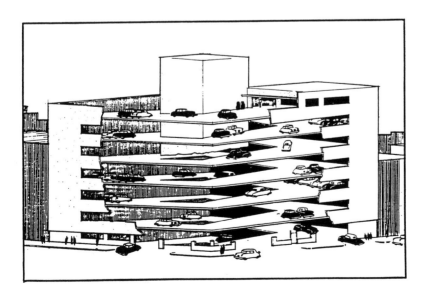

tion.[45] For downtown emporia just to "hold on" to the 11 percent share of Los Angeles County sales they had in 1948 would have necessitated a new construction campaign rivaling that of the 1920s. For them to recover the 29.6 percent share of county sales they enjoyed in 1929, retail space would have had to increase perhaps two- or even threefold. To carry out such epic expansion and yet keep the precinct relatively compact, and thus still conducive to the large-scale pedestrian movement that was essential to its functioning, development would have had to become much denser, with buildings twenty to forty stories tall replacing virtually all extant edifices—thus realizing, in effect, the futuristic visions of the 1920s. Not only would the cost of such a transformation have been enormous, but the problems of vehicular movement and storage would have intensified severalfold.

On the other hand, significant growth could have occurred laterally, as some boosters had hoped in the 1920s, on the blocks extending to the west of Broadway and to the south of Seventh Street. Taking this course, which would more or less have replicated on a much larger scale the process that had occurred during the early twentieth century, the shopping district might have grown to three or four times its then present size without a significant increase in density, but it would have lost all coherence. Pedestrians would never have traversed such distances; some form of transit would have had to supplement walking. Furthermore, it would have been difficult to reestablish a hierarchy of store locations over such a dispersed area. Most off-street parking spaces would have been eliminated; alternative storage facilities with several times the present capacity would have had to be rapidly created.

A third option lay in building a new retail district adjacent to the core area; however, this course would have rendered extant stores redundant—a huge loss in real property. Moreover, the new emporia would have been separated from movie theaters, which were heavily patronized by shoppers, and from the office blocks whence many other customers came. Parking accommodations would still have been needed in vast numbers. The best location for a new precinct was not to the south, toward an area then considered among the region's most blighted, but rather to the west, which was inhospitable topographically. And if westward expansion did occur, it would have been separated from the existing core by the Harbor Freeway, a bifurcation disadvantageous to old and new districts alike.

All scenarios for large-scale expansion of the central shopping district would have been predicated on the willingness of many thousands of new consumers to drive ever further from home along ever more crowded arterials to reach downtown—an assumption for which there was little supporting evidence. Some business leaders hoped the metropolitan freeway system then under construction would bring new life to downtown by making it easier to drive there, but much of that network was not completed until the early 1960s, and well before that time it was helping to accelerate the decentralization process far more than reinforce the existing urban structure.

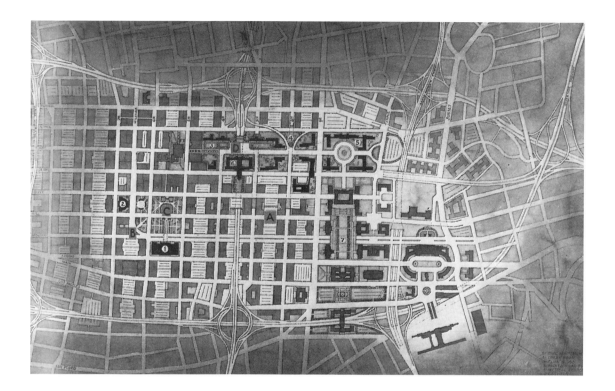

150

"Study for the Redevelopment of the Central Business District, Los Angeles," Southern California Chapter, American Institute of Architects, ca. 1942–1943; project. (Los Angeles City Planning Commission, *Accomplishments* 1943, n.p.)

At the heart of the problem lay the fact that the large downtown retail districts of Los Angeles and other cities nationwide had emerged primarily because a major share of the population could reach them with relative ease through urban rail systems. Even with the advent of widespread automobile use, downtown Los Angeles had continued to grow with the momentum gained from earlier decades as much as from any other factor. Business leaders almost never questioned whether the old order could continue; few considered that the automobile might change the form and arrangement of growth patterns.

But by the 1930s, retail development in outlying areas spawned changes that effectively altered practices across the board. The supermarket demonstrated the value of selling in volume at low prices, which necessitated a substantial amount of low-cost land. The supermarket also underscored the importance of having large areas of continuous selling space to induce customer circulation for convenience goods, just as the department store had done several decades earlier for specialty items. Achieving a configuration that was more horizontal than vertical dominated design objectives for almost every kind of retail facility by the eve of World War II. Even with a huge department store, such as the May Company Wilshire, four selling floors extending over a large area was considered far more desirable than having additional stories with a smaller floorplate. The earlier vision of a new skyscraper center, with emporia towering thirty or forty stories, would have seemed as foolish to merchants of the postwar era as the multilayered speedways running through those towers seemed to traffic engineers.

151
"Study for the Redevelopment of the Central Business District," typical "parking mall." (*Accomplishments* 1943, n.p.)

No proposal for so massive an expansion of downtown Los Angeles ever surfaced during the 1930s and 1940s because none was remotely feasible. The most sweeping plan for the business district came from members of the American Institute of Architects' local chapter, working in cooperation with the city planning department during the middle of the war when ample time existed for dreaming. The scheme introduced civic amenities long absent as well as access routes from the anticipated freeway system, but the most fundamental change was a complete reconfiguration of the business district (figure 150).[46] Under the plan, space for buildings and for automobiles was more or less evenly dispersed. The leitmotif used to create this balance came from the Miracle Mile: buildings abutted the streets, large surface lots lay to the rear (figure 151). The basic difference was that the ensemble was nodal instead of linear, with row after row of regularized Wilshire groupings from First to Ninth streets.

No one appears to have taken the proposal seriously since it would have entailed exorbitant costs without measurable gain in building area, even had the sweeping authority been mustered to effect its implementation. Besides, Wilshire Boulevard was no longer considered the optimal paradigm. Too many changes had occurred to retailing since the late 1920s. The mercantile elite that led the wave of commercial decentralization after the war sought to produce a new model. No one of them had a clear idea of what that model might be, but the years of armed conflict—as the region's population swelled, savings mounted, and the pent-up desire for new consumer goods reached an all-time high—gave retailers opportunity to think about the possibilities and to lay the groundwork for their strategic plans.

IX

MARKETS IN THE MEADOWS

When A. W. Ross predicted in 1952 that Los Angeles would have many miracle miles, he knew full well that examples could already be found in the metropolitan area and that others were planned.[1] The largest new shopping centers, like the Miracle Mile before them, were to function as "downtowns" for their respective areas. Yet most of these developments did not look anything like what Ross had created on Wilshire Boulevard. They embodied significant departures in layout, appearance, and business structure, and they were seen not just as mavericks but as harbingers of a fundamental shift in retail development.

Postwar practices drew from lessons learned during the 1920s and 1930s. Inspired by the success of the supermarket, many retailers now pursued volume sales at moderate prices using self-service and self-selection methods in big stores situated at strategic but previously isolated locations. The shopping center's rise in the prewar years fostered a widespread concern for planning. After the return of peace, ever more attention was given to analyzing the market, selecting tenants, and devising an effective management structure as well as to creating a visually unified ensemble. A layout that provided adequate parking space was also among the foremost concerns. The shopping center became a major thrust in retail development. Major complexes were built much more frequently than in earlier years. Many of the individual stores were considerably larger, and having thirty or forty of them in a complex was no longer unusual.

The sweeping changes in shopping center development led to a conscious hierarchy of types, and for the first time definitions were advanced regarding size and complexion. Larger than the neighborhood complex, the "community" or "district" center had convenience stores but also a greater range of specialty shops purveying soft (clothing, shoes, etc.) and hard (hardware, furniture) lines. Sometimes a small ("junior") department store—a limited-line business carrying mostly apparel and "soft" home furnishings, and usually oriented toward the lower end of the market—was part of the ensemble as well. These complexes contained around twenty to forty units, had a target audience of up to 100,000 people, and were intended as equivalents to the commercial center of a sizable town. The "regional" shopping center expanded the scope of merchandise by including more specialty outlets and at least one large branch of a major department store. The regional center generally had more than forty units and served a population of generally over 100,000 people. The mammoth complexes were developed to function as counterparts to the center city, much as the Miracle Mile or Westwood Village were a generation earlier.[2]

The most pronounced changes in shopping center development took place during a relatively short period between the mid-1940s and early 1950s. *Women's Wear Daily* estimated that about 100 centers of twenty or more stores and occupying more than 50,000 square feet of retail space existed in the United States by January 1953 and that only 10 percent of these had been constructed before the war. More than 50 had joined their ranks a year later, another 100 at the close of 1955.[3] The proliferation of complexes that seemed at once so new and so large elicited widespread interest among those involved in commercial development. There was no question that these "markets in the meadows," as they were described in the *Architectural Forum,* were a remarkable occurrence, one that an editor of *Chain Store Age* believed to be of paramount importance to retailing in the era. The impact also was pronounced on the urban land-

scape, shopping patterns, and the very idea of what a business center should be.[4] Nowhere was that impact so great so early as in Los Angeles, where four enormous shopping centers were operating, under construction, or on the boards by the close of 1950—all of them in "meadows" theretofore removed from concentrated settlement (figure 152).[5] All of them, too, were experiments, and underscored the challenges and risks involved in setting a course for which little precedent existed. As much as any metropolitan area, Los Angeles demonstrated at an early date that the shopping center was now a key feature of urban expansion. At the same time, an underlying strain of conservatism characterized aspects of the phenomenon locally. None of these centers emerged as a paradigm for later work, but, directly or otherwise, they left an indelible imprint on the broad patterns that eventually coalesced.

MARKET CONDITIONS

A number of factors contributed to the rapid growth of shopping centers across the country. There was a rise in population nationally (almost twenty million added between 1940 and 1950), a significantly greater percentage of which now resided in metropolitan areas (a 22.4 percent gain from 1940 to 1950). There was a huge increase in buying power ($25.20 per week in 1940, $60.00 per week in 1950) and with it greater disposable income ($979 per annum in 1940, $1,314 in 1950). With the forty-hour work week becoming commonplace, more time could be spent on leisure pursuits, shopping among them. This shift, along with the shopping center's accessibility, fostered greater family and male patronage in addition to the more customary women shopping alone.[6]

The rise of moderate-income households with disposable incomes was recognized as one of the most significant new factors in retailing and had a major impact both on the location and the nature of commercial development through the postwar years.[7] The percentage of both highest and lowest income groups had declined since 1929; more people were now considered middle class. Much of this group was upwardly mobile. Some had been victims of the depression and were on the rebound. Others were enjoying money and leisure for the first time. As the consumer market was increasing, it also shifted geographically. Along with more affluent groups, families of modest yet expanding means continued to relocate in outlying parts of metropolitan areas. A majority of the latter group now expected to live in a freestanding residence set amid a sizable yard—the low-density environment commonplace for some time in Los Angeles. From coast to coast, much of the newly settled territory lay beyond city limits. Population increases in cities themselves were often less during the 1940s than they were in the surrounding counties. There was also a substantial growth of businesses, especially industrial plants, well beyond the city center. These patterns were both fostered by, and in turn

152
Site of May Company Crenshaw store, 4005 Crenshaw Boulevard. Photo "Dick" Whittington, 1945. (Whittington Collection, Department of Special Collections, University of Southern California.)

further stimulated, automobile use. Highway building became ever more ambitious as public transportation systems suffered.[8]

These demographic changes had a great impact on both the acceptance of the shopping center as an optimal means of selling goods and on the scale at which those centers were constructed. Since mass consumer markets were being created very rapidly in new places, they could be captured most effectively by large centers because of the range of offerings they provided. Land was cheap and in many cases unencumbered by the rather mechanical zoning patterns established during the interwar decades. Many outlying business districts developed prior to 1941 were already overcrowded. Often they lacked adequate space to satisfy postwar needs, and a paucity of off-street parking made traffic congestion prevalent at prime shopping periods. Much the same conditions precluded large-scale new development from concentrating in established centers of satellite communities now being absorbed by metropolitan areas. It was far easier and cheaper to start afresh on virgin soil—in the meadows.

Development on a large scale was spurred by the realization that substantial acreage had to be dedicated to parking. Chain store companies, moreover, considered a big selling area essential for their mass merchandising techniques. The smaller, independently owned specialty shop was still seen as an important part of the tenant mix, but chain stores were now considered the foremost attractions to the vast white- and prosperous blue-collar target populations. Financial reward as well as recognition lay in creating large complexes, particularly regional centers.

Los Angeles's continued importance as a proving ground for new ideas in retail development was in large part due to the persistence of conditions that were central to shaping the metropolis during the 1920s. Southern California had suffered less and for a briefer period from the depression than did many parts of the country. By 1935 the economic climate was showing clear signs of improvement, due to a significant extent to the demand for products that comprised the backbone of local manufacturing, including petroleum, motion pictures, food, rubber, and aircraft. In 1937 the county ranked fifth nationally in the value of goods made and seventh in wages paid. The defense buildup prior to World War II and the far greater surge of wartime production dramatically increased Los Angeles's economic importance. By the opening months of 1948, the city ranked third nationally in its dollar volume of business. The prosperity that characterized the postwar years exceeded most predictions.[9]

The sustained rise in business activity was a key reason why Los Angeles continued to attract large numbers of skilled persons from other parts of the United States. The county's population increase during the 1930s was less than half that of the previous decade but still amounted to over 500,000. Between 1940 and 1950 the gain was more than 1,360,000; between 1950 and 1960, close to another two million. Well before the latter date, the metropolitan area approached that of Chicago as the country's second largest.[10]

Migration accounted for most of the population increase between 1930 and 1960, just as it had during the 1920s. Similarly, too, the dominant group was comprised of persons with white- or skilled blue-collar experience. Local business growth bolstered a broad-based prosperity among recent arrivals. By 1950, the metropolitan area possessed the highest percentage of proprietors, managers, and officials as a group in the nation as well as an unusually wide distribution of wealth.[11]

Abundant vacant land still existed in southern California to receive the new surge of migrants. As industry and other sources of employment continued to decentralize, the area's lateral, low-density patterns of residential growth were sustained, often intensified. Between 1940 and 1950, the population within an eight-mile radius of downtown increased only 39 percent, while that lying between an eight- and a twenty-mile radius rose 282 percent.[12] Inside the Los Angeles city limits, tracts in the San Fernando Valley and far to the southwest of downtown experienced some of the most intense growth. Areas outside the city, whether part of well-established communities such as Long Beach or in predominantly rural areas such as Orange County, acquired an increasingly significant place in the metropolitan realm. In 1930, residents of Los Angeles surpassed those elsewhere in the county by almost 300,000. Twenty years later, the ratio was nearly reversed, and by 1960 city dwellers comprised just slightly more than one-third the county total.

Among the most telling indicators of the character of this growth was the extent of new house construction. Even in 1935, Los Angeles ranked second to New York in construction costs estimated on building permits issued, a position the city maintained through 1941. During the same period, Los Angeles far exceeded all other cities in the number of building permits issued, the great majority of which were for single-family residences. By the close of 1939 almost 37,000 single-family houses had been erected in the city over the past six years. The *Times* repeatedly characterized the annual volume of house building as equivalent to the creation of a new city.[13] Los Angeles's leadership in residential development reinforced the belief in business circles that the 1920s boom was not an isolated occurrence but part of their city's sustained vitality. The freestanding house, which had carried particular importance as a distinctive feature of the region, gradually yet decisively usurped the vision of a towering metropolitan business center as a symbol of place.

The post-depression record of residential building was quite modest compared to the postwar years. In 1949 alone, the number of single-family houses begun in Los Angeles County exceeded 48,000. Well into the 1950s, the metropolitan area held its national lead even though many other cities were likewise experiencing a boom. Over 330,000 houses were added to the county's stock during the 1940s, more than 450,000 the following decade. The number of multiunit dwellings also increased, but most of the new buildings were still one- and two-story structures of modest dimensions and with some yard space.[14] The basic patterns of de-

velopment changed little during the mid-twentieth century; it was the sheer scale that elicited so much attention, locally and beyond.

DEPARTMENT STORES

Prior to war's end, three of southern California's leading department store companies were planning major expansion programs in response to built-up demand and the anticipated flood of residential development. Earlier branches had not served as catalysts for district growth. The Dyas Hollywood and May Company Wilshire stores were built toward the end of the principal expansion periods of their respective retail centers. Bullock's Wilshire came toward the beginning of its precinct, but the depression abruptly ended the anticipated building boom. Bullock's and other major stores were linchpins in Westwood Village's development, but they never functioned as dominant retail magnets. Elsewhere in the country, most retail executives believed that large branches were uneconomical and threatened patronage at the parent store.[15] This situation changed dramatically after the war in Los Angeles and other cities. Within a few years, the large department store branch—generally over 100,000 square feet and often 200,000 or more—became the norm for new construction, a shift that was viewed as one of the most significant changes in retailing patterns of the period.[16] Urban population dispersal, growth in disposable income and leisure time, as well as increasing mobility all affected the trend, just as they soon would propel the advent of the regional shopping center.

But one of the key factors that initially forced department store owners to expand through large branches was intense competition, mounting since the prewar years, from national chains that dealt in a wide variety of merchandise, such as Sears, and in more specialized lines as well. The influx of the chains, not only in major outlying centers but also in more localized ones such as the complex at Broadway and Eighty-seventh Street, was seen as a significant threat to the department store's future. To remain competitive, department stores adapted the chains' mass merchandising techniques to suit their own agenda. Central to that program was creating branches that, like Sears's "A" stores, were full-line outlets. The modest buildings of the prewar era were now seen as ill suited to volume sales, especially for a wide range of goods. The new generation of branches provided an enormous amount of space for customers' cars. Employing techniques pioneered by the supermarkets as well as by Sears, department stores were turning not only to self-service but also to self-selection—an approach once unthinkable, but one that many consumers preferred and that required yet more space for displays.

The huge Los Angeles department stores constructed in outlying centers during the late 1920s and 1930s were no longer seen by industry leaders as anomalies, but rather as pioneering examples from which valuable lessons could be learned.[17] Los Angeles became a national leader after the war as a result of this legacy and even more because new expansion

programs there ranked among the earliest, most ambitious, and most innovative in the field.

Bullock's was the first of the Los Angeles companies to make its intentions public, announcing plans in January 1945 to erect a store of some 250,000 square feet in Pasadena. Sumptuous in appearance and isolated from other shopping outlets, the facility was an updated version of its celebrated Wilshire emporium. Six months later, the May Company made known its $10,000,000 expansion program, reputedly then the largest ever undertaken by a single department store in the United States. Besides upgrading its downtown plant, May would add a large wing to its Wilshire store, erect a 600,000-square-foot warehouse, and build two new branches of 300,000 and 200,000 square feet, respectively.[18] Executives of the Broadway were more circumspect about their agenda, perhaps because they did not want competitors to realize how unorthodox and potentially lucrative the plan was until construction was under way. That plan entailed not just a mammoth department store but a new, fully integrated shopping center calculated to draw from a population the size of Kansas City. Located on Crenshaw Boulevard, six miles southwest of downtown, the complex dwarfed most previous undertakings in the region and was instrumental in setting new parameters nationally for large-scale retail development.

Among the three stores, the Broadway arguably had been the most aggressive in its decentralization efforts for some time, beginning with its purchase of the Dyas Hollywood store in 1931. Nine years later, the Broadway opened another store, containing nearly 100,000 square feet, in Pasadena. The operational structure of both outlets was much like that of Bullock's. Each store had its own management and purchasing offices; coordination occurred only at the top executive level.[19] The practice helped diversify trade. The Broadway's downtown store focused on a middle-income market; the Hollywood and Pasadena stores catered to a more affluent one, much as did Bullock's. As early as 1938, the Broadway began to explore the possibilities of a fourth outlet. This building, like the May Company Wilshire store, would be a very large facility that functioned as a full extension of the downtown plant. But, more than the Wilshire behemoth, this store was targeted to a middle-income audience—the swelling one in southwest Los Angeles.

CRENSHAW CENTER

The trade potential of southwest Los Angeles was enormous. Studies conducted for the company during the war indicated that 567,000 people, 15 percent of the county's total population, lived within a 20-minute driving radius of the site that was eventually selected. The combined income of these residents was $200,000,000 in 1940. The area also had the highest percentage (40.5) of homeowners in the county.[20] On the other hand, no major retail center existed below Wilshire Boulevard. For many southwest

residents, driving to Westwood or the Miracle Mile was at least as long a journey as going downtown. Outer portions of the southwest were among the most rapidly developing sectors of the metropolitan area during the 1940s, and the potential for further growth seemed limitless. Besides responding to this pent-up demand, a move to the southwest carried strategic advantages. To date, Bullock's and the May Company had concentrated on the Wilshire corridor, each focusing on a somewhat overlapping clientele. The Broadway could not only enlarge the scope of patronage but encircle the competition, as it were, to the north (Hollywood), east (Pasadena), and now the south with outlets in the region's three most lucrative trading areas aside from the Wilshire corridor.

Finding the proper site was probably the most challenging aspect of the plan since the area, which now extended well beyond the Southwest district developed during the first three decades of the century, possessed no readily identifiable center. Commercial facilities abounded but were mostly modest outlets oriented to neighborhood trade. Building a large, integrated center carried advantages but also great risks. Westwood Village and the Miracle Mile enjoyed proximity to larger affluent populations. The few neighborhood shopping centers built before the war demonstrated the efficacy of a quasi-integrated approach in less well-to-do areas, but at a much smaller scale. Furthermore, all these precursors were realized incrementally, in response to demand, and most were built by a number of second parties who bore the greatest financial burden. Most of the Broadway's shopping center had to be erected in one campaign, requiring an outlay of nearly $6,000,000. If sales failed to cover both the large initial and operational costs within the anticipated time frame, the economic consequences could be devastating, not just for the complex but for the parent company. The Broadway's executives were confident that the market existed to support their retail giant. The key problem was finding a place from which full advantage of that market could be taken.

While the precise nature of the site selection process is uncertain, contemporary accounts suggest that studies were of a new cast. The project was among the earliest, perhaps the first, of its kind to use the detailed information gathered in the 1940 census, which inaugurated the compilation of housing statistics broken down by very small geographic parcels for communities of 50,000 people or more.[21] Figures were available on such matters as the number of dwelling units (including the rate of owner occupancy), approximate age and condition of stock, and average monthly rents paid on a block-by-block basis. From this data, it was relatively simple to compute household income and correlate it with precise geographic locations. Market analysts were already adept at correlating income levels with spending habits to delineate target audiences for retailers. Now it was possible to conduct what became known as a time-distance study, pinpointing where that audience lived and how long it would take to drive to a given site.[22]

The time-distance study and related forms of market analysis drawn from the 1940 census permitted a more accurate projection of the

retail market. Previously, statistical methods employed for store location were predicated on downtown siting and thus examined factors such as pedestrian traffic volume as well as population characteristics for the community as a whole. Site selection in outlying areas often resorted to the same methods, augmented by counts of streetcar patronage and/or passing automobiles. Developers of supermarkets and other stores in more or less isolated situations gathered data about the environs from building permits, utility connections, and even newspaper circulation. Firsthand observation of residential development, taking into account such aspects as the size and character of housing, were also used.[23] All this information conveyed a reasonable sense of the market in a comparatively small area. For much larger projects, a developer such as Janss or Nichols could assume that a major share of the clientele would come from his own housing tracts. A. W. Ross could turn to no such source. The data he collected may have been more extensive than most compilations of the period; nevertheless, he also seems to have relied on an unbounded optimism, unflappable perseverance, and a good intuitive sense. Without more precise statistics, it is doubtful whether any developer would have undertaken a project of comparable size unilaterally and in a single construction campaign, as the Broadway was now planning. Even more doubtful would have been the willingness of any financial institution to fund such a venture. Acquiring a detailed statistical profile for a sizable part of the metropolitan area was an essential basis for the large shopping centers of the postwar era.

To guide their course, the Broadway's executives worked closely with one of the region's prominent commercial real estate firms, Coldwell Banker, which undertook the site search, advised on the composition of tenants, and served as broker and leasing agent. Coldwell's Frank Riley got his client interested in a thirty-five-acre tract used as a golf course, which could become available for long-term lease.[24] The property was strategically located in relation to most of the new and prosperous neighborhoods in the district. The most prestigious enclave, Baldwin Hills, was close by and could enhance the project's reputation. Crenshaw Boulevard, the major north-south route through the middle of the area, fronted the property on one side, and Santa Barbara (now Martin Luther King) Avenue, which could become an important cross street, provided equally extensive frontage on another.

The acreage Riley identified was sufficiently large and deep to allow unusual freedom in the arrangement of the complex. Los Angeles's zoning ordinance, like others nationwide, made no allowances for the creation of large new shopping centers. Land allocated for commercial use was almost always limited to the depth of properties fronting thoroughfares, a holdover from arterial development along streetcar lines. The shopping center sites at Palos Verdes and Westwood Village lay outside municipal boundaries, and hence zoning jurisdictions, when the land was so dedicated. Property could be rezoned, as it was for the Miracle Mile or for the rear parking lots of early neighborhood centers, but extending a yet greater depth from the street was often hampered by existing residen-

tial development. Both the size and shape of the Crenshaw tract may have influenced the final decision to build a complex of enormous proportions.[25] Once arrangements were made for leasing the land, planning began in earnest during the early months of 1945. Ground was broken that October. Postwar material shortages delayed progress, so that the project took more than two years to complete.

When it opened in November 1947, the Broadway-Crenshaw Center, as it was officially called, was quite unlike any other retail development in the nation (figure 153).[26] The complex had nearly 550,000 square feet of enclosed space supplemented by thirteen acres of parking lot designed to hold 2,500 cars at a time. Bigness permeated the scheme: the supermarket alone was more than 45,000 square feet, the variety store over 48,000. At 208,000 square feet, the department store ranked among the largest outlying ones in the nation.[27]

The Broadway-Crenshaw Center was not the first example of a major downtown department store branch anchoring an integrated retail complex. Marshall Field opened a shop for infants' clothes at Lake Forest's Market Square in 1928 and leased an entire building in the complex three years later. The earliest purpose-built department store erected in a shopping center was Strawbridge & Clothier's 40,000-square-foot facility of 1929–1930 at Suburban Square (begun 1927) in Ardmore, along Philadelphia's Main Line.[28] Several widely published schemes built about the same time as the Broadway-Crenshaw had a department store branch as the anchor tenant, including Bellevue (1945–1946) near Seattle and Ridgeway (1945–1947) at Stamford, Connecticut.[29] But these latter complexes were

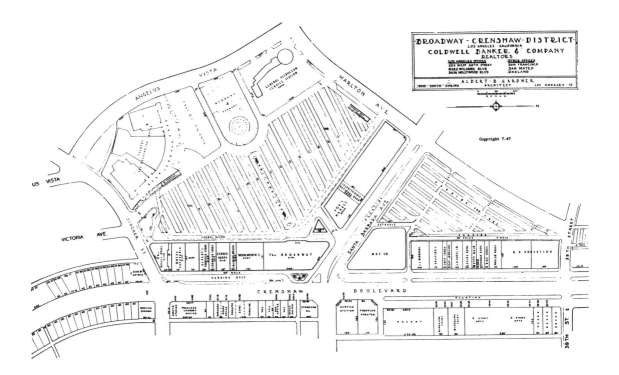

far less ambitious, with the department store in each about a tenth of the Broadway's size; indeed the combined square footage of the two shopping centers in their entirety was less than that of the Broadway's big store.

Size was not the only aspect differentiating the Broadway-Crenshaw Center from its predecessors. Most prewar branch stores and large shopping centers aside from those in Los Angeles were intended to complement more than compete with the city center. Furthermore, as the Broadway's project was targeted to a budget-conscious clientele, its size was predicated on high-volume sales, much like a supermarket or a Sears store. The ensemble was planned as a mass merchandising center, not with the exclusive aura of Westwood Village or the Miracle Mile but a grade above downtown—a balance that would characterize many postwar shopping centers but had never been realized on so large a scale before.

To achieve functional equivalence with downtown in this way, the composition of tenants broke the normative pattern as well. Branches of most leading downtown specialty stores as well as smaller, independently owned shops associated with fashionable outlying areas were excluded. Instead, the mix primarily included chain-owned outlets purveying goods and services in wide demand. Units included a variety store (F. W. Woolworth), children's clothes (Bond), women's wear (Lerner's), shoes (Chandler's), fabrics (Alpert's), men's clothing (Silverwood's), drugs (Owl and Savon), banking (Security-First), food (Von's), and automobile products and repairs (Mobil). Except for Silverwood's and the Broadway itself, the number and type of units were somewhat akin to those at the Broadway and Eighty-seventh Street center.[30] Coldwell Banker had considerable experience in assembling the tenant package for such "Main Street" developments and may well shaped the Broadway-Crenshaw's complex-

153

Broadway-Crenshaw Center, Crenshaw Boulevard, Martin Luther King Avenue and Stocker Street, Los Angeles, 1945–1947, Albert B. Gardner, architect; all but Broadway Department Store demolished 1987. General view looking east, also showing May Company department store (left), 1945–1947, Albert C. Martin & Associates, architects. Geoffrey Baker and Bruno Funaro, *Shopping Centers,* 174.)

154

Broadway-Crenshaw Center and adjacent blocks, site plan showing existing and projected store units, 1947. (*Urban Land Institute Technical Bulletin,* July 1949, 32.)

ion, determining that the department store could most effectively compete with chains through an integrated business structure. The mix provided a basis for comparison shopping, transforming two adversaries into partners. The development thus was part neighborhood center, greatly enlarged, and part downtown, but only a small slice. The conclusion that this arrangement would succeed was no doubt bolstered by Coldwell Banker's extensive work in addressing middle-class retail demands. Once in operation, the Broadway-Crenshaw Center proved a gold mine, demonstrating the importance of having major chain outlets in a regional shopping center, even though most later examples included a wider range and larger number of stores.[31] Similarly, the complex revealed to real estate and retail interests alike the value of having a large department store as an anchor. By the decade's end, there was general agreement that building lone-wolf department stores was no longer viable in most cases.

The Broadway-Crenshaw Center also established a precedent in having a major department store initiate the project and act as the controlling force in tenant selection and management—tasks previously undertaken by real estate developers. With no prior experience in such work, the Broadway relied not only on the services of Coldwell Banker but also on the Northwestern Mutual Life Insurance Company, which financed most of the construction and retained ownership of the buildings, leasing them as a unit to the Broadway. The department store, in turn, subleased to other tenants, an arrangement that allowed its merchandising objectives to be realized without the burden of ownership. Projections of income from subleases were estimated for the long run as equaling the amount the Broadway paid in rental fees for its own store.[32] At the same time, the company was beholden to no other party to ensure that the tenant mix was fully integrated to suit its own needs. The store also could exercise authority over tenants in key aspects of appearance and operation.[33] The desirability of a department store assuming this central role in shopping center development was debated among industry leaders for some years to

come; but the significance of the Broadway-Crenshaw Center as a point of departure was nationally recognized.

In its layout and appearance, the complex likewise represented an abrupt break from prevailing patterns. It retained no vestiges of the idealized town center or high-rise metropolis. Instead, most of the site was consumed by an enormous parking lot, one larger in relation to the buildings it served than those created for Wilshire department stores, and probably the biggest continuous space of its kind in the United States other than those serving recreational facilities or industrial plants (figure 154). The basic arrangement found in several of the region's prewar neighborhood centers was here expanded to a grand scale. In the eyes of many observers, adequate provision for the motorists patronizing a large center had at last been made. Equally important, the stores were oriented to that space, establishing a relationship somewhat like that of the big Wilshire emporia, but one entirely absent in the neighborhood centers (figure 155). By virtue of its integral role in the design as well as its vast dimensions, that space was given unmatched prominence. The parking lot was no longer the back yard, defined only by utilitarian needs.

Yet the Broadway-Crenshaw Center was Janus-like, for it also remained visually anchored to the street, with no clear distinctions between "front" and "rear." Stores facing Santa Barbara Avenue abutted the sidewalk, while provision was made for an access road and parallel curbside parking along the Crenshaw Boulevard elevation (figures 156, 157). The sculptural massing of the Broadway store, with its elaborate pylon rising well above the roofline, was composed to attract the eye of the motorist from some distance. Like most other retailers, Broadway executives as-

155
Broadway-Crenshaw Center, store fronts, west face. Photo author, 1986.

156
Broadway-Crenshaw Center, east face looking south. Photo "Dick" Whittington, 1952. (Whittington Collection, Department of Special Collections, University of Southern California.)

sumed that the complex would generate a considerable walk-in trade; a strong streetfront presence was deemed essential for the success of the store and for securing the right tenants. Those selected shared that view.[34]

In reality, very few pedestrians came. Force of habit—what Albert C. Martin, Jr., one of the regions' leading department store architects of the period described as "urban thinking"—among retail executives can partially explain their viewpoint.[35] Furthermore, elaborate sidewalk window displays had long been key to creating a department store's identity. During the interwar decades, Los Angeles had become a major center in the United States not only for fashion design but for the artful ways in which these goods were presented to the sidewalk pedestrian.[36] There was little inducement for any department store to abandon this basic and prestigious component of its merchandising.

Department store displays were also revolutionizing the design of specialty outlets, a trend conspicuously manifested at the Broadway-Crenshaw Center. Shortly before the war, several young New York architects—Victor Gruen, Morris Ketchum, and Morris Lapidus the most prominent among them—began to advocate adapting the theatrical character of the most sophisticated department store show windows to the entire front of small retail outlets. By having the facade serve as one large display, continuing the emphasis on dramatic presentation of goods inside and creating a sense of continuity between the two areas, it was believed that the limitations of the deep, narrow plan common to most specialty shops could be overcome. The penchant for "packaging" the storefront in a slick, streamlined veneer, popular during the 1930s, was disparaged as a superficial restyling of earlier mistakes whereby the window displays were

divorced from the interior. With exuberant interpretations of avant-garde models as well as avant-garde rhetoric, exponents referred to stores as "machines for selling" where the ensemble was a stage organized to induce purchases.[37] Yet Gruen and his colleagues studied the methods and problems of merchants to a degree few architects had previously undertaken. By the end of the war, the approach of these architects became widely accepted for stores nationwide. While New York remained the pacesetter for such work, Los Angeles emerged at an early date as a second focus after Gruen's Hollywood office, which opened in 1941, became his headquarters.

Architect and retailer alike presumed a traditional setting for such work, since the sidewalk provided the springboard in both physical and conceptual terms for the design. Once in California, Gruen modified his approach to attract the motorist no less than the pedestrian by intensifying the dramatic qualities of his fronts and often by extending the scale of this treatment to encompass a height of two or three stories.[38] The Broadway-Crenshaw Center's architect, Albert Gardner, adapted this idea, setting the storefronts at a bold scale certain to catch the motorist's eye from both street and parking lot. At the same time, Gardner emphasized unity to a degree seldom found in southern California retail developments outside the guaranteed neighborhood. But here the effect was quite different, underscoring bigness in a forthright way calculated to enhance middlebrow consumer appeal.

Since both the new merchandising ideas and design associated with them were rooted in the conventional matrix of the nucleated retail center, the Broadway's executives gave no thought to alternative layouts for their complex. Indeed, they believed one of the design's advances to be dual facades for each store, with the elevation facing the parking area identical to that facing the street. Besides its convenience value, the car lot was seen as a means of enhancing store identity, doubling the normal exterior display area. Considerable expense was incurred to realize this objective. In addition to the cost of a second front, there was the greater one of constructing a tunnel that ran nearly half a mile from end to end in which all deliveries were made. Perhaps inspired by the subterranean service entrance at the May Company Wilshire store, the tunnel carried distinct logistical advantages over the arrangement at neighborhood centers where parking lot patrons had to thread their way around delivery vehicles, piles of packaged goods, and refuse containers. The scale of the Broadway-Crenshaw development enabled a practical resolution that was widely followed in later shopping malls.[39]

Finally, the Broadway-Crenshaw Center set a major precedent in a way that was wholly unplanned: it triggered a sequence of events that would demonstrate the drawing power of two large department stores in the same location outside downtown. Having a competitor right across the street was the last thing Broadway executives desired. Such closeness was peculiar to the urban core, but even there major department stores were often situated at least a block from one another.[40] Locally and nation-

157
Broadway-Crenshaw Center, store fronts, east face. Photo author, 1986.

wide, the expansion of department stores beyond the downtown resulted in each enterprise establishing its own territory. Bullock's was now staking a claim in Pasadena where the Broadway had opened a branch in 1940; however, the two buildings were some distance apart, they had different target audiences, and Pasadena was a small city in itself. The idea of paired department stores oriented to the same clientele lying where open fields had recently spread was unthinkable during the mid-1940s—unthinkable except by the leadership of the May Company (see figure 152).

Much of the impetus for the May Company's plans may have come from the Broadway's own territorial agenda. When May announced its vast expansion program in July 1945, not only was one of the new stores (200,000 square feet) opposite the Broadway-Crenshaw Center site, but the other (300,000 square feet) was just slightly further away from the Broadway Hollywood store.[41] The initiative implied that, beyond expanding in outlying areas, May sought to keep the Broadway's share of the market in check, neutralizing if not gaining dominance over the competition. Relations between the two enterprises were hardly amiable; the Broadway's leadership had regarded May and its predecessor, Hamburger's, as a predator since the early twentieth century. If there had been any lingering doubt among Broadway executives about the commitment to build a large shopping center, it probably dissipated once May's plan became known. The competitive struggle was perhaps the main reason why the Broadway did not publicize the full scope of its project until ground was

broken, by which time May was well into its own single-store development. The May site was much smaller, precluding construction of a comparable shopping complex. Subsequently, May erected a store group, but not as an integrated center. The additional facilities at once diminished the size and intensified the use of the car lot, which was less than half the size of the Broadway's. Relations between the companies worsened when Edward Carter left a senior position at May to assume the presidency of the Broadway while the two complexes were under construction.

Unofficially, then, the Crenshaw Center became a district, bisected by the widened and now heavily traveled Santa Barbara Avenue, which separated two adversarial department stores and their attendant groups of shops (figure 158). The street hindered circulation from one side to the other on foot and by car. Poised like ancient warships about to do battle, the department stores formed a bifurcated "middle" of the precinct, rendering the locations toward either end much less desirable in terms of customer draw. Other problems arose as well. If the May lot was too small, the Broadway's was too big in that it had spaces many customers considered too far away from the stores.[42]

But despite the drawbacks, the entire district did a thriving business. Both Broadway and May executives were in fact surprised at the level of patronage. What neither company had expected was that the presence of two major stores would serve as a catalyst in much the same way as complementary stores did in a shopping center; in generating trade, the whole was greater than the sum of its parts. A correspondent for *Women's Wear Daily* believed that the addition of "Tom May's own 'baby' [was] just the beginning of a new day for the section which is veritably a small city in itself." In short order the meadow was transformed into a "new retail axis" of major proportions—a formidable competitor with downtown. From a national perspective, the ensemble was nothing short of a unique phenomenon that "far transcends that of store construction work of a majority of large cities. Persons familiar with the retail scene say they cannot recall anything quite like the Crenshaw development."[43]

Most customers were unaware of the acrimonious relationship that lay behind the scenes; they assumed the development was a single undertaking like the Miracle Mile. Once again, the emergence of so ambitious and new a solution to retail demands fueled the boosterish mystique of Los Angeles as a place where unprecedented growth occurred overnight. Even more important, the inclusion of the May Company and its flock of support stores, while not significantly expanding the scope of goods offered, further enhanced the opportunities for comparison shopping.

Within the metropolitan areas, the Crenshaw Center as a commercial district rather than the Broadway-Crenshaw Center as an integrated business development had the greatest immediate impact on other projects for at least several years. Coldwell Banker promoted business property across Crenshaw Boulevard, which made the area even more akin to arterial business nodes (see figure 153). In May 1950, yet another real es-

158
Broadway-Crenshaw Center and May Company Crenshaw store, aerial view. Photo "Dick" Whittington, 1954. (Whittington Collection, Department of Special Collections, University of Southern California.)

tate venture, sponsored by an independent company, was announced for
the block fronting Santa Barbara Avenue just to the west of the Broadway's land, with streetfront buildings on all four sides and parking in the
center, yet without an integrated tenant structure (figure 159).[44] The appeal of these tracts lay in their potential to partake in the trade drawn to
the established outlets. Newcomers, which included branches of major
downtown stores such as Barker Brothers and Desmond's as well as chain
units and independently run businesses, gave little thought to the point
at which the lack of planning or coordination might undermine the
endeavor.[45]

WESTCHESTER

The degree to which some conventional patterns of retail development
persisted in the region was underscored at the Westchester Business Center, which was among the largest complexes in acreage (73) and number
of stores (83) orchestrated by a single party in southern California during
the 1940s. The scheme was created to serve the Westchester district, a
3,000-acre, comprehensively planned development of inexpensive single-
family houses situated between the town of Inglewood and the Los
Angeles Municipal (now International) Airport at the southwestern edge
of the city. Planning began before the war by the tract's owners, Superior
Oil Company and Security-First National Bank, working in close cooperation with the city planning department. The site was then isolated from
well-settled parts of the metropolitan area, a condition viewed as advantageous. Westchester was planned as a model development for around
50,000 persons of moderate income, a place that functioned as a community in itself. Wartime needs fostered growth, owing to the site's proximity to several aircraft plants. By 1945, a major part of Westchester was
realized.[46]

Likewise conceived as a paradigm for metropolitan development,
the shopping center was a key component of the Westchester plan. Follow-

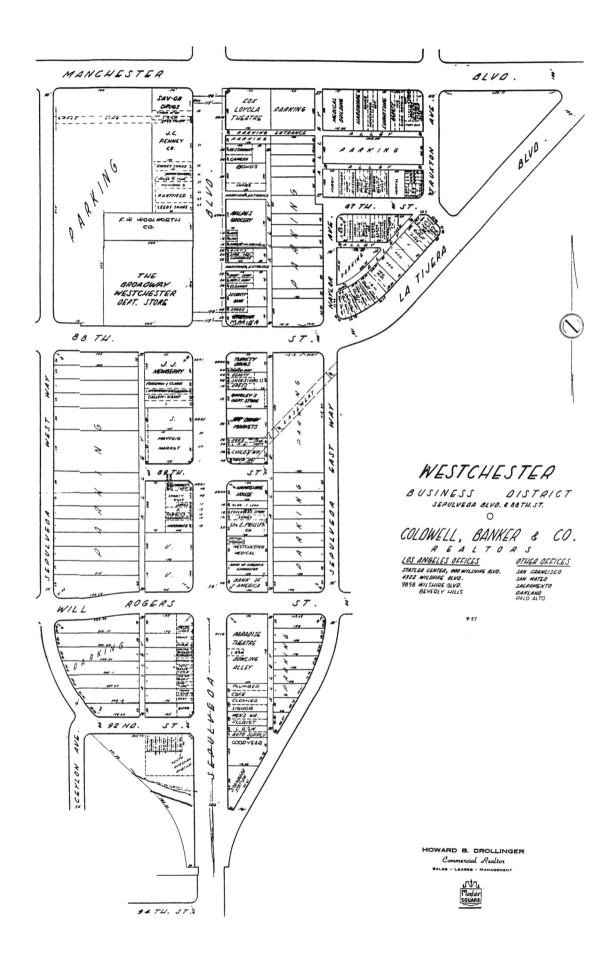

IX   MARKETS IN THE MEADOWS

ing the example of large-scale community developers such as Janss, the project's planners excluded business from the housing tracts so that it could be concentrated in a single area. Unlike at the Crenshaw Center, commerce would not continue to spread. Gordon Whitnall, director of the city planning department, believed that the project would validate his belief that a decentralized business district could be well designed. Stores, he reasoned, had to escape "the starvation conditions in the 'commercial concentration camps' and seek . . . new locations" with adequate space, but had to be contained so as never to encroach on residential property. Extensive provisions had to be made for parking, while "thoroughfares should be maintained solely for moving vehicles."[47] The proposal was unveiled in schematic form before the war as a generic solution for the metropolis, and provides a direct link between the planning of neighborhood centers of the 1930s and of the larger centers of the late 1940s and 1950s (see figure 139).

Considerable refinements were introduced to the scheme for its realization at Westchester. While drawing from the arterial vernacular, the plan sought to establish new standards for the private sector. On the east side of the complex, building lots extended a depth of 140 feet, behind which another 10 was reserved for loading and 30 for vehicular access. An additional 180 feet was to be used exclusively for parking, entered from a boundary street, designed to separate local from through traffic (figure 160). Even more space was allocated to parking on the west side. The total estimated capacity of 3,300 cars at one time was an enormous amount for the period, and was still considered excessive in the early 1950s by some out-of-town developers.[48] The scheme was intended to be just as far-sighted in its business structure, so as to satisfy most Westchester residents' needs most of the time. Frank H. Ayres & Son, a venerable Los Angeles firm specializing in commercial real estate and with a reputation that rivaled Coldwell Banker's, was given charge of developing the ensemble to ensure a high caliber of tenants, a strong tenant mix, and strategic siting of key business functions.

Ground was broken for the Westchester Business Center in August 1942; the first business, a supermarket, opened seven months later. By the war's end a block of convenience-oriented outlets was realized (see figure 166). Ayres found it difficult to secure the major stores, however. J. C. Penney was courted but rejected the overtures because the site was too close to its unit in downtown Inglewood, several miles to the east.[49] Isolated through the 1920s, that town now lay in the path of residential development. A site on the eastern edge of Inglewood's core rather than at Westchester was chosen by Sears in 1945 for one of the largest of its units in the metropolitan area.[50] Westchester was more a fringe location from the chain companies' perspective, lacking the critical mass to enable a big store to thrive on volume sales.

In the latter months of 1946, Ayres finally was able to convince Milliron's, the newly renamed Fifth Street Store, to build its first branch at Westchester.[51] Still progress was slow. The 90,000-square-foot empor-

161
Westchester Business Center, aerial view looking south, Manchester Avenue in foreground. Photo Spence, ca. 1948. (Photo archives, Department of Geography, University of California, Los Angeles.)

162
Westchester Business Center, aerial view looking south, 1964. (Courtesy Howard B. Drollinger.)

ium was relatively small by Los Angeles standards, and Milliron's lacked the drawing power of the Broadway, the May Company, or Bullock's. When the store opened in March 1949, the precinct remained mostly vacant. Only during the next decade did the business center mature (figures 161, 162).[52]

Westchester's sporadic growth stood in sharp contrast to the fast pace of development at the Crenshaw Center and indeed at many other large-scale shopping complexes of the period. The difference may be partly attributable to changes in the scale of retailing. Major stores sought an ever-larger audience to reach their mass merchandising targets. Under the circumstances, Westchester's own population could not compensate for the absence of growth potential on three sides due to topographical and land use constraints. The precinct's layout did not help either. For all the interest accorded its master plan, the arrangement was quite traditional in some respects. Business blocks and parking areas alike were subdivided by the street grid. Having developed arterial frontage since the early twentieth century, Ayres trumpeted the advantages of the project's location on a major route, Sepulveda Boulevard. This thoroughfare proved a substantial hindrance, however, to the circulation of shoppers from one side to the other. With an increasing amount of through traffic, Sepulveda was anything but a fabulous boulevard.

Ironically, a pedestrian orientation remained paramount in other aspects of the configuration. After surveying a number of "leading merchants" in the metropolitan area, Westchester's planners confirmed their belief that front parking would render display windows ineffectual and create too great a distance between the stores on either side of the street. Furthermore, "pedestrian traffic, the most valuable and important to any volume merchant, [would be] lost entirely by the front parking arrangement."[53] Just as with the Broadway-Crenshaw Center, the assumption remained that Westchester would function well as an updated Main Street so long as sufficient space was given to parking. But parking, as it turned out, did not prove adequate where it was most needed, close to the largest stores. Nor was the maximum allowed building depth enough to accommodate a behemoth on a scale now being planned elsewhere. As a result, an exemption had to be granted to Milliron's if it was to build a viable facility. Moreover, the store had to augment lot space with a costly rooftop parking deck (figure 163).

Milliron's architect, Victor Gruen, capitalized on the constraints of the program to design one of the most unorthodox and well-publicized retail facilities of the period. The Sepulveda Boulevard elevation was scaled to the pedestrian, yet given a bold composition easily discernible to the passing motorist (figure 164). At the rear, ramps of the roof deck were treated as futuristic sculptural elements to entice shoppers (figure 165).[54] Entrance to the store from the deck was through an airy penthouse, with

163
Milliron's Westchester department store, 8739 Sepulveda Boulevard, Los Angeles, 1947–1949, Gruen & Krummeck, architects; altered. Photo 1949. (Courtesy Gruen Associates.)

164
Milliron's Westchester store, detail of front elevation. Photo 1949. (Courtesy Gruen Associates.)

a restaurant, auditorium, beauty shop, and children's playroom (figure 166). Gruen was determined to make the shopping experience seem memorably new in this scheme, his first for a large store.

At Westchester, Milliron's remained an anomaly. Few other business owners expressed an inclination to develop distinctive designs; the buildings constructed during the 1950s were collectively no different from what could be found at the numerous smaller arterial business centers of the period (figure 167). Ayres focused on business objectives in selecting purchasers for each site. Once that purchase was made, designs had to be approved by an architectural review committee, just as at Westwood Village, but here the members appear to have addressed practical considerations more than artistic ones.[55]

The development process employed at Westchester did not allow full control of the tenant structure either. Some parcels were sold to the business that would occupy the site, but others were sold to third parties. Ayres maintained some oversight on the kinds of tenants selected once a building was finished and negotiated leases for a number of them, but lacked the control found at a fully integrated center.

Adhering to the tradition of multiple ownership generated more than the anticipated difficulties in creating the car lots. Each purchaser had to buy a section of the parking area equal to the width of the streetfront property and improve the parcel according to a uniform standard. At the same time, control over all these rear sections had to be turned over to the Westchester Association, whose sole responsibility was to manage, maintain, and repair them.[56] Many merchants balked at these stipulations. Complaints over improving all of a parcel at once were great enough for Ayres to devise agreements for phasing. Paying taxes on the parking area was another source of irritation. Some parties may have rejected locating at Westchester because of the arrangement. For customers, the irregular quilt of paved areas that resulted during the early years of this piecemeal process was no doubt an annoyance as well. At the Broadway-Crenshaw Center such matters were never an issue because the property was owned and operated as a single business. The large car lot was a unified entity, constructed in a single campaign in concert with the buildings. Expenses were shared by the tenants, but as part of their overall leases. In this packaged form, providing space for cars and paying for improvements did not seem as onerous as in the loosely coordinated program at Westchester.

Westchester underscored the difficulties of enlarging the neighborhood center model, as it had developed locally during the late 1930s, to address the new scale of retailing of the postwar era. Yet the conventional practices Westchester embodied—street orientation, multiple ownership, and minimal controls—continued to prevail in the metropolitan area into the 1950s. Little inducement existed to change such practices when the growth of outlying areas was so great that all but the most ill-conceived projects yielded handsome profits. Most shopping complexes were created as neighborhood or community centers.[57] Sometimes enough land was set aside to enable future growth as a major trade mag-

165
Milliron's Westchester store, ramps to roof deck. Photo 1949. (Courtesy Gruen Associates.)

net, yet the elements of the plan were nonetheless rooted in traditional patterns of localized arterial development rather than setting the framework for a new scale of operation. There is no better example of the hold these habits retained during the postwar years than Panorama City.

Situated on the former Panorama Ranch in the geographic center of the San Fernando Valley, some fifteen miles northwest of downtown Los Angeles, Panorama City was planned, much like Westchester, as a large, self-contained community for moderate-income households. Here, however, the project was developed by a single party, Kaiser Community Homes, which had been one of several builders at Westchester. Besides containing 2,000 single-family residences, the 400-acre tract was designed to support churches, schools, and recreational facilities. Unlike Westchester, the site lay not on the edge but in the middle of one of the region's fastest-growing areas. When Panorama City's master plan was created in the mid-1940s, sixteen acres were set aside for buildings and another twenty-five for parking in what was envisioned as the "downtown" of the entire valley. The Kaiser tract's first houses were completed in 1948. Within two years the development and several contiguous ones hosted an estimated population of 20,000.⁵⁸

Beyond its size, the Panorama City Shopping Center, as it became officially known in 1951, emulated the Broadway-Crenshaw development in having a single ownership and management structure. Kaiser Homes' president, Fritz Burns, had witnessed the erratic pace of Westchester's business growth and no doubt wished to avoid repeating it. On the other hand, the Panorama City complex was laid out in a standard manner along a thoroughfare, Van Nuys Boulevard, with streetfront buildings constructed on an individual basis and parking at the rear. Only the large block sizes, delineated in the master plan, differentiated the arrangement from the norm. Much as at Westchester and at Windsor Hills, which Burns and Fred Marlow, now also with Kaiser, had developed during the previous decade, the first Panorama outlet was a supermarket, completed in 1949. Around twenty businesses were operating by the early months of 1951, all purveying routine goods and services.[59]

Panorama City continued as little more than a sizable neighborhood center until a major addition was completed in 1955, the first part of the development not constructed incrementally. Anchored by a 225,000-square-foot branch of the Broadway, this new ensemble included an array of national chain stores (W. T. Grant, F. W. Woolworth, Lerner Shops, Bond Clothes, and Mandel's and Kinney shoes) as well as Silverwood's eighth unit.[60] The project required additional land for parking and had to be placed on the opposite side of Van Nuys Boulevard (figures 168, 169). By then such bifurcation was considered the worst possible arrangement for a shopping center of any size; however, executives of the Broadway and the other companies involved elected to proceed with the development because the location was central to a large middle-class population, the existing complex drew a sizable trade, and no good alternative site existed in the environs. Furthermore, the May Company was studying sites for a San Fernando Valley store and might have selected Panorama City given the chance.[61] The Broadway and its attendant stores transformed

Panorama City into a regional center that became a primary shopping magnet in the rapidly developing area. Yet the plan of nearly a decade earlier ensured permanent separation between the stores that attracted this trade and those oriented to more routine functions.

What became nationally recognized as an error in shopping center layout by the mid-1950s was not seen as such only a few years previous, at least in Los Angeles. Real estate and retail interest were wedded to the Main Street idea to such an extent that one scheme, Culver Center (begun 1949), created the arrangement where it did not previously exist. Located several blocks to the west of the commercial core of Culver City, a satellite town of the 1920s, the complex was designed to serve the now fast-growing residential areas nearby. Locally based developers, W. W. and Blake Touchstone, chose a site between two of the metropolitan area's major east-west thoroughfares, Venice and Washington boulevards, more or less equidistant from the Crenshaw Center (to the east), the Miracle Mile (north), downtown Santa Monica (west), and Westchester (south), boasting that their project would obviate the need to patronize other commercial centers, including Culver City's own modest core. The complex introduced national chains to the district, including J. C. Penney, W. T. Grant, Mode O'Day, and Karl's Shoes, but most of the merchants were local ones who moved from the town's center or established new branches.[62] Occupying twelve acres, the ensemble did not approach a regional center in its size or complexion. It did, however, cultivate the aura of a town, with stores facing a new, block-long street, almost useless for vehicular circulation—all set at right angles to the thoroughfares (figures 170, 171).

DESIGN

Most parties involved in Los Angeles shopping center development believed that if they were to succeed in creating new urban centers—new

"Main Streets"—a sense of visual coherence would be a key factor. The Culver City complex continued the common practice of facade differentiation among stores, but soon greater uniformity in massing and sometimes in detail became the norm. Such treatment could make a large shopping center seem all the more impressive to the passing motorist and also facilitate reading the signs of the major stores. The Broadway-Crenshaw Center set an influential precedent in this respect as well as in having both street and parking lot elevations embellished to more or less the same degree.

On the other hand what failed to continue was a sense of hierarchy. The major retail development became less readily distinguishable by its buildings from smaller retail districts. Tall buildings, towers, and conspicuously decorated fronts had filled this role during the interwar decades, so that the center of Hollywood, the Miracle Mile, or even the modestly scaled blocks of Westwood Village stood apart from the norm. Much of the Broadway-Crenshaw Center's distinction in this respect lay with the theatrical treatment of its anchor store. Thereafter, community-sized centers were basically akin to neighborhood ones.[63] The differences lay more in the number and range of stores than in physical character.

By the mid-1950s, when the design of shopping center exteriors became more homogeneous and a taste for neutrality in the architecture it-

168
Panorama City Shopping Center, Van Nuys Boulevard between Roscoe Boulevard and Parthenia Street, Los Angeles, begun 1949. General view showing Panorama Market (1949, Arthur Froelich, architect), in center with units dating from early 1950s to either side, and the Broadway department store (1954–1955, Welton Becket & Associates, architects), on left. Photo "Dick" Whittington, 1956. (Whittington Collection, Department of Special Collections, University of Southern California.)

169
Panorama City Shopping Center, general view showing the Broadway and other stores in the 1954–1955 addition. Photo "Dick" Whittington, 1956. (Whittington Collection, Department of Special Collections, University of Southern California.)

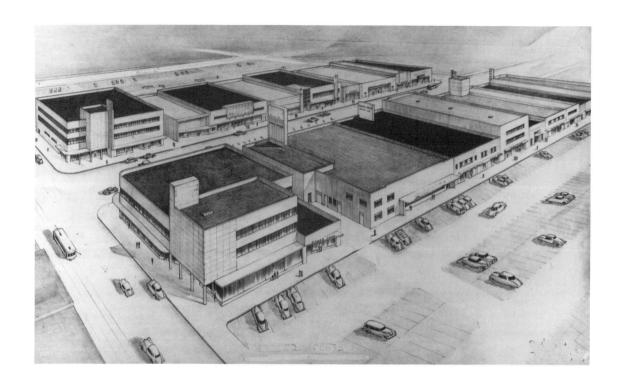

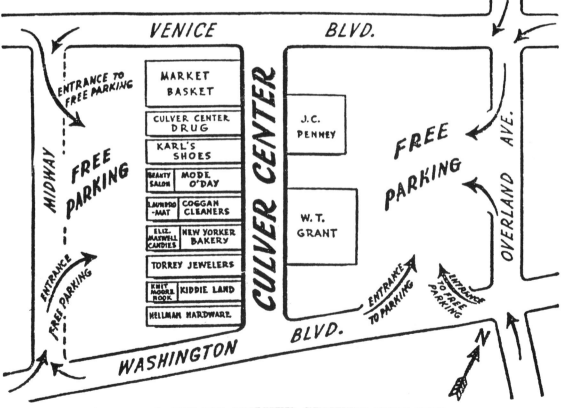

ALL ROADS LEAD TO CULVER CENTER AND VALUES!

self became prevalent, even a major complex could be unassuming, indeed uneventful, in nature. Besides large signs and a very large parking lot, the primary thing that signified a regional center's importance as a magnet of trade was the great unadorned bulk of the department store. Panorama City could not have been more different in its lack of memorable presence from the Miracle Mile, which in functional terms was somewhat equivalent.

Probably the single most important factor in this shift was the emerging belief among retailers and real estate developers that an embellished facade had little to do with sales. The brands of merchandise, pricing, the reputation of the store (especially for major chains), accessibility of the site, and adequate free parking were all now considered of greater importance to simulating trade. Furthermore, with much of the target audience now lower middle and prosperous working class, imagery associated with an elite residential enclave or an equally posh metropolitan center seemed not only superfluous but inhibiting. The atmosphere cultivated instead was more egalitarian—relaxed, convenient, but also practical and no-nonsense. The investment in appearances was concentrated inside, on product displays, fixtures, and lighting in particular.[64] At the same time, the cost of a building's infrastructure, which now always included air conditioning, was rising in proportion to that of its structural and surface components. Wartime technologies generated a plethora of new building materials, many of which could be used as relatively inexpensive veneers.[65] The minimalist aesthetic espoused by young architects, which dominated design practice in the United States by the early 1950s, lent artistic legitimacy to a shift propelled by economic considerations.

The new attitude toward store exteriors was the key to a change in thinking about how those buildings could be oriented. If exterior image no longer played a prominent advertising role, there was little justification on those grounds for keeping the front close to the street. The most compelling argument had been window displays, but the Crenshaw Center and other projects of the immediate postwar years demonstrated how little streetside pedestrian traffic was generated in new outlying areas. Furthermore, two nationally acclaimed projects with alternative configurations had recently been built in southern California, both for lone-wolf department stores by two of the industry's pacesetters in their respective areas: Sears and Bullock's.

Just as Sears had pioneered in the use of off-street parking for large commercial outlets during the 1920s, so it played a seminal role in the realignment of stores away from the street. This step was initially taken due to the very particular circumstances of a new Los Angeles unit built in 1938–1939, but the design approach of the scheme had a profound effect on Sears's subsequent work and on stores generally. The site was chosen because it fronted two major arteries (Pico and Venice boulevards), had access to a third (West Boulevard), and lay adjacent to a streetcar-bus transfer terminal of the Los Angeles Municipal Railway. Yet the property also possessed little street frontage for a big store, stood away from prime

corner lots, and was both eccentric in shape and irregular in topography. The land had never before been considered a good place for a retail outlet of consequence.

In response to these constraints, an ingenious solution was developed allowing a sizable building (202,000 square feet) containing only two stories and a basement as well as outdoor space for over 700 cars on the premises (figure 172).[66] To achieve this plan, the facility was built into the sloping terrain, occupying what would normally have been viewed as the least desirable part of the property. The configuration allowed much of the remaining flat land to be used as parking space for 455 cars. The arrangement also enabled ready access to the roof, which was designed as an additional parking area for 275 cars—one of the first such arrangements to be realized in the United States. Unusually large, two-tiered display windows ran across the Pico Boulevard elevation, but the building did not possess a clear front. Instead, the mass was treated as a piece of abstract sculpture, its forms echoing the variations of the site, its sole embellishment emanating from carefully composed elements serving utilitarian purposes (figures 173, 174). The longest and arguably the most important side faced the car lot, but probably the most memorable experience lay in driving onto the roof deck, being directed to a parking space from a public address system in a control booth, thence descending by escalator to the sales floors inside.[67] Within this experiential schema, the boulevard was reduced to a minor role.

The unorthodoxy of the design stemmed in large part from the process employed to create it. The Pico Boulevard store was the company's first major project not prepared by the architectural office of George Nimmons. Sears turned in-house to its Store Planning and Display Department, which was established in 1932 and was by now assuming a decisive role in designing facilities. Among the department's most significant innovations was eliminating exterior windows above the ground floor, a concept first implemented at its Englewood store (1934) on Chicago's south side. Although highly controversial at that time, the step proved its worth by improving methods of illumination and display as well as the efficiency of mechanical systems. Few other companies followed Sears's example during the 1930s, but the "windowless" building became a hallmark of department store design after the war.[68]

The elimination of most windows affected the approach to exterior treatment and orientation of the Pico Boulevard store. For the first time, Sears gave its department the chance to plan all aspects of a scheme from the start. The team in charge—John Raben, a specialist in store layout who developed the design concept, and John Stokes Redden, recently appointed Sears's chief architect—claimed that little attention was paid to the exterior per se; the effectiveness of the layout for merchandising overrode other considerations. As a result, "the focusing of all efforts on merchandise and none on the building would seem to sacrifice many a possibility, but such a disappearance of 'architecture,' or rather its shifting to plain performance, is a sign of maturity in retailing."[69] While discounting the traditionally decorous role of architecture, the scheme was seen by many practitioners as achieving precisely those objectives of avant-garde modernism whereby basic functional requirements served as the basis for expression. The *Architectural Forum*'s editor offered nothing but praise for

172
Sears, Roebuck & Company store, 4550 W. Pico Boulevard, Los Angeles, 1938–1939, John Stokes Redden, architect, John Gerard Raben, designer; altered. Aerial view. Photo "Dick" Whittington, 1940. (Whittington Collection, Department of Special Collections, University of Southern California.)

173
Sears Pico Boulevard store, north elevation. Photo "Dick" Whittington, 1939. (Whittington Collection, Department of Special Collections, University of Southern California.)

the solution, emphasizing that it represented maturity in design no less than in retailing. Architects' handbooks on store planning published after the war not only presented the solution as a benchmark but advocated much the same design process as that employed by the Sears team.[70]

Attention was also showered on Bullock's "store of the future" in Pasadena (1945–1947), which likewise seemed to shed all vestiges of traditional design (figure 175).[71] Described as looking more like a country club than a commercial outlet, the emporium lay in a residential area some blocks from downtown—a site company executives believed advantageous given the success of their Wilshire Boulevard store. Like the latter, the building had a conspicuous presence from the street, but both topography and landscaping separated the building from the sidewalk; the pedestrian entrance appeared incidental. Only when approached from the larger of the two parking lots did the main entry path become clear. The directness with which this arrangement was expressed elicited admiration no less than did the elegance of the store's treatment inside and out. Both the Bullock's and Sears stores were bold, singular statements—low-slung in mass, plastic in form—quite unlike the boxy piles that would come to characterize department stores in regional shopping centers by the mid-1950s. Yet the two projects demonstrated how the type need not have the traditional streetfront orientation.[72] Sears underscored the practical attributes of such thinking; Bullock's made it fashionable.

The specifics of site configuration for a lone-wolf store, of course, could not be applied to a large retail complex. Thus there remained the issue of how to organize the regional shopping center's plan so that motorists did not feel as if they were entering from the rear, and how to maximize the convenience of their movement from street to store in both physical and perceptual terms. One basic solution lay in reversing the customary order, placing the car lot in front of the buildings. This fore-

court configuration was used on a much smaller scale for many drive-in markets, popular in the region during the late 1920s. The drive-in's example inspired the use of the forecourt in some neighborhood shopping centers elsewhere during the 1930s, but this arrangement was rejected in southern California for supermarkets and shopping centers alike for a number of years.[73] Nevertheless, the forecourt eventually proved its worth as the best way to avoid the problems encountered at the Broadway-Crenshaw and Westchester centers. The initial step was taken at Valley Plaza, which, like its rival Panorama City, was planned in the late 1940s as the "downtown" for the San Fernando Valley.

174
Sears Pico Boulevard store, view from southwest. Photo author, 1986.

175
Bullock's-Pasadena department store, 401 S. Lake Avenue, Pasadena, 1945–1947, Wurdeman & Becket, architects. Street elevation. Photo author, 1986.

VALLEY PLAZA

Valley Plaza was created by Bob Symonds, a veteran of area real estate ventures since the late 1920s. Most of his experience was in selling residential lots, but Symonds had undertaken the development of a neighborhood retail center at one of his tracts, Valley Village in North Hollywood, in the late 1930s. During the war he embarked on studies for a much larger, integrated commercial development, inspired at least in part by the Country Club Plaza, which he admired for its business structure and its generous accommodation of automobiles.[74] Symonds purchased a fifty-acre tract at the intersection of Laurel Canyon and Victory boulevards, lying about an equal distance from Burbank, North Hollywood, and Van Nuys, then the three largest population centers in the valley (figure 176). The scale of the

enterprise was based not only on projected growth nearby but on that of a much larger territory. Time, not distance, was the key factor in delineating the target area.

Symonds predicated his approach on the regional plan for high-speed, limited-access freeways, which was slated for implementation after the war. The property lay adjacent to one of these routes (the Hollywood Freeway) and near two others (Ventura and Golden State freeways). Symonds was probably the first developer in southern California and one of the first in the country to recognize the significance of the freeway in making a retail complex convenient to large numbers of motorists and to move decisively in securing a strategic point along its path, well before construction, when a sizable piece of land could be obtained at relatively low cost (figure 177). Until the 1950s, most southern California developers continued to rely on boulevards as the matrix for locating large-scale commercial projects, while retailers harbored hopes that the freeways would primarily enhance patronage of downtown stores.[75]

Symonds proved no more bound by convention in the layout of his shopping center. He later claimed that around thirty designs were studied before the scheme was finalized in 1949, a process that consumed some four to five years. Several different approaches were taken, reflecting substantial changes in thought and the major shifts then occurring in the design of large shopping centers. The idea of placing the cars up front came relatively late in the sequence. One of the early proposals for Valley Plaza, probably prepared in 1945 or 1946, owed the clearest debt to J. C. Nichols in having a series of small blocks, wide interior streets, and cen-

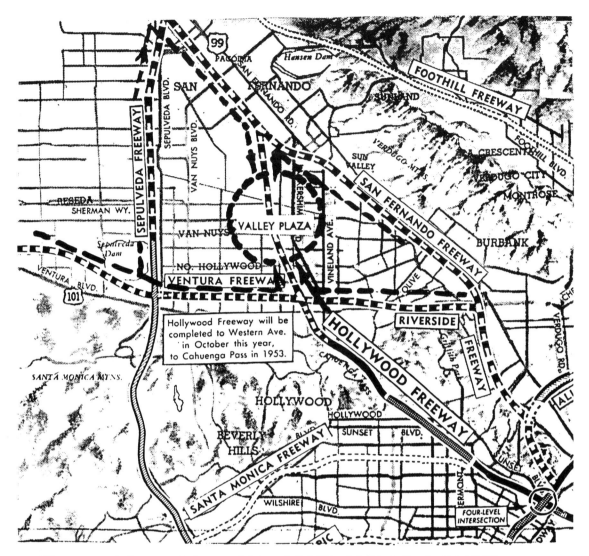

FOUR FREEWAYS TO SERVE VALLEY PLAZA

trally placed parking areas—all to facilitate vehicular movement (figure 178). Both the size and configuration of the lots precluded having large anchor stores. The ensemble may have been conceived like the Country Club Plaza in having retail outlets of a more traditional size—a center for specialty goods more than for mass merchandising. The whole concept changed substantially by the latter months of 1947 with a master plan developed by the Austin Company (figure 179). Now called the "central business district" for the San Fernando Valley, its organization was more akin to that of an existing downtown, with a crossroads as a focal point, updated by placing car lots on block interiors and at the periphery. Key sites were allocated to anchor stores, including Sears, Roebuck, which Symonds was courting.

Within a year, however, the arrangement was transformed again. Prepared by Stiles Clements, the new scheme called for a more compact configuration of stores interspersed by parking areas (figure 180). Cross

176
Valley Plaza, Laurel Canyon and Victory boulevards, Los Angeles, begun 1949. Photomontage of site plan and aerial view looking west, showing major routes and communities, ca. 1949. (Courtesy Sears Merchandise Group.)

177
Valley Plaza, diagrammatic map, showing relationship to existing and proposed freeways, ca. 1950. (Courtesy Bill Symonds.)

streets were narrowed, functioning more as access roads to maximize continuity in what had become two expansive blocks flanking Victory Boulevard. The biggest difference, however, was the 156-foot setback of all stores from Laurel Canyon Boulevard, accommodating 878 cars, nearly half the total. Only a corner extension of the huge Sears store retained its streetfront ties. Soon thereafter, this residual arm was eliminated from the plans, but Symonds had to forfeit the front lots on the southern block because owners of the corner parcels at Laurel Canyon and Victory refused to sell (figure 181). At the same time, the project gained from the emer-

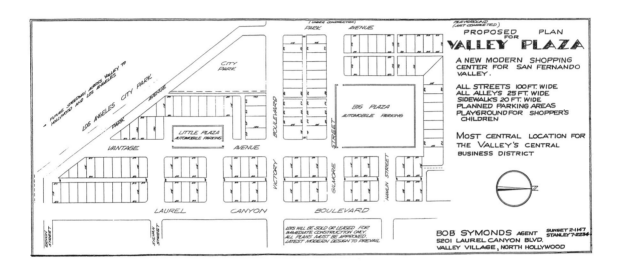

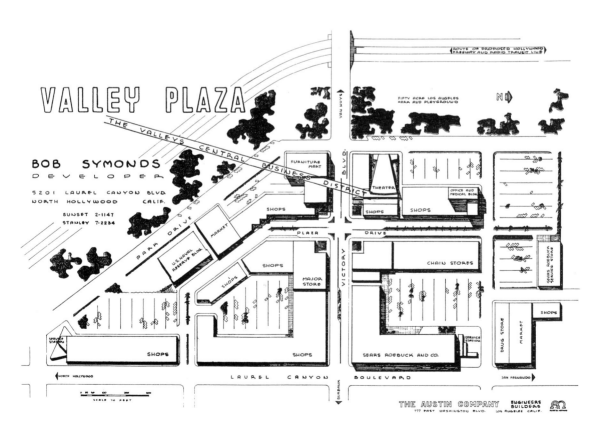

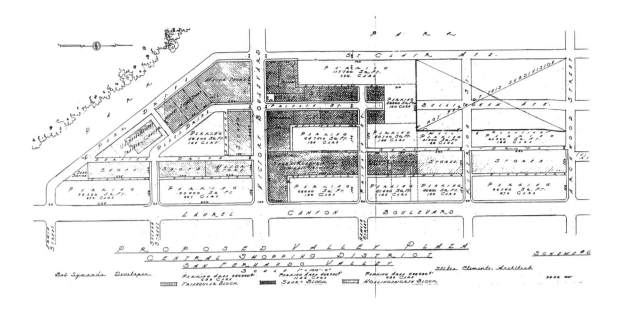

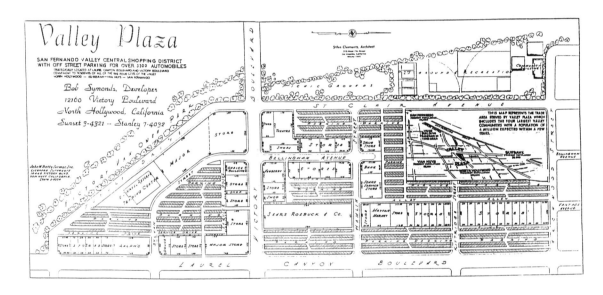

gence of a tangent retail center, developed by W. I. Hollingsworth, extending a block and a half to the north. Hollingsworth refused to cooperate with Symonds on tenancy and other business matters, but did honor the setback (now at 172 feet) and other physical aspects of the plan so that the ensemble would appear to be one.[76] This unplanned addition not only made more stores available to shoppers, it greatly enlarged the perceived size of the complex from its major north-south approaches and brought the car lot capacity to 3,300 (figure 182).

Several factors may have prompted the shift from rear to front parking. Symonds could have been influenced by recent plans for several community-sized shopping centers elsewhere, which he illustrated in a portfolio used to interest retailers in the project.[77] Sears's concerns were perhaps the decisive ones, however. Not only did the L-shaped form of the building depicted in earlier schemes impede both the internal display

178
Valley Plaza, preliminary site plan, ca. 1945–1946. (Courtesy Bill Symonds.)

179
Valley Plaza, preliminary site plan, ca. 1947, Austin Company, architects. (Courtesy Bill Symonds.)

180
Valley Plaza, preliminary site plan, 1948, Stiles Clements, architect. (Courtesy Bill Symonds.)

181
Valley Plaza, site plan, 1949, Stiles Clements, architect. (Courtesy Bill Symonds.)

of goods and customer movement that Sears or any other large-scale retailer demanded by this point, but the car lot was too small. Sears stores
had always had large parking areas of their own. Here, the lot would also
be used by patrons of the other stores. If Sears's building stretched the entire length of a front lot, by contrast, the space would remain essentially
its own. Sears may also have requested that Symonds hire Clements to
prepare the master plan since he had just designed the company's two
newest southern California stores and was well familiar with its retailing
requirements.[78]

The degree to which particular circumstances affected the use of
a large front lot at Valley Plaza was probably great, since scant precedent
existed at a comparable scale. Similar undertakings were all new; many
were under construction or in the planning stage, and thus there was no
way to measure their performance. While the forecourt was now a common feature of neighborhood shopping centers, no consensus existed for
the layout of bigger complexes.[79] The Urban Land Institute's Community
Builder's Council, comprised of real estate developers seasoned in shopping center design, stressed that an expansive front parking lot placed
buildings too far from the street and gave an unattractive impression of the
whole complex. They preferred dividing the car lot between the front and
rear of stores. Much the same view was expressed by the authors of the
most detailed study of shopping center design published before the mid-
1950s. Within a few years, attitudes would change and front lots become
the overwhelming favorite for centers of all sizes not oriented around a pedestrian mall. Merchants found it advantageous always to remain in sight
to patrons and thus not have them pass from view to a rear lot.[80] Appearance no longer seemed to matter as much as consumer convenience and direct visual ties with stores, regardless of how far back from the street they
stood. While the development of large centers was still at an early stage,
Valley Plaza helped set an important precedent.[81]

Valley Plaza was an experiment for Sears also. Never before had the company functioned as the principal retailer in the development of a shopping center from its inception. Sears had almost always located its new "A" stores away from concentrated business areas; the Westwood Village unit (1936) constituted a rare prewar exception. But the success of large shopping centers caused Sears to rethink its policies in order to stay competitive with major downtown department store companies. As early as 1946, Sears unveiled plans for a big unit at the Country Club Plaza, and more or less concurrently with the southern California project it decided to build at Cameron Village, a new "downtown" on the outskirts of Raleigh, North Carolina.[82] At Valley Plaza Sears also broke from its usual practice in setting the store back a significant distance from the street. The Compton and Inglewood units (both 1947) had the normative emphasis on frontality, with massive facades set at the property line (figure 183).[83] The considerably larger (180,000 square feet) Valley Plaza store, also designed by Clements, combined facets of his work just completed for the company with those of the Pico outlet. His scheme possessed a clear front but one more neutral in character, appearing somewhat like an immense billboard, large enough to catch the eye of the passing motorist but also serving as a backdrop to the rows of automobiles that separated it from the street (figure 184).[84]

Symonds was the first southern California real estate developer to attempt what the Broadway had achieved at the Crenshaw district; that is, to create from the outset a fully integrated regional shopping center, with a major department store as its anchor unit. Yet he possessed neither the capital nor the financial leverage enjoyed by the large corporations engaged in retailing, banking, insurance, and construction that were responsible for the Broadway-Crenshaw, Westchester, and Panorama City projects. Much like A. W. Ross, Symonds had to realize his ambition by

182

Valley Plaza, general view of east face. Photo author, 1992.

183

Sears, Roebuck & Company store, 2100 N. Long Beach Boulevard, Compton, 1947, Stiles Clements, architect; altered. Photo ca. 1947. (Courtesy Sears Merchandise Group.)

persuading others that the scheme was a sound investment. Most of the acreage reserved for buildings thus was sold to outside parties for development. At the same time, work had to conform to Clements's master plan. Symonds not only selected the businesses but retained control over building exteriors and the parking lots. To avoid the problems encountered at Westchester, all car lots, save the one fronting Sears, were held by management subsidiaries, which granted easements to businesses for use of the space.[85]

Once Sears agreed to build at Valley Plaza, other stores quickly followed. From the start, Symonds pursued a mix that entailed numerous chain companies in both convenience and specialty lines as well as independently run establishments, so that customers could have at least three stores in which to compare any type of merchandise. The first emporia opened in 1951; over fifty businesses were operating by mid-decade.[86] Symonds also planned for two other key features in the complex—a large concentration of professional offices and a second major department store—neither of which he got (figure 185). The multistory office buildings were probably dropped from the agenda as more was learned about how their parking needs significantly imposed upon space for shoppers' cars—a problem that had long existed, but was just being recognized, downtown. Only one small office tower, more a symbol than a major facility of its kind, was constructed.[87]

On the other hand, Symonds pursued a second department store vigorously, perhaps spurred by the success of the Crenshaw Center. Downtown emporia remained uncooperative with one another in this regard, but because Sears was not considered a direct competitor, the May Company agreed to locate at Valley Plaza, abandoning its long-held plans for a Hollywood store. Unanticipated complications over an exchange of public land for additional parking scuttled the new initiative, however. May next studied a site for a lone-wolf store further west on Van Nuys Boulevard.

184

Sears, Roebuck & Company store, Valley Plaza, 1949–1951, Stiles Clements, architect. Photo author, 1992.

185

Valley Plaza, aerial perspective as envisioned in 1949 master plan, Stiles Clements, architect. (Courtesy Bill Symonds.)

But by the end of the Korean War, the proliferation of regional shopping centers nationwide induced a reversal in thinking. The Broadway's plans to build at Panorama City, coupled with Symonds's successful effort to find a large tract close to Valley Plaza, led to May's decision to return. Competing with the nearby Broadway branch also may have led to an increase in the store's size to 420,000 square feet—the largest west of the Mississippi, according to its owners (figure 186). Located opposite the southern tip of Valley Plaza and occupying a twenty-six-acre tract with a 3,500-car capacity, the emporium greatly boosted the shopping center's draw. May was no less a beneficiary of the relationship and let Symonds promote his complex as if its store were an integral part.[88] Still, the arrangement all but precluded walking from one part of the ensemble to the other.

The May Company's store's location was symptomatic of problems inherent in Valley Plaza's own layout. To realize his dream, Symonds had to compromise repeatedly. There were drawbacks in adapting to a site originally intended for a different kind of retail development. A number of stores faced Victory Boulevard, which bifurcated the ensemble, even though Symonds insisted shoppers need only park their cars once to have easy access to all businesses. The interior lot south of Victory was too big to bring coherence to the buildings around it. From the vestigial side streets, Valley Plaza looked not so much like an integrated center as a town center (figure 187). The array of visually unrelated parts did little to foster perambulation. Nevertheless, Valley Plaza ranked among the largest and most heavily patronized shopping centers in the metropolitan area after only a few years of operation. Perhaps even more than the Crenshaw

Center, it had a strong impact on normative practices locally during the 1950s.

Well before Valley Plaza opened, its influence could be seen at a community-sized shopping center, Barnsdall Square, the master plan of which was completed by October 1950 (figure 188).[89] Stiles Clements may have been hired for the project because of his work for Symonds, and he clearly sought to translate lessons learned at Valley Plaza to these more modest circumstances. The site, on Vermont Avenue between Sunset and Hollywood boulevards, was an unusually large one for an area that had experienced most of its development before the war. This acreage became available due to the parceling of Olive Hill, the remarkable estate designed by Frank Lloyd Wright in 1919–1921 for Aline Barnsdall. While the location was considered desirable, its topography was not conducive to the standard streetfront layout, for a rear parking area, sandwiched between the buildings and the steep sloping terrain behind them, would seem narrow and confining.[90] A front lot extending 160 feet back from the property line—almost as much as at Valley Plaza—made the center more conspicuous, at once distinguishing it from the older streetfront buildings nearby while clearly revealing the extent of off-street parking space in a part of the city where such facilities had always been rare. The big front lot thus served as a visual means of attracting trade, not just as a utilitarian convenience.

Once the barrier imposed by conventional thinking was broken and retailers no longer conceived of a shopping center in terms of streetfront stores, the shift to large front car lots was rapid. Valley Plaza stood as an anomaly in the metropolitan area when its first units opened in 1951. Within three years, dozens of large centers that gave primary space to parking were in the course of realization.[91] Both the rapidity and the extent of this change suggest that a number of factors contributed to the process, cost no doubt among them. The dual fronts of the Crenshaw Center were expensive, not just in terms of exterior treatment but also in the allocation of interior space to public circulation end to end. That layout further posed problems for delivery access and storage of gods at ground level. A rear delivery way was a much cheaper and more effective utilization of space.

By the mid-1950s, many retailers and developers also realized that while streetfront stores, even in big complexes such as the Crenshaw Center, were not generating much pedestrian traffic, customers were inclined to circulate on foot along the front facing the car lot, where canopies could extend over the sidewalk, as long as the arrangement of stores encouraged perambulation. The size of a complex such as Barnsdall Square, which was now considered quite small, was nevertheless so much bigger than the neighborhood centers of the 1930s that the relationship between the motorist and the building was effectively altered. For many shoppers, the sequence was no longer one of merely pulling up to the front of a store and entering, but rather of leaving the car in the lot and be-

186

Valley Plaza promotional leaflet, showing plan for May Company Valley store, 1954–1955, Albert C. Martin & Associates, architects. (Courtesy Bill Symonds.)

187

Valley Plaza, general view looking south at intersection of Bellingham Avenue and Hamlin Street. Photo author, 1987.

coming a pedestrian again, going on foot to several, perhaps numerous, stores.

The turn away from streetfront centers entailed more than setting the range of stores back from the artery to provide space for cars. Planning began with the car lot to achieve the most effective means of getting customers parked and thence to the stores. At the same time, the greatly increased size of new projects made that process more difficult. By the early 1950s, most parties involved in such work agreed that the tract as a whole, not its arterial front, must provide the point of departure in both site selection and developing the design, and that the arrangement of cars, not of buildings, was the initial issue to resolve. The best building layouts would fail unless the ordering of space to serve them was well planned. Although the large parking areas that resulted tended to look spatially amorphous, they were the product of detailed study, which in turn determined all other aspects of the scheme.[92] Probably no other development contributed as much to this change in approach to the layout of shopping centers in southern California and elsewhere in the country as the regional shopping mall, which, by the early 1950s, was rapidly becoming viewed as the most important new thrust in the creation of major retail centers.

188
Barnsdall Square shopping center, 1535–1615 N. Vermont Avenue, Los Angeles, 1952–1956, 1964, Stiles Clements (and others?), architect; altered. Photo author, 1987.

X

GRASS ON MAIN STREET

Well before postwar shopping center plans such as Valley Plaza progressed beyond the broad conceptual stage, a contrasting approach to retail development was taking shape as part of a broad reform effort in architecture and community planning. The scope of that effort was epitomized by a proposal from George Nelson and Henry Wright, Jr., editors of the *Architectural Forum*. Unveiled in the May 1943 issue, the scheme called for a sweeping revitalization of downtown Syracuse, New York. The most unusual feature of the plan was a pedestrian mall extending eleven blocks through the urban core, replacing Erie Boulevard, the city's principal east-west street and a long-time spine of business activity (figure 189). The mandate for so pronounced a change, its authors asserted, stemmed from the automobile. With the widespread use of cars, "the pedestrian lost his right to do anything but dodge. Shopping developed into a hazardous, nerve-racking duty from which no one might escape." Traffic congestion was identified as a primary factor driving merchants from established business districts. Thus the Syracuse plan was practical, not utopian; decisive change was needed because "downtown merchants are becoming concerned with the loss of trade to new shopping areas where parking is less of a problem. Tax officials and investors are disturbed by the likelihood of further declines in downtown real estate. There is a very real basis for effective cooperation to remedy this situation." In diagrammatic terms, the remedy was simple enough: route through traffic around the core, develop off-street parking areas on the relatively inexpensive land between

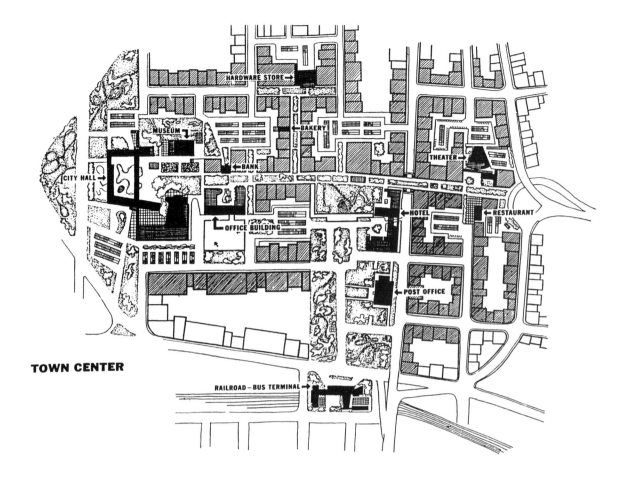

TOWN CENTER

those new arteries and the business center, then restore free pedestrian movement to the center itself. The *Forum*'s clarion call for this endeavor was no less direct: "plant grass on Main Street."[1]

The underlying reasons for the Syracuse plan were the same as those that spawned outlying centers, but it arose out of quite different concerns and priorities. Besides focusing on a traditional business district, the scheme sought to retrieve urban patterns that predated the modern era and to adapt them to rescue the purportedly decaying contemporary city. The approach rejected the notion of the fabulous boulevard as an urban spectacle unfolding from behind the windshield of a moving automobile. Instead, advocates of the mall claimed that the environment should be a more intimate one, oriented to the movement of the pedestrian, just as such settings were before the nineteenth century. The marketplaces of the preindustrial city and the commons of colonial New England villages were held to be more appropriate points of departure than any subsequent urban forms. As a concept, the pedestrian mall thus entailed a basic dichotomy. In its appearance such a place would seem very modern, differing from shopping districts of every kind, irrespective of age. On the other hand, the acknowledged origins of this new work, and the patterns of human interaction it was conceived to foster, were older than the places with which most Americans were familiar.

The *Forum* proposal reflected a widespread view among young architects, planners, and critics that prevailing forms of urban growth required fundamental change. Retail areas were a vital part of the community, but they must be contained and isolated from vehicular traffic while functioning as integral parts of a large infrastructure. The primary objective in such planning was social, not economic—to enhance the lives of residents rather than to realize the maximum profit for individual businesses. In this respect the shopping mall grew out of circumstances paralleling those that gave rise to the shopping center during the late nineteenth and early twentieth centuries. Now, as then, many new proposals, including that for Syracuse, were justified on practical grounds; but theory more than experience in real estate development served as the guiding arm. Most of the architects involved were members of the avant-garde, for whom intellectual and aesthetic as well as social values were more important than the pragmatic ones that propelled business.

More than fifteen years elapsed before a mall was realized in a city center. The first opened in 1957 as part of a master plan for Kalamazoo, Michigan, designed by Los Angeles architect Victor Gruen.[2] In the meantime, the concept was embraced as the optimal way to configure regional shopping centers lying far from the traditional core. But acceptance outside the designer's arena was not easily won. Through most of the 1940s, retail and real estate firms took scant interest in the concept. The schemes initiated prior to that time were for modest-sized complexes and were a product of artificial circumstances: federal housing projects not served by existing retail facilities. It was from these unlikely beginnings that the mall concept began to be applied to commercial development.

The initial phase of shopping mall development, extending from the mid-1930s through the mid-1940s, was a limited but national phenomenon, advanced by architects practicing in New York, Washington, Detroit, Portland, Oregon, and Los Angeles, among other places. With its benign climate, well-established patterns of outdoor activity, and unusually large concentration of avant-garde designers, southern California was a natural place for the concept to flourish. The region boasted one of the most fully developed and widely admired examples of the type built during World War II. Not long after moving his headquarters to Los Angeles, Victor Gruen also began to experiment with shopping mall design, embarking on a course that would eventually bring him renown at home and abroad. Nevertheless, the fundamental departure in thinking manifested by the mall concept required more than favorable circumstances to enter the mainstream of retail development. In southern California, as everywhere else, the initial work was merely a prelude. But the Los Angeles area was unique among metropolises in its unparalleled spectrum of prototypes—retail complexes created during the interwar decades, which in form and tenancy bore little resemblance to the malls of the mid-twentieth century, but which were significant in demonstrating the potential of a plan oriented foremost to the pedestrian and of festival qualities as a merchandising strategy.

189
Proposal for redevelopment of town center, Syracuse, New York, 1943. Site plan. (*Architectural Forum,* May 1943, 71.)

During the early 1920s, when the taste for Mediterranean allusions converged with the fast-growing demand for stores of high caliber situated
outside the urban core, southern California became a proving ground for
retail complexes organized around sheltered outdoor pedestrian space. In
configuration no less than in image these developments were intended to
underscore regional distinctiveness, proclaiming, as it were, the advantages
afforded by a salubrious climate and relaxed, domestic-oriented environment. Probably the first and certainly the most ambitious such project was
devised as part of the master plan for Carthay Center, a 136-acre subdivision south of Wilshire Boulevard and east of Beverly Hills. Designed in
1921–1922, the endeavor was conceived by real estate developer J. Harvey
McCarthy to bring high standards of planning and architecture within
reach of medium-income households. The scheme called for community
facilities, including a church, school, playhouse, and "shopping center."[3]
As in model company towns of the previous decade, these public functions were centrally grouped and given visual prominence, yet were contained so as not to encroach on residential blocks beyond (figures 190,
191). Similarly, too, little differentiation was made between the appearance of commercial and institutional components. The ensemble had a
campuslike quality and bore particular resemblance to the 1916 master
plan of the California Institute of Technology, by Bertram Grosvenor
Goodhue, with whom Carthay Center's architect, Carleton Winslow, Sr.,
was associated.[4]

Among other aspects, Goodhue's campus plan probably served as
the conceptual springboard for the most unusual aspect of Carthay Center,
its extensive use of segregated pedestrian spaces as routes for access to businesses. The spine of the complex consisted of a broad paved mall, while a
network of walkways and patios was woven through the building groups
to either side. Here was a place where shoppers could meander in an envi-

190
Carthay Center shopping district, San
Vincente Boulevard between Foster and
Carillo drives, Los Angeles, preliminary
scheme, 1923, Carleton Winslow, Sr., ar-
chitect. J. Harvey McCarthy Company
advertisement. (*Los Angeles Times,* 19
August 1923, V-6.)

191
Carthay Center, site plan, 1923, Cook &
Hall, landscape architects. (*California
Southland,* November 1923, 19.)

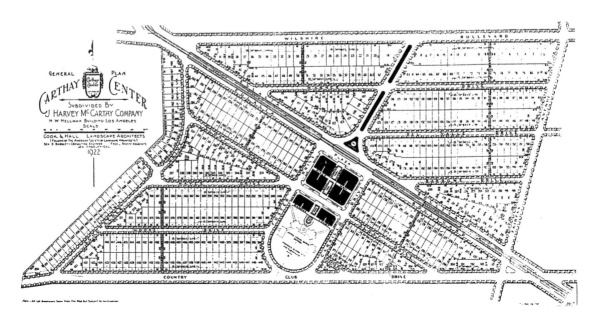

Sidewalks *above the Street* *an Exclusive feature of the*

Mercantile Arcade
"THE WONDER BUILDING OF THE WEST."

HIGH above Spring Street and Broadway and parallel with Fifth and Sixth Streets are wide, spacious sidewalks more than three hundred feet long, lined with beautiful shops in which will be found all kinds of high grade merchandise; beauty parlors, tea rooms, studios, etc.

The second and third floors of the great Mercantile Arcade offer wonderful possibilities for building up a profitable business. They will be thronged with visitors day and night. They will be the "talk of the town."

On both Broadway and Spring Street ends of the Mercantile Arcade will be great twelve story twin office buildings—edifices containing luxurious suites and offices, each an outside room, a model of modern finishing and equipment.

Mercantile Arcade is Los Angeles' newest business artery—the connecting link between the Spring Street financial district and Broadway's shopping center.

A·C·Blumenthal & Co
INCORPORATED
REALTY · INSURANCE · FINANCIAL AGENTS
611 Loew's State Building, Los Angeles
San Francisco Office—105 Montgomery St.

ronment totally divorced from the street—a setting more cloisterlike even than those proposed for Palos Verdes.

McCarthy believed that his shopping center would attract a considerable trade, since the nearest retail activity at that time lay some miles to the east along Western Avenue and scarcely less far removed to the west at the still nascent Beverly Hills Business Triangle. However, piecemeal zoning variances granted along Wilshire Boulevard nearby, including those for the Miracle Mile, scuttled the enterprise.[5] A few, convenience-oriented outlets were built at Carthay Center, but the major element was the playhouse, itself transformed during the preliminary design stage into a movie theater.[6] Had the initial scheme been realized, it might have reshaped regional patterns of retail development. On the other hand, Carthay Center might have remained an anomaly, for nothing on its scale was proposed again. Where Winslow's plan does appear to have had some local influence was in fostering the patio arrangement, which soon became a popular means for configuring enclaves of specialty shops.

Small shops—each containing only a few hundred square feet at the most and purveying a very limited stock, often unusual in nature—had seldom been able to find space in top retail locations of the modern urban core owing to the high rents those locations commanded. Usually such outlets were scattered toward the edge of downtown, frequently on side streets where leading retailers would never think of operating. The rapid expansion of city centers during the late nineteenth and early twentieth centuries meant that these tiny stores were in an ongoing state of flux. Efforts to protect small-scale merchants from ever-escalating land values and to bolster their patronage began in the 1880s by grouping a substantial number of such shops at a central site while organizing them in such a way as to minimize costs. These ends were achieved through a revival of the commercial arcade, a type well known in European cities but not found in the United States save for a handful of examples constructed in the 1820s.[7] The arcade's success depended on connecting two streets heavily traveled by pedestrians more or less at midblock. Retail space could be distributed along the arcade's entire length rather than concentrated at the streetfronts and could also be placed at one or two upper levels, enabling an affordable per-square-foot rent schedule. As long as the urban retail structure remained centralized, demand for such space remained strong. Dozens of arcades were constructed in the United States during the late nineteenth and early twentieth centuries.[8]

Los Angeles boasted one of the nation's largest examples, the Mercantile Arcade (1923–1924), which was strategically placed as "a new thoroughfare" linking the financial district on Spring Street with the shopping district on Broadway, between Fifth and Sixth streets. The complex included two ten-story office blocks rising above "a new Main Street, three stories high" and three hundred feet long (figure 192).[9] Promoters stressed that the galleria afforded welcome respite from the elements as well as from sidewalk crowds; it was destined to become a hub of commercial activity. But such ventures could not stem the swelling exodus of small

Mercantile Arcade, 538–546 S. Broadway, 539–545 S. Spring Street, Los Angeles, 1923–1924, Kenneth MacDonald, Jr., architect; altered. (*Los Angeles Times,* 24 October 1928, I-7.)

stores to less expensive and more conveniently located land removed from the city center. Even as the Mercantile Arcade opened, alternatives were being planned for the same kind of specialty shop, placing consumers out-of-doors in intimate settings that carried no vestige of their urban forebears. Some three decades later, the arcade would provide an important point of departure for the enclosed regional shopping mall.[10] During the interim, it had no distinguishable impact on tendencies to create outside-oriented havens for pedestrians, which were posited as preferable to anything found in the core.

Called shopping courts, shopping streets, and sometimes even shopping arcades, pedestrian-oriented complexes in outlying areas were modest in size and domestic in scale. Few had more than a dozen shops, cafes, and other compatible establishments, all at ground level. Sometimes a second story was included to house offices and studios. Almost all businesses faced internal open spaces—a linear walkway or a more expansive

patio—rather than the public domain. The type seems to have been introduced after the first world war, drawing from the broad historical precedent of courtyards in Latin America and the Mediterranean basin. By 1930, the Los Angeles metropolitan area spawned by far the largest number of shopping courts, although examples could be found in other regions that enjoyed mild climates as well as in cities such as Chicago where conditions were less hospitable.[11] Nevertheless, these complexes were identified foremost with southern California, where they were seen as testaments to the state's Hispanic legacy, fulfilling the contemporary quest for a distinct regional character.

Shopping courts were extolled for economic no less than for associational reasons. The arrangement provided an atmosphere conducive to consumption. The internalized setting could be completely controlled and made to suggest another world—tranquil, private, protected, intimate, close to nature, and even somewhat exotic—that stood in sharp contrast to most commercial landscapes: a place where shopping could be at once leisurely and slightly adventurous. The use of Latin imagery was praised for its links to a regional past, but for many middle-class patrons the experience may have seemed more analogous to sets from the movies, affording a passive sense of adventure marshaled to stimulate purchases (figure 193). A quantifiable advantage of shopping courts was that, like commercial arcades, they could utilize deep and often irregularly shaped parcels of land to maximum benefit for small retail outlets. Far more selling space could be gained by organizing units around a pedestrian way than to the street.[12]

Despite its attributes, the shopping court remained a limited phenomenon because the types of businesses to which it was tailored did not comprise a significant growth area in retailing. Most tenants specialized in unusual, even one-of-a-kind, craft, apparel, or accessory goods. Other occupants purveyed services for which there was never widespread demand or which were by nature small in scale. Out-of-the-ordinary functions were essential to operation, since trade was based on the reputation of individual establishments, not on widely recognized store names, advertising, or a conspicuous streetfront presence. Moreover, the diminutive size of the units ran counter to the trend toward increased dimensions for many types of retail outlets, and the secluded character of these places defied the impulse to design store facades that could capture the motorist's attention. The kinds of tenant who would find the shopping court attractive, in turn, limited the clientele to persons of some means. As a result, realized examples tended to be built near affluent residential areas (Hollywood, Beverly Hills, Pasadena) or in resort communities (Palm Springs, Santa Barbara). Yet the shopping court gained more recognition than its numbers or narrow purpose might suggest. The type not only embodied much that was seen as distinct to southern California, but helped establish the perceptual framework that contributed to the acceptance of the regional mall some two decades later. Perhaps most important, the shopping court's tenant mix and its festive atmosphere would become important features of

193
La Floreira, El Jardin Patio, 455 Main Street, Ventura; Webber, Staunton & Spaulding, architect, 1927. *Pacific Coast Architect,* July 1928, 16.)

many regional malls, balancing the larger-scale operations of chain and
major local stores.[13]

Perhaps most influential in diffusing the idea of an inward-
looking, pedestrian-oriented retail center were three much-celebrated projects, each of which was a departure in some aspects of both its appearance
and its business complexion and each of which became a major destination. The first of these was Olivera Street, which extended one block
from the Plaza, the core of the Spanish colonial settlement, lying just to
the north of downtown in an area that had long remained a center for
Mexican-Americans. By the late 1920s, most of these inhabitants had
moved further afield; storage and industrial facilities were more common
than housing. Such functions were likely to permeate the district in the future since a nearby site seemed the most probable one for a mammoth
union station.[14] The setting was an unlikely one for a retail center.

The creation of that center was propelled largely by sentimental
concerns. In 1928, condemnation of the early nineteenth-century Avila
house, thought to be one of the oldest buildings in the city, led an ardent
and socially well-placed Hispanophile, Christine Sterling, to revive her previously unsuccessful attempts to rejuvenate the Plaza area. For southern
California, she asserted, the dwelling held a historical significance equiva-

lent to that of Mount Vernon for the East. Sterling gained the cooperation of the City Council and enlisted a cadre of prominent citizens, led by *Times* editor Harry Chandler, as directors of a corporation that would restore the house and develop tangent Olivera Street into "an important Latin-American trade and social center." [15]

Opened in 1930, Olivera Street was rechristened El Paseo de Los Angeles, although it became known by the slightly abbreviated name of Olvera Street. The block was closed to vehicular traffic and lined with open-air concessions operated by Mexican-Americans. Sterling's intention was to create the atmosphere of a traditional Hispanic marketplace as well as to provide an outlet for Hispanic artisans and merchants. At a time when popular sentiment for things Spanish ran high but lay almost entirely among the Anglo population, this enterprise was both novel and altruistic in its pursuit of authenticity. At first the treatment was direct and simple, with scattered stalls on brick pavement, framed by buildings little changed for decades (figure 194). Within a few years, however, the setting became more genteel. Street fountains and sculpture were added; plantings grew more numerous; building walls were patched and painted; flags, banners, and other festive paraphernalia proliferated (figure 195). Still, with the profusion of open-air displays and people jamming the long, linear space,

194
Olvera Street, Los Angeles, as remade into pedestrian shopping area, 1929–1930. Photo "Dick" Whittington, ca. 1930. (Whittington Collection, Department of Special Collections, University of Southern California.)

195
Olvera Street. Photo "Dick" Whittington, ca. 1938. (Whittington Collection, Department of Special Collections, University of Southern California.)

Olvera Street seemed the antithesis of the store blocks popularized by Morgan, Walls & Clements, where Spanish imagery was used in a theatrical manner to provide lavish streetfront landmarks (see figure 69).

In reality, Olvera Street was almost as much a contrivance. Most of the saved buildings were part of Anglo development from the late nineteenth century and fronted parallel streets to either side. This new center of trade had functioned as a service alley for much of its existence. The stalls that now lined it bore some resemblance to the temporary booths found in Latin American cities, but one of the most basic street functions, through vehicular movement, was impeded by the plan. As the ambience became increasingly ordered and clean, Olvera Street verged on being a Hollywood interpretation of a street market. Merchants were under the strict control of Sterling's corporation. The crafts, novelty items, food, and entertainment purveyed were oriented toward the Anglo population. Thus, like the contemporary shopping court, Olvera Street was an invention of the twentieth-century city. Residual space was compressed through ephemeral adornment and in the process converted into an oasis of prime space—an outdoor corridor, stuffed with miscellany like a long-forgotten attic, stretched precariously across a long-neglected precinct. The complex was never a true Hispanic center but rather a mecca for the

"Cross-Roads of the World"
in the heart of
Hollywood, California

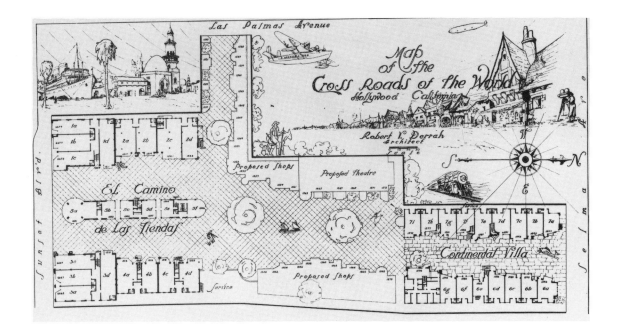

newcomer, a place so different from anything else in the region that even Angelenos could feel like tourists. Within a few years, tiny Olvera Street grew to be so important a southern California attraction that it was used as a symbol of the city itself.[16]

    One of the largest and last of the shopping courts realized during the interwar decades was equally important for the recognition it brought to pedestrian shopping. Called Crossroads of the World, the complex was built in 1936–1937 on Hollywood's Sunset Boulevard several blocks from the business core. Crossroads was intended to be an "outstanding landmark and civic attraction as well as a centralized shopping district" that would draw a markedly larger trade than other shopping courts. The project was conceived by Ella Crawford, who, like Sterling, was unbound by normative modes of retail development. While the general nature of tenancy echoed that of earlier examples—"a wide variety of high class shops, cafes and professional offices, exclusive of drug stores, grocery stores, filling stations and the like"—the appearance was more overtly suggestive of a stage set than most predecessors.[17] Building exteriors were designed as a composite, the parts alluding to the traditional architecture of England, France, the Netherlands, Sweden, Spain, Italy, Algeria, Turkey, Persia, and Mexico as well as of colonial New England. The centerpiece of this mélange was a streamlined pile suggestive of a cruise ship, its "foremast" a beacon to passing motorists (figures 196, 197). The resulting character was far less akin to earlier shopping courts than to the midway of a world's fair, especially the 1933 Century of Progress Exposition at Chicago. There, the Streets of Paris, Belgian Village, Midget Village, Oriental Village, and even a mock Hollywood stage set stood in proximity to one another, visually anchored by a rambunctious Art Deco shaft, the multi-storied Havoline Thermometer.[18] Much like a world's fair, too, the pedestrian space at Crossroads was not secluded and intimate but seemed expansive and tied to the public realm.

196

Crossroads of the World, 6665–6679 Sunset Boulevard, Los Angeles, Robert V. Derrah, architect, 1936–1937. Photo late 1930s. (Security Pacific Historical Photograph Collection, Los Angeles Public Library.)

197

Crossroads of the World, site plan. (*California Arts & Architecture,* January 1937, 24.)

Like a midway, Crossroads exuded a playfulness and exaggeration to a degree unusual even in Hollywood. Yet these qualities were devised for the pragmatic purpose of creating an indelible image in the minds of consumers. About a year after the complex opened, a writer for the real estate community observed:

[Crossroads] can not be confused in the mind of any Los Angeles resident or in the mind of any tourist or city visitor with any other project in the city. . . . It would be practically impossible to mention the place in the city to any person who would not know what you were talking about. It is the type of thing also that elicits plenty of free advertising, and shop and office tenants have the advantage of a constant stream of publicity.[19]

Crawford was as meticulous in selecting tenants as she was in creating the ambience. She successfully courted film stars, whose patronage, in turn, broadened Crossroads's popular appeal. Unlike earlier shopping courts, the wide pedestrian spaces invited people in number. Here the pedestrian-oriented retail center was no longer so exclusive and remote a place; it was more overtly commercial and public, sufficiently well known and admired to fulfill its role as a shopping destination.

Novelty was no less central a factor in the more or less contemporaneous development of another specialty center, the Farmers Market, which transformed the shopping court idea into a new kind of retail establishment. The project was conceived by Roger Dahlhjelm, a veteran of real estate and other business endeavors who had lost most of his assets in the depression. Dahlhjelm sought to provide a service for which there was substantial demand—making fresh produce and meat available to prosperous urban households—but which could be begun in a modest way. When the market opened in 1934, it consisted of just eighteen booths set in an open field, offering an array of goods far from the rural areas and wholesaling districts where they could normally be procured (figure 198). The site was strategically located in the Wilshire corridor between Holly-

wood and Beverly Hills, several blocks north of the Miracle Mile. Lack of capital was used to advantage. With little outlay, a bazaar-like atmosphere was cultivated to enhance the experience so that shopping for food would seem more akin to a leisure than a routine pursuit. Fueled by an aggressive advertising campaign, the Farmers Market began to attract an affluent trade of movie stars and others who sought the unusual goods sold there and took pleasure in the novel ambience.[20]

A swelling trade led to a sequence of enlargements, so that by 1941 eighty-five merchants were installed on the premises in a permanent structure. The range of food also was expanded to encompass many more hard-to-find items. One outlet specialized in game birds, another in corn meal and wheat flours, a third in tropical fruits. Early on, shoppers started to consume some of the foods they purchased while going from booth to booth; soon, a number of vendors began catering to them. The first of several restaurants followed not long thereafter. A host of other outlets was added as well, selling everything from pet supplies to Mexican pottery. There was a post office, telegraph office, laundry call station, and a tourist information bureau. In 1941 work began on the Gilmore Village Stores, a complex of sixty small specialty shops that lay adjacent to the market.[21] While undertaken by another business concern, the store group was planned to function as part of the ensemble, greatly increasing the range of merchandise available, drawing from and at the same time bolstering

198

Farmers Market, 633 Third Street and 140–166 S. Fairfax Avenue, Los Angeles, begun 1934. Early view, showing temporary stalls. Photo ca. 1934. (Security Pacific Historical Photograph Collection, Los Angeles Public Library.)

199

Farmers Market, as realized in permanent form, begun ca. 1935–1936, John Deleena and Edward Barber, designers. Photo "Dick" Whittington, 1941. (Whittington Collection, Department of Special Collections, University of Southern California.)

the Farmers Market as a trade magnet. The cumulative result was a retail center that combined aspects of a conventional farmers' market, a great downtown food emporium, a neighborhood shopping district, and an exclusive shopping court.

Despite its size, the scale of the Farmers Market was kept small, the atmosphere informal, with concessions remaining open-air, set in five linear ranges. Walkways were narrow, creating an intimate, festive atmosphere, much like that of Olvera Street (figure 199). Similarly, too, the design sought associations with the region's past to establish its identity. Here nineteenth-century western agrarian buildings provided the basis for a casual imagery that seemed the product of no conscious design, much as with many of the "ranch" houses well-to-do Angelenos were then building as country retreats and year-round domiciles (figure 200).[22] The configuration was equally unorthodox. The complex was neither oriented to nor conspicuous from the street, in striking contrast to siting practices of most stores in the region. Even the big "ranch" markets of the late 1930s, operated by major retailers but located along arteries in peripheral sections of the metropolitan area and built in the guise of greatly enlarged roadside stands, emphasized frontality with long curbside facades.[23]

The Farmers Market stood as an island amid a car lot more than twice its size, suggesting a circus or some other fete staged in an open field, with the surrounding acreage consumed by parked cars for the occa-

sion (figure 201). Olvera Street and other shopping courts evoked the pre-industrial city; at the Farmers Market this precedent was absorbed into a larger setting where rural associations predominated. But while both the layout and the character reinforced allusions to the countryside, only in a metropolis could one find such an array of specialized products. The basic idea of internalized pedestrian traffic surrounded by circumferential parking was a complete departure from convention. Although more an outgrowth of the complex's ad hoc beginnings than the product of a conscious plan, the arrangement would become an important characteristic of the regional shopping mall. While the regional mall did not embrace rustic allusions, it did present an atmosphere similarly emphatic in breaking from standard commerical settings.

For the present, the efficacy of Dahlhjelm's enterprise was underscored by the creation of several similar complexes. The Producers Public Market (1938) in the Southwest district emphasized product quality but also low prices, utilizing converted warehouses next to a railroad spur to generate a festival atmosphere, here calculated to attract the moderate-income families that predominated in that area. On the other hand, the Marketplace (1941) and the Town and Country Market (1941–1942) were targeted toward a more affluent clientele and included a number of non-food stores from the start. Situated just across the street from the Farmers Market, the Town and Country was particularly elaborate. Portrayed as a "small 'town' of 100 smart shops," the complex was more regular in plan and more pretentious in appearance than its progenitor (figure 202).[24] The Town and Country also gave greater emphasis to its function as a place of entertainment. Twenty-six restaurants featuring a wide choice of menus were housed within the compound, which was promoted as an ideal

200

Farmers Market, general view from Fairfax Avenue. Photo "Dick" Whittington, 1946. (Whittington Collection, Department of Special Collections, University of Southern California.)

201

Farmers Market, aerial view. Photo "Dick" Whittington, 1938. (Whittington Collection, Department of Special Collections, University of Southern California.)

place for families to spend a weekend afternoon and to bring guests from out of town.

Variations on the Farmers Market idea continued to be built in the region and elsewhere in the state through the end of the decade. By that time, the type had gained widespread recognition among Californians and food retailers nationwide.[25] Yet the specialized nature of such places, which necessitated a novel ambience and was mostly targeted to persons of some means, limited their applicability in the retail sphere. Perhaps the greatest impact the type had on broader patterns was in demonstrating that a sizable inward-looking establishment could attract a commensurate trade. It did not have to abut, or be particularly conspicuous from, the street. A lot filled with cars could catch the eye as much as a building and perhaps be an even better adverstisement. The relation of architecture to cars did not yield strong visual results, however. The character of these new complexes seemed to exist in spite of the automobile; the attractions lay in a secluded realm beyond.

Divorcing the shoppers from both the street and the parking lot proved quite another matter for outlets that were less specialized or exclusive in nature. Beyond the stillborn proposal for Carthay Center, only two others for complexes structured to meet routine shopping needs incorporated a mall as a central feature prior to World War II. Only one of these was realized. That shopping center was at Greenbelt, the prototypical Resettlement Administration town near Washington, D.C.[26]

EXPERIMENTS

The Greenbelt center epitomized what housing reformers considered an essential feature of community development, just as a previous generation

of real estate developers had advocated a retail complex for their guaranteed neighborhoods. The shared aim was to provide basic goods and services for residents in a contained area. Equally important, and unlike private-sector counterparts save at model company towns, the Greenbelt complex was an integral part of the community center, which included the school, library, swimming pool, youth hall, and municipal offices. The underlying objective differed, too, for this ensemble was to be socially regenerative, restoring a sense of civic spirit and intercourse believed to be absent in the modern city. Thus the center's foremost purpose was to provide a setting for residents to congregate. Few existing places were conducive to this aim, Greenbelt's planners believed, because of motor vehicle congestion. Preindustrial settlement patterns were believed more suited to human interaction; the mall was a means of adapting these patterns to contemporary needs. Clarence Stein, who served as an advisor to Greenbelt's planning, emphasized that the shopping center's pedestrian way was a "modern market square."[27]

Greenbelt was, of course, planned for the motorist. Those responsible for its design understood the central role of the car in population dispersal. They realized, too, that many residents would rely on their automobiles for shopping trips. Generous provision was made for off-street parking, and the shopping center was referred to as a "drive-in" facility. Yet the entire community, including its commercial core, was laid out on the assumption that people should walk more than drive. As a result, the two car lots serving the retail center were given peripheral sites at the rear (figure 203). Equally important, these lots were divorced from the

202
Town and Country Market, 350 S. Fairfax Avenue, Los Angeles, 1941–1942, Rowland H. Crawford, architect; demolished 1960. Photo Al Green & Associates, ca. 1946. (Los Angeles County Museum of Natural History.)

203
Greenbelt Shopping Center, Crescent Road, Greenbelt, Maryland, 1936–1937, Douglas D. Ellington and R. J. Wadsworth, architects, Hale Walker, planner. Preliminary site plan showing cross-axial mall (H) and arrangement of buildings (D, G) modified in execution as well as school (N) and firehouse/garage (J). (*Architectural Record*, September 1936, 197.)

mall that served as the focus; the car could not be ignored, but neither
should it be celebrated, in this schema. Stein later wrote that one of the design's most significant accomplishments was the "complete segregation" of
pedestrians from automobiles. Revealing an idealized view of the distant
past shared by many reformers of the period, he added that "even more
than in the characteristic European medieval marketplaces, there is a definite exclusion of active flow of traffic from the area of peaceful shopping." [28] Allusions to a preindustrial heritage in southern California
shopping courts were used primarily as scenographic devices for simple
commercial ends. Stein's interest in that past, on the other hand, was
spurred by a concern for human interaction.

   The Greenbelt shopping center also embodied the primacy of
open space as a means of improving community life. Providing a maximum amount of light, air, and room for movement was deemed essential
not just to stimulate outdoor recreation, socializing, and civic endeavors,
but to foster ties between rural and town inhabitants. Greenbelt would
create a local market for farm products raised nearby and serve as a community center for farmers, just as it allowed residents to partake of the
pleasures of the countryside. The model for this relationship was, once
again, based on a cleansed perspective of the past. Greenbelt was to function much like an idealized view of a traditional New England town center. In physical terms, the shopping complex and other community
buildings stood as islands, united by the open space that was to function as
a latter-day common. This model may well have been one reason why the
mall was designed as if to suggest a place developed before the buildings
on either side. The shopping center was centrally located, yet it stood at
the edge of the populated area (figure 204). The mall afforded a visual link
between the space amid the dwelling units and a more open area that was
to serve as a park, leading to the greenbelt beyond.

No clear evidence has been found documenting who introduced the mall in the Greenbelt design; however, Stein was the most likely figure. Greenbelt's planner was Hale Walker, who had worked for architect Jacques Gréber in France, then John Nolen in Boston before joining the Maryland State Planning Commission in 1930. One of the town's two architects, Douglas Ellington, had enjoyed a substantial practice in Asheville, North Carolina, before the depression. The other, Reginald Wadsworth, had worked for some of Philadelphia's leading designers of residences. In none of these cases does the record reveal much defiance of convention.[29] On the other hand, Stein had been a maverick for over a decade. As a consultant to the Resettlement Administration he had a formative influence on the Greenbelt towns program and a significant impact upon the design of Greenbelt itself, which was the least orthodox of the three realized communities.[30] Stein composed the guidelines for shopping center development in the greenbelt towns, and was highly respected among housing reformers as the authority on the subject. After Greenbelt, he was an even more vigorous champion of the mall, arguing that it should be a key component of a shopping center's plan. During the late 1940s, he worked on the design of several such complexes, most of them in southern California.[31]

The Greenbelt center had no immediate effect on retail development. Even counterparts in the two later greenbelt towns relied on less unusual configurations. Not until the early 1950s, when the mall was emerging as an important component of shopping center design, did the Greenbelt complex get recognition as an important precursor.[32] One reason for its earlier neglect may have been associational. Greenbelt was widely criticized as a government boondoggle, a project more expensive than conditions warranted, and even as a covert instrument of socialism. The shopping center was run as a cooperative enterprise, an aspect that received far more publicity than its plan.[33] Most business interests probably viewed the endeavor as utopian at best and at worst as a threat to the very foundation of their practices.

On the other hand, many young architects and planners alike considered Greenbelt a blueprint for the future. The extent to which the shopping center influenced subsequent thinking is suggested by the Los Angeles County Regional Planning Commission staff's 1941 adaptation, bereft of surrounding green space and regularized for the ubiquitous grid (figure 205). Yet it is doubtful that business interests considered such models more than wishful thinking. The mall concept might never have progressed further were it not for the unusual conditions that shaped the defense housing program during World War II. Much as with the sponsorship of Greenbelt, the pressing needs for shelter among workers at defense plants removed commercial development from its conventional sphere. Wartime housing programs had no social agenda; with few exceptions, projects were of a temporary nature—places that could be quickly built utilizing a minimum of materials required for combat purposes. A number of the architects involved, however, saw the need to create tens of thou-

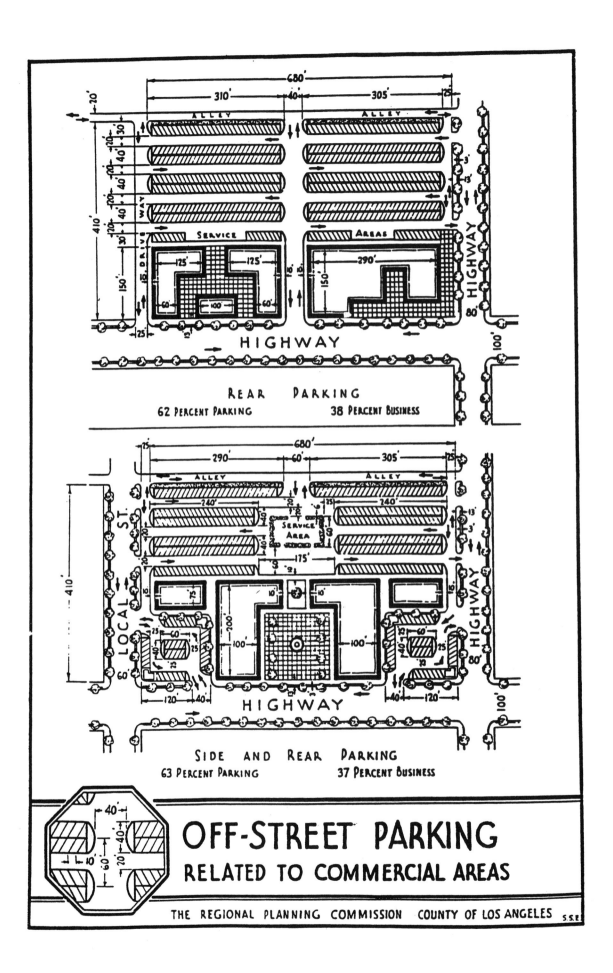

REAR PARKING

62 PERCENT PARKING   38 PERCENT BUSINESS

SIDE AND REAR PARKING

63 PERCENT PARKING   37 PERCENT BUSINESS

OFF-STREET PARKING
RELATED TO COMMERCIAL AREAS

THE REGIONAL PLANNING COMMISSION   COUNTY OF LOS ANGELES   S.S.E.

sands of dwelling units as an unparalleled opportunity to advance the cause of reform in community development. New standards set here could enter the mainstream once peace returned.

Linda Vista, located on the northern edge of San Diego and the first project authorized under the Lanham Defense Housing Act of 1940, became an important point of departure. Designed by the Public Buildings Administration in Washington, with former Los Angeles architect Gilbert Stanley Underwood as the principal in charge, the scheme entailed 3,000 dwelling units for more than 13,000 people, forming "a self-contained community."[34] Linda Vista was developed in great haste, yet unlike most of the wartime housing that followed, it was built for long-term occupancy. The master plan of Greenbelt as well as that of Radburn were clearly important sources of inspiration. Salient features included small clusters of units, many of them on cul-de-sacs, and large blocks that provided abundant open space, kept roads to a minimum, and separated pedestrian from vehicular traffic to a considerable degree. Equally distinctive was the large "commercial and administrative center" designed to address the needs of the community as a whole with two ranges of buildings that opened onto a broad, landscaped mall (figure 206).

The modest shopping center at Greenbelt provided a springboard for the Linda Vista complex only in broad conceptual terms. A counterpart planned in 1936 for the stillborn sister town of Greenbrook, New Jersey, was a more useful prototype in its scale and arrangement (figure 207). Designed by Albert Mayer (Stein's friend and kindred spirit in community

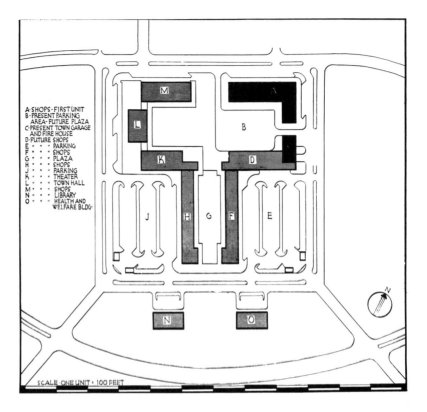

A· SHOPS· FIRST UNIT
B· PRESENT PARKING
      AREA· FUTURE PLAZA·
C· PRESENT TOWN GARAGE
      AND FIRE HOUSE·
D· FUTURE SHOPS
E· "   "   " PARKING
F· "   "   " SHOPS
G· "   "   " PLAZA
H· "   "   " SHOPS
J· "   "   " PARKING
K· "   "   " THEATER
L· "   "   " TOWN HALL
M· "   "   " SHOPS
N· "   "   " LIBRARY
O· "   "   " HEALTH AND
                WELFARE BLDG·

SCALE· ONE UNIT = 100 FEET

planning), Allan Kamstra (Stein's former employee), and Henry Wright
(Stein's former associate), the layout rendered the mall the primary space,
at once inward looking yet easily reached from all directions. The plan
was illustrated in a widely read article by Mayer, which both reiterated the
methods for shopping center development championed by Stein and provided the most detailed analysis then available in print of the approach
used in planning the greenbelt towns. Mayer's piece became an important
reference work for practitioners who sought a new course for community
development.[35]

    The Linda Vista center was more formal in arrangement, embod-
ying Beaux-Arts planning principles of axiality and hierarchy. These attributes are not surprising given the academic proclivities of the Supervising
Architect of the Treasury's office, from which Underwood was appointed
to oversee the project. Yet the importance of the mall, not just as promenade but as a major organizing element of the plan, and the balance attained between pedestrian space and convenient, accessible parking space
bear affinity to the Greenbrook scheme. Having spent most of his career
in Los Angeles, Underwood also was well aware of local precedents for
the arrangement.[36]

    While the housing at Linda Vista was completed in less than a
year, the commercial center remained on paper, a fate that would become
common with such projects. The configuration may have caused real estate developers to shy away, but, irrespective of layout, developers often
considered such ventures too risky once temporary housing became the
norm. Thus by the middle of 1942, the federal government reluctantly

committed itself to sponsor commercial facilities when outside parties could not be secured. Guidelines were prepared by Stein and Samuel Ratensky in June 1942 for the newly formed Federal Public Housing Authority, which had charge of all such federally funded projects aside from those erected by the armed services. An original provision, that stores "should front on project open spaces, reached by pedestrian paths free from traffic hazard," failed to become part of the final document, issued within a few months of the draft, perhaps because officials considered it a hindrance to securing developers.[37] Yet the idea of the mall was now sufficiently accepted among architects that it figured prominently in designs for two projects already in progress: Willow Run, near Detroit, and McLoughlin Heights near Portland, Oregon. Malls were incorporated in several other schemes planned during the months that followed. Pietro Belluschi, architect of the McLoughlin Heights center, recently recalled that "we were given only days to complete projects which would have taken normally months to plan—literally we had no time to ponder, to consult or to exchange ideas."[38]

There was no dispute that the mall was the optimal configuration among young modernist architects, who embraced Stein's community planning principles if not his somewhat more conservative approach to building design. The greenbelt towns and several other demonstration projects such as Baldwin Hills Village in Los Angeles (1938–1942) were revered as models for organizing the site as much as, it not more than, avant-garde examples abroad.[39] The mall thus continued to be part of a broader agenda of reform in development patterns that was propelled by social as well as aesthetic concerns. Wartime conditions allowed architects to employ this new approach to retail development as a matter of course even though no demand existed for it in the marketplace.

An equally important legacy of the greenbelt towns was the concept of the mall as ideal focus for community life. The generic New England common seemed a logical source of inspiration because it embodied the social vision while satisfying the avant-garde's new taste for preindus-

207
Greenbrook shopping center, Somerset County, New Jersey, 1936, Albert Mayer and Henry S. Churchill, architects, Henry Wright and Allan Kamstra, planners; project. Site plan. (*Architectural Forum*, February 1937, 128).

208
Diagrammatic sketch of New England common, ca. 1943. (*Architectural Forum*, August 1943, 67.)

trial archetypes. As a model, the common was venerated not for its picturesque attributes or romantic associations, of which eclectic architects were
so fond, but because it was purported to have an inherent utilitarian logic
manifested in elegantly simple solutions. The New England common also
was appreciated because it was seen as an American phenomenon. Three
months after publishing the Syracuse plan, the *Architectural Forum*'s editors
discussed the common as an exemplar of what community centers should
again be:

> Our colonial villages were not arranged like medieval towns, yet they too suited the
> needs of the people who lived and worked in them. Because many of the early settlers
> were refugees from religious persecution, the church was their first thought. Life was
> hard and building was a slow process, and so the church quickly became more than a
> religious edifice—it also housed the town meetings, the nucleus of our democratic
> form of government. Near the church the houses were clustered, partly for protection,
> but chiefly because people in a new and empty land wanted to live close to each other.
> It made trading, handicraft manufacture and social intercourse easier. The Common
> around which the shops, houses, church and school were grouped was a social center,
> a parade ground, a grazing field, and it gave light and air—breathing space—to the
> community [figure 208].[40]

Assumptions about the past based on functional determinism
were not by nature any more accurate than those based on sentiment that
young modernists so disparaged; nevertheless, this ahistorical perspective
emerged as a driving force behind the common's adaptation as a mall in
new commercial development. Belluschi explained:

> People learn to think of the shopping center as the focus and symbol of their commu-
> nity life, especially if in addition to the bare shopping requirements there are theaters
> and tearooms and meeting halls where people may use their leisure time in various so-
> cial and cultural pursuits. It is by speculating on the far-reaching possibilities of these re-
> newed community ties—akin to those existing in the New England towns of old with
> all their restraining as well as liberating powers—that we begin to see the appearance
> of a fully developed community life in contrast to the cruel, amorphous, and disorga-
> nized modern city.[41]

The New England common probably held appeal for more abstract aesthetic reasons as well. Besides encompassing low-density settlement around a sizable open space, this archetype was conducive to the
decomposition of parts that had long been a central characteristic of avant-
garde design. Major components could be expressed separately as freestanding pavilions, connected by canopies over walks, the ensemble unified by the mall itself. Such a relationship need not be achieved through
Beaux-Arts conventions, but rather in a more informal, relaxed vein, ostensibly guided by use, topography, and orientation but also reflecting
compositional devices that emanated from early twentieth-century abstract
art. The mall thus enabled the avant-garde to design commercial facilities
in much the same way its members had already established for schools and
other types harboring a number of related components.[42]

Wartime conditions proved beneficial to realization of mall plans
for several reasons. Few members of the avant-garde had had the opportunity to put their ideas about community design into practice during the
1930s, when responsibility for most public housing projects was delegated

to local authorities who, in turn, tended to hire large, established firms with a more conservative approach to design.[43] Now many thousands of dwelling units were needed quickly, increasing the demand for architectural services, while the draft was fast diminishing the available pool. A number of housing administrators in Washington had become partial to, or at least accepting of, the modernists' call for change in patterns of community development. Although they remained in a minority, a substantial portion of the avant-garde architects in the United States participated in the housing program.[44] When a shopping mall was included in these plans, there was little time for local groups to argue over the configuration. Retailers, so bound to streetfront orientation, were in no position to quibble either, since the projects promised a lucrative trade. The pedestrian focus also seemed more acceptable since most of the target audience lived nearby and since gas rationing meant that most consumers would be arriving on foot or by bus. Unlike Greenbelt, these wartime projects did not seem to pose much of a threat to conventional business practices. But for the architects who created them, the designs were considered of vital importance in defining priorities for the postwar era.[45] Federal sponsorship, the chaotic conditions wrought by exigency, and the idealism of the designers combined to propagate the shopping mall in a nation that might never have accepted it otherwise. Few examples were actually realized, but they had a significant impact on postwar practices. No scheme was more influential than that finally erected at Linda Vista in 1943.

209

Linda Vista Shopping Center, 1943–1944, Earl F. Gilbertson and Whitney R. Smith, associated architects, Harold Dankworth, landscape architect; altered. Site plan. (Talbot Hamlin, *Forms and Functions of Twentieth-Century Architecture,* IV: 118.)

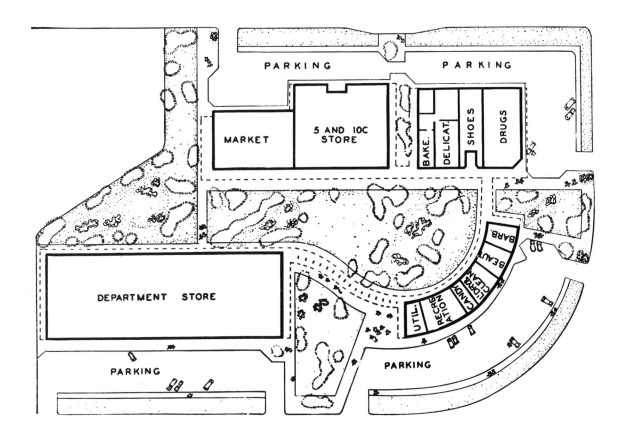

MODELS

Built according to a new design, the Linda Vista shopping center provided
the most coherent resolution to date of the mall as the central component
of a commercial facility. Unlike the initial scheme, this one had no defined front or main entrance in any traditional sense (figure 209). The perimeter was occupied almost entirely by parking. Street elevations were
treated in a matter-of-fact way to accommodate deliveries and other utilitarian functions. Perceptually, the dominant image was not a facade but
a three-dimensional play of mass and void: a broad green defined
by four buildings, each different in size and shape, and a canopied walk
connecting them (figure 210). Wide separations between the buildings
extended as walkways to the street, establishing clear ties from the approaches to the core. But the mall that occupied that core was the paramount feature, creating the sensation of a neighborhood park around
which retail services were grouped. Grass, trees, and benches invited relaxation and play (figure 211). Here, wrote Whitney Smith, the Pasadena architect who designed the complex, "instead of garish store fronts and a
raucous discord of signs there are the order and peace of an early village
green." Here, cooed the *Forum*'s editors, was "the full-dress presentation"
of the idea they had advanced for planting grass on Main Street.[46]

   At the same time, the stores were unmistakably commercial in
character, employing a minimalist vocabulary and curvilinear forms, dramatically lit at night (figure 212). The design also capitalized on wartime
building materials restrictions to exude some of the studied casualness
of the Farmers Market and its progeny.[47] Like the Farmers Market, too,
and like Olvera Street and shopping courts in the region, the mall was
a world in itself that seemed quite removed from the twentieth-century
metropolis.

The configuration of Linda Vista was justified primarily on practical grounds. A full block could be utilized to advantage; no store had a better position than another; shoppers would see all parts equally well; perambulation would be encouraged; children were safe, completely removed from vehicular traffic. Such concerns were credited with leading to a solution where civic values predominated, a solution that could improve living patterns by retrieving the ostensibly better conditions that existed before the automobile filled the streets and indeed before speculation and the drive for profit shaped communities nationwide. Smith made clear his intention of designing Linda Vista as a model for postwar development, including the rehabilitation of existing districts. Good planning was requisite. The large, undivided block of land provided the matrix for turning conventional, street-oriented development "inside out." Otherwise,

you [will] have . . . the evils of Main Street all over again. Streets too narrow. Trucks, buses, autos, and hopping pedestrians sharing the space. Stop lights choking the streets with thru traffic. No parking space for shoppers. Buildings fighting each other for light and air and attention. Business slowly mushrooming out into the residential area —shops here and there, filling stations, funeral parlors. The old story—blight, congestion, ugliness.[48]

The tenants had mixed feelings about the Linda Vista center. Some still regretted not having a streetfront store; others found the layout

210
Linda Vista Shopping Center, general view. Photo Maynard Parker, 1944. (Architectural Drawing Collection, University Art Museum, University of California, Santa Barbara.)

211
Linda Vista Shopping Center. Photo Maynard Parker, 1944. (Architectural Drawing Collection, University Art Museum, University of California, Santa Barbara.)

advantageous. Customers were pleased. Within a few years, however, parking needs began to change the situation. The center had only 216 spaces, far fewer than the standard for a complex of its size (82,000 square feet of store area) during the postwar era. Vacant lots set aside for expansion became supplementary parking areas, but they were not as convenient. Merchants began to clamor for converting the mall into space for cars. Among these priorities, the garden was no match for the machine.[49]

Most of the wartime shopping centers were modest in scale, designed to address the immediate needs of families in defense housing projects that lay beyond the easy reach of existing retail outlets. The complex proposed for Willow Run was a notable exception. Although it never advanced beyond the schematic stage, the design was among the most important examples of its kind for the regional malls planned in Los Angeles and other U.S. cities during the immediate postwar years.

Lying some twenty-five miles west of downtown Detroit, next to the bomber plant bearing the same name, the Willow Run development was to have been twice as large (6,000 dwelling units) as Linda Vista and to stand in a rural area, much like Greenbelt. Like Greenbelt, too, Willow Run was conceived as "a model American community," establishing "the level on which planners, builders, realtors and investors will have to compete in the postwar period."[50] Five "neighborhood units," each with a school and shopping facilities, were sited in an arc with the "town center" at the fulcrum. Designed by Eero Saarinen while in his father's office, this core group was to include all the features expected in a fully developed community.[51] Municipal agencies, a post office, fire and police station,

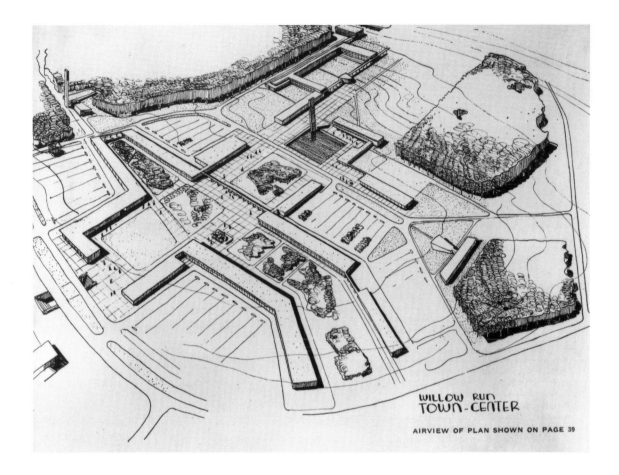

WILLOW RUN
TOWN-CENTER

AIRVIEW OF PLAN SHOWN ON PAGE 39

high school, and a utilities building rested at one end of the complex, a hotel at the other. In between lay a sizable shopping precinct, with a cruciform mall unifying the ensemble (figure 213).

Three aspects of the Willow Run plan made it an important precursor to the regional mall. First, the scheme demonstrated how a large retail complex with an inward focus could possess a clear, logical order that was not derived from a standard street plan or indeed any form of vehicular circulation system. Here it was the arrangement of the buildings and the open spaces serving them that dictated the layout of roads. A major route ran through the complex, separating the hotel from the retail area, but that path seemed of little consequence visually to the ensemble except as a means of vehicular access. Smaller roads extending around other parts of the perimeter were treated precisely for what they were: service routes, subordinate to, not determinants of, the building configuration. The most coherent aspects of the scheme lay within the core.

The second key feature was the mall's modified cruciform plan, which showed how open space could unify stores on a large scale, giving the complex a sense of centrality and avoiding a long, linear progression (figure 214). As a diagram, the scheme was multidirectional and open-ended rather than a hollow square as at Linda Vista. Finally, the design resolved the matter of peripheral parking for a complex of its size. With a car lot embraced by each L-shaped building, the distance between parked

212
Linda Vista Shopping Center. Photo Maynard Parker, 1944. (Architectural Drawing Collection, University Art Museum, University of California, Santa Barbara.)

213
Community center, Willow Run, Michigan, 1942, Saarinen, Swanson & Saarinen, architects; project. Aerial view. (*Architectural Forum,* March 1943, 37.)

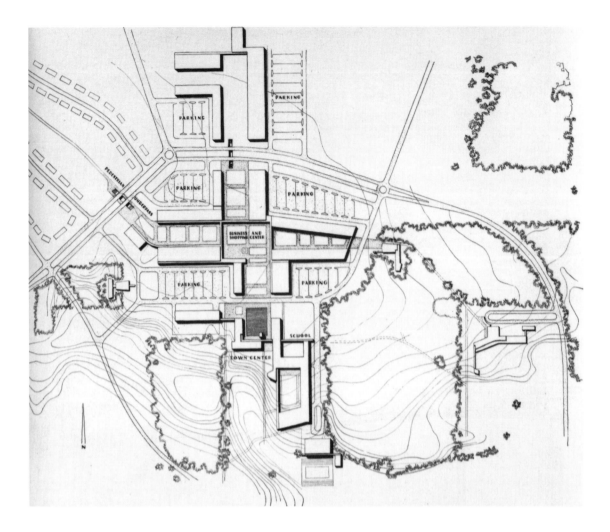

214
Community Center, Willow Run. Site plan. (*Architectural Forum,* March 1943, 39.)

215
Urban redevelopment plan for South Central district, City Planning Department, City of Los Angeles, 1943 (*Accomplishments* 1943, n.p.)

automobiles and the mall entrance was kept relatively short. Though still modest by postwar standards, a far greater percentage of space was devoted to the automobile here than at Linda Vista. Parking was no longer treated like a regrettable necessity, but rather as a key component of the plan.

Willow Run remained a preliminary design, yet it had considerable impact and was cited in texts on shopping center design over the next decade. Morris Ketchum, who would soon emerge as a leader in the creation of the regional mall, considered Willow Run a benchmark and incorporated a number of its aspects into his own work. After the war, too, Victor Gruen used the scheme as a point of departure for his first regional mall proposal, situated in Los Angeles.[52]

Willow Run was at once a catalyst and a symptom. The degree to which its characteristics embodied reform ideas that were becoming canon is evident in a plan prepared by the Los Angeles City Planning Department within months of the Michigan project's publication. Proposed to regenerate a deteriorated area just south of downtown, the design eliminated virtually all traces of the existing urban matrix to enable full presentation of contemporary planning practices (figure 215). Within each superblock, housing was clustered around parklike open spaces, two of

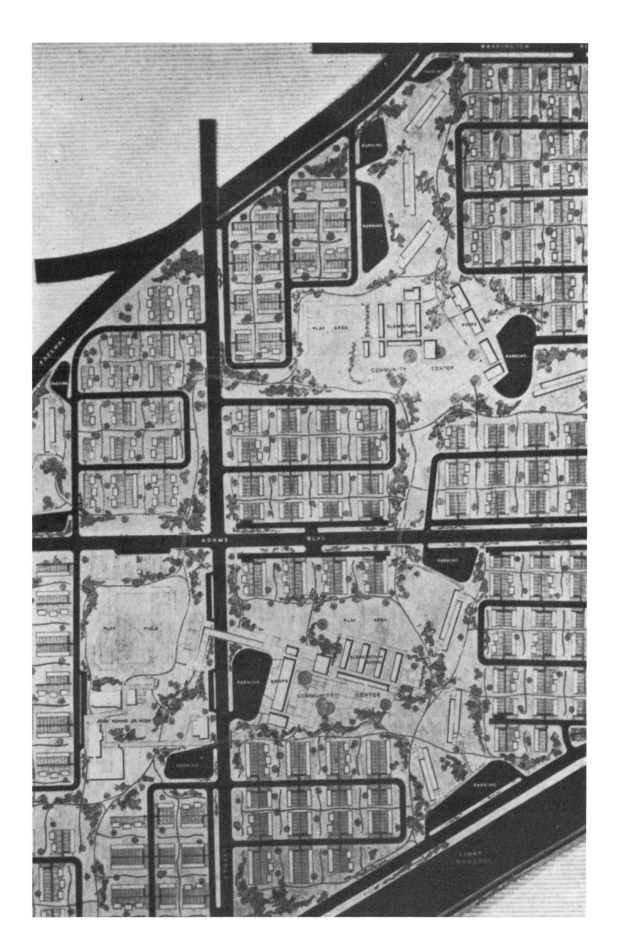

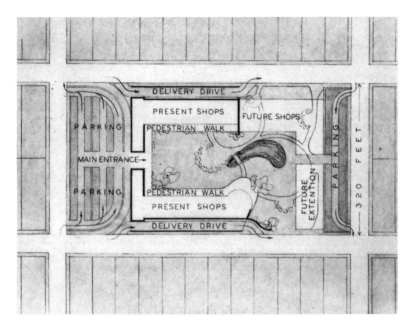

which contained community centers, comprised of elementary schools and stores. These neighborhood shopping facilities also served as a buffer between the expansive pedestrian areas and the off-street parking that served them. In a project designed less than three years after the Westchester model, both the arrangement and the thinking behind it could not have been less similar. Main Street had vanished.

An approach more suggestive of reconciliation was advanced concurrently as a model neighborhood shopping center in the *Forum*'s Syracuse plan. The editor's choice of Victor Gruen, now based in Los Angeles, to design this component was propitious. Gruen had a national reputation as a retailer's architect, whose work to date had been for specialty stores with a streetfront orientation. The fact that Gruen was now willing to embrace an "inside out" approach, positing the mall as a harbinger of future work, suggests a view predicated on commercial as well as aesthetic and social concerns. It was also an important initiation for Gruen into a new realm of retail planning, for which he would later become a prominent advocate.[53]

Diagrammatically, the layout of Gruen's complex was similar to that of Linda Vista, with all stores turned away from the street and opening onto a landscaped mall (figure 216). Parking and deliveries were peripheral, here with the car lots placed at either end, the stores serviced along the sides. On the other hand, the normative urban context of the orthogonal grid was accepted, implying at least a concern for applicability to what still constituted the vast majority of potential sites. Gruen noted that "larger centers could be built on the same principle, covering several blocks," adding that "automobile traffic could be diverted around such centers or if necessary, under them."[54]

Gruen also implied that such a center should be isolated, surrounded entirely by residences, since it would provide "all [the] necessities

of day-to-day living." Thus, like Linda Vista, the scheme was treated as a self-contained island, but one oriented entirely to the motorist. No aspect was conducive to patrons walking to the premises. Furthermore, the design possessed a distinct front, separated from the street by the car lot yet asserting its presence through Gruen's rambunctious use of large-scale forms (figure 217). Though both the mass and the vocabulary were different, the effect was much the same as at some of the exuberant drive-in restaurants erected in southern California during the previous few years. This motorist-oriented facade would have been the more prominent by virtue of its contrast with the unadorned sides where the deliveryways were screened by freestanding walls.

The commercial character of the design was further evident in its plan. Sizable areas were allocated for a market, drug store, and variety store, reflecting a concern for attracting chain companies as anchor tenants. Unlike at Linda Vista or many other planned centers, Gruen drew

216
Shopping Center for 194X, Syracuse, New York, hypothetical design, 1943, Gruenbaum & Krummeck, architects. Site plan. (*Architectural Forum,* May 1943, 101.)

217
Shopping Center for 194X, entrance front. (*Architectural Forum,* May 1943, 103.)

218
Shopping Center for 194X, general view from mall. (*Architectural Forum,* May 1943, 101.)

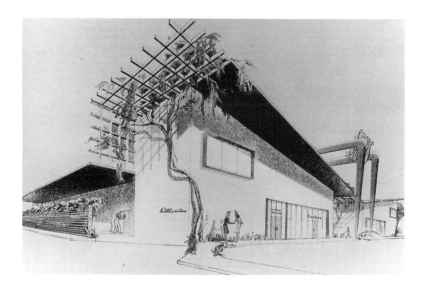

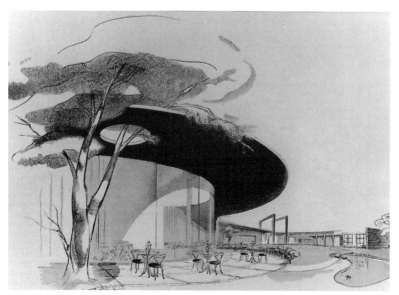

from Los Angeles's commercial vernacular: storefronts here would be individualized and the market would have an open front facing the mall, just as others of its kind in southern California opened to the street. As a controlling device, however, a wide canopy and evenly placed structural piers were conceived to unify the ensemble. Such treatment, combined with the prominence given to open space, would create an effect quite different from the accretive one common to recent arterial development in Los Angeles (figure 218). Gruen struck a balance between the identity of each store and of the complex as a whole that would become the norm for regional malls after 1950. He also matched his interest in an architecture calculated to stimulate purchases with broader objectives. From its landscaped centerpiece, the scheme imparted the feeling of a tropical resort as much as a place for buying everyday goods. A "community center," which included an assembly room, lounge, library, and post office, was an integral part of the plan. A circular restaurant opening onto an outdoor terrace lay on the opposite side. Provision was also made for doctors' and dentists' offices. Although Gruen was yet to champion commercial architecture as an instrument of fundamental change in living patterns, he now shared the housing reformers' commitment to making the retail center a magnet of communal activities—a place where purchasing goods would be "a pleasure, recreation instead of a chore."

The essential groundwork was laid for the shopping mall before the end of World War II, with a new generation of architects advocating "inside out" retail facilities. "Grass on Main Street" became a reality, albeit a tentative one. Most of the advances remained on paper. Southern California had the premier realized example at Linda Vista, yet the complex's immediate impact on the urban landscape was virtually nil. In sharp contrast to a Westwood or a Farmers Market, few members of the general public were even aware of its existence. The business community remained unimpressed. Some years elapsed before the shopping mall gained acceptance among retail and real estate interests. The drawbacks to less radical programs such as those developed at the Crenshaw Center, Westchester, and Valley Plaza had to become clear before the shift became decisive.

XI

NO AUTOMOBILE EVER BOUGHT A THING

The regional shopping mall was the most important means by which fully integrated management and merchandising techniques became institutionalized in retail development. The form of the mall alone rendered multiple ownership impractical. With stores oriented to one another as part of a contained, inward-looking landscape, the placement of each unit in relation to the others so as to encourage perambulation throughout became even more crucial than it was for shopping centers oriented to the street or car lot. Once cast in bricks and mortar, a mall left little room for correcting errors in judgment save through costly modifications. The layout also reinforced customer perceptions of the center as a single entity and therefore intensified the need for careful coordination among tenants. Likewise, retailers had to be satisfied with the mix and be willing to work as a group. The fragmented merchandising and management structures as well as piecemeal planning that resulted from multiple ownership made little sense under the circumstances.

In its physical characteristics, the regional mall broke even more abruptly from normative practices. These huge centers were perceptually disconnected from the street, creating their own environments instead. Buildings were set back and generally lacked a strong distinguishing presence from the arteries that served them. Signs and enormous expanses of parking area were more prominent than architecture as identifying characteristics from the public realm.[1] Aerial views were the only ones from

which the complex was readily comprehensible as a whole. The mall space itself was, of course, the most important part of the ensemble experienced by customers. While this precinct was frequently characterized as a street without vehicles and numerous analogies continued to be made to the marketplaces of preindustrial settlements, the new complexes seemed different from any setting familiar to their clientele. Not only was the design vocabulary derived from a nonreferential modernism, but the ambience bespoke a degree of control uncommon to retail areas, suggesting more an institution than a magnet for commerce. Cars were absent, but so were things that once had jammed trading centers: animals, carts, wagons, street vendors, and many forms of unorganized activity. Like a college campus, the mall exuded neatness, order, and perhaps some of the trappings of a park.

The automobile figured more decisively in determining the size, configuration, and the placement of each store in the regional mall than with any other form of retail development. Easy access to the buildings from every part of the car lot became as important a concern as providing adequate space for cars themselves. Never before had the design of parking been so complicated or so significant a component of site planning. Public streets dividing the car lot were considered as detrimental as those dividing store groups; thus an internal system of vehicular routes was needed so that motorists could move through the huge area with ease. Determining the most effective connections between this private network and adjacent streets also posed problems in traffic management. The site plan carried all the challenges of a small city center, while being premised on conditions that had little precedent in realized work of any sort.

The level of attention paid to vehicles was matched by a concern for separating them from the shopping environment to a degree that was even more pronounced than in early malls. The objective was to divorce customers from their automobiles as quickly as possible by making the pedestrian retail precinct a world unto itself. Dominated by stores and displays, with no perceptual ties to the outside world, the setting was analogous to those created in the shopping courts or at the Farmers Market in Los Angeles. Victor Gruen became one of the most outspoken advocates of this dichotomy, arguing that while the demands imposed by the car were of great importance in planning retail developments, the needs of people remained paramount. It was a mistake to suppose that the two were synonymous. By 1960, he could draw from two decades of practice in southern California and a dozen years of experience in regional mall design to observe: "As the retailer-automobile honeymoon comes to an end, the retailer slowly realizes that his love has been misdirected. His true love belonged not to the automobile, but to the female customer in it. No automobile—not even the elegant Cadillac—ever bought a thing."[2] The car could pose significant problems in new retail precincts just as it could in older areas developed prior to widespread automobile use. The regional mall must embody a rethinking of the problem rather than be a refinement of existing models. Malls were appearing coast to coast by the time

Gruen's remarks were published; however, those who created them were still learning how profound a change their endeavors represented.

Just as with prototypical examples, the emergence of the regional mall was a national phenomenon. During the type's formative years, from the mid-1940s to the mid-1950s, key examples were designed for numerous metropolitan areas, including Boston, New York, Detroit, Chicago, Minneapolis, Seattle, and San Francisco as well as Los Angeles. While no one place became the clearly recognized pacesetter, assuming a central role comparable to that still maintained by New York and Chicago in the design of tall commercial buildings, southern California's contribution was among the most significant. Between 1948 and 1950 alone, at least a half-dozen regional mall schemes were proposed for the Los Angeles area. Collectively, they reveal the experimental nature of thinking at the outset. The gestation period was relatively short. In 1950, construction began on Lakewood Center, one of the earliest examples to be realized in the United States, which at once reflected tendencies elsewhere and helped define many of those found in the unusually large number of regional malls erected locally over the next decade. Los Angeles affords abundant evidence with which to analyze the type during the complicated period of its early development. At the same time, the region was no longer the uncontested leader in innovation, as it had been with many other forms of retail decentralization during the 1920s and 1930s or even with the creation of regional centers immediately after World War II. The metropolitan characteristics that had once made Los Angeles conspicuously different from other cities were rapidly becoming national ones. Furthermore, a basic conservatism, evident in some aspects of the city's development for decades, may have precluded any party from taking a more adventurous, higher-risk approach at this pivotal juncture.

EMERGENCE

The first regional shopping center to employ a mall plan in the United States was designed in 1947; the first to be built was begun the following year and opened in 1950. Half a decade later, the type was viewed by the business world as well as by many planners and architects as the preeminent form of retail facility for major metropolitan areas. The transformation from a reformer's ideal to a major thrust in commercial development was remarkably swift. Compelling reasons had to exist for such a venture, with the risks it entailed, to be undertaken by numerous parties in so short a period.

The major impetus for the regional mall's ascendency stemmed from shifts in the practices of department store companies. By the early 1950s, many department store executives believed that branches built independent of other outlets no longer constituted a sound strategy for expansion. Instead of alleviating the problems that plagued downtown locations, this type of facility could duplicate them. A large store attracted other mer-

chants, which, in turn, could thwart expansion and overburden parking facilities. Stores of lesser caliber could undermine the appeal of the precinct. Even when such problems did not arise, street congestion almost always did.[3] The department store was powerless to affect the course of events unless it controlled, directly or otherwise, all of the land in question. Chain and other specialty store competition could be held in check, perhaps even turned to advantage, by the department store company's selecting only those best suited to complement its emporium.

The incentive to develop a regional center was heightened by the market demand for big facilities. Stores of 200,000 square feet or more, containing a full set of product lines found in the downtown facility, became standard in the 1950s. Increased size not only raised the level of investment but intensified the complexities of site selection and planning. Both factors made the inclusion of additional outlets more feasible and appealing. The Broadway-Crenshaw Center provided an important lesson in this respect, underscoring the difficulties created by parasite stores no less than the advantages of having a large, integrated complex where the parent company exercised control over tenancy, parking, and vehicular movement on the premises.

By the mid-1950s, a number of department store companies had followed the Broadway's example by initiating regional shopping centers. In other cases, where a real estate developer took the lead, the department store still played a key role in shaping the form and character of the project.[4] The size and scope of shopping center development had a direct bearing on configuration. Layouts satisfactory for neighborhood and community centers were far less desirable at the regional scale. The Broadway-Crenshaw Center revealed the shortcomings of a linear form: irrespective of where the department store was situated, greater distance from it meant greater disadvantage for the establishment occupying that spot. One developer spoke on the subject with an animosity that suggested he knew from experience: "these 'miracle strips' seemed to have been planned with malice afterthought [sic], and the only miracle seems to be that some of them have made money."[5]

A single file of stores also posed problems in relation to the car lot, irrespective of whether parking lay at the rear or in front. Long walks from peripheral parking spaces to the stores, as at the Broadway-Crenshaw Center, could discourage customers at peak shopping periods. At the same time, a long range of buildings, as at Valley Plaza, was not conducive to perambulation. Customers tended to seek a parking place close to their primary destination and either park anew near other stores or leave. The desire for proximity between parking and store remained a fundamental one among shoppers, and was the most thwarted precisely at times of heavy patronage, upon which merchants depended for profitable returns.[6]

The mall proved its worth by resolving problems basic to shopping center design on a large scale. The inward-looking orientation encouraged movement throughout the premises. Once divorced from their cars and walking amid what seemed like an entirely different world, cus-

tomers tended to spend greater blocks of time meandering, meeting friends, having meals, and buying goods. Patrons also were inclined to think of the complex as a whole rather than just of the one or two stores frequented on a given trip. Perambulation was further stimulated by a seeming compactness. With stores on either side of the pedestrian way, the frontage of a single-file plan could be accommodated in half the linear distance. Additional frontage was available along the access paths between the car lot and the mall proper, which proved especially good for the small outlets earlier attracted to arcades and shopping courts. Perceptually, the ends of a mall were more like portals than marginal tails. The configuration enabled all locations to be more or less equally desirable for some kind of store, recapturing the balance devised by J. C. Nichols at the Country Club Plaza.[7]

The mall also addressed vehicular problems more effectively than other shopping center arrangements. With a generally even distribution of parking spaces around the complex, the distance from the extremities of the lot to the stores was kept to a minimum. Thousands of cars could be held in a circumferential lot while retaining a maximum walking distance of 300 feet—soon the industry standard. The mall further helped to resolve the long-troublesome matter of separating deliveries from customers. The delivery tunnel devised for the Broadway-Crenshaw Center was an ideal solution save in the cost to small stores. The mall plan allowed the tunnel to be employed more efficiently because at least twice as many outlets could be reached with the same length. The arrangement also enabled a number of stores to tie into a single subterranean connection. Only the largest emporia had their own link. With these adjustments, the delivery tunnel became a standard feature of the regional mall, bringing with it the added advantage of eliminating exterior service areas.

The mall's configuration helped the retailer's basic goal of broadening customer draw in outlying areas. The range of goods, easy access, and convenient parking all contributed to more families shopping together and also more males shopping alone than was typical in downtown shopping districts. This tendency both encouraged and was encouraged by the longer operating hours made possible by the comparatively low operating costs in outlying areas. As a result, evenings and weekends became important trading periods in a way they had never previously been. At the same time, during traditional shopping periods the mall seemed a more private, predominantly female world, absent the many components of the male workforce—from corporate executives to errand boys—found in the city center. The inward-looking orientation of the mall enhanced the reputation of these complexes as destinations. An editor of *Printer's Ink,* a leading organ for advertisers, described her experience at a pioneer mall as being "just as much fun" as visiting a world's fair: "The thing that impressed me the most was the carnival air that pervades the whole place—and opens pocket books! The shoppers are . . . relaxed, thoroughly enjoying themselves." The mall truly seemed to represent "the future today."[8]

Finally, proponents believed that malls would discourage, perhaps even prevent, competing retail development nearby because of the large tracts of land they required well beyond established business districts. Many early examples occupied between forty and eighty acres; in some cases, one hundred. The inward-looking focus of the mall would further this objective.[9] As the department store company could "control" its competitors from within, so it could "control" the impact of others through exclusion. Proponents believed the size of a regional mall could extend its power no less than its customer draw over a large geographic radius. Creating a location, pioneered by the lone-wolf department store during the 1920s, was thus merged with the reform concept of contained shopping nodes. But the mall stood in isolation for economic reasons, not out of aesthetic, social, or other planning concerns. Containment was now a strategic business tool, not a protection device for the nearby homeowner. The underlying reason why the mall gained favor in the retail world so quickly, then, was that it proved to be a more effective, predictable means of generating high revenues in retailing than other large-scale methods available at that time.

STEIN

Realizing the benefits of a mall plan and understanding how it might be best configured were not insights gained easily. After World War II, many questions remained, even among proponents of the mall, as to its optimal size and form. In 1946, no one thought of complexes that approached the dimensions of those developed only a few years later. Preferences varied widely as to the arrangement of open space and stores: should the mall space be narrow or wide, mostly paved or landscaped, evocative of a street, a plaza, or a village green; should movement be linear or circuitous; should retail units face one large open area or a sequence of smaller ones? Fewer possibilities were entertained in the layout of parking, which was almost always circumferential; however, different approaches were taken in trying to relate the pedestrian way to the car lot.

Designs advanced up through 1950 represent an assemblage of singular examples, encompassing a broad range of characteristics with no clear overall pattern. In advancing new ideas, architects and planners played a central role, serving as advocates as well as designers. Southern California was one of the most important staging grounds for this experimentation, harboring more schemes than other metropolitan areas owing to its great size, continued fast pace of growth, economic strength, and low-density patterns of development. None of these projects was realized, but they stand as key documents of the transition between the modest undertakings of previous years and the emergence of the type into the forefront of retail development nationwide.

Few architects tried harder than Clarence Stein to give form and direction to the shopping mall during the late 1940s. Stein's experience

convinced him that the type would become preeminent. Three opportunities arose in southern California to put his ideas into practice. For each, he served as a consultant, recommending the size, general configuration, and tenant mix.[10] Having studied the shopping center since the early 1930s, he was among the most knowledgeable persons on the subject. Yet Stein's hopes were stillborn; two of the projects never progressed beyond diagrammatic sketches, and the third, advanced no further than detailed design development. None of this work appears to have influenced subsequent endeavors. The episodes suggest the problem of translating an idea devised for neighborhood centers to much larger complexes and of adapting a concept based on social objectives to the demands of the marketplace.

The first of Stein's California projects was for a mammoth center on Whittier Boulevard designed to serve East Los Angeles and numerous other prosperous blue-collar communities that up to then possessed only small-scale arterial development. Occupying a seventy-acre site and with some 300,000 square feet of store space, the complex would have surpassed the Broadway-Crenshaw Center in size. The sheer number of people living close at hand may have been the decisive factor in convincing the developer, Leo Harvey, that a huge shopping center oriented to volume sales would be profitable. It was estimated that 345,000 people lived within a fifteen-minute driving radius, one million within a thirty-minute radius.[11] The center would challenge downtown as a retail magnet for as many as one quarter of the metropolitan area's residents.

Stein was asked to collaborate on the project by Los Angeles architect Lewis Wilson, with whom he had worked on the celebrated design of Baldwin Hills Village (1939–1942). More than a half-dozen layouts were studied, all of which had an inward focus, with stores grouped around one or more "parks" and walkways.[12] The organization was hierarchical. A space framed by a department store and entertainment facilities lay at the core (figure 219). To either side were comparatively narrow malls, one lined by specialty shops, the other by nonretail services. A third extension, the "court of daily needs," was much larger and presumably would hold a spectrum of chain outlets similar to that at the Broadway-Crenshaw Center. Drive-in facilities—restaurant, theater, and service station—defined the boundary on one side. As at Willow Run, parking was circumferential and bracketed by the main buildings; here the distance between the two was never much more than 250 feet. Yet in contrast to Saarinen's design the spatial order was static; each area was defined as a more or less discrete zone.

The formality of Stein's plan reflected an academic approach to design learned at the outset of his career, over three decades previous, in the office of Bertram Goodhue. Much as with Carleton Winslow's design for Carthay Center, the arrangement was in a general way reminiscent of Goodhue's plans for the California Institute of Technology campus at Pasadena.[13] Stein's layout appears to have been predicated on the belief that people would require no encouragement from the configuration itself to

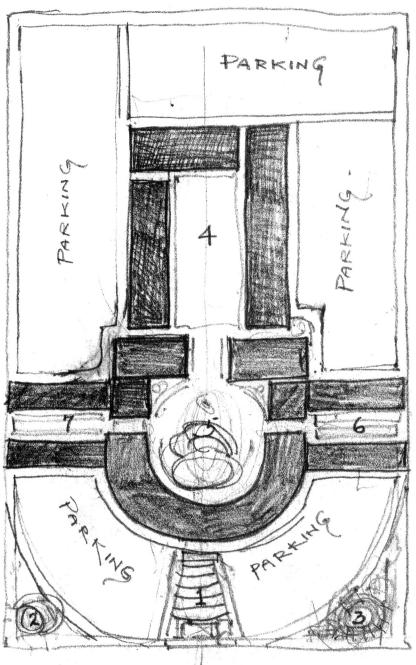

PARKING

PARKING

PARKING.

4

7

6

PARKING

PARKING.

1

2

3

1. OUTDOOR MOVIE
2. GAS STATION
3. DRIVE IN
4. COURT OF DAILY NEEDS
5. ENTERTAINMENT & DEPT STORE
6. PROMENADE OF SPECIALTIES
7. OFFICES

HEALTH CENTER
POST OFFICE
BANKS
TRAVEL.

circulate from end to end. But retail centers were hardly analogous to a campus in this respect. It would be easy for customers to patronize stores in one segment of Stein's compound and not venture into others. There was no clearly defined main circulation path, and almost every component had the potential to suffer from the consumer neglect that plagued side streets.

An awareness of such drawbacks may have led to the revisions Stein made several weeks later. While no less formal, the new scheme introduced a single open space of differentiated parts (figure 220). This large, cruciform "garden" was more accessible from the car lot, which, in turn, was more integrally related to the buildings. That Stein was beginning to address the issue of perception—how this behemoth would be experienced in the progression from street to car lot to mall—is further suggested by his ingenious varying of levels. A small cross section on the same sheet indicates that the main shopping floor and the "garden" were to rest a fully story above grade. Delivery access and storage thus could be underground without the cost of excavation. The parking lot sloped away from the center, and much of it was screened from the street by a raised perimeter service road. As a result, the buildings would be conspicuous from some distance away and the approach to the mall proper would seem more purposeful. The scheme may have proven too ambitious, however, for it did not advance beyond this exploratory stage.[14]

Less than two months later, in October 1948, Wilson again asked Stein to collaborate, this time on a more modest retail complex to be situated near Baldwin Hills Village. After inspecting the site, Stein argued that it was too small and should be combined with an adjacent parcel to form a thirty-acre tract for a regional shopping center. The architects convinced their client, Paul Trousdale, to fund a schematic plan that could be presented to the owners of the adjoining land to persuade them to cooperate. Size was crucial to the equation, Stein maintained, if the results were to be satisfactory. A complex that did not rival the Broadway-Crenshaw Center would be unable to secure tenants of high caliber. The East Los Angeles project also may have led him to believe that working at a large scale was necessary if the mall was to be developed to optimal advantage. Clearly the earlier scheme had a formative influence on the new plan (figure 221).

The importance Stein gave to the mall is evident in the argument made to his client. In expanded form, the facility would set a new standard: no "really modern shopping center . . . exists at present in . . . the Los Angeles region."[15] Beside ample parking close to all stores, the characteristics must include "complete separation of pedestrians and automobiles" and "shops and amusements facing on a pleasant park." Here the "park" was an axial extension of the "village green" in Baldwin Hills Village, and while the retail center was to serve a far broader clientele, the layout was a poignant reflection of Stein's commitment to providing communal open space secluded from its urban matrix.

219

Schematic study for shopping center, probably on Whittier Boulevard between Goodrich and Gerhart streets, Commerce, Clarence Stein and Lewis Wilson, associated architects, 1948. Site plan. (Rare and Manuscript Collections, Carl A. Kroch Library, Cornell University.)

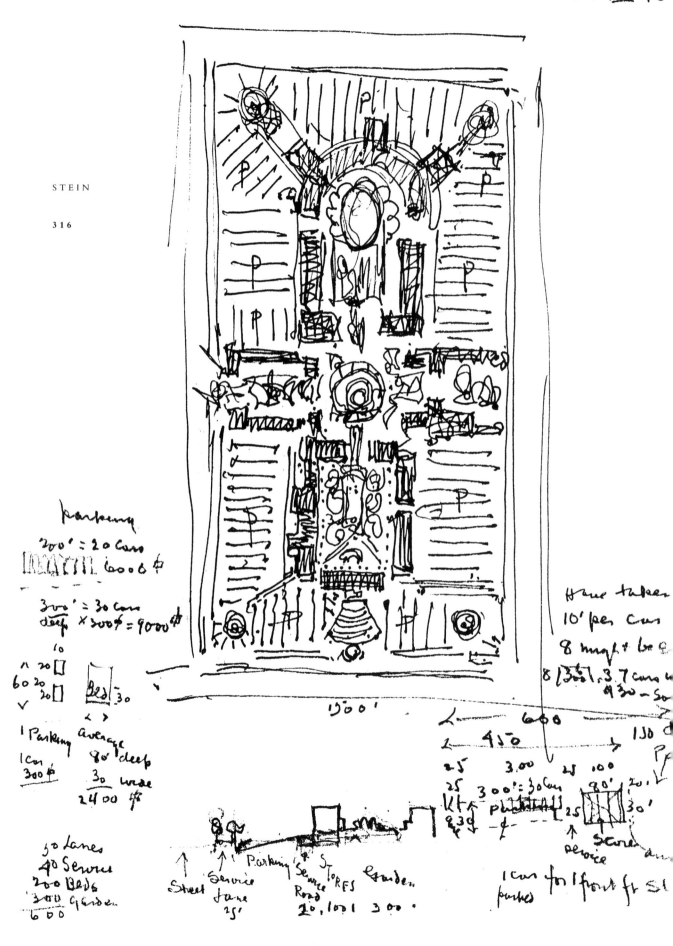

STEIN

316

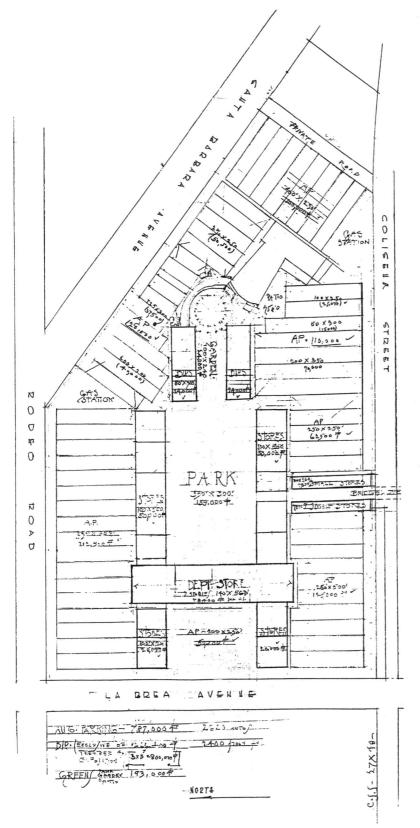

220

Schematic study for shopping center, probably on Whittier Boulevard, 1948, Stein and Wilson, associated architects. Site plan. (Rare and Manuscript Collections, Carl A. Kroch Library, Cornell University.)

221

Preliminary design for shopping center, La Brea and Martin Luther King avenues, Rodeo Road, and Coliseum Street, Los Angeles, 1948, Clarence Stein and Lewis Wilson, associated architects. Site plan. (Rare and Manuscript Collections, Carl A. Kroch Library, Cornell University.)

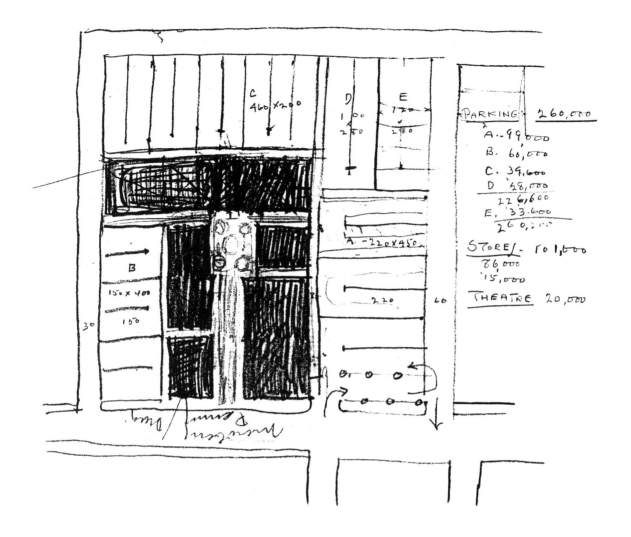

Within the sketch (handwritten annotations):

C
460×200

D
100
250

E
120
250

A -220×450

B
150×400

30   150

220   60

PARKING: 260,000
A -99,000
B. 60,000
C. 39,600
D 48,000
226,600
E. 33,600
260,200

STORE:- 101,000
86,000
15,000

THEATRE 20,000

222
Study for shopping center, Thompson Boulevard and Borchard Drive, Ventura, ca. 1948–1949, Clarence Stein, architect. Site plan. (Rare and Manuscript Collections, Carl A. Kroch Library, Cornell University.)

Remarkably, the site lay only about a dozen blocks from the Crenshaw Center. Wilson asserted that the two would not compete. The area's growth was such that "every large merchandiser in the United States will eventually be located in this area, and . . . with the proper . . . [design, the client] would be in the best position of offering them the first choice rather than Beverly Hills or Wilshire Boulevard."[16] The architects envisioned an updated Miracle Mile with branches of the region's finest stores; however, the Broadway–Coldwell Banker team had a more accurate reading of the market. Stein and Wilson's naiveté concerning both the target audience and the viability of siting a regional center so close to an existing one probably explain why their proposal advanced no further. For his part, Trousdale decided that developing land adjacent to the Crenshaw Center was the most advantageous course to take.[17]

The scale needed to justify an expansive pedestrian area in economic terms was revealed in the third of Stein's projects. Commissioned by the Los Angeles real estate developer Samuel Marks, the center was to be built at Ventura, seventy miles up the coast. Its dimensions were not much larger (101,000 square feet of store area, 20,000 square feet for a theater) than Linda Vista; however, the effect was wholly different. At Linda

Vista, primacy was given to pedestrian space; at Ventura, the objective shifted to providing adequate space for automobiles.

Minimum requirements for parking at shopping centers rose dramatically during the postwar years because many earlier calculations proved inadequate and also because of the continued increase in automobile use. By the late 1940s, the needed ratio of parking area to store area was held to be 2½:1 or 3:1, far larger than most prewar practices.[18] Focusing on in this aspect, Stein found little room left for the mall, which was

223

Shopping center, Thompson Boulevard and Borchard Drive, Ventura, ca. 1949–1950, Matthew Nowicki and Clarence Stein, associated architects; project. Site plan and section. (Rare and Manuscript Collections, Carl A. Kroch Library, Cornell University.)

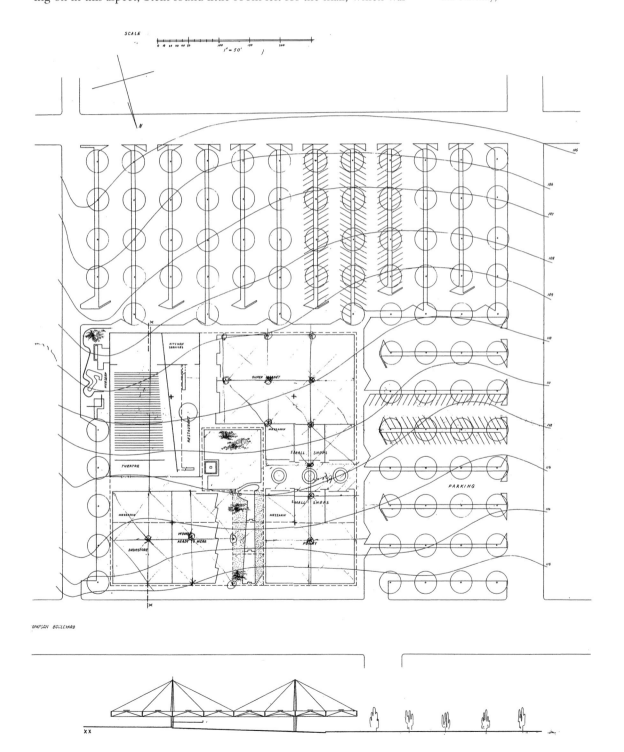

reduced to along, narrow, and potentially claustrophobic zone. Oddly it was oriented to the street, suggesting that he may still have hoped many customers would walk to the premises (figure 222).

The problem of confined space could be overcome by making it appear more expansive than it actually was, or by making confinement an attribute, as was done at the Farmers Market. A fusion of both approaches was attained in the remarkable design for the Ventura project prepared some months after the initial studies by Stein's friend and now collaborator, Matthew Nowicki. The solution was deceptively simple, exemplifying what Lewis Mumford described as Nowicki's ability to unite "law and order with adventure and freedom."[19] Four pedestrian ways, each a different width and shape, led to a central plaza (figure 223). Only the latter space and one of its approaches were left fully open, and even these were visually part of a rigorous grid established by a roof frame of precast concrete panels suspended by cables from four masts (figure 224). The absence of any other structural components enabled Nowicki to manipulate space with considerable freedom, evoking a sense of a grand promenade on one hand and a crowded bazaar on the other (figures 225, 226). The roof frame was indeed analogous to a great tent, under which a parade of wares could be strewn for perusal. Had it been realized, the design might well have had a significant impact, for it prefigured some of the ingenious spatial effects pursued with the development of enclosed malls of later years. As it was, Nowicki died in a plane crash not long after his drawings were made, and the Korean War temporarily put a halt to new construction. But the underlying problem seems to have been that the retail area could not justify the project's cost, for it never advanced further and few subsequent attempts were made to incorporate a mall into a shopping center of comparable size.[20]

If the Ventura design demonstrated how the mall could enhance a compact arrangement of retail space, a more or less concurrent proposal explored how the mall could serve as an instrument of dispersal. The scheme was developed in 1949 by Robert Alexander as a master plan for the newly incorporated community of West Covina, which lay in a fast-

224
Shopping center, Ventura, Nowicki and Stein, model. (Rare and Manuscript Collections, Carl A. Kroch Library, Cornell University.)

225
Shopping center, Ventura, sketch of mall by Matthew Nowicki. (Rare and Manuscript Collections, Carl A. Kroch Library, Cornell University.)

226
Shopping center, Ventura, sketch of mall by Matthew Nowicki. (Rare and Manuscript Collections, Carl A. Kroch Library, Cornell University.)

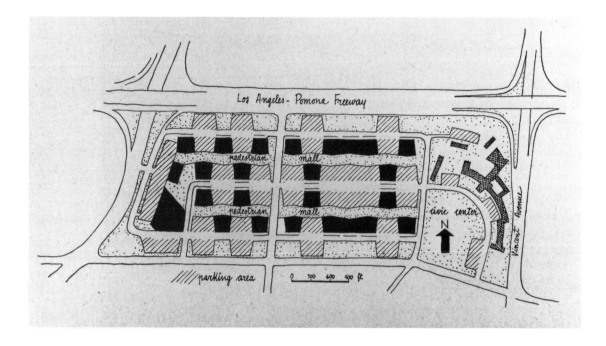

227

Study for shopping and civic center, Walnut Creek Parkway, Sunset and Vincent avenues and San Bernardino Freeway, West Covina, ca. 1949, Robert Alexander, architect; project. Site plan. (*Architectural Record,* August 1949, 114.)

expanding area some thirty miles east of downtown Los Angeles. Alexander and Wilson were partners when Baldwin Hills Village was designed and both men now lived there. That compound's layout provided the major source of inspiration for the West Covina plan, which ranked among the most unconventional in the country proposed for a shopping center of the postwar period.[21]

Given no specifics for a program by his municipal client, Alexander felt free to experiment, seeking to correct what he saw as major shortcomings in shopping center design. The distance between parked cars and stores would be reduced, all the while avoiding great expanses of asphalt, by fragmenting the parts into a checkerboard (figure 227). Two parallel malls linked the pieces and enabled extensive landscaping. These pedestrian ways converged at a plaza and department store at one end and at a "common" with municipal buildings at the other. In contrast to most mall designs of the period, this one held the potential for visually integrating architecture, automobiles, and people. Yet the decompositional approach was not conducive to circulation throughout the premises, which stretched 4,200 feet end to end. Most customers either would have made frequent stops in their cars or not gone to some portions, causing the same dual problems of congestion and underuse that plagued many traditional retail districts. The design never had the chance for refinement. After the schematic drawings were completed, the project lost its foremost proponent when the mayor died unexpectedly. Thereafter, the city council terminated the contract.

However significant their designs, neither architects such as Nowicki nor planning reformers such as Stein finally secured the shopping center's acceptance in the business world. The architects who succeeded in this were of quite a different sort. Some produced commercial, industrial, and institutional projects on a large scale. Their work was not distinguished by artistic prowess so much as by efficient, no-nonsense resolution of complex programs in which budgetary constraints were paramount. The major firms of this kind that contributed to the regional mall's early development included John Graham & Company of Seattle, designers of the first realized example, and Welton Becket & Associates and Albert C. Martin & Associates, both of Los Angeles, whose approach was influenced by Graham's prototype. Other architects who came to the fore espoused fundamental change in retail design through the adaptation of avant-garde concepts. The two most prominent figures in this arena were Morris Ketchum of New York, who was probably the first to prepare plans for a regional mall, and Victor Gruen of Los Angeles, who undertook similar work soon thereafter and eventually was seen as the nation's foremost innovator in shopping center design.

Among Gruen's strengths was his ability to translate theory into practice—to adapt the radical notions of form and space nurtured by the avant-garde to the pragmatic needs of the merchant and the investor, while making the ideas seem as if they originated with retail concerns. The downtown specialty shop was the launching pad for his career; the regional mall was the means by which he secured international renown.[22] The shift came neither quickly nor easily. The exuberant schemes Gruen designed for west coast retailers during the 1940s earned him the reputation of an eccentric in some local business circles—one reason, perhaps, why he did not see a shopping center plan materialize in southern California until the mid-1950s.[23] Nevertheless, the innovative proposals Gruen designed for malls in Los Angeles between these two phases of his career gave him the experience and perspective necessary to achieve the later work that brought him worldwide recognition.

Gruen's first opportunity to develop his ideas on a large scale came with studies for an unidentified regional shopping center in Los Angeles. Presented in mid-1948, the scheme was as ambitious as the Whittier Boulevard complex for which Stein made studied soon thereafter.[24] In every other way, the two proposals underscored the differences in approach between these architects. Gruen's design imparted a sense of formality in its arrangement, while drawing from the avant-garde's penchant for dynamic interplays between form and space (figure 228). Gruen was at once assimilating what he could from previous endeavors and creating a solution that broke new ground.

As at Willow Run, the ensemble was composed in a cruciform plan, dividing the car lot into quadrants. Yet rather than being open-ended, the complex was visually anchored to the corners of the site, its

axes arranged to tie pedestrian space to the street. A sense of order likewise pervaded those spaces as they extended toward the middle. Instead of
being treated like a garden or park, the mall was a promenade neatly defined by buildings (figure 229). This configuration allowed customers to
move easily between stores on both sides of the path. Equally important,
space gave a strong sense of unity to the sprawling complex, a relationship
enhanced by Gruen's unprecedented design for the core. In contrast to previous shopping mall plans, this central area was punctuated by an immense
(250,000 square feet) department store, circular in plan, with a seven-story
storage and utility tower at its heart. While treated as a freestanding sculptural object, the building's primary visual role was as a focal point for the
ensemble. The mass was sufficiently great that it also would serve as a beacon, identifying the complex from some distance afield even though it
was removed from the street. Gruen made the department store the linch-
pin, giving it a physical prominence commensurate with its function like
the big Wilshire Boulevard stores.

Gruen's mall encompassed much the same broad scope of establishments as Stein's Whittier Boulevard project. Besides the department
store and large chain outlets, the center included numerous small enterprises. Gruen was among the first figures to criticize the tendency in early
postwar retail developments to neglect the one-of-a-kind merchant, arguing that a shopping center should include places specifically designed
for such enterprises. Here, some of these stores were enclosed; others
formed a market, offering unusual foods that could be carried home or
consumed on the premises. The mall proper harbored kiosks, refreshment
stands, and other vending booths. A variety of restaurants likewise would
"invite people to spend many hours within the center." In its mix, the
design thus combined the big stores as at the Broadway-Crenshaw, more
diversified shopping as at Westwood Village, and the intimately scaled, ba-
zaarlike qualities of the Farmers Market and Olvera Street.

The project also addressed some of the social concerns of Stein
and other reformers. Besides a movie theater, there was an outdoor audito-

228

Shopping center, Los Angeles area, ca. 1947–1948, Gruen & Krummeck, architects; project. Aerial perspective. (*Chain Store Age,* Administrative Edition, July 1948, 22.)

229

Shopping center, Los Angeles area, view of mall. (*Women's Wear Daily,* 18 October 1949, 62.)

rium where plays, concerts, fashion shows, and other performances could be staged. These activities were complemented by others held at an exhibit hall. Meeting rooms were provided for civic groups. Municipal authorities had branch offices; parents could leave their children at a nursery. In these ways, the concept joined aspects of the downtown department store, Main Street, and the open-air market—a scope then unparalleled in any retail development, existing or proposed. The mall itself not only tied these attributes together, it created a new kind of setting, at once metropolitan and private—a place where one could partake of an array of things possible only in a great city and at the same time gain refuge from the street and all other messy aspects of urban life. Each of the four ranges would be tangent to a street, facilitating arrival by bus, but otherwise the place was divorced from its environs. Deliveries to the large stores were underground; the remaining outlets had segregated service areas. Gruen sought to create a total environment made feasible only by widespread automobile use while excluding the negative effects of traffic: "The automobile age," he concluded, "has destroyed the pleasant market place character of shopping areas as they are found in Europe and in New England. Yet this need not be so." The scale of the center and its orientation entirely to the mall enabled the experience to be both highly varied and wholly desirable. It was "more than just a place where one may shop—it shall be related . . . [to] all the activities of cultural enrichment and relaxation."[25]

When Gruen proposed his plan, few designs for shopping malls had been advanced since World War II. Among them, two unexecuted proposals by his one-time Manhattan colleague and occasional associate, Morris Ketchum, appear to have had a measurable influence.[26] Both of Ketchum's projects were widely publicized and heralded as significant steps in recasting the nature of retail development. The first was prepared in 1946 for the town center of Rye, New York, an area experiencing decline purportedly due to competition from newer, outlying retail districts. The solution drew heavily from the *Architectural Forum*'s Syracuse plan of three years previous, with the existing matrix modified to accommodate off-street parking, arterial routes beyond, and a pedestrian mall along the business coordinator (figure 230).[27] Here Ketchum developed the concept in greater detail, giving persuasive exposition of the mall as a street with-

out cars, narrow enough to retain definition as a linear path, yet wide enough to have landscaping as a major element. It was precisely this balance that Gruen employed in his Los Angeles project.[28]

Soon after the Rye plan, Ketchum was at work on the North Shore Center, sited near Beverly, Massachusetts, some eighteen miles from Boston. Unveiled in schematic form in 1946 and in a more refined vein a year later, this project was the first design for a regional mall to advance beyond the preliminary stage and presented a number of features that became hallmarks of the type. Plans called for thirty outlets and space to accommodate 3,000 cars on a sixty-two acre site, making it one of the most ambitious integrated retail facilities proposed to date (figure 231).[29] Parking formed a virtually unbroken ring around the stores, rendering the complex more a self-contained island than earlier examples and establishing what became a common pattern. The center also was completely removed from other establishments so that there would be no competition and no encroachment. The site was finalized on the basis of accessibility to households; distance from, rather than proximity to, existing businesses was the determining factor. The scheme further set a precedent by being situated adjacent to a limited-access highway (Route 128)—a relationship as rare in the East as it was in Los Angeles until the mid-1950s. The locational choice was based on an extensive study, which perhaps more than any other of the period revealed the need for detailed analysis of the market area, transportation routes, and potential locations prior to embarking on the development of a large-scale complex.

The North Shore Center also codified the role of a sizable branch of a downtown department store as the retail anchor. As initially envisioned by real estate entrepreneur Huston Rawls, the complex was to have been smaller. Harold Hodgkinson, president of Filene's in Boston, reputedly advised Rawls on expanding the project's scope and introduced him to architect Kenneth Welch. Welch, in turn, advocated a regional center and conducted the exhaustive market study to justify risking the $6,000,000 financial commitment required.[30] His writings on this project indicate a far more sophisticated approach than Stein's. At the time, there was no comparably thorough analysis in print of market potential and strat-

230
Redevelopment plan for central business district, Rye, New York, 1946, Ketchum, Gina & Sharp, architects; project. Perspective of mall. (*Architectural Forum,* August 1946, 78–79.)

egies for its capture in outlying areas. Welch contributed significantly to the advancement of the regional mall concept by delineating a clear, step-by-step method that made the investigative process comprehensible and convincing.[31] He also became the foremost advocate of siting these complexes far from established business centers and residential areas alike, determining location as much from projected growth as from existing use patterns.

Finally, the North Shore Center pioneered in uniting the hard-boiled concerns of retail development with the reformer's ideal of a center planned for social betterment. Extensive recreational facilities were included as a complementary focal unit to the department store. Surrounding acreage would be zoned to protect the residential environs as

231
North Shore Center, Route 128 and Brimbel Avenue, Beverly, Massachusetts, 1947, Ketchum, Gina & Sharp, architects, Anderson & Beckwith, associated architects, Frederick J. Adams, planner, Arthur A. & Sidney N. Shurcliff, landscape architects; project. Aerial perspective, drawing by Vincent Funro. (*Architectural Forum*, June 1947, 84.)

well as to prevent competing interests from locating nearby. Expanding on the idea of Linda Vista, the mall was cast in the mold of a village green, 100 feet wide, around which the buildings formed a modest backdrop (figure 232). The treatment of the storefronts facing the car lot was more elaborate. All aspects of the setting were designed to appeal to consumers and thus induce perambulation.

In creating his Los Angeles project, Gruen relied on the basic conceptual framework established for the North Shore Center, while striking an independent chord in many significant ways. Besides its more complex program, Gruen's scheme possessed greater clarity, with buildings arranged as if in a procession. Centrally poised, the department store held a commanding presence much like that accorded to the church in ideal city plans of the Renaissance or to the courthouse in many U.S. county seats. Yet the mall did not evoke a town street, a market square, or a village green so much as a fabulous boulevard. Later Gruen cited Vienna and other European cities he had known since youth as the ultimate inspiration for his approach to mall design. Consciously or otherwise, however, he seems to have absorbed the metropolitan aspirations embodied in outlying business districts of Los Angeles since the 1920s. Diagrammatically, his scheme was as if the composite Crenshaw Center had spawned a twin across the street, both the main and intersecting arteries had been narrowed, vehicular traffic had been barred, and the adversarial department stores had consolidated to form a new symbol of coherence. In its character, Ketchum's work still harked back to the small town and an agrarian ideal; Gruen's proposal was thoroughly of the city.

No regional mall was in operation when the Los Angeles scheme was published, so the planning of such complexes remained to a large degree theoretical. The context to which experimentation continued to mark the architect's endeavors is revealed by a second project, announced in September 1950, of the same Whittier Boulevard site for which Stein

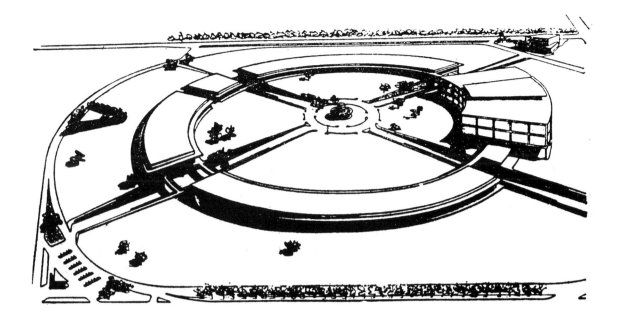

had made studies two years before. Now called the Olympic Shopping Circle, the design was the near opposite of Gruen's earlier plan (figure 233).[32] Instead of being the central focus, the department store rose toward the periphery without much architectural fanfare. The huge core was almost entirely open. Rather than developing the mall as a refuge from the parking area as well as from the street, Gruen maintained the close spatial relationship between automobiles, pedestrians, and storefronts that existed in front-lot centers. The main departure here was the circular plan, in which space existed for 2,000 cars outside the ring and an additional 1,000 within. Access routes divided the plan into quadrants and terminated at a drive-in restaurant positioned like a piece of civic sculpture. Suggestive of a traditional urban square updated for the motor age, the inner zone was clearly the most important. The pedestrian way that encircled this space was wide, tall, and sheltered—delineated by the architect to evoke an arcade bordering the marketplace of a Mediterranean city (figure 234).

Gruen advanced the hollow-core configuration as a means of minimizing the distance between parked cars and stores. Here, too, was an arrangement where the entire complex was readily comprehensible at ground level, not just from the air. Yet the plan had an insurmountable flaw: it channeled automobiles along limited paths from equally limited places of access and egress, intensifying the drawbacks of downtown street patterns. Since the inner parking area would be sought by most customers, peak shopping periods would be plagued by vehicular congestion. Neither Gruen nor his clients seemed aware of just how complicated traffic planning was at this scale. Three months before the Olympic center was announced, he unveiled a design for the even larger Eastland Plaza near Detroit, which was laid out much like the North Shore Center, but with the big interior car lot replacing the green and an even more limited vehicular circulation system (figure 235). The Korean War halted the execution

232
North Shore Center, view of mall, drawing by Vincent Funro. (*Architectural Forum*, June 1947, 91.)

233
Olympic Shopping Circle, Whittier and Olympic boulevards, Goodrich and Gerhart streets, Commerce, 1950, Gruen & Krummeck, architects; project. Aerial perspective. (*Los Angeles Times,* 22 September 1950, I-8.)

of both schemes—a fortunate circumstance for Gruen. Had either one been realized, his reputation might never have recovered.[33]

Over the next two years Gruen rethought the problem thoroughly, as if the Olympic and Eastland centers had been a necessary extreme before his approach could be cast in a fresh perspective. Thereafter he continued to experiment, producing solutions that were no less innovative but that acknowledged the need to plan in different ways for cars and people. By mid-1952 Gruen embarked on a new direction, with buildings grouped tightly around the department store. The most famous example of the so-called cluster plan of his invention was the huge (110 units, 1,192,000 square feet) Northland Center near Detroit (1952–1954), the second commission he received from J. L. Hudson.[34] But Northland was only one in a series that revealed the concept's flexibility in application.[35] The initial plan (1953) for Southdale Center near Minneapolis was similar, but with the mall set on two levels and fully enclosed.[36] With such schemes, Gruen earned his reputation as the nation's leading architect of shopping malls. However, none of this seminal work was for southern California, where patterns were developing along somewhat different lines.[37]

Had Gruen's first mall proposal been realized, Los Angeles might well have become a leading center of innovation in regional mall design. As it was, the metropolitan area was simply one of several places where the type got its initial foothold, and even though examples proliferated there to an unmatched degree by the late 1950s, none became a national model in the way Gruen's 1948 design could have been or his later work in other parts of the country actually was. The architect's questionable reputation among local retailers does not fully explain the outcome. The fact that, even when Gruen became a recognized national pacesetter in shopping center design, his Los Angeles work was relatively unadventurous reflects the persistence of the underlying conservative strain evident in the Los Angeles commercial sphere since the 1930s. The development of streetfront neighborhood centers instead of ones organized around a forecourt prior to the war, the adherence to this pattern even with postwar regional centers such as Westchester and Panorama City, the reluctance to depart from established patterns of multiple ownership—all were symptomatic of an outlook that was inclined toward the ordinary and the expected as much as to the novel. However pathbreaking other facets of its retail development were, and however strong the stereotype of Los Angeles as a harbor for unorthodoxy, local preferences often were guided by mainstream practices.

234
Olympic Shopping Circle, view of mall. (*Los Angeles Times,* 22 September 1950, I-8.)

235
Eastland Plaza, Vernier, Eight Mile, and Kelly roads, Harper Woods, Michigan, 1950, Gruen & Krummeck, architects; project. Model. (*Architectural Forum,* August 1950, 111.)

REALIZATION

While Gruen was still at the early stages of the hollow-core plan, construction was nearing an end on the first two regional malls to see three-dimensional form: Shoppers' World and Northgate. Both were of great importance in validating the mall concept on a large scale, while their fundamental differences emphasized the still tentative nature of such undertakings. Located at Framingham, Massachusetts, nineteen miles west of Boston, Shoppers' World (1949–1951) was conceived as the second unit in Huston Rawls's projected network of regional centers.[38] The basic plan developed for the North Shore Center was retained, while several important modifications were introduced. Shoppers' World was larger (550,000 square feet, forty-four stores, parking for 6,000 cars) and designed to have a major department store branch at either end—a pairing perhaps inspired by the unplanned composite at the Crenshaw Center and one that became a key feature of regional malls by the late 1950s. At the same time, the arrangement was more compact, without wide spaces between building groups. The mall itself was still a broad, parklike space; however, the dual storefront treatment of the North Shore Center was abandoned for one where all the visual emphasis was given to the inner area. Among the most pronounced departures was the two-tier placement of stores, a configuration that may have been inspired by the commercial arcade, and that here doubled the frontage possible for each linear foot of the mall (figure 236). Although it is questionable how much this solution

actually reduced the distances patrons walked, the perceived effect was of a more convenient, cohesive place. The two-story plan failed to elicit much emulation at first, but it did become a favored one for enclosed malls, of which Gruen's Southdale (1953–1956) as the first.[39]

Northgate (1948–1950), located six miles from downtown Seattle, just outside the city limits, was the first regional mall to open and proved more influential than Shoppers' World on its immediate successors, especially those on the west coast.[40] Like the Broadway-Crenshaw Center, this complex was developed under the auspices of a major department store, Seattle's Bon Marche, which proved a key factor in both the layout and tenant structure. The complex was planned foremost to support the Bon Marche branch, which occupied one quarter of its total 800,000 square feet. Rising midway along the 1,500-foot-long "Miracle Mall," the department store was also the most conspicuous feature from the primary approach route (figure 237). A junior department store, Butler Brothers, occupied space at one end, but Bon Marche's major competitor, Frederick & Nelson, was excluded. At the same time, the overall tenant structure was planned for competitive merchandising so that patrons could have a greater choice of goods among the eighty stores. Northgate also had considerable variety in the size, type, and ownership of those stores, including both sizable chain outlets and small shops such as Gruen envisioned for his complex.

The size and scope of Northgate, plans for which were announced in February 1948, may have influenced Gruen in developing his first Los Angeles project, but there were significant differences between the two. The Seattle complex was linear instead of cross-axial in its ar-

236
Shoppers' World, Worcester Road, Framingham, Massachusetts, 1949–1951, Ketchum, Gina & Sharp, architects, Arthur A. & Sidney N. Shurcliff, landscape architects; demolished 1994. View of mall. (Photo author, 1988.)

237
Northgate, First Avenue, N.E., between N. 103rd Street and Northgate Way, Seattle, Washington, 1948–1950, John Graham & Company, architects; altered. Aerial view. Photo Pacific Aerial Surveys, 1950. (*Architectural Forum,* August 1950, 117.)

rangement, and the mall itself was a narrow (forty-eight feet), paved area, which seemed the more contained as a result of canopies over the stores to either side (figure 238). The inspiration for this funnel-like space came from the narrow retail spine in downtown Seattle where the parent store was located. The effect was very different from what Ketchum had designed for Rye or Gruen for Los Angeles.[41] Here the more intimate pedestrian spaces of shopping courts were elongated and homogenized. Customers were also close to the storefronts along either side, their view of window displays interrupted by only a few, unobtrusive planting boxes.

Where Gruen and Ketchum had employed architectural variety, Northgate's buildings, save for the Bon Marche, were minimally treated, signs affording the sole departure from the expanses of unadorned wall and canopy surfaces. Differentiation between storefronts at ground level was not marked either. Neither the buildings nor the ambience competed with the window displays for visual attention. Here the regional center was established as a serious alternative through mercantile attributes alone. Neither Gruen's idea of the mall as a colorful bazaar nor the reformers' ideal of a cultural center—a place of beauty that would revitalize a sense of community life—had much impact on the plan.

Northgate's biggest contribution was to demonstrate that the regional mall could be an attractive investment without an elaborate physical plant. Soon after the complex opened, James B. Douglas, president of the parent company, Allied Stores, was asked why the center resembled the aircraft factory nearby. His response was direct: "Some centers spend a lot more on frills, but they'll never get their money back. The main thing is that Northgate makes money."[42] Sales at the Bon Marche branch ran twice as high as anticipated during its first year of operation. Shoppers' World was also successful, but due to the failure to secure a second depart-

ment store, among other reasons, its operating company declared bankruptcy several years later, severely limiting its influence.[43]

Northgate emerged as the key prototype for work of the early 1950s, not just in general terms but in such particulars as the single department store anchor, competitive merchandising among other tenants, the long and narrow paved mall, and the decisively plain treatment of its buildings. Similar schemes began to appear almost at once, including ones by two Los Angeles architects. Welton Becket incorporated a number of Northgate's features at Stonestown in San Francisco (1950–1952) and in his revised plans for Hillsdale nearby in San Mateo (1952–1954).[44] Equally strong similarities can be seen in the plan Albert C. Martin, Jr., prepared in 1950 for Lakewood Center, the first regional mall to see realization in southern California.

LAKEWOOD CENTER

Plans for Lakewood Center were announced in June 1950, when only Northgate and Shoppers' World were under construction and plans for about eight other regional malls were being prepared elsewhere in the country.[45] In this still infant state of the type's development, Lakewood

238
Northgate, view of mall. Photo Martin Mayer, 1950. (Courtesy Meredith Clausen.)

239
Lakewood Center, Lakewood Boulevard between Del Amo and Candlewood streets, Lakewood, begun 1950, Albert C. Martin & Associates, architects; altered. Aerial view, ca. 1952. (Courtesy Bill Symonds.)

ranked among the most ambitious proposals. The master plan called for
about 100 businesses and parking for 12,000 cars on a 154-acre site (figures 239, 240). Bigness permeated the scheme from the department store
(350,000 square feet) in its center to supermarkets (45,000 square feet
each) at either end.[46] The scale of Gruen's and Stein's biggest projects
here became a reality.

      The impact of Lakewood on local practices derived not just from
its unprecedented size and mall configuration, but from the fact that it was
the first large retail development in the region to be fully integrated since
the Broadway's Crenshaw complex. Probably the most important determinant in shaping Lakewood Center was that it was conceived as the business core of a huge (3,400-acre) development in which more than 17,000
single-family houses accommodating up to 70,000 people were to be constructed.[47] The undertaking departed from most of its kind, locally and nationally, in having so many units constructed by a single firm (a joint
venture company formed by Biltmore Homes and Aetna Construction)
within a short period of time (less than three years). The scheduled pace
of forty to sixty dwellings started each working day was only possible because of a carefully planned production line system in which specialized
crews performed each task in rapid sequence. Like the concurrent work of
Levitt & Sons on the east coast, Lakewood Park's unified operation created an economy of scale that enabled considerable savings in construction
costs and thus lowered the selling price of houses.[48] Much the same thinking probably guided the creation of Lakewood's shopping center. Single

ownership could render both the process of development and the operation more efficient, ultimately generating greater returns.

Lakewood Park was shaped by more than monetary concerns. The entire scheme incorporated a number of features that had been advocated by Los Angeles County planners for some twenty years but that seldom saw implementation.[49] Lakewood Park was conceived as a self-sufficient residential community with its own schools, recreation grounds, religious facilities, and civic center as well as shopping mall. The totality of this agenda exceeded those of Westchester, Panorama City, or most other postwar tracts in the metropolitan area not only in size but in scope, for Lakewood as intended to form a discrete municipal jurisdiction. The target audience, on the other hand, was typical: the many thousands of young, skilled working- and lower-middle-class families that were prospering in the region. Situated seven miles north of downtown Long Beach, Lakewood Park was in a rapidly growing area, near a Douglas Aircraft plant and within convenient driving distance of the region's primary industrial corridor as well as other centers of employment. Yet basic services were few and far between in the immediate area. Lakewood Park's developers did not have to worry about competition; any facilities provided would likely be used by most residents as well as by others less well served in surrounding tracts.

Lakewood's most striking physical departure stemmed from its comprehensive land use program. In sharp contrast to normative patterns of business development along thoroughfares, and even unlike the plans of Westchester and Panorama City where retail activity was confined to arterial nodes, Lakewood's boulevards were generously landscaped, with access roads as buffers between them and the dwellings. Trees and shrubs were planted in great number. Churches, schools, and other institutions was closely related to the housing fabric around them. Commercial activities not only were limited to a single precinct but were separated from other land uses. The guaranteed neighborhood became a product of mass consumption.

Control over land use, coupled with a huge target audience of 70,000 people soon to inhabit Lakewood Park and many thousands more soon to live in the surrounding area, justified Lakewood Center's size. At the same time, the experimental nature of this enterprise, as of the entire development, argued for careful control, with nothing left to chance. To develop Lakewood Center, a subsidiary corporation of the same name was established with Joseph Eichenbaum at its head. Eichenbaum was a veteran in the retail field, having begun his career at the family department store in Chicago and worked with a number of chain companies as a real estate broker once he moved to southern California after the war. However, Eichenbaum had never undertaken a project of his own, let alone one of this magnitude. At a very early stage in the new center's planning, he enlisted the May Company, which, in effect, became a partner in the process well before a contract was signed. The department store's president, Tom May, together with the May Company's design staff and Albert

240
Lakewood Center, site plan. (*Urban Land Institute Technical Bulletin*, July 1953, 79.)

C. Martin, Jr., whose firm had been the architect of May buildings in the region since the 1930s, were the key figures in determining the form Lakewood Center would take.

The May Company's decision to build at Lakewood entailed risks. Current and future growth in the target area was a decisive factor in selecting a branch department store site; however, the locations generally chosen up to that point were close to precincts already occupied by substantial numbers of people. The clientele for Lakewood Center, in contrast, largely consisted of projections. Building at Lakewood Park had just started and few developments around it were much further advanced. The chances that rapid growth would continue were high, so that Lakewood Center would soon stand in a pivotal location from which to draw hundreds of thousands of people from southern Los Angeles and eastern Orange counties; but the outcome was by no means assured. These circumstances may well have influenced the May Company's decision to build an enormous facility of its own and support the creation of a comparably expansive retail center as part of the package. Bigness furthered the risk but also enhanced the market appeal, as the Crenshaw Center had shown. With a number of well-known branches and chain units, a complex the size of Lakewood could draw from a great array of residential areas south of downtown Los Angeles, which had little beyond neighborhood-oriented arterial developments from previous years. The Crenshaw Center showed how strong the draw of a complex could be under those circumstances. Moreover, Lakewood could attract consumers from areas to the south at Long Beach. The latter community had its own department stores, but none matching the status of the May Company. Lakewood was close enough to be a serious competitor, and the complex had more parking space, Eichenbaum stressed, than in all of downtown Long Beach.[50]

To guide the design, "careful surveys" were reportedly made of "every major shopping center in the United States." Yet according to Martin, few of the complexes visited possessed attributes that became models for the scheme. The Crenshaw Center was among the first examined. Tom May was adamant about excluding direct competition with his store; no company would be allowed to do what his had done there. The experience at Crenshaw also made May and Martin reject a plan with rear parking and decide that the department store should have a central place surrounded by car lots. May and Martin inspected the Country Club Plaza, which, for them, affirmed the validity of creating a large, integrated center but provided no model for layout. Shopper's World failed to impress them due to the great width of the mall and the fact that the entire scheme was devised to accommodate two department stores rather than one. Both client and architect felt Northgate looked cheap and unappealing; nevertheless, it appears to have influenced Lakewood's arrangement, hierarchy of stores, and tenant mix.[51]

While similarities existed between Lakewood and Northgate, the two differed in conceptual origin. According to Martin, the decisive party

241

Lakewood Center, view of mall. (*Southwest Builder and Contractor,* 27 October 1950, 31.)

in choosing a mall plan and in determining the nature of its configuration was the May Company's store planning staff. The premise for their solution lay with the aisles of a department store along which various types of merchandise were carefully positioned so as to foster perambulation and impulse buying. Martin had worked closely with these designers on the interiors of the Wilshire and Crenshaw stores. He regarded them as masters at understanding the psychological aspects of shopping and how to induce movement of customers throughout large areas of space. Lakewood's mall was thus developed as an extension of interior planning, an externalized adaptation of the department store aisle. The notion of a downtown shopping street closed to vehicles, the inspiration for Northgate, was a less controlled setting from the retailer's perspective and does not seem to have affected the concept for Lakewood at all.[52]

In reaction to Northgate, considerabe effort was made at Lakewood not to have the experience boring. The mall was slightly wider (sixty feet) than Northgate's; yet it remained a tight, linear zone, paved and with minimal landscaping so that pedestrians could get a clear view of displays on both sides (figure 241). The main difference was that each store could have its own identity—indeed, each was designed by a party of the tenant's choosing—echoing Gruen's 1943 *Forum* proposal. Martin's office prepared plans for the building "shells," which included the canopies. Unlike at Northgate, but again similar to Gruen's scheme, the canopies were set high so that all signs and other elements related to the stores themselves could be treated as a unit below, in full view of customers and subordinate to the overall character of the precinct (figure 242). Martin fur-

ther coordinated the process by reviewing individual store designs to ensure harmonious relationships.

While the street was not an archetype for Lakewood, the results, more than at Northgate, suggested a planned urban landscape. The array of storefronts contributed to this effect; but the predominant ambience was one of order. The site plan possessed Beaux-Arts overtones in its pervasive biaxial symmetry. The complex had an equally distinct hierarchy—the size, shape, and position of each part enunciating its relative importance. However significant the mall as a merchandising space, there was no question as to which side was the front, with the vast May store dominating the ensemble and centered on the primary axis at the end of a tree-lined drive. Plantings, approach routes, and the placement of buildings also gave the complex a clear relationship with the surrounding streets and the site of the municipal center, directly across Lakewood Boulevard. The concern for visual clarity extended to such minor, albeit expensive, details as grading the front car lot on an almost imperceptible slope to give more emphasis to the buildings and less to the automobiles from the periphery—a device Stein had studied for similar reasons in his Whittier Boulevard project (figure 243). Unlike Northgate, where the Bon Marche store projected far beyond its neighbors, the stores at Lakewood had minor recesses, giving continuity to the front elevation end to end. Furthermore, in contrast to the subdued treatment of storefronts fac-

ing the car lots at Northgate and the nondescript character of those at Shoppers' World, counterparts here were much the same as those facing the mall, so that the complex seemed accessible and inviting from its approach paths (figure 244).

SEQUELS

Lakewood Center established a significant precedent in southern California for the construction of large, fully integrated retail complexes, each oriented to a pedestrian mall and conveying little semblance of a conventional urban retail district. Within the Los Angeles metropolitan area, thirteen other regional malls were open or nearing completion of their first phase by 1960.[53] Several more were community-sized centers anchored by a junior department store.[54] Indeed, after Valley Plaza, no regional center was built in the area without a mall as its spine.[55] None of the new complexes was as large as Lakewood; nevertheless, the average size was impressive. Three had between 400,000 and 450,000 square feet of retail space; three between 500,000 and 600,000; five between 675,000 and 800,000. Among the biggest, eight occupied between fifty and eighty-five acres; eight were planned for fifty or more store units; and the same number had parking lots accommodating between 5,000 and 7,000 automobiles. Three had department stores of roughly the same size as the May Company at Lakewood; at least four others had a department store of over 200,000 square feet. Nationwide, only New York rivaled Los Angeles in the number of large new shopping centers within the metropolitan area.[56]

The development of regional malls in Los Angeles occurred at a more or less even pace between the end of the Korean War and the close of the decade. Plans for at least three such complexes were announced in 1953, although construction began on only one of them. Two more were

242
Lakewood Center, detail of Bond Clothes storefront at opening, 1952. (Hearst Collection, Department of Special Collections, University of Southern California.)

243
Lakewood Center, general view showing May Company store and adjacent buildings. Photo author, 1986.

started in 1954 and in 1955; three each in 1956 and 1957, and one each in 1958 and 1959.[57] Two complexes had at least a major component of their master plan opened in 1955. They were joined by one more the following year, four each in 1957 and 1958, and two in 1960. Throughout the period, there was an overriding consistency in layout, tenant structure, and physical character. Among the shopping malls designed before the Korean War, Northgate and its immediate progeny, including Stonestown and Lakewood, were the most obvious precedents for this work. Continuity was fostered in part because two of the earliest sequels (Anaheim Plaza and Los Altos Shopping Center) were designed by Stonestown's architect, Welton Becket, and a third (Eastland) was undertaken by the same team (Eichenbaum, May, and Martin) responsible for Lakewood. Yet by the mid-1950s, the characteristics of these shopping centers reflected tendencies that were national more than particular to southern California or even the west coast.

As at Northgate and Lakewood, the tenancy of Los Angeles malls for the most part included a major department store branch as the retail anchor, balanced by an array of sizable chain outlets and smaller specialty shops. Nonretail functions tended to be limited to closely related support facilities, including restaurants, banks, a few recreational enterprises such as movie theaters and bowling alleys, and an equally modest number of offices, usually for medical and other services people were likely to combine with shopping trips. The broader planning reform agenda of creating a retail complex that also functioned as a civic and/or cultural center secured no more than token acknowledgment. The pedestrian mall in these

facilities tended to be a long and relatively narrow space where paved surfaces rather than landscaping predominated and where store windows were the primary objects of attention. Much as at Northgate, the buildings generally were treated as a neutral backdrop, without the cultivated variety of storefronts proposed in Gruen's projects and realized at Lakewood. But the most pronounced departure from Lakewood and Northgate was in the positioning of the major stores.

The layout of Lakewood was successful owing to its enormous size. All parts of the complex were considered more or less equally desirable because, in addition to the centrally placed department store, there were one or more secondary anchors—a junior department store, variety store, and supermarket—at each end. Less ambitious regional malls could not follow this tripartite arrangement with the same success since they had fewer large units. As a result, the favored layout in southern California and many other parts of the country soon became the "dumbbell" plan in which the major stores were placed at or near the ends. This configuration was planned, but not implemented, as early as 1949 at Shoppers' World. The concept gained additional publicity with an unrealized 1951 scheme undertaken by Marshall Field & Company for 1,500,000-square-foot center at Skokie, Illinois.[58] Probably the first executed dumbbell design plan was Stonestown, which opened in July 1952, not long before the planning got under way for the post–Korean War generation of shopping centers. Stonestown also provided a model in terms of the types of anchor units: a junior department store and huge supermarket, together balancing the major department store at the other end. Preliminary plans for several southern California successors called for a centrally placed department store, but almost all the executed designs utilized the dumbbell configuration.[59]

244
Lakewood Center, general view of store block. Photo author, 1986.

245
Anaheim Plaza, Santa Ana Freeway, Crescent Drive, Euclid and Loara streets, Anaheim, 1954–1957, Welton Becket & Associates, architects; later additions, demolished 1993. Aerial perspective, 1954. (Hearst Collection Department of Special Collections, University of Southern California.)

There was even greater impetus to situate the retail anchors at either end when both units were large branches of major downtown department stores and hence of equivalent stature. The idea of having dual anchors was another unfulfilled innovation of Shoppers' World, where a branch of Filene's was to have complemented that of Jordan Marsh. Most department store executives remained skeptical of such an arrangement, believing that competition should come from specialty stores instead. The closest thing to parity these companies were willing to accept was having a junior department store, as at Northgate, which would remain subordinate to the major store in the shopping center's hierarchy. Some change in thinking began to emerge during the mid-1950s, so that having dual anchors became a distinct trend, if not as yet a prevalent one, by the start of the next decade.

Among the early projects of this type to see realization was Anaheim Plaza (1954–1957), which was developed by the Broadway (figure 245). The leadership of what was by then Broadway-Hale Stores was in a good position to realize the benefits of having dual anchors from firsthand experience at the Crenshaw Center. Again working in collaboration with Coldwell Banker, Broadway executives planned to institutionalize what had occurred unexpectedly at the earlier project. There was little question as to how such an arrangement should be resolved when the entire complex was planned. The Crenshaw Center demonstrated the weaknesses of having the two major stores next to one another; the dumbbell plan was the logical alternative that could work to maximum advantage to all parties.[60] However, persistent apprehension about this concept, coupled with fears that the development of regional centers might soon oversaturate the market, prevented the Broadway's plan from being fully implemented until the 1960s.[61] Anaheim Plaza was also the first regional center in the metropolitan area after Valley Plaza to have its siting predicated on the freeway system, a factor that subsequently became key for almost every retail development of this scale.

Another important innovation in regional center design launched during the 1950s, which appears to have originated in the Los Angeles area, was the so-called "fashion square," comprised of a major department store and branch specialty stores dealing primarily in stylish clothing, accessories, and furniture. A few groupings of this kind were created during the 1940s, among the best known of which were the Miracle Mile at Manhasset, Long Island, and what later became known as the Chestnut Hill Shopping Plaza at Newton, Massachusetts.[62] However, probably the first such undertaking in the country where the complex was fully integrated and employed a pedestrian mall as a unifying feature was Fashion Square (1957–1958), a thirty-two-unit complex undertaken by Bullock's at Santa Ana, the largest community in Orange County (figure 246). More than its prototypes, the new Orange County center carried almost nothing in the way of everyday goods and services. Bullock's officials maintained that the majority of their customers made routine purchases and bought "fashion goods" on different occasions.[63] Thus, alongside the 330,000-square-foot

department store were large outlets of I. Magnin, Desmond's, Haggerty's, and numerous smaller stores. Unlike at many shopping centers, the hierarchy was less one of corporate stature than of size. The layout was more informal than at most contemporary malls, with a large, irregular court, formed by Bullock's on one side, small shops on the other, and the three medium-sized stores at the ends (figure 247).

Like the Broadway, Bullock's devised the scheme based on the success of a previous, unplanned venture. When the company's Pasadena store opened in 1947 it was wholly isolated from retail activity, yet within a few years the fronting street had become the spine of a thriving new district of prestigious shops. During the next decade, over thirty stores were built there, and while it was not an integrated development, South Lake Center, as it became known, was widely recognized as a premier retail precinct. For Bullock's the impact of this growth, all of it orchestrated by Coldwell Banker, was so positive that company executives embarked on planning a complex along somewhat similar lines, without the constraints of, or the congestion from, a bisecting street.[64] The organization that had been so instrumental in creating the lone-wolf department store now joined its competitors in pursuing the potential advantages of a fully planned business center.

The proliferation of regional malls in southern California during the 1950s underscored the pivotal place of Lakewood Center in establishing new standards of scale and planning. A decade after Lakewood was be-

246
Fashion Square, N. Main Street and Roe Drive, Santa Ana, 1957–1958, Pereira & Luckman and others, architects; altered, some parts demolished. Aerial view, 1958. (Hearst Collection, Department of Special Collections, University of Southern California.)

gun, the commercial landscape of the Los Angeles metropolitan area had changed dramatically with fourteen such complexes in operation and proposals for many more under way. Collectively this work not only addressed the demands of an ever-expanding population but posed a serious challenge to the importance of older retail districts—those cast in a traditional mold such as downtown Los Angeles, Hollywood, and Long Beach, and even somewhat newer developments such as the Miracle Mile. As a whole, the complexion was now much less hierarchical, with many places serving as primary retail destination points rather than a single, dominant core with several important but subsidiary nodes around it. Downtown's status as the principal center for retailing had completely dissipated. That district was just another among many—physically larger than any one other place, but eclipsed in sales volume and in prestige by the now greater collective galaxy of regional centers. Downtown was considered of little consequence by a great portion of area residents. Outlying developments, whose promoters had once hoped for hegemony at least in a sizable part of the metropolitan area, likewise had diminished roles. Just as Hollywood never became the preeminent retail center for the region, and no one part of the Wilshire corridor secured dominance over the others, so neither Valley Plaza nor Panorama City attained the position of "down-

town" for all the San Fernando Valley. Pioneering examples of each type reaped the rewards of novelty, drawing consumers from far afield at an early stage, but then competitors began to open, and within a decade the territory was more or less saturated.

The regional malls demonstrated that while the new commercial landscape was quite different in appearance from previous endeavors, many of its underlying aspects drew from work begun in the 1920s. Bullock's credited its Pasadena store with inspiring Fashion Square, but much the same type of district had been created along Wilshire boulevard in large part due to the unprecedented siting of its store there. If the Crenshaw Center provided the obvious antecedent for Anaheim Plaza, A. W. Ross had come close to achieving an equivalent along the Miracle Mile by securing both the new flagship store of the May Company and Coulter's sizable emporium lured from downtown. Indeed, it could be argued that the Miracle Mile also represented the dumbbell plan in embryo, with the May store at one end and a cluster of heavily used chain outlets offering a complementary balance at the other. The Farmers Market, Crossroads of the World, and earlier shopping courts revealed how a space oriented to pedestrians could serve as a significant asset in the retail field. The large chain store, which provided an essential component of the regional mall, and the anchors of less comprehensive centers were profoundly influenced by the focus on volume sales and self-service pioneered by the supermarket. Finally, there was the concept of one-stop shopping at a place where businesses operated in concert and to which one could drive, thence, park and reach the stores conveniently—an experience that regional malls and dozens of smaller shopping centers allowed Angelenos to take for granted by 1960, but which seemed very novel when it was introduced to the previous generation in the guaranteed neighborhood.

AFTERWORD

The transformation from central shopping district to regional shopping mall occurred piecemeal as a result of numerous factors that no one party could predict and over which no one party exercised control. Major department store companies emerged as the pivotal players in the development of the regional mall just as they had been in the rise of the core retail center. In Los Angeles, these firms became crucial in the decentralization process scarcely a decade after finalizing the matrix for downtown development, and they never relinquished their formative influence on patterns of commercial growth during the years that followed. Yet the big stores found that expansion into outlying areas carried the continual risk of undermining their enormous investment in the city center. Department store executives were nervous about such a fate from the earliest stages of branch development. Los Angeles companies were less cautious than most, perhaps because the diffuse nature of residential development seemed to offer no viable alternative. These companies strove to achieve a balance: to maintain big emporia both in and beyond the urban core. But the equilibrium was short-lived. At midcentury, Los Angeles led the nation in the number of large department store branches, while the city also ranked among the least active in updating its premier downtown establishments.

Department store companies expanded outside the city center in part out of fear that chain store firms would seriously undercut their hard-won share of the market if the status quo was maintained. Sears, Roebuck helped create this new, intensely competitive situation by rejecting the

retail hierarchy entrenched in the centralized urban structure. Sears gambled that customers would not feel the need to comparison-shop, as they often did downtown, if they were satisfied with merchandise and pricing. Many other chains adapted this approach, locating in small clusters where they, too, were no longer cast in the department store's shadow. Collectively, these new arterial "Main Streets" posed a threat not just to downtown emporia but to large-scale developments in outlying areas as well. After World War II, the regional shopping center became an instrument for counterattack, a means by which the department stores could regain more control over their competition. Some chain companies no doubt welcomed the regional center for the advantages it afforded, but others may have acquiesced only because there seemed no choice, paralleling the viewpoint of the department stores themselves.

Two decades earlier, the first generation of large shopping centers, epitomized by Westwood Village, bore the individual stamp of their respective developers. These were singular enterprises, much like the elite residential tracts they were built to serve, and they could be realized only because of the large amounts of capital acquired through developing those tracts. After World War II, the demand for integrated retail complexes on this scale extended well beyond the interest and the capacity of the community builders who created their predecessors. Entrepreneurs entering the field had to depend on other parties for funding and thus were beholden to major department store companies before they started to make concrete plans. The required financial commitment was greater because most, if not all, of the project had to be constructed in a short period of time rather than in modest increments as had occurred before the war. The developer was now less a visionary and more a prudent orchestrator of independent parties, few of which accorded high value to costly appearance in a retail complex.

Architects and planners ostensibly exercised greater influence in the casting of the regional mall than they had in most earlier retail centers. Both the concept of physically unified, contained ensemble of stores and that of segregating pedestrian and vehicular areas emanated from their realm. Yet the designer was no more the dominant force than the real estate developer. In much the same way, pragmatists, who could efficiently guide the design through the complex development process, never losing site of the stringent demands made by the leading stores, became the most prominent figures in the field. Acceptance of the regional mall in business circles brought modifications in both character and function to the designer's ideal. Not only did built examples tend to eschew the residential overtones of their forebears, but ties with any nearby residential enclave were rare. The mall belonged to no one place in the traditional sense, but rather to a large, rapidly growing, and continually amorphous swath of the metropolitan area. Much like downtown, the mall was a mercantile arena, not the true community center that J. C. Nichols, Clarence Stein, and Victor Gruen had envisioned.

*The primary force usually cited as shaping new retail develop-
ment was the consuming public. Population movement, increased mobility, greater disposable income, more free time, an ever-expanding middle
class—all were seen as key factors spurring change. Some consumers probably bemoaned the decline of the pampering service found at the best downtown stores. Going to the mall carried little of the drama of shopping in a
big city center, and the range of choices was never as great. But for many
people, the mall represented an improvement. Not only did it lie within
convenient reach, but its stores enabled an unprecedented independence in
the selection of merchandise. For consumers who found the rituals of service at a premier store intimidating, the self-service mode enabled greater
freedom, blistered by confidence in brand names and chain reputations.
Nevertheless, the mall failed to become* the *alternative to downtown, as
some of its proponents hoped. The many experiments undertaken as part
of the decentralization process from the 1920s on left the public with a
spectrum of options that had not existed downtown. Once exposed to this
range, consumers and merchants alike seem to have been reluctant to diminish it in favor of a single course.*

*The transformation from city center to regional mall was thus
only part of the equation. The metropolitan fabric of Los Angeles today
no less than fifty years ago documents the rich repertoire of types, which
includes the core area. While downtown was long ago displaced as the
dominant center of trade, it was never wholly abandoned. In recent decades this precinct has emerged as a regional destination for a predominantly Hispanic clientele. The stores have all changed; the market is
lower-end; nevertheless, thousands of people still travel considerable
distances to shop there.*

*Unplanned arterial development also remains a major component
of the retail landscape. In Los Angeles as in most metropolitan areas, this
genre of building is ubiquitous, both in new districts and in ones long established. Far more outlets can be found in such places than in integrated
business centers of all sizes. Often arterial development is oriented to a
localized trade, but a sizable portion is intended to draw consumers from
a distance, as the Wilshire corridor did by the 1930s. Some such centers
have even assumed the trappings of a miniature downtown, as Hollywood
and other Aladdin cities did prior to the depression. In the Los Angeles
area, Beverly Hills has not only become one of the densest business districts but also one of singular prestige—an unchallenged distinction that
eluded its Wilshire precursors.*

*Much the same has occurred with building types. The intimacy
and stage set–like ambience of the Farmer's Market or shopping courts of
the 1920s have been adapted as a basic fixture in many regional malls as
well as in other, more specialized developments. The lone-wolf store is no
longer a strategy used by the most fashionable emporia, but it retains its efficacy for a number of well-known outlets selling goods as varied as appliances, furniture, and automobiles, and the basic idea of "creating"*

location at a remove from established business areas remains fundamental to many forms of retail development, including the shopping center.

Most of the places discussed in this study no longer retain their original stature. Many have assumed marginal functions. Many, too, have sustained conspicuous physical changes. Some no longer exist. The buildings and districts alike that remain recognizable afford a haunting testament to the short life span we accord to places of commerce. Their legacy, however, transcends the sites and period involved. It has helped to recast the shape and character of the American metropolis. The patterns remain omnipresent in a landscape that some welcome, some merely accept, and others find vile, but that all of us are just beginning to understand.

NOTES

Abbreviations

JOURNALS/NEWSPAPERS

A&E	*Architect and Engineer*
AA	*American Architect*
AAG	*Annals of the Association of American Geographers*
AB	*American Builder*
ABu	*Anaheim Bulletin*
ACi	*American City*
AC	*Architectural Concrete*
AD	*Architectural Digest*
AF	*Brickbuilder/Architectural Forum*
AJ	*Appraiser Journal*
APC	*American Planning and Civic Annual*
APS	*Annals of the American Academy of Political and Social Science*
AR	*Architectural Record*
AR/WS	*Architectural Record*, Western Section
ASPO	American Society of Planning Officials, *Newsletter*
BA	*Building Age*
BHC	*Beverly Hills Citizen*
BW	*Business Week*
CS	*California Southland*
CSA	*Chain Store Age*
CSA/AE	*Chain Store Age*, Administrative Edition
CSA/DE	*Chain Store Age*, Druggist's Edition
CSA/GE	*Chain Store Age*, Grocer's Edition
CSA/GME	*Chain Store Age*, General Merchandise Edition
CSA/VS	*Chain Store Age*, Variety Store Manager's Edition
CSR	*Chain Store Review*
DGE	*Dry Goods Economist*
DSE	*Department Store Economist*
DW	*Display World*
EES	*Eberle Economic Service*
ESN	Culver City *Evening Star News* / *Star News*
GNP	*Glendale News Press* / *Glendale Evening News*
HDC	*Hollywood Daily Citizen* / *Hollywood Citizen News*
HDC/HES	*Hollywood Daily Citizen*, Home Economics Section
IDN	*Inglewood Daily News*
JAPA	*Journal of the American Planning Association*
JLP	*Journal of Land and Public Utility Economics* / *Land Economics*

JSAH	*Journal of the Society of Architectural Historians*
LAEE	*Los Angeles Evening Express*
LAEEY	*Los Angeles Evening Express Yearbook*
LAEx	*Los Angeles Examiner*
LAR	*Los Angeles Realtor*
LAT	*Los Angeles Times*
LATMN	*Los Angeles Times, Midwinter Number*
MA	*Motor Age*
MSBC	*Monthly Summary of Business Conditions*, Security-First National Bank
NRB	National Retail Dry Goods Association, *Bulletin*
NREJ	*National Real Estate Journal*
PCA	*The Architect / Building News / Pacific Coast Architect / California Arts & Architecture / Arts & Architecture*
PI	*Printer's Ink*
PIM	*Printer's Ink Monthly*
PM	*Popular Mechanics*
PP	*Pencil Points / Progressive Architecture*
PSM	*Popular Science Monthly*
PSN	*Pasadena Star News*
PVB	*Palos Verdes Bulletin*
RE	*Retail Executive*
RM	*Retail Management*
SAR	Santa Ana *Register*
SCB	*Southern California Business*
SEP	*Saturday Evening Post*
SMEO	*Santa Monica Evening Outlook*
SMM	*Super Market Merchandising*
SN	*Saturday Night*
SWBC	*Southwest Builder and Contractor*
SWW	*Southwest Wave*
ULI	*Urban Land Institute Technical Bulletin*
VNN	*Van Nuys News*
VT	*Valley Times* (North Hollywood)
WA	*Western Architect*
WHN	*Westwood Hills News / Westwood Hills Press*
WWD	*Women's Wear Daily*

CUL   Rare and Manuscript Collections, Carl A. Kroch
Library, Cornell University

LAMRL   Los Angeles Municipal Research Library

LC   Prints and Photographs Division, Library of Congress

Introduction

1

A concise debate on the subject is presented in William Sharpe and Leonard Wallock, "Bold New City or Built-Up 'Burb? Redefining Contemporary Suburbia," and responses, *American Quarterly* 46 (Mar. 1994), 1–61. Joel Garreau, *Edge City: Life on the New Frontier* (New York: Doubleday, 1991), is a supportive journalistic chronicle. A counterpoint is provided by James Howard Kunstler, *The Geography of Nowhere: The Rise and Decline of America's Man-Made Landscape* (New York: Simon & Schuster, 1993).

    Scholarly examinations of this development include: Brian Berry and Yehoshua Cohen, "Decentralization of Commerce and Industry: The Restructuring of Metropolitan America," in Louis Masotti and Jeffrey Hadden, eds., *The Urbanization of the Suburbs* (Beverly Hills: Sage Publications, 1973), 431–455; Peter Muller, *The Outer City: Geographic Consequences of the Urbanization of the Suburbs* (Washington: Association of American Geographers, 1976); Thomas Baerwald, "The Emergence of a New 'Downtown,'" *Geographical Review* 68 (June 1978), 308–318; Peter Muller, *Contemporary Suburban America* (Englewood Cliffs, N.J.: Prentice-Hall, 1981), chap. 4; Thomas Baerwald, "Land Use Change in Suburban Clusters and Corridors," *Transportation Research Record* 861 (1982), 7–12; Rodney Erickson, "The Evolution of the Suburban Space Economy," *Urban Geography* 4 (Mar.–Apr. 1983), 95–121; Rodney Erickson and Marylyn Gentry, "Suburban Nucleations," *Geographical Review* 75 (Jan. 1985), 19–31; Truman Hartshorn and Peter Muller, "Suburban Business Centers: Employment Implications," U.S. Department of Commerce, Economic Development Administration, Technical Assistance and Research Division, Nov. 1986; Christopher Leinberger, "The Six Types of Urban Village Cores," *Urban Land* 47 (May 1988), 24–27; Robert Cervero, *America's Suburban Centers* (Boston: Unwin Hyman, 1989); Truman Hartshorn and Peter Muller, "Suburban Downtowns and the Transformation of Metropolitan Atlanta's Business Landscape," *Urban Geography* 10 (July–Aug. 1989), 375–395; Thomas Stanback, *The New Suburbanization: Challenge to the Central City* (Boulder: Westview Press, 1991); and Robert Bruegmann and Tim Davis, "New Centers on the Periphery," *Center* 7 (1992), 25–43. Robert Bruegmann, "Schaumburg, Oak Brook, Rosemont, and the Recentering of the Chicago Metropolitan Area," in John Zukowsky, ed., *Chicago Architecture and Design, 1923–1993: Reconfiguration of an American Metropolis* (Munich: Prestel, 1993), 158–177, offers a very valuable historical perspective.

2

The decentralization of industry is also an important part of the equation. However, while certain kinds of manufacturing activities had gravitated to sites near the city center, others traditionally located some distance away. During the nineteenth century, industry as a whole never assumed a strong core configuration comparable to those of service, financial, retail, and other downtown functions.

3

For definitions of the shopping center in general and the regional center in particular, see chapters 6 and 9 below.

4

Pioneering studies include Arthur Grey, "Los Angeles: Urban Prototype," *JLP* 35 (Aug. 1959), 232–242; and Howard Nelson, "The Spread of an Artificial Landscape over Southern California," *AAG* 49 (Sep. 1959), 80–99. For recent examples, see Scott Bottles, *Los Angeles and the Automobile: The Making of the Modern City* (Berkeley and Los Angeles: University of California Press, 1987); Robert Fishman, *Bourgeois Utopias: The Rise and Fall of Suburbia* (New York: Basic Books, 1987), chap. 6; Edward Soja, *Postmodern Geographies: The Reassertion of Space in Critical Social Theory* (London and New York: Verso, 1989), esp. chap. 8; Rob Kling et al., eds., *Postsuburban California: The Transformation of Orange County since World War II* (Berkeley and Los Angeles: University of California Press, 1991); and Greg Hise, "Home Building and Industrial Decentralization in Los Angeles: The Roots of the Postwar Urban Region," *Journal of Urban History* 19 (Feb. 1993), 95–125.

5

For a recent case study of the latter, see Arthur Krim, "Los Angeles and the Anti-Tradition of the Suburban City," *Journal of Historical Geography* 18 (Jan. 1992), 121–138.

6

Mike Davis, *City of Quartz: Excavating the Future in Los Angeles* (London and New York: Verso, 1990), 90. The subject is discussed further in chapter 1 below. Even the historian Reyner Banham departed from conventional scholarship to write his perceptive travelogue of the city, *Los Angeles: The Architecture of Four Ecologies* (Harmondsworth, England: Penguin, 1971).

7

Recent examples of the latter include William Kowinski, *The Malling of America: An Inside Look at the Great Consumer Paradise* (New York: William Morrow, 1985); Edward Pawlak et al., "A View of the Mall," *Social Science Review* 59 (June 1985), 305–317; Jeffrey Jacobs, *The Mall: An Attempted Escape from Everyday Life* (Prospect Heights, Ill.: Waveland Press, 1988); Jeffrey Hopkins, "West Edmonton Mall: Landscape of Myth and Elsewhereness," *Canadian Geographer* 34 (Spring 1990), 2–17; Tracy Davis, "Theatrical Antecedents of the Mall That Ate Downtown," *Journal of Popular culture* 24 (Spring 1991), 1–15; issue on West Edmonton Mall, *Canadian Geographer* 35 (Fall 1991), 226–305; Margaret Crawford, "The World in a Shopping Mall," in Michael Sorkin, ed., *Variations on a Theme Park: The New American City and the End of Public Space* (New York: Hill and Wang, 1992), 3–30; Deborah Karasov and Judith Martin, "The Mall of Them All," *Design Quarterly* 159 (Spring 1993), 18–27; Jon Goss, "The 'Magic of the Mall': An Analysis of Form, Function, and Meaning in the Contemporary Retail Built Environment," *AAG* 83 (Mar. 1993), 18–47; and Witold Rybczynski, "The New Downtowns," *Atlantic Monthly* 271 (May 1993), 98–106.

Most accounts of the shopping center's history draw from a scattering of secondary sources and suffer from inaccuracy. See, for example, Kenneth Jackson, *Crabgrass Frontier: The Suburbanization of the United States* (New York: Oxford University Press, 1985), 257–261; and Peter Rowe, *Making a Middle Landscape* (Cambridge: MIT Press, 1991), chap. 4, as well as passages in several of the writings cited above.

The best historical overview is Meredith Clausen, "Shopping Centers, in John Wilkes, ed., *Encyclopedia of Architecture: Design, Engineering, and Construction,* 4 vols. (New York: John Wiley & Sons, 1989), 4:406–421. Other histories are narrower in focus: idem, "Northgate Regional Shopping Center: Paradigm from the Provinces," *JSAH* 43 (May 1984), 144–161; Howard Gillette, "The Evolution of the Planned Shopping Center in Suburb and City," *JAPA* 51 (Autumn 1985), 449–460; Richard Longstreth, "J. C. Nichols, the Country Club Plaza, and Notions of Modernity," *Harvard Architecture Review* 5 (1986), 120–135; William Worley, *J. C. Nichols and the Shaping of Kansas City: Innovation in Planned Residential Communities* (Columbia: University of Missouri Press, 1990), chap. 8; Richard Longstreth, "The Neighborhood Shopping Center in Washington, D.C., 1930–1941," *JSAH* 51 (Mar. 1992), 5–34; and Thomas Hanchett, "U.S. Tax Policy and the Shopping Center Boom of the 1950s and 1960s," *American Historical Review,* forthcoming. See also Neil Harris, "The City That Shops: Chicago's Retailing Landscape," in Zukowsky, ed., *Chicago Architecture,* 178–199; Harold Kalman, *A History of Canadian Architecture,* 2 vols. (New York: Oxford University Press, 1994), 2:833–837; and Robert Stern et al., *New York 1960: Architecture and Urbanism between the Second World War and the Bicentennial* (New York: Monacelli Press, 1995), 1063–1072.

8

Here I should state that I am personally quite partial to many forms of commercial architecture and have devoted a major portion of the past twelve years to preserving significant examples in the Washington area. Nevertheless, I have consistently sought in these endeavors to build a case on historical merit rather than on personal appreciation. See Richard Longstreth, *History on the Line: Testimony in the Cause of Preservation* (Ithaca, N.Y.: National Council for Preservation Education and National Park Service, forthcoming).

9

A sense of how wide-ranging the concern has become is indicated in the scope of recent literature, for example Constance Beaumont, *How Superstore Sprawl Can Harm Communities (and What Citizens Can Do about It)* (Washington: National Trust for Historic Preservation, 1994); "Beyond Sprawl: New Patterns of Growth to Fit the New California," San Francisco: Bank of America et al., Jan. 1995; and Jerry Adler "Bye-Bye, Suburban Dream," *Newsweek,* 15 May 1995, 40–53.

I am not defending all that has been developed in the recent past nor opposing current strategies for change; only arguing that we should not repeat the mistake of previous generations that dismissed cities of the nineteenth and early twentieth centuries as wastelands.

I The Perils of a Parkless Town

1

For a detailed recent account, see Scott Bottles, *Los Angeles and the Automobile: The Making of the Modern City* (Berkeley and Los Angeles: University of California Press, 1987), 63–91.

2

"The Perils of a Parkless Town," *LAT,* 29 Feb. 1920, II-1.

3

"No Parking Law . . . ," *LAT,* 25 Apr. 1920, VI-1, 6.

4

Bottles, *Los Angeles,* emphasizes the point; however, detailed comparative study of the subject has yet to be undertaken. For a sampling of contemporary sources, see John Gillespie, "The Automobile and Traffic," in National Conference on City Planning, *Proceedings* 1916, 57–90; Robert Whitten, "Unchoking Our Congested Streets," *ACi* 23 (Oct. 1920), 351–354; Ernest Goodrich, "The Urban Auto Problem," National Conference on City Planning, *Proceedings* 1920, 76–105; Herbert Swan, "Our City Thoroughfares—Shall They Be Highways or Garages?," *ACi* 27 (Dec. 1922), 496–500; Walter White, "How the Modern City Traffic Problem Is Affecting Your Business," *PIM* 13 (Apr. 1927), 21–22, 134, 137–138, 141–142; Floyd Parsons, "Everybody's Business," *Eastern States Building Developer* 1 (Dec. 1927), 46–47; John Miller, Jr., "The Chariots That Rage in the Streets," *ACi* 39 (July 1928), 111–114; and Robert Nau, "No Parking—a Year and More of It," *ACi* 40 (Mar. 1929), 85–88.

5

Bottles, *Los Angeles,* 32; Robert Fogelson, *The Fragmented Metropolis: Los Angeles, 1850–1930* (Cambridge: Harvard University Press, 1967), 115; James Elliott, "Los Angeles Leads . . . ," *LAT,* 17 June 1928, V-5; "Metropolitan Los Angeles," *LATMN,* 3 Jan. 1928, V-5.

6

The strategic importance of the aqueduct in the city's growth is emphasized in Steven Erie, "How the Urban West Was Won . . . ," *Urban Affairs Quarterly* 27 (June 1992), 519–554.

7

Mark Foster, "The Decentralization of Los Angeles during the 1920's," Ph.D. diss., University of Southern California, 1971, 2; idem, "The Model-T, the Hard Sell, and Los Angeles's Urban Growth . . . ," *Pacific Historical Review* 44 (Nov. 1975), 461.

8

Fogelson, *Fragmented Metropolis,* 115–134; Bottles, *Los Angeles,* 198–200; *Los Angeles County: Some Facts and Figures* (Los Angeles: Los Angeles Chamber of Commerce, 1926), 6–15; Foster, "Decentralization," 36–37; L. M. Benton, *A Study of 81 Principal American Markets* (Chicago: The 100,000 Group of American Cities, 1925), 141.

9

Los Angeles's nonwhite population in 1930 (14.2 percent) was the second highest among major cities in the nation. For a good account of the general subject, see Fogelson, *Fragmented Metropolis,* 75–84. Numerous insights are also afforded by writings of the period; see especially Albert Atwood, "Money from Everywhere," *SEP* 195 (12 May 1923), 10–11, 134, 137, 140–141, 144, 147.

10

Walter Woehlke, "How Long Los Angeles?," *Sunset* 52 (Apr. 1924), 10; Louis Adamic, "Los Angeles! There She Blows!," *Outlook and Independent* 155 (13 Aug. 1930), 594. See also Garet Garrett, "Los Angeles in Fact and Dream," *SEP* 203 (18 Oct. 1930), 138.

11

The quotations are from Woehlke, "How Long?," 10; and Joseph Lilly, "Metropolis of the West," *North American Review* 232 (Sep. 1931), 240–241, 242. See also James Collins, "Los Angeles: Ex-Crossroads Town," *World's Work* 59 (Aug. 1930), 54; Fogelson, *Fragmented Metropolis,* 81; Foster, "Decentralization," 23, 35.

12

Marrow Mayo, *Los Angeles* (New York: Alfred A. Knopf, 1933), 327–328.

13

Lilian Symes, "The Beautiful and the Dumb," *Harper's Monthly* 163 (June 1931), 32.

14

Lilly, "Metropolis," 240; Sarah Comstock, "The Great American Mirror," *Harper's* 156 (May 1928), 723, 715.

15

Carey McWilliams, "*Southern California Country* (New York: Duell, Sloan & Pearce, 1946), 12–13.

16

Cecil B. DeMille, "The Birth of a Giant," *SCB* 2 (Dec. 1923), 19; "Subdivision Situation . . . ," *EES* 8 (2 Mar. 1931), 37; Charles Clark, "Penalties of Excess Subdividing," *City Planning* 10 (Apr. 1934), 52, 54; Fogelson, *Fragmented Metropolis,* 92, 142–143; Bottles, *Los Angeles,* 32, 189; Martin Wachs, "Autos, Transit, and the Sprawl of Los Angeles . . . ," *JAPA* 50 (Summer 1984), 298–301; Authur Grey, "Los Angeles: Urban Prototype," *JLP* 35 (Aug. 1959), 233.

17

For a sampling of period accounts, see "Fact and Comment," *LAT,* 1 May 1910, V-1; "Fact and Comment," *LAT,* 5 June 1910, V-1; "Great Growth . . . ," *LAT,* 19 June 1910, VI-1; "Southern California . . . ," *LATMN,* 1 Jan. 1912, 162; and "Tremendous Activity . . . ," *LAT,* 14 July 1912, VI-1.

18

Fogelson, *Fragmented Metropolis,* 146; Bottles, *Los Angeles,* 187, 189; "Building in Los Angeles . . . ," *EES* 5 (July 1928), 167–170; "Economic and Sociological Aspects . . . ," *EES* 4(18 July 1927), 173–175. Between 1919 and 1930, 117,340 "family capacities" were provided in the new construction of single houses, 45,563 in duplexes, and 79,833 in multiunit buildings. By 1933 apartments afforded 109,026 "family capacities," single houses 231,956; see "The Housing Situation," *MSBC,* 2 Jan. 1934, n.p.

19

To my knowledge, no detailed comparative survey exists of the spatial order found in such precincts of the 1920s. The observations made in this paragraph and the one below are based on firsthand study, covering several thousand miles in the Los Angeles area and many times that elsewhere. A number of cities, particularly those in the south-central and southwestern states, acquired much the same ambience as Los Angeles, albeit on a smaller scale. The influence on places such as Phoenix and Houston exerted by practices in southern California, or vice versa, deserves further study.

20

For a contemporary account, see Marc Goodnow, "Be It Ever So Humble . . . ,"
SCB 7 (Jan. 1929), 20–21, 47, 49.

21

Bottles, *Los Angeles,* 40.

22

Ibid., 34–39.

23

Ibid., 58–59.

24

"Automobile Is Now a Necessity," *LAT,* 20 Mar. 1921, VI-3; Howard Nelson and
William Clark, *Los Angeles Metropolitan Experience: Uniqueness, Generality, and the
Goal of the Good Life* (Cambridge, Mass.: Ballinger, 1976), 277; Bottles, *Los Angeles,*
93; Benton, *81 Principal American Markets,* 141; "Traffic Proves City's Noose," *LAT,*
12 June 1938, II-1. See also Ashleigh Brilliant, *The Great Car Craze* (Santa Barbara:
Woodbridge Press, 1989); Ernest McGaffey, "The Automobile Transforms Business," *SCB* 2 (Aug. 1923), 17, 39–40; Edward Hungerford, "California Takes to
the Road," *SEP* 196 (22 Sep. 1923), 27, 108, 113–114; "California Stands . . . ,"
LAT, 4 Mar. 1928, VI-1; "Golden State Wealth . . . ," *LAT,* 9 Feb. 1930, VI-1, 3;
and Frank Snook, "Growth of Motoring in California," *California Real Estate* 10
(June 1930), 1.

25

Used cars appear to have been sold primarily direct from their owners. Numerous
advertisements appeared in *LAT* encouraging two-car families and the use of the
paper's own want ads section as a source for purchases. See, for example, 7 July
1925, I-6; 21 Nov. 1926, IV-12; 10 Mar. 1929, I-8.

26

Comstock, "Great American Mirror," 718, 720.

27

McWilliams, *Southern California,* 135.

28

Los Angeles Board of Public Works, *Annual Report* 1927–1928, 27; "Streets
Here . . . ," *LAT,* 18 Dec. 1927, V-8. For analysis of local street improvements generally, see Bottles, *Los Angeles,* chap. 4. This and other recent accounts emphasize
the inadequacies of the street system downtown and the problems with street
improvement elsewhere in the city without emphasizing the enormous amount
of work that was accomplished and its effect on driving habits.

29

Interviews with the late Regula Fybel, Los Angeles, 25 June 1987, and Albert
Frey, Palm Springs, 27 June 1987. Both recounted their own experiences driving
in the city during the late 1920s and/or 1930s.

30

Gordon Whitnall, *Municipal League of Los Angeles Bulletin* 5 (30 Nov. 1928), 3.

31

A. J. Gries, "Measuring Los Angeles Purchasing Power by Motor Car Statistics," *LAR* 2 (Oct. 1922), 23.

32

"Finding Out . . . ," *LAT,* 31 Oct. 1920, V-1; Clarence Snethen, "Los Angeles Activity Reflected . . . ," *LAR* 4 (June 1924), 31; Frederick Law Olmsted et al., *A Major Traffic Street Plan for Los Angeles* (Los Angeles: Committee on Los Angeles Plan of Major Highways and Traffic Commission of the City and County of Los Angeles, May 1924). For a sampling of period accounts of traffic problems see David Edstrom, "Congestion as Fatal . . . ," *LAT,* 13 Mar. 1921, II-2; "Los Angeles and Its Motor-Jam," *Literary Digest* 81 (26 Apr. 1924), 68–71; and Walter Woehlke, "Traffic Jams . . . ," *Sunset* 56 (Mar. 1926), 38–41, 92–93.

II The Problems Solved

1

The project is discussed in the text below. See note 64 for references.

2

Howard Nelson and William Clark, *Los Angeles Metropolitan Experience: Uniqueness, Generality, and the Goal of the Good Life* (Cambridge, Mass.: Ballinger, 1976), 191–193; Lee Phillips, "The Retail Business Section of Los Angeles," *LAR* 1 (Nov. 1921), 1; John Cooper, "Spring Street's . . . ," *LAT,* 1 June 1930, V-2; Earle Crowe, "Wall Street of the West," *LATMN,* 2 Jan. 1930, II-6.

3

"Permits for Height Limit Buildings," typescript, LAMRL, n.p.; P. R. Kent, "Los Angeles," *The Skyscraper* 1 (Feb.–Mar. 1925), 56; "The Office Building Situation . . . ," *EES* 3 (14 June 1926), 128; "City Takes High Rank . . . ," *LAT,* 1 June 1930, V-2. Readily available statistics of office space in Los Angeles are not broken down by district; nevertheless, period accounts, maps, and photographs, coupled with fieldwork in the core and counterparts across the country, leaves no doubt as to the Los Angeles core's magnitude and importance.

4

"Twenty-five Years Hence," *LATMN,* 1 Jan. 1913, 131–132. See also Heber Waters, "Hillside Life . . . ," *LAEx,* 30 Apr. 1925, IV-1; Charles Sloan, "No Prophesies . . . ," *LAT,* 6 Dec. 1925, III-26; *LAT,* 3 Apr. 1929, I-4; *LAEEY* 1930, cover; and *LAT* Fiftieth Anniversary Ed., 4 Dec. 1931, I-3.

5

Irving Hellman, "The Skyscraper's Influence on Municipal Progress," *The Skyscraper* 1 (Feb.-Mar. 1925), 6.

6

Concerning Boston, see Douglass Shand Tucci, *Built in Boston: City and Suburb 1800–1950* (Boston: New York Graphic Society, 1978), 186; concerning Washington, see U. S. Congress, House, *Building Height Limitations,* S. Report, Committee on the District of Columbia, 94th Cong., 2nd sess., 1976; concenring Chicago, see Carol Willis, "Light, Height, and Site: The Skyscraper in Chicago," in John Zukowsky, ed., *Chicago Architecture and Design 1923–1993: Reconfiguration of an American Metropolis* (Munich: Prestel, 1993), 119.

7

Department of City Planning, City of Los Angeles, "Preliminary Report, Proposed City Charter Amendment, Building Height Limits," typescript, Feb. 1956, LAMRL, 1–3; Gordon Whitnall, "Many Advantages Possessed . . . ," *LAR* 1 (Apr. 1922), 5, 24; "Building Height . . . ," *LAT,* 21 Sep. 1923, II-1, 3; "Height Limit . . . ," *LAT,* 30 Sep. 1923, V-2; Lawrence McNeil, "Should Los Angeles Maintain . . . ?," *LAR* 6 (Jan. 1927), 15, 26; Gordon Whitnall, "Building Height Limitation," *California Real Estate* 7 (Apr. 1927), 18; "Building Owners Association Oppose . . . ," *SWBC* 73 (21 June 1929), 35; "City's Skyline Plans . . . ," *LAT,* 11 Mar. 1931, II-1.

8

Concerning Hamburger's, see Alice Mary Phillips, *Los Angeles: A Guide Book* (Los Angeles: Neuner Co., 1907), 44–47; "Four Great Buildings . . . ," *LAT,* 3 Aug. 1919, V-1; and advertisements in *LAT,* 21 June 1896, 30; 26 July 1896, 30; and 1 June 1899, 9. The Broadway opened in 1895 under the proprietorship of J. A. Williams & Co. (*LAT,* 29 Aug. 1895, 9), but closed shortly thereafter. The store's lease and stock were purchased by Arthur Letts, who established a new operation but retained its predecessor's name. Much useful material on the Broadway can be gleaned from a biography of its owner, written by a chief lieutenant; see William Kilner, *Arthur Letts 1862–1923* (Los Angeles: privately published, Young & McCallister, Inc., 1927). See also advertisements in *LAT,* 8 July 1900, II-3; 2 July 1904, VI-8; and 6 Feb. 1916, II-16.

Most square footage figures given in the text here are approximations calculated from 1906 Sanborn fire insurance atlases. The estimates represent gross floor area. Space devoted to sales tended to be considerably less.

Illustrations of many early Los Angeles business buildings appear in the Sunday *LAT* from 14 June to 20 Sep. 1896. See also "Our Business Blocks," *LAT,* 1 Jan. 1896, 9.

9

Neil Harris, "Museums, Merchandising, and Popular Taste: The Struggle for Influence," in Ian Quimby, ed., *Material Culture and the Study of Amreican Life* (New York: W. W. Norton, 1978), 149–154, and William Leach, "Transformations in a Culture of Consumption: Women and Department Stores, 1890–1925," *Journal of American History* 71 (Sep. 1984), 319–342, provide introductory cultural analyses of this phase in the department store's development. Little has been written on the buildings. the most insightful overview is Meredith Clausen, "Department Stores," in Joseph Wilkes, ed., *Encyclopedia of Architecture: Design, Engineering & Construction,* 4 vols. (New York: John Wiley & Sons, 1988), 2:204–222. See also her "The Department Store: Development of the Type," *Journal of Architectural Education* 39 (Fall 1985), 20–29. For a case study of a prototypical example, see Ann Van Zanten, "The Marshall Field Annex and the New Urban Order of Daniel Burnham's Chicago," *Chicago History* 11 (Fall–Winter 1982), 130–141. Important background studies of the ascendancy of the department store as a phenomenon during the second half of the nineteenth century include Gunther Barth, *City People: The Rise of Modern City Culture in Nineteenth-Century America* (New York: Oxford University Press, 1980), chap. 4; Susan Porter Benson, *Counter Cultures: Saleswomen, Managers, and Customers in American Department Stores, 1890–1940* (Urbana and Chicago: University of Illinois Press, 1986), chap. 1; and William Leach, *Land of Desire: Merchants, Power and the Rise of a New American Culture* (New York: Pantheon, 1993). See also H. Pasdermadjian, *The Department Store: Its Origins, Evolution and Economics* (London: Newman Books, 1954), esp. chap. 2.

The best period account of the subject is Paul Nystrom, *Economics of Retailing,* 2 vols. (rev. ed., New York: Ronald Press, 1930), chap. 6. See also J. Russell Doubman and John Whitaker, *The Organization and Opertaion of Department Stores* (New York: John Wiley & Sons, 1927), esp. 9–21.

10

"Unique Ideas in Big Store," *LAT,* 14 Apr. 1906, I-6; Phillips, *Los Angeles,* 45–47; "Public Library . . . ," *LAT,* 9 Feb. 1908, V-1; "Imposing and Practical," *DGE,* 28 Nov. 1908, 111, 113, 115; *WA* 16 (Sep. 1910), 94. See also "Four Great Buildings." Hamburger's and other west coast department stores are illustrated in *PCA* 10 (Nov. 1915), pls.

11

This site and that of Bullock's, discussed in the text below, are illustrated in J. E. Scott, "Los Angeles, the Old and the New," supplement to *Western Insurance News* 8 (Nov. 1911), 54 and 50, respectively.

12

Concerning the movement of downtown retail districts, see Martyn Bowden, "Growth of the Central District in Large Cities," in Leo Schnore, ed., *The New Urban History* (Princeton: Princeton University Press, 1973), 75–109; and idem, "Persistence, Failure, and Mobility in the Inner City: Preliminary Notes," in Ralph Ehrenberg, *Pattern and Process: Research in Historical Geography* (Washington: Howard University Press, 1975), 169–192.

Concerning mid-nineteenth-century developments in New York, see Mona Domosh, *Invented Cities: The Creation of Landscape in Nineteenth-Century New York and Boston* (New Haven: Yale University Press, 1996), chap. 2. M. Christine Boyer, *Manhattan Manners: Architecture and Style 1850–1900* (New York: Rizzoli, 1985), chap. 3; Charles Lockwood, *Manhattan Moves Uptown* (Boston: Houghton Mifflin, 1976), chap. 8; and Edgar Hoover and Raymond Vernon, *Anatomy of a Metropolis* (Cambridge: Harvard University Press, 1959), 113–116.

13

Robert Twyman, *History of Marshall Field & Co. 1852–1906* (Philadelphia: University of Pennsylvania Press, 1954), 21–24; Joseph Siry, *Carson Pirie Scott: Louis Sullivan and the Chicago Department Store* (Chicago: University of Chicago Press, 1988), chap. 1; Miles Berger, *They Built Chicago: Entrepreneurs Who Shaped a Great City's Architecture* (Chicago: Bonus Books, 1992), 7–11, 77–84.

14

LAT, 29 July 1906, II-19. Different full-page advertisements appeared with some frequency in *LAT* during the months of June, July, and August. See also "Hamburgers Sell Broadway Frontage," *LAT,* 10 May 1908, V-1. Hamburger established a separate organization for the purpose, Hambuger Realty & Trust Company, which collaborated with another real estate firm, Robert Marsh & Company.

15

According to Kilner, *Arthur Letts,* 182–183, Letts financed the new establishment but did not review Bullock's plans while the project was under way. The two stores retained separate identities; the public did not become aware that they were under single ownership until years later. Conerning the facility itself, see "Tehama Building . . . ," *LAT,* 29 Apr. 1906, V-1.

16

Sherley Hunter, "Nine Acres of Service . . . ," *WWD,* Retail Merch. Sect., 8 Oct. 1915, 5; "Greater Bullock's . . . ," *LAT,* 15 Jan. 1911, V-24; "Bullock's Acquires . . . ," *LAT,* 29 June 1919, V-1. The last addition was made in 1928; see "New Six Floor . . . ," *WWD,* 28 July 1928, 6; and "Formally Open . . . ," *WWD,* 11 Sep. 1928, I-11.

17

LAT, 1 Apr. 1900, IV-5; 25 Mar. 1900, IV-5; 11 Mar. 1900, IV-3; 6 Feb. 1916, II-16.

18

"Plans for Mammoth Store," *LAT,* 29 Dec. 1912, V-1; *PCA* 10 (Nov. 1915), 154.

19

"Feels Pulse of Broadway," *LAT,* 7 June 1914, V-1.

20

"Plans Shaping . . . ," *LAT,* 24 May 1914, VI-1; H. A. Stebbins, "Splendid New Building . . . ," *WWD,* 5 June 1914, Merch. Ed., 1, 16; "Rush Work . . . ," *LAT,* 6 June 1915, V-1; "Great Palace . . . ," *LAT,* 5 Sep. 1915, V-1; Hunter, "Nine Acres of Service," 5, 12; "Architectural Treatment of a Modern Store," *PCA* 10 (Nov. 1915), 225, 234, 238. The site was proposed for this use by others as early as 1912; see "Seventh and Grand . . . ," *LAT,* 28 Jan. 1912, V-1. Concerning the earlier Robinson's store, see *LAT,* 22 Sep. 1895, 27; and *LATMN,* 1 Jan. 1897, 39.

21

Harvey Westgate, "Swarms of Jitneys . . . ," *LAT,* 3 Dec. 1916, VI-1, and sequential articles on pp. 2–3. See also idem, "L. A. Man Asks . . . ," *LAT,* 17 Dec. 1916, VI-2; and "High Above Traffic Eddy," *LAT,* 13 Sep. 1914, VI-1, 2. Earlier moves by retailers to Broadway may also have been influenced by growing streetcar congestion on Main Street, which had become so acute by 1905 that a proposal to construct elevated tracks was made. See "Streetcar Congestion . . . ," *LAT,* 10 Dec. 1905, II-1.

22

Stebbins, "Spendid New Building," 1; Hunter, "Nine Acres of Service," 5.

23

"Fact and Comment," *LAT,* 3 May 1914, V-1.

24

"Fact and Comment," *LAT,* 10 May 1914, V-1.

25

"New Block for West Seventh," *LAT,* 1 July 1917, V-1, 12; "Two Big Projects . . . ," *LAT,* 15 July 1917, V-1; "Association to Back . . . ," *LAT,* 16 Sep. 1917, V-1, 12; "New Store Ready," *LAT,* 7 Oct. 1917, V-1. The street's potential was recognized as early as 1907 when Bullock's was still under construction; see "Seventh Street . . . ," *LAT,* 24 Feb. 1907, V-22.

26

For a sampling of accounts of large Broadway stores, see "Rushing Work . . . ," *LAT,* 18 Apr. 1909, V-1; *LAT,* 18 Jan. 1914, Barker Brothers extra issue; "Contract Let . . . ," *LAT,* 10 Dec. 1916, V-1; "Millions Go . . . ," *LAT,* 22 Apr. 1917, V-1, 13.

27

These, and the general observations in the text below, are based on numerous period accounts, maps, directories, and photograph as well as on-site study.

28

"Hamburger Store Sold," *LAT,* 1 Apr. 1923, I-1, 2; "Buildings Announced," *LAT,* 29 July 1923, V-1; *LAT,* 22 June 1924, II-15; "May Co. Open . . . ," *WWD,* 10 Mar. 1925, 55; "Plan 10-Story . . . ," *WWD,* 20 Feb. 1929, 1; *LAT,* 24 Mar. 1929, III-33; *LAT,* 7 May 1929, II-8 (May Co.); "Bullock's Acquires . . . ," *LAT,* 29 June 1919, V-1; "Bullock's Plan . . . ," *WWD,* 13 Apr. 1923, 1; *LAT,* 28 July 1924, I-7; "Bullock's Open . . . ," *WWD,* 20 Nov. 1924, 41; *LAT,* Mar. 1926, II-3; "Trio of Major Units . . . ," *LAT,* 2 Oct. 1927, V-1, 2; "Bullock's Will Build . . . ," *LAT,* 26 Feb. 1928, II-1; "New Sixth Floor . . . ," *WWD,* 28 July 1928, 8; "Formally Open . . . ," *WWD,* 11 Sep. 1928, I-11; *LAT,* 6 Mar. 1932, III-1 (Bullock's).

29

"Shopping District . . . ," *LAT,* 11 Jan. 1923, II-1; *WWD,* 23 Jan. 1923, 57 (Robinson's); "Will Add . . . ," *LAT,* 9 July 1922, V-1; "Millions for New Buildings," *LAT,* 22 Apr. 1923, V-1, 19; "Work to Start . . . ," *WWD,* 1 May 1923, 42; *WWD,* 7 May 1923, 27; "Store Unveils . . . ," *LAT,* 9 Nov. 1924, II-2; "Sale at Opening . . . ," *WWD,* 17 Nov. 1924, 33; "New Floor Opened . . . ," *WWD,* 10 Feb. 1925, 65; "The Broadway Plans . . . ," *WWD,* 3 June 1929, I-13 (the Broadway); "Fifth Street Store . . . ," *LAT,* 14 Aug. 1921, V-1; "Fifth Street Store . . . ," *WWD,* 6 Feb. 1923, 55; "Seven Taken . . . ," *LAT,* 10 Mar. 1924, II-1, 2 (Fifth Street Store). Soon after the Fifth Street Store's new building was completed the name was changed to Walker's, after the company president, but reverted to Fifth Street Store in 1937. Nine years later, the name was changed once again to Milliron's. Gimbel Brothres anticipated building a large store as well; see "Hear Gimbel's Plan . . . ," *WWD,* 28 Apr. 1923, 1, 3.

30

"Will Open New Store," *LAT,* 31 Aug. 1920, I-9 (Silverwood's). Desmond's management initially planned to expand the existing facility on Spring Street ("Prepare Plans . . . ," *LAT,* 9 Jan. 1921, V-1), but soon decided to relocate in larger new quarters in the heart of the shopping district on Broadway; see "Store and Mills . . . ," *LAT,* 10 June 1923, V-1; "New Desmond . . . ," *LAT,* 16 Sep. 1924, II-3; *LAT,* 23 Sep. 1924, I-7; and *LAT,* 3 Oct. 1924, I-9. Harris & Frank's executives contemplated building a large new store as early as 1917 ("Association to Back . . . ," *LAT,* 16 Sep. 1917, V-1, 12) but completely revised the building program after World War I; see "Five Major Projects . . . ," *LAT,* 11 Jan. 1925, V-1, 2; *LAT,* 2 Nov. 1925, I-5; Olive Gray, "Years Bridged . . . ," *LAT,* 3 Nov. 1925, II-22; and *LAT,* 13 Dec. 1925, I-15. Concerning Myer Siegel, see "Six-Story Building . . . ," *LAT,* 10 Jan. 1926, V-1; "Projected Myer-Siegel . . . ," *WWD,* 19 Jan. 1926, 4; "New Block on Flower . . . ," *LAT,* 9 Jan. 1927, V-2; and *LAT,* 6 Feb. 1927, III-3.

31

LAT, 4 Jan. 1920, I-9; "Fine Buildings . . . ," *LAT,* 5 Feb. 1922, V-1, 2; *LAT,* 12 Aug. 1923, II-2; "Wurlitzer Building," *LAT,* 30 Sep. 1923, V-1; *LAT,* 6 Mar. 1927, V-2; *LAT,* 3 Jan. 1928, I-5.

32

LAT, 7 Dec. 1897, 11; *LAT,* 10 July 1898, 14; *LAT,* 6 Nov. 1903, II-7; *LAT,* 25 Feb. 1906, II-8; *LAT,* 2 Jan. 1910, III-21; *LAT,* 2 Jan. 1910, II-5; *LAT,* 13 Mar. 1910, II-11; *LAT,* 11 Apr. 1915, III-13.

33

"Rushing Work . . . ," *LAT,* 18 Apr. 1909, V-1; *LAT,* 18 Jan. 1914, I-4; *LAT,* 11 Sep. 1921, V-1; *LAT,* 21 Aug. 1921, II-7; "Big Firm . . . ," *LAT,* 11 Sep. 1921, V-1; *LAT,* 9 Oct. 1922, II-11.

34

"Sixty Million . . . ," *LAT,* 31 Oct. 1924, II-1, 2; "Los Angeles Sets . . . ," *LAT,* 13 Dec. 1924, I-13, 14; *LAT,* 28 Dec. 1924, III-32; "Rush Work . . . ," *LAT,* 8 Nov. 1925, V-1; Olive Gray, "Hospitality . . . ," *LAT,* 24 Jan. 1926, II-3; *PCA* 30 (July 1926), 20.

35

"Firm Plans . . . ," *LAT,* 14 Jan. 1924, I-4; *LAT,* 3 May 1923, I-4; "Begin Soon . . . ," *WWD,* 25 Mar. 1927, 47; *LAT,* 25 May 1927, I-7; Olive Gray, "Genius Honors . . . ," *LAT,* 4 Dec. 1927, II-9; "Skyline Buildings Rise," *LAT,* 15 Apr. 1928, V-1; *LAT,* 15 May 1928, I-9; *LAT,* 5 Oct. 1928, I-14; *AB* 45 (June 1928), 58–59 (Alexander & Oviatt); "Skyscraper Job . . . ," *LAT,* 15 Jan. 1928, V-1; *LAT,* 11 Oct. 1928, I-6, 7; Olive Gray, "New Store . . . ," *LAT,* 12 Oct. 1928, II-5; *LAT,* 12 Dec. 1928, II-20 (Foreman & Clark).

36

For a sampling of small stores in much larger office buildings, see *LAT,* 20 Oct. 1920, I-5; *LAT,* 7 Nov. 1920, III-36; *LAT,* 1 May 1921, II-3; *LAT,* 18 Nov. 1921, III-2; *LAT,* 24 May 1921, II-11; *LAT,* 10 Feb. 1922, I-5; *LAT,* 17 Oct. 1923, II-14; *LAT,* 14 Oct. 1924, II-9; *LAT,* 8 Jan. 1925, I-9; *LAT,* 13 Sep. 1925, III-13; *LAT,* 16 Sep. 1925, II-6; *LAT,* 11 Oct. 1925, III-8; *LAT,* 14 Mar. 1926, III-6; *LAT,* 16 May 1926, I-4; *LAT,* 3 Jan. 1928, III-5; *LAT,* 19 Aug. 1929, I-8; *LAT,* 15 Sep. 1929, III-9; and *LAT,* 27 Nov. 1929, III-10.

For examples of small, purpose-built retail facilities, see *LAT,* 8 Sep. 1921, III-42; "New Stores . . . ," *LAT,* 5 June 1921, V-1; *LAT,* 8 Sep. 1921, III-42; *LAT,* 13 Nov. 1921, III-1; "Big Lease . . . ," *LAT,* 27 Nov. 1921, V-1; *LAT,* 6 Nov. 1922, II-12; *LAT,* 3 Dec. 1922, II-6; "Will Open . . . ," *LAT,* 25 June 1924, V-7; *LAT,* 14 Nov. 1926, I-8; and *LAT,* 12 Dec. 1928, I-5.

37

"Downtown Congestion . . . ," *LAT,* 16 Sep. 1923, V-16; Bernard Rosenthal, "Outlook for Flower Good," *LAT,* 24 Sep. 1924, V-3.

38

LAT, 5 June 1921, III-11; "New Buildings . . . ," *LAT,* 3 July 1921, V-1.

39

"To Build on Flower," *LAT,* 7 May 1922, V-1; "To Build on Flower," *LAT,* 20 Aug. 1922, V-1; *LAT,* 19 Nov. 1922, III-19; "Valuable Addition . . . ," *LAT,* 15 Apr. 1923, V-15; *LAT,* 5 June 1923, II-7; "Shoe Store . . . ," *LAT,* 6 Dec. 1925, II-2; "Store Unit . . . ," *LAT,* 14 Nov. 1926, V-1; "Ransohoff's Unit . . . ," *WWD,* 26 Nov. 1926, 8, 53; "New Store . . . ," *LAT,* 2 Jan. 1927, III-17; *LAT,* 2 Oct. 1927, III-11; *LAT,* 30 Mar. 1930, V-2; "Tailors Pick . . . ," *LAT,* 4 Jan. 1931, II-7.

40

"Exclusive Shop . . . ," *LAT,* 25 Apr. 1926, V-11; "Building Height Extended," *LAT,* 27 Mar. 1927, V-1; Olive Gray, "Great Store . . . ," *LAT,* 11 June 1927, I-7; Olive Gray, "New Store . . . ," *LAT,* 12 June 1927, III-30. Concerning Myer Siegel, see note 30 above.

41

"Downtown Congestion . . . ," *LAT,* 16 Sep. 1923, V-16; "Flower-Street . . . ," *LAT,* 25 Nov. 1923, V-7; "Outlook . . . Good," *LAT,* 24 Sep. 1924, V-3; "Exclusive Shop Area . . . ," *LAT,* 25 Apr. 1926, V-11; "Established District . . . ," *WWD,* 15 Oct. 1926, 26. For background on N. Michigan Avenue, see John Stamper, *Chicago's North Michigan Avenue* (Chicago: University of Chicago Press, 1991). Comparable precincts in other cities include Chestnut and Walnut streets west of Broad in Philadelphia and Boylston Street in Boston's Back Bay. Most smaller cities did not have such precincts tangent to the business center. Washington's Connecticut Avenue was an exception; see Richard Longstreth, "Building for Business: A Century of Commercial Architecture in the Washington Metropolitan Area," in C. Ford Peatross, ed., *Washingtoniana: 200 Years of Architectural, Design and Engineering Drawings in the Prints and Photographs Division of the Library of Congress,* forthcoming.

42

Harris & Frank, for example, was founded in 1856, Desmond's in 1862, Barker Brothers in 1875, Parmelee-Dohrmann in 1883, and Myer Siegel ca. 1886. Leading department and dry goods stores were, on the average, somewhat newer. Jacoby Brothers was founded in 1875, Coulter's in 1878, Hamburger's in 1881, Robinson's in 1883, the Ville de Paris in 1893, the Broadway in 1895, and N. B. Blackstone in 1896.

43

The dominance of locally owned firms is noted in Ned Johnson, "Creating New Shopping . . . ," *WWD,* 14 Oct. 1927, IV-15.

44

F. W. Woolworth stores were located at 431 and 719 S. Broadway (1912), 113 N. Spring (1912; replaced by unit at 524 S. Main in 1924) and 131–135 S. Broadway (1924). The S. H. Kress store was at 621 S. Broadway (1920); the two J. J. Newberry units at 141 and 445–447 S. Broadway (1927); and those of F. W. Grand at 337 and 537 S. Broadway (1928, 1931). For general discussion of five-and-dime chain store locational practices, see Henry Wolfson, "Real Estate from the Chain Store Viewpoint," *Annals of Real Estate Practice* (Chicago: National Association of Real Estate Boards, 1929), 296–311. The chain store phenomenon is discussed further in chapter 3 below.

45

See, for example, W. Ross Campbell, "The Effect of Congestion . . . ," *LAR* 9 (May 1930), 8–9, 34; (June 1930), 8–9, 33–35; (July 1930), 9, 25–26; (Aug. 1930), 12–13, 32–34. Campbell headed one of the region's leading commercial real estate firms. Like many of his contemporaries, he did not offer a concrete solution to the problem.

Historical studies focusing on physical change in the city center due to heavy automobile traffic are few. For two exceptions, see R. Stephen Sennott, "Chicago Architects and the Automobile . . . ," in Jan Jennings, ed., *Roadside America: The Automobile in Design and Culture* (Ames: Iowa State University Press, 1990), 157–

169; and idem, "'Forever Inadequate to the Rising Stream' . . . ," in Zukowsky, ed., *Chicago Architecture,* 52–73.

46

C. A. Cooper, "Street Traffic and Parking," *LAR,* 7 (28 Mar. 1928), 44.

47

Estimates are based on a correlation of listings in city directories and in Sanborn fire insurance atlases. The boundaries chosen are somewhat arbitrary, based on walking distances averaging two to three blocks from densely developed parcels of land devoted to major downtown functions (including professional offices, theaters, financial institutions, hotels, restaurants, and stores) as of 1930.

I have established these boundaries and made independent calculations of parking lot capacity to attain a consistent comparative base from the 1920s to the early 1950s. The geographic area used in period accounts varies to a considerable degree, being often much larger and sometimes markedly smaller. Lot capacity was calculated using standard per-square-foot ratios of the period, which assumes all available space was occupied on demand. Self-service parking in such places did not become general practice until well after World War II.

Detailed information on downtown parking lot capacity prior to 1930 has yet to be found in period sources. That year, W. Ross Campbell claimed that downtown parking lots and structures could hold 25,753 cars at a time and that curbside space could accommodate another 3,200 (Campbell, "Effect of Congestion" [May 1930], 8). These tabulations were probably based on a larger area than that used in this study. For accounts of the parking lot business of the period locally, see "Develops Million Dollar Parking Business," *MA* 46 (10 July 1924), 16; and L. B. Millard, "Auto Parks," *LAR* 11 (Apr. 1931), 11, 21. For general discussion, see Charles LeCraw and Wilbur Smith, *Parking Lot Operation* (Saugatuck, Conn.: Eno Foundation, 1948).

48

According to Millard, "Auto Parks," 11, most Los Angeles car lot operators did not have definite-term leases; property owners could break the agreement with a sixty to ninety-day notice.

49

Campbell, "Effect of Congestion" (May 1930), 8–9, 34.

50

As in other cities, a number of small garages were erected in downtown Los Angeles during the 1920s, typically in peripheral locations. The buildings were seldom more than one story; most of them contained between thirty and sixty cars at a time. Many of them may have been constructed primarily for repair and maintenance services rather than for storage. Their collective impact on the downtown parking situation was never great. By 1930, the total number of cars thus housed within the 102-block core area was probably 1,500 at most.

Multistory garage construction outside downtown Los Angeles was almost nonexistent during the interwar decades due to the high cost relative to the availability of land. One facility holding up to 500 cars was constructed in the Westlake district in 1924–1925 at Sixth and Carondelet streets, principally to serve nearby apartment houses and apartment hotels; see *LAT,* 9 Nov. 1924, V-1; *LAT,* 19 Dec. 1925, I-8; and "An Eight-Story Concrete Garage," *Concrete* 30 (Feb. 1927), 45–46. A residential clientele was also the target for the Chapman Park Garage (1927) at Sixth between Normandie and Mariposa avenues, several blocks to the west; see

"Commercial Garage . . . ," *SWBC* 78 (4 Nov. 1927), 37; and *AD* 6:4 (1928), 54. A six-story garage holding 300 cars was planned but never built in downtown Beverly Hills; see "Plan Unit . . . ," *LAT,* 14 Feb. 1926, V-13.

51

"New Garage . . . ," *LAT,* 15 Feb. 1920, V-2; "Some Sidelights . . . ," *MA* 42 (12 Oct. 1922), 13. The type has yet to be the subject of detailed scholarly study. For a sampling of period accounts, see "Traffic Relief Requires More Motor Hotels," *Building Investment and Maintenance* 1 (Jan. 1926), 21–22; "Big Garage . . . ," *Building Magazine* 6 (Dec. 1926), 14; Robert Derrick, "The City Parking Garage," *AF* 46 (Mar. 1927), 233–240; "Unusual Six-Story Garage . . . ," *Building Magazine* 7 (Nov. 1927), 13; Lee Eastman, "The Parking Garage . . . ," *ACi* 40 (Jan. 1929), 156–157; "Garages," *AR* 65 (Feb. 1929), 177–196; A. E. Parmelee, "Multi-Story Garages for Mid-City Lots," *NREJ* 38 (18 Feb. 1929), 23–25; Fay Leone Faurote, "Garage Chains Excel in Personal Service," *CSR* 2 (Apr. 1929), 15–16, 30–31; "Leasehold Requirements . . . ," *WA* 38 (July 1929), 125–126; Fred Moe, "Downtown Parking Garages," *Building Investment and Maintenance* 10 (Sep. 1930), 5–7; and *AR* 69 (Apr. 1931), 309.

52

Namely, the 350-car Savoy Garage at 402–410 S. Olive (1923), the 600-car Mutual Garage at 363 S. Olive (1923–1924), a garage at 531–535 S. Maple (1924), the 500-car Auto Cleaning Company Garage at 814–820 S. Grand (1924), the 500-car Auto Center Garage at 742–744 S. Hope (1925), and the 1,000-car Hill's Garage at 413 S. Spring (1927–1928). For contemporary accounts, see *LAT,* 12 Jan. 1924, I-8; "Ramp Garage . . . ," *LAT,* 13 Jan. 1924, VI-14; *LAT,* 24 Sep. 1924, II-3; "New Garage . . . ," *LAT,* 13 Sep. 1925, VI-4; "Hugh Auto Park . . . ," *LAT,* 27 June 1926, V-7; "Downtown Section . . . ," *LAT,* 4 Mar. 1928, VI-1, 2; "New Garage . . . ," *LAT,* 7 Mar. 1928, II-9; Solving the Parking Problem . . . ," *SN* 8 (3 Mar. 1928), 2; *AA* 133 (5 Apr. 1928), 480; Harris Allen, "Industrial Architecture in California," *PCA* 33 (Sep. 1928), 14, 25; *WA* 38 (June 1929), pls. 94–95. Sanborn atlases document the location of these structures and, in most cases, their capacity.

Soon after construction began on the Grand Central Garage, plans were developed for a much larger structure of similar configuration at Hill and First streets. Capacity was projected at a whopping 4,300 cars. Both the size and location, well removed from principal downtown growth areas, probably prevented the project's realization; see "Block of Many Grades . . . ," *PM* 34 (Sep. 1920), 439. Two other garages, built by downtown stores for their patrons, are discussed in the text below.

53

Documentation on parking fees of the period is difficult to find. Rates advertised by the Auto Cleaning Company Garage—$.50 minimum, $.75 over five hours, $12.50 monthly (*LAT,* 24 Sep. 1924, II-3)—were probably competitive with other garages at that time. Car lot fees appear to have been much less, with $.25 a standard charge for several hours. Garage rates dropped as the number of off-street parking facilities grew and as economic conditions worsened. By 1931, Guasti-Giulli (Auto Center Garage) charged a $.25 minimum for up to three hours and $6.00 monthly (*LAT,* 15 Oct. 1931, I-8).

54

"Solving the Parking Problem." Total construction cost of Hill's, including land and equipment, was given as $1,250,000. The figure cited for the Grand Central Garage was $650,000, but this may have been for building construction alone. Even so, Hill's clearly was the more expensive of the two.

55

An ambitious scheme for a series of fifteen-level garages was being pursued by Merchants Parking Company, a major car lot operator in the city, during the mid-months of 1929, but it never materialized. See "New Parking Plan . . . ," *LAT,* 7 July 1929, V-3.

56

LAT, 2 Feb. 1919, VI-1; P. G. Morriss, "The Hotel Garage," *Pacific Coast Record* 28 (Aug. 1937), 8–9.

57

"Store's Garage Solves . . . ," *WWD,* 8 Mar. 1924, 14; Arthur Einstein, "Shall the Store Provide Parking Facilities?," *NRB* 6 (Jan. 1925), 36–37, 40; "Three Stores' Expeiences . . . ," *WWD,* 23 May 1925, 18; A. E. Parmelee, "Should Stores Give Customers Free Parking Space?," *DGE* 83 (19 Jan. 1929), 60–61.

58

"Store-Garage . . . ," *LAT,* 10 Oct. 1926, V-5; "May's to Build . . . ," *WWD,* 8 Dec. 1926, 1, 2; "Three Projects . . . ," *LAT,* 12 Dec. 1926, V-1; *WWD,* 22 Dec. 1926, 8; "Garage Opening . . . ," *LAT,* 4 Sep. 1927, II-10; "Garage Aids . . . ," *LAT,* 6 Nov. 1927, VI-2; "On Trial Eighteen Months . . . ," *DGE* 84 (3 Aug. 1929), 67, 78.

The May Company had already built a garage for its Cleveland store; see *WWD,* 1 July 1925, 32. For other early examples, see "Plan $500,000. . . ," *WWD,* 10 Apr. 1924, 34; "4 Seattle Stores . . . ," *WWD,* 11 Nov. 1924, 41; "Four Stores . . . ," *WWD,* 14 Mar. 1925, 15; "Sanger's, Dallas . . . ," *WWD,* 18 Apr. 1925, 23; "Store's Service . . . ," *WWD,* 20 Mar. 1926, 9; and "Garage Service . . . ," *WWD,* 28 Aug. 1926, 7.

59

"New Parking Plan Announced"; Millard, "Auto Parks," 11. For general discussion, see William Nelson Taft, "Is the Downtown Shopping District Losing Out?," *NRB* 8 (July 1926), 30–31.

60

"Big Structure Completed . . . ," *LAT,* 31 July 1921, V-1, 4; *LAT,* 22 Jan. 1922, VI-8; "Basement Garage. . . ," *PM* 37 (June 1922), 921–922; "Sixth and Olive's . . . ," *SN* 10 (30 Nov. 1929), 7. Several years later, a three-story above-ground structure was added to house company dining rooms and other support facilities; see "Down-Town Building . . . ," *SWBC* 69 (21 Jan. 1927), 44.

For general discussion, see Harvey Wiley Corbett, "Skyscraper Garages and Congestion," *AF* 52 (June 1930), 825–828; and Owen Owens, "Incorporating a Parking Garage in the Office Building," *AF* 52 (June 1930), 897–902.

61

These projects included the Standard Oil Building at 605 W. Tenth (Olympic Boulevard) of 1923–1924; Los Angeles Gas & Electric Company Building at 810–816 S. Flower of 1923–1924; West Seventh Street Building at 643–659 S. Main of 1924–1925 (125 cars); Pacific Finance Building at 621–623 S. Hope of 1924–1925; Roosevelt Building at 727 W. Seventh of 1926–1927 (350 cars); Title Insurance Building at 421–443 S. Spring of 1927–1928 (200 cars); Ninth and Broadway Building at 850–860 S. Broadway of 1928–1929 (125 cars); and Richfield Building at 555–557 S. Flower of 1929–1930.

For period accounts, see "Construction Begins Soon," *LAT,* 5 May 1923, II-1 (Standard Oil); "Parking in Basement . . . ," *HDC,* 12 Oct. 1923, 7 (Los Angeles Gas & Electric); "Announce Huge Structure," *LAT,* 4 Apr. 1926, V-1; *LAT,* 10 May 1927, I-9; "Roosevelt One of Los Angeles . . . ," *SWBC* 70 (15 July 1927), 36–37 (Roosevelt); "Splendid New Title Insurance . . . ," *SWBC* 69 (11 Feb. 1927), 36; "New Title Insurance . . . ," *California Real Estate* 7 (June 1927), 22–23; "New Height-Limit . . . ," *SN* 8 (9 June 1928), 2; *SCB* 7 (Sep. 1928), end cover; "Title Insurance Building . . . ," *PCA* 33 (Dec. 1928), 27–33 (Title Insurance); "Downtown Structure . . . ," *LAT,* 25 Aug. 1929, V-2; Harris Allen, "Terra Cotta versus Terra Firma," *PCA* 30 (Feb. 1930), 33–35, 72; and David Gebhard, *The Richfield Building 1928–1968* ([Los Angeles]: Atlantic-Richfield Co., 1970).

62

Concerning the building itself, see "Demolition of Old . . . ," *LAT,* 10 May 1908, V-1; "Modern Structure . . . ," *LAT,* 21 Feb. 1909, V-1; and *WA* 16 (Sep. 1910), 91, pl. The garage entrance is illustrated in Gebhard, *Richfield Building,* 2; however, it was constructed ca. 1930, not 1934 as stated there. Similar coversions were made to two other vintage piles, the Herman W. Hellman Building (1903) and the Alexandria Hotel Annex (1910), but their dates are uncertain.

63

LAT, 17 May 1927, I-11; *LAT,* 8 Aug. 1927, II-2; " 'X' Marks Spot . . . ," *LAT,* 1 Sep. 1930, II-2; *LAT,* 11 June 1931, I-19; *LAT,* 3 Nov. 1927, V-8.

64

"Launch Local Improvements," *LAT,* 23 Mar. 1924, V-1; *LAT,* 27 Mar. 1924, I-11.

65

Patrons left their cars at the garage portal of the Jewelers Building; storage was accomplished through an automatic elevator systemopeated by attendants at ground level. See "Skyscraper Garage . . . ," *PSM* 105 (June 1924), 42; "Autos Parked . . . ," *PM* 46 (July 1926), 438–439; Sennott, "Chicago Architects," 164–168; and Sennott, " 'Forever Inadequate,' " 62.

In 1923 an architect, Harry H. Hill, proposed an internal ramp system for core parking in skyscrapers, but the scheme possessed so many unrealistic attributes that it is doubtful whether any client had commissioned the study; see "Parking Space . . . ," *PM* 40 (Aug. 1923), 226.

66

I know of only two instances where this concept was realized. Both were by Washington developer Morris Cafritz, for the Cafritz Building (1948–1950) and Universal Building (1952–1954). Given the dates and location, it is doubtful whether these designs were directly inspired by any pre-1930 proposals. The configuration appears to have had little influence because its advantages failed to outweigh the high cost. See "Cafritz Plans . . . ," *Washington Post,* 29 Aug. 1948, R-1; *AF* 89 (Oct. 1948), 13; "Solving the Parking Problem," *Buildings* 49 (June 1949), 49; "Integrated Parking . . . ," *AR* 106 (Dec. 1949), 12; "26-Million-Dollar . . . ," *Washington Post,* 23 Nov. 1952, 1R; "Integral Parking," *Parking* 1 (Winter 1954), 49; and Geoffrey Baker and Bruno Funaro, *Parking* (New York: Reinhold, 1958), 90–91.

67

"Fifteen Floors . . . ," *SWBC* 67 (30 Apr. 1924), 43; "Downtown Garage . . . ," *LAEx,* 19 Sep. 1926, IV-3. Yet another scheme, identified only as for a Pacific

coast city, was devised the previous year; see "Office Building with . . . ," *PM* 43
(June 1925), 947.

III Westward Ho for Business

1

Ralph Ford, "Remarkable Development of One Outlying Business District," *LAR*
1 (Apr. 1922), 23; "Lilly-Fletcher Company," *LATMN,* 1 Jan. 1921, III-24. Both
accounts focus on the development of Western Avenue, discussed in the text
below.

2

Material presented in the text is derived from the classified section of city directories for 1900, 1910, and 1920 as well as that in Sanborn fire insurance atlases issued
in 1906 for the city center and its environs, and between 1919 and 1923 for areas
further afield.

Several factors make the figures cited approximate. First, precise boundaries
for the central business district are difficult to draw since geographic overlap always
occurred between functions oriented to the city population as a whole and those
serving a localized clientele. Automoble facilities were among several types that
tended to congregate on the fringe of downtown, where they were interspersed
with neighborhood outlets such as groceries and barber shops. As a result, I include businesses as part of outlying areas only when they lie beyond a radius of
about ten blocks from the core as it was then identified.

Second, it is likely that not all businesses were cited in the classified section
of city directories, a discrepancy that comes to light when listings are compared
to stores shown on Sanborn atlases, even when allowing for a predictable number
of vacancies. I have assumed, however, that the large majority of businesses of any
consequence are listed and thus that the classified section affords a relatively accurate picture.

Third, directory listings include only those businesses lying within the Los
Angeles city limits for the years in question, and thus encompass a progressively
larger area each decade. Yet, with the exception of Hollywood, most of the land
was sparsely developed when annexed by the city and thus had few or no business
activities. I have included most businesses listed, even those in places such as Owensmouth and Van Nuys that were then isolated from the rest of the city. On the
other hand, I have excluded those in San Pedro and Wilmington, which had their
own employment bases and continued to function as more or less independent
communities during this period.

3

Namely the 2200−2400 blocks of N. Broadway, 4200−4600 blocks of S. Broadway (then Moneta Avenue), 2500−2600 blocks of S. Central, 1800−2100 blocks
of E. First, Hollywood Boulevard around Highland and Cahuenga avenues,
2200−2400 blocks of S. Hoover, and 2500−2600 blocks of W. Pico Boulevard.
The estimate of the number of businesses in these precincts is rough owing to the
absence of Sanborn or comparable maps for this time frame. An extensive search
has failed to uncover street address directories published before 1935.

4

Namely the 2100−2600 blocks of N. Broadway, 4200−4900 and 5800−6200
blocks of S. Broadway, 1900−2800 and 4200−4700 blocks of S. Central, 1800−

2100 blocks of E. First, 6200–6800 blocks of Hollywood Boulevard, 2200–2500 blocks of S. Hoover, 2500–3000 blocks of W. Pico Boulevard, and 3100–3500 blocks of S. Vermont. At least six centers containing between forty and sixty businesses included a substantial range of goods and services: 5200–5500 blocks of S. Central, 1200–1500 and 3600–4000 blocks of E. First, 5400–5500 blocks of Hollywood Boulevard, 5600–5800 blocks of Pasadena Avenue, and 4600–4900 blocks of S. Vermont. Others with roughly the same number of businesses were more limited in scope. These findings are based on correlating directory listings with information in Sanborn fire insurance maps published between 1919 and 1923.

A sharp decline in residential construction occurred after 1913, from which it did not recover until after World War I. However, commercial development in outlying areas often continued in the wake of house-building booms and thus probably was sustained for a longer time in this instance.

5

Function is much more useful than density in delineating what constitutes an outlying center for Los Angeles during this period. I have defined "outlying center" as a more or less unbroken sequence of blocks where a variety of nonconvenience goods and a comparable variety of services can be procured, interspersed with other goods and services used on a routine basis. Defining a center by the concentration of businesses alone, irrespective of function, would exclude many key outlets and also fail to differentiate between major centers and ones of less importance. It is equally misleading to characterize this arterial development as an unbroken strip, since considerable variation was found in both the kinds and number of business activities along the length of a given thoroughfare.

6

Good period photographs documenting this genre of commercial development are extremely hard to find, especially ones taken before the mid-1920s. Figure 35 and several others I have used from the Whittington collection (figs. 36, 209) were shot for insurance purposes at the scene of an automobile accident. Though taken several years later, fig. 35 shows development that for the most part occurred prior to 1923. This commercial center was at the small end of the scale discussed in the text (about forty businesses in 1923), but its buildings and their arrangement exhibit the same characteristics as those of a core zone for a center with twice to three times as many businesses. For further discussion, see Richard Longstreth, "The Forgotten Arterial Landscape: Photographic Documentation of Commercial Development along Los Angeles Boulevards during the Interwar Decades," *Journal of Urban History,* forthcoming.

7

Some stretches of S. Vermont and S. Western avenues still contained exclusively residential development, affording a clear break in the pattern; however, such changes were exceptional.

8

These observations must remain tentative since so little research has been done on the subject. The one detailed historical analysis of outlying business center development in the United States prior to 1900 is Michael Conzen and Kathleen Neils Conzen, "Geographical Structure in Nineteenth-Century Urban Retailing: Milwaukee, 1836–90," *Journal of Historical Geography* 5 (Jan. 1979), 45–66. Fieldwork I have done over the past twenty-five years in a number of cities, especially Philadelphia, reinforces the Conzen's hypothesis that patterns found in Milwaukee are

typical for the period. Useful information on the subject can also be found in several studies of Baltimore, Philadelphia, and Chicago done during the 1930s: I. K. Rolph, *The Local Structure of Retail Trade,* U.S. Department of Commerce, Domestic Commerce Series No. 80 (Washington: U.S. Government Printing Office, 1933), which appears in condensed form in R. D. McKenzie, *The Metropolitan Community* (New York: McGraw-Hill, 1933), chap. 19; Malcolm Proudfoot, *Intra-City Business Census Statistics for Philadelphia, Pennsylvania,* U.S. Department of Commerce, Bureau of the Census, 1935, the findings of which are presented in idem, "City Retail Structure," *JLP* 13 (Oct. 1937), 425–428; and idem, *The Major Outlying Business Centers of Chicago* (Chicago: private ed., distributed by the University of Chicago Libraries, 1938).

A good sense of the density that outlying centers oriented toward middle-income consumers could reach in the largest U.S. cities prior to World War I is afforded by Homer Hoyt, *One Hundred Years of Land Values in Chicago* (Chicago: University of Chicago Press, 1933), 191–192, 225–227. The extent to which counterparts differed in a relatively small city such as Washington, D.C., is conveyed by a series of contemporary articles published weekly in the *Washington Post* between 21 August and 20 November 1910. Regrettably nothing approaching this level of detail can be found for Los Angeles.

9

"Valuable Sites . . . ," *LAT,* 14 Apr. 1912, V-1; "Fine Improvement . . . ," *LAT,* 22 Sep. 1912, V-1; "South Main . . . ," *LAT,* 16 Mar. 1913, V-1. Later accounts include "Half Million Paid . . . ," *LAT,* 26 Mar. 1922, V-2; "Store Alterations Rushed," *LAT,* 20 July 1930, V-3; and "Store Leases Announced," *LAT,* 12 Oct. 1930, V-3. Much of the Prager Park tract remained undeveloped for some years (*LAT,* 24 June 1928, V-6).

10

"Developments in South End," *LAT,* 17 Jan. 1909, V-21. The equivalent monthly expense of homeownership and rent was stressed in numerous real estate advertisements during the 1910s and 1920s. Concerning the popularity of apartment buildings for close-in locations, see "New Stores . . . ," *LAT,* 30 Oct. 1910, VI-1; and "Idle Lots . . . ," *LAT,* 13 Nov. 1910, VI-1.

11

"Idle Lots."

12

"Important Projects . . . ," *LAT,* 3 Oct. 1915, V-1. The size of Braun's building, with a 240-foot frontage on Vermont Avenue, also was unusual for the period.

13

Albert Fribourg, "Taxpayers Offer Profitable . . . ," *Building Investment* 4 (Mar. 1929), 27–29, provides a detailed account of economic aspects of the type's development. See also Tyler Stewart Rogers, "Good Possibilities for Profit . . . ," *Building Investment* 4 (July 1929), 27–29. Both address work in the New York metropolitan area. Accounts written almost twenty years earlier in Washington, D.C., indicate that the taxpayer's profitability was widely recognized by that time; see "One-Story Stores . . . ," *Evening Star* [Washington], 14 Jan. 1911, II-2; "Row of One-Story Stores . . . ," *Evening Star,* 22 July 1911, II-2; and "Interesting Development . . . ," *Evening Star,* 9 Nov. 1912, II-3. Comparable pieces for Los Angeles have yet to be found.

General characteristics noted in the text are based upon a random sample taken from 1928 issues of *SWBC,* analysis of historic photographs, and on-site study.

14

Fribourg, "Taxpayers," 27.

15

Otto G. Wildey, *An Approach to Business Real Estate* (Los Angeles: Otto G. Wildey Co., 1930), 6, 8; "Changes in Neighborhood Business . . . ," *EES* 4 (30 May 1927), 128. See also Leonard Hammel and S. Charles Lee, *Los Angeles Blue Book of Land Values* (Los Angeles: Land Value Book Publishing Co., 1932), 7.

16

Detailed discussion of the city's zoning ordinance and its creation as a means to enhance real estate development is found in Marc Weiss, *The Rise of the Community Builders: The American Real Estate Industry and Urban Land Planning* (New York: Columbia University Press, 1987), chap. 4.

17

Hoyt, *One Hundred Years,* 191–192, 225–227; Proudfoot, *Major Outlying Business Centers,* 7–9.

18

A map of the municipal railway system in 1898 is contained in Robert Fogelson, *The Fragmented Metropolis: Los Angeles 1850–1930* (Cambridge: Harvard University Press, 1967), 88. For the system as it existed in December 1910, see Robert Cowan, *On the Rails of Los Angeles: A Pictorial History of Its Streetcars* (Los Angeles: Historical Society of Southern California, 1917), n.p. For the post–World War I period, I used the 1924 edition of *Chadwick's Standard Los Angeles Street Guide.*

Transfers between the Los Angeles Municipal Railway and the interurban line, the Pacific Electric Railway, were not high in volume. Rather the two systems functioned more or less independently of one another. This relationship was quite different from that of the subway and elevated lines of Boston, New York, Philadelphia, and Chicago, where stations often served as major transfer points to surface rail lines.

19

See, for example, Ford, "Remarkable Development," 23; and "Western Avenue Proves Popular," *HDC,* 22 Oct. 1927, 10.

20

"Fact and Comment," *LAT,* 10 Mar. 1913, V-1; Ford, "Remarkable Development," 7, 23. See also Walter Woehlke, "How Long Los Angeles?," *Sunset* 52 (Apr. 1924), 11, 100.

21

Accounts of buildings include *LAT,* 31 Oct. 1920, V-1; "Plans Nearing Completion . . . ," *LAT,* 5 Dec. 1920, V-1; "Four-Story Building . . . ," *LAT,* 30 Jan. 1921, V-1; "Will Soon Erect . . . ," *LAT,* 5 Mar. 1922, V-1; *LAT,* 1 July 1922, II-3; Plan New Business . . . ," *LAT,* 3 Sep. 1922, V-1; "Start Hollywood Store," *LAT,* 15 Oct. 1922, V-15; *LAT,* 18 Jan. 1923, V-4; "New Projects . . . ," *LAT,* 26 Apr. 1925, V-1; and *LAT,* 25 Jan. 1931, V-2.

22

Mason Case, "Outlying Business Districts," *NREJ* 31 (15 Sep. 1930), 30.

23

"Lilly-Fletcher Company," *LATMN*, 1 Jan. 1921, 24. The firm was building apartment houses on Western Avenue for at least one investor as early as 1917; see "New District . . . ," *LAT*, 5 Aug. 1917, V-1. Not everyone was optimistic about such business districts; see, for example, Ned Johnson, "Creating New Shopping Zones . . . ," *WWD*, 14 Oct. 1927, IV-15.

Detailed accounts of the development of medium-sized outlying commercial centers are extremely hard to find. "Neighborhood" newspapers provide one of the best, albeit elusive, sources. A number of areas within the City of Los Angeles were never covered, or at least not covered in detail, by such papers. In some cases, too, publication began after the formative period of development. Finally, important periods of the paper's run may be missing from collections, as is the case with *SWW*, which covered an extensive area south of Pico Boulevard and west of Figueroa Street, prior to the 1930s. Finally, the paper itself may be lost—the apparent fate of the *Uptown Journal,* which covered much of the Wilshire district, including those blocks of Western Avenue discussed in the text above.

24

For biographical information, see *Men of California . . .* (San Francisco and Los Angeles: Western Press Register, 1925), 38. See also *LATMN*, 1 Jan. 1920, VI-13. Taft's role in the development of Hollywood Boulevard is noted in chapter 4 below.

25

"New District"; "Taft Corner . . . ," *HDC*, 6 June 1925, 7. During the early 1920s, Taft added another two-story building and two one-story buildings to the site.

26

General accounts include: "New Center . . . ," *LAT*, 17 July 1921, V-1; "Santa Monica and Western . . . ," *HDC*, 15 Apr. 1922, 1; "Western Avenue . . . ," *HDC*, 13 Oct. 1922, 1; "Rapid Growth . . . ," *HDC*, 24 July 1925, 10; M. L. Garrigue, "Santa Monica and Western Site," *HDC*, 9 July 1927, 12; and "Western Avenue . . . ," *HDC*, 22 Oct. 1927, 10. For good illustrations, see *HDC*, 8 June 1926, Hollywood Today Sect., III-n.p.

For accounts of individual projects, see *LAT*, 12 Oct. 1919, V-1; "Fine Theater . . . ," *LAT*, 24 Apr. 1921, V-3; "New Stores . . . ," *LAT*, 1 May 1921, V-3; "Pasadena Merchant . . . ," *HDC*, 6 June 1921, I-2; "New Robinson Building . . . ," *HDC*, 17 June 1921, I-4; *HDC*, 17 June 1921, I-8; *LAT*, 25 Dec. 1921, I-4; "Large Building . . . ," *HDC*, 10 May 1922, 1; 'Big New Building . . . ," *HDC*, 9 Feb. 1924, 10; "Western Avenue . . . ," *HDC*, 16 June 1924, 5; *LAT*, 21 Dec. 1924, V-1; "Pioneer Realtors . . . ," *HDC*, 24 July 1925, 9; "New Ries Building," *HDC*, 7 Nov. 1925, 2; and "Ready for Opening," *HDC*, 1 May 1926, 2.

27

"Owl Drug Re-opens . . . ," *HDC*, 15 June 1928, 13; *LAT*, 13 Aug. 1922, V-3; "Santa Monica and Western Site"; "Santa Monica–Western Bank . . . ," *HDC*, 2 Mar. 1923, 1; "Finish One Bank . . . ," *HDC*, 5 July 1923, 9. The Seelig store was one of thirty-nine he operated by 1920; see *LAT*, 19 Dec. 1920, II-10. For illustrations of other Security branches, see *LAT*, 3 Jan. 1922, I-6.

28

Godfrey Lebhar, *Chain Stores in America 1859–1950* (New York: Chain Store Pub. Corp., 1952), 63, and Paul Nystrom, *Economics of Retailing,* 2 vols., rev. ed. (New York: Ronald Press, Co., 1930), 1:229, stand among the most useful period accounts of the subject. See also William Baxter, *Chain Store Distribution and Management,* rev. ed. (New York: Harper & Bros., 1931); M. M. Zimmerman, *The Challenge of Chain Store Distribution* (New York: Harper & Brothers, 1931); and John Nichols, *The Chain Store Tells Its Story* (New York: Institute of Distribution, 1940).

Contemporary periodical literature on the subject is vast. *CSA* and the short-lived *CSR* are among the most informative sources. For a sampling of other accounts, see James Palmer, "Economic and Social Aspects of Chain Stores," *Journal of Business of the University of Chicago* 2 (July 1929), 272–290; H. M. Foster, "Have the Chain Stores Reached Their Peak?," *PIM* 20 (June 1930), 29–30, 128, 131–132, 134, 137; 21 (July 1930), 39–40, 76, 79–80, 82, 85, 114, 117; and Hugh Foster, "The Chain Store Comes of Age," *PIM* 34 (Apr. 1937), 79–94. For a recent overview, see Susan Strasser, *Satisfaction Guaranteed: The Making of the American Mass Market* (New York: Pantheon, 1989), 222–229.

29

Nystrom, *Economics of Retailing,* 1:213. Zimmerman, *Chain Store Distribution,* 23–24, considered ten units the threshold.

30

Some chain companies such as Sears, Roebuck did have two or more gradations of store, which determined the range and sometimes the quantity of stock carried. Chain outlets should not be confused with branch stores, most of which, during the period under study, were operated as extensions of the main, downtown emporium and subsidiary to it.

31

Carl Schmalz, "Independent Stores versus Chains in the Grocery Field," *Harvard Business Review* 9 (July 1931), 439.

32

See, for example, Ruth Leigh, "Mrs. Housewife, May We Present Mr. Chain Store," *Chain Store Progress* 3 (Jan. 1931), 5; and Malcolm Sweeney, "Chains Raise Standards of Store Appearance," *Chain Store Progress* 3 (Aug. 1931), 5.

33

For a sampling of accounts, see Ira Lurie, "What's the Best Location?," *System* 42 (Oct. 1922), 401–403, 446, 448, 450; "Scarcity of Chain Store Locations . . . ," *WWD,* 21 Nov. 1924, 35; Jesse Bell, "How to Determine the Comparative Rental Value . . . ," *Real Estate Brokerage* (Chicago: National Association of Real Estate Boards, 1927), 237–241; Bernard Rosenthal, "Surveys Prove Their Worth," *LAR* 6 (Sep. 1927), 14–15, 39; Frank Slosson, "Chain Store Locations," *Chicago Realtor* 40 (Nov. 1927), 9–12, 28–29; Meyer Eiseman, "Chain Store Operation . . . ," *Annals of Real Estate Practice* (Chicago: National Association of Real Estate Boards, 1928), 344–348; "Location Expert . . . ," *WWD,* 28 July 1928, 13; Henry Wolfson, "Traffic-Location-Trends . . . ," *NREJ* 30 (8 July 1929), 39–41; William Junglas, "Accessibility Is Richman's Location Key," *CSA/GME* 5 (Dec. 1929), 41–42, 66; Robert Moore, "The Relation of the Real Estate Broker to the Chain Store," *Annals of Real Estate Practice* (Chicago: National Association of Real Estate Boards, 1930), 74–81; Case, "Outlying Business Districts," 27–30; Stanley McMichael, "Chain Stores—Their Influence on Real Estate," *LAR* 10 (June

1931), 7–9, 32; Richard Ratcliff, "The Problem of Retail Site Selection," *Michigan Business Studies* 9 (1939), 77–88; and Joseph Laronge, "Traffic Counts," *AJ* 6 (Apr. 1938), 146–154.

34

"Note Invasion . . . ," *WWD,* 5 Oct. 1928, IV-5. For background, see Glen White, "Picking Sites for Penney Stores," *CSA* 1 (July 1925), 5–7, 24; H. S. Wright, "Locating Grocery Stores," *CSA* 1 (Aug. 1925), 10–11, 54–57; M. G. Gibbs, "How a Prominent Chain Picks Store Locations," *PI* 141 (10 Nov. 1927), 108–109; J. J. Witherspoon, "The Future of the Neighborhood Store," *PIM* 15 (Dec. 1927), 34–35, 88, 91–92; Eiseman, "Chain Store Operation," 347; Irving Williams, Jr., "Selecting Store Locations in Rural Districts," *CSA/GME* 4 (June 1928), 27–28; and Henry Wolfson, "Real Estate from the Chain Store Viewpoint," *Annals of Real Estate Practice* (Chicago: National Association of Real Estate Boards, 1929), 296–311.

35

For most of the 1920s, Los Angeles directories do not list chain store units, only the main office and, sometimes, the warehouse. According to contemporary accounts, in 1925 Daley's (first store 1916) had 169 units; Chaffee's (first store 1902) had 87; E. A. Morrison (first store 1909) had 50. One year later (1926) Von's had 58. No figure is given for Piggly Wiggly except statewide: 130 stores. See *LAT,* 30 Apr. 1924, I-9; Joseph Daley, "Turnover Is King," *CSA* 1 (Sep. 1925), 9–10, 42; Frank Williams, "How Joe Daley 'Makes a Hit' . . . ," *CSR* 1 (Dec. 1928), 27–30; Dorothea Howard, " 'Chaffee's' Pioneer Grocers . . . ," *HDC/HES,* 8 Jan. 1926, 1; "E. A. Morrison Co. . . . ," *HDC/HES,* 16 Oct. 1925, 1; Charles von der Ahe, "Some Things to Avoid in Operating a Small Chain," *CSA* 2 (Aug. 1926), 25–26, 59; "7 Piggly Wiggly Stores . . . ," *HDC/HES,* 25 Sep. 1925, 1; A. C. Jones, "An Analysis of Piggly Wiggly Progress," *CSA* 1 (Jan. 1926), 6–7, 38–39, 44; *LAT,* 13 Feb. 1927, I-11; *LAT,* 15 Mar. 1927, II-9; and *LAT,* 12 Apr. 1929, II-3.

Concerning the largest grocery store chain in 1925, see note 36 below. One other important local chain, Ralphs Grocery Company, built a comparatively small number of large stores.

36

Concerning Seelig, see J. Gordon Wright, "Attention to Details Spell Success for Seelig," *SMM* 3 (Jan. 1938), 30. See also his advertisements in *LAT,* 24 Oct. 1920, II-7; 19 Dec. 1920, II-10; 2 Jan. 1921, II-11; 19 Jan. 1921, II-13; 23 June 1922, I-9; 24 Sep. 1922, II-9; 1 Oct. 1922, II-6; 10 June 1924, II-9; and 19 Aug. 1924, II-9. Concerning Safeway, see Wright, "Locating Grocery Stores"; "Sixteen Safeway Stores . . . ," *HDC/HES,* 11 Sep. 1925, 1; *LAT,* 9 Nov. 1926, II-9; "West Hollywood Has . . . ," *HDC/HES,* 10 June 1927, 1; *LAT,* 28 June 1927, II-9; and *LAT,* 17 July 1928, II-7. Concerning MacMarr, see "Stores Acquired . . . ," *Oregonian* [Portland], 1 Apr. 1929, 12; "Nine Chain Store . . . ," *Oregon Daily Journal* [Portland], 1 Apr. 1929, 9; and *HDC,* 24 May 1929, 15.

37

Wright, "Locating Grocery Stores."

38

Baxter, *Chain Store Distribution,* 78.

39

Concerning Owl, see "California's Finest . . . ," *HDC,* 3 Feb. 1928, Owl Drug Sect.; "Owl Drug Stores' . . . ," *HDC,* 31 July 1930, 9. Concerning Liggett, see

"How Liggett's Opened Up the West," *CSA* 1 (May 1926), 24–25, 54–56; and "Liggett Stores . . . ," *HDC/HES,* 25 June 1926, 1.

40

Zimmerman, *Chain Store Distribution,* 40.

41

Howard Preston, "Branch Banking with Special Reference to California Conditions," *Journal of Political Economy* 30 (Aug. 1922), 494, 503–507; John Chapman and Ray Westerfield, *Branch Banking: Its Historical and Theoretical Position in America and Abroad* (New York: Harper, 1942), 84–92; John Farnham, "Making a Tour of Hollywood Banks," *Burroughs Clearing House* 23 (Sep. 1939), 31.

42

Hale Huggins, "Decentralization of Shopping," *LAR* 3 (Apr. 1924), 39; Preston, "Branch Banking," 506–512. Many early branches in Los Angeles did not provide loan services. The leader in changing this practice was Security Trust, which established as policy to have all its branches offer full banking services by 1922.

43

Quoted in "Branch Banks of Southern California," *Shapes of Clay* 2 (Jan. 1926), 2.

44

LAT, 29 Apr. 1923, V-11; *LAT,* 28 Oct. 1923, V-18; *LAT,* 24 Oct. 1926, V-7; *LAT,* 12 Dec. 1923, V-16. For a sampling of similar advertisements, see *LAT,* 8 Apr. 1923, V-8; 18 Nov. 1923, V-12; 29 Nov. 1927, I-10; and 12 May 1929, V-5.

45

Charles Cohan, "Los Angeles in 2035 . . . ," *LAT,* 2 June 1935, V-1, 2.

IV Hollywood — Los Angeles's Other Half

1

"Hollywood—Los Angeles Other Half," *LAR* 7 (Nov. 1927), 35.

2

Contemporary accounts of this phenomenon are cited in chapter 3, note 8. For a recent popular case study, see Jean Fahey Eberle, *Midtown, a Grand Place to Be!* (St. Louis: Mercantile Commerce Trust Co., 1980). Detailed historical analyses of the subject have yet to be written; however, some worthwhile background material is found in broader local studies, such as Harold Mayer and Richard Wade, *Chicago: Growth of a Metropolis* (Chicago: University of Chicago Press, 1969), 342–348.

3

For background, see Wm. McGarry, "Creating a Chain Community . . . ," *CSR* 2 (Sep. 1929), 9–11, 62, 64; and "69th St. Growing . . . ," *Philadelphia Inquirer,* 19 Feb. 1928, B16.

4

Basic information on Hollywood's development can be found in Edwin Palmer, *History of Hollywood,* 2 vols. (Hollywood: Arthur H. Cawston, 1937). Much of this material is repeated in Bruce Torrence, *Hollywood: The First Hundred Years* (New

York: Zoetrope, 1982). Contemporary accounts include Jerome Sengel, "Hollywood," *LAR* 5 (Oct. 1925), 13–14; George Coffin, "From Pasture to Metropolis," *LAR* 5 (Oct. 1925), 15; Hollywood Today Ed. of *HDC*, 8 June 1926; Hollywood issue of *LAR* 6 (Nov. 1926); and Thomas Barnett, "Hollywood—A City Within a City," *LAR* 8 (Nov. 1928), 23, 55–56.

5

As early as 1921, a promotional column in *HDC* stated that "Hollywood seems be a step from New York, if one judges distance by the styles seen in Hollywood shops" ("Helen Hollywood A-Shopping Goes," 1 Apr. 1921, II-11). By the end of the decade, the newly formed Hollywood Boulevard Association boasted that its precinct was the "style center of the world" (*HDC*, 6 Apr. 1922, 1).

Other useful accounts of the district's commercial development during the 1920s include: "Retail District . . . ," *HDC*, 4 Aug. 1922, 1, 2; "More Business . . . ," *HDC*, 16 Nov. 1922, 1; "Bigger Business . . . ," *HDC*, 2 Dec. 1922, 9; "Great Hollywood Growth . . . ," *HDC*, 2 Dec. 1922, 9, 15; "Boulevard Faces . . . ," *HDC*, 1 June 1925, 7; "Westward Trend . . . ," *HDC*, 20 Aug. 1927, 11; "Shopping Area . . . ," *WWD*, 4 Aug. 1928, 1, 16; and "Hollywood Business . . ." *LAT*, 15 Sep. 1929, V-2.

Accounts of new stores include: "Marie Company . . . ," *HDC*, 27 Feb. 1925, 2; "New Store Opens," *HDC*, 17 Apr. 1926, 2; "Movie Mode . . . ," *HDC*, 23 July 1926, 9; "Beauty and Convenience . . . ," *HDC*, 2 Sep. 1926, 7; "Bess Schlank Secures . . . ," *HDC*, 6 Aug. 1927, 17; "New Trousseau . . . ," *HDC/ HES*, 18 Nov. 1927, 1; "Stoner's to Open . . . ," *HDC*, 29 Sep. 1928, 3; and "2 Hollywood Stores . . . ," *WWD*, 14 May 1929, I-7.

6

HDC, 4 Oct. 1921, 8; *HDC*, 6 Oct. 1921, 8; "English Room . . . ," *HDC*, 21 July 1925, 2; "New Clothing Firm . . . ," *HDC*, 2 Nov. 1921, 1; *HDC*, 16 May 1922, 8; "New Store . . . ," *HDC*, 18 May 1922, 5; *HDC*, 3 Oct. 1924, Guaranty Souvenir Ed., n.p.; "Meyer, [sic] Siegel . . . ," *HDC*, 6 Nov. 1925, 6; *HDC*, 26 Aug. 1921, I-5; "Innes' Dream . . . ," *HDC*, 22 Sep. 1921, I-2; "New Business Block . . . ," *HDC*, 28 Oct. 1922, 1; "Wetherby-Kayser . . . ," *HDC*, 9 Mar. 1923, 1; "New Shoe Store . . . ," *HDC*, 2 Aug. 1923, 7; "Hollywood Branch," *HDC*, 1 June 1925, 10; "C. H. Baker . . . ," *HDC*, 28 Sep. 1928, 13; and *HDC*, 26 Sep. 1924, 2.

7

"Magnins [sic] Buy Site . . . ," *LAT*, 19 Nov. 1922, V-1; "Interior Architecture . . . ," *AA* 129 (5 Feb. 1926), 229–232; "Typical of . . . Hollywood," *HDC*, 3 Aug. 1926, 3; "Hollywood Shop . . . ," *LAT*, 13 Nov. 1927, V-1; "Magnin's Plan . . . ," *WWD*, 15 Nov. 1927, I-14; "Open Addition . . . ," *WWD*, 27 Mar. 1928, I-1, 2; "Plans for Roos' . . . ," *WWD*, 5 Sep. 1928, I-12; *HDC*, 8 Dec. 1928, 11; "Roos' Opens . . . ," *WWD*, 19 Feb. 1929, I-11; *HDC*, 13 Feb. 1929, 4; "Roos Brothers . . . ," *HDC*, 15 Feb. 1929, 5; "Throngs at New . . . ," *LAT*, 16 Feb. 1929, II-6; and *CSA* 5 (Sep. 1929), 59.

8

LAT, 20 Feb. 1921, V-2; "W. P. Fuller . . . ," *HDC*, 12 August 1921, 1; Harriet Burdsal, "Gold Rush Saw . . . ," *HDC/HES*, 7 Oct. 1927, 1; "Barker Brothers . . . ," *HDC*, 13 Aug. 1927, 1, 8; *HDC*, 7 Oct. 1927, Barker Bros. Ed.; "Frigidaire Opens . . . ," *HDC/HES*, 5 Aug. 1927, 1; "Hollywood Has General Electric . . . ," *HDC/HES*, 17 Feb. 1928, 1. For other examples, see *HDC*,

27 Sep. 1927, I-9; "Milnor Opens . . . ," *HDC*, 12 Nov. 1927, 9; and Harriet Burdsal, "Milnor's Inc. . . . ," *HDC/HES*, 28 Oct. 1927, 1.

9

"Platt Formal Re-Opening . . . ," *HDC*, 12 Sep. 1925, 2; "Many Buildings Planned," *LAT*, 15 July 1923, V-1, 8; "Paulais to Open . . . ," *HDC*, 22 Sep. 1924, 5; "Completion of Beautiful . . . ," *LAT*, 8 Oct. 1924, I-9 to 11; "Film Stars . . . ," *HDC*, 11 Oct. 1924, 3; "All World May Dine . . . ," *HDC/HES*, 15 Oct. 1926, 1; "Restaurant Men . . . ," *HDC/HES*, 21 July 1927, 1, 3; "F. & W. Grand . . . ," *HDC*, 27 July 1928, 11; "Crowds at Opening . . . ," *HDC*, 30 July 1928, 12; "Newberry to Build . . . ," *LAT*, 16 June 1929, V-1; "Newberry Store . . . ," *HDC*, 28 Mar. 1930, 12.

For general accounts, see "Great Local Shopping Center Predicted," *HDC*, 20 Aug. 1927, 11; "Westward Trend . . . ," *HDC*, 27 Nov. 1926, 10; and "The Shopping District of Northwest Los Angeles," *LAR* 6 (Nov. 1926), 28, 45.

10

"Bigger Business . . . ," *HDC*, 2 Dec. 1922, 9; "Boulevard Faces . . . ," *HDC*, 17 May 1924, 9; "Hollywood Shops . . . ," *HDC*, 7 Oct. 1927, II-2.

11

References to new buildings not cited in the notes above include: *LAT*, 31 Mar. 1918, V-1; "Rebuild Picture House," *LAT*, 19 Sep. 1920, V-1; "New Store Building . . . ," *HDC*, 8 Oct. 1920, 13; *HDC*, 18 Feb. 1921, II-6; "New Stores . . . ," *LAT*, 27 Mar. 1921, V-1, 2; "New Building . . . ," *LAT*, 10 Apr. 1921, V-2; "Automobile Club . . . ," *HDC*, 10 May 1921, I-1; *HDC*, 29 July 1921, I-7; "Fine Improvements . . . ," *HDC*, 2 Sep. 1921, I-4; "William O. Jackson . . . ," *HDC*, 5 Dec. 1921, 1; *LAT*, 8 Jan. 1922, V-9; "New Business Block," *HDC*, 20 Dec. 1922, 9; *PCA* 22 (Oct. 1922), pl. 51; "New Building . . . ," *HDC*, 18 Sep. 1924, 2; "New Projects . . . ," *LAT*, 25 Jan. 1925, V-1, 2; "Boulevard Clubhouse . . . ," *LAT*, 19 Apr. 1925, V-1; "Announce Hollywood . . . ," *LAT*, 14 Feb. 1926, V-3; *LAT*, 9 Jan. 1927, V-3; *LAT*, 3 Apr. 1927, V-9; "New Shop . . . ," *LAT*, 31 July 1927, V-2; "Hollywood Store . . . ," *LAT*, 3 Mar. 1929, V-3; "Structure Designed . . . ," *LAT*, 30 June 1929, V-3.

12

"Toberman Proves . . . ," *HDC*, 11 Aug. 1922, II-1. See also Robert Smith, "Boulevard Will Be . . . ," *HDC*, 7 Oct. 1927, II-2. Among Toberman's many other projects was the Barker Brothers building noted in the text above.

Originally the emporium was to be called Rippe's Department Store, run by Walter Rippe, who had worked for Hamburger's and the Broadway department stores; see "Break Ground . . . ," *HDC*, 3 Oct. 1921, 1. For subsequent accounts, see "Center of Big Development," *LAT*, 15 Jan. 1922, V-1, 3; "Department Store . . . ," *HDC*, 24 May 1922, 1, 2; "Wonders to Be Revealed . . . ," *HDC*, 11 Aug. 1922, II-1; *LAT*, 24 Feb. 1924, III-17; and *LAT*, 16 Mar. 1924, III-16.

13

The only other large enterprise proposed in the immediate wake of the C.R.S. store was for a facility of about the same size, situated several blocks to the east at Hollywood and Vine. The bid came not from a downtown company but from Boadway Brothers, which already operated department stores in Long Beach, Pasadena, and San Bernardino. The project never materialized, apparently due to a lack of sufficient capital. See "Big Department Store . . . ," *HDC*, 17 June 1922, 1. An advertisement run one month later (*HDC*, 20 July 1922, II-4) depicts a larger

building (six versus four stories) carrying the headline "Do You Want This Store in Hollywood?" Its purpose was to solicit investors, suggesting that attempts to date had been unsuccessful. The project seemed finalized by mid-August but never progressed further; see "Lease for Big Store . . . ," *LAT,* 13 Aug. 1922, V-1; and "Start Hollywood Store," *LAT,* 15 Oct. 1922, V-15.

14

"Report Dyas' Plans . . . ," *WWD,* 6 July 1927, 1, 23; "New Hollywood Store . . . ," *HDC,* 9 July 1927, 1, 10; "Height-Limit Unit . . . ," *LAT,* 10 July 1927, V-1; "How New Dyas Branch . . . ," *WWD,* 13 July 1927, I-6. Both Bullock's and the May Company made preliminary plans to establish large branches on Wilshire Boulevard as early as 1924, however. See chapter 5 below.

15

"New Hollywood Store." For subsequent accounts, see "Work to Begin . . . ," *HDC,* 23 July 1927, 9, 11; "Dyas Store Building . . . ," *HDC,* 8 Oct. 1927, 2; "Dyas Structure . . . ," *LAT,* 3 Jan. 1928, V-6; *HDC,* 2 March 1928, B. H. Dyas Co. Opening Ed.; and "Shop Idea Carried . . . ," *WWD,* 7 Apr. 1928, I-15.

16

"Filene's to Open . . . ," *Boston Herald,* 27 Nov. 1927, 27; "Filene's Plan Branch . . . ," *WWD,* 28 Nov. 1927, I-1; "Remodeling to Begin . . . ," *WWD,* 12 Jan. 1928, I-7; *WWD,* 12 March 1928, I-9; "Saks-Fifth Ave. . . . ," *WWD,* 13 Nov. 1925, 1, 12; "Best's to Enlarge . . . ," *WWD,* 19 Mar. 1929, I-2; Maxwell Fox, "Filene's Wellesley Shop . . . ," *WWD,* 21 June 1928, 8.

17

"Nugents' Opens Store . . . ," *St. Louis Globe-Democrat,* 13 Apr. 1913, 12. For illustration, see *St. Louis Globe-Democrat,* 23 Nov. 1929, 7. Located at Vandeventer Avenue and Olive Street, the building appears to have been erected not long before its acquisition by Nugent's. The precinct was originally referred to as being uptown, and the store was always known by that appelation. Concerning the district itself, see note 2 above.

18

"Germantown Store . . . ," *Philadelphia Inquirer,* 17 Apr. 1927, 12W; "New Store Planned . . . ," *WWD,* 20 Apr. 1927, 5; "Two Chestnut Street . . . ," *Building Magazine* 7 (May 1927), 15; *WWD,* 25 May 1927, I-6; "30,000 Attend . . . ," *WWD,* 16 Nov. 1927, I-2; "Allen's Open . . . ," *WWD,* 15 Nov. 1927, I-11; "George Allen . . . ," *Building Magazine* 7 (Dec. 1927), 19; "Moderness in Every . . . ," *WWD,* 7 Jan. 1928, I-7.

19

R. C. Markley, "Hollywood Now . . . ," *HDC,* 2 Mar. 1928, 5.

20

"The Broadway Buys . . . ," *WWD,* 2 Mar. 1931, 1, 36; "Broadway Buys . . . ," *LAT,* 3 Mar. 1931, II-1, 2; "Broadway-Hollywood . . . ," *HDC,* 9 Mar. 1931, II-13, 14.

21

"Store All Set . . . ," *HDC,* 22 June 1933, 13; "New Elevators . . . ," *HDC,* 25 Oct. 1934, 14; "Broadway-Hollywood . . . ," *WWD,* 1 June 1937, I-1; "Broadway Will Build . . . ," *HDC,* 31 Dec. 1937, 9, 14; "Broadway-Hollywood . . . ,"

WWD, 7 Jan. 1938, I-9; *HDC,* 12 Feb. 1938, 9; "Broadway-Hollywood . . . ,"
WWD, 26 July 1938, 8; Patricia Killoran, "Steady Increase . . . ," *HDC,* 15 Nov.
1938, 13; "New Broadway-Hollywood . . . ," *LAT,* 15 Nov. 1938, I-16; "Broad-
way-Hollywood . . . ," *WWD,* 21 Nov. 1938, 1, 4; "New Broadway-Hollywood
. . . ," *WWD,* 2 Dec. 1938, III-4; Patricia Killoran, "The Broadway-Hollywood's
. . . ," *HDC,* 6 Mar. 1941, 10.

22

"2 Coast Stores . . . ," *WWD,* 29 Sep. 1927, I-1, 20. Bullock's Wilshire store is discussed in chapter 5 below.

23

"Report May Store . . . ," *WWD,* 24 Feb. 1931, 1; "Hollywood Unit . . . ,"
WWD, 25 Feb. 1931, I-1; "Tom May Confirms . . . ," *WWD,* 2 Mar. 1931, 36.
Fourteen years later the May Company again announced plans for a Hollywood
store, which likewise never saw realization; see chapter 8 below.

24

"New Buildings . . . ," *LAT,* 25 Jan. 1930, II-2; "Announcements Tell . . . ," *LAT,*
26 Jan. 1930, V-1, 2. Laemmle apparently was in final negotiations with the retailer. The store's identity remains unknown. Frustratingly, too, no clue is given as
to Laemmle's architect or the collaborating Los Angeles architect. The latter could
have been Richard Neutra, who Laemmle subsequently commissioned to design a
taxpayer block on the site. See Thomas Hines, *Richard Neutra and the Search for Modern Architecture* (New York: Oxford University Press, 1982), 160–162. Neutra's
own work was considerably more sophisticated by 1930, as is evident in ibid., 62–
75. I am grateful to Thomas Hines and Isbelle Gournay for examining material on
the 1930 project in what proved a futile attempt to gain more specific information.

25

"Hollywood Establishes . . . ," *LAT,* 11 Aug. 1929, V-1; "Five-Year . . . ," *LAT,*
22 Dec. 1929, V-2; "The Hollywood-Vine . . . ," *LATMN,* 2 Jan. 1930, VI-15;
"New World Record . . . ," *LAEEY* 1930, 30. See also "Hollywood Catches
Up . . . ," *LAT,* 19 July 1925, V-7; and Gaylord Elliott, "Office Buildings of
Hollywood," *LAR* 6 (Nov. 1926), 23, 53.

26

"Toberman Proves Great Confidence." Initial plans for the bank called for a four-
story building; see "Security Trust & Savings . . . ," *HDC,* 23 July 1920, 1; and
"Big Building . . . ," *LAT,* 25 July 1920, V-2. Revised plans increased the size; see
"Security Bank . . . ," *HDC,* 8 Dec. 1920, 1; "Security Bank . . . ," *HDC,* 8 Apr.
1921, 1; and *HDC,* 3 June 1922, Security Sect. See also "Hollywood Has Banking
Center," *LAT,* 21 Oct. 1923, V-3.

27

"Start $1,000,000 Structure," *HDC,* 29 Oct. 1923, 1; *HDC,* 3 Oct. 1924,
Guaranty Building Sect.; "Flood of Lights . . . ," *HDC,* 6 Oct. 1924, 3; "New
Bank . . . ," *HDC,* 23 July 1927, 11; "Bank Announces . . . ," *LAT,* 24 July 1927,
V-3; *LAT,* 1 July 1928, V-3; "First National Bank . . . ," *HDC,* 16 Nov. 1928, 7.
Equally ambitious was the unrealized project for the Hellman Commercial Trust
& Savings Bank; see "Tallest Hollywood Building . . . ," *HDC,* 12 Oct. 1923, 1;
and *HDC,* 11 Oct. 1924, 12. Another unrealized scheme was the Federal Trust &
Savings Bank; see "Trust Company . . . ," *LAT,* 4 Mar. 1923, V-1.

28

"Buy Boulevard Site . . . ," *HDC*, 14 Oct. 1921, 1; "Big Hollywood Build-ing," *LAT*, 1 July 1923, V-1; "Taft to Build . . . ," *HDC*, 7 Sep. 1923, 9; "Taft Building . . . ," *LAT*, 17 Aug. 1924, V-2; "New Taft Building . . . ," *HDC*, 20 Aug. 1924, 7, 9; *HDC*, 14 June 1928, 2; "New Skyscraper . . . ," *HDC*, 29 Sep. 1929, 2; "Structure to Rise . . . ," *LAT*, 30 Sep. 1928, V-1; "Bank of Holly-wood . . . ," *HDC*, 17 May 1929, 8, 9; "Hollywood Bank . . . ," *LAT*, 19 May 1929, V-3; "Annex for Bank Building," *HDC*, 9 Apr. 1930, 11; and "Bank Annex . . . ," *LAT*, 13 Apr. 1930, V-2.

Hollywood also became the home of the Mountain States Life Insurance Company, which was founded in Denver and moved into its nine-story building just north of Hollywood Boulevard in 1929. See "Ground Broken . . . ," *HDC*, 17 Oct. 1928, 2; "Ground Broken . . . ," *LAT*, 28 Oct. 1928, V-3; "Suburban Build-ing . . . ," *LAT*, 28 July 1929, V-1; and "New Mt. States . . . ," *HDC*, 31 July 1929, 9, 10.

Many other tall office building projects were proposed but unrealized; see "Height-Limit Buildings," *LAT*, 16 March 1924, V-1; "Great 13-Story Build-ing . . . ," *HDC*, 3 January 1927, 2; "Plan Height-Limit Edifice," *LAT*, 27 Febru-ary 1927, V-1; "Three-Story Addition . . . ," *LAT*, 20 January 1929, V-2; "Sky-scraper Projected . . . ," *LAT*, 5 January 1930, V-1; "Medical Building . . . ," *LAT*, 31 August 1930, V-1; "New Height-Limit Building . . . ," *HDC*, 16 January 1931, 1; and "Hollywood Skyscraper . . . ," *LAT*, 18 January 1931, V-3.

29

The image was introduced during the 1927 Christmas season; see "Mary Pick-ford . . . ," *HDC*, 17 Nov. 1927, II-1. See also *HDC*, 10 Nov. 1928, 11; 15 Nov. 1928, 1; 17 Nov. 1928, I-4; and 23 March 1929, 7.

30

"Business Conditions in Hollywood," *EES*, 30 Apr. 1928, 108.

31

"New Roosevelt Hotel," *HDC*, 24 Oct. 1925, 25; "Begin Hotel . . . ," *LAT*, 25 Oct. 1925, V-1; "Fine Hollywood Hotel . . . ," *LAT*, 4 Aug. 1927, II-10; "Expect Five Thousand . . . ," *HDC*, 27 Oct. 1927, 13. The first tall building planned for Hollywood Boulevard was the Christie Hotel (1919–1921); see "Plans for Eight Story . . . ," *HDC*, 5 Dec. 1919, 1; "Million Dollar Hotel . . . ," *HDC*, 13 Aug. 1920, 1; and "Native Sons . . . ," *LAT*, 14 May 1922, V-1. Another major facility was the ten-story Hollywood Plaza Hotel (1924–1925); see *HDC*, 22 Sep. 1924, 10, and 15 Oct. 1925, 7; and "Many Difficulties . . . ," *LAT*, 15 Oct. 1925, II-10 to 12.

An even larger facility was proposed for the one corner of the Hollywood and Vine intersection that remains unoccupied by a tall building. Initially proposed in 1924 (*HDC*, 19 July 1924, 9; *LAT*, 20 July 1924, V-5), the scheme resurfaced from time to time until the depression.

32

For a sampling of accounts, see "Work Is Started . . . ," *HDC*, 7 Sep. 1923, 9; *HDC*, 8 Sep. 1923, 11; "Plan Several . . . ," *LAT*, 9 Dec. 1923, V-1, 3; *HDC*, 19 Jan. 1924, 13; *HDC*, 26 April 1924, 11; "7,500,000 Project . . . ," *HDC*, 17 May 1924, 9; "Skyscraper to Rise," *LAT*, 7 Oct. 1928, V-1; *LAT*, 5 Oct. 1929, I-8; "Hollywood Hotel . . . ," *LAT*, 2 Feb. 1930, V-1; and "Apartment Skyscraper Announced," *LAT*, 7 Sep. 1930, V-4.

33

"Plans for Athletic Club . . . ," *HDC,* 28 Aug. 1922, 1; "New Athletic Club . . . ," *HDC,* 27 Jan. 1923, 1; "New Athletic Club . . . ," *HDC,* 12 Jan. 1924, 12. Extensive coverage of Hollywood's automobile row can be found in *HDC,* particularly in the automobile sections.

34

For background on the large neighborhood movie houses of the 1920s, see Douglas Gomery, "The Picture Palace: Economic Sense or Hollywood Nonsense?," *Quarterly Review of Film Studies* 3 (Winter 1978), 23−36; and idem, *Shared Pleasures: A History of Movie Presentation in the United States* (Madison: University of Wisconsin Press, 1992), 44−47.

35

"Will Erect Theater . . . ," *HDC,* 6 Feb. 1920, 1; "Grand Grauman Ground-Breaking . . . ," *HDC,* 6 May 1921, 1, 12; *HDC,* 14 Oct. 1922, 9; "Grauman Egyptian . . . ," *HDC,* 19 Oct. 1922, 1, 2; "Old Egypt . . . ," *LAT,* 19 Oct. 1922, II-1, 2; "Chinese Theater . . . ," *HDC,* 23 Apr. 1927, 7; "Hollywood Merchants . . . ," *HDC,* 14 May 1927, 4; "Great Premiere . . . ," *Los Angeles Evening Herald,* 17 May 1927, A-18; "Grauman's Chinese . . . ," *HDC,* 18 May 1927, 5; "Portland Cement Products Enrich . . . ," *Concrete* 32 (Jan. 1928), 49−50; Terry Helgesen, *Grauman's Chinese Theatre, Hollywood,* supplement to *Console,* Journal of the American Theatre Organ Society, n.d. See also Charles Beardsley, *Hollywood's Master Showman: The Legendary Sid Grauman* (New York: Cornwall Books, 1983), 80, 82, 90−92, 110, 112.

36

"Home of Premiere," *HDC,* 8 July 1925, 6; "New Warner Brothers' . . . ," *LAT,* 22 Apr. 1928, III-11, 17; "Largest Auditorium . . . ," *HDC,* 26 Apr. 1928, 5; *LAT,* 1 Oct. 1924, I-9; "Hollywood Units Planned," *LAT,* 3 May 1925, V-1, 3; "El Capitan . . . ," *HDC,* 20 Mar. 1926, 6−7; "Hollywood's First . . . ," *LAT,* 21 Mar. 1926, III-33, 34, 35; "Thrilling Opening . . . ," *LAT,* 2 May 1926, III-23; "Theater Skyscraper . . . ," *LAT,* 23 Dec. 1928, V-1; Terry Helgesen, *The Hollywood Pantages,* Theatre Historical Society Annual, 1973.

37

"Hollywood Slated . . . ," *HDC,* 13 Aug. 1927, 9; "Hollywood Fast Becoming . . . ," *HDC,* 15 Oct. 1927, 9; and Robert Smith, "Is Hollywood . . . ," *LAR* 7 (Nov. 1927), 16−18. For other examples, see "Plans Completed . . . ," *LAT,* 18 July 1920, V-1; "Fine Theater . . . ," *LAT,* 3 Sep. 1922, V-1; "Theater Cost . . . ," *LAT,* 29 May 1923, II-1; "Hollywood's Second . . . ," *LAT,* 17 Oct. 1926, III-23; "New Theater . . . ," *LAT,* 13 Sep. 1929, V-3; and "New Playhouse . . . ," *LAT,* 1 June 1930, II-1.

38

"Mary Pickford."

39

Downtown Los Angeles's promotional pageants seem to have followed Hollywood's lead and did not occur until some years later; see chapter 7 below.

40

"Boulevard Group Forms," *LAT,* 22 Apr. 1928, V-4.

41

HDC, 23 Mar. 1929, 7; "70 Hollywood Stores . . . ," *WWD*, 26 Mar. 1929, I-2. The association advertised extensively in *LAT;* see, for example, 1 June 1928, I-9; 17 Sep. 1928, I-9; 15 Oct. 1928, I-9; 24 Oct. 1928, I-5; 12 Dec. 1928, I-14; 4 June 1929, I-11; and 20 Nov. 1929, I-7.

42

HDC, 6 June 1932, 3; *HDC*, 26 Apr. 1934, 18.

43

"Valley Traffic . . . ," *LAT*, 26 Feb. 1928, V-8; "Auto Traffic . . . ," *LAT*, 8 Dec. 1929, V-3; "Two-Year Program . . . ," *LAT*, 13 Apr. 1930, V-3; "City Embarks . . . ," *LAT*, 7 Sep. 1930, V-1, 2; "Street Concrete . . . ," *LAT*, 28 Sep. 1930, V-2; "Avenue Rezoning . . . ," *LAT*, 18 Jan. 1931, V-2; "Hollywood to Celebrate . . . ," *HDC*, 14 Mar. 1931, 13; "Fete to Complete . . . ," *LAT*, 15 Mar. 1931, V-1, 3. The routes were Yucca, Ivar, Cole, and Wilcox streets and Cahuenga Boulevard. A concurrent project entailed the widening of Sunset Boulevard.

44

"New Nisley Shop . . . ," *HDC*, 13 Nov. 1930, 11; "Two New Shops . . . ," *HDC*, 1 Dec. 1930, 9; "Chain Store Locations . . . ," *LAT*, 31 May 1931, V-2; "Sontag Drug Store . . . ," *HDC*, 16 Oct. 1931, 15; *HDC*, 27 Nov. 1931, 9; *LAT*, 3 Dec. 1931, I-8; "Style Salon . . . ," *HDC*, 31 Mar. 1932, 11; "New Hollywood Cafe . . . ," *LAT*, 10 July 1932, I-15; "Unique Hollywood . . . ," *LAT*, 23 July 1933, I-20; *HDC*, 29 Sep. 1933, 2; "New Achievement . . . ," *HDC*, 8 Nov. 1934, 17; *HDC*, 13 Apr. 1935, 11; "New Owl Drug . . . ," *HDC*, 8 Nov. 1935, 17; "Thrifty Drug . . . ," *HDC*, 21 Nov. 1935, 17; "Women's New Hat . . . ," *HDC*, 15 Feb. 1936, 11; "Modern Setting . . . ," *HDC*, 3 Apr. 1936, 5; "Pinnell of Paris . . . ," *WWD*, 28 Aug. 1936, II-66; "Los Angeles Music . . . ," *HDC*, 14 Jan. 1938, 10; "Thrifty Opens . . . ," *LAT*, 10 Dec. 1939, V-3; Patricia Killoran, "Famous Names . . . ," *HDC*, 13 Mar. 1940, Foreman & Clark Premiere Ed., 1; "Foreman & Clark's . . . ," *LAT*, 14 Mar. 1940, I-6, 7; *HDC*, 24 Sep. 1940, 5; "Shoe Store's . . . ," *HDC*, 18 Oct. 1940, 13; "Store Wins Popularity," *HDC*, 21 Apr. 1941, 14.

45

For discussion of remodeling programs, see "Local Leaders to Meet . . . ," *HDC*, 15 Feb. 1930, 2; "Boulevard Sees Activity," *LAT*, 18 Jan. 1931, V-2; "Hollywood Work Brisk," *LAT*, 11 Nov. 1934, V-1; "Boulevard Acquiring . . . ," *HDC*, 22 Jan. 1940, 9; "Boulevard Gets 'Facial' . . . ," *HDC*, 2 Mar. 1940, 9.

Concerning remodeled and new stores of established merchants, see "Matthes Opening . . . ," *HDC*, 13 Mar. 1931, 10; "Columbia Outfitting . . . ," *HDC*, 14 May 1931, 17; *HDC*, 1 June 1934, 5; "Firm Takes . . . ," *HDC*, 7 June 1934, 16; *HDC*, 22 June 1934, 2; "Renovated Boulevard . . . ," *HDC*, 5 Mar. 1935, 11; "Anderson's Knit Shop . . . ," *HDC*, 22 Mar. 1935, 11; *HDC*, 14 Dec. 1935, 7; "Opening of Mandel's . . . ," *HDC*, 18 Mar. 1938, 8; "Apparel Shop . . . ," *HDC*, 8 Apr. 1938, 13; *HDC*, 24 Mar. 1939, 7; "Leed's Shoes . . . ," *HDC*, 7 Apr. 1939, 7; "New Quarters . . . ," *LAT*, 30 July 1939, I-14; *HDC*, 24 Oct. 1939, 16; "Maison Gaston . . . ," *HDC*, 7 Dec. 1939, 16; *HDC*, 12 Mar. 1940, 12; *HDC*, 24 July 1940, 13; "Mayfair Riding . . . ," *HDC*, 9 Aug. 1940, 4.

46

Mullen & Bluett closed all its branch stores (the other two were in Pasadena and on Wilshire Boulevard) in an effort to consolidate its assets, and did not reestablish branches until after World War II. See *HDC*, 6 Apr. 1932, 5. I. Magnin expanded its Hollywood store in 1934 and undertook further alterations two years later, but closed the facility when its much larger building on Wilshire Boulevard (discussed in chapter 5) was completed in 1939. See "Boulevard Store . . . ," *HDC*, 16 June 1934, 9; "Store's Growth . . . ," *LAT*, 17 June 1934, I-21; "Shop Marks . . . ," *LAT*, 18 Nov. 1934, I-8; "Informal Opening . . . ," *HDC*, 19 Nov. 1934, 6; and "I. Magnin's New Store . . . ," *HDC*, 22 Aug. 1936, 6.

The largest store to close was Robertson's. Indicative of the shift in the district's retail complexion, the building became quarters for the J. C. Penney Company in 1936; see: "J. C. Penney Store . . . ," *HDC*, 10 Sep. 1936, 1, 18; and "Nationally Known . . . ," *HDC*, 18 Nov. 1936, 1, 2.

47

"New Building Plan . . . ," *HDC*, 13 Feb. 1932, 13; "S. H. Kress . . . ," *LAT*, 14 Feb. 1932, V-1; "Kress Speeds . . . ," *HDC*, 3 Apr. 1934, 7; *HDC*, 27 Nov. 1934, 5; "Plans Slated . . . ," *LAT*, 18 Mar. 1934, II-1; "Preview Slated . . . ," *HDC*, 21 Nov. 1935, 15. The existing Max Factor store was only seven years old, but much more pedestrian in character; see "Max Factor . . . ," *HDC*, 16 Nov. 1928, 7, 10.

48

"Here's Architect's . . . ," *HDC*, 19 May 1939, 9, 14; "New Nancy's . . . ," *WWD*, 2 June 1939, 34; "Modernistic Shopping . . . ," *HDC*, 28 July 1939, 12; "Nancy's . . . ," *HDC*, 19 Sep. 1939, 9, 14; "Hollywood Store . . . ," *LAT*, 24 Sep. 1939, V-2.

49

See note 7 on page 383.

50

A Comprehensive Report on the Master Plan of Highways . . . (Los Angeles: Regional Planning Commission, 1941), 29; *Traffic Survey, Los Angeles Metropolitan Area* (Los Angeles: Automobile Club of Southern California, 1938), 8–9.

51

Coverage of the subject in the pro-business *HDC* is slim throughout the period, affording a marked contrast to that in *BHC* from the mid-1930s on, as discussed in chapter 7 below.

52

"New Parking Spaces . . . ," *HDC*, 19 Jan. 1932, 27. Concurrently, Taft's brother was pursuing a more intense development of retailing along adjacent blocks of Vine Street. See "Vine Street . . . ," *LAT*, 17 May 1931, V-4; "Many Seek Locations . . . ," *LAT*, 21 June 1931, V-3; "Shopping Area . . . ," *LAT*, 26 July 1931, V-2; "Vine Street . . . ," *LAT*, 10 Apr. 1932, V-3; and "Vine Street . . . ," *LAT*, 31 July 1932, I-17.

53

"Business Men Signing Up . . . ," *HDC*, 30 Mar. 1939, 9; "Free Parking . . . ," *HDC*, 21 Mar. 1939, 11.

54

Charles Cohan, "Hollywood Tackles . . . ," *LAT*, 19 May 1940, V-1, 4; "New

Hollywood Plan . . . ," *LAT,* 10 Nov. 1940, V–1; "Hollywood Tackles the Parking Problem," *AR* 88 (Dec. 1940), 45–48.

55

I have yet to find an account giving the scheme's total capacity, but on the basis of available information I estimate that it was between 2,000 and 3,000 cars, an enormous number for a single plan of the prewar period. Most contemporary projects were for municipal systems, discussed more fully in chapter 7, and entailed space for fewer than 1,000 cars.

56

"Hollywood to Start . . . ," *HDC,* 6 Feb. 1941, 11; *HDC,* 7 Feb. 1941, 4; "Three Hours . . . ," *WWD,* 19 May 1941, 22–23.

V *Fabulous Boulevard*

1

Wilshire Topics, November 1930, as quoted in Ralph Hancock, *Fabulous Boulevard* (New York: Funk & Wagnalls, 1949), xii; and idem, 5, 13. While it lacks notes and bibliography, the text appears to have been based on a search through period sources (many now lost) and interviews with key figures in the corridor's development. A scholarly overview of the street's history is given in Thomas Hines, "The Linear City: Wilshire Boulevard, Los Angeles, 1895–1945," in Jan Cigliano, ed., *The Grand American Avenue 1850–1920* (San Francisco: Pomegranate Artbooks, 1994), 307–337. See also Douglas Suisman, *Los Angeles Boulevard: Eight X-Rays of the Body Public* (Los Angeles: Los Angeles Forum for Architecture and Urban Design, 1989), esp. chap. 3; Arthur Krim, "Los Angeles and the Anti-tradition of the Suburban City," *Journal of Historical Geography* 18 (Jan. 1992), 121–138; and Esther McCoy, "Faces of the City: Wilshire Boulevard," *A&E* 222 (Sep. 1961), 24–51.

2

Concerning the development of single-family houses in the area, see "From Barley Fields . . . ," *LAT,* 29 Mar. 1914, VI–1, 2; "City's Amazing . . . ," *LAT,* 20 Dec. 1914, V–1; and "Wilshire Tract . . . ," *LAT,* 9 Nov. 1914, V–4, 5. For a sampling of early multiunit residential products, see "For Wilshire Boulevard," *LAT,* 8 Mar. 1907, V–1; "Fine Hotel . . . ," *LAT,* 1 Oct. 1911, V–1; "Large Apartment House . . . ," *LAT,* 19 May 1912, VI–1; "Fact and Comment," *LAT,* 26 May 1912, V–1; "Wilshire Holding . . . ," *LAT,* 18 May 1913, V–1; "Seek Site . . . ," *LAT,* 22 Mar. 1914, V–22; "Notable Improvement . . . ," *LAT,* 2 Sep. 1917, V–1; "Hotel Plans . . . ," *LAT,* 15 Dec. 1918, V–1; "Great Hotel . . . ," *LAT,* 23 Feb. 1919, V–1; "Proposed to Build . . . ," *LAT,* 3 Apr. 1921, V–1; "To Start Work . . . ," *LAT,* 7 Jan. 1923, V–1, 2; "Plan Made . . . ," *LAT,* 4 Feb. 1923, V–1; "Many Buildings . . . ," *LAT,* 17 June 1923, V–1, 4; *LAT,* 21 Feb. 1924, I–11; *LAT,* 26 Mar. 1924, I–12; "Thousands Will Inspect . . . ," *LAT,* 9 Apr. 1924, I–10, 11; *LAT,* 6 Dec. 1925, II–5; "New Projects . . . ," *LAT,* 15 Aug. 1926, V–1; *LAT,* 19 Oct. 1926, I–4; *LAT,* 19 Jan. 1928, I–5; and *LAT,* 18 Sep. 1929, Rotogravure sect., n.p.

3

Hancock, *Fabulous Boulevard,* 156–158; "From the City . . . ," *LAT,* 7 June 1922, II–2; "Fact and Comment," *LAT,* 16 July 1922, V–1; "Save Wilshire Boulevard," *LAT,* 13 Aug. 1922, V–7, 27; and "Plan of Magnificent . . . ," *LAT,* 21 Jan. 1923, V–1, 6.

4

"'Rosy' Does the Work," *LAT,* 25 June 1922, VI-1; "Reserves Strip . . . ," *LAT,* 20 Aug. 1922, I-4; "Traffic Lanes Proposed . . . ," *LAT,* 6 Nov. 1927, V-1, 2; "Projects Aid . . . ," *LAT,* 29 Jan. 1928, V-1; "Traffic Capacity . . . ," *ACi* 38 (June 1928), 98; "Boulevard Completion Near," *LAT,* 13 Jan. 1929, V-3; "Lanes Needed . . . ," *LAT,* 24 Nov. 1929, VI-1; "Wilshire Plan . . . ," *LAT,* 27 Oct. 1929, VI-1, 4; "Step Taken . . . ," *LAT,* 7 Sep. 1930, V-1; R. T. Dorsey, "Protecting Lives on World's Busiest Boulevard," *Western City* 6 (Oct. 1930), 37–38; Walter Lindersmith, "Ironing Out the Traffic Wrinkles . . . ," *Western City* 7 (Nov. 1931), 7–8; "Heavy Traffic Stream . . . ," *ACi* 46 (Feb. 1932), 106; R. T. Dorsey, "Extra Center Signal . . . ," *ACi* 53 (Apr. 1938), 125; "Three Lanes West . . . ," *ACi* 53 (Sep. 1938), 107.

5

"Values Mount . . . ," *LAT,* 30 Nov. 1924, V-1; "Wilshire Zoning Urged," *LAT,* 11 Apr. 1926, V-1; "Urges Wilshire Zoning," *LAT,* 18 Apr. 1926, V-11; "Wilshire Boulevard . . . ," *LAT,* 25 Apr. 1926, V-1; *LAT,* 29 Apr. 1926, II-11; Harland Bartholomew, "Wilshire Boulevard . . . ," *LAT,* 27 June 1926, V-3; "Traffic Lanes Proposed," 1, 2; "Cooperative Improvements . . . ," *SWBC* 70 (25 Nov. 1927), 43; "Projects Aid . . . ," *LAT,* 29 Jan. 1928, V-1.

6

Concerning the latter, see John Stamper, *Chicago's North Michigan Avenue: Planning and Development, 1900–1930* (Chicago: University of Chicago Press, 1991).

7

For examples, see "Artistic Edifice . . . ," *LAT,* 12 Apr. 1925, V-1; "Plan Block . . . ," *LAT,* 28 Nov. 1925, V-4; "Plan Shops . . . ," *LAT,* 22 Nov. 1925, V-4; *LAT,* 6 Feb. 1927, V-5; *LAT,* 26 Feb. 1928, V-2; "New Step . . . ," *LAT,* 1 Mar. 1928, II-1; "Wilshire Unit . . . ," *LAT,* 29 July 1928, V-4; "New Buildings . . . ," *LAT,* 13 Jan. 1929, V-1, 2; "Wilshire Project . . . ," *LAT,* 23 Feb. 1930, V-3; "Manor Type . . . ," *LAT,* 27 July 1930, V-10; *LAT,* 14 Sep. 1930, V-2; "Boulevard Structure . . . ," *LAT,* 5 Oct. 1930, V-2; *WA* 39 (Dec. 1930), 210; *WA* 40 (Feb. 1931), 21. See also note 8 below.

8

"Soaring Wilshire Values . . . ," *LAT,* 8 Apr. 1928, V-7; "Wilshire Section Leads," *LAT,* 24 Mar. 1929, V-2; "Survey Discloses . . . ," *LAT,* 2 Feb. 1930, V-3; "Wilshire Paces . . . ," *LAT,* 20 Jan. 1929, V-1, 2; "Wilshire Boulevard . . . ," *LAT,* 24 Nov. 1929, V-2; "Wilshire Boulevard . . . ," *LAEx,* 28 Sep. 1929, III-1, 7; "Wilshire Building . . . ," *LAT,* 1 Dec. 1929, V-1.

Concerning the two buildings, see "Boulevard Structure Announced," *LAT,* 17 Feb. 1929, V-1; *LAT,* 7 Apr. 1929, V-2; "Theater Work Planned," *LAT,* 4 May 1930, V-1; "Theater Work Started," *LAT,* 2 Nov. 1930, V-1; "A Western 'Broadway' and 'Fifth Avenue' Combined," *PCA* 40 (Dec. 1931), 36; and F. B. Nightingale, "Castles in the Air," *A&E* 108 (Mar. 1932), 59–60. A considerably larger project was planned nearby; see "Theater-Office Plan . . . ," *LAT,* 9 Feb. 1930, V-1. See also "Fine Office Unit . . . ," *LAT,* 17 Apr. 1932, V-2.

9

The local origins of this form for commercial buildings are discussed later in this chapter.

10

One corner of Wilshire and Vermont was among the very first along the street to be developed for commercial purposes, but this project remained the exception for some years. See "To Improve Corner," *LAT,* 11 Feb. 1923, V-5, and also "Film Star to Erect . . . ," *LAT,* 16 Mar. 1924, V-5. The management of Bullock's department store purposefully avoided a site at that intersection because of anticipated traffic congestion, as noted in the text below.

11

A large building was planned for a site adjacent to Bullock's that would house a number of national chain specialty stores catering to women, but the project appears to have been shelved due to the depression; see "New Wilshire . . . ," *LAT,* 1 Sep. 1929, V-1, 2. Branches of two downtown clothing stores, Halbriter's and Mullen & Bluett, did open in the precinct; see *LAT,* 7 Oct. 1929, I-10; "Mullen, Bluett . . . ," *HDC,* 26 Apr. 1930, 7; "Clothiers to Build . . . ," *LAT,* 27 Apr. 1930, V-2; and "Fifth Mullen . . . ," *HDC,* 24 Oct. 1930, 17. For other examples, see *LAT,* 31 Mar. 1930, I-3; "Actress to Enter . . . ," *LAT,* 6 July 1930, V-3; and "Milestone Marks . . . ," *LAT,* 9 Aug. 1931, III-26.

12

This pattern, well established by the mid-1930s and strengthened over subsequent years, is clearly documented by correlating street address listings published in the Southern California Telephone Company's *Los Angeles Street Address Directory* for January 1935 and January 1942 with information on Sanborn fire insurance maps.

13

J. C. Nichols, "Planning Shopping Centers," *NREJ* 8 (22 Mar. 1926), 47.

14

Donald Marquis, "The Spanish Stores of Morgan, Walls & Clements," *AF* 50 (June 1929), 901; Harold Donaldson Eberlein, "Shop Fronts in Country Towns and Smaller Cities," *AF* 50 (June 1929), 878; M. S. C. Wood, "Shop Fronts Must Advertise," *BA* 52 (Jan. 1930), 39. See also Frank Hawkins, "Attracting Trade to the 'Neighborhood' Store," *CSA/GME* 6 (Jan. 1930), 43; W. A. Edwards, "Sales Appeal in Store Fronts," *CSR* 3 (July 1930) 37; R. W. Sexton, *American Commercial Buildings of Today* (New York: Architectural Book Pub. Co., 1928), 153–208; James Edsall, "Attractive Store Buildings . . . ," *BA* 52 (Sep. 1929), 50–52; Marc Goodnow, "Architecture for the Merchant," *A&E* 97 (June 1929), 35–40; and Harwood Hewitt, "Is Good Architectural Design a Paying Investment . . . ?," *PCA* 25 (Mar. 1924), 5–17.

15

Recognition of such factors in Los Angeles is indicated in William Garner, "City Adopts Modernism . . . ," *LAT,* 5 June 1927, V-10; and "'Moderne' Architecture . . . ," *SWBC* 74 (17 Sep. 1929), 31. See also note 14 above.

16

Recent scholarly writing on the subject includes David Gebhard, *George Washington Smith, 1876–1930: The Spanish Colonial Revival in California* (Santa Barbara: Art Gallery, University of California, Santa Barbara, 1964); idem, "The Spanish Colonial Revival in Southern California (1895–1930)," *JSAH* 26 (May 1967), 131–147; and idem, *Santa Barbara—The Creation of a New Spain in America* (Santa Barbara: University Art Museum, University of California, Santa Barbara, 1982).

17

Newness was not often explicitly addressed in accounts of the period. For exceptions, see Edward Leaf, "Southern California Architecture," *LAR* 5 (Dec. 1924), 11; Harris Allen, "Industrial Architecture in California," *PCA* 33 (Sep. 1928), 14; Harris Allen, "This California Architecture," *PCA* 33 (Oct. 1928), 11; Marquis, "Spanish Stores," 901–903, 916; and Sheldon Cheney, *The New World Architecture* (New York: Tudor Pub. Co., 1930), 268–272.

Motion picture sets may have been influential as well; see Wharton Clay, "California, the Movies and Beauty," *SCB* 2 (Nov. 1925), 17, 30. On the other hand, architectural examples may well have had a catalytic effect on cinematography. The relationship between the two demands careful study before generalizations can be made.

18

"For Commercial Uses," *LAT,* 17 Sept. 1922, V-1; "An Attractive Group . . . ," *SWBC* 62 (12 Oct. 1923), 36; "West Seventh St. Store . . . ," *SWBC* 62 (16 Nov. 1923), 36; "Center for Shopping . . . ," *LAT,* 18 Nov. 1923, V-8; "Seventh Street Store . . . ," *LAT,* 3 Feb. 1924, V-9; Hewitt, "Is Good Architectural Design," 7, 9–10, 14, 17; "Shop Building . . . ," *LAT,* 20 Apr. 1924, V-3; "Shops in Los Angeles," *PCA* 25 (Apr. 1924), 11, 13, 17; "Spanish Style Business Building . . . ," *SWBC* 63 (30 May 1924), 42–43; Arthur Duncombe, "Beautiful Architecture . . . ," *CS* 6 (Sep. 1924), 7–8; M. Urmy Seares, "The Expert Is Worthy of His Hire," *CS* 6 (Sep. 1924), 9–10; *LAT,* 14 Jan. 1925, I-10, 11; *PCA* 27 (Apr. 1925), 29, 31; Goodnow, "Architecture," 36–37; *LAT,* 19 Aug. 1926, II-6.

19

For examples, see note 7 above; also Marquis, "Spanish Stores," 907–909; *LAT,* 3 May 1931, V-2; and *PCA* 40 (Nov. 1931), 34.

20

A number of comparable examples were built in the Hollywood district during the same period, but relatively few of them were located along Hollywood Boulevard.

21

"Expansion of Bullock Store," *LAT,* 28 Apr. 1928, I-1, 2. No square footage figure for the scheme was given. The vary tall second-story zone probably would have included a mezzanine, if not a full third story. Assuming, too; that the store had a full basement, the total floor area would probably have been around 100,000 square feet. This was still a very large store of its kind for the period, as discussed in the text below.

22

"Million-Dollar Class A . . . ," *LAT,* 8 Jan. 1925, II-2; "Report Dyas' Plans . . . ," *WWD,* 6 July 1927, 23. Soon after Bullock's and May's Wilshire plan was announced in January 1925, another project, the Southern California Athletic and Country Club, was unveiled as a prototype for other buildings in the precinct; see "Structure to Be Model," *LAT,* 18 Feb. 1925, I-4; and "Club's Plans . . . ," *LAT,* 18 Oct. 1925, V-5. See also "Parking Plan Favored," *LAT,* 11 Jan. 1925, V-5; and figure 95.

23

"J. C. Haggerty Leases . . . ," *WWD,* 23 June 1928, 21; "Plans Ready . . . ," *LAT,* 1 July 1928, II-2.

24

"Bullock's Will Add . . . ," *LAT,* 13 Nov. 1928, II-9; "Revised Sketch . . . ,"
WWD, 22 Nov. 1928, I-2P; "Outlying Shops Popular . . . ," *WWD,* 11 Oct.
1929, IV-19.

25

Contemporary accounts include "New Bullock Store . . . ," *WWD,* 25 Sep. 1929,
I-9; "Bullock's Branch Store Ready Next December," *DGE* 83 (19 Jan. 1929), 68;
"Bullock's-Wilshire Ultra Modern Store," *SN* 9 (21 Sep. 1929), 7, 11; "New Bul-
lock Store . . . ," *WWD,* 25 Sep. 1929, I-9; "Bullock's Temple . . . ," *LAEE,* 25
Sep. 1929, 3; George Douglas, "Bullock's Wilshire . . . ," *LAEx,* 26 Sep. 1929,
I-8; Alma May Cook, "Art and Business . . . ," *LAEE,* 26 Sep. 1929, 16; Edith
Bristol, "So. Cal. Spirit . . . ," *Los Angeles Evening Herald,* 26 Sep. 1929, B1, B4;
Winifred Aydelotte, "Bullock's Wilshire . . . ," *Los Angeles Record,* 26 Sep. 1929, 9;
Alma Whitaker, "Bullock's in Debut Today," *LAT,* 26 Sep. 1929, II-1, 5; Olive
Gray, "Store Weds Art to Beauty," *LAT,* 26 Sep. 1929, II-6; "Bullock's Wil-
shire . . . ," *WWD,* 26 Sep. 1929, I-1, 18; *LAT,* 14 Oct. 1929, I-8; "Modern—
Beautiful—Unique! . . . ," *DGE* 84 (26 Oct. 1929), 45–49; "Art in Business,"
LATMN, 2 Jan. 1930, IV-15; Harris Allen, "A Building Designed for Today,"
and Pauline G. Schindler, "A Significant Contribution to Culture," *PCA* 37 (Jan.
1930), 20–28, 74; "Bullock's Wilshire . . . ," *AR* 67 (Jan. 1930), 54–64; "Bul-
lock's Wilshire," *DGE* 85 (Sep. 1930), 192–193; and "Eight Modern Department
Stores," *AF* 58 (May 1933), 357–358. An indication of the building's significance
for the development of the type is given in Meredith Clausen, "Department
Stores," in Joseph Wilkes, ed., *Encyclopedia of Architecture: Design, Engineering and
Construction,* 4 vols. (New York: John Wiley & Sons, 1988), 2:215–216. Bullock's
Wilshire is noted in many writings on Los Angeles architecture, but generally only
in passing. For a recent popular account, see Pauletta Finkelstein, "Bullock's Wil-
shire," *Antique Showcase* 31 (Sep. 1989), 35–40. I am grateful to Shirley Wilson of
I. Magnin Company for supplying me with additional information. In a 1963 inter-
view, Robert Field stated that he had been the principal designer of Bullock's Wil-
shire while in the employ of the Parkinsons; see Donald Shippers, "Walker &
Eisen: Twenty Years of Los Angeles Architecture, 1920–1940," *Southern California
Quarterly* 46 (Dec. 1964), 387.

26

LAT, 28 Sep. 1932, II-8. No figures for the parking lot's capacity were given at
the time of opening, and the full area may not have been used at first. If expansion
did take place, however, it probably occurred within the first decade of operation.
By the early 1950s the 375-space area was well below demand, justifying a raised
deck for an additional 300 spaces; see "Store Increases . . . ," *LAT,* 16 Apr. 1953,
II-2.

27

Compilations of the period include "The Growth of Branch Stores," *NRB* 12
(Oct. 1930), 546–547; Clinton Simpson, "How Are Department Store Branches
Operated?," *Advertising & Selling* 16 (7 Jan. 1931), 26; and Edwin D. Dibrell, "The
Effects of Branch Store Expansion," *NRB* 28 (Apr. 1946), 16–17, 54.

The earliest account I have found arguing for branch development among department stores is by John Ihlder of the U.S. Chamber of Commerce; see "Department Store of Future . . . ," *WWD,* 13 Feb. 1926, 7. Charles Mears, "Outlying
Shops Cited . . . ," *WWD,* 2 July 1927, 6, suggests some of the doubts many department store executives may have had on the matter. See also John Guernsey,
Retailing Tomorrow: Practical Retailer's View of the Future of His Profession (New York:

Dry Goods Economist, 1929), chap. 13; "Mrs. Jones Changes Her Shopping Habits," *BW,* 5 Oct. 1929, 28–30; and "Department Store Branches in Suburbs Succeed, Multiply," *BW,* 1 Oct. 1930, 10–11. Retrospective accounts of this pivotal period are often inaccurate in detail. See, for example, John Guernsey, "Suburban Branches," *DSE* 14 (July 1951), 42; and Dero Saunders, "Department Stores: Race for the Suburbs," *Fortune* 44 (Dec. 1951), 101.

28

Concerning the Fair stores, see "The Fair to Enter . . . ," *WWD,* 7 Dec. 1928, I-1; "Fair, Chicago, Plans . . . ," *WWD,* 13 Dec. 1928, I-1, 20; and *WWD,* 30 Apr. 1929, I-13.

In 1928, Marshall Field & Company opened small stores in Lake Forest and Evanston prior to embarking on plans for major outlying facilities. See "Marshall Field's Plan . . . ," *WWD,* 14 Sep. 1928, I-5; "Field's Will Have Oak Park Branch," *DGE* 83 (Sep. 1928), 67; *WWD,* 27 Nov. 1928, I-24; "Marshall Field Unit . . . ," *WWD,* 22 Jan. 1929, I-13; "Marshall Field to Build . . . ," *WWD,* 1 Mar. 1929, I-1, 15; *CSR* 2 (June 1929), 16; "Marshall Field . . . ," *Chicago Daily News,* 18 Oct. 1929, 71; "Oak Park Opens . . . ," *Chicago Daily News,* 19 Oct. 1929, 18; "Field's First Permanent . . . ," *WWD,* 21 Oct. 1929, I-1; "Evanston Branch . . . ," *Chicago Daily News,* 21 Nov. 1929, 34; "Fields Adapt French Renaissance . . . ," *DGE* 84 (23 Nov. 1929), 50–51; "35,000 at New Field . . . ," *WWD,* 25 Nov. 1929, I-2; "Similarity of Design Identifies Marshall Field Branches," *CSA/AE* 6 (May 1930) 60, 62–63; and Sally Kitt Chappell, *Architecture and Planning of Graham, Anderson, Probst and White, 1912–1936: Transforming Tradition* (Chicago: University of Chicago Press, 1992), 233–235.

29

Concerning the Bailey Company, see Victor Sincere, "Why We're Opening Branch Department Stores," *CSA/GME* 6 (Feb. 1930), 5–6, 81; *Cleveland Plain Dealer,* 10 Apr. 1930, 7; "Bailey Co. Opens . . . ," *Cleveland Plain Dealer,* 11 Apr. 1930, 11; and "Thousands at New Bailey . . . ," *WWD,* 15 Apr. 1930, I-11, 14. Concerning Strawbridge & Clothier's store, see "Strawbridge Plans Branch . . . ," *WWD,* 23 Sep. 1929, I-1, 2; "New Store Opens . . . ," *Philadelphia Inquirer,* 12 May 1930, 7; "2,000 Attend . . . ," *WWD,* 13 May 1930, I-13; "Store Building of Modern Design Completed on Ardmore Site," *Building Magazine* 10 (May 1930), 25–26; *AR* 68 (Dec. 1930), 465–466; and Alfred Lief, *Family Business: A Century in the Life and Times of Strawbridge & Clothier* (New York: McGraw-Hill, 1968), 183–186.

30

"Branch Store Growth . . . ," *WWD,* 19 Feb. 1941, 31; interview with Eaton Ballard, retired first vice president of the Broadway Company, Pasadena, 14 Nov. 1989. For a synopsis of the then prevailing attitude toward the function of branches, see "Growth of Branch Stores," 546–547.

31

"Outlying Shops Popular," IV-19.

32

See also *LAT,* 23 Jan. 1920, II-7. The company moved to new quarters more centrally located in Pasadena in 1925. I am grateful to Mary Jo Winder for additional information on the building.

33

Quoted in James Worthy, *Shaping an American Institution: Robert E. Wood and Sears, Roebuck* (Urbana and Chicago: University of Illinois Press, 1984), 83. Worthy's account and that found in Boris Emet and John Jeuck, *Catalogues and Counters: A History of Sears, Roebuck and Company* (Chicago: University of Chicago Press, 1950), chap. 21, provide valuable background on Sears's entry into the retail trade. See also General R. E. Wood, "Our Part in Chain Store Progress," *CSA/GME* 5 (Apr. 1929), 41–43, 66; and idem, "Long-Time Trends and the Retail Merchant," *CSA/VS* 13 (Dec. 1937), 20, 66.

34

"Sears-Roebuck's 2 Chicago Retail . . . ," *WWD,* 2 Nov. 1925, 2, 55; "Sears, Roebuck Says . . . ," *WWD,* 3 Nov. 1925, 34. See also "Two More Sears-Roebuck Stores Open in Chicago," *Sales Management* 9 (14 Nov. 1925), 682–683; George Nimmons, "The New Renaissance in Architecture . . . ," *AA* 134 (5 Aug. 1928), 141–148; "Decentralization in Retail . . . ," *WWD,* 27 Jan. 1930, I-10; "Class A," *Tide* 6 (Dec. 1932), 7–8; and "Sears, Roebuck and Co. . . . ," *CSA/GME* 9 (Sep. 1933), 21, 46.

35

See, for example, Leslie Janes, "Sales, Not Appearance Is Our Display Aim," *CSA/GME* 7 (Aug. 1931), 5–6, 25. Such an approach was considered heretical among leading department store executives.

36

Concerning department store executives' attitude toward Sears at that time, see Guernsey, *Retailing Tomorrow,* 61–74. Views had begun to change a decade later; see, for example, J. M. Baskin, "Leading the Field," *Retail Executive* 9 (Aug. 1939), 2, 10, which summarizes what were considered to be the most important characteristics of Sears's approach to merchandising during the interwar decades. Most postwar chronicles of the then rapid expansion of department store branches and large shopping centers credit Sears, together with the supermarket, as pioneers in the retail decentralization trend.

37

See, for example, "Sears-Roebuck Retail Stores . . . ," *WWD,* 21 Nov. 1925, 1, 5; "Sears, Roebuck New Profit . . . ," *WWD,* 23 Jan. 1928, I-1, 6. The former article noted that some of the major Chicago department stores were already planning branch stores as a result of Sears's initiative.

38

"Sears-Roebuck Plan . . . ," *WWD,* 7 Dec. 1926, 1, 63; *LAT,* 9 Jan. 1927, V-1; "New Sears-Roebuck . . . ," *WWD,* 4 Feb. 1927, 10; "Sears, Roebuck . . . ," *LAT,* 3 Apr. 1927, V-1; "Record Speed . . . ," *SWBC* 69 (17 June 1927), 36–37; *LAT,* 17 June 1927, I-8; *LAEE,* 24 June 1927, 23; "Mail-Order Plant . . . ," *LAT,* 22 July 1927, II-3; *LAT,* 31 July 1927, I-14; *LATMN,* 3 Jan. 1928, V-2; "A Mail Order Building in Los Angeles, California," *AR* 64 (July 1928), 65–69; "Sears, Roebuck Uses Futuristic Billboard Advertising," *CSA/AE* 4 (Dec. 1928), 46; "Sears, Roebuck . . . ," *LAT,* 27 June 1931, II-6; and "Free Parking Space Another Chain Store Service," *Chain Store Progress* 3 (July 1931), 5. Two additional stores were opened in Hollywood and Long Beach the following year, and a six-story addition was made to the Olympic Boulevard facility in 1929.

39

Many smaller retail operations in the metropolitan area, notably automobile service facilities and markets, included off-street parking as an integral part of the design at an earlier date.

40

Louis Bromfield, "California," *Vogue* 76 (8 Dec. 1930), 150.

41

"Beauties and Future of Wilshire Boulevard," *SN* 10 (11 Jan. 1930), 7.

42

Vague reference is made to this provision in several contemporary accounts cited in note 25 above. Blueprints of load calculation studies, dated 18 September 1928, document the extent to which vertical expansion was calculated. These materials are on file at the successor architectural firm, Parkinson Field Associates. I am grateful to William Scott Field for giving me access to this and other valuable material on the project.

43

"Suburban Branch Plan . . . ," *WWD,* 15 Jan. 1927, 1, 15; "Heavy Traffic Seen . . . ," *WWD,* 29 Nov. 1929, I-7. See also "Suburban Branches . . . ," *WWD,* 21 Mar. 1932, I-24.

44

"Best's Opens . . . ," *WWD,* 15 Jan. 1930, I-1; "Best Store to Open . . . ," *Standard Star* [New Rochelle], 15 Jan. 1930, II-1; "Best & Co.'s New Store . . . ," *Standard Star,* 25 Feb. 1930, 2; Milton Lowenthal, "The Suburban Branch Department Store," *AR* 72 (July 1932), 3, 5. The store was apparently the first branch of a major New York retailer to open in Westchester County, but was soon followed by one of B. Altman & Company in White Plains. Best's president was quite aware of both accessibility and parking as key factors; see "Parking Question . . . ," *WWD,* 14 Mar. 1930, I-7; and Philip LeBoutillier, "The Parking Question," *NRB* 12 (Apr. 1930), 199−200. Best's two other nonseasonal branches of the period, in Garden City, Long Island (1929), and East Orange, New Jersey (1930), were situated on the edge of their respective town centers.

45

"Franklin Simon Greenwich . . . ," *WWD,* 3 Sep. 1931, I-1; "Franklin Simon Announces . . . ," *Greenwich Press,* 3 Sep. 1931, 1, 8; "Franklin Simon's . . . ," *WWD,* 15 March 1932; *Greenwich Press,* 17 March 1932, fourth sect.; *Greenwich News and Graphic,* 18 Mar. 1932, Franklin Simon & Co. sect.; Lowenthal, "Suburban Branch," 9. Off-street parking of this nature was extremely rare for New York− area branch stores at that time. The only comparable instance of which I am aware was at B. Altman & Company, East Orange (1930−1931), which had a lot holding twenty-four cars off the rear alley.

46

The shopping complex was begun in 1928; Strawbridge's became involved in the development at a later date. For background, see "Now They Stop and Shop in Ardmore," *Integrity Spokesman,* Nov. 1930, [1−9]; "Shopping Center Accepts . . . ," *Evening Star* [Washington], 9 Dec. 1939, B-4; Bernard J. Birnbaum, "Shoppers' Heaven," *Liberty* 19 (19 Jan. 1946), 20−21, 75−76; and Geoffrey Baker and Bruno Funaro, *Shopping Centers: Design and Operation* (New York: Reinhold, 1951), 191−193. Concerning the store, see note 29 above.

47

The defining characteristics of a shopping center are discussed in chapter 6 below. Concerning examples in which a large department store served as anchor, see chapter 11.

48

"Another Branch for Strawbridge," *WWD,* 20 Nov. 1930, I-1; "The New Strawbridge & Clothier . . . ," *Main Line Times* [Ardmore], 4 Dec. 1930, 2; *WWD,* 8 Dec. 1930, I-6; "To Start Work . . . ," *Times-Chronicle* [Jenkintown], 4 Dec. 1930, 1, 2; "Philadelphia Store to Open Second Branch," *DGE* 85 (Feb. 1931), 161; "Strawbridge's Takes . . . ," *WWD,* 9 Sep. 1931, I-1, 5; "Strawbridge Opens . . . ," *Philadelphia Inquirer,* 10 Sep. 1931, 4; "Thousands View . . . ," *Times-Chronicle,* 10 Sep. 1931, 1, 4; "Strawbridge & Clothier's . . . ," *Times-Chronicle,* 17 Sep. 1931, 6. The store had a basement automobile service and parking facility; see *Times-Chronicle,* 4 Feb. 1932, 5.

49

Samuel Feinberg, "From Where I Sit . . . ," *WWD,* 9 Feb. 1960, 17; and 10 Feb. 1960, 10. See also Ralph Jones, "Wanamaker, Phila . . . ," *WWD,* 9 Feb. 1949, 80.

50

"Magnin Plans Big Expansion . . . ," *WWD,* 14 Feb. 1938, 1; "Magnin's Minds . . . ," *WWD,* 24 Oct. 1938, 4; "New I. Magnin . . . ," *WWD,* 10 Feb. 1939, 1, 8–9; "$3,000,000 Magnin Home . . . ," *HDC,* 11 Feb. 1939, 1, 13; "Leaders Visit . . . ," *LAT,* 11 Feb. 1938, I-7; "Thousands Greet . . . ," *WWD,* 13 Feb. 1939, 1, 23; "Beverly-Wilshire Area . . . ," *BHC,* 17 Feb. 1939, 5; "Old and New . . . ," *DSE* 2 (25 Apr. 1939), 26.

51

For accounts of the name's origins, see J. Edward Tufft, "The Miracle Mile," *NREJ* 39 (May 1938), 40; Hancock, *Fabulous Boulevard,* 154; and W. W. Robinson, *History of the Miracle Mile* (Los Angeles: Columbia Savings & Loan, 1965), 1–2. For other useful accounts, see "Wilshire Boulevard Business . . . ," *LAT,* 24 Nov. 1929, V-2; "'Miracle Mile' Noted . . . ," *LAT,* 7 Dec. 1934, I-7; "Wilshire Boulevard . . . ," *BHC,* 8 Sep. 1939, 9; "Back Door Parking for Shoppers in Los Angeles," *Freehold* 6 (15 Mar. 1940), 198–204; and Charles Cohan, "Advance of Famous 'Mile' . . . ," *LAT,* 2 Mar. 1952, V-1.

The development was called Wilshire Boulevard Center until ca. 1928. Names similar to Miracle Mile were not uncommon in real estate advertisements at that time. One company called Western Avenue the "Miracle Street" (*LAT,* 19 Mar. 1922, V-11); another referred to Downey Boulevard near the Union Pacific Railroad crossing as the "Magic Mile" (*LAT,* 28 Jan. 1923, V-10). What was unusual was that such a term would enter common parlance. Before World War II, the term was given to blocks slated for arterial development elsewhere; see, for example, E. V. Miller, "Divided Highway Enters Tucson, Arizona," *ACi* 53 (Jan. 1938), 37–38. Perhaps the best-known Miracle Mile aside from the original was that along the North Hempstead Turnpike in Manhasset, Long Island; see Baker and Funaro, *Shopping Centers,* 162–163.

52

As late as 1930, Ross's precinct was only twelve blocks long, extending west to Stanley Avenue. It is uncertain when the area was enlarged, but the process may have occurred due to the May Company's desire to locate at the Wilshire-Fairfax intersection, as discussed in the text below.

53

Hancock, *Fabulous Boulevard,* 152. In this account, which appears to be based on conversations with Ross himself, four miles is given as the determining radius; however, a number of the target areas identified lie closer to five or six miles from the development.

54

Kenneth Crist, "Miracle Mile . . . ," *LAT,* 2 Apr. 1939, V-3.

55

The practice of spot zoning was nevertheless widespread in Los Angeles by the late 1920s; see Edward Bassett, "Spot Zoning," *City Planning* 6 (July 1930), 229.

56

For a sampling of early projects, see *LAT,* 16 May 1926, V-12; *LAT,* 21 Jan. 1927, I-8; *AR* 63 (Apr. 1928), 302–303; *LAT,* 20 Aug. 1929, I-8; and "Building to Be Erected . . . ," *LAT,* 25 Aug. 1929, V-2. Another leading real estate firm, Burton & Company, held some acreage around the Wilshire–La Brea intersection; see "Wilshire Unit . . . ," *LAT,* 12 Apr. 1925, V-4; and "Wilshire Properties Sold," *LAT,* 17 May 1925, V-3.

57

"Wilshire Boulevard Wins . . . ," *LAT,* 10 Oct. 1928, II-1; "Desmond's Plan . . . ," *WWD,* 16 Oct. 1928, I-9; "Desmond's Extends . . . ," *LAT,* 15 Mar. 1929, I-7; "Desmond's Opens . . . ," *WWD,* 18 Mar. 1929, I-10; "Desmond's Extends Service . . . ," *DGE* 83 (31 May 1929), 67, 81–82. Circumstantial evidence indicates that the building was designed specifically to meet Desmond's needs, but it is unclear whether Ross first persuaded investors to underwrite the project, then secured the retailer, or vice versa.

58

For background, see "New City Hall," *LAT,* 26 Sep. 1925, II-1, 3; "Preliminary Plans . . . ," *SWBC* 66 (2 Oct. 1925), 44; "Quandary on Height . . . ," *LAT,* 12 Oct. 1925, II-1, 2; "New Hall . . . ," *LAT,* 11 Apr. 1926, II-3; "Moving Begun . . . ," *LAT,* 22 Apr. 1928, II-2; George Hales, "The Los Angeles City Hall," *PCA* 33 (May 1928), 13–37, 42–43. See also *LAT,* 6 Sep. 1921, II-4; *LAT,* 1 Jan. 1928, II-1; and *LAT,* 24 May 1931, II-9. As a municipal building, the City Hall was not subject to the height ordinance.

59

Concerning the stores, see "Firm Observes New Expansion," *LAT,* 8 Sep. 1929, V-7; "Silverwood's New Wilshire Boulevard Store," *SN* 9 (14 Sep. 1929), 7; "Merchants to Locate . . . ," *LAT,* 26 July 1931, V-3; "Myer Siegel . . . ," *HDC,* 24 Oct. 1931, 5; "New Wilshire Store . . . ," *LAT,* 25 Oct. 1931, III-17; and "Myer Siegel's . . . ," *WWD,* 2 Nov. 1931, I-7. Later, Silverwood's opened a smaller branch in Hollywood, which was closed in 1937; see *HDC,* 26 Feb. 1937, 7.

Concerning the office towers, see "Skyscraper Reveals . . . ," *LAT,* 28 July 1929, V-1, 3; "Building to Rise . . . ," *LAT,* 26 Mar. 1930, II-1; "Three Structures . . . ," *LAT,* 30 Mar. 1930, V-1; *PCA* 37 (Apr. 1930), 2; "Two Limit-Height Buildings . . . ," *LAT,* 20 Apr. 1930, V-2; "Skyscraper Completion . . . ," *LAT,* 25 May 1930, V-2; "Height-Limit Construction . . . ," *LAT,* 8 June 1930, V-1, 4; "Wings or No Wings?," *AA* 137 (Oct. 1930), 36–37; "New Wilshire Store . . . ," *SWBC* 77 (1 May 1931), 42–43; and "E. Clem Wilson Building . . . ," *HDC,* 24 Oct. 1931, 7.

60

For a good example of Ross's promotional efforts at this stage, see *LATMN,* 2 Jan. 1930, III-2. Later examples include *LATMN,* 1 Jan. 1938, I-14; *LATMN,* 2 Jan. 1939, I-17; and *HDC,* 18 Sep. 1941, 19.

61

"Skyscraper Hotel Sketched," *LAT,* 16 Aug. 1929, II-1. The building could rise to such heights because the site lay just outside what were then the city limits, probably on a large, contiguous tract of land to the north owned by Earl Gilmore. The rendering suggests the building was to be set back some distance from the street, and the accompanying text indicates Ross's plans to develop a golf course and gardens on the property. Ross was still advancing the proposal in January 1930, but deteriorating economic conditions no doubt brought its demise soon thereafter.

At least two other tall buildings were proposed for the Miracle Mile prior to World War II. One is discussed in the text below. Concerning the other, see *LAT,* 24 Mar. 1940, V-1; and David Gebhard and Harriette Von Breton, *Los Angeles in the Thirties 1931–1941,* rev. ed. (Los Angeles: Hennessey & Ingalls, 1989), 56.

62

BHC, 17 Oct. 1929, 6. This was one of a series in the paper illustrating the lavishly furnished store.

63

Citations for the Carthay Theatre are in chapter 10, note 6. Concerning the Fox Wilshire, see "Playhouse Plans . . . ," *LAT,* 2 June 1929, V-1; and Maggie Valentine, *The Show Starts on the Sidewalk: An Architectural History of the Movie Theatre, Starring S. Charles Lee* (New Haven: Yale University Press, 1994), 78–81. Beverly Hills is discussed in chapter 7 below.

64

Tufft, "Miracle Mile," 38; "Back Door Parking," 199; "Wilshire Boulevard World Wide Exemplar."

65

However, the treatment of the parking entrance here and at the Dominguez-Wilshire Building was not nearly as elaborate as could be found at Bullock's or I. Magnin; see figure 75.

66

See note 22 above.

67

After World War II, however, the precinct's parking capacity dropped well below demand; see "Off-Street Parking Facilities," *ASPO* 15 (July 1949), 59.

68

LAT, 29 Apr. 1928, V-1; Harriet Burdsal, "Thousands Enjoy . . . ," *HDC,* 21 Sep. 1928, 9; "Unit to Rise . . . ," *LAT,* 9 Aug. 1931, V-1; "Newberry Store Opens New Unit" and "Brooks Clothing . . . ," *HDC,* 24 Oct. 1931, 7.

69

"Miracle Mile of Chain Stores," *CSA/GE* [14] (Sep. 1938), 82–83, 100; "Sontag Drug Building . . . ," *HDC,* 6 Nov. 1935, 19; "Largest and Finest . . . ," *HDC,* 30 Apr. 1936, Advertising Sect. Announcements of other stores include *LAT,* 10 Mar. 1934, I-3; "Wilshire Store . . . ," *HDC,* 12 Mar. 1934, 7; *LAT,* 29 Mar. 1935,

III-sect.; *LAT,* 20 Aug. 1937, I-7; "Chandler's Wilshire Blvd. . . . ," *HDC,* 1 Apr. 1938, 7; *LAT,* 1 Apr. 1938, I-7. One national chain, Nisley's shoe store, replaced its Hollywood unit with one in the precinct; see "Wilshire Blvd. Store Opens," *HDC,* 4 Nov. 1940, 11. A downtown emporium, the Eastern furniture store, also established a branch on the Miracle Mile; see "Eastern to Open . . . ," *HDC,* 8 Aug. 1935, 13; and *LAT,* 11 Aug. 1935, I-2.

70

" 'Moderne' Architecture Meets Demand . . . ," *SWBC* 74 (17 Sep. 1929), 31. This and other accounts of the period indicate that flexibility in design was seen as encompassing capacity for change in expression over time as well as options available at any given point. For this reason, among others, it is misleading to consider Art Deco a short-lived mode that was employed during the late 1920s and early 1930s. Rather, the phenomenon should be viewed as a popular thrust in modernism that lasted for some two decades and encompassed a variety of expressive forms, including streamlining, that were allied in intent. For a good analysis of the subject, see Richard Striner, "Art Deco: Polemics and Synthesis," *Winterthur Portfolio* 25 (Spring 1990), 21–34.

71

"Latest Skyscraper Announced . . . ," *LAT,* 2 Mar. 1930, V-1.

72

"Modern Structure Planned . . . ," *LAT,* 14 Nov. 1937, V-1, 2; "Coulter's to Quit . . . ," *HDC,* 15 Nov. 1937, 15; "New Structure . . . ," *WWD,* 16 Nov. 1937, 15; *LAT,* 11 June 1938, II-3; "Coulter's to Occupy . . . ," *BHC,* 24 June 1938, 5; "Coulter's Wilshire Opens," *BHC,* 9 Sep. 1938, 5; "New $1,000,000 Home . . . ," *WWD,* 12 Sep. 1938, 1; "Los Angeles: New Store Provides for Motorized Patrons," *AR* 84 (Nov. 1938), 42–46; "Glass Tower . . . ," *HDC,* 13 Dec. 1938, 18; "The New Building . . . ," *California Plasterer* 15 (Feb. 1939), 14; "Behind the Counter," *BHC,* 28 July 1939, II-1; "Coulter's Modern Building . . . ," *RM* 37 (August 1942), 12–13, 32; Louis Parnes, *Planning Stores That Pay* (New York: F. W. Dodge, 1948), 66, 72, 122, 202–203, 250.

73

Glass block did not enter commercial production until the latter months of 1935; see Richard Longstreth, "Hecht's Warehouse: Why It Should Be Saved," *Trans-Lux,* newsletter of the Art Deco Society of Washington, 10 (June 1992), 5. For accounts of the period, see A. E. Marshall, "Future of Glass in the Building Field," *Civil Engineering* 7 (Aug. 1937), 566–567; *AF* 68 (Feb. 1938), 13–33; and "Products and Practice: Glass Block," *AF* 72 (May 1940), 327–330.

74

For example, see "Burdine's to Spend . . . ," *WWD,* 14 Mar. 1938, 1, 4, 32; "15,000 at Formal Opening," *WWD,* 29 Nov. 1938, 1, 87; "Pomeroy's after . . . ," *WWD,* 24 Jan. 1939, 10; "New Remodeled, and Future Store . . . ," *AR* 85 (May 1939), 36–39; and "New Pomeroy Home . . . ," *WWD,* 16 Nov. 1939, 1, 8, 35.

75

"May Co. to Establish . . . ," *LAT,* 20 Oct. 1938, II-1; "May Co. to Build . . . ," *WWD,* 21 Oct. 1938, I-1; "Work to Start . . . ," *LAT,* 13 Nov. 1938, V-1; "May Co. Granted . . . ," *LAT,* 1 Dec. 1938, I-8; "Putting Final Touches . . . ," *WWD,* 4 Aug. 1939, 9; "May Co. to Open . . . ," *LAT,* 3 Sep. 1939, II-2; "May Co. Chief . . . ," *HDC,* 7 Sep. 1939, 12; "May's New Coast . . . ," *WWD,* 7 Sep.

1939, 1, 32; "New May Co. Store . . . ," *LAT,* 8 Sep. 1939, I-13; *BHC,* 8 Sep. 1939, I-1, 9, II-2 to 9; "New Steps in Design," *RE,* 20 Sep. 1939, 3; "New Two-Million Dollar Store . . . ," *SWBC* 95 (20 Oct. 1939), 12–13; "May Co. Opens . . . ," *DSE* 2 (10 Jan. 1940), 34; "Department Store . . . ," *AF* 72 (May 1940), 353–357; "Store Modernization . . . ," *RM* 35 (15 May 1940), 15–17; Emrich Nicholson, *Contemporary Shops in the United States* (New York: Architectural Book Pub. Co., 1945), 142–147; Parnes, *Planning Stores,* 72, 127, 200, 203, 249. Albert C. Martin, Jr., provided me with a number of additional insights on the project (interview, Los Angeles, 7 November 1989).

76

As at Bullock's, parking was initially done by attendants who met customers at a porte-cochere on the rear side. By the postwar era, most if not all parking on the site had become self-service; see "Controlling Parking Lot Traffic," *CSA/AE* [23] (Feb. 1947), 13. A major addition was made in 1947–1948; see "May's Wilshire . . . ," *WWD,* 4 Mar. 1948, 6.

77

For background, see Meredith Clausen, *Frantz Jourdain and the Samaritaine* (Leiden: E. J. Brill, 1987), 198–203; Joseph Siry, *Carson Pirie Scott: Louis Sullivan and the Chicago Department Store* (Chicago: University of Chicago Press, 1988), 88, 101–104; Clausen, "Department Stores," 209–210; idem, "The Department Store—Development of the Type," *Journal of Architecture Education* 39 (Fall 1985), 25. See also Bruno Zevi, *Erich Mendelsohn: opera completa* (Milan: Etas Kompass, 1970), esp. 124–125, 142–151, 165–167.

78

Outside the Miracle Mile, two of the largest branches built prior to World War II were located in the Los Angeles area: I. Magnin Wilshire, discussed in the text above, and the Broadway Pasadena (1940, 95,000 sq. ft.), noted in chapter 9 below.

Outside Los Angeles, by far the most active region for branch store development was New York. For general discussion, see "Branch Stores Best . . . , *New York Times,* 19 Oct. 1930, II-18; "Plans for Expansion . . . , *New York Times,* 2 Aug. 1936, III-8; John Wingate, "Trends in the Department Store Field," *Journal of Retailing* 17 (Feb. 1941), 2–3; Selma Ruttenberg, "Branch-Store Developments among New York City Stores," *Journal of Retailing* 17 (Feb. 1941), 4–6; and Dibrell, "The Effect of Branch Store Expansion," 16–17, 54, 56–57. The five largest branches in the New York area were Macy's Parkchester (1940–1941, approx. 90,000 sq. ft.); Arnold Constable, Hempstead (1939–1940, approx. 62,000 sq. ft.); Lord & Taylor, Manhasset (1940–1941, 58,000 sq. ft.); Arnold Constable, New Rochelle (1937–1938, 51,000 sq. ft.); and Frederick Loeser, Garden City (1937, 40,000 sq. ft.).

79

Most of the new downtown stores that were built were the size of Coulter's or smaller. For examples, see *WWD,* 4 May 1937, 9; *DSE* 4 (10 Apr. 1938), 44; *WWD,* 2 Aug. 1940, 8; *WWD,* 17 Sep. 1940, 8; *WWD,* 6 Dec. 1940, 7; and "White House Takes New Home," *DSE* 4 (25 Mar. 1941), 27. Another scheme was overtly derived from the May Company exterior; see "Lichenstein's Leads . . . ," *WWD,* 9 Apr. 1941, 32.

80

The largest development on the Miracle Mile to be realized during the decade after World War II was the ten-story Prudential Building (1947–1948), occupying a seventeen-acre site that included a bank and several shops as well as a 150,000-square-foot branch of Ohrbach's, a New York–based clothing store, then just entering the West Coast market. See "Prudential Will Erect . . . ," *LAT,* 20 Mar. 1947, II-1, 8; "Ohrbach's New . . . ," *WWD,* 29 May 1947, I-4; "Prudential Opens . . . ," *LAT,* 15 Nov. 1948, II-1; "Ohrbach's Is Well Stocked . . . ," *WWD,* 26 Nov. 1948, 1, 7; "Ohrbach's Opens . . . ," *LAT,* 1 Dec. 1948, II-1; "Ohrbach's Store . . . ," *LAT,* 2 Dec. 1948, II-1; "Shoppers by Thousands . . . ," *LAT,* 3 Dec. 1948, II-1, 3; "Ohrbach's Meets Los Angeles—Head On," *Stores* 30 (Dec. 1948), 13, 32–33; Leonard Miller, "Prudential Insurance Building . . . ," *A&E* 176 (Mar. 1949), 14–20, 34; "Two Office Buildings . . . ," *AF* 90 (May 1949), 42–45; "Trends in Department Store Construction," *Stores* 31 (July 1949), 22–23; "Miracle Mile Shoe Store . . . ," *LAT,* 7 Sep. 1949, II-6; and Prudential Square . . . ," *LAT,* 8 Mar. 1950, I-11.

Several other branch and chain units were built for major clothing companies; see "Mullen & Bluett Plan . . . ," *LAT,* 12 Jan. 1948, I-7; "Young's New Shoe Store . . . ," *LAT,* 16 Dec. 1948, II-6; "Mullen & Bluett . . . ," *LAT,* 24 Feb. 1949, I-14; "Mullen & Bluett . . . ," *LAT,* 25 Feb. 1949, II-3; "New Store Stresses Informal Atmosphere," *AR/WS* 103 (Mar. 1948), 32-A to 32-C; "Clothing Store Leases . . . ," *LAT,* 17 Mar. 1949, I-9; "Remodeled Mandel Store . . . ," *LAT,* 28 Apr. 1949, II-6; "Leed's Chain Opens . . . ," *LAT,* 2 Sep. 1949, II-2; "Thrifty to Open . . . ," *LAT,* 10 May 1950, II-7; "Wilshire Store . . . ," *LAT,* 27 Apr. 1952; and *LAT,* 14 Oct. 1956, VI-7.

VI A Guaranteed Neighborhood

1

"Lunada Bay Plaza . . . ," *LAEx,* 13 Jan. 1924, IV-17.

2

LAT, 6 Apr. 1924, V-16.

3

The more precise later definition of "shopping center" owes much to the work of Kansas City real estate developer J. C. Nichols; see note 53 below.

4

Definitions did not begin to be advanced for the shopping center as an integrated business until after World War II. For early examples, see Geoffrey Baker and Bruno Funaro, *Shopping Centers: Design and Operation* (New York: Reinhold, 1951), 10; Victor Gruen and Lawrence Smith, "Shopping Centers: The New Building Type," *PP* 33 (June 1952), 71; J. Ross McKeever, "Shopping Centers: Principles and Policies," *ULI* 20 (June 1953), 6; Gordon Stedman, "The Rise of Shopping Centers," *Journal of Retailing* 31 (Spring 1955), 13–15; Jack Hyman, "Shopping Center . . . ," *WWD,* 27 Dec. 1955, II-6; and Paul Smith, *Shopping Centers: Planning and Management* (New York: National Retail Merchants Assoc., 1956), 12.

5

The displeasure residents expressed over makeshift buildings, generally located near the railroad depot, is discussed in John Stilgoe, *Borderland: Origins of the American Suburb, 1920–1939* (New Haven: Yale University Press, 1988), 212–217. For illustrations, see Michael Ebner, *Creating Chicago's North Shore: A Suburban History* (Chicago: University of Chicago Press, 1988), 115, 204–205, 232. The importance of having basic goods and services available nearby is suggested in contemporary accounts. See, for example, Sidney Maxwell, *The Suburbs of Cincinnati* . . . (Cincinnati: Geo. E. Stevens & Co., 1870), 96; and Richard Nelson, *Suburban Homes for Business Men* . . . (Cincinnati: Nelson & Bolles, 1874), 34, 43–44, 53, 72, 79, 94, 126.

6

Concerning the Riverside store block, see Richard Longstreth, "The Neighborhood Shopping Center in Washington, D.C., 1930–1941," *JSAH* 51 (Mar. 1992), 7–8, and references cited therein. Several other communities that were planned with an unusual degree of thoroughness for the period are discussed in Mary Corbin Sies, "American Country House Architecture in Context: The Suburban Ideal of Living in the East and Midwest, 1877–1917" (Ph.D. diss., University of Michigan, 1987). See also her "The City Transformed: Nature, Technology, and the Suburban Ideal, 1877–1917," *Journal of Urban History* 14 (Nov. 1987), 81–111. Often these places had no commercial facilities because they lay closer to settled areas where services were available than did Riverside.

7

For general discussion, see Marc Weiss, *The Rise of the Community Builders: The American Real Estate Industry and Urban Planning* (New York: Columbia University Press, 1987), 40–48, 53–72. Case studies include Gary Molyneaux, "Planned Land Use Change in an Urban Setting: The J. C. Nichols Company and the Country Club District in Kansas City" (Ph.D. diss., University of Illinois at Urbana-Champaign, 1979); William Worley, *J. C. Nichols and the Shaping of Kansas City: Innovation in Planned Residential Communities* (Columbia: University of Missouri Press, 1990; Roberta Moudry, "Gardens, Houses and People: The Planning of Roland Park, Baltimore" (M.A. thesis, Cornell University, 1990); Roderick French, "Chevy Chase Village in the Context of the National Suburban Movement, 1870–1900," *Records of the Columbia Historical Society of Washington, D.C.* 73–74 (1973–1974), 300–329; Margaret Marsh, "Suburbanization and the Search for Community: Residential Decentralization in Philadelphia, 1880–1900," *Pennsylvania History* 44 (Apr. 1977), 99–116; Patricia Stach, "Deed Restrictions and Subdivision Development in Columbus, Ohio, 1900–1970," *Journal of Urban History* 15 (Nov. 1988), 42–68; and Stilgoe, *Borderland*, chap 19.

8

Correspondence to and from Bouton, preserved in the Roland Park Company Records, CUL, provides the best source of information yet found on this building. For citations, see Longstreth, "Neighborhood Shopping Center," nn. 9–10.

9

For examples of the coverage Roland Park received, see W. Fawcett, "Roland Park . . . A Representative American Suburb," *House and Garden* 3 (Apr. 1903), 175–196; E. Otis Williams, "The Homebuilders' Suburb of New Baltimore: Roland Park," *Indoors and Out* 3 (Mar. 1907), 259–267; and Arthur Cranford, "A Suburb Conforming to Architectural Standards . . . ," *AF* 23 (Aug. 1914), 191–194.

10

Tuxedo Park, New York, originally laid out in 1886, was a much praised example of residential planning of the period, but its remote, mountainous site and role as a millionaires' resort limited the applicability of its plan to most metropolitan endeavors. Furthermore, the store block serving this community lay outside the entrance gates, through which only property holders, guests, and staff were admitted.

A more analogous case to Roland Park was the well-known Westchester County development of Lawrence Park (begun 1892); see Frederick Partington, "A Unique Suburb," *Indoors and Out* 2 (July 1906), 153–155. Recent English work also may have influenced American practice, especially the small, ornate store blocks at the model company towns of Port Sunlight (begun 1888) and Bournville (begun 1895), which were beginning to receive coverage in U.S. journals. See, for example, "Port Sunlight," *Architecture and Building* 30 (4 Feb. 1899, plate); and Lona Bartlett, "The Bournville Village Trust," *House and Garden* 4 (Dec. 1903), 305.

The considerably earlier commercial building at the London suburb of Bedford Park may not have been as well known by the early twentieth century. Designed in 1880 by Richard Norman Shaw, the complex included a tavern, row houses, and stores, and was far more evocative of its postmedieval prototypes than was work in the United States. The concept of commercial service it embodied, however, may have been known to the English investors who originally financed the Roland Park Company and thus may have influenced the store block there.

11

For background, see the company's own publications, including *Practical Bungalows of Southern California* (1911), *Inexpensive Bungalows . . .* (1912), and *Modern Homes of California* (1913). See also *Los Angeles, the Old and the New* (Los Angeles: J. E. Scott, 1911), 55. On the College Tract, see "Transformation in Southwest," *LAT,* 6 Dec. 1908, V-24.

12

"Growth of Southwest," *LAT,* 1 Sep. 1907, V-1; "Building-Up . . . ," *LAT,* 3 May 1908, V-18; "Attractive Southwest . . . ," *LAT,* 12 Apr. 1914, VI-13. A somewhat similar project was undertaken in 1912 by another major developer of the Southwest district, the Angeles Mesa Land Company, at Sixth Avenue and Fifty-fourth Street; see "Store Is Attractive," *LAT,* 5 May 1912, VI-17. See also *LAT,* 16 Dec. 1923, V-4.

13

"A Village Street—Before and After," *House Beautiful* 27 (April 1910), 127.

14

Ibid.

15

Peter Wight, "The New Market Square at Lake Forest . . . ," *WA* 26 (Oct. 1917), 27. This article (pp. 27–31, pls. 1–15) remains the most informative on the project. See also "Market Square and Community Center . . . ," *NREJ* 17 (Jan. 1918), 31. The importance of this undertaking for members of the real estate field is suggested in "A Pioneer Shopping Center Has 25th Birthday," *Freehold* 7 (15 Aug. 1940), 122–125. See also note 18 below. The complex is the subject of a short popular history: Susan Dart, *Market Square, Lake Forest, Illinois* (Lake Forest: Lake Forest–Lake Bluff Historical Society, 1984). See also Ebner, *Chicago's North Shore,* 203–209, although it mistakenly suggests that financial gain was a primary motivation for the venture.

16

Aldis's firm was associated with the development of some of Chicago's most celebrated late nineteenth-century office buildings. His older brother, Owen, served as agent for constructing the Montauk (1881–1882), Monadnock (1889–1892), and Marquette (1891–1895) buildings. Specializing in property management, Aldis & Co. was formed with Owen and Arthur Aldis and Anayas Northcote in 1889. See Miles Berger, *They Built Chicago: Entrepreneurs Who Shaped a Great City's Architecture* (Chicago: Bonus Books, 1992), 39–48.

The total raised through subscription was approximately $300,000. The remaining funds were secured through the bond issue. It is not certain whether the trust retained control over Market Square primarily because the enterprise became more profitable with the passage of time, or because there was fear that an outside owner might not be as good a steward of the property, or because no potential purchaser was interested in assuming title with the restrictive covenants it carried.

17

Within the first year of operation, tenants in the complex included a delicatessen, two restaurants, a market, a drug store, a millinery shop, an automobile supply store, a bank, a real estate office, public service company offices, a post office, a plumber's office, a barber shop, an American Express office, a nursery, a bakery, a confectionery, a women's apparel store, a tobacco store, and a sewing machine and music store (Wight, "New Market Square," 30–31).

18

Albert Farr, "A Plea for Better Business Centers in Our Suburban Towns," *A&E* 55 (Dec. 1918), 81–85. See also Werner Hegemann and Elbert Peets, *The American Vitruvius: An Architects' Handbook of Civic Art* (New York: Architectural Book Pub. Co., 1922), 279.

19

For background, see Margaret Crawford, *Building the Workingman's Paradise: The Design of American Company Towns* (London: Verso, 1995). See also idem, "Earle S. Draper and the Company Town in the American South," in John Garner, ed., *The Company Town: Architecture and Society in the Early Industrial Age* (New York: Oxford University Press, 1992), 139–172; Richard Candee and Greer Hardwicke, "Early Twentieth-Century Reform Housing by Kilham and Hopkins, Architects of Boston," *Winterthur Portfolio* 22 (Spring 1987), 47–80; and Richard Candee, *Atlantic Heights: A World War I Shipbuilder's Community* (Portsmouth, N.H.: Portsmouth Marine Society, 1985). Much was published on the subject at that time. See, for example, William Phillips Comstock, *The Housing Book* (New York: William H. Comstock Co., 1919); U.S. Department of Labor, Bureau of Industrial Housing and Transportation, *Report of the United States Housing Corporation,* 2 vols. (Washington: U.S. Government Printing Office, 1919); and Morris Knowles, *Industrial Housing* (New York: McGraw-Hill, 1920).

20

Shaw himself used Market Square as a model for an industrial community; see Ralph Warner, "The Town of Mark, Indiana," *Architectural Review* [Boston] 24 (Nov. 1918), 97–100.

21

For an overview, see Crawford, *Building,* chap. 7; and Leland Roth, "Company Towns in the Western United States," in Garner, *Company Town,* 173–205. See

also Irving Morrow, "Two Town Planning Projects in Arizona . . . ," *A&E* 63 (Dec. 1920), 46–87.

22

The best account of Tyrone is Crawford, *Building,* chap. 7. See also "Tyrone, New Mexico . . . , *AF* 28 (Apr. 1918), 130–134; "The New Mining Community . . . ," *Architectural Review* [Boston], n.s. 6 (Apr. 1918), 59–62; Richard Oliver, *Bertram Grosvenor Goodhue* (New York and Cambridge: Architectural History Foundation and MIT Press, 1983), 151–154; and Roth, "Company Towns," 184–187. The extent to which the scheme attracted attention in Los Angeles is suggested in "Best Known Examples . . . ," *LAT,* 25 Dec. 1921, V-1. Oliver, *Goodhue,* 109–119 and 151–158, provides an overview of the architect's contribution to California work. See also David Gebhard, "The Spanish Colonial Revival in Southern California (1895–1930)," *JSAH* 26 (May 1967), 136–138; and *Caltech 1910–1950: An Urban Architecture for Southern California* (Pasadena: Baxter Art Gallery, California Institute of Technology, 1983).

23

For background, see "Palos Verdes Carries Its Town Plan into Execution," *ACi* 33 (Dec. 1925), 666–669; "Palos Verdes Ideals . . . ," *PVB* 3 (June-July 1927), 1, 6–8; J. F. Dawson, "The Placing of Houses . . . ," *PVB* 3 (Aug. 1927), 6–8; Charles Cheney, "Where Poor Architecture Cannot Come," *WA* 37 (Apr. 1928), 75–77; Rexford Newcomb, "Palos Verdes Estates: An Ideal Residential Community," *WA* 37 (Apr. 1928), 79–82; "Californian Architecture," *PVB* 4 (Oct. 1928), 2–4; "Estate Acres . . . ," *LAT,* 11 Nov. 1928, V-4; Frederick Law Olmsted, "How We Planned Palos Verdes Hills," *APC* (1929), 227–231; "Palos Verdes Estates . . . ," *NREJ* 30 (15 Apr. 1929), 64–71; "Shore Project . . . ," *LAT,* 5 Jan. 1930, V-4; and collections of articles in *PCA* 31 (Apr. 1927), 9–20, and *A&E* 100 (Jan. 1930), 35–83.

24

By 1925, Palos Verdes was among the sites proposed for the new campus of what became the University of California, Los Angeles. In 1926, the Westwood area was chosen instead, as noted later in this chapter. Had Palos Verdes been selected, the economic base of the tract would have been considerable. To my knowledge, this was the only instance of interest in securing a major employer within the development.

25

The target audience certainly included, and may well have principally included, persons working in or near downtown Los Angeles. See, for example, *LAT,* 10 Jan. 1926, V-5. The main sales office was downtown. Others were in Hollywood, Long Beach, San Pedro, and on site.

26

"Palos Verdes Ranch . . . ," *LAT,* 4 Jan. 1914, V-1; "Palos Verdes Ranch . . . ," *LAT,* 8 Feb. 1914, VI-1; "Coast Boulevard . . . ," *LAT,* 22 Feb. 1914, V-1, 14.

27

"Coast Boulevard," 14.

28

There are few quantitative projections for Palos Verdes in the sources I have found. The first four subdivisions were to occupy about a fifth of the total area,

which was planned for a population of 160,000. If this population were divided evenly, each tract would hold 8,000 people. Period accounts suggest, however, that variation in size and density between subdivisions was anticipated. Lunada Bay was to be the most populous at 30,000.

The total projected number of stores is not given in any contemporary descriptions of the business centers. The original plan of Malaga Cove Plaza (figure 112) shows forty-three units plus a theater at ground level. This complex was somewhat smaller than the other two for which preliminary designs were prepared. Published illustrations indicate that these might have contained between fifty and seventy units.

Calculations made for shopping centers some years later estimated that a minimal population of 5,000 families was needed to sustain a complex of between twenty and forty units, and a population of between 100,000 and 250,000 people to support one having between fifty and a hundred units (J. Ross McKeever, "Shopping Centers: Principles and Policies," *ULI* 20 [July 1953], 6). However, such figures were based on the assumption that the complexes would be competing with at least some other facilities.

29

Three of the four centers envisioned for the initial developments—Malaga Cove Plaza, Lunada Bay Plaza, and Valmonte Plaza—were discussed in advertisemens. See *LAT,* 16 Dec. 1923, V-18; 13 Jan. 1924, V-2; 10 Feb. 1924, V-22; and *CS* 6 (Feb. 1924), back cover. The schemes are also illustrated in *A&E* 100 (Jan. 1930), 38, 82, 83. Further references to Malaga Cove Plaza are cited in note 31 below.

30

LAT, 26 Feb. 1922, V-10.

31

The first section (four stores) was built in 1924–1925; the second (seven units) was built in 1929–1930. For background, see *LAT,* 16 Dec. 1923, V-18; "A Town by Webber, Staunton & Spaulding, Architects," *CS* 6 (Feb. 1924), 23; "Four Projects . . . ," *LAT,* 27 July 1924, V-1; "Malaga Cove . . . ," *PVB* 1 (Dec. 1924), 1; "Dedication of First . . . ," *PVB* 1 (June 1925), 1; *PVB* 1 (Sep. 1925), 2; "Dedicate Malaga Plaza," *LAT,* 13 Sep. 1925, V-6; "Malaga Cove . . . ," *PVB* 1 (Oct. 1925), 1, 4–5; "A New Year's . . . ," *PVB* 5 (Jan. 1929), 2; "Malaga Cove . . . ," *PVB* 5 (July 1929), 1; "Community Office and Shops . . . ," *NREJ* 30 (14 Oct. 1929), 62; "The Dedication," *PVB* 6 (Mar. 1930), 1, 3–7.

32

Examples include Girard (platted 1923), a San Fernando Valley subdivision that soon gained notoriety for its isolated site ("New Townsite . . . ," *LAT,* 4 Feb. 1923, V-4; *LAT,* 18 Feb. 1923, V-16; *LAT,* 9 May 1925, I-5; *LAT,* 15 July 1923, V-10; "Girard Is Center . . . ," *LAT,* 5 Aug. 1923, V-6); Beverly Park (1923) and Hollywood Knolls (1923), two foothill tracts developed by the Taft Realty Company for the well-to-do (*LAT,* 28 Oct. 1923, V-4; "Wonders of Hollywood . . . ," *HDC,* 18 Oct. 1923, 3; "Third Unit Opened," *HDC,* 8 Mar. 1924, 9; "Purchasers Protected . . . ," *HDC,* 29 Mar. 1929, 9); and Benmar Hills (1927), near Burbank ("Tract Follows . . . ," *LAT,* 18 Sep. 1927, V-14; "Groundbreaking . . . ," *HDC,* 24 Sep. 1927, 9).

Isolated locations developed for resort purposes were sometimes more successful, although they did not spawn innovations in the commercial sphere. The most notable examples were Rancho Santa Fe (1923) (Lee Shippey, "Rancho Santa Fe . . . ," *A&E* 76 [Feb. 1924], 55–63; Hazel Boyer, "Men Who Build for the Fu-

ture," *CS* 6 [Nov. 1923], 26–27; Lee Shippey, "Spanish Grant . . . ," *LAT,* 20 June 1926, V-4; William Pollard, "Santa Fe Rancho," *Community Builder* 1 [May 1928], 40–45; M. Urmy Seares, "The Village of Rancho Santa Fe," *PCA* 38 [Sep. 1930], 28, 35, 66); and San Clemente (1925) ("Village Keeps . . . ," *LAT,* 27 Mar. 1927, V-6; "The Young Architect and the New Town," *CS* 10 [Dec. 1928], 16–19; Frank Williams, "On the Pacific Shore . . . ," *Building Developer* 4 [May 1929], 26–43; Christine Emery, "A New Town DeLuxe," *ACi* 42 [Feb. 1930], 118).

33
Although it promoted its landholdings with a vigor remarkable even by southern California standards, the Janss company revealed relatively little about its operations, including the ambitious plans prepared for the Letts tract. Among the best sources are the thousands of advertisements Janss published weekly in *LAT* and other newspapers. Advertisements for Westwood began in 1922 and continued into the next decade. Other useful accounts include William Kilner, *Arthur Letts . . .* (Los Angeles: privately printed by Young & McCallister, Inc., 1927), 172–178; "Janss Investment Corporation Success," *SN* 9 (2 Feb. 1929), 7; and Kenneth Crist, "Transformed Barley Field . . . ," *LAT,* 30 Apr. 1939, V-2. *WHN* provides many details of the developments.

34
LAT, 9 Sep. 1923, V-6; 2 Dec. 1923, V-8.

35
In 1919, the regents acquired the twenty-nine-acre campus of the Los Angeles State Normal School on Vermont Avenue south of Sunset Boulevard. The official name of the new institution was the University of California, Southern Branch. Rapid population growth soon rendered this campus, built in 1914, a temporary staging ground. Numerous real estate interests lobbied to secure a commitment from the regents to locate near their tracts; the Jansses' success was not easily won. Along with the move, the institution changed its name to the University of California, Los Angeles. The relationship between campus and residential development during the early twentieth century, an important one for many metropolitan areas, awaits focused study.

36
Useful general accounts of the complex and its development include "Fine New Plan . . . ," *BHC,* 12 Dec. 1927, 2; "Start Work . . . ," *WHN,* 13 Apr. 1928, 1; "Business Village . . . ," *LAT,* 6 May 1928, V-5; "Univ. Business District . . . ," *WHN,* 8 June 1928, 1, 8; "Business Section . . . ," *BHC,* 14 Mar. 1929, 1; "Start Village . . . ," *WHN,* 29 Mar. 1929, 1; "Ideal Westwood Center . . . ," *SN* 9 (6 July 1929), 10; L. B. Snell, "Westwood Village Is Unique Center," *WHN,* 22 Nov. 1929, 8; Katherine Doyle, "The Town Made for the Gown," *SCB* 9 (Mar. 1930), 16, 27, 35; M. Urmy Seares, "Westwood Village . . . ," *PCA* 38 (July 1930), 41–43, 70; John Steven McGroarty, "Westwood Village: A Year and a Day to Build," *A&E* 102 (Aug. 1930), 29–41; "Westwood Village . . . ," *WHN,* 6 Apr. 1934, 1, 5; Rowe Rader, "Westwood Village the Heroic Achievement . . . ," *WHN,* 8 Apr. 1938, 3, 5; "Westwood Village . . . ," *BHC,* 21 Apr. 1939, 15, 24; "From Zero to $11,000,000 . . . ," *WHN,* 19 Apr. 1940, 3A; "Village Story . . . ," *WHN,* 19 Apr. 1940, 3A, 5A.

37
The company claimed that as part of the research done for the Westwood Village plan "a survey of practically every unique business center in the nation" was under-

taken ("Two Business Blocks . . . ," *WHN,* 22 Mar. 1929, 8). What was meant by "unique" is unclear, but in all likelihood it included early examples of integrated complexes and perhaps other cases where an individual or firm played the dominant role in advancing development. See note 54 below. I am grateful to the late David Gebhard for supplying me with useful background information on Tilton.

38

"Univ. Business District," 1; "Fine New Plan"; "Westwood Village the Heroic Achievement."

39

"Westwood Village Is Unique Center."

40

No community's commercial architecture received so much coverage by the west coast architectural press during the 1920s. See Winsor Soule, "Santa Barbara Architecture," *A&E* 79 (Dec. 1924), 51–73; H. C. Nickerson, "The Rise of Santa Barbara," *CS* 7 (Aug. 1925), 9–11; Ralph Urmy, "Results of the Work of the Community," *CS* 7 (Nov. 1925), 14; Harris Allen, "The Jewel of Architectural Consistency," *PCA* 28 (Nov. 1925), 5, 27, 35, 37, 43; T. Mitchell Hastings, "The Rebuilding of Santa Barbara," *Journal of the American Institute of Architects* 13 (Nov. 1925), 408–409; "Santa Barbara Gains . . . ," *LAT,* 21 Mar. 1926, V-6; "The Santa Barbara Plan," *CS* 8 (June 1926), 26; Winsor Soule, "The New Santa Barbara," *AA* 130 (5 Jul. 1926), 1–10; Irving Morrow, "New Santa Barbara," *A&E* 86 (July 1926), 43–65; Marshall Selover, "Santa Barbara . . . ," *LAT,* 19 Sep. 1926, V-8; and M. Urmy Seares, "A Community Approaches Its Ideal," *PCA* 37 (June 1930), 19–21, 70–71. For a retrospective account, see David Gebhard, *Santa Barbara— The Creation of a New Spain in America* (Santa Barbara: University Art Museum, University of California, Santa Barbara, 1982), 20–21, 51–55.

41

"Business Section . . . ," *WHN,* 15 Mar. 1929, 2; "Construction . . . Started," *LAT,* 17 Mar. 1929, V-9; "Two Business Blocks . . . ," *WHN,* 22 Mar. 1929, 1, 8; "First Unit . . . ," *BHC,* 24 Mar. 1929, 17; "Start Village." Concerning the Allisons, see Robert Judson Clark and Thomas Hines, *Los Angeles Transfer: Architecture in Southern California 1880–1980* (Los Angeles: William Andrews Clark Memorial Library, University of California, Los Angeles, 1983), 36–41. Concerning Kaufmann, see Alson Clark et al., *Johnson Kaufmann Coate: Partners in the California Style* (Claremont, Calif.: Galleries of Pomona and Scripps Colleges, 1992).

42

The principal task of the Palos Verdes Art Jury was reviewing plans for houses and for institutional and recreational buildings. The exterior of the commercial centers was designed as part of the overall plan for each precinct. At Westwood Village, much greater latitude was apparently given to the designers of commercial work. Among all the material publicized on the center, I have yet to find indication that drawings were prepared before the fact to suggest the appearance of Westwood Village when completed.

43

"Fine New Plan"; "Desmond's Will Open . . . ," *WHN,* 1 Nov. 1929, 1; *WHN,* 22 Nov. 1929, 12; "New Desmond . . . ," *LAT,* 24 Nov. 1929, V-2; *WHN,* 14 Mar. 1930, 1; "Nine Shops . . . ," *LAT,* 16 Mar. 1930, V-4; *AD* 8:4 (1931), 47; Bullock's to Erect . . . ," *WHN,* 8 Jan. 1932, 1; "Branch Store . . . ," *LAT,* 10 Jan.

1932, V-2; "Bullock's Store . . . ," *WHN*, 15 Jan. 1932, 1; "Bullock's Opens . . . ,"
LAT, 15 Mar. 1932, V-3; "Bullock's Westwood . . . ," *WHN*, 13 May 1932; "Westwood Village . . . ," *LAT*, 1 Aug. 1937, V-2; "Myer Siegel . . . ," *WHN*, 6 Aug.
1937, 1; *WWD*, 13 Aug. 1937, I-13; "Distinguished New . . . ," *WHN*, 10 Dec.
1937, 1, 3.

44

"Newberry Store . . . ," *WHN*, 13 Mar. 1931, 1; *WHN*, 27 Mar. 1931, 1; "Sears,
Roebuck . . . ," *WHN*, 3 Jan. 1936, 1; "Community Welcomes . . . ," *WHN*,
10 July 1936, sect. II; "New Building . . . ," *LAT*, 27 Dec. 1936, V-3; "Village
Growth . . . ," *WHN*, 1 Jan. 1937, 1; "J. C. Penney . . . ," *WHN*, 8 Jan. 1937, 1;
"New J. C. Penney . . . ," *WHN*, 15 Jan. 1937, 5.

45

"Market Structure . . . ," *LAT*, 14 July 1929, V-5; "Business Units . . . ," *LAT*, 17
Nov. 1929, V-6; *LAT*, 14 Dec. 1930, V-2; "A. & P. Tea Co. . . . ," *WHN*, 20 Feb.
1931, 1, 4; "New Building . . . ," *WHN*, 21 Sep. 1934, 1; "Build Briskly . . . ,"
WHN, 16 Nov. 1934, 1; "Gala Opening . . . ," *WHN*, 11 Jan. 1935, 1; "A&P Village Store . . . ," *WHN*, 3 May 1935, 1; "Westwood Hills . . . ," *BHC*, 10 Mar.
1936, suppl.; "A. & P. Food Stores' . . . ," *WHN*, 10 July 1936, 3; "Reinforced
Concrete . . . ," *WHN*, 12 Nov. 1937, 1; "Smart New Westwood . . . ," *WHN*,
13 May 1938, 3; "Model Safeway . . . ," *WHN*, 30 Sep. 1938, 4.

46

"Many New Stores . . . ," *WHN*, 18 July 1929, 15. Periodic collective advertisements in *WHN* are invaluable in documenting the businesses established in the
complex at a given time; see 17 Jan. 1930, 8; 1 May 1931, 13; 26 May 1939,
16. See also "120 Business Firms . . . ," *WHN*, 9 Oct. 1931, 1, 8; and "Village
Rivals . . . ," *WHN*, 11 Dec. 1936, 7.

 Accounts in *WHN* of individual stores are too numerous to cite. Among the
useful descriptions of buildings erected in the center, besides those cited in notes
44–45, are: "New Westwood . . . ," *WHN*, 13 Dec. 1929, 17; "Kelly Music . . . ,"
HDC, 14 Mar. 1930, Kelly Music Sect.; "New Studio Shop . . . ," *WHN*, 21 Mar.
1930, 6; "Tea-Room Building . . . ," *LAT*, 5 Apr. 1931, V-3; "Two $40,000 Build-
ings . . . ," *WHN*, 12 June 1931, 1; "Building Spurt . . . ," *LAT*, 12 July 1931, V-
3; "Construction Started . . . ," *WHN*, 17 July 1931, 1; "Construction Well Under-
way . . . ," *WHN*, 31 July 1931, 1; "Westwood Adds . . . ," *LAT*, 20 Aug. 1933, I-
22; "Business Houses . . . ," *LAT*, 25 Oct. 1931, V-2; "El Encanto . . . ," *WHN*,
30 Oct. 1931, 5; "Craftsmen Open . . . ," *LAT*, 8 Oct. 1933, I-17; "Structure to
Be . . . ," *LAT*, 24 Dec. 1933, I-12; "La Ronda . . . Unique," *WHN*, 29 Dec.
1933, 1; "Westwood Store . . . ," *LAT*, 30 Sep. 1934, I-20; "New Structure . . . ,"
WHN, 6 Dec. 1935, 1; "Nationally Famous . . . ," *WHN*, 5 June 1936, 1; "New
Business . . . ," *WHN*, 10 July 1936, 1; "Three New Units . . . ," *WHN*, 31 July
1936, 7; "Important New Income . . . ," *WHN*, 7 Aug. 1936, 1, 7; "Twelve New
Projects . . . ," *LAT*, 23 Aug. 1936, V-3; "Important Village Building . . . ," *WHN*,
11 Sep. 1936, 3; "Geophysicist Erects . . . ," *WHN*, 2 Oct. 1936, 1, 3; "Five Businesses . . . ," *WHN*, 11 Dec. 1936, 1; "Associated to Open . . . ," *WHN*, 14 May
1937, 1; "Modern Business Building . . . ," *WHN*, 18 Mar. 1938, 1; "Potter's
Open . . . ," *WHN*, 5 Aug. 1938, 4; "New Structure . . . ," *WHN*, 6 Sep. 1940, 1;
"Chandler Boot Shop . . . ," *WHN*, 10 Oct. 1940, 5.

47

Concerning banks, see "Opening Date Set . . . ," *WHN*, 13 Dec. 1929, 1; "Westwood Village . . . ," *WHN*, 20 June 1930, 7; "Citizen's Nat'l Bank . . . ," *WHN*,

31 Oct. 1930, 1, 5; and "Bank of America . . . ," *WHN,* 18 Mar. 1938, 1, 14. Concerning recreational facilities: "Fox Will Build . . . ," *WHN,* 13 Sep. 1929, 1; "Proposed Theatre . . . ," *WHN,* 4 Oct. 1929, 19; "Theatre Plans . . . ," *WHN,* 18 Apr. 1930, 1; "Recreation Center . . . ," *WHN,* 4 July 1930, 1; "Recreation Center . . . ," *WHN,* 26 Sep. 1930, 1; "Building Projects . . . ," *WHN,* 31 Oct. 1930, 1; "Construction of Fox . . . ," *WHN,* 14 Nov. 1930, 1; "Ground Broken . . . ," *WHN,* 21 Nov. 1930, 1; "Fox Westwood . . . ," *WHN,* 13 Aug. 1931, 5, 7; "Village Theatre . . . ," *WHN,* 14 Aug. 1931, 1, 8; and "Westwood Hills' . . . ," *WHN,* 12 Mar. 1937, 1. Concerning other buildings: *WHN,* 5 Sep. 1930, 1; "Redman Warehouse . . . ," *WHN,* 16 Jan. 1931, 1; *WHN,* 28 Feb. 1936, 1; "Southern California Gas . . . ," *WHN,* 20 Nov. 1936, 1; "Ground Broken . . . ," *WHN,* 29 Apr. 1938, 1; "$75,000 Professional Building . . . ," *WHN,* 3 June 1938, 1, 2; "Large Professional . . . ," *LAT,* 23 Oct. 1938, V–2; "New Medical Building . . . ," *WHN,* 9 Dec. 1938, 2; and "Associated Telephone . . . ," *WHN,* 18 Apr. 1941, 3.

48

"First Gas Station . . . ," *BHC,* 3 Oct. 1929, 16-D; "The West's Most Unique . . .," *WHN,* 22 Nov. 1929, 1; "Big Garage . . . ," *WHN,* 10 Jan. 1930, 1; *LAT,* 25 May 1930, V–5; "Work Speeded . . . ," *WHN,* 27 June 1930, 1; "Union Oil Adds . . . ," *LAT,* 19 Feb. 1933, I–18; "Architecture of New Station . . . ," *WHN,* 24 Feb. 1933, 13; "Massey & Keating . . . ," *WHN,* 9 Mar. 1934, 1; "Massey Inaugurates . . . ," *WHN,* 14 Oct. 1938, 6, 7.

49

"Bullock's Westwood . . . ," *WWD,* 11 Oct. 1935, I–1; "Expansion for Store . . . ," *LAT,* 22 Oct. 1933, I–20; "Bullock's-Westwood . . . ," *WHN,* 24 May 1935, 1; "Bullock's Enlarged . . . ," *WHN,* 4 Oct. 1935, 1; "Prominent Dept. Store . . . ," *WHN,* 20 Jan. 1939, 1; "Bullock's Westwood . . . ," *LAT,* 22 Jan. 1939, V–2; "Bullock's Unit . . . ," *WWD,* 23 Jan. 1939, 6; "Sears, Roebuck . . . ," *LAT,* 19 Feb. 1939, I–4; "Plan Extensive . . . ," *WHN,* 24 Feb. 1939, 1; "Westwood Store's . . . ,"*LAT,* 20 Aug. 1939, V–2; "Capacity of Prominent . . . ," *WHN,* 25 Aug. 1939, 2; *WWD,* 1 Sep. 1939, 12; "New Expansion . . . ," *WHN,* 1 Sep. 1939, 2; "New Bullock's . . . ," *WHN,* 1 Mar. 1940, 1; "Bright Note . . . ," *HDC,* 1 Mar. 1940, 12; "New Bullock's . . . ," *WHN,* 1 Mar. 1940, 1, 2; "Store Addition . . . ," *LAT,* 12 May 1940, V–2; "Desmond's Westwood . . . ," *LAT,* 15 Sep. 1940, V–3; "Desmond's Hold . . . ," *WWD,* 20 Sep. 1940, 9.

50

WHN, 10 Apr. 1936, 7th Annual Village Birthday Ed., 45; Crist, "Transformed Barley Field."

51

Originally called Westwood Village Business Men's Association, the group was formed out of a Janss initiative. See "Westwood Village . . . ," *WHN,* 10 Jan. 1930, 1; "Westwood Village . . . ," *WHN,* 10 Apr. 1936, 1; "Westwood Village . . . ," *WHN,* 9 Apr. 1937, 1; "W.V.B.A.'s Fine Leadership . . . ," *WHN,* 8 Apr. 1938, 3. For a sampling of the organization's promotional activities in *WHN,* see "Plans Complete . . . ," 6 Sep. 1929, 1; 31 Jan. 1930, 10; "Village Leaders . . . ," 21 Mar. 1930, 1; 11 Apr. 1930, 6–7; "Carnival Will Draw . . . ," 11 Apr. 1930, 1; "Village Dons . . . ," 12 Dec. 1930, 1; "The Village Has It . . . ," 10 Apr. 1931, 1; 8 May 1931, 9; 22 May 1931, 9; 26 June 1931, 11; "Plan for Gay . . . ," 30 Oct. 1931, 1; "Big Contest . . . ," 15 Dec. 1933, 1; "Village Awaits . . . ," 29 Oct. 1937, 1.

52

"New Home . . . ," *LAT,* 12 Apr. 1931, V-2; "Janss' Main Office . . . ," *WHN,*
1 May 1931, 1, 8.

53

Concerning Nichols and the Country Club District, see Molyneaux, "Planned
Land Use Change"; and Worley, *J. C. Nichols.* Concerning the Plaza, see Richard
Longstreth, "J. C. Nichols, the Country Club Plaza, and Notions of Modernity,"
Harvard Architecture Review 5 (1986), 120–135; and Worley, *J. C. Nichols,* chap. 8.
      Nichols wrote two important articles on the subject in which he introduced
"shopping center" as a synonym for integrated business development at a time
when the term was still loosely used in common parlance. See "The Planning and
Control of Outlying Shopping Centers," *JLP* 2 (Jan. 1926), 17–22, reprinted as
"Planning Shopping Centers," *NREJ* 8 (Mar. 1926), 47–49; and "The Develop-
ment of Outlying Shopping Centers," in National Conference on City Planning,
Planning Problems of Town, City and Region (Philadelphia: Wm. F. Fell, 1929), 16–
36, reprinted in abbreviated form as "Developing Outlying Shopping Centers,"
ACi 41 (July 1929), 98–101.

54

The Country Club Plaza is known to have influenced the planning of at least several other sizable, integrated business developments of the period, even though
their respective designs were markedly different. Among these, the only one under
way at the time the Janss study was conducted was Shaker Heights in Cleveland
(1927–1929). For background, see "Van's to Make . . . ," *Cleveland Plain Dealer,* 20
Aug. 1928, 1-A, 12-A; "All-Chain Shopping Area . . . ," *CSA/GME* 6 (Dec.
1930), 56, 58, 60, 62; "Model Business Center," *NREJ* 31 (22 Dec. 1930), 35, 36;
Baker and Funaro, *Shopping Centers,* 184–185; and Eric Johannesen, *Cleveland
Architecture 1876–1976* (Cleveland: Western Reserve Historical Society, 1979),
172–174.

55

The best record of tenants during the early stages of the Plaza's development are
the listings of and features on stores that appeared regularly in the *Country Club District Bulletin.* A check through city directories reveals that the tenant profile did not
change much during the 1930s. Not until after World War II did the complex get
a branch of a major downtown department store (Emery, Bird, Thayer) and a large
Sears unit.

56

An immediate justification for developing the parking stations was the need to ac-
comodate patrons of the Plaza Theatre (1928), but the scope of the project clearly
extended beyond that single purpose. For background, see "A Day in Spain: An Interpretation of Plaza Theatre . . . ," brochure printed for the J. C. Nichols Companies, n.d. [1928]; M. S. Munson, "Parking Space Added Convenience of Suburban
Movie Theatre," *BA* 51 (Feb. 1929), 88–91; and Nichols, "Development of Outlying Shopping Centers," 27, 29.

57

"Univ. Business District," 8; "Approve Auto Parking . . . ," *WHN,* 12 Dec. 1930, 1;
"Members Rap . . . ," *WHN,* 25 Mar. 1932, 1, 8; "Angle Parking . . . ," *WHN,* 26
June 1937, 1; "Two Hour . . . ," *WHN,* 13 Sep. 1940, 1; "Parking Lots . . . ,"
WHN, 27 Sep. 1940, 1.

58

"New Parking Plan . . . ," *WHN,* 28 Sep. 1945, 1; "Parking System . . . ," *WHN,* 31 Dec. 1946, 1; "Angle Parking . . . ," *WHN,* 24 Aug. 1948, 1; "Business Men Get . . . ," *WHN,* 14 Sep. 1948, 1.

VII A Hindrance to Business

1

E. E. East, "Los Angeles' Street Traffic Problem," *Civil Engineering* 12 (Aug. 1942), 437. See also E. B. Lefferts, "Should Business Provide Off-Street Parking for Patrons," *1938 Proceedings* (New York: Institute of Traffic Engineers, 1939), 22.

2

"Off-Street Parking Practices," *ASPO* 15 (July 1949), 59.

3

"Petition Against . . . ," *BHC,* 17 June 1926, 1.

4

George Hall, "Beverly Hills, California—A Subdivision That Grew into a City," *American Landscape Architect* 3 (Aug. 1930), 21–26. See also J. C. Albers, "Beverly Hills, California . . . ," *Concrete Highways and Public Improvements Magazine* 12 (June 1928), 123–125; and Bryant Hall, "Beverly Hills Acquires Unique Park . . . ," *Western City* 7 (Sep. 1931), 9–12. Coverage in *LAT* affords useful insight on the plan as a central part of the developer's marketing strategy; see "Building Up Beverly," 8 Sep. 1907, V-1; "A Beauty Spot," 26 June 1910, VI-8; "Magnificent Tourist Hostelry . . . ," 14 May 1911, V-1; "Between Ocean . . . ," 12 Apr. 1914, VI-4; and a sampling of advertisements: 21 Oct. 1906, II-20; 11 Nov. 1906, II-23; 18 Nov. 1906, V-2; 20 Apr. 1907, II-8; 22 Sep. 1907, V-15; 13 Nov. 1910, VI-3; 4 Dec. 1910, V-3; 11 Dec. 1910, VI-3. See also "Beverly Hills . . . ," *LAT,* 29 Nov. 1931, V-1, 3. Two general accounts are Pierce Benedict and Don Kennedy, eds., *History of Beverly Hills* (Beverly Hills: A. W. Cawston and H. M. Meier, 1934), 60–82; and Genevieve Davis, *Beverly Hills: An Illustrated History* (Northridge, Calif.: Windsor Pubs., 1988), 45–52. Fred Basten, *Beverly Hills: Portrait of a Fabled City* (Los Angeles: Douglas-West, 1975) contains numerous period photographs.

5

"Building Up Beverly."

6

Initial plans for the bank called for a two-story building that could be expanded to the height limit when demand warranted; see *BHC,* 12 Jan. 1928, II-1. The fast growth of the Business Triangle prompted two sets of revisions, each substantially increasing the size; see "Bank Building . . . ," *BHC,* 14 June 1928, 1; "California Bank . . . ," *BHC,* 29 Nov. 1928, 1, 6; and "Bank Will Construct . . . ," *LAT,* 9 Dec. 1928, V-6. See also "Open House . . . ," *BHC,* 31 Oct. 1929, 1; and "Brilliant Opening . . . ," *BHC,* 17 Nov. 1929, 16B. Much denser development might have occurred in the immediate area without the depression. At least two other large, multistory projects were announced but never begun. One was for a facility housing a theater, stores, a hotel, and apartments ("New Theatre . . . ," *BHC,* 16 Jan. 1930, 1). The other scheme was for a department store branch for an unnamed company, which would have been almost as large as Bullock's; see *LAEx,*

7 Aug. 1931; "Trade Palace Projected," *LAT,* 7 Aug. 1931, II-1; and *LAT,* 9 Aug. 1931, V-1. Additional retail development of consequence did not occur along these blocks until the mid-1930s, as discussed in the text below.

7

The best sense of business development during this period is gleaned from coverage of individual projects in *BHC.* General accounts include: "Beverly Hills . . . ," *LAT,* 20 Dec. 1925, V-6; "Beverly Hills . . . ," *LAT,* 4 Sep. 1927, V-7; R. Ellis Wales, "Commercial Body . . . ," *BHC,* 3 Jan. 1929, I-1; Charles Robinson, "Trading Center . . . ," *BHC,* 3 Jan. 1929, I-4; "Many Firms Locating . . . ," *LAT,* 23 Feb. 1930, V-3; and "Development of West End . . . ," *BHC,* 17 Jan. 1936, 8. Unfortunately, several microfilm reels of the early volumes of *BHC* are missing, one of which includes installments of a serial on business streets. Those installments still available are "See Big Business . . . ," 11 Nov. 1926, 1, 4; and "Camden Seen . . . ," 18 Nov. 1926, 1, 4.

8

"Propose Novel Solution . . . ," *BHC,* 19 Mar. 1937, 1.

9

Orin Nolting and Paul Opperman, *The Parking Problem in Central Business Districts* (Chicago: Public Administration Service, 1938), 4. This report and Clarence Ridley and Orin Nolting, *The Municipal Year Book* (Chicago: International City Managers' Assoc., 1942), 515–521, provide two of the most detailed accounts of municipal parking lot development prior to World War II. Coverage of individual projects can be found in *ACi* and *PM.*

10

T. T. McCrosky, "Yonkers Planning Commission Recommends Municipal Parking Space," *ACi* 46 (Feb. 1932), 108–109. See also "Eliminate the Parking Toll," *ACi* 53 (Apr. 1938), 117.

11

For a sampling of accounts beyond those cited in note 9 above, see: Thomas Henry, "Strangled Cities," *Toledo Business* 17 (May 1939), 11–12; Burton Marsh, "Solving the Automobile Parking Problem," *Public Management* 23 (Jan. 1941), 10–14; Wilfred Owen, "Financing Off-Street Parking Facilities," *Public Management* 23 (Apr. 1941), 107–111; Theodore McCrosky, "Decentralization and Parking," *1941 Proceedings* (New York: Institute of Traffic Engineers, 1942), 59–63; *The Parking Problem: A Library Research* (Saugatuck, Conn.: Eno Foundation, 1942); D. Grant Mickle, "Providing Off-Street Parking and Terminal Facilities," National Safety Council, National Safety Congress, *Transactions* 1943, 60–64; D. Grant Mickle, "Local Parking Problem Solutions," University of Michigan, Annual Highway Conference, *Proceedings,* 1944, 93–117; Wilbur Smith and Charles LeCraw, *Parking* (Saugatuck, Conn.: Eno Foundation, 1946); and *Parking for Smaller Cities* (Indianapolis: Associated Retailers of Indiana, 1948).

12

Written by Carlos Valle-Riestra, one of the traffic engineers who prepared the report, the series appeared weekly in *BHC* from 15 July to 28 Oct. 1938, each installment with its own title.

13

Pertinent articles in the series include "Necessary to Find . . . ," 23 Sep. 1938, 1,

20; "Off-Street Parking . . . ," 30 Sep. 1938, 1, 18; "Best Method . . . ," 7 Oct. 1938, 1, 19; "Attractiveness of Parking . . . ," 14 Oct. 1938, 1, 12; and "Parking Solution . . . ," 21 Oct. 1938, 1, 13.

14

"Major Business Block . . . ," *BHC*, 16 May 1935, 2; "Building Boom . . . ," *BHC*, 16 May 1935, 1; "Sloane Company . . . ," *LAT*, 19 May 1935, I-12; "Store to Build . . . ," *LAT*, 13 Aug. 1935, I-37; "Sloane's to Add . . . ," *BHC*, 15 Aug. 1935, 1; "New Sloane Store . . . ," *BHC*, 28 Feb. 1936, 1; Helen King, "An Old Firm with Young Ideas," *PCA* 49 (Mar. 1936), 15–16; "New Building Project . . . ," *LAT*, 24 May 1936, V-4; *AR* 80 (Aug. 1936), 130; "Building Permits . . . ," *BHC*, 4 Sep. 1936, II-1; "Levy and Son . . . ," *BHC*, 27 Aug. 1937, 10; "To Begin Work . . . ," *WWD*, 15 Nov. 1937, 1, 12; "New York Shop . . . ," *LAT*, 16 Nov. 1937, I-9; "Saks Fifth Avenue . . . ," *BHC*, 19 Nov. 1937, 1; "Saks-Fifth Ave. . . . ," *WWD*, 10 Mar. 1938, 28; "Firm's Opening . . . ," *LAT*, 17 Apr. 1938, II-8; "New Saks Fifth-Ave. . . . ," *WWD*, 29 Apr. 1938, I-12.

15

"Beverly Hills Business . . . ," *BHC*, 12 July 1934, 1. Concerning Saks, see *PCA* 53 (June 1938), 20–21; "Saks Expansion . . . ," *WWD*, 22 Dec. 1938, 1, 28; "Plans Are Ready . . . ," *BHC*, 23 Dec. 1938, 1, 10; "New Unit . . . ," *LAT*, 1 Jan. 1939, V-1; "Saks, Beverly Hills . . . ," *WWD*, 17 Aug. 1939, 28; "Saks Largest . . . ," *BHC*, 18 Aug. 1939, 1, 2; "Saks-Fifth Ave. . . . ," *HDC*, 19 Aug. 1939, 7; "Extensive New Store . . . ," *LAT*, 20 Aug. 1939, V-2; and "New York Comes . . . ," *WWD*, 1 Sep. 1939, II-1. The Levi branch did not last long; however, the building was quickly leased by J. J. Haggerty, another prominent downtown clothier: see "New Store . . . ," *LAT*, 26 June 1938, II-3; *WWD*, 1 July 1938, 5; "September 1 Opening . . . ," *BHC*, 1 July 1938, 4; "Haggerty in New Store . . . ," *BHC*, 9 Sep. 1938, 3; and "J. J. Haggerty . . . ," *WWD*, 12 Sep. 1938, 7.

16

"Parking for Business . . . ," *BHC*, 18 Nov. 1938, 1; "Parking Lots . . . ," *BHC*, 2 Dec. 1938, 1; "First Steps . . . ," *BHC*, 9 Dec. 1938, 1; "The Parking Problem," *BHC*, 9 Dec. 1938, 36; "Solution to Parking . . . ," *BHC*, 16 Dec. 1938, 17; "City to Grade . . . ," *BHC*, 20 Jan. 1939, 1, 12.

17

"Interest Is Displayed . . . ," *BHC*, 27 Jan. 1939, 1; "New Parking Areas . . . ," *BHC*, 31 Mar. 1939, 1; "Work Nearly Completed . . . ," *BHC*, 14 Apr. 1939, 1; "Parking Plan . . . ," *BHC*, 26 May 1939, 1, 18; "Permanent Parking . . . ," *BHC*, 9 June 1939, 1; "Adequate Parking . . . ," *BHC*, 23 June 1939, 8; "Parking Plan . . . ," *BHC*, 14 July 1939, 1; "Permanent Parking . . . ," *BHC*, 21 July 1939, 1; "Parking Plan . . . ," *BHC*, 24 Nov. 1939, 1; "That Map . . . ," *BHC*, 24 Nov. 1939, 10.

18

"Parking Bill . . . ," *BHC*, 10 Jan. 1941, 1, 6; "Parking Bill . . . ," *BHC*, 20 Feb. 1941, 1; "Assembly Bill 1207," *BHC*, 28 Feb. 1941, 8; "Shall We Wait . . . ?" *BHC*, 28 Feb. 1941, 8; "Patterson in Accord . . . ," *BHC*, 21 Mar. 1941, 1, 15; "Parking Solution . . . ," *BHC*, 16 May 1941, 1, 8.

19

"Work Is Pushed . . . ," *BHC*, 8 Aug. 1941, 1, 6; "City Council Gets . . . ," *BHC*, 15 Aug. 1941, 1; "Officials Study . . . ," *BHC*, 29 Aug. 1941, 1, 7; "Beverly Hills

Considers . . . ," *Western City* 18 (Mar. 1942), 37; "Plan Utilizing Rear Alley Spaces for Car Parking," *Engineering-News Record* 128 (16 Apr. 1942), 11; "Beverly Hills Plans Rear Lot Parking . . . ," *ASPO* 8 (May 1942), 42.

20

"Traffic and Parking in Beverly Hills," *AR* 104 (Dec. 1948), 94–99.

21

For background, see Richard Longstreth, "The Neighborhood Shopping Center in Washington, D.C., 1930–1941," *JSAH* 51 (Mar. 1992), 6–7.

22

For discussion, see chapter 6 above.

23

For background, see Richard Longstreth, *Drive-Ins, Supermarkets, and Reorganization of Commercial Space in Los Angeles,* forthcoming. General studies include James Mayo, *The American Grocery Store: The Business Evolution of an Architectural Space* (Westport, Conn.: Greenwood Press, 1993), chaps. 4–5; and Chester Liebs, *Main Street to Miracle Mile: American Roadside Architecture* (Boston: New York Graphic Society, 1985), 124–135.

24

A. E. Holden, "Super-Markets on Coast Set Modernization Pace," *CSA/GE* 11 (May 1935), 58; Walter Leimert, "The Super Markets of Los Angeles," *Freehold* 4 (15 Mar. 1939), 200–201.

25

For background, see James Turnbull, "The Supermarket," *AJ* 7 (Oct. 1939), 352–353.

26

For background, see "New Surv-al Market . . . ," *HDC,* 16 May 1931, 11; "New Surv-All Food . . . ," *HDC,* 21 May 1931, 13; Charles Gormack, "Enter New Locality and Develop It . . . ," *SMM* 3 (May 1938), 6–7; J. Gordon Wright, "Belvedere Gardens Offers Best in Low Income Section," *SMM* 3 (Sep. 1938), 14, 53; and M. M. Zimmerman, "A Cross Country Impression," *SMM* 5 (Apr. 1940), 41. The reputation of Wisstein Bros. & Surval as respected innovators in the field was underscored by veteran Los Angeles food marketer Ben Schwartz (interview, Commerce, Calif., 13 Nov. 1989).

27

Interviews with a number of persons involved with commercial real estate development in the region prior to World War II revealed that such complexes were not thought of as shopping centers, at least as that term came to be used in later years. California examples were ignored by national trade journals. Neither *LAT* nor more localized papers gave these complexes much coverage either, in contrast to the attention paid by newspapers to counterparts in cities such as Houston, Detroit, and Washington. I could find no account of the Broadway and Eighty-seventh Street complex as a whole in *SWW,* which covered that area of the city. Some space was given to several individual stores, but without mention of the project in its entirety. See *SWW,* 9 Oct. 1936, S23; 22 Dec. 1936, 24; 2 Mar. 1937, 6; and 5 Mar. 1937, 2.

28

Quoted in Gormack, "Enter New Locality," 6.

29

The original tenants in the section completed in 1937 included Thrifty Drug Co., J. J. Newberry, Bud's department store, Owl Drugs, and the Foodtown supermarket. Tenants for the additional units, completed in 1939, were Lee Ann's children's clothes, Janet's Women's Clothes, and F. W. Woolworth. Directory listings for the adjacent blocks in 1938 indicate a standard range for nodes of this size. Among the outlets were four beauty shops, three furniture stores, three paint stores, two markets, four clothing stores, two cleaners, two drug stores, and a restaurant, variety store, bank, hardware store, theater, department store, shoe store, radio store, auto supply store, bakery, and jewelry store. Among these competing services, however, only one was operated by a large chain company, S. H. Kress.

30

City directory listings from which these figures were compiled also indicate how these major chain companies tended to cluster their stores. Outside of centers on Hollywood and Wilshire boulevards, nine other concentrations are distinct: the 4400–4600 and 8600–8700 blocks of S. Broadway, 5300–5400 blocks of Crenshaw Boulevard, 5700–5800 blocks of N. Figueroa, 8700–8800 blocks of W. Pico Boulevard, 5500 block of W. Santa Monica Boulevard, 5800 and 8400–8500 blocks of S. Vermont, and 4700–4800 and 5200 blocks of Whittier Boulevard. Among these, only the 4400–4500 blocks of S. Broadway, the 5500 block of Santa Monica (at its intersection with Western Ave.), and the 5700–5800 blocks of S. Vermont had a concentration of forty or more businesses in the early 1920s. Most of the others, however, had some significant grouping by the end of that decade. Not until after World War II would the convention emerge locally of developing a cluster of chain outlets within a short period on a previously isolated site.

31

For a sampling of coverage of new drug outlets, see *Tide* 7 (Aug. 1933), 20–21; "Katz's Super," *Tide* 8 (Sep. 1934), 56–57; "Makes Most of Strategic Location," *CSA/DE* [15] (Dec. 1939), 13; *CSA/DE* [16] (Mar. 1940), 109; Willis Parker, "From Pine Board to Streamlined Stores," *CSA/DE* [16] (Sep. 1940), 26–27, 72; "Drug Firm Enters Self-Service Field," *SMM* 6 (Aug. 1941), 24; "New Drive-In Store Is Semi-Self-Service," *CSA/DE* [17] (Sep. 1941), 42, 77; "New Self-Serve Stores . . . ," *CSA/DE* [17] (Dec. 1941), 14–15, 50; and "Open Display Keynotes New Store," *CSA/DE* [18] (May 1942), 32–33.

For Los Angeles area examples, see "Drug Company . . . ," *LAT,* 2 Sep. 1934, I-14; *HDC,* 20 Dec. 1935, 15; "Beach City Store . . . ," *LAT,* 28 June 1936, V-5; "Personnel of Owl Stores . . . ," *PSN,* 28 Nov. 1936, 2; "Drug Store Organization's . . . ," *LAT,* 26 Dec. 1937, V-2; "New Business Unit . . . ," *LAT,* 10 July 1938, I-14; "New Stores for 'Thrifty,'" *AC* 6:1 [1940], 34–35; "Thrifty Opens . . . ," *LAT,* 9 June 1940, V-2; "Thrifty Opens . . . ," *LAT,* 11 Aug. 1940, V-2; "Store Added . . . ," *LAT,* 22 Sep. 1940, V-3; *CSA/DE* [16] (Dec. 1940), 25; "Drug Chain . . . ," *LAT,* 22 June 1941, V-3; "Drugstore Chain Launches . . . ," *LAT,* 29 June 1941, II-2; and *SWW,* 11 July 1941, 13.

For a sampling of variety stores, see "Present Trend for Better Stores," *Chain Store Progress* 3 (Mar. 1931), 3; "1939 Store Design . . . ," *CSA/DE* [15] (Nov. 1939), 65–67; *CSA/VS* [16] (Nov. 1940), 83; "Woolworth's Largest," *CSA/VS* [16] (Dec. 1940), 22–23; "New Unit Is Woolworth's Largest Single-Floor Store," *CSA/VS* [17] (Aug. 1941), 78b–78c; *WWD,* 26 Nov. 1941, 25; and Murray Winn, "Women Like Self-Service in Variety Stores," *CSA/VS* [18] (June 1942),

26, 64, 66. For local examples, see "Chain Store Leases . . . ," *LAT,* 16 Oct. 1932, I-17; and "Ventura Blvd. . . . ," *LAT,* 31 Mar. 1940, V-4.

32

For background, see R. C. Erskine, "Valuing Business Subcenter Property," *AJ* 6 (Oct. 1938), 340–342; Joseph Hall, "What Makes the Hot Spot 'Hot?,'" *AJ* 7 (Oct. 1939), 343–347; and idem, "Business Districts in Motion," *AJ* 9 (Jan. 1941), 35–40.

33

"Shopping Centers: An Analysis," *ULI* 11 (July 1949), 9–11. Concerning the market, see "Super-Market Rises . . . ," *LAT,* 6 Oct. 1940, V-4; "Super Pledges Community Aid," *SMM* 6 (July 1941), 6, 8; and "Super Markets: The Office of Stiles Clements, Architect," *AR* 90 (Oct. 1941), 72. Concerning Windsor Hills, see *SWW,* 7 Feb. 1939, 12; and "Marlow-Burns Company . . . ," *SWW,* 11 Aug. 1939, 20. One of the project's developers, Fred Marlow, kindly supplied me with additional insights (interview, Los Angeles, 16 Nov. 1989).

34

Letter from the late S. Charles Lee to author, 15 July 1988; interviews with Philip Lyon (Los Angeles, 7 Apr. 1988), Fred Marlow, and William McAdam (Newport Beach, 8 Apr. 1988). All persons interviewed agreed that the great majority of such work occurred after World War II. The estimate, however, is my own.

Documenting these complexes is a difficult task at best, given the often fragmentary nature of their ownership, construction, and management. Besides those discussed in the text, there was one on Wilshire Boulevard in Santa Monica where a Von's supermarket served as anchor; see *LAT,* 17 Aug. 1939, IV-whole sect.; and J. Gordon Wright, "75,000 Help Celebrate Von's New Opening," *SMM* 4 (Nov. 1939), 12, 38–39, 59. Another example is illustrated in *SMM* 6 (Apr. 1941), 62.

Lee could not recall the location or developer of the project illustrated in figure 136, but believed that only a small portion was built and that no off-street parking was included in the scheme (letter to author). The scheme may be for the center he designed in Van Nuys; see "Neighborhood Center Planned," *LAT,* 24 Sep. 1939, V-2.

35

"Sontag Opens . . . ," *LAT,* 27 Oct. 1940, V-2; "Store Units . . . ," *LAT,* 17 Aug. 1941, V-3; "New Shopping Area . . . ," *WWD,* 5 Sep. 1941, 11; "Latest Store . . . ," *LAT,* 2 Nov. 1941, V-3.

36

A complex built about the same time further south on Crenshaw had a much more limited tenancy, with neither a supermarket nor a chain variety store. On the other hand, it did include units for all three of the region's leading drug store chains. The project was intended to complement another in the same precinct, which included a Woolworth unit and at least one market; see "Chain Store Deals . . . ," *LAT,* 10 Aug. 1930, V-1.

Yet another form of development occurred at Valley Village in North Hollywood, representing some of the methods used by A. W. Ross for the Miracle Mile but applied at a scale more akin to Windsor Hills. The area's principal developer, H. W. Moon, collaborated with real estate broker Bob Symonds in creating the retail node at the intersection of Magnolia and Laurel Canyon boulevards by selling to individual parties whom they believed would contribute to a strong tenant mix. Most, if not all, of the stores that opened before World War II were independently

operated, not major chain units. See "New Market to Open . . . ," *HDC,* Valley
ed., 27 Aug. 1937, 11; " 'Live and Shop' . . . ," *HDC,* Valley ed., 24 Aug. 1939, 9;
and "Plans Completed . . . ," *HDC,* Valley ed., 15 Apr. 1941, 9. I am grateful
to Bill Symonds for supplying me with additional information (interview, North
Hollywood, 4 June 1992).

37

Interviews with Philip Lyon (who was one of the Main Streeters) and William
McAdam (who was not an "official" member, but was invited to join many of
the group's meetings).

38

The group of Crenshaw Boulevard stores discussed in the text above and cited
in note 35 was used as an example of "what Beverly Hills might eventually have
in every business block"; see *BHC,* 8 Aug. 1941, 6.

39

"Master Development Plan . . . ," *LAT,* 9 Feb. 1941, V-1, 3. The Westchester development is discussed in chapter 9 below.

VIII Hold On!

1

R. F. White, " 'Hold On for Profits!' . . . ," *LAT,* 1 Jan. 1933, I-6.

2

"May Co., Los Angeles . . . ," *WWD,* 19 Aug. 1928, 15.

3

This shift was recognized early on in some circles. See, for example, "Shopping
Area . . . ," *WWD,* 4 Aug. 1928, 1, 16; and "Los Angeles . . . ," *WWD,* 20 Oct.
1930, IV-2.

4

Trade literature on the subject is vast. See, for example, Kenneth Kingsley Stowell,
Modernizing Buildings for Profit (New York: Prentice-Hall, 1935); and *52 Designs to
Modernize Main Street with Glass* (Toledo: Libby Owens Ford Glass Co., ca. 1935).

5

Egerton Shore, "Downtown: A Study of the Central Business District of Los
Angeles," printed report, March 1935, 2 (LAMRL). A systematic updating of storefronts in some of the oldest blocks of the city center was called for early on; see
"Modernization Idea . . . ," *LAT,* 13 Apr. 1930, V-2. The sentiment became widespread among retailers nationally; see, for example, Earl Burke, "Oakland Keeps
Shoppers Coming Downtown," *RE,* 21 Feb. 1940, 2–3; "St. Louis Is Aroused
about Decentralization," *RE,* 24 July 1940, 12; J. M. Baskin, "Downtown Chicago Decentralization Tide," *RE,* 20 Nov. 1940, 2, 6; and Earl Elhart, "Diagnos-
ing the Dread . . . ," *WWD,* 26 Dec. 1940, II-20, 52.

6

LAT, 17 Mar. 1933, II-5; *LAT,* 23 Mar. 1933, II-3; "Bullock's Will Erect . . . ,"
LAT, 15 July 1933, II-1; *LAT,* 3 Apr. 1934, II-3; "New Store . . . ," *LAT,* 3 Apr.
1934, II-1; *LAT,* 18 Apr. 1934, I-10; *LAT,* 28 Apr. 1934, I-12.

7

"Robinson's Store . . . ," *LAT,* 6 Aug. 1933, I-19; "Store Building . . . ," *LAT,* 4 Feb. 1934, I-15; *LAT,* 1 Mar. 1934, I-11; "Modernization Permits . . . ," *LAT,* 27 May 1934, I-13; "Store Repeats . . . ," *LAT,* 3 Sep. 1934, II-8. See also "Robinson Floor . . . ," *WWD,* 13 July 1931, I-6; *LAT,* 7 Jan. 1937, II-5.

8

LAT, 4 Nov. 1934, I-11; "The Broadway's . . . ," *WWD,* 14 Feb. 1936, I-10D; and "The Broadway . . . ," *WWD,* 21 Oct. 1939, I-13 (the Broadway); "May Co. Caters . . . ," *WWD,* 26 Oct. 1934, I-10; *LAT,* 31 Oct. 1935, I-8; *LAT,* 23 July 1936, I-12; "May Company Store . . . ," *LAT,* 3 Oct. 1937, V-3; *LAT,* 16 Jan. 1938, II-2; *LAT,* 4 Oct. 1940, I-14; and *LAT,* 15 Oct. 1940, I-10 (May Co.).

9

"Store Repeats."

10

Concerning Desmond's, see *LAT,* 27 Aug. 1933, I-20. Concerning Mullen & Bluett, see "Store Work Completed," *LAT,* 11 Oct. 1934, I-8. Subsequently, Desmond's expanded its other store, on Seventh and Hope streets, which had opened in 1928; see "Expansion of Desmond . . . ," *LAT,* 27 Dec. 1936, V-3; and "Desmond's Opens . . . ," *LAT,* 21 Oct. 1937, I-6 to 9. Mullen & Bluett likewise undertook further work: "Women's Sportswear Shop . . . ," *LAT,* 10 Aug. 1941, V-3. General discussions of such work include "Downtown Area Leads . . . ," *LAT,* 12 Aug. 1934, I-22; "Downtown Los Angeles . . . ," *LAT,* 7 Oct. 1934, I-21, 23; and "Extensive Projects . . . ," *LAT,* 23 June 1935, I-21, 23.

11

LAT, 25 Sep. 1938, IV-5, 6–8 (Barker Brothers); *LAT,* 15 Sep. 1940, I-12; "Store Fashion . . . ," *LAT,* 22 Sep. 1940, V-3; "Department Store Acquires . . . ," *LAT,* 25 May 1941, V-1 (Eastern-Columbia); "Store to Have . . . ," *LAT,* 11 Aug. 1940, V-2; *LAT,* 18 Sep. 1940, I-14; "Harris & Frank Unveils . . . ," *LAT,* 22 Sep. 1940, V-2 (Harris & Frank); "Jacoby Bros. . . . ," *WWD,* 11 Nov. 1935, I-1, 20; "Jacoby Brothers . . . ," *LAT,* 31 Jan. 1936, I-11; *WWD,* 14 Feb. 1936, I-10C (Jacoby Brothers); "Silverwood's Latest . . . ," *WWD,* 28 Aug. 1936, II-6A, 6D; *LAT,* 2 Nov. 1936, I-7; and *LAT,* 9 Mar. 1939, V-8 (Silverwood's).

For a sampling of accounts of smaller establishments, see "Store Modernizing . . . ," *LAT,* 26 Feb. 1939, V-2; *LAT,* 15 Nov. 1938, I-11; *LAT,* 26 Apr. 1931, III-5; *LAT,* 11 June 1939, I-5; "Innes Store . . . ," *LAT,* 30 July 1939, I-14; *LAT,* 13 June 1937, I-5; *LAT,* 19 Oct. 1937, I-5; and "Enlarged Wetherby-Kayser . . . ," *LAT,* 20 Sep. 1937, I-18.

12

Concerning national chains, see "Self-Service Store . . . ," *WWD,* 13 July 1931, I-6; "Grayson's Opens . . . ," *WWD,* 11 Oct. 1932, 10; "Modern New Shoe . . . ," *LAT,* 8 Mar. 1936, IV-4; "Stevens Shops . . . ," *WWD,* 25 Sep. 1936, III-4; *LAT,* 14 Oct. 1938, I-7; "Elaborate Quarters . . . ," *LAT,* 1 Oct. 1939, V-2; "Bond Clothes . . . ," *LAT,* 4 Oct. 1939, I-12; "Chain Leases . . . ," *LAT,* 1 Sep. 1940, V-3; "Eastern Shoe Firm . . . ," *LAT,* 20 Oct. 1940, V-2; and "Latest Store Architecture . . . ," *LAT,* 2 Nov. 1941, V-3.

Concerning regional chains, see "Modernization Job . . . ," *LAT,* 1 Sep. 1940, V-2; "Todd's Modernizing . . . ," *LAT,* 10 Nov. 1940, V-2. See also "Downtown Properties . . . ," *LAT,* 30 July 1939, I-14; and Lucius Flint, "How Chains Are Selecting Locations," *CSA/AE* [22] (March 1946), 10–11.

13

The major expansion downtown among variety chains was by F. W. Woolworth; see "Hill Street Structure . . . ," *LAT,* 23 Aug. 1936, V-1; "New Business Building . . . ," *LAT,* 11 Oct. 1936, V-5; "Completion of $300,000 . . . ," *LAT,* 12 Sep. 1937, V-1; and "Huge Lease . . . ," *LAT,* 27 Oct. 1940, V-2. Concerning drug stores, see "Downtown Lease Deal . . . ," *LAT,* 23 Jan. 1938, V-1; "Extensive Unit . . . ," *LAT,* 8 May 1938, I-14; "Large New Business . . . ," *LAT,* 10 July 1938, I-14; "Broadway Lease . . . ," *LAT,* 20 Aug. 1939, V-1; "Thrifty Makes . . . ," *LAT,* 14 Apr. 1940, V-2; and "Broadway Corner . . . ," *LAT,* 4 June 1939, V-2.

14

LAT, 14 Mar. 1930, I-7 (Blackstone's); "Two Bedell Stores . . . ," *WWD,* 5 Feb. 1931, I-1, 36; *LAT,* 8 Nov. 1931, II-3 (Bedell's); *LAT,* 16 July 1932, I-2; "New Capital . . . ," *WWD,* 18 Jan. 1933, 1 (Dyas); *LAT,* 6 Feb. 1933, V-5; *LAT,* 9 Mar. 1933, I-5 (Parmelee-Dohrmann); *LAT,* 14 Feb. 1933, I-5 (Alexander & Oviatt). Three large furniture retailers—Los Angeles, Birch-Smith, and Goodman-Jenkins—merged in 1933 under the name of the first concern in order to maintain operations; see "Three Pioneer . . . ," *LAT,* 15 Jan. 1933, I-21.

15

LAT, 17 Aug. 1933, I-5 (Oviatt's); "Myer Siegel Takes . . . ," *LAT,* 24 June 1934, I-14; "Store to Open . . . ," *LAT,* 2 Sep. 1934, I-15; "Innes Store . . . ," *LAT,* 2 June 1940, V-2 (Dyas building); "New Hirsch Unit . . . ," *WWD,* 10 Oct. 1939, 31; "Famous Department Store . . . ," *LAT,* 1 Dec. 1939, I-8; "New Famous Store . . . ," *WWD,* 5 Dec. 1939, 1, 28; and *WWD,* 27 Dec. 1939, II-39 (Blackstone's building).

16

Concerning Coulter's and Magnin's, see chapter 5 above; concerning Sloane's and Saks Fifth Avenue, see chapter 7.

17

William Bowden and Ralph Cassady, "Decentralization of Retail Trade in the Metropolitan Market Area," *Journal of Marketing* 5 (Jan. 1941), 270–275; Ralph Cassady and W. K. Bowden, "Shifting Retail Trade within the Los Angeles Metropolitan Market," *Journal of Marketing* 8 (Apr. 1944), 398–404; "The Pattern of Retail Trade . . . ," *MSBC* 31 (Nov. 1952), n.p.; "Department Store Sales . . . ," *MSBC* 27 (13 May 1948), n.p. See also J. George Robinson, "Suburbanization of Retailing in the Los Angeles Market," *New York Retailer* 7 (Mar. 1954), 5–6; Arthur Grey, "Los Angeles: Urban Prototype," *JLP* 35 (Aug. 1959), 235; and Scott Bottles, *Los Angeles and the Automobile: The Making of the Modern City* (Berkeley and Los Angeles: University of California Press, 1987), 194–196. For a useful national comparison, see "Local Business Measured by Department Store Sales," *Real Estate Analyst* 15 (30 Aug. 1946), 249–261.

18

George Eberle, "The Business District," in George Robbins and L. Deming Tilton, eds., *Los Angeles: Preface to a Master Plan* (Los Angeles: Pacific Southwest Academy, 1941), 129, 131–132. Similar views continued to be expressed after the war, particularly among analysts who studied retail development extensively during the 1920s and 1930s. See, for example, "The Decentralization of Downtown Districts," *Real Estate Analyst* 14 (July 1945), 187–190; Miller McClintock, "Toward Traffic-Trade Balance," *WWD,* 25 July 1946, 44; George Eberle, "Metropolitan

Decentralization and the Retailer," *Journal of Retailing* 22 (Dec. 1946), 91–94; Robert Armstrong, "What and Where to Build," *Retail Control* 20 (Mar. 1952), 7–16; and C. T. Jonassen, *The Shopping Center versus Downtown* (Columbus: Bureau of Business Research, Ohio State University, 1955), esp. 94–100.

19

"Pattern of Retail Trade"; "Department Store Sales"; "1955 Retail Sales . . . ," *MSBC* 34 (Dec. 1955), n.p; Edward Staniford, "Business Decentralization in Metropolitan Los Angeles," [Los Angeles County?] Bureau of Government Research, June 1960, typescript (LAMRL). See also "Suburbanization . . . , *WWD*, 4 Oct. 1950, I-54.

20

The initial thrust of department store expansion during the postwar era, including the Fifth Street Store's (Milliron's) branch, is discussed in chapter 9. Robinson's was not only the last of the city's major department stores to undertake branch development, but it experienced long delays in seeing that branch realized; see "Robinson Co. to Build . . . ," *LAT*, 25 July 1947, II-2; "J. W. Robinson . . . ," *WWD*, 25 July 1947, 1, 30; "Robinson Co. . . . ," *LAT*, 16 Dec. 1948, I-4; "Robinson's Branch . . . ," *WWD*, 2 Mar. 1950, 1, 46; "Beverly Hills . . . ," *LAT*, 2 Mar. 1950, II-1, 2; "Work Well Advanced . . . ," *LAT*, 1 July 1951, V-2; and "Department Store," *PP* 33 (Aug. 1952), 79–86.

21

LAT, 14 Feb. 1949, I-13; "Bond Clothing . . . ," *LAT*, 15 Feb. 1949, II-2; "New Boot Shop . . . ," *LAT*, 27 Mar. 1949, V-4; "French Consul . . . ," *LAT*, 22 May 1949, II-2; *LAT*, 27 Mar. 1949, V-6; "Thousands at Opening . . . ," *LAT*, 4 Aug. 1949, I-12; "Newberry's Opening . . . ," *LAT*, 16 Oct. 1949, I-24; "Shoe Chain Opens . . . ," *LAT*, 12 May 1949, II-6; "Richman Bros. . . . ," *LAT*, 24 Feb. 1950, II-3; "Richman Bros. . . . ," *LAT*, 12 Mar. 1950, V-3; "Store Installs . . . ," *LAT*, 2 Apr. 1950, V-6.

For accounts of remodelings by locally owned stores, see "Newly Improved . . . ," *LAT*, 25 Aug. 1946, II-2; *LAT*, 31 Oct. 1946, I-8; *LAT*, 20 Jan. 1949, III-9; *LAT*, 6 Feb. 1949, V-5; and "Silverwood's Store . . . ," *LAT*, 14 Apr. 1949, I-14.

22

"Downtown Group Names . . . ," *LAT*, 6 Apr. 1950, I-20; "City Beauty Plan . . . ," *LAT*, 13 Apr. 1950, I-2; Lester Gilbert, "Drive on to Modernize . . . ," *WWD*, 12 July 1950, 86.

23

LAT, 24 Nov. 1929, I-13; "Pageant to Thrill . . . ," *LAT*, 27 Nov. 1929, II-9, 10, 16. The event was sponsored by a consortium of organizations and individuals under the name of the Christmas Festival Committee of Los Angeles. For discussion of Hollywood, see chapter 4.

24

"Downtown Yule Decorations . . . ," *LAT*, 20 Nov. 1939, II-1; "Downtown Christmas Season . . . ," *LAT*, 23 Nov. 1939, II-1. For a sampling of *LAT* advertisements sponsored by the association, see 18 May 1935, I-5; 2 Dec. 1937, I-6; 23 Dec. 1937, II-3; 22 Nov. 1939, II-2; 5 Dec. 1939, I-8; 10 Dec. 1939, I-14; and 19 Dec. 1939, II-3. The Christmas parade appears to have become more elaborate in subsequent years; see, for example *LAT*, 19 Nov. 1940, I-9; *LAT*, 8 Dec. 1940, II-7; *LAT*, 18 Nov. 1941, I-8; "Santa's Parade . . . ," *LAT*, 19 Nov. 1941, II-1, 2; and

"Thousands Jam Streets . . . ," *LAT,* 20 Nov. 1941, II-1, 2. For a sampling of other prewar association promotions, see "Downtown Stores Thronged . . . ," *LAT,* 18 Feb. 1940, II-1; *LAT,* 31 Dec. 1940, II-3; "Dollar Days . . . ," *LAT,* 16 Feb. 1941, II-1; and "Dollar Day Shoppers . . . ," *LAT,* 14 Sep. 1941, II-1. Concerning the DBMA's reorganization, see "Downtown Business . . . ," *LAT,* 21 Aug. 1941, II-2; and "Downtown Awakens," *WWD,* 18 Dec. 1941, 35.

25
"Night Shopping Rush," *LAT,* 1 Sep. 1948, I-15; "Transit Ready . . . ," *LAT,* 5 Sep. 1948, II-6; "Stores Ready . . . ," *LAT,* 12 Sep. 1948, II-1; "Downtown Stores . . . ," *LAT,* 13 Sep. 1948, I-12; "Monday Night . . . ," *LAT,* 14 Sep. 1948, II-1, 2. For a sampling of other association promotional activities, see "Downtown Stores . . . ," *LAT,* 14 Oct. 1947, II-1; *LAT,* 13 Oct. 1947, II-10; "Home Festival Week . . . ," *LAT,* 27 Sep. 1948, II-2; "Downtown Home Festival . . . ," *LAT,* 28 Sep. 1948, I-11; "Spring Fashion . . . ," *LAT,* 15 Feb. 1949, II-1; "Father's Day . . . ," *LAT,* 6 June 1949, II-8; *LAT,* 11 Sep. 1949, I-14; "History of 'Downtown' . . . ," *LAT,* 22 Sep. 1949, I-29; "Stores Continue . . . ," *LAT,* 25 Sep. 1949, II-6; "Downtown Stores . . . ," *LAT,* 13 Feb. 1950, II-1; "Downtown Stores . . . ," *LAT,* 21 Feb. 1950, II-1; "Downtown Visited . . . ," *LAT,* 4 Apr. 1950, II-1; "Downtown Business Group . . . ," *LAT,* 21 May 1950, I-30; and "Father's Day . . . ," *LAT,* 4 June 1950, I-50.

26
Concerning the association's leaders, see "Downtown Business"; "Downtown Businessmen Elect . . . ," *LAT,* 26 June 1947, II-1; and "Corrin Re-elected . . . ," *LAT,* 1 July 1950, II-1, 5.

27
For a sampling of the numerous accounts of the subject, see John Miller, "They're All Afraid to Mention It," *Review of Reviews* 9 (Aug. 1936), 54–56; Robert Weinberg, "For Better Places to Park," *ACi* 52 (June 1937), 99–101; "But Where'll We Park?" *PIM* 35 (Oct. 1937), 12–13; Miller McClintock, "Break That Traffic Jam!" *WWD,* 28 Dec. 1937, II-60; Orin Nolting and Paul Oppermann, *The Parking Problem in Central Business Districts* (Chicago: Public Administration Service, 1938); Thomas Henry, "Strangled Cities," *Toledo Business* 17 (May 1939), 11–12; "Car Parking," *Tide* 13 (15 Aug. 1939), 36; Fred Fisch, "Should Cities Provide Off-Street Facilities for Citizens," *1938 Proceedings* (New York: Institute of Traffic Engineers, 1939), 24–26; George Becker, "Parking Lots and Garages in the Central Business District," *AJ* 8 (Jan. 1940), 62–67; Harry Koch, "Parking Facilities for the Detroit Central Business District," *1939 Proceedings* (New York: Institute of Traffic Engineers, 1940), 73–76; "Traffic Jams Business Out," *AF* 72 (Jan. 1940), 64–65; Burton Marsh, "Solving the Automobile Parking Problem," *Public Management* 23 (Jan. 1941), 10–14; John Marr, "The Parking Problem in the Business District," *Civil Engineering* 12 (Jan. 1942), 21–23; Thomas Willier, "Parking Needs of the Modern City," *1944 Proceedings* (New York: Institute of Traffic Engineers, 1945), 28–38; "Parking Jam," *AF* 85; and Jay Runkle, "Downtown Merchant Looks at the Future . . . ," *Stores* 29 (Nov. 1947), 13, 68, 70.

28
"Store Building to Be Changed"; see also *LAT,* 3 Mar. 1938, I-7. Prior to this plan, the store had validated customer tickets from the Auto Center Garage nearby on Hope Street. After the war, the company added a remote car lot four blocks away on Francisco Street between Eighth and Ninth, providing patrons with limousine service to the store; see *LAT,* 7 Sep. 1948, 6.

29

Concerning the May Company garage, see chapter 2.

30

For background, see Bottles, *Los Angeles,* chap. 9, esp. 222–223, 226–227.

31

For discussion, see chapters 4 and 7 above.

32

"Huge Parking Plan . . . ," *LAT,* 17 Jan. 1941, II-1. The spokesman for the scheme was Hayden Jones, who chaired the taxation committee of the California Real Estate Association.

33

Downtown Los Angeles Parking Study (Los Angeles: Downtown Business Men's Assoc., 1945); Seward Mott and Max Wehrly, eds., "Automobile Parking in Central Business Districts," *ULI* 6 (July 1946), 8–10.

34

"Levy for Downtown Chain . . . ," *LAT,* 15 Jan. 1946, I-2; "New Parking Plan . . . ," *LAT,* 21 Mar. 1946, II-1; *Parking and Parkway Lighting in the Los Angeles Area* (Los Angeles: Central Business District Assoc., 1946); "Los Angeles Takes Step . . . ," *WWD,* 28 May 1946, 51; "Four-Front Attack . . . ," *LAT,* 20 Aug. 1946, II-1; "Off-Street Parking in California," *Western City* 24 (May 1948), 19. An important background document is *Interregional Highways* (Washington: National Interregional Highway Committee, Jan. 1944).

35

Later accounts indicate that a proposal for underground parking on the site was advanced as early as 1928 and that three were made in 1931 and 1932 ("Work Starts on Underground Pershing Square Garage . . . ," *A&E* 184 [Mar. 1951], 14). I have found descriptions of only one of these schemes; see "Pershing Park . . . ," *LAT,* 11 Mar. 1931, II-1, 2; and "Square Proposed as Traffic Aid," *Western City* 7 (Apr. 1931), 25, 47. The late S. Charles Lee informed me that he had devised a plan for such a project at that time (interview, Beverly Hills, 26 June 1987). A somewhat similar scheme was more or less concurrently advanced for downtown Detroit; see *ACi* 44 (Jan. 1931), 133; "Underground Garage . . . ," *PM* 55 (Feb. 1931), 180; and "A Sub-Surface Parking Plan," *NREJ* 32 (30 Mar. 1931), 32–34. Another was proposed for Cleveland as early as 1924; see "City Plans Underground . . . ," *PSM* 102 (Feb. 1923), 57. Earlier proposals included using Pershing Square for the city library ("Where Shall We Put . . . ?" *LAT,* 21 Aug. 1921, II-1) and as an interurban railway terminal ("Pacific Electric . . . ," *LAT,* 17 Mar. 1923, II-1, 18; "Diagram of Subway . . . ," *LAT,* 22 July 1923, II-1, 2).

36

For background, see "Pershing Park Garage . . . ," *LAT,* 21 Jan. 1947, II-1; "Pershing Square . . . ," *LAT,* 27 Jan. 1947, I-3, II-1; "Subterranean Garage . . . ," *LAT,* 28 July 1948, II-1; "Problem of the Garage . . . ," *LAT,* 20 Aug. 1948, II-4; "Pershing Square Garage . . . ," *LAT,* 23 Aug. 1948, II-2; "Pershing Square Bids . . . ," *LAT,* 21 Oct. 1949, II-7; *LAT,* 23 Jan. 1950, I-3; "Pershing Square . . . ," *LAT,* 2 Feb. 1951, II-1, 2; "Huge Garage . . . ," *LAT,* 25 May 1952, V-1, 5; *Parking— How It Is Financed* (New York: National Retail Dry Goods Assoc., 1952), 23–24; "Work Starts . . . ," 12, 15, 26; and Dietrich Klose, *Metropolitan Parking Structures:*

A Survey of Architectural Problems and Solutions (New York: Praeger, 1965), 190–191. The primary model for the scheme was acknowledged to be the underground garage at Union Square in San Francisco, which opened in 1941; see Geoffrey Baker and Bruno Funaro, *Parking* (New York: Reinhold, 1958), 60–61.

37

Sanborn atlases reveal three such structures standing in 1953: a private garage for the Southern California Edison Co. at 432 S. Hope holding 180 cars, a two-level garage at 432 S. Olive (both built 1931), and a garage at 537 S. Grand holding 100 cars (1939). Others may have been constructed during the 1930s and dismantled by the early 1950s; however, the dearth of new construction downtown during the period renders such instances unlikely.

38

For discussion, see "Parking 'Decks' Urged . . . ," *Detroit News,* 10 Jan. 1937, I-8; Hunley Abbott, "Low Cost Off-Street Parking," *AC* 4:1 [1938], 6–8; W. S. Wolfe, "Shoppers Parking Deck—Detroit," *AC* 5:2 [1939], 24–26; *AR* 85 (May 1939), 46–47; Hunley Abbott, "Metropolitan Store Parking—Philadelphia," *AC* 7:3 [1941], 32–34; "How Stores in Seven Cities Help Customers Park Their Cars," *RM* 36 (15 Mar. 1941), 8, 44; *AR* 87 (Oct. 1941), 68–69; *The Parking Problem: A Library Research* (Saugatuck, Conn.: Eno Foundation, 1942), 18–20; Wilbur Smith and Charles LeCraw, *Parking* (Saugatuck, Conn.: Eno Foundation, 1946), 99–101; and "Evolution . . . ," *Parking* 1 (Winter 1954), 19. The type grew in popularity after the war. For a sampling of accounts, see "Logical Relief of Downtown Congestion," *ACi* 63 (Mar. 1948), 133–134; Fred Moe, "What Is a Practical Parking Facility?" *ACi* 63 (Dec. 1948), 139, 141, 143; "Mid-town Parking Garages," *AC,* no. 49 [1949], 12–13; "Stop Fooling with the Parking Problem," *ACi* 64 (Dec. 1949), 133, 135; and "What's Being Done about the Parking Problem?" *NREJ* 51 (Nov. 1950), 30–31. The increase in scale of such structures by the 1950s is well documented in Baker and Funaro, *Parking,* 64–71, 78–80, 86–89, 136–141, 148–151, 154–163.

39

I have not included in this tally underground garages constructed as integral parts of commercial buildings. For background on the General Petroleum project, see "'Spiral' Garage . . . ," *LAT,* 13 Feb. 1948, II-8; *AR/WS* 104 (Jul. 1948), 32-12, 32-13; "Spiral Garage . . . ," *LAT,* 3 Oct. 1948, V-1; "Two Office Buildings in Los Angeles," *AF* 90 (May 1949), 92; *Off-Street Parking* (Washington: Chamber of Commerce of the United States, 1949), 6; *Parking—How It Is Financed,* 10; and Baker and Funaro, *Parking,* 152–153. A 1,000-car structure designed in 1952 for a site at Sixth Street and Grand Avenue was never realized; see "Plans Are Completed . . . ," *LAT,* 13 Apr. 1952, V-3. The first executed scheme after General Petroleum's was built by the Standard Oil Company of California at Wilshire Boulevard and Flower Street in 1953; see "Pigeon Hole Parking . . . ," *LAT,* 24 May 1953, V-5.

40

Located at Eighth and Flower streets, the site lay adjacent to the former quarters of Parmelee–Dohrmann, an apt reflection of Flower's demise as a fashionable shopping corridor.

41

"Model of Los Angeles Statler . . . ," *LAT,* 15 June 1946, II-1; "Statler Hotel . . . ," *LAT,* 17 Sep. 1946, I-6; "Statler Bids . . . ," *LAT,* 1 Jan. 1948, II-1; "Hotel Statler . . . ," *LAT,* 9 Oct. 1949, II-5; "Statler's June Start . . . ," *LAT,*

16 Apr. 1950, V-1, 6; "Statler Center . . . ," *AR* 97 (June 1951), 89–104; and "Statler Center . . . ," *AR* 99 (May 1953), 127–136.

42

See chapter 2 for discussion of boundaries and sources that provide the basis for estimates cited in the text.

43

One account noted that in 1937 at least half a dozen new car lots had been created in the core area; see "Los Angeles Parking . . . ," *LAT,* 12 Dec. 1937, V-1. A detailed study of parking conditions downtown was made that same year; see *Traffic Survey, Los Angeles Metropolitan Area . . .* (Los Angeles: Automobile Club of Southern California, 1938), 21–22. By that point the land devoted to parking in the central business district was said to equal that devoted to buildings. See also E. B. Lefferts, "Should Business Provide Off-Street Parking for Patrons," *1938 Proceedings* (New York: Institute of Traffic Engineers, 1939), 19–23. For accounts of old buildings demolished for car lots, see "Downtown Los Angeles . . . ," *LAT,* 27 Aug. 1939, V-3; Edwin Schallert, "Old Lyceum Theater . . . ," *LAT,* 17 Mar. 1941, II-1, 3. Not all buildings demolished were of modest size or dated from the nineteenth century. The Telephone Exchange Building at 622 S. Hill Street was constructed in 1898 but completely reconfigured as a ten-story office block in 1921; see "Wreck First Building . . . ," *SWBC* 79 (11 Mar. 1932), 36. Another new facility, at 122–134 S. Broadway, replaced the six-story Southwest Building, which was constructed in the early twentieth century. Known as Walt's Auto Park, the project had a basement garage as well as the surface area, the latter fronted by a small block of store units; see *LAT,* 9 Feb. 1936, V-1; and *LAT,* 16 July 1936, I-6. The scope of the development made it an exception locally.

44

See chapter 7.

45

Grey, "Los Angeles: Urban Prototype," 234, 242.

46

For additional illustrations, see Los Angeles City Planning Commission, *Accomplishments 1943,* n.p.

IX Markets in the Meadows

1

Charles Cohan, "Advance of Famous . . . ," *LAT,* 2 Mar. 1952, V-1.

2

No two definitions developed for shopping centers during this period were precisely the same. The characteristics noted in the text above are derived from several sources: Geoffrey Baker and Bruno Funaro, *Shopping Centers: Design and Operation* (New York: Reinhold, 1951), 10; J. Ross McKeever, "Shopping Centers: Principles and Policies," *ULI* 20 (July 1953), 6; Gordon Stedman, "The Rise of Shopping Centers," *Journal of Retailing* 31 (Spring 1955), 14–15; Jack Hyman, "Shopping Center Here to Stay," *WWD,* 27 Dec. 1955, II-6; Paul Smith, *Shopping Centers: Planning and Management* (New York: National Retail Merchants

Assoc., 1956), 12; Eugene Kelley, *Shopping Centers: Locating Controlled Regional Centers* (Saugatuck, Conn.: Eno Foundation, 1956), 5–7; and J. Ross McKeever, "Shopping Centers Re-Studied: Emerging Patterns and Practical Experiences," *ULI* 30 (Feb. 1957), I: 9–10. Not surprisingly, definitions based on both size and scope of services were created after a number of examples of the new types could be found. Accounts written prior to the 1950s do not make such distinctions. See, for example, John Mertes, "The Shopping Center—A New Trend in Retailing," *Journal of Marketing* 13 (Jan. 1949), 375–376; and *The Community Builders Handbook* (Washington: Urban Land Institute, 1950), pt. IV.

3

"Shopping Center Boom . . . ," *WWD,* 28 Dec. 1953, II-32–34; Hyman, "Shopping Center," II-6, 34, 40. The prewar estimate is low.

4

"Markets in the Meadows," *AF* 90 (Mar. 1949), 114; S. O. Kaylin, "The Planned Shopping Center," *CSA/AE* [30] (May 1954), 13. Contemporary literature on the subject is extensive. Besides sources cited in notes 2 and 3 above and writings cited in chapter 11, see Joseph Reiss, "Shopping Centers . . . ," *PI* 220 (12 Nov. 1947), 31–33, 85, 88, 90, 93; Harry Fawcett, "Your Key to a Profitable Shopping Center," *NREJ* 49 (Sep. 1948), 14–18; Kenneth Welch, "Regional Shopping Centers: Some Projects in the Northwest," *JAPA* 14 (Fall 1948), 4–9; Seward Mott, "Recent Developments in Suburban Shopping Centers," *AJ* 17 (Jan. 1949), 39–44; Henry Gallagher, "Merchandising Moves to the Suburbs," *American Business* 19 (Feb. 1949), 30, 32, 56–57; Bob Fawcett, "How to Develop a Profitable Shopping Center," *NREJ* 50 (Nov. 1949), 14–17; Howard Fisher, "The Impact of New Shopping Centers upon Established Business Districts," *APC* 1950, 144–155; "What's Needed in a Shopping Center," *BW,* 4 Mar. 1950, 66, 68; "Shopping Centers . . . ," *PI* 230 (9 June 1950), 23–25, 44, 47; "Shopping Center Round-Up," *CSA/AE* [26] (July 1950), 26–29; "Easy Comparative Shopping . . . ," *WWD,* 24 July 1950, 40; Tom McReynolds, "Planning Suburban Shopping Centers," *Appraisal Bulletin* 20 (28 Feb. 1951), 85–122; Kenneth Welch, "Regional Shopping Centers," *AR* 109 (Mar. 1951), 121–131; Myron Heidingsfield, "The Suburban Shopping Center," *Economic and Business Bulletin,* School of Business and Public Administration, Temple University, 3 (Mar. 1951), 3–12; Howard Fisher, "Shopping Centers Lure Customers . . . ," *American Business* 22 (Mar. 1952), 16–17, 50; "The Marketing Revolution III . . . ," *Tide* 26 (26 Sep. 1952), 36–39; "Planned Postwar Shopping Centers . . . ," *BW,* 11 Oct. 1952, 124–125; Arthur Rubloff, "Regional Shopping Centers and Their Effect on the Future of Our Cities," *APC* 1953, 45–49; S. O. Kaylin, "The Impact of Recent Development in Retailing," *25th Annual Boston Conference on Distribution,* 1953, 76–78; "Will Today's Shopping Centers Succeed?" *NREJ* 54 (Feb. 1953), 22–29; Karl Van Leuven, "From Joe's Hot Dog Stand to a Regional Shopping Center," *ACi* 68 (Apr. 1953), 98–99; "Shopping Centers," *AR* 114 (Oct. 1953), 178–201; C. R. Palmer, "The Shopping Center Goes to the Shopper," *New York Times Magazine,* 29 Nov. 1953, 14–15, 37, 39–40, 42, 49; Genevieve Smith, "Regional Shopping Grows Fast," *PI* 247 (14 May 1954), 37–40, 74–75. A detailed account that includes views of the then recent past as well as of current tendencies is the 110-entry series by Samuel Feinberg in his column, "From Where I Sit . . . ," *WWD,* 19 Oct. 1959 to 25 Mar. 1960.

The development of postwar shopping centers has been the subject of several recent scholarly accounts, most notable among them: Meredith Clausen, "Northgate Regional Shopping Center—Paradigm from the Provinces," *JSAH* 43 (May

1984), 144–161; Howard Gillette, Jr., "The Evolution of the Planned Shopping Center in Suburb and City," *JAPA* 51 (Autumn 1985), 449–460; and Meredith Clausen, "Shopping Centers," in Joseph Wilkes, ed., *Encyclopedia of Architecture: Design, Engineering and Construction,* 4 vols. (New York: John Wiley & Sons, 1989), 4: 412–415. A valuable study of the context in which this phenomenon occurred is James Vance, "Emerging Patterns of Commercial Structure in American Cities," in Knut Norborg, ed., *Proceedings of the IGU Symposium in Urban Geography, Lund, 1960* (Lund, Sweden: C. W. K. Gleerup, 1962), 485–518.

5

Four of these, the Broadway-Crenshaw Center, Westchester Center, Panorama City Shopping Center, and Valley Plaza, are discussed in this chapter. They were planned in the 1940s, but the latter three were in large part developed during the next decade. Lakewood Center and Olympic Shopping Circle are discussed in chapter 11. They were planned in 1950; the Olympic center was never built. The only two metropolitan areas then to approach Los Angeles's scale of shopping center development were New York and Chicago, which had four and three comparably sized complexes, respectively, operating by 1957.

6

R. W. Welch, "Convenience Is King in the New Shopping Centers . . . ," *PI* 241 (12 Dec. 1952), 51.

7

Much discussion of this shift occurred in trade journals of the period. See, for example, William Snaith, "Redistribution of Shopping Areas," *WWD,* 22 Nov. 1950, 53, as well as references cited in notes 4 and 8. The difficulties in identifying market demands as a result of this shift were also frequently noted; see, for example, Eldridge Peterson, ed., "Retailing in Ferment," *PI* 241 (12 Dec. 1952), 41–54; and "Shopping Centers . . . ," *Tide* 28 (24 Apr. 1954), 21–23.

8

Among the most useful contemporary analyses of the subject are Snaith, "Redistribution"; Baker and Funaro, *Shopping Centers,* 4–6; Stedman, "Rise of Shopping Centers," 11–12; "Shopping Spreads Out . . . ," *U.S. News & World Report* 33 (7 Nov. 1952), 58, 60, 62–63; Peterson, ed., "Retailing in Ferment"; Malcolm McNair, "Improving the Dynamics of Retailing . . . ," *25th Annual Boston Conference on Distribution,* 1953, 57–61; "The Lush New Suburban Market," *Fortune* 48 (Nov. 1953), 128–131, 230–232, 234, 237; Samuel McMillan, "Decentralization of Retail Trade," *Traffic Quarterly* 8 (Apr. 1954), 213–223; and Feinberg, "From Where I Sit . . . ," 2 Nov. 1959, 12; 3 Nov. 1959, 12, 17.

9

John Parke Young, "Industrial Background," in George Robbins and L. Deming Tilton, eds., *Los Angeles: Preface to a Master Plan* (Los Angeles: Pacific Southwest Academy, 1941), 69; *MSBC* 27 (10 Feb. 1948), n.p.

10

Edwin Cottrell and Helen Jones, *Metropolitan Los Angeles: A Study in Integration, I. Characteristics of the Metropolis* (Los Angeles: Haynes Foundation, 1952), 58–59; B. Marchand, *The Emergence of Los Angeles: Population and Housing in the City of Dreams 1940–1970* (London: Pion, 1976), 70.

11

For background, see Mel Scott, *Metropolitan Los Angeles: One Community* (Los Angeles: Haynes Foundation, 1949), 45–50; Howard Nelson, "The Spread of the Artificial Landscape over Southern California," *AAG* 49 (Sep. 1959), 80; Marchand, *Emergence,* 42, 69–70; and Constantine Panunzio, "Growth and Character of the Population," in Robbins and Tilton, eds., *Los Angeles,* 30–34.

12

J. George Robinson, "Suburbanization of Retailing in the Los Angeles Market," *New York Retailer* 7 (Mar. 1954), 5.

13

Articles by Charles Cohan, real estate editor of the *LAT,* present numerous revealing insights as well as statistics on the subject. See, for example, "New Population Gain . . . ," 2 Aug. 1936, V-1; "Review Shows . . . ," 31 Jan. 1937, V-1; "This City Leads . . . ," 17 Oct. 1937, V-1; "Nation Learns . . . ," 24 Oct. 1937, V-1; "This Region Sets . . . ," 12 Dec. 1937, V-1; "City Tops Detroit . . . ," 26 Feb. 1939, V-1; "City Gains . . . ," 2 April 1939, V-1, 3; "Los Angeles Building . . . ," 31 Dec. 1939, I-10; "Residence Building . . . ," 2 July 1940, V-1, 4; and "Southlands Building . . . ," 10 Aug. 1941, V-1. For comparisons nationally, see "Residential Construction in 140 Metropolitan Areas," *Real Estate Analyst* 17 (28 Feb. 1948), 37–52.

14

Writings by Cohan are again a useful source; for example: "The Boom in Home Building," *LATMN,* 2 Jan. 1947, I-13; "Construction Climbs . . . ," *LATMN,* 3 Jan. 1948, IV-3; "Dawn of 1950 . . . ," *LAT,* 1 Jan. 1950, II-8; "Surge of Building . . . ," *LAT,* 25 Feb. 1951, V-1; "Construction Here . . . ," *LAT,* 1 Apr. 1951, V-1; "L.A. Building . . . ," *LAT,* 2 Dec. 1951, V-1; "Los Angeles Building . . . ," *LAT,* 3 May 1953, V-1; "Building of Homes . . . ," *LAT,* 9 Aug. 1953, V-1, 5; and "L. A. Retains Leadership," *LAT,* 3 Jan. 1954, I-22. Marchand, *Emergence,* affords a detailed analysis of relationships between housing stock and population between 1940 and 1970. Greg Hise, "Home Building and Industrial Decentralization in Los Angeles . . . ," *Journal of Urban History* 19 (Feb. 1993), 95–125, provides an important historical perspective.

15

For discussion, see chapters 4, 5, and 6.

16

A useful overview of the subject from an operational perspective is Clinton Lewis Oaks, "A Critical Analysis of Selected Problems in the Development, Organization, and Control of Large Suburban Branches of Pacific Coast Department Stores," Ph.D. diss., Stanford Univ., 1955. Contemporary accounts are numerous, including Kenneth Welch, "Where Are Department Stores Going?" *AR* 96 (Nov. 1944), 91–96; "Stores to Expand," *BW,* 23 Mar. 1946, 80–81, 84; "Department Stores Hurrying to Suburbs," *BW,* 4 Oct. 1947, 24–26; E. B. Weiss, "How to Sell to and through the *New* Department Store," *PI* 221 (28 Nov. 1947), 31–34, 72, 76, 78; idem, "Department Stores Are Becoming Chain Stores," *PI* 221 (5 Dec. 1947), 39–40, 62, 66, 68; "Business Firms Following Suburban Trend," *Automobile Facts* 6 (Dec. 1947), 8; E. B. Weiss, "The Importance to Department Stores of Strong Resources," *PI* 222 (2 Jan. 1948), 36–37, 58–59; E. Paul Behles, "Branch Stores," *RM* 43 (Feb. 1948), 21–22, 45; E. B. Weiss, "Self-Service, Self-Selection and Robot Selling," *PI* 224 (11 June 1948), 42–43, 72, 74; "Big Department

Stores Are Threatened," *Changing Times* 3 (Aug. 1949), 19–21; Isadore Barmash, "Depreciation Factors Minimized . . . ," *WWD*, 1 Mar. 1950, 58; Faye Henle, "Branches Broaden Department Store Scope," *Barron's* 30 (17 Apr. 1950), 19; Malcolm McNair, "The Future of the Department Store," *Stores* 32 (May 1950), 15–19, 81; Paul Mazur, "The Department Store . . . ," *Stores* 32 (Nov. 1950), 22–26; Dero Saunders, "Department Stores: Rush for the Suburbs," *Fortune* 44 (Dec. 1951), 98–102, 164, 166, 168, 170, 173; John Guernsey, "Suburban Branches," *DSE* 14 (June 1951), 30–31, 114, 120; (July 1951), 42–43, 78, 111; (Aug. 1951), 32–34, 52, 112; (Sep. 1951), 41–43, 100, 102; Milton Brown, "The Trend in Branch Stores," *Twenty-Fourth Annual Conference on Distribution*, 1952, 77–81; Milton Brown, *Operating Results of Department and Specialty Store Branches . . .* , Bureau of Business Research, Bull. no. 136, Graduate School of Business Administration, Harvard University, 1952; E. B. Weiss, "The Revolution in Retailing," *Commercial and Financial Chronicle* 176 (16 Oct. 1952), 4–5; and E. H. Gault, "Suburban Branches: A New Trend in Retailing," *Michigan Business Review* 4 (Nov. 1952), 9–13. For useful lists of branch department and specialty stores, see "Main Plants Sprout . . . ," *WWD*, 7 Sep. 1948, I-70, 71; and "Branch Store Bonanza . . . ," *WWD*, 27 Dec. 1955, II: 14, 35, 41. For a recent case study, see Richard Longstreth, "The Mixed Blessings of Success: The Hecht Company and Department Store Branch Development after World War II," in Elizabeth Cromley and Carter Hudgins, eds., *Perspectives in Vernacular Architecture, VI* (Knoxville: University of Tennessee Press, forthcoming).

17

Los Angeles examples were frequently cited in a number of the articles listed in note 16 above. See also "Branch Store Growth in Los Angeles . . . ," *WWD*, 19 Feb. 1941, 31; and D. L. W., "Park Here," *WWD*, 2 Nov. 1950, 1.

18

Concerning Bullock's, see note 71 below. Concerning the May Company, see "May Co., to Build . . . ," *LAT*, 7 June 1945, I-6; "The May Company's Expansion Program," *DSE* 8 (July 1945), 62–63, 67; "May Co. Starts . . . ," *LAT*, 2 Nov. 1945, II-2; "Store Modernization," *RM* 40 (Dec. 1945), 29; "Retail Rush," *AF* 85 (Oct. 1946), 10–11; "6 Acres to Shop In," *RM* 43 (Jan. 1948), 32–34; and Edwin Wooten, "How Service and Delivery Are Expedited at the May Co.," *RM* 43 (Feb. 1948), 16–19.

19

As is too often the case, company records of the period are either destroyed or lost. I am grateful to Eaton Ballard, retired senior vice president of the parent company, Carter Hawley Hale Stores, who joined the Broadway in 1947, for a wealth of insights concerning the business from the 1930s to the 1950s (interview, Pasadena, 14 Nov. 1989).

   Concerning the Pasadena store, see "The Broadway to Open . . . ," *WWD*, 14 May 1940, 1, 28; "New Broadway-Pasadena . . . ," *WWD*, 2 Aug. 1940, 27; "Bright New Store . . . ," *PSN*, 13 Nov. 1940, 3; "Broadway-Pasadena Ready . . . ," *PSN*, 14 Nov. 1940, 8; "Store to Open . . . ," *LAT*, 14 Nov. 1940, II-2; *WWD*, 25 Nov. 1940, 6; *WWD*, 28 Nov. 1940, 9; *WWD*, 29 Nov. 1940, 29; "$1,000,000 Baby," *DSE* 3 (25 Dec. 1940), 28, 31; "Access by Autos . . . ," *WWD*, 9 Jan. 1941, 55; "New Merchandising Center," *PCA* 58 (Feb. 1941), 26–27; Albert Gardner, "Broadway Store for Pasadena," *AC* 7:3 [1941], 12–14; and "Broadway Gets . . . ," *WWD*, 25 July 1946, 1, 8.

20

One account, probably based upon information supplied by the company, noted that the latter instituted "a series of exhaustive surveys of the Crenshaw section" in 1938, two years before building the Pasadena store; see Carl Jackson, "Modern Display Facilities Mark the Broadway-Crenshaw," *DW* 52 (Feb. 1948), 26. See also "Broadway-Crenshaw: A Combination of Beauty and Functionalism," *RM* 43 (Mar. 1948), 24–27, 30.

21

Although the census itself is not cited, contemporary accounts suggest that it was an important source of information. See "One-Stop Centers Continue Growth," *CSA/AE* [22] (Sep. 1946), 24; Jackson, "Modern Display Facilities," 26; Albert Gardner, "Broadway-Crenshaw Sponsors . . . ," *SWBC* 111 (26 Mar. 1948), 8; and Baker and Funaro, *Shopping Centers,* 176. The uncertainty of siting these complexes due to a lack of precedent is emphasized in S. O. Kaylin, "The Impact of Recent Developments in Retailing," *25th Annual Boston Conference on Distribution,* 1953, 76–78.

22

Two period accounts that underscore the importance of detailed market analysis for major developments in outlying areas are Homer Hoyt, "Market Analysis of Shopping Centers," *ULI* 12 (Oct. 1949), whole issue; and Baker and Funaro, *Shopping Centers,* 17–19. See also chapter 11 below.

23

Accounts of site selection methods during the interwar years are numerous. See, for example, Ira Lurie, "What's the Best Location?" *System* 42 (Oct. 1922), 401–403, 446, 448, 450; Paul Nystrom, *Retail Store Operation,* rev. ed. (New York: Roland Press Co., 1937), chap. 17; and Richard Ratcliff, "The Problem of Retail Site Selection," *Michigan Business Studies* 9 (1939), 79–82.

24

Concerning Coldwell Banker's role, see "New Broadway-Crenshaw Store . . . ," *SWBC* 108 (23 Aug. 1946), 8; Gardner, "Broadway-Crenshaw," 8; and Jo Ann Levy, *Behind the Western Skyline: Coldwell Banker, the First 75 Years* (Los Angeles: Coldwell Banker and Co., 1981), 88–89. I am grateful to William McAdam, retired chairman of the board of Coldwell Banker, and Brent Howell, first vice president and national marketing director for commercial properties, for additional information (interviews, Newport Beach, 8 Apr. 1988, and Los Angeles, 21 July 1987, respectively).

25

Site selection was a principal determinant of the size of what became the nation's first realized regional shopping mall; see Clausen, "Northgate," 150.

26

Besides sources cited in notes 20, 21, and 24 above, contemporary accounts include "Broadway Begins Store . . . ," *LAT,* 30 Oct. 1945, I-6; Albert Gardner, "Broadway Department Store . . . ," *AC* 12:1 [1946], 21; "Shopping Centers . . . ," *WWD,* 6 Feb. 1946, 70; "Store Heads Dedicate . . . ," *LAT,* 27 Feb. 1946, I-8; "New Broadway-Crenshaw Store," 8–12; *RM* 41 (July 1946), 32; "Tunnel to Route . . . ," *WWD,* 17 Oct. 1946, 57; *SWW,* 9 Nov. 1947, 13; *LAT,* 13 Nov. 1947, I-7; "Woolworth Unit . . . ," *WWD,* 14 Nov. 1947, 3; "Broadway Crenshaw Store . . . ," *WWD,* 19 Nov. 1947, 36; "Broadway's New . . . ," *LAT,* 21

Nov. 1947, II-1; "Broadway-Crenshaw . . . ," *LAT,* 22 Nov. 1947, II-1; "New
Faces . . . ," *WWD,* 26 Nov. 1947, 50; *The Broadway World* 38 (30 Nov. 1947),
1–9; *Stores* 29 (Dec. 1947), 48; *SWW,* 12 Dec. 1947, 10; *LAT,* 18 Dec. 1947, I-3;
SWW, 29 Jan. 1948, 17; Lucius Flint, "Giant Shopping Center Takes Shape,"
CSA/AE [24] (Feb. 1948), 16–17, 40; "Shopping Is Modernized by New Stores
in Los Angeles," *DSE* 11 (Feb. 1948), 118; "New Von's among Nation's Largest,"
SMM 13 (Feb. 1948), 134; "Von's New Market in Los Angeles," *SMM* 13 (Mar.
1948), 144–145; "Phone Company . . . ," *LAT,* 13 Apr. 1948, I-5; *AR/WS* 103
(May 1948), 32-10, 32-12, 32-14; *LAT,* 18 Aug. 1948, I-13; "Owl-Rexall
Store . . . ," *LAT,* 20 Aug. 1948, II-2; "Designed to Serve 8000 Cars a Day," *AR/
WS* 104 (Oct. 1948), 32-6; "Silverwood's to Open . . . ," *WWD,* 4 Nov. 1948,
40; Nathan Zahm, "Functionalism and Beauty . . . ," *WWD,* 23 Feb. 1949, 70;
"Silverwood's to Open . . . ," *LAT,* 8 Apr. 1949, II-16; *LAT,* 11 Apr. 1949, III-20;
Seward Mott and Max Wehrly, eds., "Shopping Centers: An Analysis," *ULI* 11
(July 1949), 32–33; "Von's Crenshaw . . . ," *LAEx,* 13 Oct. 1949, III-12; Baker
and Funaro, *Shopping Centers,* 174–179; and "A Center's Financial Case History,"
CSA/AE [30] (May 1954), 27, 87.

Throughout, the complex is referred to as the Broadway-Crenshaw Center,
while the business district of which it was a part is referred to as the Crenshaw
Center.

27

Published figures vary; I have used the ones that appear to be the most accurate.
"A Center's Financial Case History," 87, cites space used for the retail units, restaurant, and bank at 482,303 square feet, the automobile service station at 9,970
square feet, and the office building at 57,300 square feet.

The only single off-street parking area integral to a planned shopping center
that I have found to be of comparable size at that time was at Hampton Village
(begun 1939) in St. Louis. There, space was originally created for 1,000 cars, but
parcels were added for another 1,500 by mid-1947; see *Building: The National
News Review* 3 (14 Apr. 1939), 12; Robert Latimer, "St. Louis Launches Shopping
Center," *SMM* 5 (Feb. 1940), 14, 33–34; "Forum: Hampton Village," *Freehold* 6
(15 June 1940), 412–413; "$11,000,000 St. Louis . . . ," *WWD,* 29 Jan. 1947, 54;
"Hampton Village . . . ," *RM* 42 (June 1947), 14–15, 41; "Shopping Center in
St. Louis," *DSE* 10 (Sep. 1947), 30–31; and Baker and Funaro, *Shopping Centers,*
188–190.

28

Market Square is discussed in chapter 6, Marshall Field and Strawbridge & Clothier in chapter 5.

29

"Shopping Center," *AF* 83 (Dec. 1945), 107–110; "Frederick & Nelson . . . ," *RM*
41 (Aug. 1946), 28; "First Suburban Store," *DSE* 9 (Oct. 1946), 28–29; "Shopping Center in Bellevue . . . ," *AF* 86 (Apr. 1947), 76–78; "Remedy for a Common Commercial Ailment," *AR* 102 (Dec. 1947), 112–114; Mott and Wehrly,
"Shopping Centers," 22–23; Baker and Funaro, *Shopping Centers,* 130–133, 222–
231; and Pietro Belluschi, "Shopping Centers," in Talbot Hamlin, ed., *Forms and
Functions of Twentieth-Century Architecture,* 4 vols. (New York: Columbia University
Press, 1952), 4: 116–117, 122–123. A department store, though not a branch
of a major downtown concern, was also included in the much heralded wartime
shopping center at Linda Vista near San Diego; see chapter 10.

30

For discussion, see chapter 7.

31

"A Center's Financial Case History," 27, 87.

32

Ibid.; Saunders, "Department Stores," 166; Stedman, "Rise of Shopping Centers," 16; "The Broadway Sells . . . ," *WWD,* 22 Apr. 1947, 1, 47.

33

The extent to which the Broadway planned to control tenancy and operations was apparently not as great in the initial program. Soon after Edward Carter became president of the company in the spring of 1946, he worked with Coldwell Banker to make the scheme more fully integrated. He also demanded modifications to the department store interior. Both initiatives delayed completion of the center for about six months (Ballard interview).

34

Ballard interview.

35

Interview with Albert C. Martin, Jr., Los Angeles, 7 Nov. 1989. Martin did extensive work for the May Company, including its Wilshire Boulevard store and that on Crenshaw Boulevard described in the text below.

36

See, for example, "Romance of Gown Design . . . ," *LAT,* 27 Mar. 1932, V-2; "Country Has Come . . . ," *WWD,* 21 Mar. 1937, III-2, 3, 4, 5; Charles Cohan, "Los Angeles Fast . . . ," *LAT,* 18 June 1938, V-1; Carlyle Roberts, "Why California Display Is Different," *DW* 53 (Oct. 1948), 42–43, 74, 76, 78. Los Angeles, New York, and Chicago were the three cities from which storefront displays were regularly featured in *DW,* the principal organ of the field.

37

Periodical literature on the subject is vast. A number of books also were published, including Emrich Nicholson, *Contemporary Shops in the United States* (New York: Architectural Book Pub. Co., 1945); Morris Ketchum, *Shops & Stores* (New York: Reinhold, 1948), esp. chap. 4; Louis Parnes, *Planning Stores That Pay* (New York: F. W. Dodge, 1948), esp. chap. 6; and Jose Fernandez, *The Specialty Shop* (New York: Architectural Book Pub. Co., 1950).

38

Grayson's Santa Monica store (1940) was probably Gruen's first work in southern California; see "Grayson's 'Most Unique Store' . . . ," *SMEO,* 29 Nov. 1940, 17; and "Novel Design . . . ," *WWD,* 24 Feb. 1941, 26. Gruen continued to design in much the same vein for at least several years after the war even when stores were in isolated locations and targeted mostly to a motorist trade. See "Furniture Store in Los Angeles . . . ," *AF* 86 (Apr. 1947), 88; and "Store Designed to Draw . . . ," *SWBC* 109 (27 June 1947), 24, 26.

39

The tunnel proved to be a financial burden to the smaller tenants. Each unit had a service elevator that was costly to operate and consumed valuable space (Martin interview). In most later examples, only the large stores had this feature.

40

Such was the case with downtown Los Angeles department stores, as discussed in chapter 2. In other cities, these emporia were sometimes directly across the street from one another, but then they were generally somewhat different in customer orientation, as was the case with Strawbridge & Clothier, Gimbel's, and Lit Brothers in Philadelphia. John Wanamaker, which came closest to Strawbridge & Clothier in the nature of its goods, was situated several blocks away.

41

See note 18 for references to the announcement. The big Hollywood store was never built and the remodeling downtown was less extensive than planned. For accounts of the Crenshaw project, see "May Co.'s Crenshaw Store . . . ," *SWBC* 102 (23 Aug. 1946), 13; "May Crenshaw Branch . . . ," *WWD*, 9 Oct. 1947, 4; "Opening Set . . . ," *LAT*, 9 Oct. 1947, I-7; "May Crenshaw . . . ," *WWD*, 9 Oct. 1947, 4; "New May Co. . . . ," *LAT*, 10 Oct. 1947, II-1, 3; "Residential Community . . . ," *WWD*, 15 Oct. 1947, 61; "May Co. Branch . . . ," *WWD*, 20 Oct. 1947, 10; "Modern Design . . . ," *SWBC* 110 (24 Oct. 1947), 22, 24; "Architect and Contractor Unite . . . ," *SWBC* 110 (28 Oct. 1947), 38, 40, 42, 44; *Stores* 29 (Dec. 1947), 48; Albert Martin, "Department Store in Suburban Los Angeles . . . ," *AC* 14:1 [1948], 2–5; "6 Acres to Shop . . . ," *RM* 43 (Jan. 1948), 32–34; Carl Jackson, "May Company-Crenshaw Geared to Sell," *DW* 52 (May 1948), 68–69, 176; and "A Department Store . . . ," *AF* 88 (May 1948), 108–109.

42

Interviews with Joseph Eichenbaum, codeveloper of Lakewood Center (Los Angeles, 11 Apr. 1988), Eaton Ballard, and Albert C. Martin, Jr., confirmed the extent to which the layout of the entire complex was considered a poor one. Passing references to the subject are also made in a number of accounts published during the late 1940s and early 1950s. A good synopsis can be found in Clausen, "Northgate," 153; however, she addresses the Broadway-Crenshaw Center exclusively, without indicating that some problems stemmed from the larger ensemble.

43

"May Co. Branch"; Ballard interview.

44

Barker Brothers purchased a parcel on the tract well before plans were unveiled for a multiunit development; see "Formal Opening . . . ," *LAT*, 22 Mar. 1948, I-9; and "Ground Broken . . . ," *LAT*, 23 Mar. 1948, II-1. For a preliminary design of the overall project, see "Baldwin Hills Work . . . ," *LATMN*, 3 Jan. 1949, IV-10. Concerning the final scheme, see "Greater Crenshaw Hub . . . ," *LAEx*, 21 May 1950, VII-4; "New Business Development . . . ," *SWW*, 21 May 1950, 16; and "Four Business Blocks . . . ," *LAT*, 21 May 1950, V-5. The company's advertisement in the same section of *LAT* (V-7) reads in part:

> In little more than 3 years, Crenshaw Center . . . has out-miracled the world-famous Miracle Mile. It has shattered just about every growth and business record known to merchandising history for any comparable sub-business center in the nation. . . . This is why the Capital Company has planned its new shopping center directly adjoining. . . . MERCHANTS, INVESTORS, BUILDERS are all invited to join the expansion of Greater Crenshaw Center through purchases of business frontage NOW. . . . Every lot buyer receives a stock interest in the parking corporation owning and operating a 9-acre free parking area.

45

Concerning Barker Brothers, see note 44 above. Concerning Desmond's, see "Desmond's Crenshaw . . . ," *LAEx*, 13 Mar. 1953, II-5; and "Desmond's Tells . . . ,"

SWW, 15 Mar. 1953, 6. Richman Brothers clothing store opened a unit in the group adjoining the May Company ("Clothing Chain . . . ," *LAT,* 10 Sep. 1948, I-24), as did J. J. Newberry. See also "Pep Boys . . . ," *LAT,* 29 Sep. 1949, I-28; and *LAT,* 20 Apr. 1950, I-40.

46

Hise, "Home Building," 108–110, and idem, "The Airplane and the Garden City: Regional Transformations during World War II," in Donald Albrecht, ed., *World War II and the American Dream: How Wartime Building Changed a Nation* (Washington: National Building Museum, and Cambridge: MIT Press, 1995), 154–159, provide useful background on the community.

47

Gordon Whitnall, "Disintegrating Commercial Centers," *AJ* 9 (Jan. 1941), 14–15. See also chapter 7, note 39.

48

The most useful piece on the intentions behind the scheme is a prospectus, "Westchester, the *Planned* Business Development," printed ca. 1945–1946 by Frank H. Ayres & Son, brokers for the project. I am grateful to Bill Symonds of Symonds Real Estate, Inc., in North Hollywood for sharing his copy of this rare surviving document of the period. Westchester is discussed in Mott and Wehrly, "Shopping Centers," 34–36; and *Community Builders Handbook,* 124–128. Additional insights were provided by Howard B. Drollinger, president of H. B. Drollinger Co., whose mother was the first to develop commercial property at Westchester and who himself has been involved in the center for over half a century (interview, Los Angeles, 19 June 1992); and also by Fred Marlow, one of the house developers at Westchester (interviews, Los Angeles, 20 July 1987 and 16 Nov. 1989). Whitnall did not see his hope for streets unimpeded by parking realized; space for 460 cars was available curbside.

49

Drollinger interview; Helen Holmes, "Ground Broken . . . ," *Los Angeles Downtown Shopping News,* 15 Aug. 1942, 12. I have yet to locate a run of this important paper, and am grateful to Greg Hise for sharing his copy of this article with me.

50

IDN, 17 Apr. 1947, 5; "Sears to Open . . . ," *IDN,* 30 Apr. 1947, 1; "Sears Postwar Expansion . . . ," *WWD,* 30 Apr. 1947, 102; "Sears Plans . . . ," *LAEx,* 4 Oct. 1949, I-1; "Sears-Inglewood . . . ," *AR/WS* 103 (June 1948), 32-2, 32-4.

51

The name was changed with the idea of establishing branches in mind; see "Milliron's New Name . . . ," *WWD,* 25 Apr. 1946, 1, 45. The building was among the most publicized commercial projects of the period; see "Suburban Unit . . . ," *WWD,* 23 Dec. 1946, 1, 32; "Future Westchester Development . . . ," *SWBC* 109 (23 May 1947), 16–17; Abbot Kinney, "Shape of Suburban . . . ," *WWD,* 30 July 1947, 49; Victor Gruen, "Problem of Store Design," *SWBC* 111 (23 Jan. 1948), 14–18; "Modelled for Traffic Flow," *CSA/AE* [24] (Mar. 1948), 17; "Ground Broken . . . ," *LAT,* 16 Mar. 1948, II-1; "Milliron's New Store . . . ," *AR/WS* 104 (Aug. 1948), 32-1, 32-2; "New Milliron's Branch . . . ," *WWD,* 22 Dec. 1948, 1, 10; *WWD,* 5 Jan. 1949, I-13; "Milliron's to Open . . . ," *IDN,* 4 Feb. 1949, 3; "Milliron's Westchester . . . ," *IDN,* 3 Mar. 1949, 9; "Milliron's Westchester . . . ," *IDN,* 16 Mar. 1949, 3; "Milliron's New Store . . . ," *LAT,* 16 Mar. 1949, I-9;

"Milliron's Opens . . . ," *IDN,* 17 Mar. 1949, 2; "Store Design," *Stores* 31 (Mar. 1949), 20–21; *WWD,* 5 Apr. 1949, 50; *WWD,* 20 Apr. 1949, 64; Victor Gruen, "Architect's Complete Control . . . ," *SWBC* 113 (22 Apr. 1949). 8–9; "New L.A. Store . . . ," *BW,* 23 Apr. 1949, 86–87; "Something New in Stores," *AF* 90 (June 1949), 105–111; "A New Suburban Department Store," *PCA* 75 (June 1949), 39–41; Carl Jackson, "New Milliron's Designed with Display in Mind," *DW* 54 (June 1949), 34–35, 90; Victor Gruen, "Triple Target for Economy," *CSA/AE* [25] (July 1949), 18–19, 63–64; "Suburban Store Solves Parking Problem," *NREJ* 50 (Aug. 1949), 51; "Department Store of Tomorrow . . . ," *Interiors* 109 (Oct. 1949), 112–119; "Milliron's Department Store . . . ," *A&E* 179 (Nov. 1949), 20–27; Baker and Funaro, *Shopping Centers,* 168–170; and idem, *Parking* (New York: Reinhold, 1958), 133–135.

Milliron's soon found itself overextended and sold the store to the Broadway; see "Broadway Dept. Store . . . ," *Westchester World,* 6 July 1950, 1; "Westchester Unit . . . ," *WWD,* 10 July 1950, 2; "Broadway to Open . . . ," *Westchester World,* 17 Aug. 1950, 1; *WWD,* 21 Aug. 1950, 9; and "New Broadway Unit . . . ," *WWD,* 21 Aug. 1950, 1, 36. Apparently the plan possessed significant flaws, yet market demand in the area was sufficiently strong to render the store profitable (Ballard interview).

52

Accounts of other buildings in the development include *IDN,* 27 Feb. 1947, 3, 14; "Building Rising . . . ," *LAT,* 9 Oct. 1949, V-1; "Ralphs Purchases . . . ," *LAT,* 9 Apr. 1950, V-3; "New Theater . . . ," *LAT,* 16 Apr. 1950, V-4; "Western Auto Supply . . . ," *Westchester World,* 13 July 1950, 4; "Westchester Theater . . . ," *LAT,* 18 Aug. 1950, I-28; "New Paradise . . . ," *Westchester World,* 24 Aug. 1950, 1; *LAEx,* 12 Dec. 1954, III-12; and *LAT,* 8 June 1958, VI-8.

53

Community Builders Handbook, 127. The authors proceed on the next page with the general recommendation of front parking for most, if not all, cars, intimating that Westchester was no longer considered part of mainstream practice.

54

Rooftop parking was only undertaken for a store when available land was so limited that no other option was prudent. Locally, the approach was pioneered at the Sears Pico Boulevard store discussed in the text below. Sears repeated the arrangement in its Wisconsin Avenue store in Washington, D.C. (1940–1941), and a postwar San Francisco store; see "Retail Store in Washington D.C.," *AF* 76 (Apr. 1942), 213–216; "Shopping Conveniences . . . ," *CSA/AE* [18] (June 1942), 8–9; John Stokes Redden, "Sears' Store for Washington . . . ," *AC* 8:4 [1942], 10–13; and "Selecting the Surface Texture . . . ," *Concrete* 51 (Feb. 1943), 5–6. Parking for customers of the Marshall Field Evanston store was placed atop the nearby Firestone auto service center in 1937 ("Parking on the Roof," *Engineering News Record* 119 [9 Dec. 1937], 939–941). As the Milliron's scheme was being designed, much publicity was given to the rooftop feature at Macy's Jamaica store (1946–1947), which became a well-known symbol of postwar retail expansion; see "Macy's Opens . . . ," *DSE* 10 (Oct. 1947), 85; "Macy's Jamaica . . . ," *RM* 42 (Oct. 1947), 13; "Macy's Jamaica . . . ," *AF* 88 (Feb. 1948), 100–104; and Parnes, *Planning Stores,* 75, 128. No other scheme approached the theatricality of Gruen's design.

55

According to Howard Drollinger, members of the architectural review committee consisted of Donald Ayres, president of the company; Hayden Worthington, head of Ayres's commercial property division and the key figure attracting well-known retailers to Westchester; Martin Hausman, a financial officer at Security Bank who subsequently joined the Ayres firm; and Charles Crawford, secretary to the Los Angeles Extension Company.

56

Drollinger interview.

57

Several examples are discussed in the text and/or notes below. For others, see *LATMN,* 1 Jan. 1949, 31; *VNN,* 24 Mar. 1949, II-1; "John Kurkjian . . . ," *VNN,* 2 May 1949, 7; "Roxbury Center . . . ," *LAT,* 7 Aug. 1949, V-4; "Community Shopping Center . . . ," *ESN,* 30 Aug. 1949, Progress Ed., 8; "Huge Community . . . ," *ESN,* 8 Aug. 1949, 2; "Encino Park Shopping . . . ," *LAT,* 16 Oct. 1949, V-2; "Construction Under Way . . . ," *VNN,* 6 Apr. 1950, I-4; "Extensive New Apartment . . . ," *LAT,* 9 Apr. 1950, V-1; "Business Center . . . ," *LAT,* 14 Oct. 1951, V-5; *LAT,* 8 June 1952, V-6; and "New Shopping Center . . . ," *LAT,* 2 Oct. 1952, V-6.

58

Hise, "Home Building," 95–96, 115–117, provides a good overview of the development. For period accounts, see "Built-in Salesmanship . . . ," *AF* 90 (Apr. 1949), 118–122; "Panorama City . . . ," *LAT,* 16 Oct. 1949, V-3; Frederick Faulkner, "Panorama City . . . ," *HDC,* 15 Sep. 1950; Ada Banks, "Infant of the Valley . . . ," *VT,* n.d. (ca. 1960), clipping in the collection of Bill Symonds, North Hollywood. For background on Kaiser Homes, see "Greatest House-Building Show on Earth," *AF* 86 (Mar. 1947), 105–113, 152, 154, 156.

59

The supermarket operation was owned by Morris Wisstein, co-owner of the facility at Windsor Hills. For discussion, see chapter 7. Burns's approach to shopping center development is discussed in "Greatest House-Building," 154.

  For accounts of early businesses, see "Distinctive New Panorama . . . ," *VNN,* 11 July 1949, 5; *LAT,* 5 Nov. 1949, I-7; "New Panorama Theater . . . ," *VNN,* 14 Nov. 1949, 2; "Work Starts . . . ," *VNN,* 27 Oct. 1949, II-2; "Panorama Theater . . . ," *VNN,* 26 Nov. 1949, I-2; "Panorama Cleaners . . . ," *VNN,* 15 Dec. 1949, 8; "Distinctive Panorama Theater . . . ," *VNN,* 19 Dec. 1949, I-1, 2, 4; "Panorama City . . . ," *LAT,* 8 Jan. 1950, V-2; *PCA* 77 (June 1950), 2; "Thrifty to Have . . . ," *LAT,* 17 Sep. 1950, V-3; "Thrifty Opening . . . ," *VNN,* 12 Mar. 1951, 7A; "Open New Stores . . . ," *VNN,* 7 May 1951, 1; *VNN,* 18 Mar. 1951, 1C; "Panorama Furniture Mart . . . ," *VNN,* 6 May 1953, 27; and "Security Bank . . . ," *VNN,* 8 May 1954, 1.

60

"Plans for $6,000,000 . . . ," *LAT,* 18 Apr. 1954, I-25; "Broadway Plans . . . ," *VNN,* 18 Apr. 1954, 1, 5; "Property Approved . . . ," *VNN,* 23 May 1954, 1; *LAT,* 9 Sep. 1955, I-29; "New Valley Development . . . ," *LAT,* 11 Sep. 1955, V-20; "Mandel Shoe Salon . . . ," *VNN,* 5 Oct. 1955, 17; "New Broadway Store . . . ," *LAT,* 5 Oct. 1955, I-18; "$6 Million Broadway-Valley . . . ," *VT,* 8 Oct. 1955, 3; "Silverwood's-Valley . . . ," *VT,* 8 Oct. 1955, 3; *LAT,* 10 Oct. 1955,

I-13; and McKeever, "Shopping Centers Re-Studied," 66–68. Later, a Robinson's branch was added; see "Opening of Robinsons . . . ," *VNN,* 25 June 1961, 22A.

61

Ballard interview. A more or less identical Broadway store opened concurrently at Anaheim that was more reflective of contemporary planning, though, since it was part of a regional mall; see chapter 11. The eastern part of the San Fernando Valley had a strategically located branch of the May Company, built at the same time, which precluded the Broadway from a site too far afield of Panorama City. The May Company store is discussed in the text below.

62

"New Shopping Center . . . ," *LAT,* 17 Oct. 1948, II-1; "$5,000,000 Shopping Center . . . ," *LAEx,* 17 Dec. 1948, I-9; "New Culver Center . . . ," *ESN,* 18 Dec. 1948, 2, 3; "Ground Broken . . . ," *ESN,* 12 Jan. 1949, 1; *ESN,* 30 Aug. 1949, 14; "First Stores . . . ," *ESN,* 30 Aug. 1949, 16; "New $5,000,000 . . . ," *ESN,* 28 Sep. 1949, 1; "Culver Center . . . ," *ESN,* 5 Oct. 1949, sect. 1; "Culver Center Opens . . . ," *LAEx,* 6 Oct. 1949, II-5; "Hordes of Culver Center . . . ," *ESN,* 6 Oct. 1949, 1; "Culver Center . . . ," *ESN,* 7 Oct. 1949, 1; "Six New Stores . . . ," *ESN,* 8 May 1950, 1; "Huge Grant Store . . . ," *ESN,* 10 May 1950, Culver Center Sect.; *LAT,* 12 May 1950, III-20.

63

Good examples include: the Bixby Knolls Shopping Center on Atlantic Avenue in Long Beach (begun 1948; see "New Bixby Knolls . . . ," *LAT,* 31 Oct. 1948, V-4; "$1,000,000 Store . . . ," *Long Beach Press Telegraph, Southland Magazine,* 21 May 1950, 12; and "Bixby Knolls . . . ," *Long Beach Independent,* 21 May 1950, 19-A); Pico-Westwood Shopping Center at Pico and Westwood boulevards in Los Angeles (1948–1950; see "Large Pico Shopping . . . ," *WHN,* 1 July 1947, 1; "New $5,000,000 . . . ," *LAT,* 14 Nov. 1948, V-1, 2; "Work to Start . . . ," *WHN,* 18 Nov. 1948, 1, 6; and "New Shopping Center . . . ," *SWBC* 114 [25 Nov. 1949], 30); and Rancho Santa Anita Shopping Center on W. Huntington Drive in Arcadia (1948–1950; see "Rancho Santa Anita . . . ," *LAT,* 14 Mar. 1948, 6; "Shopping Center Gives . . . ," *LAT,* 20 May 1950, I-14; *LAT,* 21 May 1950, V-7; and Baker and Funaro, *Shopping Centers,* 140–141).

64

This shift was more a matter of degree than of a fundamental change in thinking, and was seldom, if ever, stated explicitly in trade literature. The idea of the exterior as a neutral container is nonetheless intimated in numerous articles on the subject by the mid-1950s and often is overtly revealed in accompanying illustrations. In one handbook, Parnes, *Planning Stores,* the building exterior is not included among the topical categories of the text. Instead, the discussion addresses "zones," technics, and the "show window." Albert C. Martin, Jr., emphasized to me the change that occurred in the demands of many of his retail clients during the postwar years for as little expenditure as possible for building materials and far more attention on creating effective displays.

65

Concise synopses of this subject are Meredith Clausen, "Department Stores" and "Shopping Centers," in Wilkes, ed., *Encyclopedia,* 2: 217–218 and 4: 411, resp.

66

For contemporary accounts, see "Sears Store . . . ," *LAT,* 18 Oct. 1939, I-10; *LAT,* 19 Oct. 1939, IV-whole sect.; "Sears Largest . . . ," *BHC,* 20 Oct. 1939, 8; "Upside Down Has Parking On Roof," *CSA/AE* [16] (Jan. 1940), 16–17; "Store Building for Sears . . . ," *AF* 72 (Feb. 1940), 70–76; *A&E* 140 (Feb. 1940), 10; "Sears, Roebuck . . . ," *RM* 35 (15 Apr. 1940), 15–16; and Oliver Bowen, "Store for Sears in Los Angeles," *AC* 6:2 [1940], 7–9. The store was featured as a landmark of modernism in Elizabeth Mock, ed., *Built in U.S.A., 1932–1944* (New York: Museum of Modern Art, 1944), 110.

67

I am grateful to David Cameron for bringing to my attention the system used to facilitate rooftop parking at peak hours. The May Company's Wilshire Boulevard store also had a public address system—and uniform attendants stationed in each lane of the parking lot—to help customers find spaces; see "Controlling Parking Lot Traffic," *CSA/AE* [23] (Feb. 1947), 13.

68

An overview of the department's work during the prewar years is given in Boris Emet and John Jeuck, *Catalogues and Counters: A History of Sears, Roebuck and Company* (Chicago: University of Chicago Press, 1950), chap. 28. Concerning the Englewood store, see "Chain Stores Set the Pace . . . ," *CSA/GME* 10 (April 1934), 96; "Sears Builds Windowless Store," *CSA/GME* 10 (July 1934), 22–23, 54; "No Windows," *A&E* 120 (Feb. 1935), 35–38; and "Without Windows," *AF* 62 (Mar. 1935), 206–211. Albert C. Martin, Jr., noted that, in his office, windows were considered a nuisance in department store planning by the 1930s. His firm's approach for the May Company Wilshire store was to use peripheral areas for storage, dressing rooms, and other spaces that did not require natural light (interview). Stiles Clements used much the same technique in his design for Coulter's.

69

"Store Building for Sears," 74. Raben was given credit in contemporary accounts for the design concept of the store. He had worked in the department almost from its inception. Previously he worked for Jock Peters on the interiors of Bullock's Wilshire and for Universal Studios; see "Sears' Own Designers . . . ," *LAT,* 19 Oct. 1939, IV-7.

External appearance seems to have been considered more than the designers would later admit. At the time of announcement, not long before construction began, the elevations were far more conventional in nature. Since the configuration was essentially the same in the executed scheme, formal design concerns probably had a decisive effect on the outcome. See "New Sears Unit . . . ," *WWD,* 2 Dec. 1938, 1, 20; and "Store Project . . . ," *LAT,* 4 Dec. 1938, V-2.

70

Coverage in postwar books includes Ketchum, *Shops & Stores,* 262–265; and Parnes, *Planning Stores,* 75, 114–155, 190–191.

71

"Bullock's Pasadena . . . ," *SWBC* 105 (5 Jan. 1945), 33–34; "Store of the Future," *DSE* 8 (Mar. 1945), 43; "Bullock's-Pasadena . . . ," *WWD,* 22 Aug. 1947, 7; "Bullock's New Pasadena Store . . . ," *LAT,* 10 Sep. 1947, II-1; *AD* 12 (Sep. 1947), 103–124; "Bullock's Pasadena . . . ," *SWBC* 110 (26 Sep. 1947), 8–11, 22; "A Store for the Carriage Trade . . . ," *AF* 88 (May 1948), 102–105; Ketchum,

Shops & Stores, 260–263; Baker and Funaro, *Shopping Centers,* 164–167; idem, *Parking,* 128–129.

72

Another important design in this regard was the considerably smaller facility erected by Lord & Taylor near White Plains, New York; see "Lord & Taylor's Westchester Store," *AR* 103 (Apr. 1943), 111–122; "Parking Area Determines Store Location," *DSE* 11 (May 1948), 74–75; and Baker and Funaro, *Shopping Centers,* 167.

73

For background, see Richard Longstreth, "The Perils of a Parkless Town," in Martin Wachs and Margaret Crawford, eds., *The Car and the City: The Automobile, the Built Environment, and Daily Urban Life* (Ann Arbor: University of Michigan Press, 1992), 141–153, 310–313; idem, "Innovation without Paradigm: The Many Creators of the Drive-In Market," in Thomas Carter, ed., *Images of an American Land: Vernacular Architecture Studies in the Western United States* (Albuquerque: University of New Mexico Press, forthcoming); and idem, *Drive-Ins, Supermarkets, and Reorganization of Commercial Space in Los Angeles,* forthcoming).

74

Some background is given in Jackson Mayers, "Development of Valley Plaza . . . ," *VT,* 1 May 1956, 5. I am grateful to Bill Symonds for providing many additional insights on his father's career and on the development of Valley Plaza (interviews, Los Angeles, 4 and 11 June 1992). As part of the Symonds Real Estate company records, Bill Symonds and his brothers have saved a large collection of plans, photographs, promotional materials, and texts of presentations related to the first decade of Valley Plaza's development. This material affords a rare view of both the design's evolution and its developer's concerns. Mr. Symonds generously gave me free access to the contents.

Bob Symonds visited the Country Club Plaza (discussed in chapter 6), but no evidence has surfaced indicating when. His presentation texts confirm a veneration of the Kansas City shopping center. He could have learned about the complex prior to a visit from the extensive coverage it received in national real estate and building magazines.

A portfolio, ca. 1947, entitled "A Major Trend in Merchandising and Distribution Casts Its Shadow," which Symonds assembled to help persuade retailers and others to participate in the Valley Plaza project, discusses a number of examples, including the North Shore Center near Beverly, Massachusetts (discussed in chapter 11); Bellevue Square, near Seattle; the Broadway-Crenshaw Center; Ridgeway Shopping Center in Stamford, Connecticut; City Line Center in Philadelphia; and Hillsdale Shopping Center in San Mateo, California, among others. With the exception of Bellvue, all the examples were either in the planning or construction stages when the material was gathered.

75

To my knowledge, freeway location did not again become a central factor in siting a regional shopping center in the metropolitan area until after the Korean War, as discussed in chapter 11. One of the very few early regional centers planned elsewhere with freeway location in mind was the North Shore Center cited in note 74 above.

76

According to Bill Symonds (interviews), Hollingsworth purchased the tract from a house builder who had already started work on some dwellings. Hollingsworth had extensive real estate holdings throughout the region and considered Symonds an inferior, even though his own project would derive much of its trade from the groundwork Symonds had created. For his part, Symonds included the Hollingsworth tract in figures of Valley Plaza's acreage, stores, and car lot capacity. In 1954, Hollingsworth sold the half-block south of Kittridge Street to Philip Lyon, formerly one of the Main Streeters, who worked cooperatively with Symonds in both developing and managing the parcel. I am grateful to Philip Lyon for sharing insights on this aspect of the complex (interview, Los Angeles, 7 Apr. 1988).

For contemporary accounts of the Hollingsworth project, see "New Structure Rising . . . ," *LAT,* 5 Aug. 1951, V-7; "Building Will Be . . . ," *LAT,* 2 Sep. 1951, V-10; and "Thrifty Opens . . . ," *LAEx,* 7 Aug. 1952, I-16. Concerning Lyon's development, see "Valley Plaza . . . ," *LAT,* 13 June 1954, V-7; and "Giant Plaza . . . ," *LAEx,* 13 June 1954, III-1, 8.

77

Namely the City Line Center at Philadelphia and the Shore Shopping Center at Euclid, Ohio. See Baker and Funaro, *Shopping Centers,* 134–136; Harry Martin and Vincent Kling, "Shore Shopping Center . . . ," *CSA/AE* [23] (May 1947), 14–17; and Ernest Payer, "Euclid's New Shopping Center," *SMM* 12 (July 1947), 60–62, 64. See also note 81 below.

78

According to Philip Lyon, Sears played a decisive role in determining Valley Plaza's layout. Bill Symonds, on the other hand, primarily recalled Sears's coy attitude toward his father's overtures for several years. The company had not agreed to build before the development of Clements's plan. Symonds had to petition for a zoning change in order to provide the front lots, a move that appears to have been closely related to Sears's final commitment to proceed. See "Zoning for $20,000,000 . . . ," *VT,* 19 Nov. 1948, 1; and "25,000,000 Store Center . . . ," *VNN,* 28 Mar. 1949, 6.

79

Concerning the smaller complexes, see Richard Longstreth, "The Neighborhood Shopping Center in Washington, D.C., 1930–1941," *JSAH* 51 (March 1992), 5–34.

80

Community Builders Handbook; Baker and Funaro, *Shopping Centers,* 31–32; Smith, *Shopping Centers,* 68. Valley Plaza included "rear" lots, but the arrangement primarily served a second group of stores, not the front range.

81

For other contemporary examples, see "One-Stop Centers," 24; "Pace-Setters for Shopping," *NREJ* 52 (July 1951), 20–21; "Selling on a Curve," *CSA/AE* [26] (Oct. 1950), 49; Baker and Funaro, *Shopping Centers,* 118–121, 124–125; and Arthur Rubloff, "Design for Shopping," *NREJ* 53 (Mar. 1952), 26–28.

82

Concerning the Westwood store, see chapter 6. Concerning the Country Club Plaza unit, see *WWD,* 17 Apr. 1946, 47. On the Cameron Village store (1949–1950), see [Raleigh] *News and Observer,* 15 Nov. 1949, 1; *News and Observer,* 17

Nov. 1949, II-whole sect.; Baker and Funaro, *Shopping Centers,* 147–160; and McKeever, "Shopping Centers Re-Studied," 90–92. Sears continued to be somewhat cautious about expanding into the shopping center arena. By December 1955, the company had stores in only a few additional centers: one in the Los Angeles area, two in the Midwest, and three in southeastern Pennsylvania. See Hyman, "Shopping Center," II-6, 34, 40. Not until the 1960s was such development pursued aggressively; see Gordon Weil, *Sears, Roebuck, U.S.A.: The Great American Catalogue Store and How It Grew* (New York: Stein and Day, 1977), 115–116.

83

Concerning the Compton store, see "Sears, Roebuck . . . ," *LAT,* 1 May 1947, I-6; *LAT,* 2 Sep. 1947, I-7; and "Sears Constructs Modern Machine for Selling," *CSA/AE* [23] (Sep. 1947), 14–17, 43. Concerning the Inglewood store, see note 50 above.

84

For contemporary accounts, see "Sears Will Build . . . ," *VNN,* 15 Jan. 1949; "Break Ground . . . ," *VNN,* 19 May 1949; "Start Work . . . ," *VT,* 17 June 1949; "Contract Let . . . ," *LAT,* 23 May 1950, II-8; "A Store and a Community," *VT,* 25 Aug. 1951, 10; "New Structure Rising . . . ," *LAT,* 5 Aug. 1951, V-7; "Conveyor Belt Aid . . . ," *VT,* 6 Sep. 1951, 10; "Wednesday Opening . . . ," *LAT,* 9 Sep. 1951, II-8; "Preview Staged . . . ," *LAT,* 12 Sep. 1951, I-25.

85

Sears owned its front lot and gave Symonds legal assistance in establishing the Valley Plaza Improvement Association, which oversaw operation, maintenance, and improvement of all lots north of Victory Boulevard. A similar group, the Valley Plaza Triangle Association, was created for the large lot south of Victory (Symonds interviews). Retention of control over building exteriors by Symonds Real Estate, Inc., has enabled Valley Plaza to remain one of the least altered shopping centers of the period in the United States.

86

For contemporary accounts, see "Valley Plaza Expected . . . ," *Valley Advertiser,* 1 Feb. 1951, 1; "Huge Valley Plaza . . . ," *North Hollywood Chamber of Commerce News* 4 (June 1951), 1, 2; "M'Daniel's Will Open . . . ," *LAT,* 12 Sep. 1951, I-31; "New Bank Approved . . . ," *VT,* 11 Dec. 1952, 1, 2; "Occidental Bank . . . ," *VT,* 23 June 1953, 3; "Work Starts . . . ," *LAT,* 28 June 1953, I-9; "Huge Development . . . ," *HDC,* 4 Mar. 1955, 1; and "Construction Begins . . . ," *LAT,* 1 Sep. 1957, II-18.

87

"9-Story Tower . . . ," *LAT,* 24 Jan. 1960, VI-4. Each office floor in the Valley Plaza Tower had only around 800 square feet of usable office space, rendering the scheme a latter-day version of the Wilshire Tower Building on the Miracle Mile, discussed in chapter 5. Office facilities were developed by others in the vicinity, however, as a result of Valley Plaza's draw.

88

Symonds interviews. For accounts of the store, see "May Co. to Construct . . . ," *VNN,* 25 Feb. 1954, 1; "Commission Delays Decision . . . ," *VNN,* 7 Mar. 1954, 1; "Plan Immediate . . . ," *VNN,* 28 Mar. 1954, 1, 4B; "May Co. Starts . . . ," *VT,* 26 June 1954, 2; "May Co. Starts . . . ," *VNN,* 27 June 1954, 1, 3. Three years later, Symonds secured plans for a 100,000-square-foot J. C. Penney store on the

site once reserved for May; see "Large Structure . . . ," *LAT,* 20 Oct. 1957, VI-17; "New Store . . . ," *LAT,* 13 Apr. 1958, VI-18; and *LAEx,* 29 Jan. 1959, I-10.

89

"Parking Area Gets Approval," *LAT,* 29 Oct. 1950, V-8. Restrictions on building materials during the Korean War probably led to a delay in the project, which began some two years later; see "Construction to Start . . . ," *LAT,* 8 Oct. 1952, V-2. Units were added to the complex ca. 1954, ca. 1956, and ca. 1964.

90

The complex has often been criticized for intruding on the estate. Wright's plans for the property called for a range of artisans' shops and apartments fronting Hollywood Boulevard. A theater was to be in the area later occupied by Barnsdall Square; see Kathryn Smith, *Frank Lloyd Wright, Hollyhock House and Olive Hill* (New York: Rizzoli, 1992), chap. 9.

91

See, for example, "Parklabrea's Final Unit . . . ," *LAT,* 9 Mar. 1952, V-4 (also by Clements); "Contract Given . . . ," *LAT,* 16 Nov. 1952, V-1; "New Shopping Center . . . ," *LAT,* 2 Oct. 1952, V-6; "Whittier Area . . . ," *LAT,* 24 Jan. 1953, V-9; "Large Business Area . . . ," *LAT,* 12 Apr. 1953, V-5; "$6,000,000 Shopping Center . . . ," *LAT,* 18 Oct. 1953, V-9; "New Shopping Center . . . ," *LAT,* 6 Dec. 1953, V-9; *LAT,* 13 Dec. 1953, V-7; "Large Shopping Center . . . ," *LAT,* 10 Jan. 1954, V-12; "Valley Shopping Center . . . ," *LAT,* 7 Feb. 1954, V-9; "First Unit . . . ," *LAT,* 16 May 1954, V-16; "$2,000,000 Shopping Center . . . ," *LAT,* 20 June 1954, V-4; "Plans Prepared . . . ," *LAT,* 18 July 1954, V-13; "New $2,000,000 Center . . . ," *LAT,* 25 July 1954, V-11; and "Further Development . . . ," *LAT,* 12 Sep. 1954, V-1, 6.

92

The interdependence of factors affecting the development of a shopping center plan as well as the importance of parking as a primary determinant are clearly indicated in trade literature of the early 1950s, such as *Community Builders Handbook,* 99–156; Baker and Funero, *Shopping Centers,* 28–54; McKeever, "Shopping Centers," 15–23; *Home Builders Manual for Land Development,* rev. ed. (Washington: National Assoc. of Home Builders, 1953), 180–198; and Smith, *Shopping Centers,* 31–33, 50–73. Such concerns are also reflected in numerous articles, such as Davis Jackson, "Parking Needs in the Development of Shopping Centers," *Traffic Quarterly* 5 (Jan. 1951), 32–37; McReynolds, "Planning Suburban Shopping Centers," 90–104; Kenneth Welch, "Regional Shopping Centers," *AR* 109 (Mar. 1951), 128–129; Victor Gruen and Lawrence Smith, "Shopping Centers: The New Building Type," *PP* 33 (June 1952), 82–90; "Shopping Center Requires . . . ," *WWD,* 20 Nov. 1953, 42; and Harry Martin, "Parking Points That Make the Difference," *CSA/AE* [30] (May 1954), 20–25.

X *Grass on Main Street*

1

The quotes are drawn from two related articles: the piece focusing on Syracuse ("New Buildings for 194X," *AF* 78 [May 1943], 70, and one focusing on a southern California complex that is discussed at length toward the end of this chapter ("'Grass on Main Street' Becomes a Reality; Shopping Center, Linda Vista, Cali-

fornia," *AF* 81 [Sep. 1944], 83). The introductory paragraphs of the latter were clearly written as a restatement of ideas presented in the former, and thus I have taken the liberty to intersperse them.

The Syracuse plan was cosponsored by the *Forum* and *Fortune* and involved a number of national as well as local organizations; see "Syracuse Plans Its Future," *Planning 1944* (Chicago: American Society of Planning Officials, 1944), 182–194.

2

Gruen's plan is illustrated in Ogden Tanner, "Closed to Traffic," *AF* 110 (Feb. 1958), 93. For a useful catalogue of executed urban malls, see Roberto Branbilla et al., *American Urban Malls: A Compendium* (Washington: Government Printing Office, 1977). See also chapter 11 below.

3

LAT, 31 July 1922, I-7; *LAT,* 13 Aug. 1922, V-7; *LAT,* 20 Aug. 1922, V-5; *LAT,* 10 Sep. 1922, V-4; *LAT,* 24 Sep. 1922, V-6; *LAT,* 1 Oct. 1922, V-7; *LAT,* 20 May 1923, V-6; *LAT,* 19 Aug. 1923, V-6; Ellen Leech, "Land Development— Carthay Center," *CS* 5 (Nov. 1923), 19; "Carthay Is Lauded . . . ," *LAT,* 30 Sep. 1923, V-7; "Store Center . . . ," *LAEx,* 30 Mar. 1924, IV-5; *LAT,* 6 Apr. 1924, V-5.

4

Concerning the Caltech plan, see Richard Oliver, *Bertram Grosvenor Goodhue* (New York and Cambridge: Architectural History Foundation and MIT Press, 1983), 156–158; and *Caltech 1910–1950: An Urban Architecture for Southern California* (Pasadena: Baxter Art Gallery, California Institute of Technology, 1983). Winslow was associated with Goodhue on the 1915 Panama-California Exposition in San Diego and the Los Angeles Public Library (1921–1926). Winslow surely would have been familiar with the Tyrone plan discussed in chapter 6.

5

These precincts are discussed in chapters 2, 7, and 5, respectively.

6

Concerning the theater, see *LAT,* 1 June 1924, V-6; "Wilshire Gets . . . ," *LAT,* 22 Feb. 1925, V-5; "New Theater . . . ," *LAT,* 16 Aug. 1925, V-1; "Theater Work . . . ," *LAT,* 6 Dec. 1925, V-3; "Pioneer Spirit . . . ," *LAT,* 16 May 1926, III-19, 21; "Carthay Center . . . ," *BHC,* 20 May 1926, I-1; Dwight Gibbs, "The Carthay Circle Theatre," *A&E* 95 (Jan. 1928), 63–66; Harris Allen, "Theatrical Theaters," *PCA* 35 (Jan. 1929), 18–20; and "Fox Carthay Circle . . . ," *BHC,* 12 May 1939, 16. McCarthy vehemently opposed zoning changes on Wilshire discussed in chapter 5.

7

For background, see Johann Friedrich Giest, *Arcades: The History of a Building Type* (Cambridge: MIT Press, 1985), although the focus there is primarily on Europe. Giest lists four U.S. examples from the 1820s, in Providence, New York, Philadelphia, and Stonington, Connecticut.

8

Little research has been done on the subject. Giest, *Arcades,* cites seven U.S. examples: two in Cleveland, and one each in Cincinnati, Indianapolis, New York, St. Paul, and the company town of Pullman in Chicago. Other examples were built in Portland, Maine; Philadelphia; Washington, D.C.; Dayton, Ohio; Lexington, Kentucky; Aurora, Illinois; Kansas City and St. Louis, Missouri; and San Fran-

cisco, in addition to the Mercantile Arcade in Los Angeles, discussed in the text below. Systematic survey would no doubt reveal many others. The Cleveland Arcade is the best known among them; see Geist, *Arcades,* 237–244; and Eric Johannesen, *Cleveland Architecture 1876–1976* (Cleveland: Western Reserve Historical Society, 1979), 32–37. Concerning others, see Geist, *Arcades,* 283–284; Edward Wolner, "Design and Civic Identity in Cincinnati's Carew Tower Complex," *JSAH* 51 (Mar. 1992), 44; "The Scarritt Arcade," booklet, Landmarks Commission of Kansas City, Missouri, ca. 1980; Robert Stern et al., *New York 1900: Metropolitan Architecture and Urbanism 1890–1915* (New York: Rizzoli, 1983), 194–195; "Plan Shopping Arcade," *Washington Post,* 21 July 1907, III-3; "Evans Building Arcade . . . ," *Evening Star* [Washington], 5 Aug. 1911, II-2; "New Four Story . . . ," *WWD,* 31 May 1924, 18; "Chapman Arcade . . . ," *WWD,* 6 Oct. 1924, 26; "Denton-Ross-Todd Co. . . . ," *WWD,* 3 Nov. 1924, 24; "3-Story Block . . . ," *WWD,* 26 Nov. 1924, 38; "New Philadelphia Arcade . . . ," *WWD,* 14 Apr. 1926, 6; "Erection of Arcade . . . ," *WWD,* 30 Oct. 1926, 3; "Walnut Street Lot . . . ," *Philadelphia Inquirer,* 20 Feb. 1927, 20W; "Open-Air Business . . . ," *Philadelphia Inquirer,* 24 Apr. 1927, 16W; *WWD,* 10 Aug. 1927, 10; and "Surplus Space . . . ," *WWD,* 23 June 1928, 13. In its revived form, the arcade seldom, if ever, attained the high status enjoyed by counterparts in cities abroad such as Milan, Prague, or Vienna.

9

The quotes are taken from advertisements in *LAT:* 27 Sep. 1927, II-8; 12 Oct. 1923, II-8; 18 Oct. 1923, II-8; 24 Oct. 1923, I-7; and 1 Jan. 1924, V-32. Accounts of the scheme include "Arcade Design Received," *LAT,* 10 Jan. 1923, II-1, 3; *LAT,* 14 Jan. 1923, V-1; "Mercantile Building . . . ," *LAT,* 21 Oct. 1923, V-3; "To Be Opened . . . ," *LAT,* 10 Feb. 1924, V-7; "Great Arcade Opens . . . ," *LAT,* 15 Feb. 1924, I-9 to 13; and "New Big Arcade . . . ," *WWD,* 25 Feb. 1924, 41.

10

For discussion, see chapter 11.

11

The origins of shopping facilities arranged with stalls opening onto some form of passage used principally, if not exclusively, by pedestrians can, of course, be traced to antiquity. I am unaware, however, of any permanent building complexes built in the United States prior to World War I that were designed as a whole and arranged around open spaces from which vehicles were excluded. Two projects were undertaken in the 1920s by Addison Mizner in Palm Beach; see Donald Curl, *Mizner's Florida: American Resort Architecture* (New York and Cambridge: Architectural History Foundation and MIT Press, 1984), 112–115. See also John Stamper, *Chicago's North Michigan Avenue: Planning and Development, 1900–1930* (Chicago: University of Chicago Press, 1991), 110–113.

12

For discussions and examples, see "The Use of the Patio . . . ," *CS* 6 (Sep. 1924), 25; G. Whitecross Ritchie, "A New Type of Shops," *AA* 129 (5 Feb. 1926), 245–249; "Studio Shops . . . ," *HDC,* 21 Mar. 1925, 8; "Arcade Building . . . ," *SWBC* 68 (16 July 1926), 43; "Shops on New Building . . . ," *BHC,* 26 May 1927, 4-B; "Studio Building . . . ," *LAT,* 3 July 1927, V-8; "Shopping Court . . . ," *HDC,* 23 July 1927, 10; "Thompson Spanish Shopping Court . . . ," *HDC,* 25 July 1927, 9; "Spanish Shopping Center . . . ," *HDC,* 6 Aug. 1927, 13; "Greer, Inc. . . . ," *WWD,* 15 Aug. 1927, I-2; "Mary Helen Tea Room . . . ," *HDC/HES,* 4 Nov. 1927, 9; Zoe Battu, "In Discussion of Shop Courts," *PCA* 33 (July 1928), 15–22,

47; *SWBC* 72 (10 Aug. 1928), 37; Perry Newberry, "El Paseo Building at Car-
mel," *A&E* 95 (Oct. 1928), 99–101; Zoe Battu, "The Court 'El Paseo' of Car-
mel," *PCA* 33 (Oct. 1928), 35–38, 48; "The Influence of Old Spain as Reflected
in Modern California Architecture," *AA* 134 (20 Dec. 1928), 811–816; Hunter
Scott, "How Natives Live," *LATMN,* 1 Jan. 1929, I-19, 20; Marc Goodman, "An
Architect's Studio," *A&E* 99 (Dec. 1929), 90–97; "El Paseo Shops and Studios,
Palm Springs," *PCA* 39 (Feb. 1931), 45, 61; "Early California Patio . . . ," *LAT,*
5 Apr. 1931, V-3; "Business Court . . . ," *LAT,* 28 June 1931, V-4; "Building
Spurt . . . ," *LAT,* 12 July 1931, V-3; *A&E* 106 (Sep. 1931), 31; "Unique
Shops . . . ," *LAT,* 11 Oct. 1931, V-2; and *AF* 55 (July 1931), 27–30.

Among the earliest and most celebrated examples was El Paseo at Santa Barbara (1922–1923); see Irving Morrow, "A Step in California Architecture," *A&E*
70 (Aug. 1922), 102–103; Mrs. James Osborn Craig, "The Heritage of All California," *CS* 4 (Sep. 1922), 7–9; M. U. Seares, "Building de la Guerra Plaza . . . ," *CS*
6 (Apr. 1924), 13; Harris Allen, "The 'Street in Spain,' Santa Barbara, California,"
PCA 27 (Mar. 1925), 23–29; *CS* 7 (June 1925), 7; "Santa Barbara's Street in
Spain," *CS* 8 (Mar. 1926), 15–18; "Santa Barbara Realizing . . . ," *LAT,* 6 Feb.
1927, II-1, 2; David Gebhard, *Santa Barbara—The Creation of a New Spain in
America* (Santa Barbara: University Art Museum, University of California, Santa
Barbara, 1982), 18, 42–43; and Kevin Starr, *Material Dreams: Southern California
through the 1920s* (New York: Oxford University Press, 1990), 282–283.

Another scheme was designed with the rather awkward combination of patio
and driveway to a rear parking area; see "Arcade Brings Tenants of Character,"
PSN, 6 Dec. 1927, 30–31; "Original New Arcade Attracts Shoppers," *California
Life,* 1 Jan. 1928, 22–23; V. Cahalin, "Adding Romance to Trade," *Building Age* 50
(Apr. 1928), 217–219; and R. W. Sexton, *American Commercial Buildings of Today*
(New York: Architectural Book Pub. Co., 1928), 199, 202.

13

Variations on the shopping court idea were built in southern California through
the 1940s; see, for example, "Arts and Crafts Center," *PCA* 66 (Dec. 1944),
32–33; *LAT,* 9 Jan. 1949, V-4; and Geoffrey Baker and Bruno Funaro, *Shopping
Centers: Design and Operation* (New York: Reinhold, 1951), 102–103. The intimate
spaces of the shopping court were combined with the larger scale and tenant mix
characteristic to many postwar shopping centers in the Town & Country Village
Shops at Sacramento (1945–1947); see "Making Your Shopping Center Distinctive," *NREJ* 49 (Apr. 1948), 24–25; and Baker and Funaro, *Shopping Centers,*
98–101.

14

Locating a union station adjacent to the Plaza was proposed as early as 1911 but
was not finalized until 1939; see Scott Bottles, *Los Angeles and the Automobile:
The Making of the Modern City* (Berkeley and Los Angeles: University of California
Press, 1987), chap. 5; and Bill Bradley, *The Last of the Great Stations: 40 Years of
the Los Angeles Union Passenger Terminal* (Glendale, Calif.: Interurban Publications,
1979), chap. 3.

15

W. W. Robinson, *Los Angeles from the Days of the Pueblo,* rev. ed. (San Francisco:
California Historical Society, 1981), 101. See also Christine Sterling, *Olvera Street,
Its History and Restoration* (Los Angeles: Adobe Studios, 1933); Charles Hosmer,
Preservation Comes of Age: From Williamsburg to the National Trust, 1926–1949, 2
vols. (Charlottesville: University Press of Virginia, 1981), 1: 423–425; "El Paseo's

Fete . . . ," *LAT,* 19 Apr. 1930, II-1; "Throngs Inspect . . . ," *LAT,* 20 Apr. 1930, II-1, 3; Dorothea Oyer, "El Paseo de Los Angeles Is Restored," *PCA* 38 (Oct. 1930), 46–47, 51, 52; "Los Angeles Reaches 150," *National Republic* 19 (Sep. 1931), 28–29; *LAT,* 12 Dec. 1934, II-2; *LAT,* 13 Dec. 1934, II-9; and *LAT,* 14 Dec. 1934, II-12.

16

By 1935, Olvera Street was used along with a view of Seventh and Broadway as icons of Los Angeles for the *WWD* masthead in the section on regional trends. See also *LAT,* 31 July 1946, I-7.

Repeated efforts, many of them spearheaded by Sterling, were made to expand the precinct to include the other blocks around the Plaza. See "Historic Links . . . ," *LAT,* 27 Aug. 1934, II-1, 2; "Revised Plaza . . . ," *LAT,* 3 Feb. 1947, II-1, 3; *LAT,* 3 Mar. 1947, I-3; "Olvera Street . . . ," *LAT,* 12 Apr. 1948, II-1, 2; *LAT,* 22 July 1949, I-3; "Romantic Adobes . . . ," *LAT,* 22 July 1949, II-1, 2; "Historic Lugo House . . . ," *LAT,* 26 July 1949, II-1, 6; "Many Agencies . . . ," *LAT,* 29 July 1949, II-1; and "Saving the Los Angeles Plaza," *LAT,* 23 Mar. 1950, II-4.

Olvera Street also provided a source of inspiration for at least two other thematically organized commercial development projects nearby, Japanese Town and China City, neither of which was realized. Sterling was involved in devising the latter, which was to rise one block from Olvera Street. See "Picturesque Japanese Town . . . ," *LAT,* 4 Aug. 1935, I-16, 17; *LAT,* 17 Aug. 1937, II-1; and "Harry Carr Memorial . . . ," *LAT,* 3 Oct. 1937, V-1, 3.

17

Robert Derrah, "Unique Architectural Treatment . . . ," *SWBC* 88 (13 Nov. 1936), 13. For other contemporary accounts, see "Construction Nearing . . . ," *HDC,* 16 Oct. 1935, 13; "'Cross-Roads of the World' . . . ," *HDC,* 11 Feb. 1936, 9; "World Crossroads Project . . . ," *LAT,* 13 Oct. 1936, V-5; "'Crossroads of the World' . . . ," *HDC,* 28 Oct. 1936, 9; "Cosmopolitan Wares . . . ," *HDC,* 29 Oct. 1936, 11; *LAT,* 29 Oct. 1936, I-6; "'Crossroads . . . ,'" *WWD,* 13 Nov. 1936, I-10A; *LATMN,* 1 Jan. 1937, IV-20; *PCA* 51 (Jan. 1937), 24–25; "First Anniversary . . . ," *HDC,* 27 Oct. 1937, 11; and J. Edward Tufft, "A Unique and Successful Shopping Center," *NREJ* 39 (Mar. 1938), 46–47. Among the original tenants were A. J. Mathieu Co. (wine, liqueurs, imported foods), Peasant House and Garden (imported furnishings, gift items), Jack B. Rohan (foreign and domestic newspapers and magazines), Ann Herbert (chocolates), DuLaine-Bennati (women's clothing, fabrics), Marcy de Paris (perfume), Fashion-Fold (men's handkerchiefs), Macdonald-Meyers (oriental art, gifts, wallpaper), Worthwhile Hand Knitting Shop, the Barber of Seville, El Fumador De Seville (tobacco), Billie's (women's wear), A Bit of Sweden (restaurant), Traders in Treasures (art, jewelry), Don's Beauty Salon, Jax Secretarial Service, Pan-American Fellowship, and Burr McIntosh—"the cheerful philosopher."

18

For illustration, see *Official Pictures of a Century of Progress Exposition* (Chicago: Reuben H. Donnelley Corp., 1933), n.p. Trade literature of the period makes clear that the Chicago exposition had a consequential impact on retail architecture of the 1930s, especially on the acceptance of streamlined imagery. The importance of earlier midway attractions for roadside commercial architecture is discussed in Barbara Rubin, "Aesthetic Ideology and Urban Design," *AAG* 69 (Sep. 1979), 339–361; reprinted in Dell Upton and John Michael Vlach, eds., *Common Places: Readings in American Vernacular Architecture* (Athens: University of Georgia Press,

1986), 482–508. The impact that world's fairs may have had on the shopping mall deserves further study.

The fact that Crossroads lay near to several movie studio sets may also have contributed to the design. See, for example, "Lost Glories of Filmland . . . ," and "Fox Building 'Dream House,'" *HDC,* 3 Nov. 1932, 3, 7.

19

Tufft, "Unique and Successful," 46.

20

For background, see William Koch, "Farmers Market Defies Tradition," *SMM* 6 (June 1941), 8–10, 12; "A Dozen Restaurants under One Roof," *Pacific Coast Record* 40 (Sep. 1949), 29–33; Ralph Hancock, *Fabulous Boulevard* (New York: Funk & Wagnalls, 1949), 279–282; and Baker and Funaro, *Shopping Centers,* 94–95.

21

The scheme was originally conceived as a sizable, cash-and-carry department store; see "Unique Gilmore Village . . . ," *BHC,* 29 Nov. 1940, 14; "Gilmore Area . . . ," *LAT,* 1 Dec. 1940, V-1; and "Retail Revolution?" *BW,* 21 Dec. 1940, 31–32. Over the next several months, the project was completely recast; see "Work Progressing . . . ," *BHC,* 11 July 1941, 1; and "Stores Project . . . ," *LAT,* 13 July 1941, V-2.

22

For examples, see Editorial Staff of Sunset Magazine and Books, *Western Ranch Houses by Cliff May* (Menlo Park, Calif.: Lane Pub. Co., 1958); and David Gebhard and Harriette von Breton, *L.A. in the Thirties, 1931–1941* (Santa Barbara and Salt Lake City: Peregrine Smith, 1975), 110–111, 125, 131, 134.

23

For examples, see "Pacific Ranch Market . . . ," *SWW,* 6 May 1938, 23; Willis Parker, "'Farm' Super-Markets Catch Suburban Highway Trade," *CSA/GE* 14 (Aug. 1938), 18–19, 36, 38; *SWW,* 25 Aug. 1939, 21; and "Ranch Market Opening Lively Event," *SMM* 4 (Dec. 1939), 12.

24

Concerning the Producers Public Market, see "Sooner or Later . . . ," *SWW,* 2 July 1937, 6, 7; *SWW,* 29 June 1937, 6; *LAT,* 19 Sep. 1937, I-5; *SWW,* 30 Nov. 1937, 7; and "Long Beach Farmers . . . ," *SWW,* 29 Apr. 1938, 161. On Marketplace, see "Huge Market Project . . . ," *BHC,* 20 Oct. 1939, 1; *BHC,* 30 May 1941, II-5; "Work Starts . . . ," *BHC,* 6 June 1941, II-6; and *BHC,* 12 Dec. 1941, 7. On the Town and Country, see *HDC,* 30 Aug. 1941, 8; "Work Will Start . . . ," *LAT,* 31 Aug. 1941, I-10; *LAT,* 7 Sep. 1941, V-3; Charles Cohan, "Fairfax Ave. . . . ," *LAT,* 14 Sep. 1941, V-1; *BHC,* 1 May 1942, 58–59; "Novel New Market . . . ," *BHC,* 15 May 1942, 10; *BHC,* 22 May 1942, 5; *BHC,* 29 May 1942, 8; "Community of Markets," *PCA* 59 (May 1942), 42–53; *BHC,* 12 June 1942, II-10; *BHC,* 26 June 1942, II-12; Will Rutledge, "100 Shops Form Cooperative Super," *SMM* 7 (Aug. 1942), 52–53; and *LAT,* 17 Feb. 1949, I-20.

25

For other examples, see "Super Develops New Advertising Approach," *SMM* 6 (Mar. 1941), 8, 10, 12, 14; "Market Town," *VNN,* 6 Oct. 1947, 3; "200,000 Visitors . . . ," *VNN,* 9 Oct. 1947, I-1, 8, 18, 19; "California Does It Again," *SMM* 13

(Sep. 1948), 114, 116; "Country Mart . . . ," *WHN,* 4 Nov. 1948, 6, 12; *WHN,*
11 Nov. 1948, 17; *LAT,* 5 Dec. 1948, V-2; *LAT,* 24 Feb. 1950, I-17; and Baker
and Funaro, *Shopping Centers,* 96–99.

26

The other scheme was for the unrealized Resettlement Administration community
at Greenbrook, New Jersey, discussed in the text below.

27

Clarence Stein, *Toward New Towns for America,* reprint ed. (Cambridge: MIT Press,
1971), 150. The most definitive scholarly account of Greenbelt is Joseph Arnold,
The New Deal in the Suburbs: A History of the Greenbelt Town Program 1935–1954
(Columbus: Ohio State University Press, 1971). See also Leslie Gene Hunter,
"Greenbelt, Maryland: A City on a Hill," *Maryland Historical Magazine* 65 (June
1968), 105–136. Stein's retrospective view in *Toward New Towns* (118–177) is of
great value. Other important accounts by participants are O. Kline Fulmer, *Greenbelt* (Washington: American Council on Public Affairs, 1941); and George Warner,
Greenbelt: The Cooperative Community (New York: Exposition Press, 1954). Some
contemporary writings that shed light on the ideas that lay behind the project and
how the results were received positively include: Albert Mayer, "Green-belt
Towns for the Machine Age," *New York Times Magazine,* 2 Feb. 1936, 8–9, 18;
Albert Mayer, "The Greenbelt Towns: What and Why," *ACi* 51 (May 1936),
59–61; Henry Churchill, "America's Town Planning Begins," *New Republic* 87 (3
June 1936), 96–98; Duncan Aikman, " 'Tugwelltown' . . . ," *Current History* 44
(Aug. 1936), 96–101; John Dreier, "Greenbelt Planning . . . ," *PP* 17 (Aug. 1936),
400–419; "Greenbelt Towns," *AR* 79 (Sep. 1936), 215–222; Gordon Eames
Brown, four-part series on Greenbelt, *Evening Star* [Washington], 13 Sep. 1936, B-
1; 14 Sep. 1936, A-2; 15 Sep. 1936, A-2; and 16 Sep. 1936, A-4; *Greenbelt Towns*
(Washington: Resettlement Administration, 1936); Rexford Tugwell, "The Mean-
ing of the Greenbelt Towns," *New Republic* 90 (17 Feb. 1937), 42–43; Felix Belair,
"Greenbelt—an Experimental Town—Starts Off," *New York Times Magazine,* 10
Oct. 1937, 3, 21; and John Walker, "Life in a Greenbelt Community," *Shelter* 3
(Dec. 1938), 16–23. The most useful pictorial reference is Mary Lou Williamson,
ed., *Greenbelt: History of a New Town, 1937–1987* (Norfolk and Virginia Beach:
Donning Co., 1987). Susan Klaus, *Links in the Chain: Greenbelt, Maryland, and the
New Town Movement in America, an Annotated Bibliography . . .* (Washington: Center
for Washington Area Studies, George Washington University, 1987), provides a
useful survey of many pertinent sources.

28

Stein, *Toward New Towns,* 150.

29

Walker, "Technical Problems," 34–37, is the best published account of the plan
from Walker's own perspective, but it does not indicate which members of the
team may have been responsible for specific aspects of the design. Concerning
Walker, see his obituary, *Journal of Housing* 24 (Aug. 1967), 365. I am grateful to
Calvin Corell of Greenbelt, who supplied me with much additional information
on him. Concerning Ellington's work, see Douglas Swaim, ed., *Cabins & Castles:
The History & Architecture of Buncombe County, North Carolina* (Asheville: Historic Resources Commission of Asheville and Buncome County, 1981), 52, 93–94, 171–
172. Concerning Wadsworth, see George Koyl, ed., *American Architects Directory*
(New York: R. R. Bowker Co., 1955), 580.

30

K. C. Parsons, "Clarence Stein and the Greenbelt Towns: Settling for Less," *JAPA* 56 (Spring 1990), 174. See also the essays concerning his career in *AIA Journal* 65 (Dec. 1976), 17–33. I am grateful to K. C. Parsons for sharing additional findings of his research on Stein. Unless new material is found on the subject, it is doubtful whether credit for the mall idea at Greenbelt can be assigned more precisely.

31

See chapter 11. Stein's best-known writing on the subject was Clarence Stein and Catherine Bauer, "Store Buildings and Neighborhood Shopping Centers," *AR* 75 (Feb. 1934), 175–187.

32

Baker and Funaro, *Shopping Centers,* 232–235. Surprisingly, however, the complex has not continued to be known for its pioneering role. The only prewar account I have found suggesting Greenbelt's importance is one by Carl Feiss, "Shopping Centers," *House and Garden* 76 (Dec. 1939), 48–49, 60. Not only is the Greenbelt center illustrated, but there is a lead illustration of a neighborhood center "specially designed by HOUSE & GARDEN" that is oriented to a landscaped park at the rear.

33

"Government Backs Cooperatives," *BW,* 11 Sep. 1937, 30–31; *Time* 30 (13 Sep. 1937), 16; "'Tolerance' . . . Urged," *WWD,* 28 Sep. 1937, 1, 43; "Greenbelt Food . . . ," *WWD,* 2 Nov. 1937, 4; "Cooperative Retail . . . ," *New York Times,* 26 Nov. 1937, 39; "Co-op Stores Grow in Greenbelt," *BW,* 14 May 1938, 17–18; "Greenbelt, One Year Old . . . ," *Evening Star* [Washington], 9 Oct. 1938, B-7; "Co-op Transfer," *BW,* 3 Feb. 1940, 35; Victor Bennett, "Consumers and the Greenbelt Cooperative," *Journal of Marketing* 6 (July 1941), 3–10; Fulmer, *Greenbelt,* 27–31; John Norman, "Consumer Co-Op . . . ," *WWD,* 6 Aug. 1947, 85; and Warner, *Greenbelt,* chap. 10. Fostering cooperatives was an important part of the Resettlement Administration's agenda; see Rexford Tugwell, "Cooperation and Resettlement . . . ," *Current History* 45 (Feb. 1937), 71–76. Outlets included a market, drug store, beauty parlor, barber shop, laundry call station, shoe repair shop, movie theater, and filling station. A chronicle of the center's early stages is given by the *Greenbelt Cooperator,* a weekly news sheet published by town residents. For a sampling of the negative coverage, see Warren Bishop, "A Yardstick for Housing," *Nation's Business* 24 (Apr. 1936), 29–31, 69–70; and George Morris, "$16,000 Homes for $2,000 Incomes," *Nation's Business* 26 (Jan. 1938), 21–23, 93.

34

Donald Cameron and Gerard Beeckman, "Linda Vista: America's Largest Defense Housing Project," *PP* 22 (Nov. 1941), 697. See also "3000 Living Units for Defense on Kearney Mesa," *PCA* 58 (Sep. 1941), 33–36, 38, 45; and "War Housing," *AF* 76 (May 1942), 272–280.

35

Albert Mayer, "A Technique for Planning Complete Communities," *AF* 66 (Jan. 1937), 19–36; (Feb. 1937), 126–146. The late Frederick Gutheim emphasized the importance of this piece at that time as a key reference on the subject (interview, Washington, D.C., 20 Sep. 1990).

36

For background on the architect, see Joyce Zaitlin, *Gilbert Stanley Underwood, His Rustic, Art Deco, and Federal Architecture* (Malibu, Calif.: Pangloss Press, 1989).

37

Clarence Stein and Samuel Retensky, "Commercial Facilities in Defense Housing Projects: A Definition of the Problem and Proposed Method of Solution," typescript, 3 June 1942, 3, Stein Papers, CUL. For the published guidelines, see "Shopping Facilities in Wartime," *AR* 92 (Oct. 1942), 68–70.

38

Letter from the late Pietro Belluschi to author, 26 Nov. 1990. Willow Run is discussed in the text below. Concerning McLoughlin Heights, see "Shopping Facilities in Wartime," *AR* 91 (Nov. 1942), 66–67; "Vancouver . . . Solves Its Critical Housing Shortage," *PCA* 64 (August 1943), 45–63; Elizabeth Mock, *Built in U.S.A.—1932–1944* (New York: Museum of Modern Art, 1944), 106–107; Morris Ketchum, *Shops & Stores* (New York: Reinhold, 1948), 268–269; Pietro Belluschi, "Shopping Centers," in Talbot Hamlin, ed., *Forms and Functions in Twentieth-Century Architecture,* 4 vols. (New York: Columbia University Press, 1952), 4: 124, 130–131; Jo Stubblebine, ed., *The Northwest Architecture of Pietro Belluschi* (New York: F. W. Dodge, 1953), 64; and Meredith Clausen, *Pietro Belluschi, Modern American Architect* (Cambridge: MIT Press, 1994), 115–117. For other examples, see A. D. Taylor, "Kingsford Heights," *PP* 23 (Oct. 1942), 58, 64–65; "Two Shopping Centers," *AR* 91 (May 1943), 60–61; "A Satellite Town in the Detroit Area," *AF* 79 (Oct. 1943), 94, 96–97; "Birthplace of the Atomic Bomb," *AR* 98 (Sep. 1945), 12–13; "Atom City," *AF* 83 (Oct. 1945), 103–107; and Baker and Funaro, *Shopping Centers,* 129, 242–245. Not all commercial shopping complexes designed by members of the avant-garde incorporated a mall. See, for example, "Channel Heights," 66, 74, and "Public and Commercial Structures, Chabot Terrace . . . ," *PP* 25 (Oct. 1944), 79–84.

39

Whitney Smith, designer of the most publicized and praised of the wartime shopping malls, discussed in the text below, stressed the breadth of planning concerns shared by many of his generation. He emphasized that the design of a shopping center as a mall was merely an application of a holistic approach to community planning. Telephone interview, 1 Feb. 1991.

40

"Planning with You," *AF* 79 (Aug. 1943), 66–67. See also Joseph Hudnut, "The Art in Housing," *AR* 93 (Jan. 1943), 57–62. Belluschi confirmed the importance of Greenbelt on his thinking (letter to author).

41

Belluschi, "Shopping Centers," 129. Concerning his mall design, see note 38 above.

42

A good sense of this design characteristic is given by competition entries for institutions of the period; see, for example, James Kornwolf, ed., *Modernism in America 1937–1941* (Williamsburg: Joseph and Margaret Muscarelle Museum of Art, College of William and Mary, 1985). By the early 1950s, the affinity between the layout of shopping malls and institutional work is quite apparent. Numerous pertinent illustrations can be found in books such as Lawrence Perkins and Walter Cocking, *Schools* (New York: Reinhold, 1949), and William Caudill, *Toward Better School Design* (New York: F. W. Dodge, 1954).

43

Historical studies addressing the physical aspects of government-sponsored housing programs of the 1930s and 1940s include: Roger Montgomery, "Mass Producing Bay Area Architecture," in Sally Woodbridge, ed., *Bay Area Houses* (New York: Oxford University Press, 1976), 231–242; Richard Pommer, "The Architecture of Urban Housing in the United States during the Early 1930s," *JSAH* 37 (Dec. 1978), 235–264; Richard Plunz, *A History of Housing in New York City* (New York: Columbia University Press, 1990), chaps. 7–8; Wim de Wit, "The Rise of Public Housing in Chicago, 1930–1960," in John Zukowsky, ed., *Chicago Architecture and Design 1923–1993: Reconfiguration of the American Metropolis* (Munich: Prestel, 1993), 232–245; Greg Hise, "From Roadside Camps to Garden Homes: Housing and Community Planning for California's Migrant Work Force, 1935–1941," in Elizabeth Cromley and Carter Hudgins, eds., *Gender, Class, and Shelter: Perspectives in Vernacular Architecture, V* (Knoxville: University of Tennessee Press, 1995), 243–258; and Peter Reed, "Enlisting Modernism," and Greg Hise, "The Airplane and the Garden City: Regional Transformations during World War II," in Donald Albrecht, ed., *World War II and the American Dream: How Wartime Building Changed a Nation* (Washington: National Building Museum, and Cambridge: MIT Press, 1995), 2–41, 144–183, respectively.

44

Conversations or correspondence with the late Frederick Gutheim, Julian Whittlesey, the late Pietro Belluschi, and Whitney Smith, as well as a review of literature on World War II housing programs, indicates that there was no one person or group in the federal government that was instrumental in fostering the avant-garde's participation. On the other hand, Gutheim suggested that since a number of federal authorities in the housing field by 1942 had previously worked in the Farm Security Administration's migrant housing program, the Greenbelt towns program, or the Tennessee Valley Authority, there was probably greater receptiveness to new ideas in planning and expression during the war than there had been during the 1930s (interview).

Among the avant-garde architects involved in wartime housing projects were Pietro Belluschi; Vernon De Mars; Franklin & Kump; Walter Gropius and Marcel Breuer; Howe, Stonorov & Kahn; Mayer & Whittlesey; Richard Neutra; Antonin Raymond; Eliel and Eero Saarinen; Skidmore, Owings & Merrill; Hugh Stubbins; and William Wilson Wurster. For examples, see "Low-Cost Houses," *AF* 73 (Oct. 1941), 211–241; Antonin Raymond, "Working with USHA under the Lanham Act," *PP* 22 (Nov. 1941), 690–695; William Wilson Wurster, "Carquinez Heights . . . ," *PCA* 60 (Nov. 1941), 34–37; Vernon De Mars, "Duration Dormitories," *PCA* 60 (Dec. 1941), 34–35; "Defense Housing: New Construction Techniques," *PCA* 61 (Feb. 1942), 30–31; Fred Langhorst, "Experiment . . . ," *PCA* 61 (Apr. 1942), 28–30; "War Housing," *AF* 76 (May 1942), 281–284, 296–298, 308–311, 328–331, 334–337; "Vallejo War Housing Case History," *PCA* 62 (Dec. 1942), 22–25; "People Make Production . . . ," *PCA* 63 (June 1943), 33–50; "Housing Projects at Benecia, California," *PCA* 64 (July 1943), 36–37; "Channel Heights Housing Project," *AF* 80 (Mar. 1944), 65–74; and Mock, *Built in U.S.A.,* 64–71. Such work constituted a minority of war housing projects, yet received a major portion of the publicity given to the subject, especially in architectural journals devoted to advancing avant-garde design.

45

See, for example, Richard Neutra, "Governmental Architecture in California," *PCA* 60 (Aug. 1941), 22–23, 36–37; and idem, "People Can Gain from War's

Forced Changes," *PP* 23 (Nov. 1942), 28–41, as well as a number of the articles cited in note 44 above.

46

Whitney Smith, "No Cars on Main Street," *Better Homes and Gardens* 23 (Jan. 1945), 20; "'Grass on Main Street,'" 85. See also "Commercial Center, Linda Vista, California," *PCA* 61 (Nov. 1944), 26–29; Dorothy Ducas, "Is Your Daily Shopping Work?" *House Beautiful* 88 (Aug. 1946), 40–41; Ketchum, *Shops & Stores*, 267–270; Baker and Funaro, *Shopping Centers*, 236–241; and Belluschi, "Shopping Centers," 118. Whitney Smith graciously supplied me with additional information; letter to author, 12 Jan. 1991, telephone interview, 1 Feb. 1991.

During the mid-1930s, Smith worked for the Farm Security Administration in San Francisco and Washington; thus he had firsthand acquaintance with some of the most important avant-garde initiatives in community design of the prewar period. Smith was associated with San Diego architect Earl Gilberson on the Linda Vista shopping center. Both contemporary accounts and the salient qualities of the scheme itself suggest that Smith was the designer, a responsibility he acknowledges (letter to author).

In his letter, Smith also emphasized the importance of general rather than specific influences on the mall concept—a referential framework that is typical of the avant-garde: "I imagine that subconsciously almost all the historical architectural material that related the pedestrian to the merchant would qualify as an influence, which basically would include the entire world before 1900."

47

Smith indicated that he was unaware of the 1941 proposal for the shopping center at Linda Vista. Regarding the Farmers Market, he stated: "I don't consider the L.A. Farmers Market to be basically any different than hundreds of farmers markets in Mexico" (letter to author).

48

Smith, "No Cars," 20.

49

"'Grass on Main Street,'" 91; Smith, "No Cars," 67; Baker and Funaro, *Shopping Centers*, 237. Baker and Funaro also lamented the utilitarian character of the street elevations: "It is unfortunate that the passer-by on the road, and the arriving automobile shopper, are both presented with a sorry spectacle of service entrances and garbage cans. This is quite a heavy price to pay for the pleasant quiet charm which suffuses the pedestrian courtyard inside."

Smith indicated that persuading Safeway to accept the mall plan was crucial to implementing the scheme and that the enormous market demand was an important factor in the company's decision to accept the unorthodox arrangement (letter to author).

50

"The Town of Willow Run," *AF* 78 (Mar. 1943), 37. See also "What Housing for Willow Run?" *AR* 92 (Sep. 1942), 51–54; Alan Mather, "Backhousing for Bomber Plants," *PP* (Dec. 1942), 69–74; Tracy Augur, "Planning Principles Applied in Wartime," *AR* 93 (Jan. 1943), 72–77; and Mel Scott, *American City Planning since 1890* (Berkeley and Los Angeles: University of California Press, 1971), 394–396.

51

Architects for the initial three neighborhood units were Mayer & Whittlesey; Skidmore, Owings & Merrill; and Stonorov & Kahn. Julian Whittlesey confirmed that it was Eero Saarinen who had charge of the town center's design (interview, Wilton, Conn., 22 Sep. 1990). I am grateful to David De Long and Peter Papademetriou for additional insights on this project and its relation to Saarinen's other work of the period.

52

Ketchum, *Shops & Stores,* 271–273. Gruen's scheme is discussed in chapter 11.

53

"New Buildings for 194X," 101–103. The similarities in basic layout between this scheme and Linda Vista may be more than coincidental, but Gruen could only have known about the San Diego design through direct contact with Smith or some other party involved in its planning. No evidence has been found either to confirm or deny such a connection. Gruen's store designs are discussed in chapter 9.

54

Ibid., 101. Quotes cited in the paragraphs below are from the same page.

XI No Automobile Ever Bought a Thing

1

This characteristic has been noted for other types of retail outlets; see Chester Liebs, *Main Street to Miracle Mile: American Roadside Architecture* (Boston: New York Graphic Society, 1985), 90–93.

2

Victor Gruen, "Retailing and the Automobile: A Romance Based upon a Case of Mistaken Identity," *AR* 127 (Mar. 1960), 199. A similar conclusion was reached by another, less well-known designer of regional centers; see Howard Fisher, "Traffic Planning Opportunities in Shopping Center Design," *Traffic Quarterly* 5 (Oct. 1951), 384–385.

3

See, for example, E. B. Weiss, "The Importance to Department Stores . . . ," *PI* 222 (2 Jan. 1948), 36–37, 58–59; John Guernsey, "Suburban Branches," *DSE* 14 (July 1951), 42; Dero Saunders, "Department Stores: Race for the Suburbs," *Fortune* 44 (Dec. 1951), 102; Ed Stanton, "Parent Trees Have Divergent Opinions on Branch Locations," *WWD,* 5 Feb. 1954, 40; and Paul Smith, *Shopping Centers: Planning and Management* (New York: National Retail Merchants Assoc., 1956), 19. Among the most discussed cases in retail circles was the Hecht Company Silver Spring store (1946–1947); see Richard Longstreth, "Silver Spring: Georgia Avenue, Colesville Road, and the Creation of an Alternative 'Downtown' for Metropolitan Washington," in Zeynep Celik et al., eds., *Streets: Critical Perspectives on Public Space* (Berkeley: University of California Press, 1994), 253–254; and idem, "The Mixed Blessings of Success: The Hecht Company and Department Store Branch Development after World War II," in Elizabeth Cromley and Carter Hudgins, eds., *Perspectives in Vernacular Architecture, VI* (Knoxville: University of Tennessee Press, forthcoming).

4

From the start of the regional mall's development, there was considerable difference of opinion among retailers as to whether such projects should be undertaken by department stores or by real estate interests. Both courses proved successful; each had its staunch advocates; neither appears to have become dominant at an early date. The debate continued through the 1950s. See, for example, Guernsey, "Suburban Branches," 43, 100; Saunders, "Department Stores," 166, 168; Larry Smith, "Department Store Trends in the Development of Shopping Centers," *Urban Land* 11 (Mar. 1952), 1, 3–6; and Samuel Feinberg, "From Where I Sit . . . ," *WWD,* 24 Nov. 1959, 12; 2 Dec. 1959, 8, 17; and 3 Dec. 1959, 14.

5

J. R. Owen, "Shopping Centers: The Boom Raises Problems," *Engineering News-Record* 153 (29 July 1954), 21.

6

For a sample of contemporary accounts of parking layout, see "Markets in the Meadows," *AF* 90 (Mar. 1949), 117–118; Geoffrey Baker and Bruno Funaro, *Shopping Centers: Design and Construction* (New York: Reinhold, 1951), 43; Betty Shapiro, "Three Traffic Requisites . . . ," *WWD,* 19 Nov. 1952, I-78; *Community Builders Handbook* (Washington: Urban Land Institute, 1954), 117–180; and Smith, *Shopping Centers,* 31–32.

7

Detailed discussions of the mall's advantages are unusual save within the context of covering individual examples. For an exception, see J. Ross McKeever, "Shopping Centers: Principles and Policies," *ULI* 20 (July 1952), 24–26. The Country Club Plaza is discussed in chapter 6 above.

8

Carroll Swan, "What's New About the New Shopping Centers? . . . ," *PI* 237 (9 Nov. 1951), 37. The complex referred to was Shopper's World, discussed in the text below. See also "Shopping Spreads Out . . . ," *U.S. News & World Report* 33 (7 Nov. 1952), 60; and R. W. Welch, "Convenience Is King . . . ," *PI* 241 (12 Dec. 1952), 51.

9

The prevention of encroaching development was an explicitly articulated objective at that time. Contemporary accounts suggest that it was often achieved, at least during the initial years of operation. See, for example, Herman Radolf, "Shopping Centers Need Protection," *WWD,* 12 Nov. 1952, 115. However, surrounding acreage often tended to see a substantial buildup of commercial facilities in later years. Today many regional centers are but one part of a much larger retail area. For a case study, see Peter Rowe, *Making a Middle Landscape* (Cambridge: MIT Press, 1991), 15–18.

10

Stein's work for the first of the projects discussed below was delineated in a letter to the client:

I will submit to you my recommendations of a basic layout for buildings and ground development for the whole of the property over a period of time, together with a report recommending types of commercial and recreational enterprises, their groupings, approximate size and general character, arrangement of facilities and space requirements for automobile parking, servicing of commercial or recreational enterprises or buildings, the type and general organiz-

tion of roads and paths, the general character and treatment of landscaping and a program of the order in which the proposed buildings might be constructed and developed.

His fee for these services was $10,000. Letter from Clarence Stein to the Harvlan Co., Los Angeles, 27 July 1948, Stein Papers, CUL. Correspondence concerning the other two projects indicates a similar role in each. Unless otherwise noted, all material on this work has been gleaned from the Stein Papers. I am grateful to Michael Tomlan of Cornell University and to his research assistant, Anna Pehoushek, for gathering this material on my behalf.

11

These statistics were cited in September 1950 announcements when the project was revived; see note 32 below. Probably much the same figures were used at the time Stein was involved.

12

The drawings that provide the basis for the discussion in the text are not identified save for the generic "Shopping Center Diagram" and, in several cases, dates corresponding to the time when Stein was at work on the Whittier Boulevard project. The site as depicted in the first of these studies is similar to that on Whittier Boulevard. These drawings also appear to be the basis for notes taken by Stein and identified as "LA REGINAL [sic] STORE CENTER COMMENTS ON MY STUDIES SUMMER '48," Stein Papers. This circumstantial evidence, combined with the absence of any other known project for which the drawings could have been prepared, make it likely that they were for the Whittier Boulevard site.

13

For illustration, see Richard Oliver, *Bertram Grosvenor Goodhue* (New York and Cambridge: Architectural History Foundation and MIT Press, 1983), 111–118, 153, 155, 157. Stein worked in Goodhue's office from 1911 to 1917. Concerning the importance of that experience for his career, see K. C. Parsons, "Clarence Stein and the Greenbelt Towns: Settling for Less," *JAPA* 56 (Spring 1990), 174. Carthay Center is discussed in chapter 10 above.

14

Planning for a regional center on the site was revived by Harvey ca. 1949–1950, this time with Victor Gruen as architect. An earlier scheme by Gruen may also have been for this complex. Both are discussed in the text below.

15

Draft of letter from Stein to unnamed party, presumably the Baldwin Hills Co., Nov. 1948, Stein Papers. Numerous accounts exist of Baldwin Hills Village. Stein's own is in his *Towards New Towns in America,* reprint ed. (Cambridge: MIT Press, 1971), chap. 9.

16

Draft of letter from Lewis Wilson to unnamed party, presumably the Baldwin Hills Co., Nov. 1948, Stein Papers.

17

Concerning the realized complex, see chapter 9. In addition, a neighborhood center, designed by Wilson's former partner, Robert Alexander, was constructed across the street from the original site, adjacent to Baldwin Hills Village. See "Baldwin Hills Builds a Shopping Center," *House & Home* 1 (June 1952), 149–153. That article noted: "Present focus of regional shopping, and a large factor in considering

Baldwin Hills's retail expansion, is the giant Crenshaw Center only 1¼ mi. to the southeast. Here the big May Co. and Broadway department stores handle most of the area's demand for heavy durable goods, and a large supermarket and other outlets satisfy the immediate vicinity's lighter merchandise needs" (149).

A shopping center had been planned by the Baldwin Hills Co. on the site from the start; see "Development of Extensive . . . ," *LAT,* 9 Oct. 1939, V-1, 3; and "Work Gets Under Way . . . ," *LAT,* 10 Mar. 1941, V-1, 11.

18

Sources focusing on parking requirements are cited in note 6 above.

19

Lewis Mumford, "The Life, the Teaching and the Architecture of Matthew Nowicki," *AR* 114 (July 1954), 134. Mumford's four-part essay (June 1954, 139–149; July 1954, 128–135; Aug. 1954, 169–176; Sep. 1954, 153–159) remains the most insightful assessment of the architect's work. See also Bruce Harold Schafer, *The Writings and Sketches of Matthew Nowicki* (Charlottesville: University Press of Virginia, 1973). The Ventura shopping center is illustrated in both publications. The Stein Papers contain copies of a number of sketches by Nowicki that show that the final scheme was derived from Stein's previous studies. The date of Nowicki's design is uncertain; 1949 is given in an account prepared in conjunction with a Museum of Modern Art exhibition shortly after his death ("From the Legacy of Matthew Nowicki," *AF* 92 [Oct. 1950], 201). According to the chronology in Schafer, *Writings and Sketches,* xii, the scheme was done during the summer of 1950, right before his death.

20

For an exception, see the unrealized design for the Maybrook Shopping Center in Maywood, New Jersey: *AR* 103 (Mar. 1948), 10; and Baker and Funaro, *Shopping Centers,* 30.

21

To my knowledge, nothing but the caption accompanying the drawing illustrated in figure 227 was published. I am grateful to the late Robert Alexander for details of the project (letter to author, 3 Dec. 1990).

22

For references on Gruen's store designs, see chapter 9, notes 37–38.

23

Interview with William McAdam (retired chairman of the board, Coldwell Banker), Newport Beach, 8 Apr. 1988. Gruen's early regional malls in the area include the master plan of Riverside Plaza at Riverside (1955–1956); all but the major department store at South Bay Center at Redondo Beach (1955–1958, prepared in collaboration with Jones & Emmons); and Conejo Village at Thousand Oaks (1959–1960). Gruen also was responsible for the master plan and many of the buildings at La Mirada Shopping Center in Orange County (begun 1956), which was the size of a regional center but did not include a major department store. The scheme prepared in collaboration with S. Charles Lee for the Hollypark Shopping Center in Los Angeles (1954) was never realized. See *LAEx,* 28 Aug. 1955, III-1; *CSA/AE* [31] (Sep. 1955), 62; *LAT,* 11 Sep. 1955, V-18; "$9.5 Million . . . ," *LAT,* 8 Oct. 1959, VI-17 (Riverside Plaza); "Big Shop Area . . . ," *LAEx,* 6 Feb. 1955, III-1, 2; "Multipurpose Center . . . ," *LAT,* 6 Feb. 1955, V-16; and "$15 Million Shop Center . . . ," *LAT,* 16 Sep. 1956, VI-1, 6 (South Bay

Center); "First Phase . . . ," *LAT,* 18 Oct. 1959, VI-2; Al Johns, "West Valley Construction . . . ," *LAT,* 13 Dec. 1959, VI-1, 6 (Conejo Village); "Huge Business Center . . . ," *LAT,* 15 Jan. 1956, V-6; "La Mirada's Progress . . . ," *LAT,* 29 July 1956, VI-12 (La Mirada); "Grading May 1 . . . ," *LAEx,* 25 Apr. 1954; *LAT,* 27 June 1954, V-9; and "Work on $100,000,000 . . . ," *LAT,* 5 Dec. 1954, V-13 (Hollypark). Additional material is in Gruen's scrapbooks at LC.

24

Gruen described the scheme at length in "What to Look for in Shopping Centers," *CSA/AE* [24] (July 1948), 22, 63–66, and noted it again in "What's Wrong with Store Design?" *WWD,* 18 Oct. 1949, 62. Beyond indicating that it was to be built in Los Angeles, he gave no clue as to site or client. The amount of study and design development required for this scheme make it unlikely that the undertaking was a hypothetical one. Circumstantial evidence suggests that the project may be the same as Stein's on Whittier Boulevard. The size and scope of the proposed center, along with the shape of its site, are similar in each case. Furthermore, Gruen did prepare a design for this location two years later, which is discussed in the text below. I have yet to find any documents that would shed further light on the subject, including those in Gruen's papers at LC or in the Gruen office archives. I am grateful to Stuart Lottman of Gruen Associates for checking in the latter files.

25

Gruen, "What to Look for," 66, 64.

26

The three others I have been able to identify were redevelopment schemes for Flushing in New York (1946), Grand Haven, Michigan (1947), and Park Forest Plaza (1947–1951) at Park Forest, a planned community outside Chicago. The Flushing design may have been an important prototype for urban renewal projects of the next decade, but it had little bearing work in outlying areas. For background, see "Model Retail Center Planned for Flushing," *BW,* 17 Aug. 1946, 20; "Unique Shopping Center Proposed," *ACi* 61 (Sep. 1946), 117; "Retail Shopping Center Deluxe," *NRB* 28 (Oct. 1946), 20; "$50,000,000 Retail Center . . . ," *AF* 85 (Nov. 1946), 100–105; and Robert Hallett, "Dream Shopping Center . . . ," *Christian Science Monitor,* Magazine Sect., 2 Nov. 1946, 10–11. The Michigan design seems inspired by Ketchum's Rye plan discussed in the text below and by an earlier scheme published in *AF* discussed in chapter 10; See "Redevelopment Plan for Grand Haven," *AR* 103 (Feb. 1948), 92–97. Concerning Park Forest, see Neil Harris, "The City That Shops: Chicago's Retailing Landscape," in John Zukowsky, ed., *Chicago Architecture and Design 1923–1993: Reconfiguration of an American Metropolis* (Munich: Prestel, 1993), 183–185.

Ketchum was associated with Gruen on some of his earliest store designs. For background, see Kenneth Reid, "Perspectives—The Modernist from Wainscott: Morris Ketchum, Jr.," *PP* 25 (August 1944), 65–66; and Morris Ketchum, *Blazing a Trail* (New York: Vantage Press, 1982).

27

For background, see "Shopping Center," *AF* 85 (Aug. 1946), 76–79; Leonard Harrison, "Rye Aims at City Planning Leadership," *ACi* 61 (Oct. 1946), 88–89; "Rye Plan Approved," *ASPO* 14 (Oct. 1948), 82; and Morris Ketchum, *Shops & Stores* (New York: Reinhold 1948), 281, 284–285. The most detailed account of the scheme and of the attempt to implement it is in the *Rye Chronicle* between 28 June and 8 Nov. 1946.

28

Gruen would indeed become recognized as the leader in using the pedestrian mall as an agent of urban renewal. His role in this capacity has been succinctly outlined in Howard Gillette, "The Evolution of the Planned Shopping Center in Suburb and City," *JAPA* 51 (Aug. 1985), 545–547. For a sampling of contemporary accounts, see Ogden Tanner, "Closed to Traffic," *AF* 110 (Feb. 1958), 88–95; "Fresno Downtown: Pedestrian Preserve," *A&E* 219 (Mar. 1960), 12–13; "Heart of Gruen's Fresno Plan," *PP* 46 (Jan. 1965), 184–185; "Upgrading Downtown," *AR* 137 (June 1965), 175–190; and Eduardo Contini, "Anatomy of the Mall," *AIA Journal* 47 (Feb. 1969), 42–50. While the shopping center was almost entirely an invention of the United States, the downtown pedestrian mall was based to a considerable extent on postwar European work. Contemporary accounts make clear that architects such as Gruen and Ketchum viewed the shopping center in outlying areas and the remaking of urban cores as two sides of the same coin.

29

For background, see "$2,500,000 Business Center . . . ," *WWD,* 30 Oct. 1946, 4; "For Easy Shopping . . . ," *BW,* 9 Nov. 1946, 24; "'Recentralization' . . . ," *WWD,* 20 Nov. 1946, 71; "Shopping Center," *AF* 86 (June 1947), 84–93; Morris Ketchum, "Regaining Advantages of Related Retailing Now Lost in Main Streets' Jungles," *CSA/AE* [23] (July 1947), 16–17; "Modern Theory Is Used in Beverly . . . ," *ACi* 62 (July 1947), 124–125; "Recentralization Is Growing," *RM* 43 (Apr.–May 1948), 32–37; "Centers Planned . . . ," *WWD,* 23 June 1948, I-54; Morris Ketchum, *Shops & Stores* (New York: Reinhold, 1948), 272–281; and Pietro Belluschi, "Shopping Centers," in Talbot Hamlin, ed., *Forms and Functions in Twentieth-Century Architecture,* 4 vols. (New York: Columbia University Press, 1952), 4: 134, 135. See also note 27.

North Shore Center was to have been the prototype for a series built by the developer. The only one realized was Shoppers' World in Framingham, Massachusetts, discussed in the text below. Other centers were to have been located in northern New Jersey; White Plains, New York; and Cleveland. See "A Mammoth New Shopping Center," *ACi* 64 (Feb. 1949), 78–79; and "Trust Rides Shopping Center Boom," *BW,* 22 July 1950, 80–81, 84.

30

Saunders, "Department Stores," 164.

31

Kenneth Welch, "Regional Shopping Centers," *AR* 109 (Mar. 1951), 121–131; idem, "Location and Design of Shopping Centers," *APC* 1951, 131–138. See also his "Convenience vs. Shopping Goods," *WWD,* 26 Dec. 1946, II-82, 96; "The Relocation of Commercial Areas," *Planning* 1948, 101–110, reprinted in *AJ* 17 (Jan. 1949), 45–52; and "More Modern Shopping Centers Needed," *WWD,* 6 Apr. 1949, 52.

32

"Big New Shopping District . . . ," *LAT,* 22 Sep. 1950, I-8; "New Shopping Center . . . ," *LAEx,* 22 Sep. 1950, III-1; "$20 Million . . . ," *Los Angeles Herald Express,* 22 Sep. 1950, B1.

33

This scheme was the first of Gruen's to receive much national publicity, and marked the beginning of a working relationship with Detroit's J. L. Hudson Co. that proved key to his rise as a leading designer of regional malls. For background,

see "Hudson's First Branch . . . ," *WWD,* 5 June 1950, 1, 50; "Hudson's Finally Goes Suburban," *BW,* 10 June 1950, 80–81; *AF* 93 (July 1950), 13; "Suburban Retail Districts," *AF* 93 (Aug. 1950), 106–107, 110–115; "Detroit Suburban Shopping Center," *ASPO* 16 (Aug. 1950), 70; and Baker and Funaro, *Shopping Centers,* 200–207.

A regional shopping center was never realized on the Whittier Boulevard site, probably because no department store company was willing to locate there. By the early 1950s, residential development further east for households of somewhat more means reduced the site's value for retail uses. Eastland in West Covina (1955–1957) became the principal new shopping magnet for this part of the metropolitan area. In Detroit, the J. L. Hudson Co. postponed plans to build its Eastland Plaza until work got under way on a still larger complex, Northland, discussed in the text below. Hudson's Eastland was completed according to a different design in 1957.

34

"Huge New Shopping Center . . . ," *Automobile Facts* 12 (Dec. 1953), 4–5; "Hudson's Northland Shopping Center," *WWD,* 5 Feb. 1954, 1, 39; "Northland: A Regional Shopping Center . . . ," *Michigan Society of Architects Monthly Bulletin* 28 (Mar. 1954), 33–45; Victor Gruen, "The Chain's Stake in Planning the Center," *CSA/AE* [30] (May 1954), 34–41; "Northland: A New Yardstick for Shopping Center Planning," *AF* 99 (June 1954), 103–117; and "Northland Regional Shopping Center . . . ," *Bauen und Wohnen* 10 (Apr. 1956), 109–112.

35

Examples include Woodlawn Shopping Center at Wichita, Kansas (1952, project); an unnamed center for Gimbel Brothers near Philadelphia (1953, project); an early design for Bay-Fair Shopping Center at San Leandro, California (1953); Woodmar Shopping Center near Chicago (1953–1954); and Glendale Shopping Center at Indianapolis (1954–1956). Concerning Woodlawn, see "Two-Level Shopping Center," *House and Home* 2 (Sep. 1952), 140–143; concerning Woodmar, see "Pentagon—End Mall—Bent Strip," *AR* 117 (May 1955), 200–202. Further coverage of this work can be found in Gruen's scrapbooks at LC. Some of the schemes are illustrated and the ideas behind them are discussed in contemporary articles by Gruen, including "Shopping Centers: The New Building Type," *PP* 33 (June 1952), 66–92 (coauthored with Lawrence Smith); "Basic Planning Concepts . . . ," *SWBC* 121 (27 Mar. 1953), 2–6; "Planned Shopping Centers," *Dun's Review* 61 (May 1953), 36–37, 113–114, 116–122; "A Shopping Center Is More Than a Collection of Stores," *Practical Builder* 18 (Oct. 1953), 64–67; and "Twelve Check Points . . . ," *WWD,* 26 Dec. 1953, II-35. Victor Gruen and Larry Smith, *Shopping Towns USA: The Planning of Shopping Centers* (New York: Reinhold, 1960), provides a valuable synopsis of the architect's views at the decade's end.

36

Concerning the original plan for Southdale, see "Winter or Summer . . . ," *AF* 97 (Mar. 1953), 126–133. Gruen's first plan for an enclosed mall, albeit not one on two levels, was an unrealized design for the Montclair Shopping Center in Houston, designed in collaboration with local architect Irving R. Klein; see "First Part of $12 Million . . . ," *Houston Post,* 17 Dec. 1950, III-10; and Mickey Jones, "109-Store Houston . . . ," *WWD,* 3 Jan. 1951, 85.

37

Gruen's southern California projects of the 1950s are cited in note 23 above.

38

For background, see *WWD*, 12 Mar. 1948, I-46; "Break Ground . . . ," *WWD*, 27 Apr. 1949, 10; Baker and Funaro, *Shopping Centers*, 198–199; "'Shoppers' World' at Framingham Applies New Ideas," *AR* 110 (Nov. 1951), 12–13; Swan, "What's New," 37–39, 72, 74, 76, 79; "Shoppers' World," *AF* 95 (Dec. 1951), 180–184; Sidney Shurcliff, "Shoppers' World: The Design and Construction of a Retail Shopping Center," *Landscape Architecture* 42 (July 1952), 144–151; "Shopping for Tomorrow," *Coronet* 34 (Oct. 1953), 30–33; and Samuel Feinberg, "From Where I Sit . . . ," *WWD*, 9 Dec. 1959, 1, 8, 45; 10 Dec. 1959, I-8; 11 Dec. 1959, 6.

39

Concerning Southdale as realized, see "A Controlled Climate for Shopping," *AR* 120 (Dec. 1956), 193–195; and "Brisk Business for a Bright Shopping Center," *Fortune* 55 (Feb. 1957), 141–144.

40

The complex is the subject of a pathbreaking study: Meredith Clausen, "Northgate Regional Shopping Center—Paradigm from the Provinces," *JSAH* 43 (May 1984), 144–161. Additional information can be found in contemporary accounts, including "Bon Marche to Build . . . ," *WWD*, 24 Feb. 1948, 1, 63; "Bon Marche to Start . . . ," *WWD*, 24 Dec. 1948, 1, 24; "Shopping Center: 1949 Model," *BW*, 22 July 1949, 47, 49–50; "Northgate Shopping Center, Seattle, Washington," *AR/WS* 106 (Nov. 1949), 36-1 to 36-3; "Expect Seattle Store Center . . . ," *WWD*, 18 Jan. 1950, 5; *Time*, 8 May 1950, 83–84; Howard Jackson, "Display Is Different at the Bon Marche–Northgate," *DW* 57 (July 1950), 26–27, 84; Millie Proctor, "New Bon Marche . . . ," *WWD*, 9 Aug. 1950, 54; "Suburban Retail Districts," *AF* 93 (Aug. 1950), 116–117; Arthur Priaulx, "Northgate—Suburban Shopping Center . . . ," *A&E* 182 (Sep. 1950), 14–20; Baker and Funaro, *Shopping Centers*, 218–221; Constance Patterson, "Northgate . . . ," *WWD*, 23 Jan. 1953, 52; and McKeever, "Shopping Centers," 43–45, 47.

41

Clausen, "Northgate," 151.

42

As quoted in "Shopping Centers: A Way to More Sales . . . ," *Tide* 28 (24 Apr. 1954), 21.

43

Concerning the Bon Marche, see "Suburban Retail Districts," 116; Saunders, "Department Stores," 101; and Patterson, "Northgate." Concerning Shoppers' World, see "Center in a Fix," *BW*, 23 Jan. 1954, 51–52; Maurice Sagoff, "Other Centers Can Learn . . . ," *WWD*, 10 Feb. 1954, 71; and Meredith Clausen, "Shopping Centers," in Joseph Wilkes, ed., *Encyclopedia of Architecture: Design, Engineering and Construction*, 4 vols. (New York: John Wiley & Sons, 1989), 4: 415.

44

For background, see "Stonestown Shopping Center . . . ," *AR* 109 (Mar. 1951), 132–136; "The Big 'E' Flies . . . ," *Stores* 32 (Apr. 1952), 55, 79; Baker and Funaro, *Shopping Centers*, 210–211; "New Shopping Magnets . . . ," *AF* 97 (Mar. 1953), 143–145; McKeever, "Shopping Centers," 50–51, 59–61, 63; and Gruen and Smith, *Shopping Towns*, 228–229. Both schemes had significantly different preliminary designs; see "Shopping Center Round-Up," *CSA/AE* [26] (July 1950),

29; and McKeever, "Shopping Centers," 60. Northgate's influence on these centers is noted in Clausen, "Northgate," 160.

45

The other examples I have been able to document are the four envisioned by Suburban Centers Trust, Stonestown, the Olympic Shopping Circle in Los Angeles, and Eastland in Detroit, all cited in the text and/or notes above; and the Cross County Shopping Center in Yonkers, New York. Several more years would elapse before the type began to proliferate.

46

For background, see "May Co. Signs . . . ," *LAT,* 29 June 1950, II-1, 8; "Coast May Co. . . . ," *WWD,* 29 June 1950, 1, 48; "Begin Saturday . . . ," *WWD,* 12 Oct. 1950, 8; "Work Started . . . ," *LAT,* 9 Nov. 1950, V-13; "Market Chains . . . ," *LAT,* 19 Nov. 1950, V-13; *Stores* 32 (Nov. 1950), 17–19; "4 New Coast Units . . . ," *WWD,* 1 Dec. 1950, 2; "Opening of Extensive . . . ," *LAT,* 4 Nov. 1951, V-4; "Butler's Opens . . . ," *WWD,* 8 Nov. 1951, I-47; "Accent on Parking . . . ," *WWD,* 2 Jan. 1952, 35; "May Co.'s Lakewood Store . . . ," *LAT,* 17 Feb. 1952, II-1; "New Shop Leases . . . ," *LAT,* 28 June 1953, V-1; *LAEx,* 4 Oct. 1952, I-6; and McKeever, "Shopping Centers," 78–80. Many additional insights were gleaned from interviews with Joseph Eichenbaum (Los Angeles, 11 Apr. 1988) and Albert C. Martin, Jr. (Los Angeles, 7 Nov. 1989). I am also grateful to Kenneth Caldwell, who in his former capacity as Communication Manager of Albert C. Martin & Assocs. gave me access to material remaining in the office files.

The master plan for Lakewood Center called for numerous freestanding buildings to occupy the eastern half of the site. These facilities were planned to address a wide range of community needs and included a motel, sports arena, bowling alley, automobile showrooms, and club buildings. This aspect of the scheme was the most modified in later years. See "Big Development . . . ," *LAT,* 3 Jan. 1960, VI-1, 3.

47

Concerning Lakewood Park, see "Foundations Placed . . . ," *LAT,* 26 Mar. 1950, V-4; "Large New Lakewood . . . ," *LAT,* 9 Apr. 1950, V-1, 2; "Lakewood Development . . . ," *LAT,* 16 Apr. 1950, V-2; "Lakewood Dwellings . . . ," *LAT,* 23 Apr. 1950, V-2; "Lakewood Homes . . . ," *LAT,* 30 Apr. 1950, V-2; "Sales Total . . . ," *LAT,* 7 May 1950, V-2; "Lakewood Developers . . . ," *LAT,* 14 May 1950, V-2; "Second Lakewood Unit . . . ," *LAT,* 4 June 1950, VI-2; "Constructing 100 New Homes Per Day," *SWBC* 115 (9 June 1950), 11–14; "Lakewood Development . . . ," *LAT,* 18 June 1950, V-3; "Lakewood Park's Home . . . ," *LAT,* 4 Mar. 1951, V-1; and "Lakewood Park Tract . . . ," *LAT,* 2 Sep. 1951, V-5.

48

For a succinct account of Levitt & Sons' projects, presented within the context of postwar housing development nationally, see Kenneth Jackson, *Crabgrass Frontier: The Suburbanization of the United States* (New York: Oxford University Press, 1985), 234–238. According to Jackson, Levittown, New York, was "the largest housing development ever put up by a single builder" (p. 235). Lakewood came very close but received much less publicity at the national level. The sources cited by Jackson (p. 370) give a good sense of how much attention Levitt developments attracted.

49

The subject is addressed within the postwar context in Mel Scott, *Metropolitan Los Angeles: One Community* (Los Angeles: Haynes Foundation, 1949), chap. 8.

50

"Accent on Shopping," 35.

51

"Work Started," 30; Martin interview.

52

Martin interview. Period literature on department store layout is vast. For a succinct account, see E. B. Weiss, "New Concepts of Store Architecture . . ." *PI* 222 (26 Mar. 1948), 42, 46, 48–49, 52.

53

Namely: Anaheim Plaza (originally Broadway–Orange County Shopping Center) at Anaheim (1954–1957), Buena Park Mall at Buena Park (begun 1956), Conejo Village at Thousand Oaks (1959–1960), Del Amo Center at Torrance (1958–1961), Eastland at West Covina (1955–1957), Honer Plaza at Santa Ana (1957–1959), Indian Hill Village (originally Pomona Valley Center) at Pomona (1954–1956), Los Altos Shopping Center at Long Beach (1953–1956), Riverside Plaza at Riverside (1955–1956), Santa Ana Fashion Square at Santa Ana (1957–1958), South Bay Center at Redondo Beach (1956–1958), Stonewood Center at Downey (1957–1958), and Whittwood Center at Whittier (1956).

This listing as well as the data enumerated in the text and notes below have been derived from several sources, including *Directory of Shopping Centers in the United States and Canada,* vol. IV, 1961 ed. (Chicago: National Research Bureau, 1960); *Los Angeles Shopping Centers, 1971–1972* (Los Angeles: Marketing and Research Dept., Los Angeles Times, 1971); "Regional and Community Shopping Centers: Map of Los Angeles and Orange Counties" (Coldwell Banker Commercial Brokerage Co., 1983); and entries too numerous to cite culled from the Real Estate Sect., *LAT,* weekly between 1950 and 1960. I have visited many of the sites; however, most of these complexes have experienced major alterations. The figures cited in these sources often vary; those in the text are approximations.

Several complexes built in stages were not as yet true regional centers by 1960, but I have included them if they were planned as such from the start and attained that rank within a few years thereafter. Several other regional malls were planned but never executed according to the proposed design, including ones in Torrance (*LAT,* 8 May 1955, V-1, 4); Westminster (*LAT,* 30 Oct. 1955, V-18); and Vina Vista (*LAT,* 19 Aug. 1956, VI-1, 6).

54

These include El Monte Mall at El Monte (1956–1958), Fontana Square at Fontana (begun 1954), and Orange County Plaza at Garden Grove (begun 1955). La Mirada Shopping Center at La Mirada (begun 1956) should also be grouped in this category. Even though it was much larger (750,000 square feet of retail area by 1971), it did not have a major department store branch.

55

Among the numerous community-sized centers that were erected in the metropolitan area during the decade, most had stores oriented to a large front parking lot, following the predominant national trend. These complexes tended to have between 150,000 and 300,000 square feet of retail space and between 30 and 40 store units. A few community centers such as La Mirada, cited in note 54 above, and Crenshaw-Imperial Plaza at Inglewood were considerably larger. More typical examples include Alhambra Valley Shopping Center at Alhambra, Foothill Center at Azuza, Fremont Square at Oxnard, Garden Square at Garden Grove, Harbor

Shopping Center at Costa Mesa, Lincoln Park Shopping Center at Buena Park, Live Oak Shopping Center at Arcadia, Orangefair Center at Fullerton, Skylark Shopping Center at Garden Grove, and Westminster Center at Orange.

56

Here I have relied primarily on retail area as an index, drawing from the *Directory of Shopping Centers,* 1961 ed. The list is not limited to regional centers with malls, but most of the complexes of 400,000 square feet or greater did incorporate that feature. The New York region was the only one comparable to Los Angeles. Two others were not far behind: San Francisco and Dallas–Fort Worth.

Metropolitan Region	Number of Regional Centers, by Size of Retail Area (sq. ft.)			
	400,000– 499,999	500,000– 599,999	600,000– 699,999	700,000 and greater
Los Angeles	7	4	2	5
New York	9	3	1	5
San Francisco	4	3	3	3
Dallas–Ft. Worth	3	6	0	4
Detroit	3	0	1	2
Chicago	3	2	0	3
Philadelphia	5	2	2	0
Houston	1	2	1	3
Boston	3	2	0	0

The Los Angeles metropolitan region includes Orange and portions of Riverside, San Bernardino, and Ventura counties; the New York region includes Westchester, Nassau, and portions of Suffolk counties, portions of Fairfield County, Conn., and Bergen, Passaic, Essex, and portions of Union counties, N.J.; the San Francisco region includes San Mateo, Santa Clara, Alameda, and portions of Contra Costa, Solano, and Marin counties; the Dallas–Ft. Worth region includes Dallas, Fort Worth, and surrounding communities; the Detroit region includes Macomb, Oakland, Livingston, Washenaw, and portions of Monroe counties; the Chicago region includes Du Page, Lake, and portions of Kane and Will counties; the Philadelphia region includes Montgomery, Delaware, Chester, and portions of Bucks counties, and Burlington, Camden, and Gloucester counties, N.J.; the Houston region includes Houston and surrounding communities; the Boston region includes portions of Norfolk, Middlesex, and Essex counties.

57

Announcements documenting either the intention to construct a regional mall or commencement of its construction include "$6,000,000 Shopping Center . . . ," *LAT,* 29 Mar. 1953, V-9; "Work Started . . . ," *LAT,* 1 Dec. 1957, VI-13 (Stone-wood Center); "Plans for Large Shopping Center . . . ," *LAT,* 19 June 1953, V-4; "Large Shopping Center . . . ," *LAT,* 25 Aug. 1957, VI-9 (Honer Plaza); "Shopping Area . . . ," *LAT,* 19 July 1953, V-13; *LAT,* 2 Aug. 1953, V-9 (Los Altos Shopping Center); "Huge Shopping Center . . . ," *LAT,* 4 July 1954, I-22; "Big Project . . . ," *LAT,* 13 Feb. 1955, VI-1, 13 (Eastland); "Further Development . . . ," *LAT,* 12 Sep. 1954, V-1, 16 (Indian Hill Village); "Multipurpose

Center . . . ," *LAT,* 6 Feb. 1955, V-16; "$15 Million . . . ," *LAT,* 16 Sep. 1956, VI-1, 6 (South Bay Center); "Construction to Start . . . ," *LAT,* 17 May 1955, V-17; "Construction Starts . . . ," *LAT,* 12 Feb. 1956, V-20 (Whittwood Center); "Big Shopping Center . . . ," *LAT,* 8 Apr. 1956, V-22 (Buena Park Mall); and "First Phase . . . ," *LAT,* 18 Oct. 1959, VI-2 (Conejo Village).

A persuasive argument that accelerated depreciation significantly fostered shopping center development after its introduction to the Internal Revenue Code of 1954 is made in Thomas Hanchett, "US Tax Policy and the Shopping Center Boom of the 1950s and 1960s," *American Historical Review,* forthcoming. I am grateful to the author for sharing a copy of his manuscript with me.

58

Concerning the Skokie complex, see "Marshall Field's New Shopping Center . . . ," *AF* 95 (Dec. 1951), 185–199.

59

Preliminary plans for Los Altos Shopping Center and Stonewood Center bear affinity to Lakewood; see *LAT,* 2 Aug. 1953, V-9; and "$6,000,000 . . . ," *LAT,* 29 Mar. 1953, V-9.

60

Interview with Eaton Ballard (retired senior vice-president of Carter Hawley Hale Stores), Pasadena, Nov. 1989. Ballard confirmed that a dual anchor arrangement was planned from the start and the important role the Crenshaw Center played in the company leadership's thinking. The complex was built in increments, beginning with the department store. The mall was not open until 1957. Contemporary accounts include "Broadway to Build . . . ," *ABu,* 7 July 1954, 1; "Broadway Describes Development," *SAR,* 8 July 1954, A20; "Two Extensive Stores . . . ," *LAT,* 5 Dec. 1954, V-1, 14; "Broadway-Anaheim . . . ," *ABu,* 13 Oct. 1955, 1; "Broadway to Open . . . ," *LAT,* 14 Oct. 1955, I-38; "Work Begun . . . ," *LAT,* 12 Aug. 1956, VI-17; "Ralphs Anaheim Store . . . ," *ABu,* 10 Oct. 1956, 7; "Sav-on Drug Store . . . ," *ABu,* 24 Oct. 1956, 22; "Shopping Area Purchased . . . ," *LAT,* 9 Dec. 1956, VI-12; "Security Bank Opens . . . ," *ABu,* 21 Mar. 1957, 9; *LAT,* 24 Mar. 1957, VI-10; "Leeds to Open . . . ," *ABu,* 15 May 1957, 15; "Shoe Company Opens . . . ," *LAT,* 19 May 1957, VI-19; *LAT,* 16 Nov. 1958, VI-13; "Big Shopping Center's . . . ," *LAT,* 17 Nov. 1957, VI-8; and "Broadway–Orange County . . . ," *ABu,* 18 Nov. 1957, 9. See also "Broadway-Hale . . . ," *WWD,* 17 Nov. 1954, 21.

61

Eaton Ballard also stressed the degree of skepticism that met the Broadway's plans to build large stores at Anaheim and Panorama City. Many retailers felt that the market would not be sufficient to sustain such projects because their location was too peripheral. Circumstances proved such thinking wrong within a few years; however, the episode underscores how new the concept of the regional shopping center still was in the mid-1950s and that it was not at all uncommon to believe that even the largest metropolitan areas could support only a small number of them. Those questioning whether too many regional centers were being constructed too fast during the 1950s included some shopping center developers, most notably Arthur Rubloff of Chicago. See Arthur Rubloff, "Regional Shopping Centers and Their Effect on the Future of Our Cities," *APC* 1953, 45–49; J. M. Baskin, "Shopping Center 'Craze' . . . ," *WWD,* 28 June 1954, 1, 25. See also "Too Many Shopping Centers?" *BW,* 17 Nov. 1956; and Hanchett, "US Tax Policy."

The second anchor that finally joined the Broadway at Anaheim Plaza was J. W. Robinson. By the mid-1950s, a number of regional malls had dual anchors of more or less equal-sized branches of major downtown department stores, including Westgate Shopping Center near Cleveland (completed 1954), Cross County Center at Yonkers (1955), Old Orchard Shopping Center at Skokie, Illinois (1956); Seven Corners near Washington, D.C. (1956); and Southgate Center near Minneapolis (1956). See McKeever, "Shopping Centers," 77–78, 56–58, 46–47, 70–72, and 59–61, resp.

62

The Miracle Mile was created under the aegis of a single developer, Sol Atlas, but was located on scattered sites along the North Hempstead Turnpike. Contemporary accounts include "Lord & Taylor Suburban Apparel Shop . . . ," *AR* 89 (June 1941), 41–47; "'Country Modern' . . . ," *DSE* 4 (10 June 1941), 33; "Suburban Stores Pay," *RM* 42 (Nov. 1947), 17; "Three Stores," *PP* 29 (Feb. 1948), 55–60; "New Mary Lewis . . . ," *WWD*, 3 Sep. 1948, 30; and Baker and Funaro, *Shopping Centers,* 162–163. The Chestnut Hill group was initiated by two developers working independently of one another; see Smith, *Shopping Centers,* 21–22; and Samuel Feinberg, "From Where I Sit . . . ," *WWD*, 9 Dec. 1959, 8.

63

"Old California Influence . . . ," *SAR,* 14 Nov. 1957, C1; "Target Completion Date . . . ," *ABu,* 15 Nov. 1957, 9; "Fashion Square Idea . . . ," *SAR,* 28 Feb. 1958, B1; *LAT,* 6 Apr. 1958, VI-9; "Haggerty's Construction Starts . . . ," *SAR,* 17 Apr. 1958, B2; "$50,000 Store . . . ," *LAT,* 20 Apr. 1958, VI-9; "$140,000 Bank . . . ," *LAT,* 13 July 1958, VI-4; "New Bullock's Facility . . . ," *LAT,* 24 Aug. 1958, VI-7; "Final Stage Reached . . . ," *SAR,* 24 Aug. 1958, B3; "Fashion Square Opens . . . ," *SAR,* 16 Sep. 1958, B-whole sect.; "New Concept of Shopping . . . ," *LAT,* 16 Sep. 1958, III-1, 28; "New Santa Ana Bank . . . ," *LAT,* 30 Nov. 1958, VI-10; and "Fashion Square Observes . . . ," *LAT,* 17 Sep. 1964, RA-2 to RA-10.

Not long after the project got under way, plans were developed independently for Metcalf Plaza, a shopping center oriented more to everyday needs, on adjacent land; see "Shop Center Plans Told," *LAT,* 11 Aug. 1957, VI-11; "Ground Breaking . . . ," *LAT,* 17 Nov. 1957, VI-10; "Large New Store . . . ," *LAT,* 28 Sep. 1958, VI-10; and "Work to Start . . . ," *LAT,* 21 June 1959, VI-16. Another shopping center, Town and Country Plaza, had been built directly across the street some years earlier. Thus Fashion Square could draw upon people who wished to patronize its stores while on routine shopping trips as well as people who had its outlets as their exclusive destination.

64

"New Concept of Shopping," III-28. The status of the precinct was such that it ranked among the very few unplanned complexes listed in the annual *Directory of Shopping Centers,* beginning with its first volume in 1957. Other stores included Desmond's, Gump's, Haggerty's, Ciro Jewelers, I. Magnin, and Silverwood's. Concerning Bullock's Pasadena, see chapter 9 above.

BIBLIOGRAPHICAL NOTE

Scholarly studies of subjects central to this book—retail architecture, out-lying business centers, and Los Angeles—are relatively few. My research had to rely primarily on a wide range of period accounts, most of them very limited in nature. The process, then, in large part entailed gathering small particles of information in sufficient number and scope to gain an ac-curate perspective on the complex shift from city center to regional mall.

Under the circumstances, offering a subject guide to the hundreds of sources cited in the notes seems a more useful instrument of reference than the conventional form of bibliography. The subject categories entail some overlap. I have erred on the side of redundancy where I thought it was useful. References to major department stores in southern California shopping centers, for example, are listed under both "department stores" and "shopping centers," but not under "commercial architecture, miscella-neous" or "retailing." Citations addressing material in locations outside southern California as well as in the nation generally are grouped under "U.S." in the listings. Roman numerals refer to chapters; the following arabic numerals refer to individual notes.

Identifying key material proved a challenging task in its own right. Subject headings one might first think of as points of depar-ture—"shopping center," for example—yield almost nothing for the pe-riod in question. The probe had to proceed incrementally, for some time without a clear sense of the extent, nature, or range of publications that would be essential to consult. Only through what seemed like an almost random path could the search become systematic and conclusive.

Among the wide array of sources examined, trade periodicals proved some of the most informative, chronicling then current tendencies in considerable detail. Beyond business magazines aimed at a broad audience, such as Business Week *and* Fortune, *are numerous specialized ones for retailers (e.g.,* Chain Store Age, Department Store Economist, Super Market Merchandising*).* Women's Wear Daily *is perhaps the single most valuable in this latter category, offering abundant insight on stores, companies, retailing concerns, and trends in urban development. Journals produced for advertisers (*Printer's Ink, Tide*), appraisers (*Appraiser Journal*), property owners (*Building Investment*), and real estate developers (*National Real Estate Journal, Freehold*), among other fields, add necessary perspectives. Likewise, periodicals directed to architects (e.g.,* Architectural Forum, Progressive Architecture*), builders (e.g.,* Building Age*), and planners (e.g.,* American City*) add essential pieces of the picture.*

Periodicals with a regional focus are substantially fewer. Among the most informative for the subject are Architect and Engineer of California, Los Angeles Realtor, *and* Southwest Builder and Contractor. *Two newsletters,* Eberle Economic Service *and the Security-Pacific Bank's* Monthly Summary of Business Conditions, *provide important statistical data and analysis.*

The other principal source for this study is local newspapers. Among the city papers, the Los Angeles Times *gives the most extensive coverage to architectural, retailing, and urban development matters. Neighborhood papers (e.g.,* Hollywood Daily Citizen, Southwest Wave, Valley Times*) as well as those of satellite communities (e.g.,* Beverly Hills Citizen, Glendale News Press*) afford a wealth of detail not found elsewhere.*

Many other sources were tapped as well, including municipal reports, city and telephone directories, Sanborn fire insurance atlases and other maps, photographic collections, and company archives, as well as interviews with a number of retired architects, planners, real estate developers, and retailers.

COMMERCIAL ARCHITECTURE, MISCELLANEOUS, SOUTHERN CALIFORNIA

II   *3, 5, 25–26, 30–36, 38–40, 61–64*

III   *12, 21, 25–27, 35–36, 39, 43*

IV   *5–11, 25–28, 31, 35–37, 44–48*

V   *7–8, 10–11, 14–19, 23, 50, 56–57, 59, 61, 63, 68–69, 71–72, 80*

VI   *32, 40*

VII   *6, 14–15, 23–24, 26, 31, 34–36*

VIII   *10–15, 21, 41*

IX   *38, 44–45, 73*

X   *6, 9, 12–13, 15–17, 20–21, 23–25*

INDEX

In this index, cities, districts of cities, and towns are listed by name, as are a relatively small number of individuals, agencies, and publications. Other proper names are grouped under the following broader categories: architects; banks; business associations; commercial districts, outlying; commercial/office buildings; commercial/store buildings; expositions/world's fairs; hotels; parking; pedestrian malls; planned communities; planners/landscape architects; real estate agents/brokers; real estate developers; residential tracts; retailers; shopping centers; shopping courts; stores, clothing/dry goods; stores, department; stores, drug; stores, furniture; stores, grocery/markets; stores, miscellaneous; stores, variety; and theaters. The index also includes general topics such as architectural design, automobiles, retailing, and traffic congestion. Page numbers in italics indicate material in illustrations.

E

East Los Angeles, 313, 315

Eberle, George, 204–205, 206, 210

Eberlein, Harold, 108

El Monte, Calif., 463 (n. 54)

Euclid, Ohio, 441 (n. 77)

EXPOSITIONS/WORLD'S FAIRS

140, 311

    Century of Progress, Chicago, 1933, 201, 281, 447 (n. 18)

    Exposition des Arts Décoratifs, Paris, 1925, 39

    Panama-California Exposition, San Diego, 1915, 153, 444 (n. 4)

F

Farm Security Administration, 452 (n. 44), 453 (n. 46)

Federal Public Housing Authority, 293

Filling stations.
  See Gasoline/service stations

Flintridge (Los Angeles County), 105

Fontana, Calif., 463 (n. 54)

Fortune, 444 (n. 1)

Framingham, Mass., 332, 459 (n. 29)

Fullerton, Calif., 464 (n. 55)

Furniture stores.
  See Stores, furniture

G

Garages.
  See Parking: garages

Garden City, N.Y., 401 (n. 78)

Garden Grove, Calif., 463 (n. 54), 464 (n. 55)

Gasoline/service stations, 139, 168, 231, 281, 297, 313, 450 (n. 33)

Gilmore, Earl, 399 (n. 61)

Glendale, Calif., 6, 66, 82, 94

Graumann, Sid, 94

Greenwich, Conn., 123

Grocery stores/markets.
  See Shopping courts; Stores, grocery/markets

L

Laemmle, Carl, 89, 384 (n. 24)

Lake Forest, Ill., 150–152, 180, 230, 394 (n. 28)

Lalique, René, 39

La Mirada, Calif., 463 (n. 54)

Landscape architects.
   See Planners/landscape architects

Lanham Defense Housing Act, 291

Lexington, Ky., 444 (n. 8)

Long Beach, Calif., 6, 154, 225, 337, 338, 346, 382 (n. 13), 406 (n. 25), 438 (n. 63), 463 (n. 53)

Los Angeles

   downtown, 3, 5, 15, 16, 19–55, *20, 21, 22, 32,* 57, 58, 61, 66, 67, 68, 74, 77, 82, 83, 85, 86, 87, 89, 93, 94, 95, 96, 98, 100, 103, 106, 119, 121, 128, 129, 131, 134, 138, 154, 170, 172, 177, 178, 199–218, *206,* 227, 228, 231, 246, 256, 278, 300, 338, 346, 349, 351, 406 (n. 25), 426 (n. 43), 434 (n. 40)

   freeways, 210–211, *212,* 216, 218, *237,* 256, 440 (n. 75)

      Golden State Freeway, 256

      Harbor Freeway, 213, 216

      Hollywood Freeway, 256

      Ventura Freeway, 256

   land area of, 6, 81–82, 83, 128

   land values in, 27, 33, 44, 66, 71, 89, 106, 108, 165, 172–173, 187–188, 256

   manufacturing, 6–7, 10–11, 79, 83, 224, 337

   parks

      Pershing Square, 213

      Plaza, 278, 446 (n. 14), 447 (n. 16)

      Sunset (Lafayette), 104

      Westlake (MacArthur), 104, 106, 109, 177

   population of, 6, 7, 83, 224–225, 227

   port of, 6

   residential development in, 9–13, *10, 11,* 19, 20, 23, 24, 59–60, 62, 63, 67, 83, 99, 104–105, 127, 128, 225–226, 300, 302, 360 (n. 18)
   (*see also* Residential tracts)

   streets

      Adams Avenue, 31

      Beverly Boulevard, 81

      Boyle Avenue, 121

      Broadway, 5, *20,* 23, 24, 27, 28, 29, 31, 33, 34, 35, 36, 37, 43, 50, 53, 59, 66, 68, 86, 94, 112, 139, 204, 206, *206,* 213, 216, 275, 365 (n. 21), 373 (nn. 3, 4), 417 (n. 30), 426 (n. 43), 447 (n. 16)

      Cahuenga Boulevard, 83, 387 (n. 43)

      Carondelet Street, 369 (n. 50)

      Central Avenue, 66, 373 (nn. 3, 4), 374 (n. 4)

      Cole Street, 387 (n. 43)

Los Angeles Municipal Airport, 238

Los Angeles Police Department, 174

Los Angeles Public Library, 444 (n. 4)

Los Angeles Realtor, 81

Los Angeles River, 121

Los Angeles State Normal School, 408 (n. 35)

Los Angeles Times, 3, 5, 12, 20, 21, 32–33, 57, 62, 77, 79, 199, 208, 210, 225, 279, 416 (n. 27)

Owensmouth (Los Angeles), 373 (n. 2)

Owens Valley Aqueduct, 6

Oxnard, Calif., 464 (n. 55)

P

S